THE GEORGIA LAND LOTTERY PAPERS
1805 – 1914

Genealogical Data From the Loose Papers Filed in the Georgia Surveyor General Office Concerning the Lots won in the State Land Lotteries and the People who won Them.

Compiled by
Robert S. Davis, Jr.
and
Rev. Silas Emmett Lucas, Jr.

Copyright 1979
      By: Southern Historical Press, Inc.

All rights reserved. No part of this publication may be reproduced, stored in a retrieval system or transmitted in any form or by any means without the prior permission of the publisher.

Please direct all correspondence and orders to:

SOUTHERN HISTORICAL PRESS, Inc.
PO BOX 1267
375 West Broad Street
Greenville, SC 29601

ISBN # 0-89308-156-6
ISBN # 978-0-89308-156-0

Portrayal of the Land Lottery drawings done by George I. Parrish, Jr. This painting is in the Surveyor General Office at the Georgia Department of Archives and History, Atlanta. Photograph of the painting courtesy of the Georgia Surveyor General Department.

MAP SHOWING THE LAND AREA AND THE COUNTIES FORMED IN EACH OF THE SEVEN LAND LOTTERIES, AND THE HEADRIGHT-BOUNTY GRANT LANDS. See next page for more details.

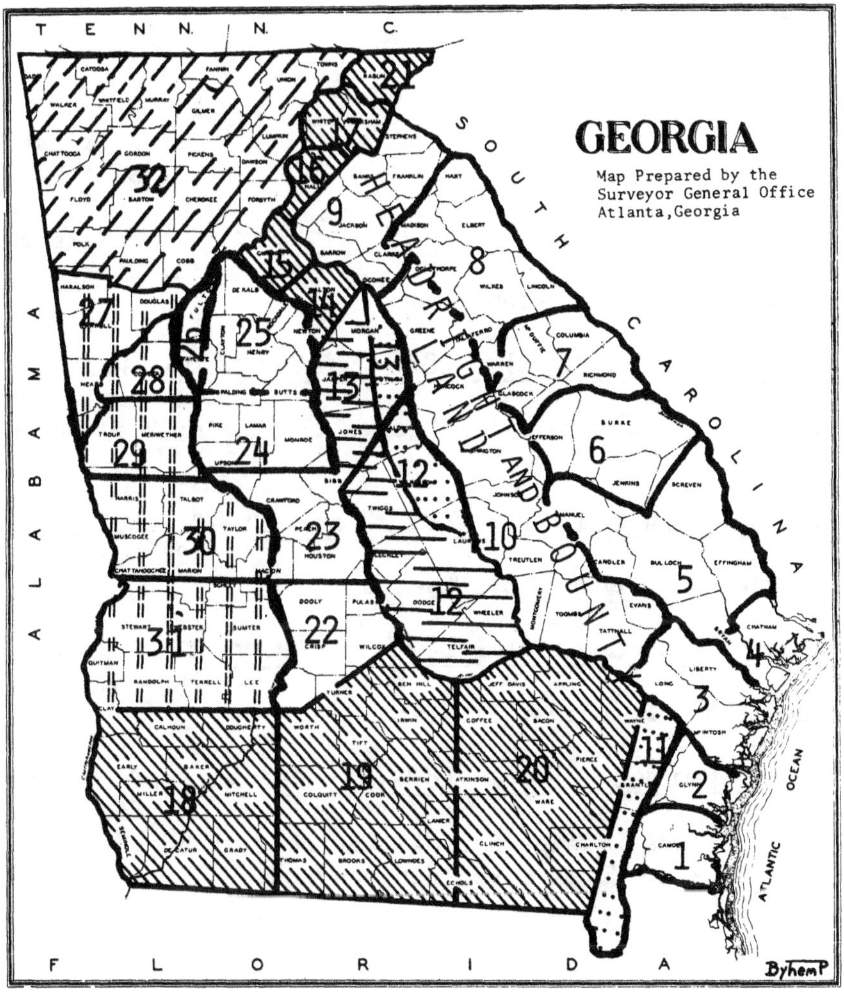

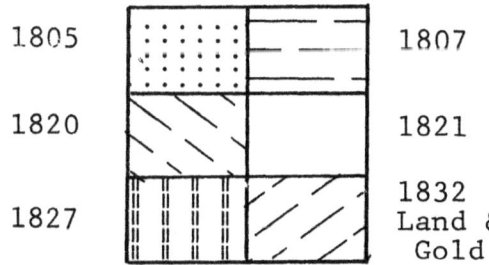

1805			1807
1820			1821
1827			1832 Land & Gold

GEORGIA'S ORIGINAL 32 COUNTIES

Counties formed from the HEADRIGHT and BOUNTY GRANTS: 1. Camden; 2. Glynn; 3. Liberty; 4. Chatham; 5. Effingham; 6. Burke; 7. Richmond; 8. Wilkes; 9. Franklin; 10. Washington.

Counties Formed in the 1805 Lottery: 11. Wayne; 12. Wilkinson and 13. Baldwin.

Counties Formed in the 1807 Lottery: The remainder of 12. Wilkinson; and the remainder of 13. Baldwin.

Counties Formed in the 1820 Lottery: 14. Walton; 15. Gwinnett; 16. Hall; 17. Habersham; 18. Early; 19. Irwin; 20. Appling; 21. Rabun.

Counties Formed in the 1821 Lottery: 22. Dooly; 23. Houston; 24. Monroe; 25. Henry; 26. Fayette.

Counties Formed in the 1827 Lottery: 27. Carroll; 28. Coweta; 29. Troup; 30. Muscogee; 31. Lee.

Counties Formed in the 1832 Lotteries: 32. Cherokee which was divided into Cass (later Bartow), Cherokee, Cobb, Floyd, Gilmer, Lumpkin, Murray, Paulding and Union.

Dedicated to

John Elzie Ladson, Jr., Janice Gayle Blake
and Marion R. Hemperley for their kind help
and continuous encouragement

Georgia
Richmond County } Be it known that I have this day appointed William R. McLaws, Esqr. of the County aforesaid my lawful Attorney to apply for and take out of Office the grant for Lot No. 58 in the 23d District 2nd Section in the County of _____ and to do all such matters and things as I could do as Administrator of the Estate of William H. Dill decd in the premises were I present at the doing thereof.

In witness whereof I have hereto affixed my hand and Seal this the first day of June 1843

Signed Sealed and
acknowledged in presence of }   Robert S Dill Admr.
William R. McLaws N.P.R.C.

Georgia Richmond }
County } Personally appeared before me Robert S. Dill who being Sworn Says that he is the Administrator on the Estate of Wm H Dill and is the proper person to take out grant for Lot No. 58 in the 23d District 1st Section in the County of _____ the grant for which is applied for by him under the provision of an act assented to Dec. 28th 1822

Sworn and Subscribed before }   Robt S Dill
me this first June 1843 }
    William R. McLaws
        N.P.R.C.

Example of a Loose Land Lottery Paper from Which This Book is Compiled.

The State of Alabama }
Chambers County } Know all men by these presents that Mr. Wm. N. Curry in right of his wife Lucinda formerly Lucinda Farrar and John Sharman in right of his wife Elizabeth Jane formerly Elizabeth Jane Farrar and Peter Farrar lawful heirs of Robert Farrar deceas'd have for certain good causes and reasons them thereunto moving constituted and appointed & by these presents do hereby constitute and appoint Amelia Torrance of the County of Baldwin and State of Georgia our true and lawful attorney in fact to grant in our name and for our use a certain lot of Land situated in the Cherokee region of Country and known and distinguished by the Number four hundred and fifty six (156)— in the fourteenth (14). District and third (3). Section which lot of Land was drawn by the orphans of Robert Farrar of Jones County Georgia, which orphans are the said Lucinda, Elizabeth Jane, & Peter Farrar as above mentioned. And we the said Wm. N. Curry in right of his wife Lucinda John Sharman in right of his wife Elizabeth Jane & Peter Farrar orphans of said Robert Farrar do hereby authorise the said Amelia Torrance to grant said land firmly as aforesaid and do all such things in connexion therewith as is required of us by law to do were we personally present, hereby ratifying and confirming all of his acts as such. As Witness we have here unto set our hands and seals this 8th day of March 1843—

Wm. N. Curry {seal}
in right of his wife Lucinda Curry

Georgia }
Jefferson County } Personally appeared before me Thomas Maddin a Justice of the peace duly sworn deposeth and saith that he is the lawful owner of a certain tract of Land drawn by Nancy Sammons widow— No 204 — Spring in the 8th district 2nd Section Cherokee County — also the lawful owner of Lot No 1152 Second 2nd District 4 Section Cherokee ___ — and that he was the drawer of said Lot

Sworn to and Subscribed before
this 2nd day of June 1843 — Seaborn ✕ Simmons
Pleasant Walden J.P.   mark

INTRODUCTION

The Georgia Surveyor General Department has thousands of loose documents connected with the state land lotteries of 1805, 1807, 1820, 1821, 1827, and 1832. Among these papers are the petitions, also refered to as oaths, of the "fortunate drawers", or their heirs, for formal grants to lots; letters by civil officials to correct misspellings on the lists of winners before the lists were published; signed statements by Indian agents that certain lots did or did not have Cherokee Indian "improvements"; records of Cherokees who attempted to return to Georgia; and other miscellaneous papers concerning the lots won and the people who won them.

Only a fraction of these records are of obvious genealogical value, and thus were abstracted for this volume. These include examples of almost every type of personal or family relationship, ranging in research value from simply naming the executor of an estate to detailed family information on people who lived in a county whose records have since been destroyed by fire to lengthy personal histories.

The Georgia legislature passed an act in 1842 that nullified any claims to lots not claimed in the land lotteries prior to 1821 and set a deadline of July 1, 1843 for taking out grants on lots won in the lotteries of 1821, 1827, and 1832. Orphans were exempted from the deadline, being allowed until their 21st birthdays to take out their grants. Most of the papers of genealogical value were filed by heirs of the original winners in the lotteries, just before the 1843 cut off date for taking out grants for lots won in the later lotteries. Hence, the reason that most of the documents abstracted herein are dated more than ten years after the last land lotteries.

At the present time, the loose land lottery papers are not available for use by researchers and the Georgia Surveyor General Department will not conduct searches in these thousands of papers for specific individuals or lots. Their staff, however, have begun to organize these records in files by county, section, district, and lot. When this project is completed, a patron will be able to look up the designation of a lot won by an individual and then request that the file for that lot be checked for loose land lottery papers. Using this system, genealogists will be able to examine the records not abstracted in this volume for particular information of special value to their research, such as tieing an ancestor to a certain critical date or place. Researchers writing county historians will be provided with a means of checking the lots of an entire area for the lots that had "Cherokee improvements".

Not every lot has loose papers, however. Many of these records have been stolen or destroyed in the years before the present Georgia Surveyor General Department came into existence. The papers for the older lotteries are particularly incomplete.

For many years, these records were stored in three large boxes, in no particular order. Starting in 1971, The Georgia Genealogical Magazine began publishing abstracts by Rev. Silas E. Lucas,Jr. of the papers in one of these boxes. His abstracts are part one of this present volume. The documents in the remaining two boxes were abstracted after the Georgia Surveyor General Department be-

i

gan their present system of organizing these papers by lot designations. The new abstracts are part two of this volume and were written with their system in mind.

The published lists of drawers in the Georgia land lotteries provide valuable census like data for the period 1805 to 1832, and, in the later lotteries, proof of service in the American Revolution. For information on these volumes, write for the catalogue of the Southern Historical Press.

Robert S. Davis, Jr.

April 7, 1979

CONCERNING THE USE OF THE ORIGINAL OATH'S IN THE SURVEYOR GENERAL OFFICE.

Mr. Marion Hemperley, Deputy Surveyor General has requested that each reader of this bookbe advised that these original documents are not in order and have not been cataloged for public use. Therefore, under no circumstances can they be made available to the public until such cataloging and possible lamination.

The Surveyor-General Department does not have the staff to receive requests to make a search through these records. At some point in the future these Xerox copies of the originals will be placed in the Ladson Memorial Library of the Vidalia-Toombs County, Georgia Library so that individuals may see copies of the original oath's.

Other records of interest to genealogists in:

Georgia Surveyor General Department
Georgia Archives Building
330 Capitol Avenue
Atlanta, Georgia 30334
(open Monday through Friday, only)

* Surviving colonial and state land grant and plat books (also available on microfilm, the Microfilm Library, Georgia Department of Archives and History).

* Loose warrants, certificates, and other land records, including certificates of service in the American Revolution and the Oconee War, filed alphabetically by name of claimant.

* Georgia Map collection, including published catalogue of pre-1800 maps.

* Dr. John H. Goff Collection of files on Georgia forts, ferries, and roads.

* Published abstracts of Georgia colonial land grants and plats, by parish.

Part I

From: The Georgia Genealogical Magazine

The following are all Georgia counties. For people living in other states, see back of this section with states listed in alphabetical order.

GEORGIA:

TALBOT COUNTY: Know all men by these presents that I. D. W. TOMME, the legal representative of one of the orphans of JOSEPH DIGBY of county and state afsd....do appoint JOSEPH EDGE of the County Chambers and State of Alabama my true and lawful attorney....to grant my interest in a certain lot of land lying in the 13th Dist. of Irwin county, No. (427)...... drawn by the orphans of JOSEPH DIGBY.
Dated: 26 Aug. 1841
Signed: D. W. TOMME   J. C. GOODWIN, J. P.

MORGAN COUNTY: Know all men by these presents that we the orphans of AUSTIN CLEMEN/CLEMENTS being all of age, have appt'd THOMAS V. ALLEN our true and lawful attorney....to take out Plat and Grant for Lott of land drawn by us as orphans of AUSTIN CLEMENTS, dec'd of Morgan co.....Lot No. (66) in Muscogee co., originally but now Marion.
Dated: 5 May 1843, in the presence of _____ THOMPSON, R. A. PRIOR, J. P.
Signed: MATILDA WILLIS, formerly Clements, PERMELIA BROOKS, formerly Clements, NANCY WHITLOCK, formerly Clements, LILLY ANN STEWART, formerly Clements, ROBERT H. CLEMENTS. Sworn to in Baldwin co., Ga. by THOMAS V. ALLEN, lawful agent for the owners, 8 May 1843, bef. ALFRED M. HORTON, J.P., Baldwin county.

STATE OF GEORGIA: Know all men by these presents that I, ELIZABETH G. LAWRENCE of the County of Columbia and state afsd. for divers good causes there unto me moving have this day appt'd CHARLES E. RYAN of Baldwin county my lawful Att'y to take out a lot of land in the Cherokee Purchase cont. 160 acres drawn in my name and also to take out a Gold Lot in sd. Cherokee drawn by the orphans of WILLIAM LAWRENCE (I being their guardian)....etc.
Dated: 8 May 1843
Signed: E. G. LAWRENCE (L.S.)
Wit.: JNO. A. STAPLER, J.I.C.

BALDWIN COUNTY....CHAS. E. RYAN....lawful agent of owner of Lot 386 in 12th Dist., 1st Sect. in originally Cherokee county. Grant applied for Dec. 28, 1842. Dated: June

13, 1843. Wit.: J. R. ANDERSON (J.P.?).

RICHMOND COUNTY: Be it known that I, SAMPSON McCARTY and
                    GREEN B. RED have this day appointed AL-
FRED M. HORTON the Surveyor of the State of Ga. at Milledgeville
our lawful Att'y to take out grants for the several lots of land
described in the foregoing affidavit.....etc.
Signed: SAMPSON McCARTY (L.S.) G. B. RED (L.S.)
Wit.: JOHN SHLY, Judge, Superior Ct., Milledgeville, Ga.

MORGAN COUNTY: Personally appeared before me JOHN C. REES
                    who being duly sworn saith that he is the
proper owner of Lot #244 in 14th Dist., Dooley county and also
lots #1281 in 2nd Dist. of third section and Lot #112 in 11th
Dist. of 3rd section of Cherokee, originally and said last two
lotts was drawn by SUSANNAH M. FURLOW, Widow with whom I have intermarried since the drawing of the same and he applies for the
grant under Act of Legislature 28 Dec. 1842.
Signed: JNO. C. REES.
Wit.: 24 May 1843, ELIJAH E. JONES, J.I.C.

BURKE COUNTY: Personally appeared JAMES HAMPTON who be-
                    ing duly sworn saith he is the owner of a
Lot of land in one of the Land Lotteries drawn by his wife NANCY
HAMPTON (formerly NANCY BROOKINGS, orphan) and believes it is No.
126 in 3rd Dist. of Dooley county.
Signed: JAMES HAMPTON
Wit.: 1 June ____, JAS. JONES, (JICBC)......"I hereby authorize
and empower W. JAMES LAVATEN of County of Burke, Ga. to grant the
land ment. in the above affidavit. It Wit. I set my hand and seal
this 1 June 1843. JAMES HAMPTON (L.S.)
Wit.: JA'S W. JONES J.I.C. B.C.

RICHMOND COUNTY: Personally appeared before me REBECCA
                    CAMFIELD who being duly sworn says that
she is the proper agent and Gdn. of ELIZABETH I., MARY, REBECCA,
JOHN, LYDIA OCTAVIA and SARAH CAMFIELD, orphans of ABIEL CAMFIELD
for Lott #1140 in 2nd. Dist., 2nd Sect. of Cherokee and now in
Cherokee County.....acc. to Act. of Dec. 28, 1842.
Signed: REBECCA CAMFIELD, agent and gdn. of the orphans of ABIEL
CAMFIELD.
Wit.: 3 June 1843, RICHARD ALLEN, J.P.

MONROE COUNTY: Personally came before me JAMES NORRIS a
                        Justice of the Peace for sd. county, HIL-
LARY M. PRATT who being duly sworn sayeth that he is the husband
of PERMELIA KING by intermarriage with her who drew lot of land
cont. 40 acres in 4th dist. and 1st sect. Cherokee and that sd.
PERMELIA KING drew lot as the orphan of JOHN KING of Bibb county,
it being Lot 657 and that he wants Plat and Grant to issue to
him in right of his wife PERMELIA.
Signed: HILLARY M. PRATT.
Wit.: 3 June 1843, JAMES NORRIS, J.P.
                        MONROE COUNTY ....HILLARY M. PRATT husband
of PERMELIA KING of county and state afsd.....app't JOSEPH GRAY
of County of Monroe his true and lawful att'y....to receive the
Plat and Grant of lott of land cont. 40 acres in 4 Dist., 1st
Sect. of Cherokee, No. 657.
Signed & Ack. bef. JAMES NORRIS, J.P.
Signed: HILLARY M. PRATT

BURKE COUNTY: Personally appeared before me JOHN ROGERS
                        who being duly sworn that he is the owner
of Lot. #923, 19th District, 2nd Section Cherokee, drawn by JOHN
CONNER of Rogers District, Burke county. Also that he is the
owner of Lot. #77, 18th Dist., 2nd Sect. drawn by JOHN VAUGHN,JR.
(but published in the printed list JOHN VAUGHN, SENIOR), 72nd.
Dist., Burke county and no lot has come out from the drawing
which deponent has seen, to the name of JOHN VAUGHN, JNR. before
selling same to me, I consider the same as my own....but if any
lot has been drawn by JOHN VAUGHN, JUNR., besides the one attended to carrying out in the name of JOHN VAUGHN, SENR. is the Lot
owned by me, and for which I consider myself the owner and pray
grant to issue for. Also that said JOHN ROGERS is a Judgement
Creditor of BENJAMIN OLIVER of said county who drew (in the sd.
72 Dist. of sd. county, Lott No. 233, 2nd Dist., 3rd Sect., also
Lot 339, 15 Dist., 2nd Sec. (Affidavit says Burke county in reference to 72nd Dist.)
Signed: JOHN ROGERS. Sworn to 6 June 1843, SIMEON BELL, J.P.
                        GEORGIA, BURKE COUNTY : Know all men by
these presents that I, JOHN ROGERS of county and state afsd.
have appt'd and hereby authorise EDMOND B. GRESHAM of Co. and
State afsd. to take out for me the grants for the tracts and Lots
of land as specified in annexed affidavit.
Dated: 6 June 1843, SIMEON BELL, J.P. Signed: JOHN ROGERS (L.S.)

TWIGGS COUNTY: In person appeared before me GREEN ALLEN
who being duly sworn says on oath that he
is the lawful owner of the undivided half lot of land #86 in the
12th Dist., 5th Sec. now Carroll county drawn by the orphans of
WILLIAM ALLEN of said county and that he is the only one of the
heirs now living and that he is now over 21 years of age.
Signed: GREEN (his mark) ALLEN. Sworn to June 7, 1843, PEYTON
REYNOLDS, J.I.C.
            TWIGGS COUNTY,....GREEN ALLEN of said county appoints ELIJAH E. CROCKER of said state his true and lawful
attorney in fact to take _____ for the plat and grant of land
No. 80 in 12th Dist. & 5th Sect. now Carroll County drawn by the
orphans of WILLIAM ALLEN of sd. county of Twiggs.
Signed: GREEN (X) ALLEN (L.S.) In presence of PEYTON REYNOLDS,
J.I.C........June 7, 1843 ELIJAH E. CROCKER acknowledges he is
lawful attorney for GREEN ALLEN.

BURKE COUNTY: Personally appeared before me GEORGE W.
EVANS a Justice of the Inferior Court of
said county and state, Mrs. MARTHA LEQUEUX who upon oath says
that she is the widow of PETER LEQUEUX late of said county and
state and that her said late husband drew lands in the lotteries
of this state and that said lands do belong to her and she the
said MARTHA LEQUEUX prays that all ungranted lands drawn by her
late husband on what was originally Carroll county may be granted
to her.
Signed: MARTHA LEQUEUX. Sworn, Subscribed & Erased before me
this 5 June 1843, GEO. W. EVANS, J.I.C.B.C., W. W. HUGHES, J.I.
C.B.C.
            BURKE COUNTY: MARTHA LEQUEUX of state
and county afsd. constitutes WM. C. POWELL her true and lawful
attorney to take out grant of land drawn by PETER LEQUEUX.
Dated: June 5, 1843, W. W. Hughes, J.I.C.B.C.; GEO. W. EVANS,
J.I.C.B.C. MARTHA LEQUEUX.

COLUMBIA COUNTY: Be it known that I have this day appointed
SHADRACK A. GIBSON of county afsd. my
true and lawful Attorney as Executor to the Last Will of WALTER
JONES, dec'd. to apply for me and take out of office the Grant
for Lot #575, and to do all such matters and things touching the
premises as I could do.
Signed: ISAAC W. JONES (L.S.)   (cont'd next page)

Sworn to June 7, 1843. H. W. GERALD, ED. BALLARD, J.I.C.

COLUMBIA COUNTY: ISAAC W. JONES makes affidavit he is Executor of Last Will of WALTER JONES, dec'd and is true owner of Lot #575 - 12- 1.
Dated: June 7, 1843

CLARK COUNTY: Personally appeared before me JOHN JOINER of said county and being duly sworn saith that he is the owner of one undivided half of 2 lots of land drawn by FRIDERICK TILLARS orphans, he having married one of the orphans who own said lots of land....the same being #803 in 17th Dist., 2nd Sect. & #254 in 5th Dist. & 2nd Sect., as he is informed and believing that he claims and is the owner of one undivided half of whatever lot or lots of land were drawn by said orphans, and that he applies for the grants to said lots of land or any that said orphans may have drawn.
Signed: JOHN (X) JOINER. Sworn to June 9, 1843 before M. C. GREER, JOHN G. FERGERSON and WILLIAM NABERS, J.P.

CLARK COUNTY: JOHN JOINER of said county appointed CHARLES DAUGHARTY and JAMES CAMACK of sd. county his lawful attorneys to apply and take out grants of said land of orphans of FREDERICK TILLARS.
Signed: JOHN (X) JOINER, June 9, 1843 before J. M. C. GREER, JOHN G. FERGERSON and WILLIAM NABERS, J.P.

MORGAN COUNTY: Personally appeared before me JOHN J. WALKER a Justice of the Peace for said county....WILLIAM H. WILSON who being duly sworn saith that Lot of Land #157 in 25th Dist. & 1st Sect., formerly Lee county....was drawn by the orphans of THOMAS STOVALL of Decalb county....and that by intermarriage with one of said orphans has become, and is now the owner of said land in part.
Sworn and subscribed before JOHN J. WALKER, June 10, 1843.
Signed: WILLIAM H. WILSON

TALBOT COUNTY: Before me in person came JAMES JOHNSTON who being duly sworn saith that he is one of the legal heirs of JOHN JOHNSTON, dec'd. who drew a lot of land in Dooly county (Lot #115, 10 ____ and District no recalled) that JOHN JOHNSTON lived in Coopers or Vinenns Dist. of Putnam county at the time of giving in for a draw.
Signed: JAMES JOHNSTON. Sworn June 10, 1843. C. H. McCALL, J.P.

TALBOT COUNTY: A. G. PERRYMAN is hereby authorised to take out a grant for Lot. No. ___ in the ___ Dist. of Dooly co. for the heirs of JOHN JOHNSTON, dec'd.
Signed: JAMES JOHNSTON (L.S.)
Test.: C. H. McCALL, J. P. and ALEX JOHNSTON.

TWIGGS COUNTY: Personally came before me NANCY GANDY and after being duly sworn deposeth and sayeth on her oath that she is the widow of GRIFFIN GANDY (deceased) and that he drew Lot #46 in 21st Dist. of Lee county and that she now applyeth for the Plat and Grant of said lot for No other purpose but her own benefit and use.
Signed: NANCY (X) GANDY. Sworn to June 12, 1843, before ABISHA ANDREWS, J.P. (Note underneath: GRIFFIN GANDY PEARSON Twiggs. 46 -)

OGLETHORPE COUNTY: Personally appeared before me SUSAN ARNOLD THOS. R. ARNOLD, JOHN T. ARNOLD and MOSES ARNOLD who being duly sworn say that they are the proper owners of Lot #743 in 72nd Dist. and 1st Sect. in county of (originally Cherokee) the grant of which is applied for by them under the Provisions of an Act. of Dec. 28, 1842. Sworn to June 12, 1843 before MOSES WRIGHT, J.P.
Signed: SUSAN (X) ARNOLD, THOMAS R. ARNOLD, JOHN T. (X) ARNOLD, MOSES (X) ARNOLD.
OGLETHORPE COUNTY: JOSEPH H. ECHOLS has appt'd lawful attorney to apply for and take out Grant for Lot 743 in 12th Dist. of 10th Sect. in county (originally Cherokee). Sworn June 12, 1843.
Wit.: _____ COBB, MOSES WRIGHT, J.P. (Signed as above by the heirs.)

WARREN COUNTY: Personally came before me WILLIAM FOWLER, Esqr. who being duly sworn on oath, deposeth and saith that he is one of the lawful heirs of ZAPHANIAH FOWLER, late of Warren county, dec'd, and that he is by the Will of said dec'd, left Executor and that the Will of said dec'd has not been proven, neither can it by law be proven and admitted to Record so that this deponent cannot be qualified as Executor before the time appearing for the taking out grants under the late laws for taking out grants in all the Late Lotteries and deponent further swearing that the said ZAPHANIAH FOWLER, dec'd was the

drawer of Lot of Land No. 59 in 16th Dist., Dooly county and that said dec'd died in possession of the said lot of land, so far as rights concerning it except obtaining the grant. Sworn to June 16, 1843 before ADAM JONES, J.I.C.
Signed: WILLIAM FOWLER.

WARREN COUNTY: JESSE M. ROBERTS of said county appointed as lawful attorney to take out grant for Lot 59 in 16th Dist. Dooly co. drawn by ZEPHANIAH FOWLER, late of Warren county, dec'd.
Signed: 16 June 1843, WILLIAM FOWLER (L.S.)

CHATHAM COUNTY: Before me personally appeared ELIZABETH S. SHICK, JANE C. CLINE and AGNES CLINE, orphans of JONATHAN CLINE, who being duly sworn deposeth and saith that they are the drawers and proper owners of Lot. #135 in 20th Dist. and 2nd Sect. in Land Lottery of 1827, the grant for which they apply for under provisions of Act of Dec. 28, 1842. Sworn 16 June 1843, ISAAC RUSSELL, J.P.
Signed: ELIZABETH S. SHICK, JANE C. CLINE, AGNES CLINE

RICHMOND COUNTY: Personally appeared before me MARY BOLAN who being duly sworn says that she and her son MICHAEL I. BOLAN, widow & only child of RICHARD BOLAN, dec'd. are the lawful owners of Lot #199 in the 13th Dist. of Dooly county in said state drawn by RICHARD BOLAN....and that the said son for whom she is guardian is an infant. Sworn 17 June 1843 bef. A. J. MILLER, N.P.
Signed: MARY (+) BOLAN

PUTNAM COUNTY: Personally appeared before me a J.P. for and in said County, Mrs. VIRGINIA CAMPBELL of said county who on oath says she is the widow....legal representative of GRIFFITH CAMPBELL, dec'd. who drew gold lot #117-4-1, Lumpkin county and land lot 292 - 28 in   Sect.   County formerly Cherokee. Sworn 17 June 1843.   Bef. FRANCIS S. HEARN, J.P.
Signed: VIRGINIA CAMPBELL

PUTNAM COUNTY: Power of Attorney given by VIRGINIA CAMPBELL to THOMAS D. SPEER to take out Plat and Grant for God lot above described. Sealed: 17 June 1843 bef. BRONSON TROTTER and FRANCIS S. HEARN, J.P.

FAYETTE COUNTY: Before me G. C. KING a J.P. in and for sd. county, personally came WILLIAM MILES, Ex'r. of the estate of AARON TILMAN, dec'd. and after being duly sworn deposeth & sayeth that AARON TILMAN, dec'd. drew Lots of land to Wit: #255 in 16th Dist. & 1st Sect. and Lot #808 in 2nd Dist. & 3rd Sect. of the Cherokee County and that said lots is now the property of the said AARON TILMANS ESTATE and that he applys for the Grant as Exec. of sd. Est. under Act Dec. 28, 1843. ......list of drawing in sd. Lottery to be drawn by AARON S. TILLMAN SHOULD BE AARON TILMAN as there has never been such a man living in Lamberths Dist. of Fayette County which was the Dist. and county that AARON TILMAN gave in and as this deponent believes is a mistake the clerkes of said Lottery or the printer of the List of the said Lottery. Sworn to 21 June 1843 before G. C. KING, J.P.
Signed: WM. MILES, Exec.

RICHMOND COUNTY: Personally appeared before me Mrs. GENEVIVE R. SAFITTE, who being duly sworn says she is the widow of the late JAMES B. SAFITTE who died possessed of Lot #181 in the 10th Dist. of Dooly county and that she is the owner or part owner of said lot the Grant of which is applied for under the provision of Act of Dec. 28, 1842.
Signed: GINEVIVE R. SAFITTE.
Sworn to 24 June 1843.   BENJ. HALL, J.P.
            RICHMOND COUNTY: Be it known that I.... GENEVIVE R. SAFITTE have this day appt'd WILLIAM H. PRITCHARD of the County of Baldwin my lawful attorney...to apply for and take out....Grant for Lot No. 181 in 10th Dist. of Dooly county.
Signed: GENEVIEVE R. SAFITTE   Dated: 24 June 1843, BENJAMIN HALL, J.P.

TALBOT COUNTY: Personally appeared before me GEORGE W. TOWNS who after being sworn says that he as Exor. of last will and testament of JOHN TOWNS, dec'd., late of Heard County is the proper owner of the lot of land drawn by sd. JOHN TOWNS, dec'd. in the_____District_____Section of Carroll, number not known by me (inserted was 39 - 8 Carroll). Said JOHN TOWNS gave in Monroe county as a Revolutionary Soldier the grant for which is applied for by him under Provisions of Act of Dec. 28, 1842.
Signed: GEORGE W. TOWNS. Dated June 24, 1843, JOSEPH JACKSON, JP

TOWNS (cont'd):   TALBOT COUNTY: Know all men by these presents that I, GEORGE W. B. TOWNS as Exor. of Last Will & Testament of JOHN TOWNS deceased of Heard county have appointed MARION BETHUNE of this County of Talbot my lawful agent....and to apply for Grant ....under Prov. of Act, Dec. 28, 1842.
Signed: GEORGE W. TOWNS.   Dated: 24 June 1843, before us, ... JAMES L. STEPHENSON and JOSEPH J. JACKSON, J.P.

RICHMOND COUNTY: Personally appeared before me WILLIAM G. LARK who being duly sworn says that he is the husband of MILDRED ANN LARK (formerly MILDRED ANN DILLON), daughter of WILLIAM C. DILLON, late of said county, dec'd who in his lifetime was the proper owner of Lot No. 930 in 18th Dist., 2nd Sect. of originally Cherokee county, the Grant which is applied for by him under Prov. of Act 28 Dec. 1842.
Signed: W. G. LARK   Sworn to 27 June 1843, BENJAMIN B. RUPELL, N.P., Rich. Co.

RICHMOND COUNTY: Be it known that I, WILLIAM G. LARK have this day appt'd WILLIAM H. PRITCHARD of Baldwin County my lawful Att'y to....for the Grant for Lot #930 in 2nd Sect. of 11th Dist. in County, originally Cherokee.
Signed: W. G. LARK   Dated: 27 June 1843, BENJAMIN B. RUPELL, N.P., Richmond County.

MORGAN COUNTY: Personally appeared before me ALLEN WEATHERS who being duly sworn deposeth and saith that he is the proper owner of Lot #93, First Dist. and 1st Sect. of County of Forsythe and that he is the owner of same by intermarriage with one of the orphans of DANIEL TAYLER, dec'd. and dated 27 June 1843.
Signed: ALLEN WEATHERS.   JOHN J. WALKER, J. P.

RICHMOND COUNTY: Personally appeared before me JOHN TAYLOR, one of the orphans of JOHN TAYLOR, formerly of Dunns District in Elbert County, this deponent being now of age do solemnly swear that he is duly authorised to make application for the Grant of tract of Land drawn to the same of same orphans, which Lot is known and designated as Lot 53, 12th Dist, 1st Section, originally Lee County.....also he swears that as the orphan of JOHN TAYLOR he now makes application for the Grant of the tract of land drawn to his name as an orphan at the time of giving in his name in Wilkes County, Georgia, which Tract of

land originally Cherokee and known as 1st, 4th Dist., 273....
Signed: JOHN (his x mark) TAYLOR.   Dated: 24 June 1843, J. W. MEREDITH, J.P.

RICHMOND COUNTY: Know all men by these presents that I, JOHN TAYLOR in behalf of himself and as one of the orphans of JOHN TAYLOR formerly of Elbert County for them and myself do hereby authorize and empower WILLIAM H. PRITCHARD now of Baldwin County my lawful Att'y to take out Grants for the Lots of Land described in above affidavit.
Signed: JOHN (X) TAYLOR   J. W. MEREDITH, J.P.

RICHMOND COUNTY: Personally appeared before me now a Notary Public for county afsd., ANN McKINNE who being duly sworn saith that she is the Administrix on the Estate of her dec'd husband, BARNA McKINNE and is the proper owner of a lot of land lying in Cherokee County, No. 440, Dist. 2, Sect. 2, County and also a lot of land lying in Cherokee No. 356, 21 Dist. 2nd Sect., County of _____, the application for grant of land is now much made under the Act of the Gen. Assembly posted 28 Dec. 1842 and deponent is Admnx. as aforesaid of Estate of the BARNA McKINNE.
Signed: ANN McKINNE   Dated: 28 June 1843, WILLIAM R. McL__ ___(illegible), N.P., Richmond Co.

TO: Mr. WILLIAM H. PRITCHARD....I send you the application of my Mother as Admnx. on the Estate of BARNA McKINNE for Grant of 2 Lots of land as described above also and on the opposite page drawn by my brother and myself of which I am sole owner. You will confer a very great favor on me by granting them and holding the Plats until I visit Milledgeville next week, when I will then take up and pay you any consideration you may owe Mr. PARK of your plans to purchase #444-2-2 drawn by B. M. McKINNE, and if I should not possibly see you in the course of next week or you shall not hear from me, of course you can make the money out of that over and doing this you will confer a great favor on Your Obb. Serv't.   Signed: JNO. McKINNE, JR.

RICHMOND COUNTY: Personally appeared before me THADDEUS S. STORY who being duly sworn that he is the Administrator on the Estate of ABIGAIL STORY, dec'd., late of Richmond County who was the proper owner of Lot #515 in 16th Dist. 2nd Sect. of originally Cherokee County....the Grant for which is now applied.

Signed: THAD. S. STORY (L.S.)   Dated: 29 June 1843, GEORGE W. SUMMERS, N.P.

BIBB COUNTY: Personally appeared before me ANN G. SANDERS, widow of the late DENIS D. SANDERS who being duly sworn sayeth on oath that she is the proper owner of Lott No. 482, 12th Dist., Sect. 1, Cherokee Purchase and drawn by said DENIS D. SANDERS, which Plat and Grant is now applied for by me.
Signed: ANN G. SANDERS.   Dated: 29 June 1843, W. H. BRANTLY, J.I.C.

COWETA COUNTY: Personally appeared before me (ALZOR - illegible) YOUNG acting Justice of the Peace for said County and State, YOUNG W. RAY who being duly sworn deposeth and saith on oath that a certain Lot or Tract of land ... known and distinguished as Lot #1149 in 12th Dist. of 1st Sect. formerly Cherokee, now Lumpkin County is the property and of right belongs to DEMPSEY I. RAY, the brother of this deponent who is absent from the State and further saith on oath that he the said YOUNG W. RAY is acting agent for his brother.
Signed: YOUNG W. RAY   Dated: 4 July 1844, A(illegible)YOUNG, J.P.

TALBOT COUNTY: Personally appeared before me RICH'D HOLT a Justice of the Peace of the 757th Dist. and M. BARTLEY McCRARY who being duly sworn says that he on$\underline{z}$ half of Lot of Land No. 155 in the 12th Dist. of Muscogee, now Marion County, drawn by ELIZABETH JENKINS Illegitimates, Hall Dist., Wilkinson County and A. McCANTZ owns the other half and they have a Bonifide title to said Lot.
Signed: BARTLEY McCRARY.   Dated: 1 June 1848, RICH'd HOLT, J.P.

MORGAN COUNTY: Personally appeared before me MILTON C. TURMAN one of the orphans of MARTIN TURMAN, dec'd. who being duly sworn saith on oath that him with G. A. & NANCY W. TURMAN were the bonifide drawers of Lot of Land No. 502 in the 16th Dist., 2nd Sect., lying in Cobb County and sd. State' and that they are the owners of said Lot and has not sold or disposed of the same to any person whatsoever.
Signed: MILTON C. TURMAN.   Dated: 6 Dec. 1849, WILLIAM B. ARNOLD.

TALBOT COUNTY: Personally appeared before me JOHN P. RILEY and being duly sworn saith in the year 1839 he purchased fraction No. 188 in 10th Dist. of Muscogee co. of one HENRY L. DENSTER....and that he has peaceable and continuous possession of it from that time up to the present day...... that the certificate of sd. fraction never has been in the possession of this deponent......that....that....deponent has searched all places and made enquiries of all persons who and ..he had any reason to believe he could find or procure it...that entertaining a belief he could find the Cert. in the possession of one ANDREW B. GRIFFIN, this deponent not long since went to the residence of sd. GRIFFIN in the State of Alabama to procure the same of him or to procure such information respecting it has he could obtain from sd. GRIFFIN...and sd. GRIFFIN then and there informed the deponent that he did not have the Cert.....that it once had been in his possession....& that it was either lost or destroyed or was consumed by fire at the burning of the Court House in Muscogee County, and that the said Griffin there and then gave this deponent his affidavit in writing stating therein the loss or destruction of sd. Cert. as afsd. which affidavit this deponent has either lost or mislain.
Signed: JOHN P. RILEY   Dated: April 30, 1850, JOHN C. MOUND, J.P.

MUSCOGEE COUNTY: Bef. me ROBERT W. CARNES J.P. for sd. County, came JOHN P. RILEY, who being sworn, saith there was a mistake made in his the within affidavit with regard to the No. of the Dist.....it should be Fraction #188 in the 10th Dist. of said county, and that he hereby attests & corrects same.
Signed: JOHN P. RILEY   Dated: June 8, 1850.   ROBERT W. CARNES, J.P.

WARREN COUNTY: Personally appeared before me CHARLES COLSTON who being duly sworn says that in with ELIZA HOLDER are the proper owners of Lot 1225 in 2nd Dist. of 2nd Sect. of Cherokee, drawn by the orphans of WILLIAM HOLDER the grant which is applied for by him under Act of Dec. 28, 1842.
Signed: CHARLES H. COLSTON   Dated: June 28, 1843, STODDARD W. SMITH, J.P.

RICHMOND COUNTY: Personally appeared before me SAMPSON McCARTY one of the orphans of MICHAEL J. McCARTY formerly of Jefferson County but now of Richmond County

who being duly sworn saith that as the authorised agent of sd. orphans he now makes application for the tract drawn to the name of MICHAEL J. McCARTY orphans, Ross Dist. and known as N. 11,4,5, originally Carroll....and the deponent further says that as one of the orphans of sd. McCarty & duly authorised he is duly authroised and has made application for the Grant for the tract drawn to McCartys (3) orphans, drawn to their names in the 123rd Dist. Richmond County, which Lot is known as N.114...21 Dist., 2nd Sect., originally Cherokee County.
Signed: SAMPSON McCARTY
Dated: June 10, 1843, JOHN SHLY, Judge, Superior Court, Middle Dist., Georgia.

MORGAN COUNTY: Personally appeared ADAM G. SAFFOLD being duly sworn before me JOHN S. WALKER, Justice of the Peace of said county, Deponeth and said that on Apr. 29, 1835 he sold to DANIEL A. MOBLEY fraction #136 in 4th Dist. of Walton County and gave to said Mobley his deponent's obligation to turn over the certificate for said fraction to said Mobley when the purchase money has been paid and application made for the certificate.....and this deponent has made expected search for the certificate without being able to find it and believe that it has been torn or destroyed by time.
Dated: November 2, 1839 Sworn to before ADAM G. SAFFOLD

RICHMOND COUNTY: Personally appeared before me WILLIAM S. PORTER who being sworn, saith that the Lot of land drawn to the name of SYLVESTOER PORTER.....Richmond County and lying and being at the time of the drawing is the 12th Irwin, No. 118....is the property of this deponant and his brother EDWIN R. PORTER who is now absent and he verily believes cannot be heard from in time to comply with the act of the last Legislature .....extending the time for taking out Tracts to the 1 Sept. 1841 .....the grant now applied for is the joint property of this deponant and the sd. EDWARD R. PORTER....who as the sole heirs of sd. SYLVESTER PORTER, now dec'd. and is taken out for our mutual benefit.
Signed: WM. S. PORTER   Sworn before me Aug. 25, 1841, J. M. MEREDITH, J.P.

MONROE COUNTY: Personally appeared bef. me LUCRETIA SHARP wid. of the 4_7th Dist., Commanded by J.M.

(illeg. but looks like MAIENE or MEUENE) Capt....and saith that
she is proper owner and drawer of Lot No. 834 in 3rd Dist. and
4th Sect. of Cherokee purchase.
Signed: LUCRETIA (X) SHARP
Sworn to bef. WILLIAM J. HEAD, J.P., 15 June 1843
                    MONROE COUNTY: LUCRETIA SHARP appoints
LITTLE JOHNSTON of Co. and State afsd. her lawful attorney to apply for the grant.
Wit.:   JAMES PONDER, WILLIAM HEAD, J.P.

JACKSON COUNTY: Personally appeared before me JONATHAN
                       BETTS who being duly sworn he is proper
owner of Lot No. 740 in 3rd Dist. of 4th Sect. of Paulding co.,
originally Cherokee, drawn by SION HILL of Walton county..grant
applied for under Act of Dec. 28, 1842.
Sworn to 31 May 1843 before JOHN G. HOUSE, J.P.
Signed: JONATHAN BETTS
                    JACKSON COUNTY: ....on May 31, 1843,
ROBERT MOON of Jackson co. appt'd lawful attorney for JONATHAN
BETTS to apply for grant.
Wit.:   JOHN (X) O'SHIELDS, JOHN G. HOUSE, J.P.

NEWTON COUNTY: Before me COLUMBUS D. PACE a J.P. of the
                       county came THOMAS NELMS of the same
place....and said that Gold Lot No. 982 in the 3rd Dist., 4th
Sect. is owned by the Estate of SIMEON S. WORRILL, dec'd, and
that no person has administered on sd. Estate and that I am a
Judgement Creditor of sd. Estate and makes application for the
grant as a Judgement Creditor.
Sworn to 19 June 1843.   THOMAS NELMS

DOOLY COUNTY: Personally appeared before me OLIVER H.
                       ROWELL...who says that he is the legal
heir of JOAB T. & RICHARD ROWELL, and that he is the legal heir
of lots of land No.'s 162,965 in the 2nd Dist., 4th Sect.,drawn
by JOAB T. ROWELL of Petersons Dist., Burke County..and no. 12,
26th Dist., 2nd Sect. drawn by RICHARD ROWELL of 516 th. Dooly
County.
Signed: OLIVER H. ROWELL
Sworn to 14 June 1843 before WILLIAM C. GREER, J.P. On 14 June
1843 OLIVER H. ROWELL appt's ALFRED M. HORTON of Baldwin co. his
lawful attorney to apply for grant.

CHATHAM COUNTY: Personally appeared before me WILLIAM H.
                           KELLEY....who says he is proper owner of
Lot No. 1244 in 3rd Dist., 2nd Sect. in Gold Lottery and Lot No.
408 in 2d Dist., 4th Sect. Gold Lottery, and that he is agent of
the owner of Lot No. 87 in 27th Dist., 2nd Sect. Cherokee County
and Lot No. 933 in 4th Dist., 1st Sect.   County - (the 2 former drawn in the name of MARY A. KELLEY, widow).
Signed: WM. H. KELLEY, before ____ RAIFORD, J.P.   WILLIAM H.
KELLEY appt's ISAAC NEWELL of Baldwin co. his lawful attorney to
apply for grants on 6 June 1843.

HABERSHAM COUNTY: Personally appeared before me an acting
                           J.P. for said county, PHILLIP HUDGINS who
being duly sworn saith on oath that lots No. 77-5-1 drew by deponent 290-2-4 drew by ABSALOM WILLIAMS of co. afsd. and No. 232-
6-1 drew by JAMES HUDGINS also of co. afsd. is deponents own property.
Signed: PHILLIP HUDGINS, before LOVEN J. KEEL, J.P. 4 Sept.1844
On 4 Sept. 1844, PHILLIP HUDGINS appt's W. H. MITCHELL of Baldwin co. his lawful attorney to apply for grants.
Wit.: BENJ. CLEVELAND, LOVEN J. KEEL, J.P.

BALDWIN COUNTY: Personally appeared before me JAMES M. BUL-
                           LARD who being duly sworn says that he is
the Administrator on the Estate of ANDREW JOHNSON, dec'd, who was
the proper owner of lots No. 248, 2nd Dist., 4th Sect., 295, 5th
Dist., 1st Sect., 323, 17th Dist., 2nd Sect. of originally Cherokee. Sworn to 26 June 1843 before R. MICKLEJOHN. J.P.
Signed: JAMES M. BULLARD

RICHMOND COUNTY: Know all men by these presents that I.
                           ROBERT D. GLOVER of Co. and state afsd.,
appoint HENRY F. YOUNG of Baldwin co. my lawful attorney.....to
cause to be granted a certain tract situate in 2nd Dist., 4th
Sect. of Cherokee county by the No. of 145, and drawn by MARTHA
A. COOMBS, orphan of Rich. co. and now my wife. 28 April 1843
before DAVIS BOTTOM, C. DICKINSON.
Signed: ROBERT D. GLOVER

FORSYTH COUNTY: Before me B. J. RICE a J.P. for said co.,
                           personally came OBEDIAH LIGHT who being
duly sworn...that he is proper agent appt'd the heirs of JOHN

MOOR, dec'd, to Grant Lot No. 4 in 27th Dist. of 3rd Sect. of originally Cherokee, now Walker county.
Dated: 29 May 1843
Signed: OBADIAH (X) LIGHT   On May 29, 1843 OBADIAH LIGHT appt'd RAYMON SANFORD of Hall county his lawful agent to apply for said grant in presence of JOSEPH MARTIN and B. J. RICE, J.P.

CHATHAM COUNTY: Personally appeared before me MARY GRIFFITH who being duly sworn says she is the proper owner of Lot 137 in 4th Dist., 4th Sect. of Cherokee co.
Signed: MARY GRIFFITH
Dated: 23 June 1843 before ____ RAIFORD, J.P. On same date, MARY GRIFFITH appt'd JOHN G. PARK, Esq., her lawful attorney to apply for grant.

BIBB COUNTY: Know all men by these presents that I, JAMES GATES, SR. do hereby app't JAMES GATES, JR. of County of Bibb and state afsd. my lawful attorney to take out grants of following lots lying in Cherokee Purchase. 2nd Dist. and 4th Sect., Lot No. 413...also Lot No. 132 lying in 17th Dist., 3rd Sect.
Signed: JAMES GATES, SENR.
Dated: 17 June 1843 before LUIS VALENT(INO or URO), MILES N. YOUNG, J.P.

BRYAN COUNTY: No. 13, 2nd Dist., 4th Sect. Personally appeared before me JAMES SHUMAN an acting J.P. for county afsd., A. J. BUTLER who being duly sworn says that the grant to above lot is made as Bonafide owner in communion with JOHN BUTLER for sd. lot.
Signed: A. J. BUTLER
Sworn to 3 Dec. 1853 before JAMES SHUMAN, J.P.

TALBOT COUNTY: Personally appeared before me JOHN H. WALLACE, a J.P. for said county, DOLLY WALLACE who being sworn says she is lawful owner of Lot No. 244 in 2nd Dist., and 4th Sect....Sworn to 11 March 1843 bef. JOHN H. WALLACE J.P.
Signed: DOLLY (X) WALLACE   On March 11, 1843 DOLLY WALLACE appt'd BENJAMIN R. SCEARCEY of Talbot co. her lawful attorney to apply for sd. grant.
Wit.: TURNER M. WALLACE, JOHN H. WALLACE, J.P.

DOOLY COUNTY: Personally appeared before me MILLS ROUN-
                        TREE who being sworn says he is a* legal
heir (*should be the) of ARTHUR ROUNDTREE and that he is the own-
er of lot No. 6 in 3rd Dist. and 4th Sect. the grant for which
is applied for by his attorney in fact.
Signed: MILLS (X) ROUNTREE.
Dated: 14 June 1843. On same date MILLS ROUNTREE appt'd ALFRED
M. HORTON of Baldwin co. to apply for sd. grant in Cherokee co.
Wit.: THOS. H. KEY, WILLIAM C. GREER, J.P.

JEFFERSON COUNTY: Personally appeared before me LEMON RUFF
                        one of the distributees of the Estate of
WILLIAM ROLLINS, dec'd of Burke County, Georgia, whose estate is
unadministered and who is the owner of lot No. 91-3-4....and Lot
No. 186-17-4 Dist. of Cherokee county.
Signed: LEMON RUFF
Dated: June 26, 1843 before THOMAS W. BATTEY, J.I.C.   On same
date LEMON RUFF appt'd BENNETT CROFTON of Jefferson county his
lawful attorney to apply for grant.
Wit.: EBENEZER BOTHWELL, THOMAS W. BATTEY, J.I.C.

PULASKI COUNTY: Personally appeared before me MATTHEW
                        GRACE one of the Justices of the Peace in
and for said county, J. B. TROY JOHNSON who being sworn saith he
is one of the heirs in right of his wife to lot of land No. 101-
3-4 drawn by orphans of AMOS WINGATE, Dilmans Dist., Pulaski co.
and further saith he is granted the land as one of the heirs &
as a friend to the other heirs & for their benefit and use.
Signed: J. B. TROY JOHNSON (his x mark).
Wit.: MATTHEW GRACE, J.P.

HARRIS COUNTY: Personally appeared before me WM. DAVEN-
                        PORT, Justice of the Inferior Court THOMAS
CUMMINGS who saith he is one of the bonafide owners of a Gold Lot
No. 238 in part in 3rd Dist., 4th Sect. of Floyd county. He the
said CUMMINGS became owner in part....by being one of the Lega-
tees of GIDEON CUMMING, dec'd of _____ County.
Sworn to 16 Nov. 1850.
Signed: THOMAS CUMMINGS.
Wit.: WM. DAVENPORT (Written underneath is "Gideon Cummins orps.
Griffins Dist., Fayette co.").

HANCOCK COUNTY: I do certify that I am the owner of Lot of
                       land No. 258, 3rd Dist., and 4th Sect.....
originally Cherokee which was drawn by BENJAMIN WILSON of Han-
cock co.
Sworn to 26 June 1843.
Signed: WM. L. WILSON.   Same date WILLIAM L. WILSON appt's JAS.
D. SMITH his lawful attorney to take out grant of land.
Wit.: WM. RACHEL.

THOMAS COUNTY: Know all men by these presents that I.
                       JOHN L. Mac INTYRE in my individual capa-
city and as executor deson tort of HANNAH Mac INTYRE, dec'd,(the
said HANNAH MacINTYRE dying intestate and no administration having been had upon her estate and the said JOHN MacINTYRE being
one of the heirs) of the Co. and state afsd. for divers good
causes and considerations...do app't CHARLES A. NELSON of Baldwin co. my true and lawful attorney....to grant a certain parcel
of land being originally in Cherokee county known as Lot No. 1002
in 2nd Dist. and 4th Sect. of the Gold Lottery and also for me
and in my name as Exec. de son tort and for proper use and benefit of the heirs of afsd. estate in originally county of Cherokee known as Lot No. 266 in 3rd Dist. and 4th Sect. of Gold Lottery. Dated 10 June 1843 bef. (illegible but looks like MO.
MILL, J.I.C.)
Signed: JOHN L. MacINTYRE
                       THOMAS COUNTY: On another separate sheet
is sworn statement of JOHN NUTT (the name that was illegible a-
bove) Justice of Inf. Crt. that JOHN L. MacINTYRE appeared before
him claiming ownership of above tracts of land and dated 10 June
1843.

FRANKLIN COUNTY: Personally appeared before me MARION T.F.
                       CAPE...being duly sworn says he is proper
owner of No. 16 in 2nd Dist., 2nd Sect. of originally Cherokee
co. drawn by JOHN SHERIDEN the grant for which is applied for by
heirs under act of Dec. 28, 1842.
Signed: T. F. M. CAPE   On 30 May 1843 T. F. M. CAPE appt'd
THOMAS KING of same county his lawful attorney to apply for the
above grant.

WARREN COUNTY: Know all men by these presents that I,
                       TAMSY MARTIN (widow of JOHN (S. or L.,

19

hard to read) MARTIN...do app't ADAM JONES of same state and co. my true and lawful attorney to take out a grant to a gold lot drawn by my husband JOHN (S? - L?) MARTIN in his lifetime, drew supposed to be lot No. 1204 in 2nd Dist. and 4th Sect. originally Cherokee.
Signed: TAMSY (X) MARTIN.
Dated: 13 June 1843 before JAMES BRADDY, J.P.

BALDWIN COUNTY: Personally came before me JACOB WITT who being duly sworn says he is the Adm'r of MARTIN WITT who is proper owner of Lot No. 1234, 2nd Dist., 4th Sect., No. 123-27, 2nd Sect. of orig. Cherokee co.
Sworn to 27 June 1843 before ALFRED M. HORTON, J.P.
Signed: JACOB WITT

CHATHAM COUNTY: Personally appeared before me LEONIDAS WYLLY, J.P., THOMAS GREEN who being duly sworn says he is lawful guardian of the orphans of JOHN GREEN, late of screven county, state afsd....and sd. orphans are proper owners of Lot No. 883 in 2nd Dist., 4th Sect., Cherokee (Gold)
Dated: 14 June 1843
Signed: THOS. GREEN. On same date THOMAS GREEN appt's ASA HALL of City of Savannah his lawful Att'y. to take out above grant.

JONES COUNTY: Personally came before me WILLIAM MARSHALL who being duly sworn saith he is lawful Gdn. for HENRY ONEAL, orphan of this county, and sd. orphan drew Lot No. 865 in 2nd Dist., 4th Sect. of late Cherokee purchase.
Dated: 20 June 1843 before ALEXANDER ODEN. J.P.
Signed: WILLIAM MARSHALL

LINCOLN COUNTY: Personally appeared before me WM. HARPER, JUNR. and being duly sworn sayeth he is one of the proper owners of Lot No. 791, 2nd Dist., 4th Sect.... drawn by WM. HARPER, SENR. of the above county and that he is legally authorised by the balance of the Legatees of the sd. WM. HARPER, SENR., dec'd to apply for sd. grant.
Signed: GEORGE HARPER
Wit.: 24 June 1843 THOMAS PSALMONDS, J.P. On 24 June 1843 he appoints JOHN R. ANDERSON of Baldwin co. his lawful attorney to secure the above grant in Paulding county.

MERIWETHER COUNTY: Personally appeared before me ADAM RAG-
                       LAND an acting J.P. for sd. co. MILTON
CLAYTON who being duly sworn saith that he is the proper owner
of a certain tract of land in originally Cherokee, No. 664, 2nd
Dist., and 4th Sect.....sd. lot was drawn by myself (MILTON CLAY-
TON) residence, Hillsborough, Jasper county at time of drawing.
Sworn to 3 June 1843 before ADAM RAGLAND, J.P.
Signed: MILTON CLAYTON. On same date he appoints ELISHA TRAM-
MEL his lawful attorney.

MORGAN COUNTY: Personally appeared before me JAMES TAR-
                       ELL he being duly sworn says he is the
proper owner as legal heir with others of Lot 149, 1st Dist.,and
4th Sect. of the County of Palding, the grant of which is applied
for by him as the legal leir and representative of EDY TERRILL
his mother who is dead.
Dated: Dec. 28, 1842.
Signed: JAMES TARRELL, before ELIJAH E. JONES, J.I.C. On 30
June 1843 he appoints DAVID (DEMERST?) his lawful attorney to
take out grant for above lot and also Lot 150, 15th Dist., 1st
Sect. in Lumpkin co. drawn by EDY TERRELL widow and mother who
is dead.

COBB COUNTY: Before me CRAWFORD TUCKER an acting Jus-
                       tice of the Inf. Crt. came WILLIAM BARBER
of sd. co. and being duly sworn saith he applied for grant to
Lot No. 3 in 28th Dist., 3rd Sect. of orig. Cherokee now Walker
county, and that he is bonafide owner of sd. Lot which was drawn
by CHARLES AVERY's orphans of Fayette county.
Signed: WILLIAM BARBER
Sworn to 14 January 1845, CRAWFORD TUCKER, J.I.C.

JACKSON COUNTY: Personally appeared before me RUBIN NASH
                       who being duly sworn saith that he is the
lawful agent for ELIJAH NASH who .....drew the following lots:
(4 lots are named but not county). Sworn to: 15 June 1843 bef.
J. B. NABERS, J.P.
Signed: REUBIN NASH

UPSON COUNTY: Personally appeared before me JAMES H.
                       BLACK a J.P. for sd. co. CARY STRICKLAND
who says he was the lawful agent for MILZY STRICKLAND of State

of Alabama until his death and that sd. MILZY departed this life
about the 5th day of this month intestate....as the deponent has
been informed and that no administrator had been appt'd in Geo.
to administer on his estate and this deponent... and further
this deponent says that said MILZY STRICKLAND drew lots of land
No. 258 in 28th Dist., 3rd Sect. of Cherokee and which is now
applied for.
Dated: 14th June 1843, JAS. H. BLACK, J.P.
Signed: CARY STRICKLAND. On same day CARY STRICKLAND appt's
JAMES W. GREENE of (illegible) County his attorney to apply for
grant.

CHATHAM COUNTY: Personally appeared before me HARRIET M.
COOK (late HARRIET M. SCHRODER) who being
duly sworn says that she drew Lot No. 16, 25th Dist., 3rd Sect.
Cherokee (now Walker) county and she is now the wife of NATHAN-
IEL M. COOKE who now applies for the grant.
Sworn to 1 June 1843 before ____ RAIFORD, J.P.
Signed: HARRIET M. COOKE   On same date she appt's ABRAM B.
FANNIN her lawful attorney.

LEE COUNTY: This is to certify that I, LEMUEL LONG of
co. and state afsd. do constitute and ap-
point DAVID N. JAMES of same co. and state my agent in the co.of
Walker, known and distinguished in the plan of sd. co. by No.297
26th Dist., 3rd Sect. of sd. Lot of land was drawn by the orphans
of STAFFORD LONG of Baker co., Hatton's Dist.
Signed: LEMUEL LONG
Dated: 3 May 1843, A. G. JAMES, J.P.

DE KALB COUNTY: Before me JNO. N. BELLINGER an acting
Justice of the Inf. Crt. in and for said
county, personally app'd REBECCA BALLINGER and being duly sworn
says she is the proper owner of Lot No. 276 in 26th Dist., 3rd
Sect. cont. 160 acres more or less, drawn by sd. REBECCA BALLIN-
GER, widow of DeKalb county the grant for which is applied for.
Dated: 27 June 1843 before JNO. N. BELLINGER, J.I.C.
Signed: REBECCA (X) BALLINGER

WAYNE COUNTY: Personally came before me Mrs. MARY ROOKS
the widow of JOHN ROOKS a Revolutionary
Soldier and declareth...she drew the following lots of land in

Cherokee, viz. No. 275 in 8th Dist., 1st Sect. and also No. 267 in 26th Dist. and 3rd Sect. and at this time she is the proper owner of sd. lots of land.
Dated: 9 June 1843, JOHN BROWN, J.I.C.W.C.
Signed: MARY (X) ROOKS

Attached to this oath was following: B. B. SMITH, Esq., I wish to attend to the business for Mrs. ROOKS and you will confer a favor on me and I will return the same to you should a chance ever happen. Yours with due esteem in haste, HEROD RAULERSON. Address the grants, Mrs. MARY ROOKS, Waynesville, Wayne Co.

DECATUR COUNTY: Know all men by these presents that I, JESSE C. SMITH of sd. Co. have this day ordained and appt'd SPENCER RILEY of Co. of Bibb in sd. State to ask for a grant from the State to DAVID PATES, orphans for Lot No. 238 in 26th Dist., 3rd Sect. of orig. Cherokee, now Walker Co., the sd. land being my bonafide property and the sd. Spencer Riley to rec. the grant as my agent.
Signed: J. C. SMITH
Dated: 9 June 1853

MERIWETHER COUNTY: Personally appeared before me A. L. ANTHONY a J.P. for said county came Mrs. FORTUNE BURKS and being duly sworn saith that Lot No. 236 in 26th Dist., 3rd Sect. of orig. Cherokee acc. to the return was drawn by her and that she is the proper owner of sd. lot.
Sworn to 26 June 1843
Signed: FORTUNE (X) BURKS. (Underneath is written: "FORTUNE BURKS, Widow, Norman's Dist., Wilkes). On above date FORTUNE BURKS appt's JOHN P. ANDERSON of Baldwin co. her lawful attorney to take out a grant. WILEY P. BURKS and A. L. ANTHONY, J.P.

A seperate sheet attached has the following: "Maj. J. P. ANDERSON, Dear Sir...Your letter of the 14th June directed to my brother in Washington was remailed and sent to me My Mother living with me and I have aided my mother in making what I suppose to be the necessary papers and having forwarded them to you...Enclosed you will find $5 for the grant fee. Yours with considerations of high Respect, WILEY P. BURKS."

GREENE COUNTY: Personally came before me DAVID ALLISON, and being duly sworn saith that MARTHA AL-

LISON widow of a Revolutionary Soldier drew a lot of land No. 170 Dist. 26, Sect. 3 and that sd. MARTHA has departed this life without a will or any person administering on her estate and he further saith that he is a Legatee of sd. MARTHA.
Sworn to 18 April 1843, before JAS. W. GODKIN, J.I.C.
Signed: DAVID ALLISON

OGLETHORPE COUNTY: Before me PETER W. HUTCHESON a Justice of the Inf. Crt. personally came LEWELLEN W. LLOYD and JARED G. LLOYD who being duly sworn say that previous to the land and gold lottery of 1832 and at time of taking names for sd. lottery they were Orphans, living in the (404) Dist. in Gwinette co. that their names as each Orphans were given in by their Mother MARY LLOYD and that they drew Lot No. 45 in 26th Dist., 3rd Sect. of Cherokee....that sd. lot has never been gtd. them and they are the bonafide and only owners of sd. lot.
Signed: LEWELLIN W. (X) LLOYD, JARED J. LLOYD.
Sworn to 21 April 1849 before PETER W. HUTCHESON, J.I.C.

CHATTOOGA COUNTY: Personally came before me JAMES A. BARREN an acting J.P. for sd. Co. JOHN MONTGOMERY who being duly sworn says that he is the owner of four fifths of Land No. 39 in 26th Dist., 3rd Sect. org. Cherokee now Walker co. ...said lot having been drawn by ELISHA DELONGS orphans...that he is the owner of four forths of sd. lot of land and that he makes application for the benefit of sd. orphans as well as for himself.
Signed: JOHN MONTGOMERY   Dated: 26 May 1853, JAS. A. BARRON, J.P.

CRAWFORD COUNTY: Before me JOHN HATCHER a J.P. for sd. co. MARY SLAUGHTER who being duly sworn saith she is the rightful and legal owner of a cert. tract of land situate in Co. orig. Cherokee, now Floyd in the 16th Dist., 4th Sec. known as Lot No. 85...and deponent further saith that she claims sd. tract as widow and representative of THOMAS P. SLAUGHTER,.. dec'd, who in his lifetime bought of JOHN FORD drawer of sd. land all his rights and title and interest. Sworn to 8 March 1843 before JOHN HATCHER, J.P.
Signed: MARY (S) SLAUGHTER

BUTTS COUNTY: Personally came before me SETH K. ADAMS a

J.P. for said County CATHARINE BREWER who being duly sworn saith she is the proper owner of Lot No. 65 in 16th Dist., 4th Sect., Cherokee, drawn by JAMES BREWER of the 108th Dist., Hancock co. Sworn to 22 June 1843 before SETH. K. ADAMS, J.P.
Signed: CATHARINE BREWER

On same date CATHARINE BREWER appr'd DAVID J. BAILEY of Baldwin co. her lawful attorney to take out grant.

FLOYD COUNTY: Before me came ROBERT G. FOSTER who being duly sworn saith he is the legal owner as Trustee for PEGGY FOSTER and her children of Lot No. 47 in 3rd Dist., 4th Sect. of orig. Cherokee, now Floyd, drawn by THOMAS PARNELLS orphans of Cobb county.
Sworn to Dec. 3, 1852 before JNO. H. LUMPKIN, J.I.C.
Signed: ROBERT G. FOSTER (Note: This name could be FORTER, as was difficult to distinguish between a lower case R and S.)

RICHMOND COUNTY: Personally appeared before me WILLIAM B. SAVAGE who being duly sworn say that he is the Executor of the Estate of DANIEL SAVAGE whose Orphans are the owners of Lot No. 157, 16th Dist., 4th Sect. of Cherokee, the grant for which is applied for by WILLIAM H. PRICHARD my lawful agent.
Dated 17 June 1843.
Signed: WM. B. SAVAGE

GREENE COUNTY: Personally appeared before me RICHARD J. WILLIS who being duly sworn says that he is the qualified Administrator on the Estate of GEORGE W. WILLIS of Wilks County and that the sd. GEORGE W. WILLIS is the proper owner of Lot No. 161 in 15th Dist. and 4th Sect. of orig. Cherokee. Signed: RICHARD J. WILLIS.
Dated: 6 June 1843, THOMAS STOCKS, J.I.C.

CHATTOOGA COUNTY: (Georgia, Chattoogaville), Personally came before me A. H. RINCHART an acting J.P., JEREMIAH W. HENDERSON one of Orphans of DAVID HENDERSON, dec;d, of sd. state and saith that JEREMIAH W. HENDERSON, ROBERT S. T. HENDERSON, with their sister H. A. T. E. J. BELLE was the orphants of DAVID HENDERSON afsd. and are rightful owners of Lot No. 79, 15th Dist., 4th Sect.
Dated: 13 Sept. 1850. Signed: J. H. HENDERSON. Bef.: A.K.Rinchart

DECATUR COUNTY: Personally appeared before me AUGUSTUS J.
                    BELL, Adm'r. on the Estate of MARGARET
BELL, dec'd, who being duly sworn says dec'd was the proper owner of Lot No. 333 in 16th Dist., 4th Sect., the grant for which is applied for by him.
Dated: 23 June 1843
Signed: AUGUSTUS J. BELL.   CANNETH W. T. SWAIN, J.P.

MORGAN COUNTY: By CARTER (or CARTEN) SHEPHERD one of the
                    J.P.'s of sd. Co. personally came FRANCIS
A. (CHEANY?), Adm'r. on Estate of RICHARD L. MC GUIRE, dec'd and saith on oath he is the legal Adm'r of sd. RICHARD L. MC GUIRE, dec'd. and sd. R. L. MAGUIRE drew a lot of land No. 336-16-4 and sd. has never been granted.
Dated: 13 June 1843
Signed: F. A. CHENY, the Adm'r of R. L. MAGUIRE, Dest. Dibo non.

APPLING COUNTY: Personally appeared before me WILLIAM WIL-
                    LIAMS a J.P. of Inf. Crt. for sd. County,
JESSE SUMMERALL, Adm'r of NIL W. SUMERALL, dec'd, and saith on oath he as Adm'r of sd. NEIL (?) W. SUMERALL claims title to Lot No. 415 in 15th Dist. and 1st Sect., drawn to the name of ELHANAN MC CALL, the title of ELHANAN MC CALL being in possession of this deponent, also Lot No. 346 in 16th Dist., 4th Sect. drawn by JOHN BROCK, which he also claims as Adm'r. of sd. NEIL W. SUMERALL.
Signed: JESSE SUMMERALL, Adm'r of N. W. SUMERALL.
Dated: 10 June 1843 before WILLIAM WILLIAMS.

RICHMOND COUNTY: Personally came before me J. W. MEREDITH,
                    a J.P. of afsd. Co. HENRY GABLE being
sworn saith that the application for the grant of Lot No. 291 in 17th Dist. and 4th Sect. orig. Cherokee is made by him for the benefit of JAMES TARMEAN the only heir living child of JOEL C. TARMEAN, dec'd. and that sd. JAMES TARMAN being a youth about 14 years of age has resided with this deponents family since the death of his mother in 1840 and continues to reside.
Dated: Jan. 18, 1853   Signed: HENRY GABLE

COBB COUNTY: Before me JAMES W. MURPHY a J.P. within
                    and for sd. Co., personally came GEORGE W.
FLOURNOY of sd. Co. who being duly sworn says he is the owner, as-

signee and controls a Deed from SAMUEL LINDSEY, PALMYRIA LINDSEY, MARTHA D. LINDSEY, FRANCES LINDSEY (& JAMES SULLIVAN), THOMAS LINDSEY's Orphans: that he is the agent, fully authorised in the premises, to grant Lot of Land No. 242 in 17th Dist., 4th Sect. of orig. Cherokee but now Polk co....and that he makes this application in good faith and the owner of sd. Lot, he having the Deed of the sd. Orphans executed in Lee County in sd. State and dated 10 June 1853, and sd. orphans are the drawers of sd. Lot.
Dated: 4 March 1854.
Signed: GEO. W. FLOURNOY

SUMTER COUNTY: Know all men by these presents that I, CHARLOTTE WHEELESS of sd. Co. do make, constitute and app't WILLIAM H. PHILPOT of sd. Co. my true and lawful agent...to take out the grant of a gold lot which I drew while living in Underwood's District, Putnam County, Georgia, the No. being 178 in 17th Dist., 4th Sect., formerly Cherokee, of which I am the legal drawer and holder and have never sold it.
Dated: June 22, 1843
Signed: CHARLOTTE (X) WHEELESS, before ANDREW J. WILLIAMS, E.H. WILLIAMS.

OGLETHORPE COUNTY: Know all men by these presents that I do ordain and app't JACOB EBERHEART my lawful attorney to take out the grants for those whom I am a Judgment Creditor, that is: JEFFERSON CULBERTSON, No. 390-4-1; JAMES PAUL, No. 680-21-2; JAMES PAUL, No. 62-17-4; WM. T. CULBERTSON, JUNR., No. 102-17-4; GEORGE EASCO, No. 255-21-2....and also to act for me on the Power of Att'y to me by JOHN S. SORROW and JOEL BUTLER. 27 June 1843
Signed: WM. (P.?) CULBERTSON. (Note: the WILLIAM T. CULBERTSON, JUNR. may have had P. as middle initial, as was difficult to determine). Sworn to before MARTIN LILL(ES?), J.P.

FRANKLIN COUNTY: Personally appeared before me SAMUEL MOSELY, JR., who being duly sworn says he is proper owner as Adm'r of the Estate of SAMUEL MOSELY, SENR. (the drawer) of Lott 66 in 17th Dist., 4th Sect. orig. Cherokee co., the grant of which is applied for.
Dated: 25 May 1843
Signed: SAMUEL MOSELY (Note: Underneath this Oath is a form signed but not filled in with persons name, giving Power of At-

torney to take out this grant.)

TWIGGS COUNTY: Personally came before me JOHN A. NELSON, one of the Justices of the Inf. Crt. of sd. Co., JAMES M. DAVIS and BENJAMIN DAVIS who being sworn sayth that they together with MARIA DAVIS drew as a family of orphans (the orphans of JOHN DAVIS of Bibb County), Lot 48, 17th Dist., 4th Sect. of Cherokee Co.....and further saith that sd. orphans are all of age....and that the sd. BENJAMIN and JAMES M. DAVIS now apply for the Lot and grant for themselves and MARIA DAVIS and no other use.
Dated: 3 June 1843
Signed: JAMES M. DAVIS, BENJAMIN DAVIS before JOHN A. NELSON, J.I.C.

DE KALB COUNTY: Personally appeared before me WYLLYS BUEL a J.P. of State and Co. afsd., SARAH J. BETTISON and JOHN S. BETTISON and being duly sworn depose and say that they are the orphan children of SAMUEL D. BETTISON and the fortunate drawers of Lot No. 147, 19th Dist., 4th Sect., and No. 113, 16th Dist., 2nd Sect., both of orig. Cherokee....and bonafide owners of sd. land.
Dated: 30 Nov. 1849
Signed: S. J. BETTISON, JOHN S. BETTISON

DE KALB COUNTY: Personally appeared GEORGE J. BOOTH who being duly sworn deposeth and saith he is one of the legatees of GEORGE BOOTH late of Elbert Co., dec'd. and that he wishes to take out the plat and grant for Lot of land No. 140 in 19th Dist., 4th Sec't Cherokee, drawn by orphans of sd. GEORGE BOOTH of WHILHITE's Dist. for the benefit of sd. orphans.
Dated: 4 Oct. 1852
Signed: GEORGE (X) BOOTH. (Note: Underneath this oath he writes dated same from Atlanta sending $5.00 for taking out this grant and here he signs his name GEORGE J. BOOTH and not by mark.)

BIBB COUNTY: Personally came before me NANCY BRADY who says on her oath that she is the only surviving orphan of JOSEPH BRADY and as such makes application thru' SPENCER RILEY, who she has employed as her agent to take out grant to Lot No. 132 in 19th Dist., 4th Sect., drawn by the or-

phans of JOSEPH BRADY in Cherokee Co., when drawn now in Dade co.
Dated: 6 Sept. 1853, before KEELIN COOK, J.I.C.
Signed: NANCY (X) BRADY

HARRIS COUNTY: Before me CALVIN HUMPHREY a J.P. for said County came NANCY COLLINS and being sworn saith that the drawee of Lot of land No. 25 in 13th Dist., 4th Sect. of Cherokee has dissiased (deceased?) and that this deponent is past twenty one years of age and is the only heir to the estate of sd. drawee and that there is neither Exor. nor Adm'r. to sd. Estate and deponent further saith that the plat and grant has not been taken out for Lot 25 in 13th Dist., 4th Sect.
Dated: 25 May 1843
Signed: NANCY (X) COLLINS. CALVIN HUMPHRIES, J.P.

EARLY COUNTY: Personally came before me D. G. KILLINGSWORTH a J.P. for said county, LUCRETIA MILLER who being sworn saith that THOMAS MILLER, HENRY MILLER, WILLIAM S. GRAY the husband of the former FRANCES MILLER and WM. G. GILMON the husband of the former LUCINDA MILLER are the lawful owners of Lots of land numbers 141, 16th Dist., 1st Sect. of Union Co., and also of No. 269, 10th Dist., 4th Sect. of Dade co. and that deponent is the mother of the said THOS. MILLER, HENRY MILLER, FRANCES MILLER and LUCRETIA MILLER who as orphans drew said lots of land, they being the orphans of LEWIS MILLER of Early County.
Dated: __th day Jan. 1854
Signed: LUCRETIA (X) MILLER.

BALDWIN COUNTY: Personally appeared before me JOHN H. BROWN who being duly sworn says he is the surviving Exor. of GEORGE A. BROWN, dec'd. who was the proper owner of lots No. 217-10-4 and No. 604-19-3 of orig. Cherokee the grants for which are now applied for.
Dated: 23 June 1843
Signed: JOHN H. BROWN, before R. MICKLEJOHN, J.P.

MERIWETHER COUNTY: Personally came before me REUBEN J. STROZER who being duly sworn says he is the proper owner of Lot No. 122 in 10th Dist., 4th Sect. of original Cherokee, the grant for which is applied for.
Dated: 2 June 1843 before ED__Y L. VARDAMAN, J.P.   (cont'd)

29

Signed: REUBEN J. STROZER. On same date he appoints THOMAS M.
COOK of County of Baldwin to act as his agent. (Note: At top
of this oath is the following which has been written at another
date in pencil, "JOHN STROZER's orphans LUNCEFORD WILKY".)

LAURENS COUNTY: Personally appeared before me, BENJAMIN
                        H. HORN who being duly sworn says he makes
application for the grant to Lot No. 233 in 5th Dist., 4th Sect.
originally Cherokee as one of the bonafide owners of said Lot...
that he is one of the minor heirs and one of the legal distributees of the law drawn by JOSIAH HORN's orphans.
Dated: 16 August 1848 before ROBERT RIGDON, J.P.
Signed: BENJ. H. HORN

CHATHAM COUNTY: Personally appeared before me LEONIDAS
                        WYLLY, a J.P. for said County, CATHERINE
BAGSHAW, lawful agent of SUSAN ANN CANT (or CANS), the said SU-
SAN ANN CANT is the lawful heir of SARAH H. ASH orphan, which sd.
SARAH H. ASH orphan as afsd. is now dead and who drew and was
the proper owner of Lot No. 28 in 5th Dist., 4th Sect. in County
of Floyd.
Dated: 5 June 1843
Signed: CATHERINE BAGSHAW. On same date CATHERINE BAGSHAW ap-
pointed JOHN W. EXLEY of Effingham county, Ga. her lawful att'y
to take out grant.

HENRY COUNTY: Personally came before me JAMES W. EDWARDS
                        and being duly sworn saith that himself,
WILLIAM Y. EDWARDS and THOMAS J. EDWARDS and MARTHA EDWARDS or-
fins of LITTLEBERRY EDWARDS, dec'd. did draw a lot of land No.
109 in 5th Dist. and 4th Sect. of Cherokee Purchase now Walker
County.
Dated: 5 June 1843
Signed: JAMES W. EDWARDS. Underneath is written LITTLEBERRY
EDWARDS orphans, DERRICKS HENRY. On same date, JAMES W. EDWARDS
appt's JOAB COOK of Henry Co. as lawful att'y. ISAIAH HAND, J.P.

WASHINGTON COUNTY: Personally appeared before me BENJAMIN
                        HARRIS and WILEY HARRIS and after being
duly sworn says that they are the proper owner of Lot No. 16 in
9th Dist. of 4th Sect. of Cherokee original, and sd. Lot was
drawn to the names of CHURCHWELL HARRIS orphans of Haygoods Dist.

of said County and that they are now of age, and that there were
no other orphans of said CHURCHWELL HARRIS at the time of giving
in their names and they apply for grant.
Dated: 19 (June?) 1843
Signed: BENJ. HARRIS, WILEY HARRIS. On same date they app't
SOLOMON D. BRANTLEY as lawful agent.

JEFFERSON COUNTY: Personally appeared before me MARGARET
MANSON who being duly sworn says that she
is the Adm'x of the Estate of HUGH MANSON late of said County,
dec'd. and the parent of the orphans of said HUGH MANSON, dec'd.
who drew Lot No. 270 in 8th Dist., 4th Sect. of Cherokee Co. at
the time of the drawing of the same.
Dated: 19 May 1843 before MYRIOTT CASON, J.P.
Signed: MARGARET MANSON. On same date she appt'd ALFRED M. HOR-
TON of Baldwin co., her lawful Att'y to take out grant, and this
was Wit. by ANDERSON McDONALD.

WARREN COUNTY: Personally appeared before me ANTHONY
JONES who being duly sworn says that he
is the Guardian of the heirs of ALFRED LONG, dec'd. and is there-
by legally authorised to grant a lot of land drawn by said heirs
in Cherokee Co. No. 232-11-4, given in Lynns Dist., Warren Co.,
Ga.
Dated: 29 May 1843
Signed: ANTHONY JONES

PIKE COUNTY: Personally appeared before me JAMES L.
ALEXANDER, a J.P. for said County, MARTHA
ALEXANDER, Guardian of the property of the orphans of ADAM ALEX-
ANDER, dec'd, who being duly sworn says that she is the proper
owner as Gdn. afsd. of lot of land No. 213 in 11th Dist., 4th
Sect. of Walker County.
Dated: 17 June 1843.
Signed: MARTHA ALEXANDER. She appt'd JOHN W. COPPEDGE of Pike
Co. her lawful att'y. on same date.

MONROE COUNTY: Personally appeared before me JOHN JAMES
who being duly sworn says that he is the
proper owner of Lot No. 7 in 21st Dist., 3rd Sect. of original
Cherokee Co., also of Lot No. 10 in 11th Dist., 4th Sect. of o-
riginal Cherokee Co., which said two lots were drawn by MARY

JACKSON formerly widow now his wife. Also of Lot No. 22 in 11th Dist., of Dooly County.
Dated: 13 May 1843.
Signed: JOHN (X) JAMES. Wit.: ZACH. HARMAN, J.P.

JACKSON COUNTY: Personally appeared before me WILLIAM Mc-ELROY who being duly sworn says that he is proper owner of one third and lawful agent of SARAH McELROY and ROBERT G. McELROY there of Lot No. 78 in 12th Dist., 4th Sec. orig. Cherokee County.
Dated: 29 Dec. 1843
Signed: WILLIAM M. McELROY. On same date he appt's NATHANIEL C. TARRETT of Jackson County his lawful Att'y. Test.: NATHAN J. SHARP, THOMAS L. MOSSLER, J.P.

STEWART COUNTY: Know all men by these presents that I, ELBERT A. BOON hath this day made and appointed JAMES O. BOON my true and lawful attorney to apply for grant to Lot of lands No. 170 in 13th Dist. of orig. Cherokee co.
Dated: Jan. 19, 1844 before ROBERT BURKS, J.P.
Signed: ELBERT A. BOON

COWETA COUNTY: Personally appeared before me WM. B. BROWN a J.P. of said Co., DOCTOR W. DIAL who being duly sworn saith that he is the proper owner of fractional lot of land No. 199 in 14th Dist., 4th Sect. of orig. Cherokee co., drawn by TEMPERANCE DIAL of (Madison?) County.
Dated: 14 June 1843
Signed: DOCTOR W. DIAL. On 15 June 1843 he appt'd H. R. HARRISON of Coweta co. as lawful Att'y.

UPSON COUNTY: Know all men by these presents that I, MARY OWEN of said State and county do hereby app't ALLEN F. OWEN of the Co. of Talbot and sd. state my lawfuf Att'y to take out grant of land No. 182 in 14th Dist., and 4th Sect. of orig. Cherokee now Floyd Co.
Dated: 8 June 1843 before C. J. WALLACE and DAVIS DAVISON, J.P.
Signed: MARY OWEN. On seperate sheet ALLEN F. OWEN appt's MANA BETHUNE of Talbot Co. lawful attorney of sd. MARY OWEN under me to apply for grant and dated 8 June 1843.
Signed: ALLEN F. OWEN, Att. for MARY OWEN. Wit.: C. R. WYNN.

GREENE COUNTY:	Before me personally came ALBERT JERNIGAN who being duly sworn says that he is the Qual. Adm'r. on the Estate of JOHN E. JERNIGAN late of said Co., dec'd. and that the sd. JOHN E. JERNIGAN is the proper owner of Lot No. 58 in 4th Dist., 4th Sect. orig. Cherokee.
Dated: 14 June 1843 before JAMES TWILLEY, J.P.
Signed: ALBERT JERNIGAN.

EXECUTIVE DEPT.
MILLEDGEVILLE. GA.	20 May 1833, It appearing satisfactory that CYPRIAN MAYO of Peaces Dist., Wilkinson County, is the drawer of Lot 59 in 6th Dist., 4th Sect., instead of CYPROP MAYO. Ordered that grant be issued to said CYPRIAN MAYO on payment of fees.
Signed: WILLIAM J. M. WELLBORN, Sec'y. E.P.

CARROLL COUNTY:	Before me ISAIAH BECK a J.P. for sd. Co., personally appeared JAMES M. TREADAWAY, who after being duly sworn saith that he is the owner of lot of land No. 140 in 2nd Dist., 4th Sect. orig. Cherokee now Polk co., which sd. Lot was drawn by RICHARD MILLER's Orphan of Campbell Co., Ga.
Dated: 9 June 1852.
Signed: JAMES M. TREADAWAY.

FORSYTH COUNTY:	Personally appeared before me MADISON C. CHASTAIN who being duly sworn says that the application for the grant to the above lot is made as the "Guardian" of the drawer of sd. lot to wit. BENJAMIN T. CHASTAIN (Lunatic) Daniels Dist. Hall County.
Dated: 2 July 1850 before CURTIS GREEN, J.P.
Signed: MADISON C. CHASTAIN

LUMPKIN COUNTY:	Before me came J. S. CHASTAIN agent for E. W. CHASTAIN who being duly sworn says from a Deed of Conveyance made to the sd. E. W. Chastain for lot No. 222 in 6th Dist. and 4th Sect., he believes sd. lot to belong to the sd. E. W. Chastain and that he wishes to grant the same.
Dated: 13 June 1843 before M. H. GATHRIGHT, J.I.C.
Signed: J. S. CHASTAIN

MORGAN COUNTY:	Know all men by these presents that I.

PETERSON TAYLOR of the Co. and state afsd. for divers good causes etc., ordain and app't JAMES M. SE_____ (water marked) of the Co. of Morgan my true and lawful Att'y.....to apply and rec. the plat and grant of land drawn by MARK P. JACKSON of Morgan Co. in the 3rd Dist. of 4th Sect. No. 650.
Dated: 18 June 1843 before JOHN JOHNSON, J.P.
Signed: PETERSON TAYLOR. Underneath is written Guardean, and also "I do certify that MARK P. JACKSON is dead and that PETERSON TAYLOR is appt'd Gdn. for his orphans and signed by JOHN JOHNSON."

CAMDEN COUNTY: Personally appeared before me JAMES THOMPSON who being duly sworn says that he is the lawful Exor. of JAMES C. SCOTT, dec'd. who was the lawful owner of Lot No. 1068 in 4th Sect. 3rd Dist. of Co. of Cherokee.
Dated: 19 June 1843 before JOHN MIGILL, J.P.
Signed: JAMES THOMPSON. On same date he appt's ALFRED M. HORTON of Baldwin Co., Ga. his lawful Att'y.

BALDWIN COUNTY: Personally appeared before me JOHN R. ANDERSON a Justice of the Inf. Crt. of sd. Co., SOLOMON D. BETTEN (diff. to read this last name. Could be BELTON) who being duly sworn saith that he is one of the legal heirs of SOLOMON D. BETTEN who drew Lot No. 533, 3rd Dist., 4th Sect.
Dated: 9 June 1843.
Signed: SOLOMON D. BETTEN.

NEWTON COUNTY: Personally appeared before me JESSE L. BAKER who being duly sworn saith he is the Att'y for the Legatees of ELIZABETH HARPER, dec'd. and that said legatees are all of age and that sd. ELIZABETH HARPER while in life drew Lot No. 603 in 3rd Dist., 4th Sect., the plat and grant which is now applied for.
Dated: 28 May 1843.
Signed: JESSE L. BAKER. On same date he appt'd JAS. R. McCALLA his lawful Att'y and agent.

GREENE COUNTY: Personally appeared before me DAVID ALLISON who being duly sworn says that he is the lawful agent of REUBEN ALLISON the owner of Lot 317 in 3rd Dist., 4th Sec. of original Cherokee, the grant now applied for.

Dated: 26 June 1843.
Signed: DAVID ALLISON

CHATHAM COUNTY: Personally came before me L. W. SMITH, J.P. of sd. Co., Mrs. ELLEN BARTON of City of Savannah who being duly sworn saith that she was the wife of JOHN B. BARTON, that she was married to him in Charleston, S. C.,that she is now the widow of sd. JOHN B. BARTON, that he died in Liberia in Africa where he was sent by the American Colonization of the Methodist Episcopal Church, and that she the sd. ELLEN BARTON is the lawful heir of the sd. JOHN B. BARTON, dec'd. and the sd. John B. Barton was the drawer and proper owner of Lot No. 103, 4th Dist., 4th Sect. Cherokee now Floyd Co.
Dated: 12 May 1843.
Signed: ELLEN BARTON

JASPER COUNTY: Personally appeared WILLIAM P. HARDY who being duly sworn saith he is the agent of LEE SWAN of the State of Alabama who is the proper owner of Lot 432 in 13th Dist., 1st Sect. and No. 189 in 27th Dist., 3rd Sect. of orig. Cherokee County.
Dated: 28 June 1843 before JOHN H. KING, J.P.
Signed: WM. P. HARDY.

DE KALB COUNTY: Personally appeared before me JOSEPH PITTS who being duly qual. and sworn saith that a cert. lot of land lying in the 4th Sect. and 4th Dist. No. 41 in the Cherokee Lottery now Chattogy County drawn by JAMES R. M. ROBERSON is his own rights and property and that the above is for the purpose of obt. a grant from the state.
Dated: 30 May 1843.
Signed: JOSEPH PITTS.   Wit.: JAS. WILSON, J.P.

MORGAN COUNTY: Personally appeared before me CHARLES M. FURLOW who being duly sworn says that his application for the grant of Lot No. 235 in 27th Dist., 3rd Sect. of orig. Cherokee now Walker Co. is made by him both as bonafide owner of an undivided one fourth interest in sd. lot and as the friend of the other drawers in good faith. The sd. lot having been drawn by him self, REBECA A. HOLLINGSWORTH (wife of J. H. HOLLINGSWORTH of Morgan Co.) formerly REBECCA A. FURLOW, EDWARD A. FURLOW and MARGARET M. FURLOW orphan children of CHARLES FUR-

LOW late of Morgan Co., dec'd. and being undivided and owned in common by the drawers.
Dated: 6 July 1850 before JOHN L. WALKER, J.P.
Signed: C. M. FURLOW

CHEROKEE COUNTY: Personally appeared before me NICY FOWLER guardian of WILEY FOWLER's orphans who being duly sworn says that she is the lawful guardian of said orphans who are the owners of Lot No. 238, 27th Dist., 3rd Sect. the grant for which is applied for.
Dated: May 5, 1843.
Signed: NICY (X) FOWLER, before RUSSELL JONES, J.P. On same date she appt'd CHARLES NELSON of Baldwin Co. as lawful Att'y which was wit. by CHARLES (+) BURTON.

RICHMOND COUNTY: Personally appeared before me WILLIAM SCHLY who being duly sworn saith as Exor. of the Last will and Testament of MICHAEL FLECK he is the proper owner of Lot No. 1238 in 3rd Dist., 4th Sect. of Floyd Co.
Dated: 5 June 1843, before RICHARD ALLEN, J.P.
Signed: WILLIAM SCHLY.

FRANKLIN COUNTY: Personally came before me Mrs. HENRIETTA HEMPHILL who being duly sworn says that she is the proper owner of Lot No. 1227 in 3rd Dist., 4th Sect. orig. Cherokee Co.
Dated: 2 June 1843 before R. A. _____, J.I.C.
Signed: HENRYETTA (+) HEMPHILL. On same day she appt'd THOMAS KING of Franklin Co. her lawful Att'y. to obtain grant, which was witnessed by LEVI SEWELL.

MORGAN COUNTY: Before me ELIJAH E. JONES a Justice of the Inf. Ct. personally came HUDSON WADE and being duly sworn saith that MARY WADE a widow late of Morgan co. drew a gold lot of land, 1221-3-4, and that there is no legal Adm'r. or Exor. of the Estate of sd. MARY WADE, dec'd. the former Exor. having fully executed his duties of his Executorship with the exception of disposition of this lot of land....and Ex'r having long since moved out of the state, the sd. HUDSON WADE being one of the legatees of the Est. of the sd. MARY WADE applies for the grant to the Gold lot.
Dated: 16 June 1845. Signed: HUDSON WADE

MORGAN COUNTY: Personally came before me E. E. JONES a
Justice of the Inf. Ct. in the sd. Co.,
JOHN S. COLBERT who being duly sworn says that he is one of the
Exor's of JOHN G. COLBERT, dec'd. , that as such Exor. he is desirous of granting lot of land No. 1137-3rd dist., 4th sect., orig. Cherokee purchase, that JOHN G. COLBERT was the drawer of the
sd. lot and that he the sd. Exor. with his Co-Exor. JOHN G. FLOYD
are the proper owners.
Dated: 3 June 1843
Signed: JOHN S. COLBERT

WILKES COUNTY: Personally appeared before me FELIX WELL-
MAKER who being duly sworn says that he
is the proper owner of Lot No. 718, 11th Dist., 1st Sect. (Gold)
and that he is the lawful and legal guardian of the owner of lot
No. 386, 3rd Dist., 4th Sect. drawn by the orphans of JOHN WELL-
MAKER the grants for which is applied for.
Dated: 2 May 1843 before LEWIS S. BROWN, J.I.C.
Signed: FELIX (+) WELLMAKER. On the same date he appt's LEWIS
S. BROWN of Wilkes Co. his lawful Att'y. to take out sd. grants.
Wit.: A. S. WINGFIELD, J.I.C.

JEFFERSON COUNTY: Know all men by these presents that I.
SAMUEL S. OATES of the Co. of Burke and
state afsd. have appt'd. PATRICK (B.?) CONNELLY for and in my
name to ? JASON WORNACK and for our benefit....illig.....grants
a cert. tract of land cont. (40 or 50?) acres in the late gold
lottery....lot of land being drawn by the (crisslons?...illig..)
of (BUGIL or BURGIS?) WORNACK, then residing in the Co. of Burke.
Dated: 6 June 1843.
Signed: SAMUEL S. OATES. Lot 521-3-4.

CHATHAM COUNTY: Personally appeared before me MARY DOTY
who being duly sworn says that she is the
proper owner of Lot No. 837 in 3rd Dist., 4th Sect. Floyd Co.
the grant of which is applied for.
Dated: 1 June 1843.
Signed: MARY DOTY. On same date she appt'd JOHN W. EXLEY her
lawful Att'y.

RABUN COUNTY: Personally appeared before me CLEVELAND
COFFEE who being duly sworn says he is the

proper owner of Lot No. 748 in 3rd Dist., 4th Sect., orig. Cherokee but now Floyd Co.
Dated: 29 May 1843
Signed: CLEVELAND COFFEE before JOEL COFFEE, J.P. On same date he appoints EDWARD COFFEE of Rabun Co. his lawful Att'y. Wit.: THOS. W. H. GARRISON.

WALTON COUNTY: ELIZA ELDER was sworn and says she is the widow of JAMES ELDER who drawed Gold Lot No. 1039, 3rd Dist., 3rd Sect. and she applies for grant with her children, the orphans of sd. JAMES ELDER.
Dated: 27 June 1843
Signed: ELIZA (X) ELDER. Wit.: GEORGE J. HURST

MUSCOGEE COUNTY: EZEKIEL CALHOUN was sworn that he drew lot of land in 3rd Dist., of 3rd Sect., Lot No. 1151 of orig. Cherokee and that he drew same as a resident of Bazemore's Dist., Jones County and that he is present owner of same.
Dated: May 9, 1844
Signed: EZEKIEL CALHOUN. Wit.: GEORGE W. TURENTINE, J.P.

WASHINGTON COUNTY: ELIZABETH REAVES of Hancock Co., Ga. was sworn that she drew in her own name and right, No. 329-3-3.
Dated: June 27, 1843
Signed: ELIZABETH (X) REAVES. Wit.: A. J. RAY, J.P.

COWETA COUNTY: HILLSBERRY R. HARRISON, Clerk of Court of Ordinary certifies that WOOTSON RAINEY is Exor. of Last Will and Testament of MATHEW RAINEY, dec'd formerly of Oglethorpe Co., as appeared from records of file in my office.
Dated: 22 April 1843
Signed: HILLSBERRY R. HARRISON, C.C.O.

MUSCOGEE COUNTY: STRIBLING F. GRIMES made oath that he is agent of THOMAS P. GRIMES the owner of Lot No. 168 in 5th Dist., 2nd Sect. (this latter description was struck through, Ed.) of Cherokee and Gold Lot 295 in 3rd Dist., 3rd Sect. of Cherokee, grant for which is applied.
Dated: 29 May 1843 (cont'd next page)

Signed: STRIBLING F. GRIMES. Wit.: GEO. W. TURENTINE. (Note: This name STRIBLING is difficult to read....it might be STRIBIND)

BALDWIN COUNTY: JAMES W. TINSLEY was sworn that he is admr on estate of JAMES W. TINSLEY, dec'd. who was adm'r. of Estate of EDWARD SWEARINGIN and Exor. on estate of ABRAHAM GOGGINS who were proper owners of Lots No. 27-1-4 and No. 285-21-3, orig. Cherokee, grants for which are applied.
Dated: 27 June 1843
Signed: J. W. TINSLEY. Wit.: R. MICKLEJOHN, J.P.

JONES COUNTY: CULLEN WHITEMAN son of CHRISTOPHER WHITMAN, dec'd. was sworn that he is interested as one of owners of No. 594 in 3rd Dist., 3rd Sect. formerly Cherokee Co. and sd. lot drawn by CHRISTOPHER WHITMAN.
Dated: .....
Signed: CULLEN WHITMAN. Wit.: BALAAM PETUS, J.P.

MURRAY COUNTY: BENJAMIN A. DAVIS of Bradly Co., E. Tennessee was sworn that lot No. 93 in 13th Dist., 2nd Sect. of Cherokee Co. is his property lawfully, which lot was drawn by GEORGE W. GLOVE (GLORE?) (here is diff. to read but looks as if next word is part of last name and would seem to be GIVENS,.....) Decalb Cty.
Dated: 7 April 1843
Signed: B. A. DAVIS. Wit.: M. VARNELL, J.P.

COBB COUNTY: CRAWFORD B. WILLIAMS was sworn that he was bonafide owner of Lot No. 1290 in 21st Dist., 2nd Sect. of orig. Cherokee, now Cobb Co., drawn by PRICE PAUL's orphans of Habersham Co., the grant for which is now applied for.
Dated: 24 Sept. 1844
Signed: CRAWFORD B. WILLIAMS. Wit.: JESSE DOBBS. On 24 Sept. 1844 he appt'd WALTER H. MITCHELL his lawful att'y to take out sd. grant and Power of Att'y. was wit. by J. H. HIGHSMITH, JESSE DOBBS, J.I.C. (Note: written in pencil at a later date is "BRICE PAUL's orh. WHIPPLES, WILKINSON").

COBB COUNTY: HENRY COLLINS was sworn that he is lawful adm'r. of estate of JOURDAN JACKSON, dec'd and sd. JACKSON drew Lot 1020 in 21st Dist., 2nd Sect. orgi. Cher-

okee, and sd. COLLINS, adm'r. now applies for same.
Signed: HENRY COLLINS. Wit.: SAML. K. OLIVER, J.P.
Dated: 14 June 1843. On 14 June 1843 he appt'd DAVID GROOVER
his lawful att'y. to take out grant for him.
Signed: HENRY COLLINS

PUTNAM COUNTY: MARGARET HEATH of sd. Co. appt's BUSH(__D) W. SANFORD of sd. Co. her true and lawful att'y. to take out grant to cert. tract cont. 40 acres, No. 943 in 21st Dist., 2nd Sect. formerly Cherokee Co. which I am the drawer and legal holder.
Dated: 15 April 1843
Signed: MARGA<u>NT</u> (X) HEATH. Wit.: THOMAS B. HARWELL, J.P. Margaret Heath swore to her ownership on 29 March 1843 before J. W. SANFORD, J.I.C.

BIBB COUNTY: SARAH Q. FLUKER, Gdn. for orphans of B.F. FLUKER who being duly sworn that she is lawful agent thereof of Lots No. 172 in 17th Dist., 3rd Sect.; No. 65 in 21st. Dist., 2nd Sect.
Dated: 14 June 1843
Signed: SARAH Q. FLUKER. Wit.: EDWARD _____ Judge Sup. Ct.
She appt'd JAMES M. ELLIS her lawful atty on 14 June 1843 in Bibb County.

FORSYTH COUNTY: SAMUEL C. BENNETT was sworn that he was one of the legal owners of Lot drawn by WILLIAM PENDER in 21st Dist., 2nd Sect. orig. Cherokee, No. 369 and he authorizes JOHN CAIN, JUN. to act for him.
Dated: 26 June 1843
Signed: SAMUEL C. BENNETT. Wit.: JOSEPH K. THOMPSON, J.I.C.
Underneath appears "Please inquire whether grant of Lot 188, 2nd Dist., 1st Sect. is taken out and if not left that."

MADISON COUNTY: WILLIAM W. POWER was sworn that he was lawful Exor. of orphans of JOHN W. DAVID who is lawful owners of Lot No. 101, 4th Dist., 3rd Sect. orig. Cherokee.
Dated: 22 June 1843
Signed: WILLIAM W. POWER. Wit.: JAMES McCURDY, J.P.

CHATHAM COUNTY: MORDICA MYERS appeared, General Assignee

in Bankrupcy in Dist. Ct. for Dist. of Ga. and being sworn that he was the legal owner of following lots of land drawn by WILLIAM RAWLINGS of Washington Co., Ga., a decreed Bankrupt in sd. Court: No. 78-21-3 Cherokee Co.; 13 (4 or 6)-45 Carroll Co.
Signed: M. MYERS. Wit.: MULFORD MARSH, N.P.
Dated: 13 June 1843

HOUSTON COUNTY: CATHERINE ROBERSON of Co. afsd. appoints THOMAS WORTHY of County of Lawrence (Laurens) and state afsd. her lawful Att'y. to receive cert. land in County orig. Cherokee, Lot No. and Sect. not known, cont. 40 acres more or less.
Dated: 17 May 1843
Signed: CATHARINE (X) ROBERSON. Wit.: CALVIN LEARY, J.P.

EARLEY COUNTY: RICHARD GRIST swore that he was lawful heir and distributee of Estate of SUSANNAH BRYAN late of sd. Co., dec'd. and is therefore lawful owner of more moiety or share of Lot No. 51 in 21st. Dist. and 3rd Sec. orig. Cherokee the grant for which is applied.
Dated: 22 March 1843
Signed: RICHD. GRIST. Wit.: WILLIAM CASTLEBERRY, J.I.C. On same date RICHARD GRIST appt'd BOLLING H. ROBINSON his lawful att'y. to apply for grant. Wit. before WILLIAM CASTLEBERRY and JNO. H. JONES.

RICHMOND COUNTY: Power of Attorney by JOSEPH MILLIGAN to WM. H. PRITCHARD of Baldwin Co., Ga. and in my name as attorney for WILLIAM A. CAMFIELD to take out grant for Lot 353 in 21st. Dist., 3rd Sect. Cherokee, now Paulding co.
Dated: 13 June 1843
Signed: JOSEPH MILLIGAN. Wit.: RICHARD ALLEN, J.P.

MORGAN COUNTY: JOSEPH HEARD Exor. of FALKER HEARD does app't as Exor. of FALKNER HEARD, dec'd., DAVID (DERNERAST?) his true att'y. to take grant for Lot 496, 21st Dist., 3rd Sect. of Cherokee Purchase, drawn by FALKNER HEARD's orphans of Morgan Co.
Dated: 16 May 1843
Signed: JOS. HEARD, Exor. Wit.: ELIJAH E. JONES, J.I.C.

TROUP COUNTY: Power of Attorney by JAMES EBERHART to

HENRY T. SMART of Chambers Co., Ala. to apply for grant for Lot No. 1223 in 20th Dist., 3rd Sect. of Paulding Co.
Dated: 23 June 1843
Signed: JAMES EBERHART. Wit.: LORANA (her X mark) WYATT, THOMAS M. WYATT, J.P.

JASPER COUNTY: ELIAS OZBURN being sworn says he is proper owner of Lot No. 168, 19th Dist., 3rd Sec. of original Cherokee Co.
Signed: ELIAS OZBURN. Wit.: WM. CONNAWAY, J.P. ELIAS OZBURN appt's. JOHN BASS of Newton Co., Ga. his lawful attorney to apply for sd. land. Wit.: May 6, 1843 before DAVID KOLB, WM. CONNAWAY, J.P., CHARLES OZBURN.

CHATHAM COUNTY: MARY TIMMONS sworn that she was a proper owner of Lot No. 334 in 19th Dist., 3rd Sect. Paulding Co.
Signed: MARY TIMMONS. Wit.: June 1843 before M. O. DILLON, J.P. She appt'd WILLIAM ROBINSON of Chatham Co. her lawful attorney to apply for grant on 13 June 1843.

BALDWIN COUNTY: MARIA McDONALD swore that she and CATHERINE McDONALD are judgement creditors of JOHN WILLIAMS late of Baldwin Co. and apply for a grant for Lot. No. 359 in 19th Dist., 3rd Sect. of Cherokee, drawn by sd. JOHN WILLIAMS.
Dated: 14 June 1843 Wit.: J. U. HORNE
Signed: MARIA McDONALD

PUTNAM COUNTY: BYRD WHITLEY swore that in the late Gold Lottery that NATHAN MARCHMAN then in life but since dead drew Lot No. 1114 in 20th Dist., 3rd Section of formerly Cherokee, now Paulding Co. and that previous to death sd NATHAN MARCHMAN, he the sd. WHITLEY bought sd. land from sd. MARCHMAN.
Signed: BIRD WHITLEY. Wit.: 28 June 1843 before O. W. SANFORD, J.I.C.

MADISON COUNTY: SILLY (SILBEY?) A. SMITH was sworn that she was lawful administrator of estate of BENJAMIN SMITH, dec'd. the owner of lot No. 1160 in 20th Dist., 3rd Section for which grant is applied.

Dated: 29 May 1843 and wit. before JAMES McCURDY, J.P.
Signed: SILLY S. SMITH

CUTHBERT, April 2, 1849: Dear Sir: I enclose $3.00, I wish to grant Lot No. 935 in 18th. Dist., 3rd Sec. drawn by MILSEY L. EDWARDS orphan of this county, I am now the legal owner. Please mail the grant to me soon as possible at Rome, Floyd County. Yours WM. N. BARTON. WILLIAM N. BARTON appeared before ZADOCK SAWYER, J.I.C. in Randolph County, Ga. on April 2, 1849 and swore he was legal owner of above land. N.B. please mail the grant to me at Rome, Floyd Co., Ga. There may be a mistake in the No. or Dist., if so grant whatever No. EDWARDS drew, viz. a 40 acre lot. I own the 160 lot that he drew but has the grant of it. Be sure to mail it to Rome as I will be there in 10 or more days. W. H. BARTON

TALBOT COUNTY: ANDREW M. CANTS being sworn that the orphans of ALEXANDER F. M. CANTS dec'd. did draw Lot No. 179-12-3 of Cherokee and he is lawful Gdn. of said orphans and now applies for grant as agent.
Signed: ANDREW M. CAMTS.
Dated: March 29, 1843. Wit.: RICHD. HOLD, J.P.

CASS COUNTY: HENRY (?) GODWIN and JONATHAN H. GODWIN two of heirs of BARNABAS GODWIN dec'd, being sworn that they are proper owners of Lot No. 297 in 12th Dis. 3rd Sec. of Murray Co. the grant for which is applied.
Dated: 30 May 1843. Wit.: JAMES STOVALL, J.P.
Signed: J. H. GODWIN, HENRY (F. or J.?) GODWIN

PAULDING COUNTY: CICERO L. CALLOTT being sworn that he is legal (heirs - this is very diff. to read at this point) that drew Lot No. 197-6-1 drawn in name of JOHN COLLOTT's orphans of Allens Dist., Henry County.
Dated: 18 Dec. 1851. Wit.: D. W. ROSS, J.P.
Signed: CICERO L. COLLET.

THOMAS COUNTY: JOHN JONES, JR. being sworn that himself and his sister ANN JONES now ANN MILLER by her intermarriage with JAMES MILLER are the proper owners of following Lots of land, to Wit.: 1011-19-3 of orig. Cherokee, also Lot No. 205-7-2 of sd. Cherokee and they draw the same as

JAMES JONES orphans and that JAMES JONES had no other child or children at the time.
Dated: 20 March 1843.   Wit.:   JNO. NUTT, J.I.C.
Signed: JOHN JONES, JR.

MADISON COUNTY: MARY CARRINGTON being sworn that ORSBURN CARRINGTON her husband drew Lot No. 1118-19-3 Cherokee when drawn and sd. ORSBURN CARRINGTON departed this life intestate and that above named Lot properly belongs to the sd. MARY CARRINGTON and his children legal representative of the sd. dec'd.
Dated: May 8, 1843   Wit.: JAMES R. WHITE, J.P.
Signed: MARY (X) CARRINGTON.

HARRIS COUNTY: ISAAC ALMAND being sworn that he is one of heirs of ANN ALMAND, dec'd. and sd. ANN died intestate and there has been no adm'n on Estate. He also with other legatees are all of age and wish to obtain grant for 134-23-3 which was drawn by ANN ALMAN widow of William Dist. Elbert Co.
Dated: May 3, 1843. Wit.: A. H. (TUTT?), J.P.
Signed: ISAAC ALMAND

RABUN COUNTY: REBECCA PRICE was sworn that she is natural Gdn. and mother of JESSE PRICE, Idiot who is proper owner of Lot No. 959 in 21st Dist., 3rd Sect. orig Cherokee but now Paulding Co.
Dated: May 30, 1843
Signed: REBECCA (X) PRICE. Wit.: W. M. JOHNSON, J.P. She appt's EDWARD COFFEE of Rabun Co. her lawful att'y to apply for sd. grant on same date. Power of Att'y. was also wit. by SILAS B. P._ILE.

MONROE COUNTY: JOHN K. TIMMONS was sworn that he is legal owner of Lot No. 107 in 19th Dist., 2nd Sect. of Cherokee, now Cobb Co., and further that he is legal representative of his father WILLIAM SIMMONS formerly of Jones Co. and he sd. WILLIAM TIMMONS, dec'd. drew Lot No. 965-21-3 in Cherokee. Wit.: JAS. HARDIN, J.P.
Dated: 14 April 1843
Signed: J. K. (T?)IMMONS. He appt's JOSHUA LEE his lawful atty. to take out grant on same date. Signed: J. K. SIMMONS (Note: in

the main body of the oath his last name looks like TIMMONS but
signature is definitely SIMMONS...Ed.)

MORGAN COUNTY: STERLING ATAWAY was sworn that he is one
                        of legatees of JAMES JONES, dec'd. of Put-
nam Co., Paces Dist. on whose estate their never has been any administration and acc. to list of drawing he has drawn No. 533 in
19th Dist., 3rd Sect. of Cherokee Co. and No. 263 in 7th Dist.,
2nd Sect., Cherokee Co.
Dated: 15 June 1843.   Wit.: JOHN D. WELLS, J.P.
Signed: STERLING (X) ATAWAY.

SUMTER COUNTY: Know that on this day I do app't. WILLIAM
                        MIMS of sd. Co. my lawful att'y. to take
out grant which HENRY DYKES now dec'd. drew he gave in Goodwin's
Dist., Houston Co., Ga. 690-19-3.
Signed: GEORGE DYKES on Estate of HENRY DYKES, dec'd. Wit.:
IRVIN D. HEATH, ROBERT N. McLIN.
Dated: May 31, 1843

STEWART COUNTY: YOUNG H. GRESHAM deputy Clerk of Ct. of
                        Ord. of Stewart Co. certifies that DELITHA
NOX has been appt'd. Gdn. of the person of MARTHA F. McCANT and
she has given her Sec. Bond for faithful performance of her duty
as such.
Dated: 10 Sept. 1847.
Signed: YOUNG H. GRESHAM, D.C.C.O.

CAMPBELL COUNTY: PEGGY THORNTON being duly sworn that she
                        is proper owner of Lot No. 798-19-3 of or-
iginal Cherokee and applies for grant through her att'y.
Dated: 29 May 1843.   Wit.: LEWIS MILES, J.P.
Signed: PEGGY (X) THORNTON. On same date she gave power of at-
torney to JOHN CARLTON of sd. county. This was also wit. by WM.
A. VESTAL.

BIBB COUNTY: LUCY H. JOHNSON being sworn that she is
                        proper owner of Lot No. 20 in 12th Dist.,
3rd Sect. of Cherokee Co.
Dated: 28 June 1843 before W. H. CALHOUN, J.I.C. On same date
she appt'd. ROBERT JOHNSON of Bibb Co. her lawful att'y.

FLOYD COUNTY: JOHN M. EDGE, Adm'r. of Estate of JOHN
                      EDGE, dec'd. who being sworn that the within-
named lots belong to and are under the control of the estate
of JOHN EDGE, dec'd.
Dated: June 5, 1843 before W. R. BERRYHILL, J.P.
Signed: JOHN M. EDGE   (note on margin 638-21-3)

GREENE COUNTY: OSBORN S. FURLOW was sworn that he is the
                      qualified Exor. of DAVID FURLOW, dec'd.
who is proper owner of Lot No. 177-6th Dist. and 1st Sect. orig.
Cherokee Co.
Dated: June 12, 1843 before JAMES MOORE, J.P.
Signed: O. T. FURLOW

FLOYD COUNTY: Know all men by these presents that I,
                      JOHN M. EDGE, Adm'r. of estate of JOHN
EDGE, dec'd., app't N. V. M. MILLER of above named Co. my lawful
att't. to apply for grant for 2 certain lots of land. One in 3rd
Dist., 4th Sect. orig. Cherokee, now Floyd Co. known as No. 944.
The other in 21st Dist., 3rd Sect. Lot No. 638 each cont. 40 acres
Dated 5 June 1843, before W. (N. or R.) BERRYHILL, J.P.
Signed: JOHN M. EDGE, Adm'r.

MERIWETHER COUNTY: DAVIS C. GRESHAM heir at law of ELIZABETH
                      WATTS, dec'd. who being sworn says that
ELIZABETH WATTS in her life time was the proper owner of Lot No.
688 in 21st Dist., 3rd Sect. orig. Cherokee and he applys for a
grant as heir at law.
Dated: 2 Feb. 1843 before ADAM RAGLAND, J.P.
Signed: DAVIS C. GRESHAM. On same date he appt's. THOMAS M.
COOK of Baldwin Co. his lawful att'y. to apply for sd. grant. Wit.
L. M. ADAMS, ADAM RAGLAND, J.P.

FAYETTE COUNTY: JOSIAH F. REAVES, Gdn. for THOMAS WILSON,
                      JOSEPH WILSON and NANCY WILSON the orphans
of WILLIAM P. WILSON, dec'd. is the proper owners of Lots of Land
to wit: No. 471-21-3 and No. 378-13-1 of the Cherokee Country,
drawn by WILLIAM P. WILSON of Fayette Co., Griffin's Dist. for
which he applies for grants.
Dated: 23 June 1843 before G. C. King, J.P.
Signed: J. F. Reaves, Gdn.

GREENE COUNTY: GEORGE HALL being sworn says he is the Qual. Exor. of JOHN SLAUGHTER late of Greene Co., dec'd. and sd. JOHN SLAUGHTER is the proper owner of Lot 711-21 Dist., 3rd Sect. of orig. Cherokee Co.
Dated: 6 June 1843   Wit.: JAS. W. GODKIN?, J.I.C.
Signed: GEORGE HALL

MONROE COUNTY: GEORGE DOUGLAS was sworn that he is agent for NANCY C. STRONG widow of ALLEN B. STRONG of Bibb Co., dec'd. and sd. NANCY C. STRONG has authorized him to take out plat and grant.
Dated: June 2, 1843   Wit.: JAMES NORRIS, J.P.
Signed: GEORGE DOUGLAS

LEE COUNTY: ELIZABETH GILBERT, Extrx. on Estate of ALLEN GILBERT, dec'd. being sworn that she is sole Exor. on above and estate is rightful owner of 1117-11-1 and 894-21-3.
Dated: 27 June 1843 before AMBROSE H. GRANT, J.I.C.
Signed: ELIZABETH J. GILBERT, now ELIZABETH J. DAVIS (in one place it looks as if it could DIVES. She appt'd ALPHEOUS DICKERSON of Hancock Co., Ga. her lawful att'y. to apply for grant on same date.

COWETA COUNTY: THOMAS SMITH was sworn that he is proper owner of the law as the agent on the owner of Lot No. 310 in 11th Dist., 2nd Sect. in the late (Chinniaker?)
Dated: May 27, 1843 before JOHN CRAVEN, J.P.
Signed: THOMAS (X) SMITH

RICHMOND COUNTY: WILLIAM E. JACKSON was sworn that SARAH F., HENRY J. and JOHN S. PORTER, Minor Children of JOHN S. PORTER, dec'd., for whom deponent is Gdn. and the proper owners of Lot No. 45 in 11th Dist., 2nd. Sect. of Gilmer Co.
Dated: 25 May 1843 before J. W. MERIDITH, J.P.
Signed: WILLIAM E. JACKSON

TATNALL COUNTY: SIMON SMITH was sworn that he lawful Admr. of Estate of WILLINGTON SMITH late of Bulloch Co., dec'd. and says that Lots No. 874-3-3 and No. 305-5-1

are property of said Estate.
Dated: 9 June 1843 before JOHN A. ROGERS, J.P.
Signed: SIMON SMITH

MORGAN COUNTY: WILLIAM G. EVANS was sworn that he is the lawful agent of JAMES EVANS, the lawful owner of Lot No. 1219, 5th Dist., 1st Sect. of Cherokee Purchase.
Dated: 3 June 1843 before ELIJAH E. JONES, J.I.C.
Signed; WILLIAM G. EVANS

NEWTON COUNTY: SARAH FIELDS was sworn that she is proper owner of Lot No. 1140 in 5th Dist., 1st Sect. of Cherokee County.
Dated: 20 June 1843 before JAMES M. SMITH, J.P.
Signed: SARAH (X) FIELDS

EARLY COUNTY: JANE SPENCE was sworn that she is drawer and owner of Lot No. 929 in 5th Dist.,1st Sect. of Cherokee.
Dated: 17 May 1843 before DANIEL M. JORDAN, J.P.
Signed: JANE SPENCE (Note at top of Oath reads "929 JANE SPENCE (Wid.) 430 Dist. Early").

MONROE COUNTY: JAS. H. MAYS was sworn that he is lawful owner of Lot No. 824 in 5th Dist., and 1st Sect. and that he is Adm'r. on Estate of MARY MAYS, dec'd. and she drew Lot No. 11 in 6th Dist., 1st Sect.
Dated: 8 June 1843 before JAS. HARDIN, J.P.
Signed: JAMES H. MAYS

WASHINGTON COUNTY: WILEY MEEKS was sworn that he is rightful owner of Lot of Gold No. 312 in 5th Dist., 1st Sect. drawn by the orphans of WILLIAM BROWN, Garner's Dist. of sd. County.
Dated: 15 May 1848
Signed: WILEY MEEKS. Wit.: JOHN D. BROWN, J.P.

GREENE COUNTY: GEORGE G. MATHEWS was sworn that he is the Exor. on Estate of JONAS FANCH (or FAUCH?) late od sd. Co., dec'd. and sd. JONAS FANCH was drawer of Lot No. 263 in 5th Dist., 1st Sect. orig. Cherokee.
Dated: 2 Feb. 1843 bef. J. R. Hall, J.I.C. Signed: GEO. G. MATHEWS

WARREN COUNTY: SARAH FRENCH being sworn that she is the proper owner of Lot No. 47 in 5th Dist., 1st Sect. of Cherokee in her right, occasioned by the death of her husband, WILLIAM FRENCH.
Dated: 26 July 1844 before SPIVEY FULLER, J.P.
Signed: SARAH (X) FRENCH

CHEROKEE COUNTY: Personally came before me EDMUND SEBASTIAN a Justice of the Peace for sd. Co., JOHN CARR (or CORR) who being duly sworn saith he is the proper owner of Lot No. 210 in 3rd Dist., 4th Sect. drawn to the name of JOSEPH CORR in the late Gold and Land Lottery.
Dated: 15 June 1843
Signed: JOHN (X) CORR

COBB COUNTY: (Note: there is some question if this is Cobb or not, as the Oath was watermarked and difficult to read, but this is the only County it looks like it could have been.) Personally appeared before me WOODLEY A. THOMAS in rite of his wife SARY GATEWOOD formerly but now SARY THOMAS and after being duly sworn says that he is the proper owner by the intermarriage with SARY GATEWOOD of Lot No. 170 in 7th Dist., 4th Sect. and county of Walker.
Dated: 13 June 1843 before DAVID MORROW, J.P.
Signed: WOODLEY A. THOMAS

WILKINSON COUNTY: Personally came before me SAML. J. BURK a J.P. for sd. Co., SAMUEL BEALL and on an oath sayeth that he is the Judgment Creditor agst. WILLIAM F. BONDS and that he the sd. WILLIAM F. BONDS was the proper owner of the Lots of land herein named (14 Lots are given).
Dated: 26 June 1843
Signed: SAML. BEALL

GREENE COUNTY: SAMUEL M. FINDLEY, Adm'r. of ROBERT FINDLEY, dec'd. who swore that he is proper owner as Adm'r. of ROBERT FINDLEY, dec'd. of Lot No. 321, 12th Dist., 2nd Sect.
Dated: 6 June 1843 Wit.: J. R. HALL, J.P.
Signed: SAMUEL M. FINDLEY

HARRIS COUNTY: JOHANNAH EMBREY, Extrx. of JOEL EMBREY, dcd

was sworn that JOEL EMBREY, dec'd. drew Lot 205 in 13th Dist., 2nd. Sect. of Cherokee and she applies for same.
Dated: 17 June 1843 Wit.: A. H. SCOTT?, J.P.
Signed: JOHANNAH EMBREY

JASPER COUNTY: W. B.? AARON, who being duly sworn that he and JAMES C. AARON, SUSANANN AARON and ELIZABETH AARON are the orphans of JOHN AARON's and are the proper drawers of Lot No. 126 in __ Dist. and 2nd Sect. of original Cherokee County and apply for same.
Dated: 29 May 1843. Wit.: CHARLES F. WALTHALL, J.P.
Signed: W. (B. or H.?) AARON

WARREN COUNTY: LAWSON D. WRIGHT was sworn that he is the proper owner of Lot No. 2, 12th Dist., 1st Sect. and Lot No. 152, 22nd Dist. and 2nd Sect. and Lot No. 222, 10th Dist. and 2nd Sect., all drawn by MILLICENT WRIGHT (Wid.), Dated: 3 June 1843 before WILLIAM CASTLEBERRY, J.I.C., Early Co., Georgia.
Signed: LAUSON D. WRIGHT

BALDWIN COUNTY: THOMAS M. MANN was sworn that he is proper owner of following Lots as the Adm'r. of Estate of ISHAM WEST, dec'd.: 1054-3-1; 475-13-1 and 43-10-2.
Dated: 20 June 1843 before ALFRED M. HORTON, J.P.
Signed: THOMAS M. MANN, Adm'r.

UPSON COUNTY: DRAKEFORD L. TRAMMELL who saith he is the owner of following Lots of Land: No. 244, No. 246, No. 267, No. 231, No. 255 and No. 248 all lying in the 10th Dist. of orig. Monroe Co., but now Upson Co.
Dated: 29 May 1843
Signed: D. L. TRAMMEL. Wit.: JAS. H. BLACK, J.P.

PUTNAM COUNTY: THOMAS G. SANFORD, Adm'r. of JAMES JORDAN, dec'd. who says that Lot No. 224 in 12th Dist. and 2nd Sect. of orig. Cherokee Co. was drawn by orphans of sd. Dec'd. and he is their legal representative.
Dated: 2 June 1843
Signed: THOS. G. SANFORD Wit.: T. B. HARWELL, J.P.

THOMAS COUNTY: MATTHEW C. DUKES was sworn that he is the

natural Guardian of SARAH ANN HANDLEY, orphan who drew and is proper owner of Lot No. 42 in 13th Dist., 2nd Sect. of Cherokee Co.
Dated: 13 June 1843 before HORACE (LANTON?), J.I.C.
Signed: MATTHEW C. DUKES

FLOYD COUNTY: JAMES DUKE being sworn that he legally purchased from the children of ROGERS, Hampton's Dist., Newton Co., Lot of Land No. 161 in 23rd Dist., and 3rd Sect. orig. Cherokee now Floyd and now applies for same to procure a legal title....he has paid a valuable consideration for same land and the name for giving the draws in the Cherokee Land Lottery was given (either THUS. or THOS.?) ROGERS children, F. A. HAMPTON's, Newton.
Dated: 31 Jan. 1851   Wit.: F. J. SULLIVAN, J.P.
Signed: JAMES DUKE

WALTON COUNTY: BENJAMIN STEVENS was sworn that he is the lawful Guardian of orphans of WM. H. DAVIS the drawer of Lot 194 in 24th Dist., 2nd Sect. and No. 157 in the 3rd Dist., 4th Sect. Cherokee the grant for which is applied.
Signed: BENJAMIN (B.) STEVENS. Wit.: W. H. BRINBERRY, dated 28 Dec. 1843. On 2 May 1843 he appt'd. WARREN J. HILL of Walton Co. his att'y to take out grants.

TWIGGS COUNTY: GIDEON BEDINGFIELD appeared before MABRY (SALCRUON?), Justice of Inf. Ct., and was sworn that he is father of HIRAM BEDINGFIELD of sd. Co., dec'd. and further that HIRAM was drawer of Lot No. 100 in 23rd Dist., 3rd Sect. Cherokee County and sd. HIRAM died seized of sd. land, and sd. deponent makes application for sd. tract, since HIRAM died intestate and there has been no adm'n. on the estate of the dec'd.
Dated: 17 June 1843.
Signed: GIDERN BIDINGFIELD.   Wit.:HENRY SOLOMON, J.I.C. (This last name could be TOLERMAN, instead of SOLOMON, as was very difficult to read...Ed.)

CHATHAM COUNTY: ANN WARD was sworn that she is proper owner of Lot No. 216 in 23rd Dist. and 3rd Sect. of Floyd Co. and Lot No. 602 in 4th Sect. and 2nd Dist. of Palding Co., grant for which is applied. (cont'd):

Signed: ANN WARD   Wit.: WM. T(HANNE?) WILLIAMS, J.I.C.C.C.
On 1 June 1843 she appt'd. JOHN W. EXLEY of Chatham Co. her atty.

CLARKE COUNTY: THOMAS E. WILLIAMSON was sworn that he is
                       lawful Adm'r. of ANOW E. WILLIAMSON, dec'd
the drawer of Lot No. 259 in 23rd Dist. 3rd Sect. County of ____
and applies for grant.
Signed: THOS. E. WILLIAMSON.
Dated: 28 Dec. 1842. Wit.: THOMAS F. SOUR, N. P. (LOT? instead
of SOUR?). On 31 May 1843 he appt's. JOHN H. SOUR (LOW?), Sr. of
Clarke Co. his lawful att'y. Wit.: WILLIAM HOLLANDS, THOMAS F.
SOUR.

OGELTHORPE COUNTY: WHITFIELD LANDRUM was sworn that he makes
                       application for grant to above as friend
of the orphans of RICHARD DERBY the drawer of above lot in good
faith and for benefit of orphans.
Dated: 2 May 1848.
Signed: WHITEFIELD LANDRUM. Wit.: _ F. PLOTT, J.I.C.

CAMPBELL COUNTY: MARGARET CALDWELL acting agent for SARAH
                       & ANN CALDWELL, orphans of WILLIAM CALD-
WELL late of Campbell Co., dec'd. who drew Lot No. 60 in 22nd
Sect., 3rd Dist., cont. 160 acres...and also that no adm'n. on
estate of sd. dec'd. has taken place.
Signed: MARGARET (+) CALDWELL, Agent.
Dated: 7 June 1843 before FREDERICK BEALLE, J.P. On 7 June 1843
she appt's. BENJAMIN MISONEY her att'y. of sd. Co. afsd.

FORSYTH COUNTY: JOHN HENDERSON was sworn that he is Exor.
                       and legal representative of ROBERT HENDER-
SON, JR., dec'd. and that he is rightful owner of Lot No. 533 in
20th Dist., 3rd Sect. the grant for which is applied.
Signed: JOHN HENDERSON
Dated: __ June 1843 before WILLIAM STOVALL, J.P. On same date
he appt's. JAMES A. GREEN of sd. county his lawful agent or atty.
Wit.: LEWIS STOVALL, WILLIAM STOVALL, J.P.

HEARD COUNTY: MENOAH D. ROBINSON was sworn that he is
                       lawful owner of Lot No. 175 in 12th Dist.
of orig. Lee Co., drawn by HEZEKIAH ROBINSON of Richmond Co. and
that he is the Admn'r. of the Estate of JOHN ROBINSON, dec'd. ..

which estate is lawful owner and drawer of lot of land No. 57 in 22nd Dist., 3rd Sect. orig. Cherokee Co.
Dated: 27 June 1843 Wit.: BENJ. B. W. DENT, J.P.
Signed: M. D. ROBINSON

DeKALB COUNTY: ROBERT D. GREEN was sworn that he is lawful agent for JOHN IRBY's orphants of Lot No. 205 in 22nd Dist., 3rd Sect. of Cherokee, sd. lot drawn by sd. orphants.
Dated: 2 Nov. 1849. Wit.: J. B. WILSON, J.P.
Signed: R. D. GREEN

FRANKLIN COUNTY: JACEL PURCELL was sworn that he is lawful agent of ABRAHAM PURCELL of Lot No. 211 in 22nd Dist., 3rd Sect. orig. Cherokee Co., now Cass Co., and the sd. ABRAHAM PURCELL having died without making a will or letting or impowering any other person -----?---- apply for grant of sd. lot.
Dated: 15 May 1843. Wit.: R. A. _____.
Signed: JACEB (L?) (her + mark) PURCELL. On 15 May 1843 TEMPLE F. CAPER of afsd. Co. appt'd. att'y. to obtain grant. Wit.: JARRETT PURCELL, R.A. _____?, J.I.C.

RICHMOND COUNTY: FRANCES C. V. HILL, widow and sole heiress of CHARLES M. HILL, late of Columbia Co., dec'd. and Adm'r. on his Estate, was duly sworn before WILLIAM DOYLE, J.P. for 119th Dist. of Co. afsd. and saith that her late husband, CHARLES M. HILL, then a resident of Burke Co., Ga. was orig. drawer of Lot No. 592 in 20th Dist., 3rd Sect. and No. 663, 1st Dist., 4th Sect. orig. Cherokee Co.
Dated: 17 June 1843 before WILLIAM DOYLE, J.P.
Signed: FRANCES C. V. HILL. She appt'd. ISAAC A. HIBLER or JAMES W. JONES or both of them her true and lawful att'y. to take out grants. Wit.: LEON P. PUSSAS. No date shown for Power of Attorney.

CLARKE COUNTY: JOANNAH SIMS was sworn that she is proper owner as lawful widow and also Extrx. of ROBERT SIMS late of sd. Co. dec'd. of Lots No. 528 in 20th Dist., 3rd Sect. of Cherokee and Lot No. 331 in 2nd Dist. and 4th Sect. grants for which are applied.
Dated: 28 Dec. 1842. Wit.: BEDFORD LANGFORD. (cont'd)...

Signed: JOANNAH (+) SIMS. On 29 May 1843 she appt'd. THOMAS A. TUCK of Clarke Co. her lawful att'y. This was wit. by GEO. M. LANIER, BEDFORD LANGFORD, J.I.C.

JONES COUNTY: WILLIAM MORELAND, Adm'r. on Estate of LUCY ADKINSON late of sd. Co., dec'd. who was sworn that LUCY ADKINSON in her lifetime drew lot of land No.460 in 20th Dist., and 3rd Sect. of Cherokee Co. and the deponent is Adm'r. of Estate.
Dated: 10 June 1843. Wit.: JAMES GRAY, J.O.C.
Signed: WILLIAM MORELAND

MONROE COUNTY: CARY COXE who was sworn that he is drawer of Lot in Gold region No. 981, 21st Dist., 3rd Sect. and also the legal heir of REBECCA BURGE, dec'd. who drew a Lot No. 1179, 3rd Dist., 2nd Sect. of Gold region and is owner of sd. lot. Wit.: J. D. CALAWAY, J.P.
Dated: 12 June 1843
Signed: CARY COXE. Same date he appt's. LEONARD T. DOYLE, his att'y. to apply for grants.

RICHMOND COUNTY: JAMES PANNELL one of the orphans who drew Lot 660 in 21st Dist., 2nd Sect. of orig. Cherokee and was sworn that he applies for grant of above land as one of owners of same.
Dated: 20 Nov. 1852. Wit.: RICHARD ALLEN, J.P.
Signed: JAMES PANNELL

JONES COUNTY: STERLING W. SMITH, Exor. of HARRISON SMITH late of Talbot Co., dec'd. who being sworn says that sd. HARRISON SMITH in his lifetime drew Lot No. 627 in the county, 1st Dist., and 2nd Sect. Cherokee and sd. deponent is Exor. of same and proper owner.
Dated: 10 June 1843
Signed: STERLING W. SMITH, SENR. Wit.: WILLIAM MORELAND, J.P.

JACKSON COUNTY: MALINDA FRIDGES being sworn that she is one of the heirs of STEPHEN FRIDGES late of Jackson Co., dec'd. and is entitled to a portion of lot drawn by sd. orphans No. 754 in 21st Dist., 2nd Sect. of orig. Cherokee Co. when drawn.
Dated: 26 May 1843. Wit.: J. B. NABERS, J.P. (cont'd)...

Signed: MALINDAY (X) FRIDGES. On same date she appt's. JAMES B. NABERS her lawful att'y. Wit.: W. S. SHAU (SSAN?), JOHN J. Mc-CULLOCH.

OGLETHORPE COUNTY: PRIER L. DAVIS was sworn that he is lawful agent of owners of Gold Lot orig. Cherokee Co., drawn by WILEY SIMS orphans, Oglethorpe Co., Hardman's Dist. No. 791-21-2, grant for which is applied. Wit.: GEORGE W. O'KELLEY, J.P.
Dated: 18 Sept. 1844.
Signed: PRIER L. DAVIS. On same date he appt's. WILLIAM S. WHITWORTH of Madison Co. his lawful att'y. Wit.: RAIFORD E. HITCHCOCK, GEORGE W. O'KELLEY, J.P.

HANCOCK COUNTY: June 13, 1843 know that I have this day appt'd. JOHN B. THOMAS of Baldwin Co. my lawful att'y. to apply for grant to Lot No. 798, 21st Dist., 2nd Sect.
Signed: SARAH (X) WILSON. Wit.: SEABORN HUTCHINGS, JAS. M. PALMER, J.P.

BRYAN COUNTY: WM. PATTERSON being sworn that he is trustee under the will of JOHN DAVID MORGIN who was proper owner of Lot No. 518 in 17th Dist. and 2nd Sect. of Cherokee Co., the grant for which is applied.
Dated: 28 Dec. 1843 Wit.: CHARLES A. HARDIN, J.P.
Signed: WM. H. PRITCHAN for WM. PATTERSON. On May 13 1843 W. PATTERSON (who signs as bef. shown) appt's. WM. H. PRICTHARD of Baldwin Co. his lawful att'y.

RICHMOND COUNTY: JOHN P. KING Guardian of MARY M. KNIGHT, (GAZAMAY?) B. KNIGHT, WOODWARD KNIGHT, WILLIAM KNIGHT and SUSAN KNIGHT being the orphans of ENOCH KNIGHT who being sworn says the said orphans are owners of Lot No. 33, 20th Dist., 2nd Sect. orig. Cherokee the grant for which is applied.
Dated: June 10, 1843. Wit.: MICH. F. BOISDAIN, N.P. R.C.G.
Signed: JOHN P. KING
Another Oath headed Richmond Co., Ga. says JOHN P. KING was sworn that he is proper owner of Lot. No. 219-4-4- of Co. orig. Cherokee, grant for which is applied. Dated June 10, 1843. Signed: JOHN P. KING. Wit.: MICH. F. BOISDAIN,NP

MUSCOGEE COUNTY: EZEKIEL CALHOUN being sworn that he drew lot in 3rd Dist. of 3rd Sect. of orig. Cherokee, Lot No. 1151 and that he drew same as a resident of Bazemore's Dist., Jones Co.
Dated: 9 May 1844. Wit.: G. W. TURENTINE, J.P.
Signed: EZEKIEL CALHOUN

FAYETTE COUNTY: MARTHA CORDEMON the widow of FREDRICK CORDEMON, dec'd. and being sworn that Lot No. 537 in ___ Dist., 3rd Sect. drawn by sd. FREDRICK CORDEMON is the lawful property of the Estate for which she applies for the grants by her lawful agent JAMES JOHNSON.
Dated: 1 June 1843. Wit.: G. C. KING.
Signed: MARTHA (+) CORDEMON

TALBOT COUNTY: MARY CASTENS who being sworn that she is proper owner of Lot of land drawn by herself, supposed to be No. 675 in 20th Dist., 3rd Sect. of orig. Cherokee Co.
Dated: ___ June 1843. Wit.: JOSEPH JACKSON, J.P.
Signed: MARY CARTEN   On same date she appt'd. MARION BETH her lawful att'y. to apply for grant. Wit.: E. B. ROBINSON, JOSEPH JACKSON, J.P.

BURKE COUNTY: ZACH D. F. TOMLIN was sworn that he is drawer of Lot in Gold region Lot No. 447-21-3.
Dated: 17 June 1843.
Signed: Z. D. F. (X) TOMLIN. Wit.: JOHN B. GORDON, J.P. June 17, 1843 ZACH. L.F. TOMLIN being sworn says he is guardian of FORNEY GEORGE orphan that drew a lot of land in Gold region and who is proper owner of same. No. 59-19-3. Wit.: JOHN B. GORDON, J.P.   Also on June 17, 1843, ZACHARIAH L. F. TOMLIN of Burke co. appt's. GREEN B. POWELL his lawful att'y. to apply grant to 477-21-3 Gold and 59-19-3. Wit.: JOHN B. GORDAN, J.P.

DeKALB COUNTY: NATHANIEL WHITE being sworn that he is the proper owner of lot No. 79 in 10th Dist., of Carroll Co. cont. 202 ½ acres, drawn by deponent of Franklin Co. and also Gold Lot No. 1025 in 20th Dist., 3rd Sect. orig. Cherokee, now Paulding Co. cont. 40 acres.
Dated: 29 May 1843. Wit.: J. N. BELLINGER, J.I.C.
Signed: NATHANIEL WHITE

COBB COUNTY: SIMON FRASER being sworn that he is proper owner of following Lots to wit: No. 310-25-3 and No. 487-21-2 Cherokee Co. originally drawn by ELIZABETH NELM, Widow of Baker's Dist., Liberty Co., Ga.
Dated: 25 April 1843.
Signed: S. FRASER. Wit.: SAML. K. OLIVER, J.P. On same date he appt's. BARRINGTON KING his lawful att'y.

(NO COUNTY HEADING FOR THIS:) ELIZA HEGGENS (formerly) now ELIZA ROWE, who being sworn that she is bonafide owner of afsd. lots, (which are at top of the Oath and are: Lot Nos. 145-13-3 Murray Co. and 544-21-2 Cherokee Co.)
Dated: 10 August 1852. Wit.: SARAH L. QUARTERMAN, (T.N.?) QUARTERMAN, J.P.
Signed: ELIZA A. (+) ROWE.

CHATHAM COUNTY: WILLIAM ROBINSON was sworn that he drew Lot No. 563 in 21st Dist., 2nd Sect. of Cherokee County.
Dated: 24 March 1843. Wit.: ROBERTS RAIFORD, J.P.
Signed: WM. ROBINSON

PUTNAM COUNTY: MARGARET HEATH appt's. BUSHROD W. SANFORD her lawful att'y. to grant a cert. tract of land cont. 40 acres, Lot No. 943-21-2, formerly in Cherokee co. of which she is the drawer and legal holder thereof.
Dated: 15 April 1843. Wit.: J. F. HARWELL, THOMAS B. HARWELL, J.P. Signed: MARGANT (X) HEATH.

PIKE COUNTY: JAMES MAXWELL sworn that he is lawful husband of SARAH A. W. MAXWELL, formerly SARAH A. W. KIRK one of the orphans of THOMAS KIRK, dec'd. and the only one of sd. orphans now surviving, the others having died intestate and without issue and that he has employed Mr. JOHN T. THWEATT of sd. Co. to apply for the grant drawn by sd. orphans in orig. Cherokee now Paulding Co. and that as husband of sd. orphan he is bonafide owner of sd. land.
Dated: 7 Nov. 1850. Wit.: JASON BURR, J.P.
Signed: JAMES MAXWELL

LIBERTY COUNTY: A. C. DUNHAM was sworn that he is one of the proper owners as an heir of J. H. DUN-

HAM, dec'd. of Lot No. 1273 in 21st Dist., 3rd Sect. of orig. Cherokee, grant for which is applied. Wit.: ____ DUNHAM, J.I. C.L.C.
Dated: 25 June 1843. Signed: A. C. DUNHAM.
On same date he appt'd. C. N. NELSON of Baldwin Co. his lawful att;y. to apply for sd. grant. Wit.: EDWARD QUARTERMAN, (CLEON) DUNHAM, J.I.C.L.C. (Note: underneath is written: "JACOB H. DUNHAM, 15th Dist. Liberty Co."...Ed.)

BURKE COUNTY: ELIZABETH SUMNER, widow being sworn that she is drawer of 2 Lots of land, one of Gold designeated by No. 1294-21-3 and one of land, No. 269-22-2.
Dated: 17 June 1845.
Signed: ELIZABETH SUMNER. Wit.: JOHN B. GORDON, J.O. On same date she appt'd. GREEN B. POWELL of Burke Co. her lawful att'y. to apply for sd. grants.

CHATHAM COUNTY, CITY
OF SAVANNAH: OCTAVIA J. STEBBINS and FRANCES C. STEB-
BINS, who being duly sworn says they are the proper owners of No. 1266, 20th Dist., 3rd Sect. Paulding co. drawn by EDWARD STEBBINS, orphans of Savannah.
Dated: 24 June 1843. Wit.: ____. ANSELL, J.P.
Signed: OCTAVIA JUDICE STEBBINS , F. C. STEBBINS. On same date they appt. THOMS. B. STUBBS, Esq., of Milledgeville their lawful attorney.
Chatham County, Ga., CATHERINE A. STEBBINS was sworn that she is the mother and natural guardian of orphans of EDWARDS STEBBINS who drew Lot 1266 above. Dated: 29 June 1843 Wit.: ____ RAIFORD, J.P. Signed: C. A. STEBBINS.

COWETA COUNTY: SARAH BACHUS, widow and representative of heirs of WILLIAM BACKUS dec'd of co. afsd.
....and she appt's. SAMUEL HOUSTON of sd. state and county her lawful att'y. to receive grants for gold lots Nos. 1233 in 12th Dist., 3rd Sect. and No. 558 in 4th Dist., 1st Sect. Cherokee co.
Dated: 24 May 1843. Wit.: WESTERN BACKUS, WM. A. SPEAR, J.P.
Signed: SARAH (+) BACHUS. The oath on a seperate sheet from the above Power of Att;y. refers to her a representative of her children the heirs of WILLIAM BACHUS, dec'd. Dated: 23 May 1843 bef. WM. A. SPEAR, J.P.

CASS COUNTY: JOSEPH CHAPMAN and AUTHANIUL CHANDLER who

who being sworn say they are proper owners of Lot No. 1073 in 20th Dist., 3rd Sect. of Paulding Co., grant for which is applied.
Signed: JOSEPH CHAPMAN, ARTHUR (X) NIAL (Note: this name perhaps correct instead of Chandler...Ed.)
Dated: 5 June 1843. Wit.: WILLIAM LATIMER, J.P. (Note: underneath says "Lot No. 1973-20-3 drawn by WRIGHT's orphans of Caroll.)

MUSKOGEE COUNTY: PRUDENCE RUNNELLS was sworn that she was the wife of RICHARD RUNNELLS formerly of Upson Co. who is now dead and that she is now his widow and with his children entitled to the tract of land No. 23 in 20th Dist., 3rd Sect. of formerly Cherokee and that she is the mother of WILLIAM RUNNELLS formerly of Upson Co. who died intestate having never been married and that she and her children his brothers and sisters are to be owners of Lot No. 76 in 11th Dist., __ Sec. of formerly Cherokee drawn by him.
Dated: 21 June 1843. Wit.: JNO. W. BETHUNE, J.I.C.
Signed: PRUDENCE (X) RUNNELLS

JONES COUNTY: CULLEN WHITMAN son of CHRISTOPHER WHITMAN dec'd. who being sworn that he the deponent is interested as one of the owners of Lot No. 594 in 3rd Dis. and 3rd Sec. formerly Cherokee Co. drawn by sd. CHRISTOPHER WHITMAN.
Dated: 27 June 1843 before BALAAM PETERS, J.P.
Signed: CULLEN WHITMAN

HARRIS COUNTY: JOHANNAH EMBREY, Extrx. of JOEL EMBREY, dec'd. and was sworn that JOE EMBREY drew Lot No. 205 in 13th Dist., 2nd Sect. Cherokee, grant for which is applied.
Dated: 17 June 1843 before A. H. SCOTT, J.P.
Signed: JOHANNAH EMBREY

GREENE COUNTY: SAMUEL M. FINDLEY, Admn'r. of ROBERT FINDLEY, dec'd. who was sworn that he is proper owner as Admn'r. of ROBERT FINDLEY of Lot No. 321-12-2, grant for which is applied.
Dated: 2 Dec. 1842 before J. R. HALL, J.P.
Signed: SAMUEL M. FINDLEY.

MURRAY COUNTY: BENJAMIN A. DAVIS of Bradley County, East
                        Tenn., was sworn that Lot No. 93 in 13th
Dist., 2nd Sect. Cherokee Co. is his property lawfully, which
lot of land was drawn by GEORGE W. GLOVE (looks like "Girens
Estr.") Decalb Cty.
Dated: 7 April 1843 before M. VARNELL, J.P.
Signed: B. A. DAVIS

JASPER COUNTY: WM. H. AARON was sworn that he and JAMES
                        C. AARON, SUSAN ANN AARON and ELIZABETH
AARON are the orphans of JOHN AARON's and are proper drawers of
and proper owners of Lot No. 126 in 10th Dist., 2nd Sect. of the
orig. Cherokee Co., grant for which is applied.
Dated: 28 Dec. 1842 before CHARLES F. WALTHALL, J.P.
Signed: WM. H. AARON

WARREN COUNTY: LAWSON D. WRIGHT who was sworn that he is
                        owner of Lot No. 2, 12th Dist., 1st Sect.
and Lot No. 152, 22nd Dist., and 2nd Sect. and Lot No. 222-10th
Dist. and 2nd Sect. all drawn by MILLICENT WRIGHT (Wid.).
Dated: 3 June 1843 before WILLIAM CASTLEBERRY, J.I.C.
Signed: LAWSON D. WRIGHT

BALDWIN COUNTY: THOMAS M. MANN who was sworn that he is
                        proper owner of following lots as Admn'r.
on Estate of ISHAM WEST, dec'd.: 1054-3-1, 475-13-1 and 43-10-2.
Dated: 20 June 1843 before ALFRED M. HORTON, N.P.
Signed: THOMAS M. MANN, Admn'r.

UPSON COUNTY: DRAKEFORD L. TRAMMELL who was sworn that
                        he is owner of following lots of land:
No. 244, 246, 247,231, 255 and 268 all lying in 10th Dist. of
orig. Monroe County but now Upson County.
Dated: 29 May 1843, before JAS. H. BLACK, J.P.
Signed: D. L. TRAMMELL

WALTON COUNTY: Mrs. ELIZA ELDER was sworn that she is the
                        widow of JAMES ELDER, who drew Lot 1039-
3rd Dist. 3rd Sect. and she applies for grant as owner in part
with her children the orphans of sd. JAMES ELDER.
Dated: 27 June 1843, before GEORGE J. HURST, J.P.
Signed: ELIZA (X) ELDER

MADISON COUNTY:　　　　　WILLIAM W. POWER was sworn that he is lawful Exor. of orphans of JOHN W. DAVID who is lawful owner of Lot 101 in 4th Dist., 3rd Sect. Cherokee originally and grant applied for.
Dated: 28 Dec. 1842 before JAMES McCURDY, J.P.
Signed: WILLIAM W. POWER

COWETA COUNTY:　　　　　I, HILLSBERRY R. HARRISON Clerk of Court of Ordinary for sd. County certify that WOOTSON RAINEY is Exor. of the Last Will and Testament of MATTHEW RAINEY, dec'd. formerly of Oglethorpe Co., Ga.
Dated: 22 April 1843.
Signed: HILLSBERRY R. HARRISON

WASHINGTON COUNTY:　　　　　ELIZABETH REAVES of Hancock Co., Ga. was sworn that she drew land in her own right and was Lot No. 329-3-3.
Dated: 27 June 1843 before A(J.?) RAY, J.P.
Signed: ELIZABETH (X) REAVES

MORGAN COUNTY:　　　　　Personally came before me J. R. BROWNING ....saying that he the lawful owner of Lot No. 157 in the 24th Dist., 2nd Sect. Cherokee purchase drawn by CHARLES, NANCY, ELIZABETH, CHARLOTTE, WILLIAM and MATILDA ADISON. Father absent of Albenson'd Dist., Walton Co. and do authoriz(sic) the sd. ALEXANDER PHARR to grant the sd. lot for me. J. R. BROWNING. Sworn to this 20th June 1843 before JOHN J. WALKER, J.P.

CASS COUNTY:　　　　　Personally appeared before me NATHANIEL GRANT, an acting Justice of the Peace in and for sd. county, SARAH HAMILTON who saith that she is the lawful owner of Lot No. 149, 24th Dist., 2nd Sect. and it was drawn by "DAVID CROMPTON's elphants (orphans) of twigs county".
Dated: 21 March 1843.
Signed: SARAH HAMILTON (her x mark). NATHAN GRANT, J.P.

BALDWIN COUNTY:　　　　　Personally appeared W. T. P. FLEMING who says that he is the proper owner in part as one of the Orphans of JAMES FLEMING of Lot No. 119, 24th Dist. 2nd Sect. of orig. Cherokee.
Dated: 15 June 1843　W. T. P. FLEMING. EMMER(?) BAILS, J.P.

PUTNAM COUNTY: ELISABETH L. JORDAN of Co. and state afsd.
                        appoint WILEY B. JORDAN of same my true
and lawful attorney to take out a Plat and Grant for Lot No. 53,
22nd Dist., 2nd Sec. of Cherokee, 160 Acres drawn by me.
Dated: 28 June 1843
Signed: ELIZABETH GORDEN (JORDAN?) (L.S.)

BALDWIN COUNTY: Personally appeared before me...WILEY B.
                        JOURDAN who is the lawful agent of the
owner of Lot No. 53, 22nd Dist., 2nd Sect.
Dated: 29 June 1843
Signed: WILEY B. JORDAN, AM. M. HORTON, N.P., Baldwin County

BIBB COUNTY: Before me MORTIN N. BURCH, a Justice of
                        the Peace in and for afsd. county, person-
ally appeared WESLEY F. SMITH who saith that Lot No. 17, 19th
Dist., 2nd Sect. Cherokee now Cobb County, containing 40 acres,
drawn by HIRUM HILES, orphans, Crawfords County.
Dated: 12 May 1849
Signed: WESLEY F. SMITH, MORTIN N. BURCH, J.P.

CHATHAM COUNTY: Before me JOSEPH FELT, a Justice of the
                        Peace in and for sd. co., personally came
Mrs. MARIA R. DAVIS, Adm'x. of JOHN SPEAKMAN, late of sd. county
and mother and guardian of his orphans, says that the sd. orphans
are the owner of Gold Lot No. 798, 2nd Dist., 3rd Sect. and Land
Lot No. 289, 7th Dist., 1st Sect.
Dated: 2 June 1843
Signed: MARIA R. DAVIS, JOSEPH FELT, J.P.

CHATHAM COUNTY: I have this day appointed JOHN WESLEY of
                        Effingham County my lawful attorney, for
Lot No. 798, 2nd Dist., 3rd Sect. (Gold) and Lot No. 289, 7th
Dist., 1st Sect. (Land).
Dated: 2 June 1843
Signed: MARIA R. DAVIS, JOSEPH FELT, J.P.

WARREN COUNTY: Personally appeared before me SARAH FRENCH
                        who says that she is the proper owner of
Lot No. 7, 5th Dist., 1st Sect. of Cherokee in her own right,
ecaisioned(sic) by the death of her husband WILLIAM FRENCH.
Dated: 26 July 1844   Signed: SARAH (X) FRENCH, SPIVY FULLER,J.P.

CASS COUNTY: Personally appeared before me WILLIAM SY-
                        LAR, a Justice of the Peace for sd. Co.,
JESSE P. JONES, the Adm'r. of THOMAS SANFORD, late of DeKalb co.,
dec'd.....dec'd. was proper owner of Lot No. 773, 2nd Dist., 3rd
Sect. of Cobb County.
Dated: 30 May 1843.
Signed: J. P. JONES, WILLIAM SYLAR, J.P.

COWETA COUNTY: FRANCIS HESTERLY of Co. and State afsd.,
                        heir and representative of MARY BATES,wi-
dow of a Revolutionary Soldier for divers good causes and consideration appoint SAMUEL HOUSTON of sd. State and County, my
true and lawful attorney for me...Gold Lot No. 835, 2nd Dist.,
3rd Sect. of Cherokee.
Dated: 20 May 1843
Signed: FRANCIS HESTERLY (Seal). Before us A. BENTON, WM. A.
SPEAR, J.P.

COWETA COUNTY: Before WILLIAM A. SPEAR, a Justice of the
                        Peace came FRANCIS HESTERLY who saith he
is the only heir and legal representative of MARY BATES, widow
of a Revolutionary Soldier, drawer of Gold Lot No. 835, 2nd Dist.
3rd Sect. Cherokee.
Dated: 20 May 1843
Signed: FRANCIS HESTERLY, WM. A. SPEAR, J.P.

BALDWIN COUNTY: Personally appeared SAMUEL M. STRUT, a
                        citizen of the county of McIntosh who
saith that he is part owner of Lot No. 543, 2nd. Dist.,3rd Sec.
40 acres....drawn by THOMAS WILLCOX of Telfaire County...deed
for sd. lot sold by THOMAS WILLCOX dated 3 May 1837...SAML. M.
STRUT.
Dated: 23 Dec. 1843 before me, A. M. HORTON, N.P.

EFFINGHAM COUNTY: Court of Ordinary: March Term 1837...PAUL
                        MARLOW and BEAL EDWARDS, were duly quali-
fied Ex'rs. of Last Will and Testament of JOHN DUGGER, JR.,dec'd.
on that part of sd. will admissable by Law...JOHN CHARLTON,Clk.
of Court of Ordinary certify the above to be a true copy from
minutes of sd. court.
Dated: 7 August 1843
Signed: JNO. CHARLTON,Clk.

LAURENS COUNTY: Personally appeared before me WILLIAM R.
HESTER, a Justice of the Peace in and for
sd. county, JOHN LOVE, who says that he is the lawful attorney
for SAMUEL RICHARDSON, only surviving heir of DAVID RICHARDSON,
dec'd., late of Emanuel County of sd. state....Lot No. 44, 2nd
Dist., 3rd Sect., Cherokee.
Dated: 5 June 1843
Signed: JOHN LOVE before me W. R. HESTER, J.P.

LAURENS COUNTY: I appoint JOHN G. FONDREN my lawful agent
as att'y. for SAMUEL RICHARDSON, heir of
DAVID RICHARDSON, dec'd....Lot No. 44, 2nd Dist., 3rd Sect. of
Cherokee.
Dated: 5 June 1843
Signed: JOHN LOVE Wit.: (illegible)

CHATHAM COUNTY: Personally appeared before me JANE BARIN-
GER, who says that she is the widow of
THOS. DARINGER and the Guardian of their children WILLIAM and
ELIZABETH....Lot No. 653, 2nd Dist., 3rd Sect. Cherokee County,
drawn by THOMAS BARINGER of Valleans(?) Dist. in the City of Sa-
vannah.
Dated: 1 June 1843 before R. RAIFORD, J.P.
Signed: JANE S. BARINGER   I have appointed ABRAHAM B. FANNIN
of Chatham Co., my lawful att'y. Signed: JANE S. BARINGER 1 June
1843, R. Raiford, J.P.

CHATHAM COUNTY: Personally appeared before me SARAH BIRD,
who says that she is the Adm'x. of LEWIS
BIRD, the drawer of Lot No. 230, 26th Dist., 3rd Sect. Cherokee
(now Walker co.)....SARAH BIRD (Signed) before me 27 May 1843,
R. Raiford, J. P.   I have appointed E. M. COWLES of Baldwin co.
my lawful att'y. Signed: SARAH BIRD 27 May 1843. R. Raiford

FRANKLIN COUNTY: Personally appeared before me GREEN B.SEW-
ELL...he is the proper owner of Lot No.82,
2nd Dist., 3rd Sect., Cherokee, drawn by sd. SEWELL.
Dated: 25 June 1843
Signed: GREEN B. SEWELL   R. A. R. NEEL(?) J.I.C.

FRANKLIN COUNTY: ...APP'd SAMUEL SEWELL who says he is the
proper owner of Lot No. 242, 19th Dist.,

3rd Sect. and Lot No. 1260, 2nd Dist., 2nd Sect.
Dated: 25 June 1843 bef. R. A. R. NEEL(?), J.I.C.
Signed: SAMUEL SEWELL

<u>LAURENS COUNTY</u>:   In person, appeared JEREMIAH H. YOPP(?),
                     Adm'r. of Estate of ZACHARIAH F. BURCFIELD
before the Subscriber a Justice of the peace in sd. county..legal owner as Adm'r. of Lot in 2nd Dist., 3rd Section of the Gold REgion of the Cherokee No. 1274.
Dated: 17 June 1843
Signed: J. H. YOPP, Adm'r.

<u>COBB COUNTY</u>:   Before me appeared NOEL B. KNIGHT who deposes that he is the duly constituted agent of WASHINGTON BEDINGTON orphan of WILLIAM BEDINGTON and sd. WASHINGTON BEDINGTON applies for the grant of Lot No. 2, in the 2nd Dist., 3rd Section of Paulding County.
Dated: 23 Feb. 1854
Signed: NOEL B. KNIGHT before me JAW S. MURPHY, J.P.

<u>FAYETTE COUNTY</u>:   Came before me C. M. DODSON, a J.P. in sd.
                   county, came SEABORN A. LEE, saith that he is the proper owner of Gold Lot No. 186 in the 2nd Dist., 3rd Sect. of Cherokee now Cobb co.
Signed: SEABERN A. LEE before me 25 April 1843. C. M. DODSON, J. P.
                   I appoint JOHN P. DODSON my true and lawful agent to apply for grant. SEABERN A. LEE (L.S.) Wit.:JOHN FULLER (O), C. M. DODSON, J.P.

...............co.?   Personally appeared before me WILLIAM P.
                     TAYLOR who says that he is the lawful Gdn. for the heirs of ABSALOM TAYLOR, dec'd. of Lot No. 1162, 2nd Dis. 3rd Sec....drawn by sd. ABSALOM TAYLOR.
Dated: 12 June 1843
Signed: WILLIAM P. TAYLOR, ELBERT L.? TAYLOR, J.P.

<u>BURKE COUNTY</u>:   I have this day appointed WM. H. PRITCHARD
                     of Baldwin co., my lawful att'y. to apply for the grant for Lot No. 1142, 2nd Sect., 3rd Dist.
Dated: 12 June 1843
Signed: WM. P. TAYLOR (LS), ABSALOM TAYLOR,YOUNGS JEFFERSON. Wit.

N. W. TAYLOR, ELBERT C.? TAYLOR.

GREEN COUNTY: Personally appd bef. me JOSHUA BARNES, the legal adm'r. on his fathers estate and say that his Father is the legal owner and drawer of two lots in Cherokee, one the gold lot the other a lot of land...the gold lot known by Lot No. 1248, 3rd Sec....Land Lot No. 73, 9 Sect......
NOAH BARNES is owner of above lots, but now dec'd.
Dated: 24 June 1843
Signed: JOSHUA BARNES, NATHAN BARNES. JOHN P. HOWELL, J.I.C.

RICHMOND COUNTY: Personally app'd bef. me JAMES W. DAVIS, who says that Gold Lot No. 495, 2nd Dist. 3rd Sect. belongs to the Estate of Mrs. ELEANOR L. NESBITT,dec'd. late of sd. county and that he is the legal representative of sd. Estate, the grant of which is applied by WILLIAM H. PRITCHARD,my lawful agent.
Dated: 29 June 1843
Signed: JAMES W. DAVIES, BENJ. HALL, J.P.

COWETA COUNTY: Personally came bef. me ALARSON(?) BOWEN, a J.P. of sd. co., ALEXANDER FLOYD, saith that the is lawful gdn. for Doctor W. DIAL and the sd. DIAL did draw Lot No. 121 9th Dist., 3rd Sect. of Cherokee now Murry co.
Dated: 27 March 1843
Signed: ALEXANDER FLOYD   A. BOWEN, J.P.

I have appt'd. LEVI NEWTON of co. afsd. my true and lawful att'y. to take out the plat and grant for Lot No. 121, 9th Dist., 3rd Sect. of Cherokee now Murry Co.
Dated: 27 Mar. 1843
Signed: ALEXANDER FLOYD,(L.S.) A. BOWEN, J.P.

GORDON COUNTY: Bef. me GEORGE W. RANSOM, a J. P., app'd. FRANCIS M. REESE who saith that he is one of the orphans of REDMAN REESE of Warrent (Warren?) Co., dec'd. who drew Lot No. 121, 8th Dist., 3rd Sect. and that the other orphans of drawers of sd. Lot are the brothers and sisters of this deponent and that he makes application of sd. Lot for benefit of sd. orphans.
Dated: 12 Feb. 1853
Signed: F. M. REESE, C. W. RANSOM, J.P.

HOUSTON COUNTY: CHARLES H. RICE, adm'r of estate of FAUNT-
                       LEROY F. CHAIN, late of sd. county, dec'd.
....app't. EZRA DAGGETT of Baldwin Co. my lawful att'y. to apply
to the proper offices at Milledgeville and take out the grant of
Lot No. 90, 8th Dist., 3rd Sect. of (now) Murry County, drawn by
FAUNTLEROY F. CHAIN.
Dated: 15 May 1843
Signed: CHARLES H. RICE (Seal), Wit.: EPHR. KENDRICK, E. MOUN-
GER(?), J.I.C.

DeKALB COUNTY: Personally app'd. bef. me HANNAH TATE who
                       says that she is the proper owner of two
lots of land...Lot No. 41, 8th Dist., 3rd Sect. of Cherokee (also Lot No. 220, 12th Dist., of Lee county--stricken)
Dated: 1 June 1843
Signed: HANNAH TATE, J. B. WILSON, J.P.

HOUSTON COUNTY: Bef. me EDWIN MOUNGER, a J. P. of the Inf.
                       Crt. came CHARLES H. RICE who says that he
believes that FAUNTLEROY F. CHAIN was the drawer of Lot No. 90,
8th Dist., 3rd Sect. now Murray Co.
Dated: 15 May 1843
Signed: C. H. RICE, E. MOUNGER, J.I.C.

                       I do hereby app't I. M.(?) HORNE, Esqr. of
Baldwin co. at Milledgeville, State of Ga., my lawful att'y. to
apply for and take out the Grant for the following lots.: Nos.
47 & 66 of the 8th and 3rd Sec., and Nos. 278 & 297 of the 9th
and 3rd Sect.
Dated: 13 June 1844
Signed: ROBERT ANDERSON (LS), L. D. CLARKE, J.P.

BALDWIN COUNTY: Personally app'd. bef. me PLENEY A. TURK
                       who says that he is the lawful agent of
the owner of Lot 34 in 8th Dist., 3d Sec. of orig. Cherokee co.
Dated: 4 March 1843
Signed: ALFRED M. NORTON, N.P. Baldwin Co....PLINEY A. TURK.

JACKSON COUNTY: SAMUEL KNOX of Chattooga county, app't.
                       PLINEY A. TURK of Jackson county, my law-
ful att'y. to apply for grants for two Lots drawn by myself,
samuel knox, jr. being in the Late Land Obtained from the Chero-

kee Indians in the 3rd Section, 13th Dist., No. 101 and also one drawn by SAMUEL KNOX, SR., who is now Dead and left me as one of his executors.
Dated: 27 Feb. 1843 - No. 34, 8th Dist., 3rd Section. ..SAMUEL KNOX   ROBERT PRUITT, J.B. NABERS (?), J.P.

JACKSON COUNTY: Personally came before me PLEYNEY A. TURK and saith that he is the lawfull attorney of SAMUEL KNOX
Dated: 27 Feb. 1843
Signed: PLINEY A. TURK, J. B. VABUS (?), J.P.

TOTTNALL(?) COUNTY: Before me JOHN J. GRAY, a Justice of the Peace, personally came THOMAS BURKE who saith that he is an heir of THOMAS J. BURKE, dec'd. who drawed Lots No. 6 in 8th Dist., 3rd Section and No. 65 (63?) in 2nd Dis. 3rd Section....and Lot No. 415, 18th Dist., 2nd Section
Dated: 10 June 1843
Signed: THOMAS BURK   JOHN H. GRAY, J.P.

RANDOLPH COUNTY: Personally appeared before me, GREEN B. LEWIS, an acting Justice of the Peace, JOHN WOOD one of the survin(sic) orphans of JOSEPH late of ____ who being duly sworn saith that No. 305 in the 7th Dist., 3rd Sec., and No. 64, 23rd Dist., 3rd Sec. of orig. Cherokee County .....he and sister LOVICA WOOD: and sister ELIZABETH WOOD is dead and that they are the children of JOSEPH WOOD, dec'd. of Houston county, Ga.
Dated: 20 Apr. 1843
Signed: JOHN WOOD   GREEN B. LEWIS, J.P.

RANDOLPH COUNTY: We, JOHN WOOD & LOVICA WOOD app't. SOLOMON P. BETTEN our true and lawful att'y. to apply for grants (above mentioned).
Dated: 20 April 1843
Signed: JOHN WOOD (Seal), LOVICA WOOD (Seal), by her agent JOHN WOOD: W. J. BALLARD, GREEN B. LEWIS, J.P.

TELFAIR COUNTY: Before me WM. R. MANNING a Justice of the Peace came BENJAMIN McLENDON who saith he is the friend of MARY CRADDICK now MARY McLENDON who drew a lot of land in Cherokee Co. number & district not known to which he now seeks to obtain a grant....BENJAMIN McLENDON (his x mark),WM. R. MANNING, J.P.

BIBB COUNTY: Personally came before me EUGENIUS A. NISBET who saith that he is the Guardian of MILES C. NISBET and that sd. orphan is the drawer and owner of Lot No. 372 (392?), 2nd Dist., 3rd Sect. Gold region in the co. of Paulding...also No. 54, 7th Dist., 3rd Sect. Mundy Co.
Dated: 26 June 1843
Signed: EUGENIUS A. NISBET   JESSE L. OWEN, J.P.

MORGAN COUNTY: MARY NELSON appoints AZARIAH B. BOSTWICK of Co. and state afsd. my true and lawful att'y. to take out Grants for the following: No. 88, 7th Dist., 3rd Sect.; No. 204, 11th Dist., 2nd Sect.
Dated: 16 Dec. 1843
Signed: MARY (X) NELSON (L.S.)   Test.: WILLIAM SIMS, A. B. BOSTWICK, J.P.

MURRY COUNTY: Personally came bef. me A. T. SMITH, an acting Justice of the peace for sd. co., WILLIAM BYROM and NANCY BYROM, saith that they are joint owners of Lot No. 72, 7th Dist., 3rd Sect. of orig. Cherokee lying now in the counties of Cass and Murray.
Dated: 20 May 1843 bef. A. T. SMITH, J.P.
Signed: NANCY BYROM (her x mark) (L.S.), WILLIAM H. BYROM (L.S.)

MURRAY COUNTY: We, WILLIAM H. BYROM and NANCY BYROM appt. JACKSON FITZPATRICK our lawful att'y. to take out grant (for above lot).
Signed: NANCY BYROM (X)(LS), WM. H. BYROM (LS), Test. A. T. SMITH, J.P.

CRAWFORD COUNTY: Personally appeared bef. me VANN HOLTON and sayeth that he is the rightful and proper owner of part of such land as was drawn by the Orphans of STEPHEN HOLTON, Washington Co., Haygoods District, 11 April 1843. Nos. 293-5-3 and 238-5-3 Cherokee.
Signed: E. JOYNER, J.P.   VAN HOLTON

CRAWFORD COUNTY: I. VANN HOLTON, being ot age, have appt'd. MATTHEW J. JORDAN my lawful att'y. (cont'd

Dated: 11 April 1843
Signed: VAN HOLTON (LS.), HILLIS TAYLER, E. JOYNER, J.P.

CHEROKEE COUNTY: Before me ELIJAH HILLHOUSE, a justice of the peace, came DENNIS FOWLER who saith that Lot No. 216, 5th Dist., 3rd Sect., drawn by A. BROWN of Habersham is his own right and property.
Dated: 14 June 1843
Signed: DENNIS (X) FOWLER, ELIJAH HILLHOUSE, J.P.

WILKINSON COUNTY: Personally appear BRYANT ROBERTS before me WILLIS ALLEN, a justice of the peace, who saith that he is one of the orphans of WILLIAM ROBERTS, of Smith district, Wilkinson county and that sd. orphans drew Lot No. 142, 5th Dist., 3rd Sect. of Cherokee.
Dated: 11 Dec. 1848
Signed: BRYANT ROBERTS (X), WILLIS ALLEN, J.P.

WILKINSON COUNTY: I. SARAH LINDSEY of Co. and state afsd., have appt'd. ISAAC LINDSEY of same, my lawful att'y. to act for me to apply for Grants for Lots No. 139 in the 5th Dist., 3rd Section Cherokee, and Lot. No. 86, 13th Dist., of Carel (Carroll) Co. and No. 245 in the 3rd Dist., of Muscogee Co.
Dated: 23 June 1843
Signed: SARAH (X) LINDSAY, H. WHITAKER, S. J. BUSH(?), J.P.

MONROE COUNTY: Personally came THOMAS BANKS who saith he is in right of his wife who was an orphan of ISAAC WILMOT by name of ESTHER ANN WILMOT, and who lived at the time of drawing in Elbert Co., in Clarke District and who drew Lot No. 42, 5th Dist., 4th Sect. of the drawing in the year 1832 and 33. Sworn to 16 Feb. 1843.
I. THOMAS BANKS hereby empower WILLIAM L. COOK as my lawful agent to apply for grants for Lots No. 45,-9-1 and No. 42-5-4 drawn by THOMAS BANKS and by ESTHER ANN WILMOT his wife.
Dated: 13 Mar. 1843
Signed: THOMAS BANKS (Seal), DOLPHIN FLOYD, J. A. BANKS, J.I.C.

HALL COUNTY: Before MOSES BREAN, a J.P. of sd. county came ELIZABETH GILMER & saith that she is

owner of Lot No. 41, 5th Dist., 3rd Sec. orig. Cherokee now Cass county.
Dated: 14 June 1843
Signed: ELIZABETH (X) GILMER, MOSES BREAN, J.P.
ELIZABETH GILMER appt's. EZEKIEL BUFFINGTON of Co. and State afsd. lawful att'y. 14 June 1843.
ELIZABETH (X) GILMER (Seal). Wit.: JAMES GILMER, MOSES BRIAN,J.P.

PAULDING COUNTY: Personally came before me GARRETT H. SPINKS an acting J. P. for sd. Co., JAMES COLE, who saith that he is the legal owner of Lot No. 29, 18th Dist., 3rd Sect. of orig. Cherokee, now Polk Co.....he purchased sd.Lot of JAMES STANTON, JOHN STANTON & BURREL STANTON, orphans of JONATHAN STANTON, dec'd.
Dated: 4 Aug. 1853
Signed: JAMES COOL. G. H. SPINK, J.P.

CHATHAM COUNTY: Savannah - Personally appeared M. MEYERS General or Official assignee in Bankruptcy for the Dist. of Ga....he is the proper owner of Lots No. 120-18-3 and No. 322-28-3 drawn by PHILIP R. YONGE a decreed and discharged Bankrupt Act.
Dated: 29 June 1843
Signed: JOSEPH FELT, J.P. M. MEYERS.

CHATHAM COUNTY: Bef. me CHARLES HUTCHINGS one of the Justices of the Inf. Crt. of sd. County came DAVID E. BLUNT who saith that he is the Adm'r. on the Estate of JOSEPH J. HAMILTON, dec'd. and the sd. HAMILTON in his life time drew Lot No. 157-18-3 of orig. Cherokee now Paulding Co.
Dated: 26 June 1843
Signed: CHARLES HUTCHINGS, J.I.C., DAVID E. BLUNT

CHATHAM COUNTY: I have appt'd. JAMES H. R. WASHINGTON, Esq of Baldwin Co. my att'y. to apply for grant for Lot No. 120-18-3 and for Lot No. 322-28-3.
Dated: 30 June 1843
Signed: M. MYERS (LS), JOSEPH FELT, J.P.

BALDWIN COUNTY: Before me personally appeared M. DENMARK, who says that he applys in good faith as the friend of DAVID GROOVER, SR. to take out grant for Lot No.225

18th Dist., 3rd Section of Bullock County.
Dated: 22 Dec. 1843
Signed: ALFRED M. HORTON, Notary Public   M. DENMARK

JACKSON COUNTY: Personally appeared before me WILLIAM M.
                         LESTER, who saith that he is the owner of
half of Lot No. 189-18-3 of original Cherokee County when drawn
by WILLIAM WOODS orphans of Jackson County, the grant for which
is applied for.
Dated: 19 April 1843
Signed: WILLIAM M. LESTER, JAS. B. NABERS, J.P.
                         JAMES B. NABERS of Jackson County is here-
by appt'd. my true and lawful agent to apply for grant for (lot
above named). 19 Apr. 1843 WILLIAM M. LESTER (SL), JOHN HORTON,
J. B. NABERS, J.P.

ELBERT COUNTY: Personally came before me JOSEPH SEWELL,
                         a J. P. for sd. county, THOMAS BURTON who
sayeth that he together with the other legal heirs of THOMAS S.
BURTON, dec'd. are the proper owners of Lot 297-18-3 originally
Cherokee County.
Dated: 6 June 1843
Signed: THOMAS BURTON, JOSEPH SEWELL, J.P.

COLUMBIA COUNTY: Personally before me THOS. H. WHITE who
                         saith that he is the lawful agent of LID-
IA DODSON of Warren County who drew Gold Lot No. 250-18-3 of the
Cherokee Co....THOS. H. WHITE before me DAVID HOLLIMAN, J.P.
Dated: 26 June 1843
                         I have this day appt'd. WILLIAM H. PRITCH-
CHARD of Bauldwin Co. my lawful agent to apply for grant for Gold
Lot (No. above).
Dated: 26 June 1843...THOS. H. WHITE, DAVID HOLLIMAN, J.P.

CHATHAM COUNTY: We, ISAAC D'LYNN, ANNA D'LYNN, REBECCA
                         D'LYNN and MORDECAI J. D'LYNN, Heirs and
distributees of ABRAHAM D'LYNN, late of sd. county, dec;d., appoint ABRAHAM BALDWIN FANNIN, Esqr. of same co., to receive the
grant for a tract drawn by sd. ABRAHAM, No. 325-118-3.
Dated: 2 June 1843
Signed: ISAAC D'LYNN, LEVI S. D'LYNN, M. S. D'LYNN (LS), in the
presence of ALEX. DRYSDALE, N.P.

WILKES COUNTY: Personally appeared before a Justice in and for sd. county, ELIZABETH W. MOSS who says she is the proper owner (as Guardian for JOHN MOSS's orphans of Benson District, Lincoln County) of Lot No. 1107-17-3 of Gold and Land Lottery (county not known). E. W. MOSS, 2 May 1843 ISAAC A. McLENDON, J.P.

I have this day appointed WM. H. PRITCHARD of Baldwin Co., my lawful att'y. E. W. MOSS (LS), ISAAC A. McLENDON, J.P.

HENRY COUNTY: Personally appeared before me THOS. E. HICKS, a Justice of the Peace in and for sd. county, DAVID KNOTT who says that he is the proper owner of Lot No. 1064-17-3 of orig. Cobb now Paulding County drawn by JAMES KNOTT of Clarke County, 40 acres.
Dated: 3 June 1843
Signed: DAVID KNOTT, T. E. HICKS, J.P.

I appoint ALLEN E. JOHNSON my lawful atty. DAVID KNOTT (LS)...3 June 1843, CHARLES McDONALD, T. E. HICKS, JP

RICHMOND COUNTY: Personally appeared before me THOMAS HICKLE who saith that he is the surviving person who drew the tract of land in the late Land Lottery, Lot No. 978-17-3 drawn in the name of JESSE & THOMAS HICKLE orphan; 119 Dist., Richmond County....THOMAS HICKLE. 30 May 1843 J. W. MEREDETH, J.P.

I, THOMAS HICKLE have appt'd. WILLIAM H. PRITCHARD of Baldwin Co., my lawful att'y. THOMAS HICKLE, J.W. MEREDITH, J.P. 30 May 1843.

JEFFERSON COUNTY: We, ARTHUR S. CLARK, ELIZA F. ANDREWS of co. and state afsd. app't. BABB L. LEMLE our lawful att'y. to take out the grants for certain lots drawn as the orphans of DAVIES(?) CLARK of Richmond Co.
Signed: A. S. CLARKE (LS), ELIZA F. ANDREWS (LS). Test.: H. POTHILL(?), N. P...Lot of Land No. 278-10-3. Lot of Land, No. 1-10-4. Lot of Gold No. 508-21-3.

ELBERT COUNTY: Personally appeared before me WILLIAM D. CAMPBELL, Exr. of JAMES DILLARD, dec'd., who was the proper owner of Lot No. 765-3-2 of Cherokee Co. and Lot No. 1023-14-1 Forsyth Co. (cont'd)

Dated: 15 May 1843. Signed: WILLIAM D. CAMPBELL, Z. SMITH,J.P.

JEFFERSON COUNTY: Before me THOMAS H. POLHILL, a Notary Public. for sd. county personally appeared ARTHUR S. CLARKE who saith that the above lots drawn by the orphans of DAVID (?) CLARK, dec'd. of Richmond County.
Dated: 16 June 1843
Signed: A. S. CLARK, T. POLHILL, ____.

COWETA COUNTY: Came before me a Justice of piece(sic).. for sd. county, LITTLEBERRY HUDGINS who sayeth that he is one of Legatees of SAMUEL WRIGHT formerly of Troup County, McGees district and became a fortunate drawer of a lot in the 3rd sect., 10th dist., No. 120, now Murray County... 160 acres. Signed: LITTLEBURY HUDGINS (X), A. BOWEN, J.P.

GLYNN COUNTY: Appeared in person before me SAMUEL M. BURNETT who says that he is the Adm'r. of the Estate of WILLIAM F. BURNETT, late of sd. county/ owner of Lot No. 111, 2nd Dist., of Coolly (?) County.
Dated: 9 June 1843
Signed: SAML. M. BURNETT, A. G. BURNETT, J.I.C.

GLYNN COUNTY: SAMUEL BURNET, Adm'r. of ABSOLUM HALLS appeared before me in person and says he is the proper owner as Adm'r. of Lot 309, 18th Dist., 3rd Section, now Cobb County, formerly Cherokee.
Dated: 28 Dec. 1843
Signed: SAML. M. BURNETT, Adm'r., A. G. BURNETT, J.I.C.
            I have this day appointed W. A. SANFORD of Baldwin, my lawful att'y. for Lot No. 111-3- and Lot No. 309-18-3. Dated: 9 June 1843. Signed: SAML. M. BURNETT, A. G. BURNETT, J.I.C.

JACKSON COUNTY: No. 166, 10th Dist., 3rd Section originally Cherokee, now Murray County...personally appeared before me JOHN VENABLE, who says that he is one of the Bona fide owners of the above lot, one of the minor heirs of NATHANIEL VENABLE late of Jackson County, dec'd.
Dated: 23 July 1853.
Signed: JOHN VENABLE.   N. H. PENDERGRASS, J.P.

BUTTS COUNTY: In person came WILLIAM F. CLARK who saith
                     that he is one of the owners by intermar-
riage of Lot No. 179-10-3, of Cherokee County drawn by a family
of orphans WILLIAM HOLLAWAYS.
Dated: 20 May 1843
Signed: WILLIAM F. CLARK, G. HENDRICK, J.I.C.
                     I, WILLIAM F. CLARK, do authorise AUGUS-
TUS CARGILE to grant Lot No. 179-10-3, Cherokee....30 May 1843.
WILLIAM F. CLARK (LS), G. HENDRICK, J.I.C.

BALDWIN COUNTY: Personally came before me ELI MANER of
                     Houston County who says that he is the
Ex'r. of the Last Will and Testament of RACHEL CULPEPPER, dec'd.
and the proper owner of Lots No. 822-2-3 and No. 182-10-3.
Dated: 19 Jun. 1843
Signed: ELI MANER, JAMES A. WASHINGTON, J.I.C.B.C.

JASPER COUNTY: Before me a justice of the Inferior Crt.
                     of sd. county came JEREMIAH PEARSON, Admr.
of EARNEST S. YOUNG, late of Bibb County, dec'd....is the owner
of Lot No. 1004, 18th Dist., 3rd Section Cherokee.
Dated: 8 June 1843
Signed: JEREMIAH PEARSON, D. A. REES(?), J.I.C.
                     1004-18-3, EARNEST L. YOUNG, Ellsworth,
Bibb County.

CARROL COUNTY: Personally appeared before me SEXTON HAR-
                     PER, who saith that he is one of the Leg-
al Heirs of HANNAH HARPER, widow of DAVID HARPER and that he is
the legal owner of Land No. 1232 in the 3rd Dist., 2nd Section,
Cherokee.
Dated: 17 Sept. 1844
Signed: SEXTON (X) HARPER, R. N. C. RUFFIN.

(Incomplete..)   Lot No. 1004-18-3, Cherokee...8 June 1843
                     JEREMIAH PEARSON (Seal), Wit.: C. L. GOOLS-
BY, D. A. REESE, J.I.C. Given in Ellsworths Dist., Bibb County.

PULASKI COUNTY: Personally came before me JOHN BOZEMAN,
                     a Justice of the Inferior Court, JOHN DOKE
and saith that he is the lawful owner of the larges(sic) portion
of Lot No. 315-10-1, Cherokee, drawn by JOHN F. SIMMONS orphans,

Wilkinson County...JOHN DOKE, 17 June 1843...JOHN BOZEMAN,J.I.C.

LAURENS COUNTY: Personally appeared before me PERMELIA
WINDHAM who says that she is the proper owner of Lot No. 1004-18-3, Cherokee. 24 June 1843...PERMELIA WINDHAM (X), DRURY F. SCARBOROUGH, J.P.
   I have appointed DANIEL WINDHAM my lawful att'y. ..24 June 1843. PARMELIA WINDHAM (X) (LS) Wit.: FRANCIS HILLIARD, DRURY F. SCARBOROUGH, J.P.

TROUP COUNTY: Personally came ELIJAH W. CHRISTIAN, JR. who saith that he is the proper owner of Lot No. 285-8-2, Cherokee and that he is agent for WILLIAM CHRISTIAN who drew Lot No. 316-12-1, Cherokee and that he makes application through JOHN HARDEN (his agent).
Dated: 29 May 1843
Signed: ELIJAH W. CHRISTIAN (name of J.P. cut off).

WASHINGTON COUNTY: Personally appeared before me JABEZ JOINES who says that he is the proper owner of Lot No. 220-13-3, Cherokee, as Ex'r. of Last Will and Testament of NATHANIEL OFFUTT(?) late of Washington Co., which lot was drawn is sd. NATHANIEL OFFUTT's name of Williams Dist., in said county.
Dated: 21 June 1843
Signed: JABEZ JOINES, A. GIBS, J.P.

JONES COUNTY: Personally came before me G. B. WILLIAMSON a Justice of the peace for sd. county, NANCY PITTS the natural Guardian of LIZZA PITTS, Idiot or lunatic and saith that she is the proper and Bonefide owner Lot No. 183-160 A.   10 June 1843. NANCY (X) PITTS, Gdn. of E. PITTS. GREEN B. WILLIAMSON, J.P.

DeKALB COUNTY: Before me JOHN H. BELLINGER an acting Justice of the Inf. Crt. came EDWARD L. JONES Adm'r. of DAVID THURMAN dec'd. and that he is the proper owner of Lot No. 128-13-2 Cherokee, 160 Acres, drawn by DAVID THURMAN,dec'd of DeKalb Co.
Dated: 1 June 1843 before J. N. BELLINGER, J.I.C. E. K. JONES

COBB COUNTY: Personally came before me JAMES W. GROVES,

an acting Justice of the sd. county, DAVID W. LINDSEY who sayeth that he is one of the Lawful heirs of JOHN LINDSEY, dec'd. of Irwin County...Gold Lottery No.124, 13th Dist., 3rd Section of Cherokee, now Murry County.
Dated: 28 Jan. 1850
Signed: DAVID W. LINDSAY

EMANUEL COUNTY: Personally appeared before me ABRAHAM L. KIRKLAND, who says that he is a judgement Creditor of RUNION(?) DREW, who drew Lot No. 900, 3rd Dist., ___ Section.
Dated: 23 June 1843
Signed: ABRAHAM L. KIRKLAND, __IS BEACHAM, J.P.

COBB COUNTY: Personally appeared bef. me N. B. GREEN, one of the Justices of the Inf. Crt. for sd. Co., CHARLES W. STONE, who says that the application for grant to Lots No. 269-5-2 and No. 24=13-3, is made as one of the orphans of JOSHUA STONE and for the benefit of sd. orphans.
Signed: CHAS. W. STONE before me 18 Mar. 1848, N. B. GREEN,J.I.C.

P. M. COMPTON, Esqr., Surveyor
Gen'l State of Geo.: Dear Sir, Enclosed I hand you Five dollars and affidavit as per form which you furnished you will please forward by return mail the Grants to me at the place, Yrs. very respectfully M. MYERS for HENRY MYERS, Marietta, March 17, 1848.

GWINETT COUNTY: Personally appeared bef. me ASA GOBER,Exr. of the est. of WM. Y. GOBER dec'd. who says that he is the proper owner of Lot 187-11-3.
Dated: 28 Dec. 1842 Signed: ASA GOBER, LOT NOWDEN, J.P.
I have this day appt'd. SAMUEL MARTIN my lawful att'y. ...ASA GOBER (Seal) Wit: WM. CROWD, LOT NOWDEN, J.P.

PUTNAM COUNTY: Personally appeared ROBERT S. DENHAM and WILLIAM D. BEVIL and saith that they are the Legal owners of Lot No. 129-11-3 of Cherokee, now Murray Co., drew by JOSEPH BARNET of Taylors Dist., Putnam County, these deponents having intermarried with the two orphans.
Dated: 25 Nov. 1845 R. S. DENHAM, W.D. BEVIL Wit.JAS. WRIGHT,JR

FAYETTE COUNTY: Before me G. C. KING, J.P., personally
                       came LORENZO D. PADGETT and sayeth that
he is the proper owner of Lots: No. 287-11-3 drawn by PENELOPE
HUDLES, widow of Fayette Co., Nickols Dist...and Lot ___Fraction
Number ____ drawn by ALEXANDER STEWART of Fayette County.
Dated: 23 Jan. 1843
Signed: L. D. PADGETT, G. C. KING, J.P.

FRANKLIN COUNTY: WILLIAM W. MITCHELL, being sworn says he
                       is a lawful legatee of CATHERINE MOLDEN(?)
dec'd. who was the proper owner of Lot No. 19, 11th Dist., 3rd
Sect. of Cherokee, now Walker Co.
Dated: 22 May 1843
Signed: WM. W. MITCHELL, NOAH LOONEY, J.P.
                       I have appt'd. TEMPLE F. CASPER of Frank-
lin Co. my att'y. WM. W. MITCHELL (Seal) Test: E. B. DUMASS.

MUSCOGEE COUNTY: STUBIND (STRIBLIND?) F. (GRIMES?) who on
                       oath says he is agent of THOMAS P. GRIMES
the owner of Lot 168-5-2 (Crossed out) and Gold Lot 295-3-3 of
Cherokee grant for which is applied.
Dated: 29 May 1843 bef. G. W. TURRENTINE, J.P.
Signed: STRIBLIND F. GRIMES

BALDWIN COUNTY: JAMES W. TINSLEY was sworn that he is Ad-
                       mn'r. on estate of W. TINSLEY, dec'd. who
was Admn'r. on estate of EDWARD SWEARINGIN and Exo'r. on estate
of ABRAHAM GOGGINS who were proper owners of Lot No. 27-1-4; No.
223-3-3 and No. 285-21-3 of orig. Cherokee, grants for which he
now applies.
Dated: 27 June 1843 bef. R. MICKLEJOHN.
Signed: T. W. TINSLEY

RICHMOND COUNTY: WILLIAM E. JACKSON was sworn that SARAH F.,
                       HENRY J. and JOHN S. PORTER, minor child-
ren of JOHN S. PORTER, dec'd. for whom the deponent is Gdn. are
the proper owners of Lot No. 45 in 11th Dist., 2nd Sect. of Gilmer Co., grant for which is applied.
Dated: 28 Dec. 1842 before J. W. MEREDITH, J.P.
Signed: WILLIAM E. JACKSON

UPSON COUNTY: D. L. TRAMMELL was sworn that he is agent

of LEROY McCOY, who is Admn'r. of DANIEL HICKS (CROSSED OUT),SU-
SAN HICKS, widow who drew Lot No. 296-12-2 and applied for grant.
Dated: 29 May 1843 before JAS. H. BLACK, J.P.
Signed: D. L. TRAMMELL

PUTNAM COUNTY: THOMAS G. SANFORD, Adm'r. of JAMES JORDAN
dec'd. was sworn that Lot No. 224-12-2 of
orig. Cherokee Co. was drawn by orphans of sd. deceased and he
is their legal representative as adm'r. of estate.
Dated: 2 June 1843 before T. B. HARWELL, J.P.
Signed: THOS. G. SANFORD

TATNELL(TATTNALL) CO. SIMON SMITH was sworn that he is lawful
Adm'r of estate of MILLINGTON SMITH (the
M could be a W(illington) late of Bulloch County, dec'd. and that
Lot No. 874-3-3 and No. 305-5-1 is property of estate of MILLING-
TON SMITH, dec'd.
Dated: 9 June 1843 before JOHN A. ROGERS, J.P.
Signed: SIMON SMITH

COWETA COUNTY: THOMAS SMITH was sworn that he is proper
owner of the lawful agent an the owner
thence of Lot No. 310-11-2 of late Cherokee Co. grant for which
is applied.
Dated: 28 May 1842 before JOHN CRAVEN, J.P.
Signed: THOMAS (X) SMITH

THOMAS COUNTY: MATTHEW C. DUKES was sworn that he is the
natural Gdn. of SARAH ANN HANDLEY orphan
who drew and is proper owner of Lot No. 42-13-2 Cherokee Co.when
surveyed, grant for which is applied.
Dated: 13 June 1843
Signed: bef. HORACE LANTON, J.I.C. MATTHEW C. DUKES

MORGAN COUNTY: WILLIAM G. EVANS who was sworn that he is
lawful agent of JAMES EVANS the lawful own-
ner of Lot No. 1219-5-1 of Cherokee Purchase.
Dated: 3 June 1843 before EILJAH E. JONES, J.I.C.
Signed: WILLIAM G. EVANS

NEWTON COUNTY: SARAH FIELDS was sworn that he is proper
owner of Lot No. 1140-5-1 Cherokee County

when surveyed by purchase. Dated: 20 June 1843 before JAMES M. SMITH.
Signed: SARAH (X) FIELDS

EARLY COUNTY: JANE SPENCE was sworn that she is the drawer and owner of Lot No. 929 - 5 - 1 of the Cherokee...grant for which is applied.
Dated: 17 May 1843 before DANIEL M. JORDAN, J.P.
Signed: JANE SPENCE

WARREN COUNTY: SARAH FRENCH who was sworn that she is the proper owner of Lot No. 47 in 5th Dist., 1st Sec. of Cherokee in her own right occasioned by the death of her husband WILLIAM FRENCH, the grant for which is applied.
Dated: 26 July 1844 before SPIVEY FULLER, J.P.
Signed: SARAH (X) FRENCH

MONROE COUNTY: JAMES H. MAYS was sworn that he is lawful owner of Lot No. 824 in 5th Dist., 1st Sect. and that he is Adm'r. on estate of MARY MAYS, dec'd. and that she drew Lot No. 11-6-1.
Dated: June 8, 1843 before JAS. HARDIN, J.P.
Signed: JAMES H. MAYS

WASHINGTON COUNTY: WILEY MEEKS was sworn that he is rightful owner of Gold No. 312 in 5th Dist. and 1st Sec. drawn by the orphans of WILLIAM BROWN, Garner's Dist. of sd. county.
Dated: 15 May 1848 before JOHN D. BROWN, J.P.
Signed: WILEY MEEKS

GREENE COUNTY: GEORGE G. MATHEWS was sworn that he is Exr. of estate of JONAS FANCH, late of sd. cty. dec'd., and sd. JONAS FANCH was drawer of Lot No. 263, 5th Dist., 1st Sect. of orig. Cherokee Co.
Dated: 2 Feb. 1843 before J. R. HALL, J.I.C.
Signed: GEO. G. MATHEWS

PAULDING COUNTY: CICERO L. COLLOTT was sworn that he is one of the legal and joint aires(sic) that drew Lot No. 197-6-1 drawn in the name of JOHN COLLOTT's orphans of Allens Dist., Henry Co. (cont'd.)...

Dated: 18 Dec. 1851 before D. W. ROSS, J.P. Signed: CICERO L. COLLO<u>T</u>.

GREENE COUNTY: OSBORN S. FURLOW was sworn that he is the Qualified Exor. of DAVID FURLOW, dec'd.... who is proper owner of Lot No. 177 in 6th Dist., 1st Sect. orig. Cherokee County, grant for which is applied.
Dated: 12 June 1843 before JAMES MOORE, J.P.
Signed: O. T.(here it looks like T. rather than S.) FURLOW

COBB COUNTY: GEORGE B. T. MADDOX was sworn that he is proper owner of Lot No. 109-20-2 of Cobb Co. drawn by MARTHA MADDOX, Greene Co., Ga., grant for which is applied. Dated: 13 June 1843 before BENSON ROBERTS, J.I.C. Signed: GEORGE B. T. MADDOX. On same date he appt's. NOEL B. KNIGHT of Cobb Co. his lawful att'y. to apply for grant and wit. before HENRY THOMPSON and BENSON ROBERTS, J.I.C.

GREENE COUNTY: EDWARD CROSSLEY and MARY BREWER who being sworn say they are the brother and sister of JOHN CROSSLEY and entitled to their part, viz. two fifths of lot of land drawn by sd. JNO. CROSSLEY now dec'd. Lot known as 239 in 20th Dist., 2nd Sect. Cherokee and that LEMUEL CROSSLEY is duly authorized to take out plat and grant.
Dated: 20 June 1843 before ROBT. F. GRIFFIN, J.P.
Signed: MARY (+) BREWER, EDWARD CROSSLEY

RICHMOND COUNTY: MARGARET BAILEY was sworn that she is the proper owner of Lot No. 248 in 20th Dist., 2nd Sect. of Cherokee originally the grant for which is applied.
Dated: 21 June 1843 before J. C. GREEN, J.P.
Signed: MARGARET (X) BAILEY

PIKE COUNTY: MARTHA ALEXANDER was sworn that she is proper owner of Lots of land No. 269-20-12 orig. Cherokee, now Cobb Co. and No. 907-5-1 of orig. Cherokee, now Lumpkin Co. grants for which are applied.
Dated: 17 June 1843 before JAS. L. ALEXANDER, J.P.
Signed: MARTHA ALEXANDER. On same date she appoints JOHN W. COPPEDGE of Pike Co. her lawful attorney.

CHEROKEE COUNTY: Personally appeared before me M. W. THWEATT who being duly sworn says that he is the drawer of Lot No. 629, 2nd Dist., 4th Sect. and is still the proper owner. Dated: 19 June 1843. Signed: M. W. THWEATT. He appoints PETERSON THWEATT or in his absence JOHN G. THWEATT his lawful Atty's.

RICHMOND COUNTY: Personally appeared before me HENRY MADDOX who being duly sworn says he is the proper owner of Lot No. 1276 in 2nd Dist. 4th Sect. of Cherokee Co., the grant for which is applied for.
Dated: 18 June 1843. Signed: HENRY (X) MADDOX before JAMES HARPER, J.I.C.R.C. Witness present, PHINEUS BUTLER. On same date he appt's. A. M. HORTON of Baldwin Co. his lawful att'y.

STEWART COUNTY: Personally app'd. bef. me JAMES G. PEEL who being duly sworn says he is the lawful owner (as agent of Lot No. 1149-2-4 Cherokee) the grant for which is applied for. Dated: 10 June 1843. Signed: JAMES G. PEEL. On same date he appt's. CHARLES A. BELL of same Co. his lawful Att'y. Wit.: C. M. STAPLETON, L. D. STAPLETON, J.P.

CHATHAM COUNTY: Pers'y. app. bef. me LEONIDAS WYLLY a J.P. for sd. Co. THOMAS GREEN who being sworn says he is the proper owner of Lot No. 788 -15-2 in Cherokee Gold the grant for which is applied. Dated: 15 June 1843.
Signed: THOS. GREEN. On same date he appt's. ASA HALL of City of Savannah his lawful att'y.

BIBB COUNTY: I, GEORGE WALKER, Ex'r. of JOHN MARTIN's will, appoint JAMES SMITH, att'y. for me to obtain grant for Lot No. 1-14-3 in Murray Co. 2 June 1843.
GEORGE WALKER, Exr. (LS), Test.: JAMES DENTON, J.P.

BALDWIN COUNTY: Personally appeared BENJAMIN N. WILKINSON who says he is interested in part ownership in Lot No. 498-3-2 Cherokee and makes application for grant. B. N. WILKINSON, 29 June 1843, J. R. ANDERSON, J.I.C.B.C.

BIBB COUNTY: Appeared GEORGE WALKER, Exr. of L. W. & T. of JOHN MARTIN, dec'd. who says that said MARTIN was the owner of Lot No. 1-14-3, Murray County.
Dated: 2 June 1843
Signed: GEORGE WALKER, Exr.   JAMES DENTON, J.P.

BIBB COUNTY: CHLOE C. COLLIER appoints CURTIS LEWIS of
                          state and County afsd. lawful attorney.
Aug. 9, 1841...C. C. COLLIER (LS) Wit.: HEMAN MEAD, C. A. HIG-
GINS, J.P. & N.P.
                          We hereby certify that the foregoing power
of attorney is a true copy of the original...Griffin, March 6,
1843. M. P. LUCK(?), N.P., A. A. GAULDING, J.P.
                          I do hereby swear that Mrs. CHLOE C. COL-
LIER formerly Greensborough, Green County, Ga. and now living at
Holly Springs, Marshall County, Mississippi, is the true and law-
ful owner of Lot No. 299 in the 20th District and 2nd Section,
Cherokee, and that I am her legally authorized agent.....CURTIS
LEWIS. Wit: A. A. GAULDING, J.P.

FRANKLIN COUNTY: Before me appeared RUTHA MILLS...she is
                          one of the heirs of JOHN MILLS and is the
proper owner of a part of Lot No. 335, 20th Dist., 2nd Sect. of
orig. Cherokee, now Cobb County, drawn by heirs of sd. Mills.
                          Grant is applyed for by her under the pro-
visions of an Act attended to Dec. 28, 1842. Sworn to this 2 day
of June 1843.
R. A. MEAL(?)   RUTHA MILLS

FRANKLIN COUNTY: Know that THOMAS KING of Co. and state
                          afsd. is hereby appointed my lawful atty.
to apply for the grant for Lot No. 335, 20th Dist., 2nd Section
of originally Cherokee now Cobb County, drawn by heirs of JOHN
MILLS, dec'd. June 2, 1843.
RUTHA (X) MILLS (Seal) Wit: LEVI SEWELL, R. A. MEAL(?)

THOMAS COUNTY: I, JAMES BLOUNT of Co. and state aforesaid
                          appoint JOHN BLEWETT of Decater County, my
true and lawful attorney to apply for the grant of Lot No. 833,
17th Dist. of Cherokee County...

BALDWIN COUNTY: Personally app'd. bef. me JOHN BLEWETT,
                          says he is the lawful agent of the owner
of Lot No. 833, 17th Dist., 2nd Sect. of orig. Cherokee Co.
May 30, 1843   JOHN BLEWETT, ALFRED M. HORTON, N.P., Baldwin Co.

COBB COUNTY: Personally app'd. bef. me RILEY GOSS who
                          says he is the lawful agent of the owner
of Lot No. 622, 17th Dist., 2nd Sect. Cobb County. (cont'd)....

Dated: 28 June 1843
Signed: RILEY GOSS, E. W. MABLEY, J.P.

WALKER COUNTY: Personally app'd. bef. me MARY KENNEMUER who says she is the proper owner of Lot No. 622, 17th Dist., 2nd Sect., Cobb County.
Dated: 20 May 1843
Signed: MARY (X) KENNEMUER, THOS. MANNING, J.P.

COBB COUNTY: Personally app'd. bef. me RILEY GOSS, who says he is the agent of the owner of Lot. No. 622 in the 17th Dist., 2nd Sec., Cobb Co.
Dated: 28 June 1843
Signed: RILEY GOSS, E. W. MOBLEY, J.P.

COBB COUNTY: Be it known that I have appointed J. G. PARK or J. M. A. SANFOR(?) of the county of Baldwin my lawful att'y. to apply for the grant for Lot No.622 in 17th Dist., 2nd Sect. of Cobb Co.
Dated: 28 June 1843
Signed: RILEY GOSS, M. L. RUFF, E. W. MOBLEY, J.P.

COBB COUNTY: Before me NAPOLEON B. GREEN an acting Justice of the Inferior Court of sd. county, in person came SOLOMON KEMP, who says he is the legal owner of Lot No. 192, 20th Dist., 2nd Sect. of Cherokee County originally, which said lot now drawn by DAVID M. STEWART's orphans of House's District, Henry County....he desires the grant for sd. lot of land. 6 Jan. 1849....SOLOMON KEMP, N. B. GREEN, J.I.C.

TALBOT COUNTY: Personally app'd. bef. me EPHRAIGM MAGEE who saith that a certain lot of land in the 17th Dist., 2nd Sec., No. 203 of orig. Cherokee, drawn by REUBEN MAGEE is his deponents own property. 23 March 1843.
Signed: EPHRAIM MAGEE, J. J. JAMISON, J.P.

TALBOT COUNTY: I, EPHRAIM MAGEE app't. WILLIAM SEAVEY(?) my lawful att'y. to take out the grant of Lot No. 203, 17th Dist., 2nd Sect. Cherokee, drawn by REUBEN MAGEE and is at this time my own bonafide property. 23 March 1843.
EPHRAIM MAGEE, Test.: J. I. JAMISON, J.P.

CHEROKEE COUNTY: Personally came bef. me, JAMES A. MADDOX, agent for GEORGE COX (who now resides in the state of Tennessee) saith that he the sd. GEORGE COX is the proper owner of Lot No. 229-10-2 formerly Cherokee Co., now Gilmer. 4 May 1843. JAMES A. MADDOX, GEO. S. HOYL, J.I.C.

JEFFERSON COUNTY: Know that we ABRAHAM BEESLEY & JAMES ANDERSON both of state and county afsd. have app'td. JAMES ANDERSON, JUNR. of Jefferson Co. our lawful att'y. to take out and grant 40 acre Lot No. 861-15-2 in the gold region drawn by ABRAHAM BEESLEY also to grant 40 acre Lot No. 868-2-3 in Cherokee purchase drawn by VINEY PHILLIPS, widdow, not the lawful wife of JAMES ANDERSON, SR....13 March 1843. ABRAHAM BEESLEY, JAMES AN......., JAMES STAPLETON, J.P.

BALDWIN COUNTY: Personally app'd. JAMES ANDERSON, JUNR., says he is the lawful agent of Lot No. 861 in 15th Dist, 2nd Sect. orig. Cherokee County. 15 March 1843....JAMES ANDERSON, ALFRED M. HORTON, N.P.,Baldwin County.

ELBERT COUNTY: Personally app'd. bef. me THOMAS J. TURMAN says he is the adm'r. of WILLIAM PULLIAM, dec'd. who was the proper owner to two lots, No. 758, 20th Dist., 3rd Sect., Paulwing(?) Co., the other No. 767, 15th Dist., 2nd Sect. in Cheroke Co. 26 May 1843.
Signed: THOMAS J. TURMAN, Adm'r. , Z. (?) SMITH, J.P.

Lots not Granted belonging to Mrs. RUTHERFORD
Land 40, 20th Dist., 2nd Sec.)
Gold 71, 20th Dist., 3rd Sec.) JAMES COX drew these lots
Land 128, 7th Dist., 2nd Sec.)
Land 138, 22nd Dist., 3rd Sec.) drawn by CHS. BRADLEY
Mrs. RUTHERFORD....personally appeared before me the 7th June of 1843 saith that the above four lots, two drawn by JAMES COX and two by CHARLES BRADLEY that the grants belong to himself that he is the rightful owner and that the grant should issue accordingly. ...Mrs. Rutherford...Sworn to bef. me 7 June 1843. ALFRED M. HORTON, Notary Public.

Memo of Granted or ungranted Lands belonging to the Estate of SOLOMON GROVE of Bibb County, deceased. (cont'd. next page)...

GRANTOR: FRANCIS L. BENTON: No. 468; Dist. Gr.; County: Cherokee purchase; Acres: 40 more or less.
" ELIZABETH HOOD: No. 1098; Dist.: 21; Sect.: 2; County: Cass; Acres: 40 not Gr JOEL HO___
" ISAAC JONES: No. 256; Dist.: 23; Sect.: 3; County: Cherokee purchase; Acres: 160
" MARY GLOVER: No. Drawn by J. GLOVER
" SALIBA F. GLOVER: No. 1146; Dist.: 16; Sect.: 2; Co.: Cobb; Acres: 40 more or less
" JOHN P. HARVEY: No. 761; Dist.: 18; Sect.: 3; County: Cherokee purchase; Acres: not gr. JAMES COLE Putnam
" G. C. BRASSWELL: No. 74; Dist. 6; Sect. 3; Co.: Cass; Acres: 160 more or less
" G. C. BRASSWELL: No. 743; Dist.: 3; Sect.: 4; County: Cherokee purchase; Acres:...BENJ. CORNER Herrings Dist. Twiggs.
" DANL. ADAMS: drawn by M. T. JONES
" BENJ. B. SMITH: No. 752; Dist.: 21; Sect.: 2; County: Cherokee purchase; Acres: 40 more or less
" CHAS. Y. BROOKS: No. 793; Dist.: 16; Sect.: 2; County: Cobb; Acres: 40 Gr.
" ANDREW OWENS: No. 1024; Dist.: 4; Sect.: 1; County: Cherokee purchase; Acres: 40 not Gr. ___?
" WILLIAM BROWN: No. 160; Dist.: 26; Sect.: 2; Co.: not Gr. PACES Dist., Wilkinson Co.
" GEORGE NORTHERN: No. 114; Dist.: 5; Sect.: 2; Acres: 160 Gr.
" RICHD. DRAWHORN: No. 8; Dist.: 26; Sect.: 3; Co.: Walker; Acres: 160 Baismores Dist.
" RICHD. DRAWHORN: No. 392; Dist.: 21; Sect.: 2; County: Cherokee; Acres: 40 JONES not Gr.
" PHILIP H. BROOKS: No. 573; Dist.: 21; Sect.: 2; Co.: Cass Mary?; Acres: 40 Holmon Wilder
" JAMES HIGHTOWER: No. 1159; Dist.: 2; Sect.: 4; Co.: Cherokee purchase; Acres: 40 ___ Dist.
" ALEX.(?) JOHNSON: No. 106; Dist.: 6; Sect.: 2; County: Groces Dist.; Acres: 53 Bibb not Gr.
" BARNETT HA---: No. 76; Dist.: 11; Sect.: 2; Co.: Baigmers Dist.; Acres: no Gr.
                  No. 37; Dist.: 13; Sect.: 3 ...Gr.
                  No. 252; 3rd. dooly Not Gr.
" SOLM. GROCE drawer lived in Pr------bert dist., Jones County....Dooley

BIBB COUNTY: Personally came bef. me P. P. ATWOOD, a Justice of the Peace for the state and co. afsd., THOMAS A. BROWN, Adm'r. on Est. of SOLOMON GROCE, late of Bibb County, dec'd., saith that the annexed memo is a just and true schedule of certain granted or ungranted lots of land belonging to sd. estate, as appears by papers and deeds in his possession. THOS. A. BROWN...Sworn bef. me 17 (month not given) 1843. PHILP. P. ATWELL, J.P.

(.pparently the last part of a letter)....if it has not been granted, you must take it out under the application there made. I recollect distinctly giving the memorandum to Judge HORTON and stating to him the fact, that the district was divided into North and South half. It is a Cherokee lot...you will be able to find it from his name and place of giving in. Please take these grants and I will pay when I see you. I have several applications but that infernal provision in the law which requires an affidavit will give us much trouble. Respectfully, N. G. FOSTER

PAULDING COUNTY: On the __ day of Dec. 1851 personally appeared bef. me an acting J. P. in and for sd. co., CICERO L. COLLATT who sayeth that he is one of the legal and joint _aires_ that drew Lot No. 197-6-1 drawn in the name of JOHN COLLATT's orphans of Allens Dist., Henry Co. Dated: 18 Dec. 1851...Signed: CICERO L. COLLAT....D. W. ROSS.JP

BIBB COUNTY: Personally came bef. me CHARLES W. BROWN, one of the orphans of CHARLES BROWN, late of Harris County, dec'd., who saith that the orphans of sd.CHAS. BROWN was the fortunate drawers of a certain lot of land known as Lot No. 755-15-2. April 1848.....C. W. BROWN, KEELIN COOK, J.I.C.

BIBB COUNTY: I, CHARLES W. BROWN do authorise SPENCER RILEY to take out the grant to any lot or lots that may be drawn by the orphans of CHARLES BROWN late of Harris Co. April 1848..C. W. BROWN (LS), KEELIN COOK, J.I.C.

MUSCOGEE COUNTY: Personally app'd. bef. me CANOT WOODRUFF, says he is the lawful agent of PHILO. D. WOODRUFF the owner of Lot No. _99-15-2, the grant for which is applied for....CARNOT WOODRUFF. June 22, 1843. JOHN J. McKENDRE (?), J.P.

MARION COUNTY: I do app't. THOMAS BIVIN my lawful attorney to grant all the lands drawn to my name in Marion Co. in the late Cherokee Land and Gold Lottery, also one lot in the 11th Dist. of Dooly Co. drawn by THOMAS SHERILS (?) orphans of Columbia Co., my wife being the younger one of sd. orphans. 5 May 1843...D. N. BURKHALTER (LS) Test.R. W. MASTON, J.P.
Before me RANDAL W. MASTON a Justice of the Peace for Marion co. personally came D. H. BURKHALTER saith he is the legal owner of the lands refered to in the above power of attorney...5 May 1843 D. N. BURKHALTER, R. W. MASTON, J.P.

HARRIS COUNTY: Personally app'd. bef. me ARCHIBALD H.
                        SCOTT, a J. P. for sd. co., WILLIAM KING,
Guardian of SARAH A. BURHAM and WILLIAM L. BURHAM orphans of LY-
MAN BURHAM, dec'd. and made oath that the lot of land in the Cher-
okee Co., 2nd Sect., 15th Dist., No. 516 that was drawn by them
in the lottery has not been conveyed to any other persons....
WM. KING, 12 June 1843 (?)...A. H. SCOTT, J.P.

BALDWIN COUNTY: Personally app'd. bef. me JOHN G. SAPP,
                        who says that he is the Adm'r. of DELANY
SAPP who drew lots No. 382-1-2 and No. 468-15-2 and applies for
grants...23 Dec. 1843...JOHN G. SAPP, bef. me A. M. HORTON, N.P.
No. 382-1-2 granted 5 March 1833 No. 468-15-2 DELANY SAPP Lot-
tory (may be HOTTORY?) BAKER.

Vienna, Ga. 26th 1843...Sir: Therewith send my Power of attorney
to grant a certain lot of land in the Cherokee Country, drawn by
my Brother EDWARD COBB of Dooly. You will please look to the
Dooly book at the letter C and place the number in my affidavit
in the power of Att'y. WILY COBB, Guardian of the orphans of
EDWARD COBB, dec'd.
DOOLY COUNTY   Personally app'd. bef. me WILEY COBB Gdn.
                        of orphans of EDWARD COBB, dec'd. who drew
a certain lot in the Cherokee County...No. 417-15-2.
28 Dec. 1842...Sworn to bef. me 26 June 1843 WILLIAM C. GREER, JP
.....WILEY COBB.

DOOLY COUNTY: Be it known that I have this day appt'd.
                        ALFRED M. HORTON, Esqr. of Baldwin Co.,
for me as Guardian of the orphans of EDWARD (COBB), dec'd. 26
June 1843...WILEY COBB, Wit.: THOS. J. KEY, WILLIAM C. GREER, JP

MARION COUNTY: Personally app'd. WM. A. BLACK who saith
                        he is the Adm'r. of WILLIAM TOMPKINS, dec'd
who was the drawer of Lot 223-15-2 Cherokee...9 Feb. 1843...WM.A.
BLACK bef. me _____ J.P.

MARION COUNTY: I make and app't. THOMAS BASELTON(?) my
                        lawful att'y. in my name as Adm'r. of est.
of WILLIAM TOMPKINS, dec'd. to apply for and receive grant for
Lot No. 223-15-2 Cherokee...WM. A. BLACK.

Executive Department Georgia
Milledgeville 5th Sept. 1833

    It appearing to the Executive from an examination of the original Return of the names of persons entitled to draws in the late Gold Lottery in the County of Franklin that a mistake has been made in transcribing from sd. return the name of NATHANIEL R. HOOD of Davids Dist., in sd. Co., the same having been written on the Lottery book, NATHANIEL R. WOOD, ordered therefore that the Surveyor General issue the plat of sd. lot to the sd. NATHANIEL R. HOOD and that the Lottery Books be corrected accordingly.

Attest L. D. BUCKNER

TROUP COUNTY: Personally app'd. bef. me THOMAS M. LIGHTFOOT, who says he is the proper owner (as one with other Legatees of the Estate of WILLIAM G. SIMONTON,.. dec'd.) of Lot No. 160-15-2 Cherokee Co., THOS. H. LIGHTFOOR.. Sworn bef. me 21 June 1843   THOS. M. WYATT, J.P.
No. 160-15-2 WM. G. SIMONTON   Nesbets Newton

MUSCOGEE COUNTY: Personally app'd. bef. me WILLIAM T. DIMON who says he is the proper owner of Lot No. 144-14 but it drawn on the last day, by WILLIAM T. DIMON of Talbot Co. of Capt. KELM's Dist. also one other lot No. 50-15-1 was drawn by ABEL DIMON (Depoint father) of DELM's Dist., Talbot co. WILLIAM T. DIMON...Sworn bef. me 15 June 1843   GEO. W. TURENTON (?), J.P.

MUSCOGEE COUNTY: I have this day app'td. KENNETH McKENZIE of Muscogee Co. my lawful att'y. to apply for Grants of above...15 June 1843...WILLIAM T. DIMON (Seal),.. GEO. W. TURENTON (?), J.P.

JONES COUNTY: I. JOHN R. WYCHE is the proper owner of Lot drawn by SUSANAH WYCHE, dec'd., No.64-14-2 of Cherokee purchase.   JOHN R. WYCHE (LS), Attest: DANIEL SCOTT, J.P., June 14, 1843

TELFAIR COUNTY: Personally came bef. me KENNETH McLEMORE one of the Justices of the Inf. Crt. for sd. co., WASHINGTON ROGERS of sd. co. who saith that he married the Widdow of ALFRED QUINN, dec'd. of sd. co., and thereby became the owner of Lot No. 3-14-2 Cherokee Co., drawn by ALFRED QUINN, dec'd., believes that the sd. QUINN gave in the co. of Bibb.   9 June 1843...WASHINGTON ROGERS, KEMMETH McLEMORE, J.I.C.

BALDWIN COUNTY: In person app'd. bef. me C. S. HAMMOND a
                        Justice of the Inferior Court, co. afsd.
MEREMIAH BEALL, he is one of the heirs of THAD. A. BEALL, late
of the Co. of Walton, dec'd....that the sd. T. A. BEALL owned &
possessed in his own right lot No. 10-15-2 Cherokee...JR. BEALL
8 June 1843...C. S. HAMMOND, J.I.C.

BALDWIN COUNTY: Personally came bef. me, RANDOLPH H. RAM-
                        SEY who saith that he is the proper owner
of Lot given in at Augusta, Ga., Walkers Dist., known as Lot No.
136-14-2. R. H. RAMSEY (LS), sworn before me 28 June 1843, JOHN
S. THOMAS, J.I.C.

WASHINGTON COUNTY: Personally app'd. bef. me THOMAS SALTERS
                        who says he is the proper owner of Lot No.
259-14-2 Cherokee as Adm'r. of TALIAFERRO B. SALTER, who intermarried with SARAH BROWN orphan and who died anterior to the sd.
T. B. SALTER to whose name the sd. lot of land was drawn, then
of William's Dist. of the sd. co. of Washington...24 June 1843,
THOMAS S. (X) SALTER, bef. me GREEN WHITDON, J.P.

No. 77, District 14, Section 2
Morgan County   Personally app'd. bef. me LOVICK L. WIT-
                        TICH says the application for the grant
of the above lot is made ad the "Bona Fide owner" of a portion of
the aforesaid lot, having purchased the interest of one of the
orphans of sd. lot...LOVICK L. WITTICH, bef. me 24 March 1847,
JOHN ROBSON, J.I.C.

WASHINGTON COUNTY: Clerks Office, Court of Ordinary, I, HAY-
                        WOOD BROOKINS, Clerk of sd. court, for sd.
county, do certify that THOMAS SALTER is the Adm'r. of <u>TEOLIVER</u>
B. SALTER, late of sd. co.   27 June 1843. HAYWOOD BROOKINS,Clk.

JASPER COUNTY: I. DAVID MERWETHER executor of THOS. MERE-
                        WETHER, dec'd., do app't. S. B. TANSLEY of
Milledgeville, my att'y. to grant for me Lot No. 31-14-2 Chero-
kee drawn by THOS. MEREWETHER, dec'd. 27 April 1843...DAVID
MER<u>I</u>WETHER,(Seal), bef. us H.(?) LOOLSBY(?), D. A. RUSE, J.I.C.

JASPER COUNTY: Personally came bef. me a J. I. C. DAVID
                        MERIWETHER who saith he is the ex'r. of

90

THOS. MERIWETHER, dec'd, who drew Lot No. 31-14-2, Cherokee....
27 Apr. 1843...DAVID MERIWETHER, D. A. RUN(?), J.I.C.

FLOYD COUNTY: Personally app'd. bef. me MOSES M. LIDDELL
                     and JOSEPH J. BUCKANNON who says that they
are the proper owners of Lot No. 8-14-2 of Cherokee Co.
Moses M. Liddel, Joseph J. Buchannon...Before me 21 May 1843,
THOS. E. BUCKANNON, J.P.

FLOYD COUNTY: THOS. PULLUM of Floyd co., is app'd. our
                     lawful att'y. to apply for the grant for
Lot No. 8-14-2 Cherokee   MOSES M. LIDDELL(LS) JOSEPH J. BUCHAN-
NON (LS), Wit.: THOMAS H. CURYLER(?), THOS E. BUCHANNON, J.P.

DeKALB COUNTY: We, LODOWICH TUGGLE and THOMAS S. TUGGLE
                     have appt'd. J. W. BUCHANNON of Co. and
state afsd. our lawful att'y. for certain lots of land, viz.
Lot No. 1013-15-2 Cherokee now Cobb Co., and the other Lot No.102
-15-2, Cherokee now Gilmer Co.
6 June 1843...LODOWICK TUGGLE, T. P. TUGGLE.. Test.: J. T. CAINE,
J. P.

JACKSON COUNTY: Personally app'd. bef. me S. J. NIBLACK
                     who saith that he is Adm'r. on est. of
WILLIAM M. NIBLACK, dec'd. is the proper owner of Lot No. 1179-
15-2 Cherokee...22 May 1843 S. L. NIBLACK, J. B. LOWERY, J.P.

JACKSON COUNTY: J. B. NABERS of Jackson Co. is hereby ap-
                     pointed my lawful att'y. to apply for the
grant for Lot No. 1179-15-2 Cherokee...22 May 1843..S. J. NIBLACK
(LS), Wit.: POLLY LOWREY, A. B. LOWREY, J.P.

CHATHAM COUNTY: Appeared bef. me LEONIDAS WYLLY a Justice
                     of and for sd. Co., WILLIAM CONDON agent
and acting Guardian of MARY FOLLOM, JAMES FULLOM, and JOSEPH
FULLOM, orphans and lawful heirs of LUKE FULLOM, who saith that
the late LUKE FULLOM was the lawful owner of Lot No. 1000-15-2
Cherokee Co. ..WM. CONDON, bef. me 5 May 1843 LEONIDAS WYLEY,J.P.

CHATHAM COUNTY: I have appointed WILLIAM H. PRITCHARD of
                     Baldwin Co., my lawful att'y.for Lot No.
1000-15-2 Cherokee, in the name of MARY FULLOM, JAMES FULLOM &

JOSEPH FULLOM, legal heirs of LUKE FULLOM, dec'd. 5 May 1843...
WM. CONDON, Wit: LEONIDAS WYLLY, J.P.

BALDWIN COUNTY: Personally app'd. bef. me JOHN Y. RHODES, who says he is the lawful agent of Lot No. 467, sworn to June 19, 1843 A. M. HORTON, Notary Public, Baldwin Co....J. Y. RHODES

TROUP COUNTY: I have this day appointed JOHN Y. RHODES of Chambers Co., Ala., my lawful attorney to apply for and take out the grant for Lot No. 467-1-3 drawn by REBECCA RHODES, Jones Co., Allsebrook Dist., June 27, 1843. REBECCA (X) RHODES, HARY(?) P. ANDERSON, J. M. HARRINGTON, J.P.

FAYETTE COUNTY: Bef. me, G. C. KING, a J. P. for sd. co., personally came TABITHA STEEN, the widow of JAMES STEEN, sayeth that lot of land No. 58-1-3 was drawn by JAMES STEEN and is now the property of his estate . June 14,1843 TABITHA (X) STEEN, G. C. KING, J.P.

UNION COUNTY: I. THOMAS PASS, have appointed my son, THOMAS S. PASS, my true and lawful agent and att'y. to transact my business in the State of Georgia.. in making application to the land office for obtaining a grant to a lott of land drawn in my name, 27th Dist., 2nd Section, No. 177. June 17, 1843...THOMAS PASS (SEAL), TAYLOR M. NOBLE, J.P.

UNION COUNTY: Bef. me TAYLOR McNOBLE, a J.P. for sd. co. personally came THOMAS PASS and makes oath that he drew Lot No. 177-27-2, June 17, 1843...THOMAS PASS (SEAL) TAYLOR McNOBLE, J.P.

ELBERT COUNTY: Personally came bef. me JESSE DOBBS, J.P. in and for sd. co., JOHN GORDEN, who says he is the Ex'r. of the estate of ANGUS McCURRY, SNR., dec'd. and that the sd. dec'd. drew Lot No. 40=1-3 orig. Cherokee. JOHN GORDON , Mar. 23, 1843, bef. me JESSE DOBBS, J.P.

NEWTON COUNTY: Before SHELBY DOURES, acting J.P. JAMES W. BLACK who sayeth he is the proper owner of Lot No. 111-27-2 Cherokee now Gillmore Co., drawn by MURPHEY's minors, Nesbet Dist., Newton Co., Ga. 5 May 1852. JAMES W.

BLACK...SHELBY DOURES, J.P.

CHATHAM COUNTY: Personally app'd. bef. me WILLIAM HUNTER and says he is the lawful agent of Mrs. ELIZABETH STURGES, owner of Lot No. 30-27-2 Gilmer County. WM. HUNTER, before me May 11, 1843, B. (?), RAIFORD, J.P.

BALDWIN COUNTY: No. 78, Dist. 27, Gilmer County...JESSE C. FARRAR says he is owner in part of sd. lot...Aug. 7, 1853...W. N. MITCHELL, N.P.....JESSE C. FARRAR.

CHATHAM COUNTY: I have appt'd. Col. A. H. KENON of Baldwin Co., my lawful att'y. to apply for and take out the grant for Lot No. 30-27-2 Gilmer Co., and Lot No.219-26-2 Walker Co. May 11, 1843 WM. HUNTER, B.(?) RAIFORD, J.P.

DeKALB COUNTY: JESSE C. FARRAR is authorized to take out Grant of No. 78-27-2 Gilmer Co., for the heirs of PRESLEY HOLLEY formerly of Laurens Co., Ga. but now of Huery(?) Co., Alabama...31 Oct. 1853...H. W. McDANELL, Atlanta, Geo. Lawrenseville.

Executive Department Ga.
Milledgeville, 7 March 1833

Ordered
        That the grant issued to WILLIAM MOORE of Peaces district Washington County be corrected so as to read WILLIAM MOORE of Peaces district Wilkinson County.
                        WM. J. W. WELLBORN S.E.D.

OGLETHORPE COUNTY: I. MARY PINSON, widow of the Co. and state afsd. app't. THOMAS A. TUCK of Clark Co. my lawful att'y. to apply for me the grant for Lot No. 14-26-2 Cherokee...May 29, 1843...MARY (X) PINSON (Seal) Wit: RICHARD T. TRIBLE, WILEY CARTER, J.P.

OGLETHORPE COUNTY: Personally app'd. bef. me MARY PINSON and saith that Lot No. 14-26-2 in Cherokee is her own right and property, May 29, 1843. MARY (X) PINSON, WILEY CARTER, J.P.

JONES COUNTY: Personally app'd. bef. me ANN CHESTNUT, widow of DANIEL CHESTNUT, dec'd. formally of Putnam Co., orph. dest., deposith that she is the legal gdn. of sd. orph. dest. and she is the proper owner of Lot 18-26-2....

Dated: 17 June 1843...ANN (X) CHESTNUT, JOHN WILLIAMS, J.P.

JONES COUNTY: I have this day appt'd. JOHN WILLIAMS, of Jones Co., my lawful att'y. the grant for Lot No. 18-26-2 ...June 17, 1843...ANN (X) CHESTNUT (LS), JOHN WILLIAMS, J.P.

BUTTS COUNTY: Personally app'd. bef. me ROBERT P. MAYO, LAWSON UNDERWOOD who says that they are the proper owners of Lot No. 312-23-2 and No. 909-17-2 of orig. Cherokee Co., both of sd. lots drawn by GILLIM (?) PRESTON's orphans...ROBERT P. MAYO, LAWSON UNDERWOOD, bef. me April 18,1843, FURMAN WALLHALL(?) J.I.C.

BUTTS COUNTY: We, R. P. MAYO and LAWSON UNDERWOOD have this day appt'd. JOSIAH UNDERWOOD our lawful att'y. for Lots No. 312-23-2 and _____, orig. Cherokee Co., April 18, 1843. ROBERT P. MAYO (SEAL), LAWSON UNDERWOOD (SEAL), FURMAN WATEHALL, J.I.C.

GWINNETT COUNTY: Bef. me JESSE MURPHY, a J. P. for sd. co. personally appeared DAVID W. SPENCE, who saith that AMANDA TURNER who has intermarried with LODOWICK M. CATES, SOPHIA TURNER who has intermarried with deponent, SARAH TURNER who has intermarried with THOMAS M. CUNNINGHAM and MARGARET TURNER who has intermarried with WILLIAM H. GINN(?), were the only orphans of JOHN W. TURNER of Lawlesses Dist., in sd. Co. who drew Lot No. 173-19-2 orig. Cherokee, now Cobb County. D. W. SPENCE, before me April 4, 1850, JESSE MURPHY J.P.

BALDWIN COUNTY: Personally app'd. bef. me ARMON H. GEIGER who says he is the lawful agent of the owner of Lot No. 275-19-2 orig. Cherokee Co....Mar. 16, 1843.... HARMAN H. GEIGER ...ALFRED M. HORTON, NP, Baldwin Co.

JASPER COUNTY: I, ANN GLENN, SEN., of Co. and state afsd. have appt'd. H. H. GEIGER my lawful atty. to receive the grant for Lot No. 275-17-2, 40 acres more or less. March 1, 1843...ANN GLENN, SEN.(her x mark) (LS), bef. me MAT. WHITFIELD, J.P.

JASPER COUNTY: ...ANN GLENN, SENR. who saith that she is

now the Lawful owner of Lot No. 275, 19th Dist., 2nd Section of Cherokee Co. March 1, 1843...ANN (X) GLENN, SENR. Before me MAT WHITFIELD, J.P.

CHATHAM COUNTY: Personally app'd. bef. me ANN PAULLEN, widow of the late JOHN PAULLEN of the Co. afsd. who says that she is the proper owner of Lot No. 109-26-2 Gilmer County...June 15, 1843...ANN PAULLEN, bef. me JOSEPH FRET (?).

TROUP COUNTY: Personally app'd. bef. me SAML. LANE, a J.P., SILAS N. DAVIS, agent for JANE DAVIS widow, and saith that the afsd. JANE DAVIS is the proper owner of Lot No. 100-26-2 Cherokee...applied for by WILLIAM B. SMITH, Esq., as agent for sd. SILAS N. DAVIS.....Signed: S. NEWTON DAVIS...SAML. LANE, J.P.

WALTON COUNTY: In person appeared bef. me NEHEMIAH JOHNSON, one of the Justices of the Inferior Court, ELIZABETH BEALL who deposeth that she is the bonafide owner of Lot No. 247-27-2 of Cherokee. Dated: _____ 1843.

CASS COUNTY: Bef. the Subscriber a Justice of the Peace, Z. G. TURNER, personally came ROBERT M. PUCKETT, & AARON B. PUCKETT who say that they are the drawers of Lot No. 114-26-2 of orig. Cherokee but now Gilmer Co., drawn to the name of AARON B. PUCKETT's orphans of Gwinnett County. Signed: ROBT. M. PUCKETT, AARON B. PUCKETT, bef. me 18 Sept.1844 Z. G. TURNER, J.P.

CASS COUNTY: JOSEPH JENKINS of Co. of Cass is hereby appt'd. out true and lawful att'y. to pass the grant for Lot No. 114-26-2 Cherokee now Gilmer Co...18 Sept. 1844...ROBT. M. PUCKETT, AARON B. PUCKETT (LS), Wit: MILES MULLINS, Z. G. TURNER, J.P.

COBB COUNTY: We, HENRY R. BEAVERS, WILLIAM C. BEAVERS, & REBECCA NEWSOM formerly REBECCA BEAVERS, have appt'd. THOMAS H. MOORE of Marietta, Ga. our lawful att'y. to receive the plat and grant for Lot No. 122-26-2 of Gilmer co. 3 Nov. 1853...HENRY R. BEAVERS (LS), WILLIAM C. BEAVERS (LS), REBECCA NEWSOM (LS) Wit.: J. M. A. JOHNSTON, B. TOLLESON, N.P.

OGLETHORPE COUNTY: Personally came bef. me, MARY PINSON, and saith that Lot No. 148-26-2 of Cherokee is her own right and property. June 26, 1843...MARY (X) PINSON, WILEY CARTER, J.P. Hargroves Dist., Oglethorpe Co.

SUMPTER COUNTY: Personally came bef. me TIMOTHY RENEW who says that he is the proper owner of Lot No. 157-26-2 .....TIMOTHY RANEW, JUNR. (his x mark), before me 7 March 1843 WRIGHT MIMS, J.P.

SUMPTER COUNTY: I have this day appt'd. WILLIAM MIMS of Sumpter Co. my lawful att'y. to apply for and take out grant for Lot No. 157-22-2 in _____ Co. March 7, 1843....TIMOTHY RANEW JR. (his x mark) (LS) Before me WRIGHT MIMS J. P.

BULLOCK COUNTY: No. 307, 26 Dist., 2nd Section....Personally appeared bef. me, CHAS. E.,S. E., D. R. GROOVER, WM. SHEFFIELD & JOHN GOODMAN, who says that the application for the grant to the above lot is made as the bonafide owners of the afsd. lot...CHAS. E. GROOVER, S. E. GROOVER, D. B. GROOVER, WM. SHEFFIELD, JOHN GOODMAN. Before me Jan. 19, 1854, AUGUSTUS LANIER, J.P.

LINCOLN COUNTY: Personally appeared bef. me MARK BOND,who says he is the Guardian of the orphans of THOMAS BOND and that they are the proper owners of Lot No. 82-23-2 Cherokee Co...MARK (X) BOND. Before me June 16, 1843, WM.M. McCARLEY, J.P.

LINCOLN COUNTY: I have this day appt'd. JOHN R. ANDERSON of Baldwin Co., Ga. my lawful att'y. to apply for the grant for Lot No. 82-23-2 in Cherokee. June 16, 1843, MARK (X) BOND, Wit: WM. M. McCARLEY, J.P...BEN B. MOORE.

RICHMOND COUNTY: I have this day appt'd. WILLIAM R. McLAWS Esq., of co. afsd. my lawful att'y. to apply for and take out grant for Lot No. 58-23-2. June 1, 1843. Signed: ROBERT S. DILL, Adm'r. of Est. of WILLIAM H. DILL. Wit: WILLIAM R. McLAWS, N.P. R.C.

RICHMOND COUNTY: ...bef. me ROBERT S. DILL who says that he

is the Adm'r. on Estate of WM. H. DILL and is the proper person
to take out grant for Lot No. 58-23-2....ROBT. S. DILL, before
me WILLIAM R. McLAWS, June 1, 1843.

NEWTON COUNTY: Personally came bef. me FRANKLIN BARNES
who says he is the joint and lawful owner
with CLARISSA BARNES of Lot No. 120-23-2 of Cherokee now Cass co.
grant is applied for...June 16, 1843...FRANKLIN BARNES, COLUMBUS
D. PAGE, J.I.C.

NEWTON COUNTY: I have this day appt'd. THOMAS F. JONES
of Newton Co., my lawful att'y. to apply
and take out grant for Lot No. 120-23-2 Cherokee now Cass Co.
16 June 1843, FRANKLIN BARNES, WILLIAM H. E. PACE, COLUMBUS D.
PACE, J.I.C.

COBB COUNTY: Personally came bef. me JOHN ANDERSON, an
acting J.P. of sd. co., WILLIAM BARNWELL
and saith he is the proper owner of Lot No. 123-23-2....
Dated and signed: June 3, 1843, WILLIAM BARNWELL, bef. me JOHN
ANDERSON, J.P.

Executive Department, Ga.
Milledgeville Dec. 14, 1832
It appearing to the Executive that a mis-
take has occured in returning...in Allens Dist., Henry County,
EDMUND BROWN instead of EDMUND BROOM...being entitled to a draw
or draws in the land and Gold lotteries of Cherokee County.....
Lots No. 214-23-2///change to EDMUND BROOM...Attest: WM. J. W.
WELLBRON, S.E.D.

GREEN COUNTY: March 7, 1843: Personally came before me
W. D. MADDEN, an acting J.P. of 149 Dis-
trict of sd. Co., MARTHA MADDEN and sayeth that she is the lawful
drawer of Lot, 40 acres, No. 389, 1st Dist., 3rd Section.
Signed: MARTHA MADDON, W. D. MADDEN, J.P. (LS)

CHATHAM COUNTY: I have appt'd. JOHN W. EXLEY of Effingham
co. my lawful att'y. for Lot 963-2-2 of
Cherokee and Lot 263=1=3 Cobb or Paulding Co. May 27, 1843.
THOS. H. KRUGER, B. RAIFORD, J.P. Granted Dec. 11, 1841

CHATHAM COUNTY: Personally app'd. bef. me THOMAS L. FULTON
who says he is one of the legatees of THOM-
AS FULTON, dec'd. and agent of ELIZABETH C. FULTON, Adm'x. of sd.

Estate, who drew and is the proper owner of Lot No. 201-1-3 Cherokee Co., THOS. L. FULTON, before me June 2, 1843...B. RAIFORD, J.P.

CHATHAM COUNTY: I have appt'd. JOHN W. EXLEY, my lawful att'y. ...Lot No. 201-1-3....June 2, 1843. THOS. L. FULTON (SEAL) B. RAIFORD, J.P.

MUSCOGEE COUNTY: Bef. me personally app'd. LORENZO D. MONROE, who is the guardian of orphans of JACKSON A. MONROE and that a 40 acres lot 316-11-1 drawn by JACKSON A. MONROE of McGUIRES dist. of Gwinnett co., and he is lawful owner of Lot 304-27-1. L. D. MONROE, bef. me June 2, 1843. AUGUSTUS ABBOTT, J.P.

PIKE COUNTY: WILSON POORE personally app'd. bef. me, and saith that he is the owner (proper) of Lot No. 19-25-2 orig. Cherokee Co., orphan of WILLIAM POORE. WILSON POORE, bef. me June 14, 1843. JOHN MAYS, J.P.

PIKE COUNTY: I have appt'd. JAMES WHATLEY my lawful att'y....lot No. 19-25-2 orig. Cherokee. Dated: June 14, 1843...WILSON POORE, JOHN MAYS, J.P.

RICHMOND COUNTY: Personally app'd. bef. me, ALLEN C. YOUNG husband and ELIZABETH YOUNG, whose maiden name was ELIZABETH DYE and who was the daughter of BENJAMIN DYE, one of the orphans of Benjamin Dye who drew lot No. 247-25-2, orig. Cherokee...Signed: ALLEN C. YOUNG, bef. me 7 Dec. 1852. RICHARD ALLEN, J.P.

HOUSTON COUNTY: Know that I RACHEL WAY of Co. and state afsd. have appt'd. BENJAMIN B. SMITH of Baldwin Co., my lawful att'y. Lot No. 273-25-2 of Cherokee. June 15, 1843. RACHEL (X) WAY (SEAL) Wit: SILUS RAWLS, J.P. RACHEL WAY, J. A. GOODWINS(HOUSTON) co.

BULLOCK COUNTY: Personally app'd. bef. me, JAMES KIRBY, a J.P. for sd. Co., MARY WILLIAMS who saith Lot No. 306-25-2 was drawn by her. May 30, 1843. MARY (X) WILLIAMS, JAMES KERBY, J.P. B.C.

BALDWIN COUNTY: Personally appeared bef. me, B. B. SMITH, who says he is the lawful agent of the owner of Lot No. 273-25-2 . Dated and signed: June 30, 1843. B. B. SMITH, bef. me J. R. ANDERSON, J.I.C. Baldwin Co.

HABERSHAM COUNTY: I. JOHN J. HIGGINS, have appt'd. E. S. BANLEY, of Habersham Co., my lawful att'y. lot No. 283-24-2 drawn by JOHN J. HIGGINS of Habersham Co., Brocks Dist....May 29, 1843. (LS) Before me THOMAS BROCK, J.P.

BIBB COUNTY: This day app'd. GEORGE WALKER, Ex'r. of Last Will and Testament of JOHN MARTIN, dec'd., who saith that JOHN MARTIN was the time of his death the owner of Lot No. 1-14-3 Murray County.
Dated and Signed: GEORGE WALKER, Ex'r., 2 June 1843, JAMES DENTON, J.P.

ELBERT COUNTY: Personally app'd. JOHN M. CARLSTON, who says he is the Executor of the Estate of STEPHEN CARLESTON, dec'd. and that Lot 518-3-2 in Cherokee co., was drawn by sd. deceased. 1 May 1843, JOHN M. CARLETON, P. B. ROBERTS, J.P.

JONES COUNTY: NANCY PITTS appoints HENRY CHILDS of co. and state afsd. my true and lawful att'y. to take out plat and grant for following tracts: Lot No. 75-14-3, also Lot No. 529-20-3, 40 acres.
10 June 1843, NANCY (X) PITTS, (LS), before us, THOS. J. MIDDLEBROOKS, GREN (?) B. WILLIAMS, J.P.

ELBERT COUNTY: Personally came bef. me WILLIAM EAVES, a Justice of sd. co., BENJAMIN THORNTON, the Adm'r. on Est. of JOHN THORNTON, dec'd., and sd. dec'd. was the owner of Lot No. 17-3-2. 2 May 1843. BENJAMIN THORNTON, Adm'r. WILLIAM EAVES, J.P.

BALDWIN COUNTY: Personally app'd. bef. me W. C. DAWSON, who says he is the agent of PETER CLARK, who drew Lot No. 448-17-3 and Lot No. 1239-3-3. 28 Dec. 1843, sworn to bef. me, 5 June 1843. W. C. DAWSON, J.R. ANDERSON, J.C. B.D.

ELBERT COUNTY: I, WILLIAM B. NELMS, Clerk of the court of

Ordinary for sd. county, do certify that BENJAMIN THORNTON is the Adm'r. on estate of JOHN THORNTON. 2 May 1843. WM. B.NELMS, C.C.O.

CASS COUNTY: Personally app'd. ROBERT G. MORROW, who says he is the judgement creditor of ABRAHAM GARRETT, the drawer of Lot No. 193-14-3 orig. Cherokee,now Cass County. 18 May 1843, ROBERT G. MORROW, WILLIAM LATIMER,JP? I appoint CORNELIUS D. TERHUM as my lawful agent or att'y. drawn by ABRAHAM GARRETT. ROBERT G. MORROW (SEAL), before A. A. TERHUM, WM. LATIMER, J.P.

CHEROKEE COUNTY: Bef. me ALLEN GILLELAND, an acting Justice of the peace, appeared JACOB FREEMAN and sayeth that Lot No. 49-3-2 drawn by DANIEL HUNT of Coweta Co. 20 Feb. 1843. ALLEN GILLELAND, J.P. JACOB FREEMAN.

TROUP COUNTY: Personally app'd. bef. me THOMAS J. THORNTON, who sayeth he is the lawful and proper owner of Lot No. 283-13-3 of Cherokee Co., which lot of land he reard(?) as a part of his present wife MARTHA THORNTON, formerly MARTHA CASE(?), drawn by THOMAS CASE(?), her former husband. 27 May 1843.
THOMAS J. THORNTON, JOHN DOUGLAS, J.I.C.

TROUP COUNTY: Personally app'd. bef. me JAS. M. BEALL, a Justice of the Inf. Crt., CLARA HARRIS, widow of Tallys Dist., Troup County, who says she is the owner of Lot No. 643-3-2, of the Cherokee purchase.
CLARA (X) HARRIS, JAS. M. BEALL, J.I.C. 8 May 1843.

WASHINGTON COUNTY: Personally app'd. bef. me MORGAN BROWN, who says he is the lawful agent or att'y. of the drawer of Lot No. 263-13-3, Cherokee Co., the grant of which is applied for by him., 24 April 1843.
M. BROWN, NICHOLAS HARDEN, J.P.

LOWNDES COUNTY: Before me DAVID HOWELL, one of the Justices of the Peace for sd. county, personally came HAMILTON W. SHARPE, who says that the following tracts belong to the estate of _____ FOLSEM, late of sd. county, dec'd. and that he is the acting admr. of estate. No. 250, 9th Dist. of Lee County; No. 408, 14th Dist. of Early County; No. 133, 15th Dist, 2nd Section; No. 578,2nd Dis.

4th Section; No. 261, 13th Dist., 3rd Section; No. 285, 9th Dist. 3rd Section; No. 317, 1st Dist., 1st Section; No. 140, 9th Dist., 1st Section; No. 1185, 3rd Dist., 1st Section; No. 290, 2nd Dist. 2nd Section.   Dated and signed: 1 April 1842, J. H. HAMLE (?), J.P. HAMILTON W. SHARPE, Adm'r. of P. FOLSEM.

COWETA COUNTY: Personally came bef. me WOOTSON RAINEY, who says that he is the Ex'r. of the est. of MATHEW RAINEY, dec'd. of Oglethorpe Co., and applies for Grant to Lot No. 325-3-3, Cherokee.
Dated and Signed: 11 May 1843. WOOTSON RAINEY, ____ PERRY,J.P.
I have appt'd. WILLIAM F. S. POWELL of Coweta Co., my lawful attorney. WOOTSON RAINEY, bef. J. J. PENSON, WM. B. BROWN, J.P. Boling Green, Oglethorpe co.

BALDWIN COUNTY: Personally app'd. bef. me, COLIN MURCHISON, who says he is the lawful agent of the owner of Lot No. 284-3-3 orig. Cherokee County.
Dated & Signed: 11 May 1843, ALFRED M. HORTON, C. MURCHISON.

UPSON COUNTY: I, WILLIAM MURCHISON of Co. afsd., appoint my brother, COLEN MURCHISON of Crawford co., state afsd., to take out grant of a 40 acre lot, No. 284-3-2. Dated and signed: 2 May 1843, WILLIAM MURCHISON (LS) Before EDMUND STEWART, J.P.

ELBERT COUNTY: Personally app'd. bef. me, NANCY RAMSEY, who says she is the proper owner of Lot No. 629-14-1 of orig. Cherokee co. Dated and signed: ____Mar. 1843. NANCY (X) RAMSEY, BARNABAS BARRON, J.P.

TROUP COUNTY: Personally app'd. bef. me JOHN DOUGLASS, one of the Justices of the Inf. Ct., HUGH A. HARALSON who says he is the proper owner of Lot No. 261-3-3 drawn by JOSEPH M. COOPER, and bought by sd. HARALSON at Bankrupt sale in town of La Grange,..2 Feb. 1843. H. A. HARALSON, 21 Mar. 1843, JOHN DOUGLASS, J.I.C.

TROUP COUNTY: Personally app'd. bef. GILLUM SCOGIN, an acting Justice of the peace, JOHN M. FORBES who says he is the proper owner of Lot No. 574-3-3 also in the name of CATHARINE FORBES; Lot No. 91-3-2 all in Cherokee Lottery, grants applied for by WILLIAM B. SMITH,Esq.

agent for JOHN M. FORBES. Dated and signed: 29 May 1843. JOHN M. FORBES, GILLUM SCOGIN, J.P.

NEWTON COUNTY: Personally app'd. GEORGE BUCHANAN, before KENNEDY H. BLAKE, a J. P. who saith that he is the Legal Drawer of Lot No. 978-3-3, and was a citizen of Wallton County, but given in Gwinnett County, Lovelesses Dist., 17 May 1843, GEORGE BUCHANAN, K. H. BLAKE, J.P.
I have this day appointed JAMES R. ALDADGE (?) my true and lawful agent to take out the plat and grant for my lot No. 978-3-3.

PULASKI COUNTY: Personally app'd. bef. me D. C. McFAIL, an acting J. P., JAMES HOLLAND and sayeth he considers himself the legal agent for his mother, her husband, SOLOMON BREWER of Pulaski Co., Walding Dist., dec'd., my mother, CHARITY BREWER. 27 May 1843. JAMES (X) HOLLAND, D. C. McFAIL,JP

TALBOT COUNTY: Personally app'd. bef. me ELIJAH M. LAURENCE, and saith he is the proper owner of Lot No. 944-3-3 of Cherokee, also Lot No. 215-4 of Dooly, drawn by JULIA ANN SHERRARD, orphan who resided in Twiggs Co., when she drew the Dooly lot and in Talbot when she drew the Cherokee Lot, sd. LAWRENCE is the husband of sd. orphan. 25 Jan. 1843. E. LAURENCE, WM. HOLT, J.I.C.

EMANUEL COUNTY: JEPTHA PURVIS, Ex'r. to the estate of WM. PURVIS, dec'd., applies for grants for Lot in 3rd Dist., 3rd Section, Cherokee County Lot No. 897 and one other tract drawn by WM. HYLTON in Cherokee, 40 acres, Lot No. 159-16-4 deeded by sd. HYLTON to sd. WM. PURVIS, now held by sd. JEPTHA PURVIS.

BULLOCH COUNTY: Personally app'd. bef. me THOS. C. LANIER, a J. P. for sd. co., JEPTHA PURVIS and saith the above is a true extract from the Books, 20 June 1843. JEPTHA PURVIS, THOS. C.LANIER, J.P.

UNION COUNTY: Personally came bef. me, CARY COX, an acting J. P., FRANCIS DANIELLY that she is the owner of Lot in the Gold region No. 5-15-1. 12 June 1843. FRANCIS DANIELLY, CARY COX, J. P.

MONROE COUNTY: I. FRANCIS DANIELLY, appoint LEONARD T.
                      DOYAL to apply for grant. 12 June 1843.
Signed: FRANCIS DANIELLY (LS).

The following oaths are from counties in the state of ALABAMA:

CHAMBERS COUNTY: Be it known that I have this day appt'd.
                      ANDW. G. LaLASTE of the county of Baldwin
and state of Georgia my lawful att'y. to take out the grant for
Lot No. 533-12-1 in County of Lumpkin and do such matters and
things as I could do in the premises were I present. Signed and
Sealed: 12 June 1843, THOMS. J. STEWART (Seal)
                      Chambers county, Alabama: Personally ap-
peared bef. me JOHN APPLEBY a J.P. for sd. Co., THOMAS J. STEW-
ART who being duly sworn, deposeth and saith that he believes
that he is the proper owner and drawer of Lot 533-12-1, Lumpkin
Co. ...by Act. of Dec. 28, 1842. And that he resided in Capt.
Maddin's District of Pike co., Georgia at the time of giving in
for draws in the Cherokee Land Lottery and that he knew no man
by name of JOSEPH J. STEWART living in Maddin's Dist. before,at
the time, or since, that Capt. Maddin has left Pike County, Ga.
and gone to parts unknown to deponent so that he can not prove
his affidavit and that he has given and paid tax fpr sd. lot.
Sworn to 12 June 1843. JOHN APPLEBY, J.P. Signed: THOS. P.
STEWART.

MACON COUNTY: No. 13, 2 Dist., 4 Sect. Personally app'd.
                      bef. me SAMUEL REID an acting J.P., JOHN
BUTLER who being duly sworn...says the application for grant to
above lot in connection with A. J. BUTLER of the afsd. lot in
complyance with the requisitions of an act. assented to Dec. 21,
1843. JOHN BUTLER. Sworn to 22 Nov. 1853, SAM. REED, J.P.

DALLAS COUNTY: Bef. me an acting J.P. in and for sd. co.
                      appeared ALVIN O. HAYNES who being sworn
says being a citizen of the state of Georgia sometime about the
year 1835, the deponent drew a lot of land under the laws of Ga.
in what was orig. Cherokee Country, being the country lately before then occupied by the Cherokee Indians and then ceded and in
possession of the State of Georgia. That sd. lot as near as deponent recollects was either Lot No. 316 in 26th Dist. and 3rd
Sect., that he has herin transferred saith lot in every way is
gtd. and conveyed his interest therein to any person but the same

still believes bonafide to this deponent. Sworn to before L. ROBERTS, J.P. 13 June 1843. Signed: A. O. HAYNES.

PIKE COUNTY: Before me, CHARLES A. DENNIS, Judge of the County Ct. in and for sd. Co., JOHN G. ROBERTSON who being sworn saith he drew by lottery in the State of Georgia the following described Lot or parcel of land to wit: Lot No. 64-11-4 in Cherokee Dade County of sd. state of Georgia and that JENNETT EVANS now the wife of him the said JOHN, drew by lottery as an orphan of STEVEN EVENS, dec'd. the following described Lot or parcel to wit: No. 275-17-4.
Dated: 5 June 1843. Signed: JOHN G. ROBERTSON.

COOSA COUNTY: Bef. me LEWIS KENNEDY a J.P. for sd. Co. app'd. HARRIETT E. SMITH who on oath deposeth ...Lot No. 131-18-1 in the Cherokee land dist. of the State of Georgia was drawn by the orphans (or orphan children) of JOSIAH BOSWELL, dec'd. that they are minors and that the HARRIETT E. SMITH as the Extrx. of the goods and chattels rights and credits which were of the sd. JOSIAH BOSWELL, dec'd. is entitled to the grant of sd. land by virtue of her sd. office of Extrx. of sd. Estate of the sd. JOSIAH BOSWELL, dec'd.
Dated: 4 Nov. 1844 bef. L. KENNEDY. Signed: HARRIET E. SMITH. On a separate sheet from the Oath is a Power of Att'y. made in Coosa Co., Ala. in which she appt's. IVERSON L. HARRIS of Baldwin Co., Ga. as her lawful Att'y. and it mentions Josiah Boswell was late of Elworth Dist., Bibb Co., Ga. and this letter was wit.by JAS. A. LOFTIN, JOHN H. CONANT.

RUSSELL COUNTY: Bef. me ABRAM P. WATT, a J.P. of sd. Co. came GEORGE C. KING, Guardian for the heir of the late WILLIAM CLEMMOND, dec'd. who being........that when the people of Jones Co., Ga. was giving their names for draws in the Land Lottery of what was then known as the Gold and Land Region in the State of Georgia, he was a citizen of Jones Co., Ga. and give in the names of MARTHA CLEMMOND and ELIZABETH CLEMMOND, then minors and orphans of the late WILLIAM CLEMMOND, dec'd. and the only children of the dec'd. now in life, as her step father and guardian in Capt. Baizmores Dist. in sd. Co. and that she did draw a lot of land of 160 acres in her name as orphan in the sd. lottery. Dated: 27 June 1843. bef. ABRAM P. WATT, J.P. Signed: GEORGE C. KING (Note: Reading this oath would indicate that only one child is mentioned. However, in reading this oath ELIZABETH CLEMMONDs name is on the line with rest of oath, while MARTHA CLEMMOND's name has been written in smaller print above hers.)

CHAMBERS COUNTY: Personally app'd. bef. me WILIE ALFORD who being duly sworn says he is the proper owner and drawer of Lot No. 503-3-4 now Floyd Co. Dated 20 June 1843. Signed: WILIE ALFORD. On same date he appt's. JOSEPH T. (BYRN?) his lawful att'y. Wit.: STEPHEN CHAFFIN, J.P.

MACON COUNTY: JOHN U. BROWN was sworn that the Lot No. 68, 3rd Dist., 3rd Sect. was what he drew and is still his. Dated: 17 June 1843. Signed: JNO. U. BROWN Wit: JOHN N. N. COLQUITT, J.P.

MACON COUNTY: J. B. HADDOCK appt's. CASWELL HADDOCK of Jones Co., Ga. his att'y. to take out Lot No. 1117-21-2 of Cherokee in with my wife formerly CYNTHIA PROSSER now CYNTHIA HADDOCK, orphan of JOHN PROSSER. Dated: 3 Feb. 1854. Signed: J. B. HADDOCK. Wit.: J. Z. C. HARRIS, J.P. on 6 April, 1854 CASWELL HADDOCK appt'd. JOHN S. WALKER of Jones co. to apply for grant. Signed: CASWELL HADDOCK.

BARBOUR COUNTY: JAMES CLARK, an acting J.P. for afsd. co. had to appear bef. him J. M. CALEB WILEY one of the firm of Tompkins and Wiley who being sworn says they are owners of Lot 527-21-2 cont. 40 acres in Cherokee Co....... and that they purchased same land from MARK S. EL(UM?) the orig. drawer for a valuable consideration. Signed: J. M. CALEB WILEY Wit.: JAMES CLARK, J.P. Dated: 21 March 1843. J. LEDBETTER, Clerk of Co. Ct. of Barbour Co., Ala. swears that JAMES CLARK was acting J. P. at time of signing.

COTTONVALLY, (ALA.) March 11, 1849: To Mr. P. M. CAMPTON, Sir I have heard that you were comtroller general and would attempt to forwarding of plat and grants for land in Ga. and that your charge is $1.00 and price of grant is $2.50 which amt. I will remit in such form as I have understood was lawful which is to get a J.P. to certify that I am the man known as J. T. WARREN...I left Troup Co. 8 years ago and know little of the form of giving grants in the 656 Dist. of Troup Co. No.

41-21-3. Signed: JESSE T. WARREN. I do cert. that JESSE T. WARREN is of lawful age that is he is 21 years of age and is own guardian and live in county of Macon of Alabama. Dated: 11 Mar. 1849. Signed: A. J. CRAWFORD, J.P. Forward to Cottonvaley P. O. in Macon Co., Ala.

TALLAPOOSA COUNTY: JOHN CARGILE swore bef. Justice of Peace for sd. state and co. that he is lawful owner of following lots, viz: No. 33-12-4 of Cherokee, now Walker Co.; Lot No. 85-1-2 of orig. Cherokee, now Cobb Co.; Lot No. 1052 in 20th Dist., 3rd Sect. orig. Cherokee, now Paulding. Signed: JOHN CARGILE. Wit.: 20 June 1844, NICHOLAS DYER, J.P.

RUSSELL COUNTY: WILLIAM PETERS being sworn that he is one of orphans of WILLIAM PETERS dec'd. of Olivers, Twiggs Co., Ga. and he is one of the drawers of Lot No. 131-12-3 Cherokee, the grant for which is applied. Dated: 13 Aug. 1846. Wit.: DAVID KNOX, J.P. Signed: WM. PETERS. On same date he appt'd. THOMAS M. COOK his lawful att'y. of Milledgeville.

MONTGOMERY COUNTY: ALFRED P. KING of afsd. have appt'd. ALFRED M. HOUGHTON of Baldwin Co., Ga. my lawful att'y. to apply for 2 grants drawn by sd. ALFRED P., one being No. 175-9 of Carroll...the other is No. 1228-19-3 in what is called Gold region of County now Cobb and that I the sd. Alfred P. gave in to JOHN BETHUNE in Greensborough in Greene Co. at one time-Dist. not recollected and at another in Sparta Hancock Co. Dist. not recollected, which lands remain ungtd. Dated: 19 June 1843. Signed: ALFRED P. KING. Wit: 20 June 1843 bef. JOS. F. HOPPER clerk of county of Montgomery, Ala.

BENTON COUNTY: S. OWDONIS being sworn that he is one of orphans of J. OWDONIS, dec'd. of Habersham Co., Ga. and that he is one of the drawers and owners of Lot No. 136-12-3 in Cherokee, Ga., grant now applied for. Dated: 9 Sept. 1846. Wit.: JESSE PAGE, J.P. Signed: SAMUEL OWDONIS. On the same date he appt'd. THOMAS M. COOK of Milledgeville, Ga. his att'y.

CHAMBERS COUNTY: HENRY G. TURNER appeared bef. HIRAM BENTLEY, acting J.P. of sd. Co. and was sworn

that he was proper owner of Lot No. 971-3-3 of formerly Cherokee
now Cobb Co. and sd. HENRY G. TURNER gave his draw in Jasper Co.
Hillsborough Dist. Signed: HENRY G. TURNER. Wit: HIRAM BENT-
LEY, J.P. Dated: 5 June 1843.

COOSA COUNTY: JAMES TRIMBLE being sworn says he was a
drawer of Lot No. 235-21-2 and is yet the
owner...affiant further state that lands AMANDA WHATLEY, orphan
of MICHAEL WHATLEY was drawer of Lot No. 216-13-3 and by virtue
of his intermarriage with sd. SARAH AMANDA WHATLEY claims her sd.
land. Dated: 8 June 1843. Wit.: SETH P. STORRS, Commissioner
in State of Alabama to adm'r. oaths. Signed: JAMES TRIMBLE.

CHAMBERS COUNTY: HENRY G. TURNER was sworn that he is proper drawer of Lot No. 971-3-3 of formerly
Cherokee now Cobb Co. and sd. HENRY G. TURNER gave in his draw
in Jasper Co., Ga., Hillsborough Dist. Dated: 5 June 1843 bef.
HIRAM BENTLEY, acting J.P. Signed: HENRY G. TURNER.

MACON COUNTY: JOHN U. BROWN was sworn that Lot No. 68-
3-3 which I drew is still mine. Dated:
17 June 1843 bef. JOHN H. H. COLQUITT, J.P. Signed: JNO. U.BROWN

BENTON COUNTY: WILLIAM RUCKS, Guardian for JANE CANNON
says that JAMES CANNON (whose father is
dead) was the drawer and rightful owner of Lot No. 147-24-2 in
Cherokee Co., Ga. 20 June 1843 WILLIAM RUCKS, W. H. ESTILL,
(?), J.P.
M. M. HOUSTON, Clerk of Co. Court of Ben-
ton Co., certify that WM. H. ESTILL whose name appears to the
above affidavit is Justice of the Peace and was at the time of
signing. 20 June 1843 M. M. HOUSTON, Clerk C.C. of Benton Co.
E. T.SMITH, Judge of the County Court of
Benton County do hereby certify that M. M. HOUSTON ...the same
clerk. 20 June 1843. E. T. SMITH (SEAL)

MACON COUNTY: Personally came bef. me WM. B. FILES, an
acting J.P. of sd. Co., GRANVILLE WHITE,
who sayeth he is the drawer of Lot No. 116-22-2 Cherokee purchase
as Gdn. of WILLIAM N.(?) STEPHENS, orphan of BERY STEPHENS, decd.
Dooly County, Ga. is the drawer of Lot No. 282-13-3 of sd. Cher.
purchase. GRANVILLE WHITE. 22 June 1843, WM. R. FILES, J.P.

RANDOLPH COUNTY: JOSEPH BENTON, Judge of Court of Probate
                     for Co. afsd. hereby certify the ROBERT
LEVENS whose genuine Signature appears on the foregoing attached
addicavit is an acting Justice of the Peace in and for sd. co.
1 Dec. 1853. JOSEPH BENTON, Judge.

BARBOUR COUNTY: Personally app'd. bef. me JAMES CLARK, an
                     acting J.P., J. M. CALEB WILY, one of the
firm of TOMPKINS & WILEY who saith they are the owners of Lot 49
-7-3 Cherokee Co. Ga. 21 Mar. 1843. J. M. CALEB WILY JAMES
CLARK, J.P.

BARBOUR COUNTY: JOHN LEDBETTER clerk of the county court,
                     sd co., cert. JAMES CLARK is now and was
....J.P. 21 Mar. 1843. J. LEDBETTER, Clerk.

CHAMBERS COUNTY: I, EDWARD CROFT, Clk. of Ct. of sd. Co.,
                     cert. that JOHN FLETCHER whose name ap-
pears to the within affidavit of MOSES WHEAT. Signer J.P. is now
and was at the date thereof an acting J.P. in and for sd. co.
4 May 1843 EDWARD CROFT, Clk.

CHAMBERS COUNTY: I, EVAN G. RICHARDS Judge of Co. Ct. of
                     sd. Co., cert. that EDWARD CROFT is clk.
of sd. co. 4 May 1843. EVAN G. RICHARDS, Judge C.C.C.C, Ala.

CHAMBERS COUNTY: I have this day appt'd. JOHN G.(?) PARK,
                     of Baldwin Co., Ga. my lawful att'y. for
me to apply for the grant for Lot 998-15-2 Cherokee Co.
1 May 1843. MOSES WHEAT....JOHN FLETCHER, J.P.

CHAMBERS COUNTY: Personally app'd. JOHN FLETCHER, a J.P.,
                     MOSES WHEAT and say that he is the proper
owner of Lot 998-15-2 Cherokee Co. 1 May 1843. MOSES WHEAT,
JOHN FLETCHER, J.P.

CHAMBERS COUNTY: Bef. me JOHN J. HUSSEY an acting J.P. in
                     sd. Co., came JAMES S. HUSSEY who saith
he is the proper owner of Lot No. 213-15-2, Cherokee Purchase,
drawn by JAMES S. MOSS. 5 June 1843. JAMES S. HUSSEY, J.J. HUS-
SEY, J.P.

MACON COUNTY: Personally app'd. bef. me WILLIAM ALEXAN-

DER, an acting Justice of the Peace in and for sd. county, JAS-
PER N. DENNORD, who says he is the proper owner of Lot No. 490-
1-3 county not recollected, drawn by J. W. THRELKILL, the grant
for which is applied for....JASPER N. DENNORD, Sworn before me
June 20, 1843, WILLIAM ALEXANDER, J.P.

MACON COUNTY: I have appt'd. this day, JOHN W. A. SAN-
FORD of Baldwin Co., Ga., my lawful atty.
to apply for the grant for Lot No. 490-1-3.
Dated and signed: June 20, 1843...JASPER N. DENNORD (LS), Wit:
WILLIAM ALEXANDER, J.P.

CHAMBERS COUNTY: Before me JOHN APPLEBY, Justice of the
peace, in and for sd. co., JACOB LIKES
personally appeared and saith that he is the proper owner of lot
No. 431-1-3 of orig. Cherokee Co. JACOB LIKES...bef. me, June
28, 1843. JOHN APPLEBY, J.P.

CHAMBER COUNTY: I have this day appt'd. A. G. LaGASTE (or
LaLASTE?) of Baldwin Co., Ga. my lawful
att'y. to apply for and take out the grant for Lot No. 432 -1-3
of Cherokee Co., Ga.
Dated and signed: 28 June 1843...JACOB LIKES, in presence of
JOHN APPLEBY, J.P.

CHAMBERS COUNTY: I, EDWARD CROFT, Clk. of Co. Ct., do certify that JOHN APPLEBY whose name appears
attesting the within affidavit and Power of Att'y. of JACOB LIKES
is an acting J.P....28 June 1843, EDWARD CROFT, Clerk.

BARBER COUNTY: We, GEORGE WALKER and wife MARY M. WALKER
and JOHN HOLLEY, formally orphans of PRES-
LY HOLLEY do authorise HENRY W. McDANIEL to take out the plat &
grant as we have this day sold to him the Lot of land No. 78-27-
2. Dated: 15 Oct. 1853. Signed: GEORGE WALKER, JR., MARY M.
(X) WALKER, JOHN HOLLEY,...Test: JOHN G. HOLLEY, JAMES WATKINS,
PRESLEY HOLLS, orphans Baileys, Laurens Co.

TALLAPOOSA COUNTY: Before me JO. A. JOHNSON, an acting J.P.
for sd. Co., appeared AARON BROOKS, who
saith Lot No. 223-27-2 was drawn by THOMAS EWING, JOHN EWING, &
SARAH V. EWING, orphans of JAMES EWING of Newton Co., Brackett's

Dist., Georgia...sd. deponent saith he is the owner of sd. lot by fair purchase. A. BROOKS. before me Nov. 13, 1852, JO. A. JOHNSON, J.P.

TALLAPOOSA COUNTY: I. MARCUS C. LANE, Judge of the Probate Court, do certify that JOSEPH A. JOHNSON, Esqr. was on the day of the affadavit an acting J. P. of ...12 Nov. 1852. M. C. LANE, Judge of Probate.

COFFEE COUNTY: KADER J. POWEL, appoint ALFRED M. GEORGE of Baker Co., Ga. my lawful att'y., to take out grant for 40 acres, Lot No. 890=3=3 Cherokee, drawn by myself and my sister MARY POWEL as orphans of ELEANY POWELL. 14 Mar. 1854. KADER POWEL (X) (LS) Attest: WM. F. BEARD, F. McGAMMER(?).

JAMES CLAXTON, Probate Judge of sd. Co., do certify that KADER P. POWELL did execute the foregoing power of attorney...14 Mar. 1854, JAMES CLAXTON.

TERRITORY OF FLORIDA:

JACKSON COUNTY: Personally came before me R. BALLARD an acting Justice of the Peace, WILLIAM E. FULGHAM, saith that he is the representative of HARDY FULGHAM, dec'd. formerly of Burke Co., Ga. and that the sd. WILLIAM is the proper and legal agent for the Heirs of sd. HARRY FULGHAM, dec'd. Lot No. not known in the gold region of Cherokee Country and Lot No.____, 160 A having lost the numbers. 2 June 1843. WILLIAM E. FULGHAM, R. BALLARD, J.P. (SEAL)

STATE OF MISSISSIPPI:

(ARUBA?) COUNTY: JOHN DAVIS was sworn that he was formerly of Hancock co., Ga. but now resident of Miss. and that he drew Lot No. 318-2-2 (crossed out) Sect. in the Land Lottery and No. 580-20-3 of Gold Lottery and that he appoints IVERSON L. HARRIS of Baldwin Co., Ga. to take out plat & grants for same. Dated: 8 Feb. 1843 bef. ANDERSON W. DABNEY, J.P. Signed: JNO. DAVIS

COUNTY ____: JOHN DAVIS formerly of Hancock Co., Ga., but now a resident of in this state and county who was sworn that while a resident of Georgia he became entitled to several chances in the land and Gold Lottery in the then Cherokee Nation and he was informed and believe he drew Lot No. 318-20-2 in the Land and Lot No. 580-20-3 of Gold Lot...and he appt's. IVERSON L. HARRIS of Baldwin Co., Ga. to take out the plats and grant for said land. Dated: 8 Feb. 1843 bef. ANDERSON M. DABNEY, J.P. Signed: JNO. DAVIS. On Feb. 9, HEZEKIAH W. (FOULE?), Clerk of Cir. Ct. of sd. Co. in Miss. did certify that ANDERSON M. DABNEY was acting J.P.

STATE OF SOUTH CAROLINA:

CHARLESTON DIST.: JOHN R. HAYES was sworn that by the last Will and Testament of GEORGE HAYES, a citizen of Thomas Co., Ga., JAMES T. HAYES and himself were appt'd. Exors. and MARY HAYES Extrx. of the sd. GEORGE HAYES now dec'd. and that sd. GEORGE HAYES in his life time was fortunate drawer of Lot No. 361-21-3 Cherokee Purchase, and sd. lot has not been sold and that he for himself and in behalf of other Exor. and Extrx. appoints WILLIAM C. POWELL legal atty. to receive grant. Signed: JNO. R. HAYES, Exor. of GEO. HAYES, dec'd. Wit: A. G. (MAVUTH?), Magistrate. Dated: 15 June 1843.

EDGEFIELD DIST.: Personally appeared bef. me ROBERT ANDERSON, saith on oath that he applys for the Grants of the following lots of land: Nos. 26,244 and 260 of the 8th Dist., and 3rd Section, originally Cherokee Co., Ga. Signed: ROBERT ANDERSON, bef. me 9 May 1844. WM. CRAPON, J.P.

STATE OF TENNESSEE:

SHELBY COUNTY: Power of Attorney made by WM. A. CAMFIELD of Shelby Co., Tenn. to Doctor JOSEPH MILLIGAN of Richmond Co., Ga. to take all lands to which he has a claim. Signed: WM. A. CAMFIELD. Dated: June 12, 1843.

PART II

To locate the original of a document abstracted in this section, ask the Georgia Surveyor General Department for the file with the lot designation used in the beginning of the abstract you are interested in.

STATE OF GEORGIA:

COBB COUNTY: Lot No.1065-7-3 Cherokee. Bef. me app'd. DUWIN(?) IRWIN as agent and friend of JOHN WHITE, SENR., FRANCIS IRWIN, EDWARD PENNUAD(DENNUAD?), ANDREW F. WOOLY, and for myself. For WHITE he applies for grants to Lots No. 1065,1236,1166,1167,1140,1213 and 1066 in 17th Dist., 3rd Sect.; for FRANCIS IRWIN...Lots No. 17,54,55,56,57,89,90,91 and 128 in 4th Dist., 3rd sect. orig. Cherokee, now Cass Co.; for PENNUAD..Lot No. 333,20th Dist., 2nd Sect.; for WOOLY..Lot No.217 16 Dist.,3rd Sect...(the rest of the manuscript is missing.)

PULASKI COUNTY: Lot No. 532-3-3 Cherokee. Personally appeared HENRY B. HATHAWAY, Adm'r. for Est. of JAMES C. HALL, dec'd. of Laurens Co. for grants for Lots No. 532-3-3 and No. 1074-3-3, drawn by JONAS JOHNSON of Washington Co., also for two lots drawn by JAMES C. HALL, designation not known. Signed: H. B. HATHAWAY bef. JOHN BRZMAN, J.I.C. Dated: 16 June 1843. (Also includes appt'mt. of AUGUSTIN H. HANSELL as att'y. to take out grants.

MORGAN COUNTY: Lot No. 486-3-3 Cherokee. Personally appeared MARY WALTON, Extrx. of the Estate of JOSEPH W. WALTON, dec'd. for grant to Lot No. 486-3-3 in Cherokee Co. Signed: MARY (X) WALTON bef. JOHN J. WALKER, J.P. Dated: 23 May 1843. (Includes app't. of WILLIAM O. PAFFORD as att'y.

SUMTER COUNTY: Lot No. 917-3-3 Cherokee. Personally appeared EBENEZER J. COTTLE, Adm'r. of the Estate of JOHN J. COTTLE, dec'd. for grant for Lot No. 917-3-3. Signed: EBENEZER J. COTTLE bef. EASAW SMITH, J.I.C. Dated: 22 June 1843. Includes app't. of WILLIAM W. BARLOW as att'y. bef. WM. MIMMS and EASAW SMITH, J.I.C.

PIKE COUNTY: Lot No. 396-4-3 Cherokee. Personally appeared JAMES EPPINGER to apply for grants for Lot No. 396-4-3 in Cass Co., drawn by BARTHOLOMEW MASTERS, part of lots No. 105-8-1 in Union Co. drawn by JOSEPH OSBORNE; Lot No. 195-8-1 Union Co. drawn by PIERCE B. PENDERGAST; and Lot No. 4-12-4 in Walker Co. drawn by JOHN S. FOSTER. He also app's. for as agent for his mother, Mrs. HANNAH E. EPPINGER, for Lot No. 614-2-1. Signed: JAS. EPPINGER bef. ALLISON SPEIR, J.P. Dated:

27 May 1843. Includes app't. of JOHN NEAL as Att'y. and brief letter from JAS. EPPINGER to JOHN NEAL, enclosing $20.00 in Bank notes, Zebulon, 27 May 1843.

HANCOCK COUNTY: Lot No. 287-4-3 Cherokee. JAMES H. MIDDLEBROOK claims grants for Lot No. 287-4-3 and as Adm'r. of the Estate of MESHACK HOWELL, Lot No. 666-5-1. Signed: JAS H. MIDDLEBROOK bef. BENJAMIN F. LATIMER, J.P. 5 June 1843. Includes app't. of WASHINGTON H. BRANTLEY as Att'y.

SCREVEN COUNTY: Lot No. 244-4-3 Cherokee. WILLIAM JENKINS appt's. JOHN ROBERTS as his Att'y. to receive grant for Lot No. 244-4-3 and also for Lot No. 88-6 Dist. in Muscogee Co. that was drawn by his brother OWEN JENKINS, since dec'd. Signed: WILLIAM JENKINS bef. AUGS. SEABORN JONES and ELIJAH ROBERTS, J.P. 27 May 1843.

RICHMOND COUNTY: Lot No. 264-4-3 Cherokee. Personally appeared ANDREW J. MILLEN, Ex'r. of Estate of ROBERT MILLEN (DILLON?), dec'd. for the grant to Lot No. 260-4-3 in Cherokee Co. Signed: A. J. MILLEN bef. T. W. MILLER, N.P. 17 June 1843. Includes app't. of WILLIAM H. PRITCHARD as Att'y.

GWINNETT COUNTY: Lot No. 1190-3-3 Cherokee. Personally appeared JULIAN A. JUHAN for grant to Lot No. 1190-3-3 as a orphan of DANIEL B. JUHAN, dec'd. of Jones Co. for himself and his brothers and sisters. Signed: JULIAN A. JUHAN (by mark) bef. FRANCIS P. JUHAN, J.P. 13 Dec. 1845.

GWINNETT COUNTY: Lot No. 710-3-3- Cherokee. Personally appeared JOHN BANKSTON for grant to Lot No. 710-3-3 as the son of the drawer, JOHN BANKSTON, SR. Signed: JOHN BANKSTON bef. SILAS LAWRENCE, J.P., 15 Mar. 1843. Includes app't. of THOMAS JOHNSON as Att'y.

FRANKLIN COUNTY: Lot No. 371-3-3 Cherokee. Personally appeared MICAJAH MARTIN, Ex'r. of the Est. of JAMES MARTIN, SR., for grant to Lot No. 371-3-3 drawn by JAS. MARTIN, SR., dec'd. Signed: MICAJAH MARTIN bef. R. A. N. NAIL (?), J.I.C. 20 June 1843. Appt. of CHARLES H. NELSON of Baldwin Co. as Att'y.

CHATHAM COUNTY: Lot No. 1007-2-3 Cherokee. Personally appeared CLAIBORN A. WATKINS for grant to Lot No. 1007-2-3 and also to Lot No. 143-18-2 as sole heir of his brother JOHN R. WATKINS, dec'd. Signed: CLAIBORN A. WATKINS before ISAAC RUSSELL, J.P. 30 May 1843. Includes app't. of PIKE WILLIAMS as Att'y.

CHATOOGA COUNTY: Lot No. 232-6-3 Cherokee. Personally appeared JOHN MONTGOMERY, Ex'r. of WILLIAM FOULER of Gwinnett Co., drawer of Lot No. 232-6-3 of Cherokee co. to apply for the grant. Signed: JOHN MONTGOMERY bef. ELIJAH WYATT, J.P. 20 May 1843. Includes app't. of WILLIAM D. FULTON as Att'y., bef. JOHN KELLETT and ELIJAH WYATT, J.P.

LOUNDES COUNTY: Lot No. 216-6-3 Cherokee. Personally appeared BERRIEN M. C. LEWIS who claims he is an heir to Lot No. 216-1-3 Cherokee Co. drawn by the orphans of WILEY LEWIS of Thomas County. Signed: BERRIEN M. C. LEWIS bef. HAMILTON W. SHARP, J.I.C. 19 June 1843. Includes app't. of ENOCH HALE as Att'y.

TROUP COUNTY: Lot No. 1274-4-3 Cherokee. Personally appeared GEORGE HEARD as guardian and agent for GEORGE F. HEARD, who is now in Texas, to take out a grant for Lot No. 1274-4-3 and he does app't. Major O. H. BULL Att'y. to do the same. Signed: GEO. HEARD bef. JAS. M. BEALL. 1 June 1843.

MERRIWETHER COUNTY: Lot No. 653-4-3 Cherokee. WILLIAM McKISSACK, WILLIAM P. GLASS, and BENJAMIN BLISSIT app't. ALFRED M. HORTON of Milledgeville as their att'y. to take out grants for Lot No. 653-4-3 Cass Co., drawn by FRANCIS LEWIS of Pike Co.; Lot No. 178-17-2 Cobb Co., drawn by WILLIAM P. GLASS of Jasper Co.; and Lot No. 65-13-2, drawn by JOHN HUDSON. Signed: WILLIAM McKISSACK, WILLIAM P. GLASS, BENJAMIN BLISS. bef. WALTER R. POPE, J.P. 23 June 1843.

TROUP COUNTY: Lot No. 294-17-3 Cherokee. SARAH FULTON and R. L. FULTON appt. AARON M. SMITH of Baldwin Co., Ga., Att'y. to receive grants for SARAH FULTON's Lot No. 294-17-3 and R. L. FULTON's Lot No. 196-26-2. Signed: SARAH (X) MARK, R. L. FULTON before WM. S. KELLY, J.P. 24 June 1843.

HALL COUNTY:(PUTNAM CO. was marked out). Lot No. 1013-21-3 Cher.

Personally appeared H. W. COZART for the grant to Lot No. 1013-21-3 of Cherokee and as Adm'r. of the Est. of PLEASANT H. ROGERS, dec'd. for Lot No. 270-26-2 in Cherokee. Signed: H. W. COZART bef. JORDON REESE, J.I.C. 19 June 1843. Also includes app't. by HUBBARD W. COZART of Putnam Co., Ga. of ISAM BROOKS of Baldwin Co. as Att'y., Signed bef. P. M. ARMOR & JORD<u>A</u>N REESE, J.I.C. 19 June 1843.

OGLETHORPE COUNTY: Lot No. 321-1-3 Cherokee. Personally appeared BENJAMIN F. HARDEMAN to claim Lot No. 321-1-3 as Adm'r. of the Estate of ASA W. VEAL(VIAL?) of Madison Co., Georgia, now deceased. Signed: BENJ. F. HARDEMAN bef. JESSE MANCEY, J.P. 28 June 1843. Includes app't. of CHAR. V. CHAMBERLESS as Att'y.

WILKES COUNTY: Lot No. 96-7-3 Cherokee. Personally appeared JOHN D. REEVES to claim Lot No. 96-7-3, orig. of Cherokee, now Murray County, drawn by RICHARD WOODRUFF, Revolutionary War soldier, which REEVES claims as Adm'r. of WOODRUFF's Estate and also Lot No. 5-25-2 orig. in Cherokee and now in Murray County. Signed: JOHN D. REEVES, 21 June 1843. Not attested to. Includes app't. of JOHN R. ANDERSON as Att'y.

HANCOCK COUNTY: Lot No. 1018-17-3 Cherokee. Personally appeared ALBERT HENRY to claim Lot No.1018-17-3 drawn by the heirs of JOSEPH HENRY. Signed:ALBERT (X) HENRY bef. R. BURNEY, J.I.C. 17 June 1843. Includes app't. of JOHN D. BISHOP of Warren Co. as Att'y. for the minor heirs of JOSEPH HENRY.

SCREVEN COUNTY: Lot No. 112-17-3 Cherokee. Personally appeared GEORGE F. SIMONS who claims Lot No. 112-17-5 for the Estate of SAMUEL SIM<u>MONS</u> , dec'd., "there being no legal Executor or Administrator to the Estate". Signed: GEO. F. SIM<u>MONS</u> bef. CHARLES EVANS, J.I.C. 15 June 1843. Includes appt. of CUYLER W. YOUNG as Att'y.

TALIAFERRO COUNTY: Lot No. 114-17-3 Cherokee. Personally appeared WILLIAM B. MOORE, lawful agent of the guardian of the heirs of THOMAS GUEST, to claim Lot No. 114-17-3 in Cherokee County. Signed: W. B. MOORE bef. JESSE WOODALL, J.P. 5 June 1842. Includes app't. of ALEXANDER H. STEPHENS as

Attorney, signed by W. B. MOORE before I. J. MOORE and JESSE WOODALL, J.P.

LUMPKIN COUNTY: Lot No. 218-17-3 Cherokee. Personally appeared SHADRACK DEAN, Adm'r. of the estate of his brother NIMROD DEAN, dec'd., to claim Lot No. 218-17-3 in original Cherokee. Signed: SHADRACK DEAN before M. H. GUTHRIGHT, J.I.C. 14 June 1842. Includes app't. of EZEKIEL BUFFINGTON of Hall County as Att'y.

JASPER COUNTY: Lot No. 314-17-3 Cherokee. Personally appeared JOSEPH I. W. CARGILE and RUNN B. M. CARGILE as proper owners of Lot No. 314-17-3 in orig. Cherokee County. Signed: J.I.W. CARGILE and R.B.M. CARGILE before CHARLES JORDAN, J.I.C., 25 Feb. 1843. Includes app't. of THOMAS M. COOK of Baldwin County as Att'y.

LINCOLN COUNTY: Lot No. 560-17-3 Cherokee. Personally appeared MARK BOND, Guardian of THOMAS BONDs orphans, to claim Lot No. 560-17-3 of Cjerokee County. Signed: MARK (my mark) BOND bef. WM. M. McCARLEY, J.P., 16 June 1843. Includes app't. of JOHN R. ANDERSON of Baldwin County as Att'y. MARK (X) BOND, bef. BEN. B. MOORE and WM. M. McCARLEY, J.P.

WALTON COUNTY: Lot No. 782-3-3 Cherokee. Personally appeared JOHN BUCKUS to claim Lot 782-3-3, and as Ex'r. of Estate of JOHN BUCKUS, SR., Lot 587-17-3 in orig. Cherokee Co. Signed: JOHN BACOUS bef. W. H. BRIMBERRY, J.P., 13 June 1842. Includes app't. of JAMES Z. LOCKLIN of Hall Co. as Attorney.

HANCOCK COUNTY: Lot No. 695-17-3 Cherokee. SARAH H. ALFRIEND, acting Extrx. of ABRAM ALFRIEND, dec'd., claims Lot No. 695-17-3 Cherokee County. Signed: SARAH H. ALFRIEND bef. THOMAS COLEMAN, J.P. 22 June 1843. Includes app't. of ALFRED M. HORTON of Milledgeville as Att'y.

OGLETHORPE COUNTY: Lot No. 720-17-3 Cherokee. JAMES B. SMITH appoints JAMES HUFF Att'y. to receive Lot No. 720-17-3 which he purchased from ELIZABETH DAVIS of Walton County. Signed: JAMES B. SMITH bef. THOS. L. WALTON, J.P. 26 June 1843.

NEWTON COUNTY: Lot No. 829-17-3 Cherokee. Personally appeared LUCINDA L. DUKE, widow of GIPSON DUKE, to claim the lot he drew in the late Cherokee and Gold Land Lotteries. Signed: LUCINDA S. DUKE bef. JOSIAH BROWN, J.P. 2 Jun. 1843. Includes appt. of SEABORN J. CLARK, att'y.

HEARD COUNTY: Lot No. 876-17-3 Cherokee. Personally appeared NANCY PEDDY guardian of the minors of WILLIAM PEDDY, dec'd. and one of the heirs of his estate, to claim Lot No. 876-17-3 and Lot 4-5-3. Also Lot 1208-21-3, drawn by WM. H. CORDELL of Heard Co. Signed: NANCY PEDDY (by mark) bef. WM. B. W. DENT, J.P. 31 May 1843. Includes app't. of GILES S. THOMPKINS as att'y., signed bef. JOSEPH E. DENT and WM. B. W. DENT, J.P.

RANDOLPH COUNTY: Lot No. 976-18-3 Cherokee. Personally appeared MATTHEW BAILEY, as administrator of the estate of JAMES BAILEY of Houston County to claim Lot No. 511-5-1 Cherokee. Signed: MATTHEW BAILEY bef. ROBERT MARTIN, J.P. 21 Sept. 1844.
         Personally app'd. JOSIAH BAILEY to claim Lot No. 976-18-3 of Cherokee. Signed: JOSIAH BAILEY (by mark) bef. ROBERT MARTIN, J.P., 21 September 1844.

WARREN COUNTY: Lot No. 998-18-3 Cherokee. Personally appeared DOROTHY HILL to claim Lot 998-18-3 drawn by herself and, as natural guardian of the orphans of MOUNTAIN HILL, lot 1269-13-3. Signed: DOROTHY HILL bef. SPIVEY FULLER, J.P. 6 June 1843. Includes app't. of JAMES A. CHAPMAN as att'y., signed bef. JOHN J. PILCHER and Spivey Fuller, J.P.

WARREN COUNTY: Lot No. 929-18-3 Cherokee. Personally appeared MARSHALL H. WELLBORN claims Lot 929-18-3 of orig. Cherokee Co., as part owner in right of his former wife, ADALINE L. WELLBORN (formerly ADALINE L. HILL), one of the orphans of THEOPHILUS HILL. Signed: MARSHALL N. WELLBORN bef. STODDARD W. SMITH, J.P. 28 June 1843. Includes app't. of A. B. ROSS as att'y., signed bef. NELSON SPAIN and Stoddard W. Smith, J.P.

CASS COUNTY: Lot No. 785-18-3 Cherokee. Personally appeared LINDSAY OGLESBY to claim above Lot

orig. Cherokee, now Paulding County, drawn by his father THOMAS
OGLESBY of Elbert County. He claims land as agent "for the rest
of the children there being no Ex'r. nor Adm'r. to said estate."
Signed: LINDSAY OGLESBY bef. JOHN MILLICAN, J.P. 12 June 1843.
Includes app't. of JOHN JOHNSON, att'y., signed bef. ROBERT HUT-
SON and John Millican, J.P.

TROUP COUNTY: Lot No. 658-2-3 Cherokee. JOHN McLEAN
                       appoints HENRY T. SMART of Chambers Co.,
Alabama, att'y. to take out grants for Lot 658-2-3 now in Paulding County; Lot 445-4-3 in Cass County; Lot 606-18-3 and Lot
447-2-4. Signed: JOHN McLEAN bef. PASCAL E. WARD and THOMAS
M. WYATT, J.P., 23 June 1843.

MORGAN COUNTY: Lot No. 406-18-3 Cherokee. Personally ap-
                       peared ABNER R. HILL, Ex'r. of the estate
of JOHN HIGH, dec'd. to claim Lot (above). Signed: ABNER R.
HILL bef. JOHN JOHNSON, J.P., 23 June 1843. Appt's. JAMES M.
SHEPHERD as Att'y.

MONROE COUNTY: Lot No. 433-18-3 Cherokee. Personally ap-
                       peared CELA FLEMING, Extrx. of the Estate
of JAMES FLEMING, dec'd., to claim Lot 433-18-3 and Lot 750-3-4.
Signed: CELA (by mark) FLEMING bef. LAMAR, J.P. 2 June 1843.
App't. of JAMES LAMAR as Att'y.

MONTGOMERY COUNTY: Lot No. 625-20-3 Cherokee. Personally ap-
                       peared JESSE M. WALL to claim Lot 625-20-
3 of orig. Cherokee that was drawn by BENJAMIN VAUGHN, but sold
to claimant's father WILLIAM D. WALL, who sold it to the claimant
in 1838. Signed: JESSE M. WALL bef. HENRY WOOTTEN, J.P. 13
June 1843.
                       Personally app'd. DANIEL D. WALL to claim
Lot No. 90-12-2 in formerly Cherokee Co. Signed: DANIEL D. WALL
bef. Henry Wootten, J.P., 13 June 1843. Includes app't. of
CHRISTOPHER McRAE of Baldwin Co. as att'y. for Jesse M. Wall and
Daniel D. Wall, signed bef. ALEXANDER McARTHUR and Henry Wootten.

MONROE COUNTY: Lot No. 920-20-3 Cherokee. Personally ap-
                       peared IRWIN H. and OWEN S. WOODWARD for
Lot 920-20-3 and Lot 180-10-2 drawn by them individually.
Signed: IRWIN H. WOODWARD and OWEN WOODWARD bef. JAS. HARDIN,J.P.

Dated: 17 June 1843. Includes app't. of their brother JOHN L. WOODWARD as attorney.

JASPER COUNTY: Lot No. 264-17-3 Cherokee. Personally appeared BENJAMIN F. WARD to claim Lot 264-17-3 of orig. Cherokee, now Cass County, and as Ex'r. of the estate of ROBERT HUMBER, dec'd. of Butts County, Lot 130-3-1 and Lot 296-2-3. Signed: B. F. WARD bef. CHAS. JUDAN, J.I.C., 23 June 1843. Includes app't. of ALFRED M. HORTON as att'y.

JONES COUNTY: Lot No. 183-13-3 Cherokee. NANCY PITTS, natural guardian of LIZA PITTS, appt's. "HENRY CHILDS (BENNETT BRIDGES)" attorney to take out grant for above lot. Signed: NANCY PITTS (by mark) bef. THOS. J. MIDDLEBROOKS and GREEN B. WILLIAMSON, J.P. 10 June 1843.

COBB COUNTY: Lot No. 18-13-3 Cherokee. Personally appeared EVAN PARSONS, of Paulding Co., one of the legal heirs of PETER GRAHAM of Harris County, to claim Lot 18-13-3 and appt's. JOHN ROWE his att'y. Signed: EVAN PARSONS bef. M. V. NORTON, J.P., 17 June 1843.

RICHMOND COUNTY: Lot No. 280-11-3 Cherokee. Personally appeared JAMES L. COLEMAN to claim Lots 280-11-3 and 1276-2-3 and as heir of his mother, the late SARAH COLEMAN, dec'd, lot 13-7-2. Signed: JAMES L. COLEMAN bef. WARREN, J.I.C. 10 June 1843. Includes app't. of WILLIAM H. PRITCHARD of Baldwin Co. as att'y.

HARRIS COUNTY: Lot No. 98-11-3 Cherokee. Personally appeared DUNCAN CASE, heir to Lot 98-11-3 Cherokee and Lot 54-9-2, one drawn by said DUN<u>LY</u> and other by ROBERT, orphans, to claim grants. He appt's. JOHN MORGAN, his att'y. Signed: DUNCAN CASE (by mark) bef. AARON GOODMAN, and JOHN MORGAN, J.P., 31 May 1843.
Personally app'd. AARON GOODMAN to claim Lot 163-14-2. Signed: Aaron Goodman bef. HAYWOOD BARROW and John Morgan, J.P., 27 May 1843.

CARROLL COUNTY: Lot No. 13-11-3 Cherokee. Personally appeared WM. SMITH, to claim Lot 13-11-3 for himself and the other orphans. Signed: WILLIAM SMITH bef. MAR-

TIN HOLCOMB, J.P., 13 May 1843. Includes app't. of SAMUEL C. CAND-
LER as attorney.

JEFFERSON COUNTY: Lot No. 123-9-3 Cherokee. Personally appeared JOHN M. HAYLES to claim his half of Lot 123-9-3 and as agent of THOMAS A. GOULDING, the owner of the other half. The lot was drawn by PETER J. GOULDING's orphans of Peterson's Dist. of Burke County, Georgia. Signed: JOHN M. HAYLES bef. S. ARMINGTON, J.I.C., 21 March 1843. Includes app't. of ALFRED HORTON, surveyor general of Baldwin Co., as att'y.

HENRY COUNTY: Lot No. 70-9-3 Cherokee. Personally appeared JOHN ROWAN, one of the legal heirs by marriage of WILLIAM FOSTER, dec'd. and thus owner of half of Lot 70-9-3, as one of the two heirs. Lot was won by WILLIAM FOSTER's orphans. Signed: John Rowan bef. THOS. E. HICKS, J.P., 2 May 1843. Includes app't. of JOHN HAIL as att'y.

WILKES COUNTY: Lot No. 316-7-3 Cherokee. Personally appeared JOHN H. DYSON Adm'r. "Deboris non" of the estate of ANDREW G. SIMMS dec'd. to claim Lot 316-7-3. Signed: JOHN H. DYSON bef. A. S. WINGFIELD, J.I.C., 19 June 1843. Includes app't. of JOHN R. ANDERSON as att'y., wit: GEORGE DYSON.

OGLETHORPE COUNTY: Lot No. 186-7-3 Cherokee. Personally appeared PERRY D. SORROW, ANDREW J. SORROW, SUSAN SORROW, LUCINDA SORROW and GEORGE P. SORROW, children of JOSHUA SORROW, dec'd., to claim Lot 186-7-3 in orig. Cherokee but now Cass County as minors and orphans of JOSHUA SORROW. Signed by each of the heirs by mark bef. WILEY CARTER, J.P. on 20 April 1844.

HALL COUNTY: Lot No. 916-17-3 Cherokee. Personally appeared ANNA PEW, agent for the heirs of ISAAC PEW, dec'd., to claim Lot 916-17-3 ..Signed: ANNA PEW (by mark) bef. JACOB ROGERS, J.P., 30 May 1843. Includes appt'd atty. JOSEPH DUNAGAN, bef. Wm. ROGERS.

JEFFERSON COUNTY: Lot No. 712-2-3 Cherokee. MARY CLARK, WILLIAM CLARK and RICHMOND ALLEN, lawful heirs of THOMAS CLARK, dec'd. appoint BENJAMIN R. PENDUE as their atty. to receive Lots 712-2-3 and Lot 174-15-1. Signed: MARY CLARK (by mark), WILLIAM CLARK and RICHMOND ALLEN bef. JAMES STAPLETON,JP, 20 June 1843. Includes statement by MARY CARTER that she was the wife of THOMAS CLARK,.dec'd.

TWIGGS COUNTY: Lot No. 23-2-3 Cherokee. Personally appeared LEWIS SOLOMON to claim Lot 23-2-3 and Lot 10-7-3 having married one of the orphans of ELIJAH LINGO, dec'd. and with the consent of JOSEPH J. CHAPPELL of Twiggs Co., guardian of the orphans. Signed: LEWIS SOLOMON bef. PEYTON REYNOLDS, acting Justice of the Inferior Court, 16 June 1843.

LUMPKIN COUNTY: Lot No. 202-25-3 Cherokee. Personally appeared JOSEPH GLAZE as agent for JACOB GLAZE to receive Lot 202-25-3 and Lot 121-2-3. Signed: JOSEPH GLAZE bef. M. H. GUTHRIGHT, J.I.C., 2 Feb. 1843. Includes app.t. of C. HIBBERTS as att'y.

CLARK COUNTY: Lot No. 357-2-3 Cherokee. Personally appeared ASA VARNUM as qualified executor of the estate of ELIZABETH HERD, dec'd. of Jackson Co. to apply for the grant to Lot 357-2-3. Signed: ASA VARNUM bef. SAML. FROST, J.P., 20 June 1843. Includes app't. of WILLIAM M. VARNUM of Lumpki County as att'y, bef. REOSS CRANE.

GWINNETT COUNTY: Lot No. 143-10-3 Cherokee. Personally appeared JOHN MILLS, Ex'r. of the estate of JOHN F. WASSON, dec'd., to claim Lot 143-10-3 in Murray County and Lot 761-19-3 in Paulding County. Signed: JOHN MILLS before W. S. IVIE, J.P., 15 June 1843. Includes app't. of THOMAS W. ALEXANDER as att'y., bef. JAMES P. SIMMONS.

RICHMOND COUNTY: Lot No. 277-8-3 Cherokee. Personally appeared ROBERT ANDERSON as a friend of WILLIAM HARRISON's orphans of Columbia County to apply for their claim to Lot No. 277-8-3 in Murray County. Signed: ROBERT ANDERSON bef. FOSTER BLODGET, J.I.C., 7 May 1853.

HANCOCK COUNTY: Lot No. 79-18-3 Cherokee. Personally appeared WILLIAM ASKEW, as Adm'r. of JAMES M. ASKEW, dec'd., who with said WILLIAM and JOHN ASKEW, RICHARD ASKEW, and BENJAMIN F. ASKEW was one of the orphans of JAMES ASKEW, dec'd. who drew Lot 70-8-3 and Lot 6-11-3 . Signed: WILLIAM

ASKEW before H. W. HENDRICK, J.I.C., 24 June 1843.

CRAWFORD COUNTY: Lot No. 978-18-3 Cherokee. Personally appeared HILLIARD CRUTCHFIELD to take out a grant for Lot 978-18-3, as Ex'r. of ROBERT M. WRIGHT, dec'd. Signed: HILLIARD CRUTCHFIELD before JOHN WALPOLE, J.I.C., 26 May 1843. Includes app't. of JEREMIAH C. HARVEY as att'y.

CAMDEN COUNTY: Lot No. 517-18-3 Cherokee. Personally appeared RICHARD N. GREEN, son and legal heir of JOHN GREEN, dec'd. to claim Lot 517-18-3. Signed: RICHARD N. GREEN bef. JOHN MIZELL, J.P., 17 June 1843

TALBOT COUNTY: Lot No. 539-18-3 Cherokee. Personally appeared G. L. TAYLOR, Ex'r. of the estate of SARAH TAYLOR, dec'd., to claim Lot 539-18-3 and he appoints JAMES STALLINGS as his lawful att'y. Signed: GEORGE L. TAYLOR bef. JOSEPH B. SWARM, J.P., 12 August 1844.

APPLING COUNTY: Lot No. 315-13-3 Cherokee. Personally appeared SILAS OQUIN to claim Lot 315-13-3 as husband of NANCY OQUIN, formerly NANCY CRUMNEY, heir of REBECCA CRUMNEY, dec'd. who drew the lot. Signed: SILAS OQUIN bef. CARLETON B. COLE, J.I.C., 9 June 1843.

NEWTON COUNTY: Lot No. 713-18-3 Cherokee. Personally appeared MARY SENTELL to claim Lot 713-18-3 for herself and her minor children. The land was drawn by NATHAN SENTELL of Newton Co., dec'd. and she is his Admtrx. Signed: MARY SENTELL bef. COLUMBUS D. PACE, J.I.C., 9 June 1843. Includes app't. of JOHN WILLIAMSON as att'y. to receive her husband's lot. signed bef. WILLIAM W. C. PACE.

BALDWIN COUNTY: Lot No. 809-18-3 Cherokee. Personally appeared ANDERSON W. REDDING to claim for widow EDNY T. ROBERTSON, now the wife of WILLIAM C. RUTLEDGE, lot No. 809-18-3. The widow lived in Talbot Co. when she drew the lot. Signed: A. W. REDDING bef. A. M. HORTON, notary public, 11 January 1844.

HOUSTON COUNTY: Lot No. 60-5-3 Cherokee. Personally appeared SANDERS D. OUTLAW, for himself and

MATILDA M. OUTLAW and JOICE E. OUTLAW, orphans of BRUTLEY OUTLAW, dec'd. to claim Lot 60-5-3 in orig. Cherokee now Cass County. Signed: SANDERS D. OUTLAW bef. THOS. B. ALDRIDGE, J.P. 10 Sept. 1847.

CHATHAM COUNTY: Lot No. 325-18-3 Cherokee. ISAAC D'LYON, LEVI S. D'LYON, ANNA D'LYON, REBECCA D'LYON and MORDECAI S.D'LYON, heirs of ABRAHAM D'LYON, dec'd. appoint ABRAHAM BALDWIN FANNIN as their att'y. to take out a grant for Lot 325-18-3. Signed: ISAAC D'LYON, LEVI S. D'LYON, and M. S. D'LYON before ALEX. DRYSDALE, N.P., 3 June 1843.

CASS COUNTY: Lot No. 48-17-3 Cherokee. Personally appeared C. D. TEVHUNE to petition that the grant be made for Lot 48-17-3 of orig. Cherokee now Cass County, to the CHRISTIAN's orphans of Jones District of Madison County so that title may be "perfected" to him. Signed: C. D. TEVHUNE bef. ISAAC DAVIS, J.P., 15 March 1850.

CLARKE COUNTY: Lot No. 3-17-3 Cherokee. RICHARD RICHARDSON, Adm'r. of ROBERT LIGON, dec'd., appoints RANSOM A. WHITEHEAD as att'y. to take out a grant for Lot 3-17-3. Signed: RICH. RICHARDSON bef. SAMUEL P. THURMOND and M. M. SHEATS, J.P., 15 May 1843.

MUSCOGEE COUNTY: Lot No. 77-6-3 Cherokee. Personally appeared JAMES H. SHORTER, who, with SOPHIA H. SHORTER, is adm'r. of the estate of ELI. S. SHORTER to claim Lot 77-6-3 in orig. Cherokee, now Cass Co., and Lot 244-7-4. Signed: JAMES H. SHORTER bef. JOHN J. McKENDEN, J.P., 8 June 1843.

PIKE COUNTY: Lot No. 605-17-3 Cherokee. Personally appeared WILLIAM H. STONE to claim Lot 605-7-3. Signed: WILLIAM H. STONE bef. A. A. GOULDING, J.P., 9 June 1843. Includes appt. of HARRISON J. SARGENT as att'y.

BALDWIN COUNTY: Lot No. 869-17-3 Cherokee. Personally appeared BENNETT BRIDGES, as Ex'r. of the owner of Lot 869-17-3 and Lot 487-16-2 to claim said lots. Signed: BENNETT BRIDGES bef. ALFRED M. HORTON, N.P., 15 June 1843.

LEE COUNTY: Lot No. 297-26-3 Cherokee. LEMUEL LONG as

part owner and agent for the other owners, appoints DAVID N. JONES as agent to receive the grant for lot 297-26-3, drawn by the orphans of STAFFORD LONG of Baker County. Signed: LEMUEL LONG bef. A. G. JONES, J.P., 31 May 1843.

WILKES COUNTY: Lot No. 587-21-3 Cherokee. Personally appeared G. F. BUCHANAN, Adm'r. of the est. of B. MULLIKIN, dec'd. to claim Lot 587-21-3. Signed: GEORGE F. BUCHANAN, bef. LEWIS S. BROWN, J.I.C., 2 June 1843.

SCREVEN COUNTY: Lot No. 195-1-2 Cherokee. JOHN DENTON appoints JOHN ROBERTS as his att'y. to take out grants on Lot 195-1-2 and Lot 23-7-2, the latter he drew as a resident of Savannah in Chatham County. Signed: JOHN DENTON before THOS. GROSS and W. I. LAWSON, J.P., 1 June 1843.

MARION COUNTY: Lot No. 302-2-2 Cherokee. Personally appeared H. K. LAMB to claim Lot 302-2-2, drawn by the orphans of HINCHEN McKINNEY of Warren County. Sign'd by H. K. LAMB bef. R. W. MASTON, J.P., 15 June 1843. Includes app't. of JOHN CAMPBELL as att'y., wit: N. BURKHALTER.

MONROE COUNTY: Lot No. 534-18-2 Cherokee. JAMES HOWELL, orphan of JAMES HOWELL, SR. of Walton co., dec'd., appoints SYLVANUS W. BURNEY att'y. to take out grant for Lot 534-18-2. Signed: JAMES HOWEL bef. A. M. SPEER, 28 May 1843.

WARREN COUNTY: Lot No. 1225-2-2 Cherokee. Personally appeared CHARLES COLSTON who says he and ELIZA HOLDER are the owners of Lot 1225-2-2. Signed: CHARLES H. COLSTON bef. STODDARD W. SMITH, J.P., 28 June 1843.

CLARK COUNTY: Lot No. 853-17-2 Cherokee. Personally appeared JOHN JOINER to claim two lots drawn by the orphans of FREDERICK TILLARS, he having married one of the orphans. The lots are No. 853-17-2 and No. 254-5-2. Signed: JOHN JOINER (his mark) bef. JNO. C. GREER, JOHN G. FERGUSON and WM. NABERS, J.P., 9 June 1843.

RICHMOND COUNTY: Lot No. 930-18-2 Cherokee. Personally appeared WILLIAM G. LARK, husband of MILDRED ANN LARK (formerly DILLON, daughter of WILLIAM C. DILLON, dec'd.)

to claim Lot 930-18-2. Includes app't. of WILLIAM H. PRITCHARD of Baldwin Co. as att'y. Signed: W. G. LARK bef. RICHMD. CUTY & BENJAMIN B. RUSSELL, N.P., 27 June 1843.

CAMPBELL COUNTY: Lot No. 943-19-2 Cherokee. Personally appeared JOHN BOYLE, a heir of the estate of HANNAH BOYLE of Floyd county, dec'd. to claim Lot 945-19-2.; also, lots that he owns including No. 1227-3-3; No. 1022-19-3 (drawn by ___ ROW of Early County); No. 1019-18-2 (drawn by TILMON HARRISON of Jackson co.); No. 762-17-2 (drawn by BURNS CROW of Campbell co.); No. 77-20-2; No. 1104-18-2; No. 496-19-3 and No. 166-7-Coweta Co. Includes app't. of HUGH MONTGOMERY of Floyd Co. as att'y. Signed: JNO. BOYLE bef. ADNASTUS BEALL (by mark) and FREDK. BEALL, J.P., 20 April 1843.

NEWTON COUNTY: Lot No. 509-18-2 Cherokee. Personally appeared MARY ESTES, the wife and legal representative of JAMES ESTES, dec'd, who was the owner of Lot 509-18-2 in orig. Cherokee co. and Lot 18-17-of Early now Thomas co. Signed: MARY ESTES (by mark) bef. GEORGE NEAYS, J.P., 22 June 1843.

MUSCOGEE COUNTY: Lot No. 464-16-2 Cherokee. Personally appeared SAMUEL McGEE to claim Lot 464-16-2, as he has married ELIZA CREW, the orphan who drew the lot. Includes app't. of JOHN W. A. SANFORD as att'y. Sgn'd: SAMUEL McGEE before AUGUSTUS J. ABBOTT, J.P., 16 June 1843.

HALL COUNTY: Lot No. 106-16-2 Cherokee. Personally appeared JEREMIAH F. TROUT to claim Lot 106-16-2, as one of the legatees of his mother widow SARAH TROUT, deceased of Jackson County. Includes app't. of JOSEPH DUNAGUN as att'y. Signed: J. F. TROUT bef. E. W. JOHNSON & JORDON REESE, J.I.C.,...2 June 1843.

HENRY COUNTY: Lot No. 652-2-2 Cherokee. Personally appeared ZABUD LITTLE to claim Lot 652-2-2 that he purchased from SUSAN STOCKS of Fayette Co. Includes appointment of JOAB COOK as att'y. Signed: ZABUD LITTLE before HANNAH L. HAND, ISAIAH HAND, J.P., 5 June 1843.

BALDWIN COUNTY: Lot No. 1061-3-2 Cherokee. Personally appeared WILLIAM G. ANDREWS as one of the heirs of the owner to claim Lot 1061-3-2. Signed: WM. G. ANDREWS before ALFRED M. HORTON, N.P., 20 April 1843.

JASPER COUNTY: Lot No. 254-7-1 Cherokee. Personally appeared DANIEL McDOWELL to claim Lot 254-7-1 as Ex'r. of MARY ANN McDOWELL, dec'd. Signed: DANIEL McDOWELL and SILAS GRUBBS, J.P., 25 April 1843.

WASHINGTON COUNTY: Lot No. 275-7-1 Cherokee. Personally appeared JOHN W. GRAYBILL to take out a grant for Lot 275-7-1 as agent for the heirs (orphans) of JONATHAN HARTS. Signed: JOHN W. GRAYBILL, 31 July 1850.

UPSON COUNTY: Lot No. 1182-2-2 Cherokee. NANCY C. EUBANK, guardian of the orphans of EDWARD EUBANK, dec'd. appoints ELBERT HUTCHINGS of Jones Co. as att'y. to take out grant for Lot 1182-2-2. Signed: NANCY C. EUBANK$\underline{S}$ before. SUSAN M. DUNCAN & JAMES DUNCAN, J.P., 19 May 1843.

WASHINGTON COUNTY: Lot No. 751-16-2 Cherokee. Personally appeared JOHN H. DAVIDSON to claim the lot drawn by ASA DAVIDSON's orphans of Jefferson Co., Ga.; Lot 751-16-2. Signed: J. H. DAVIDSON bef. NICHOLAS HARDEN, J.P. Dated: 26 June 1843.

WASHINGTON COUNTY: Lot No. 621-16-2 Cherokee. Personally appeared REUBEN MAY & JETHRO MAY, Ex'rs of EDMUND MAY, SENR., to claim Lot 621-16-2. Signed: REUB$\underline{IN}$ MAY & JETHRO MAY bef. JOHN CURRY, J.P., 25 May 1843

WASHINGTON COUNTY: Lot No. 934-2-2 Cherokee. Personally appeared LUTITIA A. G. GREENWOOD to claim Lot 934-2-2 and Lot 144-2-4 that were drawn by her late husband BENJAMIN L. GREENWOOD of Baker County, for herself and his other heirs. Includes app't. of JOHN L. HUDSON as att'y. Signed: L.A.G GREENWOOD bef. J. T. YOUNGBLOOD & JAS. F. NORTHINGTOR,J.P. 30 June 1843.

.... Lot No. 517-1-2 Cherokee. GUSTAVIS MORRIS, Ex'r. of the estate of PETER MORRIS of Savannah, appoints JOHN EVERTSON (husband of his sister LAURA,

one of the heirs of the sd. estate) of St. Augustine, Florida
Territory, as att'y. to receive the grants to lot 517-1-2 in
Cobb County, and Lot 6-21-3 in Paulding County. Signed: G. MORRIS
bef. JNO. M. CLARK, N.P., 14 January 1843.

CHATHAM COUNTY: ROBERT W. POOLER, clerk of the superior
court certifies that the above is a copy
of the original filed in the clerk's office. Signed: RBT. W.
POOLER, 21 Feb. 1843.

TALIAFERRO COUNTY: Lot No. 879-1-2 Cherokee. CHARLES MORRIS
app'ts. ALEXANDER H. STEPHENS his att'y.
to apply for the grant to lot 879-1-2 that was drawn by SIMON
MORRIS, dec'd, CHARLES MORRIS & SIMON MORRIS, JR., Ex'rs. 8 June
1843. Signed: CHARLES MORRIS bef. WM. MATTOX & ARCHD. GRESHAM.

TROUP COUNTY: Lot No. 172-10-2 Cherokee. Personally appeared WILLIS B. STERLING to claim lot
172-10-2 as husband of the Admtr'x. of the estate of BENJAMIN
BAKER, dec'd. and guardian of the children of the dec'd. 7 June
1843. Signed: WILLIS B. STERLING bef. JAS. M. BEALL, J.I.C.

TROUP COUNTY: Lot No. 1014-18-2 Cherokee. Personally appeared GEO. W. McGHEE, agent and att'y.
for MARY McGHEE, Admtr'x. of LEVIN McGEE dec'd. to claim lot
1014=18-2. 6 August 1844. Signed: GEORGE W. McGEE bef. JAS. M.
BEALL, acting Justice of the Inf. Ct.

TALBOT COUNTY: Lot No. 38-16-2 Cherokee. Personally appeared SARAH WOODALL, guardian of the es-
tate of ABNER WOODALL to claim lot 38-16-2. Signed: Sarah Woodall
bef. JACOB DENNIS, J.P., 18 June 1843. Includes app't. of WILLIAM
F. BROOKE of Talbot County as att'y.

PUTNAM COUNTY: Lot No. 903-16-2 Cherokee. THOMAS J. DAVIS
appoints CLEMENT R. ZACHARY of Morgan Co.,
as att'y. to receive the grant for Lot 903-16-2 drawn by THOMAS
J. DAVIS, orphan of THOMAS DAVIS, dec'd. Signed: Thomas J. Davis
bef. JOHN A. COGBURN, J.P., 8 June 1843.

COBB COUNTY: Lot No. 454-15-2 Cherokee. Personally appeared ROSWELL KING to app't. BARRINGTON

KING his agent for taking out grant to Lot 454-15-2. Signed: ROSWELL KING bef. SAML. K. OLIVER, J.P., 1 March 1843

BALDWIN COUNTY: Lot No. 612-16-2 Cherokee. Personally appeared GEORGE SPENCE to claim lot 612-16-2 as owner in part. Signed: GEORGE SPENCE before ALFRED M. HORTON, N.P., 14 January 1843.

SCREVEN COUNTY: Lot No. 812-15-2 Cherokee. Personally appeared HENRY McGEE to claim the lot drawn by the heirs of HENRY McGEE in Tatnall County. Signed: Henry H. McGee before WILLIAM IVEY, J.P., 22 June 1843.

BALDWIN COUNTY: Lot No. 726-16-2 Cherokee. Personally appeared LOVEL SMITH to claim lot 726-16-2 as Adm'r. of the owner. Signed: Lovel Smith (by mark) before ALFRED M. HORTON, Notary Public, 28 June 1843.

BALDWIN COUNTY: Lot No. 256-16-2 Cherokee. Personally appeared JOHN H. BROWN to claim lot 256-16-2 as Ex'r. of the drawer. Signed: John H. Brown before Alfred M. Horton, Notary Public, 24 April 1843.

BALDWIN COUNTY: Lot No. 753-16-2 Cherokee. Personally appeared A. A. J. RIDDLE to claim lot 753-16-2 as part owner. Signed: A. A. J. Riddle before P. M. COMPTON, Notary Public, 14 March 1848

BALDWIN COUNTY: Lot No. 268-14-2 Cherokee. Personally appeared ALBERT PARIS to claim lot (above) and No. 568-15-2 as owner in part. Signed: Albert Paris before R. MICKLEJOHN, J. P., 20 June 1843.

HANCOCK COUNTY: Lot No. 237-14-2 Cherokee. Personally appeared NICY CHAMBERS who claims that she is the owner in part of lot 237-14-2 drawn by MARTHA DICKSON, widow of Talbot County. Signed: Nicy (by mark) Chambers before FREDERICK TRAWICK, J.P., 12 April 1843.

BALDWIN COUNTY: Lot No. 253-14-2 Cherokee. Personally appeared WILLIAM BRYCE to claim lot 253-14-2 as Executor of the estate of the drawer. Signed: William Bryce before ALFRED M. HORTON, Notary Public, 1 June 1843.

BALDWIN COUNTY: Lot 99-27-2 Cherokee. Personally appeared WILLIAM G. ANDREWS to claim Lot 99-27-2, in part as one of the heirs of the owner. Signed: Wm. G. Andrews before Alfred M. Horton, N.P., 20 April 1843.

THOMAS COUNTY: Lot 263-23-2 Cherokee. Personally appeared GEORGE YARBY to claim lot 263-23-2 as the guardian of NANCY SEEON. Signed: George Yerby before HORACE LAWTON, J.I.C., 9 June 1843.

COBB COUNTY: Lot 28-19-2 Cherokee. Personally appeared JOHN L. CLARK who claims lot (above) ... having bought the lot from the orphans of JORDAN ANDERSON of Pulaski County. Signed: John L. Clark before NATHANIEL HAWTHORN, J.P., 20 October 1849.

BURKE COUNTY: Lot 147-26-2 Cherokee. Personally appeared WILLIAM LESSETER to claim Lot (above) as guardian of FRANCIS C. DUNN, minor of ANN H. DUNN, dec'd. Signed: William Lessester before HOMER V. MULKEY, J.P., 20 June 1843.

BURKE COUNTY: Lot 148-23-2 Cherokee. Personally appeared THOS. DRAKE and MILLY DRAKE, orphan heirs of ELIAS DRAKE, dec'd. to claim the lot they drew in the land lottery. Signed: AMILLIA DRAKE and THOMAS DRAKE before ANDERSON LAMBERT, J.P., 13 June 1843.

GREENE COUNTY: Lot 186-23-2 Cherokee. Personally appeared SAMUEL D. DURHAM to claim above lot and also Lot 637-19-2. He also claims, as legal representative of A. J. BROUCH, dec'd. Lot 557-17-3. Signed: Samuel D. Durham before JAMES M. DAVISON, J.P., 29 May 1843.

TROUP COUNTY: Lot 98-15-2 Cherokee. Personally appeared WILLIAM W. PALMER Adm'r. of LAZARAUS ATKINSON, dec'd. to claim above lot and fractional lot 288-1-3. Signed: William W. Palmer, before NATHAN L. ATKINSON, J.P. 15 April 1843.

RICHMOND COUNTY: Lot 272-25-2 Cherokee. Personally appeared REBECCA CAMFIELD guardian of the orphans of ABIEL CAMFIELD, namely: ELIZABETH J., MARY, REBECCA, JOHN, LYDIA, OCTAVIOUS and SARAH...claims Lot 272-25-2 orig. in Cherokee now in Gilmer. Signed: REBECCA CAMFIELD before RICHARD ALLEN, J.P., 3 June 1843.

SUMTER COUNTY: Lot 317-22-2 Cherokee. Personally appeared JOHN J. HODGES guardian to MARY ANN FAIRCLOTH, to claim lot 317-22-2 ...Signed: JOHN J. HODGES before D. H. BROWN, J.P. 30 October 1849.

BALDWIN COUNTY: Lot 244-3-1 Cherokee. Personally appeared RIAL GILSTRAP, Adm'r. of the estate of LAWSON CLINTON, dec'd. of Burke County, to claim Lot 244-3-1. Signed: R. W. GILSTRAP before ALFRED M. HORTON...19 June 1843.

COWETA COUNTY: Lot 425-3-1 Cherokee. Personally appeared WILLIAM CLIFTON to claim, as part owner, lots drawn by THOMAS CLIFTON. The lots are 425-3-1 and 895-20-3 ....He is the Adm'r. of the estate of THOMAS CLIFTON. Signed: WM. CLIFTON bef. JOHN F. DAVIS, J.P. 12 June 1843.

THOMAS COUNTY: Lot 565-3-1 Cherokee. Personally appeared GEORGE YERBY, lawful heir of MARY YERBY, widow and dumb, dec'd., to claim lot 565-3-1. Signed: GEORGE YERBY before HORACE LAWTON, J.I.C...9 June 1843

COWETA COUNTY: Lot 464-18-2 Cherokee. Personally appeared WELCOME PARKS to claim lot 464-18-2 in right of his wife, the Ex'r. of CHARLES SMITH, dec'd. Signed: WELCOME PARKS before K. W. PERRY, J.P...19 May 1843. Includes app't. of WM. F. S. POWELL as att'y., wit: JOHN L. ELDER.

COWETA COUNTY: Lot 1083-19-2 Cherokee. Personally appeared JOHN M. THOMAS, guardian of ELIZA J. MACKAY and JOHN T. MACKAY, orphans and minors of LITTLETON P. MACKAY, dec'd., claims lots 1083-19-2 and 314-23-2. Signed: JOHN M. THOMAS before B. H. CONYERS, J.P. 3 Sept. 1844. Includes appm't. of DANIEL METHVIN as attorney.

COWETA COUNTY: Lot 707-1-2 Cherokee. Personally appeared MARY PHILLIPS, ZACHARIAH PHILLIPS, JR.,& WILLIAM T. WILLIAMSON to claim lot 707-1-2 in orig. Cherokee and

now Cobb County, drawn by ZACHARIAH PHILLIPS, dec'd. MARY PHILLIPS, ZACHARIAH PHILLIPS, JR., EDMUND G. PHILLIPS, EMILY M. PHILLIPS, JANE L. PHILLIPS, and LOUISA M. PHILLIPS are the only legal heirs of ZACHARIAH PHILLIPS, dec'd. WILLIAM J. WILLIAMSON married EMILY M. PHILLIPS, CONSTANTINE W. BUCKLEY married JANE T. PHILLIPS and MATHEW D. ECTOR married LOUISA M. PHILLIPS and because of these marriages MARY PHILLIPS, ZACHARIAH PHILLIPS, JR., EDMUND G. PHILLIPS, WILLIAM T. WILLIAMSON, CONSTANTINE W. BUCKLEY, and MATHUS D. ECTOR are the owners of sd. lot. Signed: Mary Phillips, Zachariah Phillips and William T. Williamson before JOHN CRAUN, J.P...19 June 1843. Includes app't. of CHARLES H. NELSON of Baldwin Co. as att'y.
"Gen'l. Nelson
    Dear Sir
        Seeing your very liberal offer to all those who may be interested in having lands granted in the Cherokee Country I have taken the liberty to enclose you the grant fee accompanied with an affidavit and power of attorney to grant for the legatees of the late ZACHARIAH PHILLIPS the above described no. which by doing I fear I have intruded on your generousity, however if I have you must excuse me on the grounds of hard times and the sage Franklin's motto a penny saved is a penny made. I do not know whether this affidavit and power of attorney is in due form or not if it is not I hope the state house officers will not be over scrupulous as we live where lawyers are scarce and have no correct form by giving you punctual attendence to this you will confer a singular favor and place me under the most lasting obligations to you I am very respectfully your most obed't Servant. WM. T. WILLIAMSON
To C. H. NELSON
Direct your reply with the grant to Lodi, Geo. I could not make the change and have sent you three dollars specie funds.
        WM. T. WILLIAMSON"

CRAWFORD COUNTY: Lot 696-1-2 Cherokee. Personally appeared OLIVE COOK, admt'rx. of the owner of lot 696-1-2. Signed: OLIVE COOK before E. B. WALLACE, J.P. 30 May 1843. Includes app't. of JAMES T. CARTARPHER as att'y. Wit: C.C. LUCIS.

COBB COUNTY: Lot 779-16-2 Cherokee. Personally appeared JESSE C. FARROW, agent of "JOHN HARRIS.. Plaintiff in Execution, vs. TIMOTHY WHITE, Adm'r. of PHINNY WHEELER late of Columbia County, dec'd.", to claim Lot 779-16-2 in orig. Cherokee now Cobb County and that he is the owner of "an execution vs. PATRICK W. FLYNN of Muscogee County. GILBERT D. JOHNSON vs. PATRICK W. FLYNN" and therefore claims lot 274-11-3 in orig. Cherokee now Murray County. Signed: JESSE C. FARRAR before T. M. KIRKPATRICK, J.I.C. 24 December 1843.

CLARKE COUNTY: Lot 1062-17-2 Cherokee. Personally appeared GEO. W. KING and AGNES B. KING, heirs of SARAH KING, dec'd., to claim lot 1062-17-2. Includes appointment of J. D. FRIERSON as att'y. Signed: G. W. KING and AGNES B. KING before W. M. STOCKTON and SAML. FROST, J.P. 17 June 1843.

JACKSON COUNTY: Lot 1023-21-2 Cherokee. Personally app'd. THOMAS L. STAPLER to claim lot 1023-21-2 as owner of one half of the lot and as agent for WILLIAM N. STAPLER, owner and proper drwee of the other half. Includes att'mt. of REUBIN NASH as att'y. Signed: THOMAS L. STAPLER before JAMES H. WILLS and ABNER WILLS, J.P. 14 June 1843.

ELBERT COUNTY: Lot 904-3-2 Cherokee. Personally appeared NICHOLAS BRUTON, Adm'r. of the estate of JOHN NUNALLEE, to claim the lot NUNALLEE drew. Signed: NICHOLAS BURTON before JNO. D. WATKINS, J.P. 27 May 1843.

RICHMOND COUNTY: Lot 1160-21-2 Cherokee. Personally app'd. ELIZA OWENS, guardian for SUSAN OWENS' orphans, to claim lot 1160-21-2. Signed: ELIZA OWENS before JOHN C. LEITNER, N.P. 19 June 1843.

LUMPKIN COUNTY: Lot 970-21-2 Cherokee. Personally app'd. GEORGE HENDRICK, Adm'r. of the estate of HENRY JENNINGS, to claim lot 970-21-2. Signed: G. HENDRICK bef. ALFRED HARRIS, J.P. 24 May 1843.

CHEROKEE COUNTY: Lot 511-21-2 Cherokee. Personally app'd. McANDERSON KEITH to claim lot 511-21-2 for himself, MATTHEW KEITH and JOHN W. KEITH. Signed: M. A. KEITH before GEO. L. HOYL, J.I.C. 30 May 1843.

BALDWIN COUNTY: Lot 532-21-2 Cherokee. Personally app'd. HENRY H. ROSS to claim lot 532-21-2, as owner in part. Signed: HENRY H. ROSS bef. ALFRED M. HORTON, N.P. 22 June 1843.

TWIGGS COUNTY: Lot 16-20-3 Cherokee. Personally appeared THOMAS JEF. JOHNSTON to claim lot 16-20-2 as orphan of JAMES JOHNSTON, dec'd. Signed: TH. JEF. JOHNSTON and JNO. G. SLAPPY, J.P. 5 June 1843.

HEARD COUNTY: Lot 721-17-2 Cherokee. Personally appeared B. R. CROSBY, guardian of the orphans of LEWIS L. DAVIS, dec'd., to claim lot 721-17-2. Signed: B. R. CROSBY before A. CORRY, J.P. 7 December 1847.

BALDWIN COUNTY: Lot 86-8-2 Cherokee. Personally appeared WILLIAM SANFORD SMITH to claim lot 86-8-2. Signed:WILLIAM S. SMITH before ALFRED M. HORTON, N.P. 22 Dec. 1846.

WARREN COUNTY: Lot 261-8-2 Cherokee. Personally appeared ROBERT RONEY, in rite of his wife FRANCING WALTON, now RONEY, to claim lot 261-8-2. Also for URIAH WALTON & LURENIA WALTON, now LAURENIA BROOKS. Signed: ROBERT (by mark) RONEY before ELISHA PERRYMAN, J.P. 24 January 1850.

BALDWIN COUNTY: Lot 215-12-2 Cherokee. Personally app'd. ARTHUR I. BUTTS to claim lot 215-12-2 as Ex'r. of the drawer. Signed: ARTHUR I. BUTTS bef. ALFRED M. HORTON, N.P. 12 June 1843.

PAULDING COUNTY: Lot 1094-2-2 Cherokee. Personally app'd. JAMES M. WARE, Adm'r. of JAMES WARE, decd. od Floyd County, to claim lot 1094-2-2. Includes app't. of CHARLES H. NELSON of Milledgeville as att'y. Signed: JAMES M. WARE before JOHN A. JONES, J.I.C. 20 June 1843.

LUMPKIN COUNTY: Lot 286-5-2 Cherokee. Personally app'd. JOHN ABERCRUMBIE, agent for REBECCA CAVENDER, widow of CLEMMETH CAVENDER of Hall County, to claim lot 286-5-2 and Lot 773-2-2. Signed: JOHN ABERCROMBIE before ISAAC HEAD, acting Justice of the Inferior Court. 21 May 1843.

MONROE COUNTY: Lot 1151-2-2 Cherokee. Personally app'd. J. D. PEABODY to claim lot 1151-2-2 as legal heir, with WILLIAM CALLAWAY, orphans of BENJAMIN CALLAWAY; and with DANIEL CALLAWAY, NANCY CALLAWAY, LEVICY EDWARDS, SARAH BROWN, ANNA CALLAWAY, and SARAH CALLAWAY, heirs of JONATHAN CALLAWAY, dec'd. (the drawee of the lot). Signed: JOSIAH D. CALLAWAY before CAMPBELL RAIFORD, J.P. 12 June 1843.

MUSCOGEE COUNTY: Lot 56-2-2 Cherokee. Personally appeared

EWENA NORMAN, widow of WILLIAM M. DOWNEY of Upson County, to claim lot 56-2-2. Signed: EMMA NORMAN (by mark). before JNO. W. BETHUNE, J.I.C. 21 June 1843.

FRANKLIN COUNTY: Lot 65-23-2 Cherokee. Personally appeared JAMES RICE to claim: Lot 65-23-3 drawn by him; Lot 135-6-1 drawn by JAMIAH HENDRICK; Lot 729-1-4 drawn by RICHARD W. ROYSTON; Lot 61-9-1 drawn by ISAAC M. ADDERHOLD; Lot 895-2-3 drawn by LEWIS D. HOLSOMBAKE; Lot 225-13-1 drawn by LEWIS D. HOLSOMBAKE; Signed: JAMES RICE before ZECHARIAH THOMAS, J.P. 21 June 1843.

HENRY COUNTY: Lot 134-23-2 Cherokee. Personally appeared ELIJAH FOSTER to claim lot 134-23-2 drawn by ILSEY A. ROWNEE, deaf and dumb,...Includes app't. of JOHN HAIL as att'y. Signed: ELIJAH FOSTER before THOS. E. HICKS, J.P. 2 May 1843.

JONES COUNTY: Lot 238-27-2 Cherokee. JOHN B. DANE appt's HENRY G. DANE his lawful att'y. to take out the grant for Lot 238-27-2. Signed: JOHN B. DANE before ABINGTON BARRON and ROBERT CALDWELL, J.P. 29 June 1843.

CHATHAM COUNTY: Lot 171-24-2 Cherokee. Appeared SARAH JANE HOBKIRK to claim lot 171-24-2 for herself and her two sisters. Includes app't. of JOHN W. ELRY of Effingham County as att'y. Signed: SARAH JANE HOBKIRK before L. S. RUSSELL, J.P. 6 June 1843.

CHATHAM COUNTY: Lot 85-72-2 Cherokee. Personally appeared MARGARET C. WORTHINGTON, att'y. for PETER WORTHINGTON (her husband) to claim for him and for WALTER WALLACE, R. SMITH, MARGARET IAN SMITH, MARION HELEN SMITH, HENRY MONTGOMERY SMITH and CAROLINE VIRGINIA SMITH, minor orphans of WALTER SMITH, dec'd. of whom PETER WORTHINGTON is guardian to claim lot 85-12-2 in Gilmer County, and lot 249-3-4 formerly in Hall Co., now in Newton. Includes app't. of W. A. PRITCHARD of Milledgeville as att'y. Signed: M. C. WORTHINGTON bef. (illegible). 27 June 1843.

WILKINSON COUNTY: Lot 255-10-2 Cherokee. Personally app'd. MICAJAH PAULK, guardian of the orphans of

JOHN PAULK, dec'd., to claim lot 255-10-2. Signed: MICAJAH PAULK before S. J. BUSH, J.P. 13 June 1843.

NEWTON COUNTY: Lot 228-10-2 Cherokee. Personally app'd. SANFORD SPARKS, an heir with LOUISA SPARKS and KANZADA SPARKS (now KANZADA DENNARD) of LEVEN SPARKS, dec'd. to claim lot 228-10-2 and lot 477-20-3. Includes app't. of NICHOLAS P. HUNTER as att'y. Signed: SANFORD SPARKS before THOMAS W. DENNARD and COLUMBUS D. PACE, J.I.C. 2 June 1843.

MUSCOGEE COUNTY: Lot 194-10-2 Cherokee. Personally app'd. JAMES MONROE to claim lot 194-10-2 drawn by HENRY LUNDY and as representative of JOHN MONROE, dec'd, lot 595-4-1 drawn by E. R. SPURGERS. Includes appt. of ALEXANDER McDOUGALD as att'y. Signed: JAMES MONROE before F. F. ABBOTT and AUGUSTINE J. ABBOTT, J.P. 24 June 1843.

WARREN COUNTY: Lot 11-10-2 Cherokee. Personally app'd. CLABORN THIGPIN to claim: Lot 11-10-2 drawn by THOMAS ARNETT; Lot 88-9-1 drawn by SARAH RHODES, widow of JAMES RHODES; Lot 328-18-2 drawn by the heirs of THOMAS RHODES. Includes app't. of JAMES BEARFIELD as att'y. Signed: CLABORN THIGPIN (by mark) before LINSON BRADDY and JAMES BRADDY, J.P. 26 June 1843.

WILKES COUNTY: Lot 64-11-2 Cherokee. Personally appeared GEORGE DYSON for himself and MARTHA DYSON to claim lot 64-11-2 drawn by JOHN DYSON, ..includes app't. of JOHN R. ANDERSON from Baldwin Co. as att'y. Signed: GEORGE DYSON before JOHN H. DYSON and A. S. WINGFIELD, J.I.C. 14 June 1843.

MONROE COUNTY: Lot 74-11-2 Cherokee. Personally appeared PERRY H. FLEMING, in right of his wife, SAMANTHA J. FARLEY and MATTHEW T. FARLEY, orphans of ALEXANDER FARLEY, dec'd. to claim lot 74-11-2. Includes app't. of JAMES TUMN as att'y. Signed: PERRY H. FLEMING and MATHEW FARLEY before JAMES TUMN, J.P. 31 May 1843.

JACKSON COUNTY: Lot 78-11-2 Cherokee. Personally appeared JOHN HOGON, agent of SHADRACK HOG<u>A</u>N of Mississippi to claim lot 78-11-2. Includes app't. of JOSEPH T. CUNNINGHAM of Jackson Co. as att'y. Signed: JOHN HOG<u>A</u>N before

MILES WILSON (by mark) and JAMES B. WILSON, J.P. 9 June 1843.

COWETA COUNTY: Lot 147-19-2 Cherokee. Personally app'd.
ZIMRI ROBERTS guardian of ABSOLEM V. ROBERTS, ELIZABETH ROBERTS, LURANA ROBERTS and DELILA ROBERTS, orphans of WILLIAM ROBERTS, dec'd. to claim lot 147-19-2. Signed: ZEMRI ROBERTS before A. GRAY, J.P. 28 June 1843.

JONES COUNTY: Lot 247-11-2 Cherokee. Personally app'd.
JOHN F. COMER, Adm'r. of HUGH M. COMER, dec'd., to claim lot 247-11-2; Lot 145-27-3; Lot 582-1-2. Signed: JOHN F. COMER before CARY DAVISON, J.P. 22 Feb. 1843.

OGLETHORPE COUNTY: Lot 218-14-2 Cherokee. Personally app'd.
THOMAS E. R. HARRIS & BENJAMIN F. HARDEMAN to claim lot 918-14-2 drawn by the orphans of STEPHEN W. HARRIS, dec'd. The orphans were ANN MARCH HARRIS (now ANN MARCH ALEXANDER, wife of ROBERT B. ALEXANDER), STEPHEN W. HARRIS, SUSAN M. HARRIS (now the wife of WILLIAM T. BALDWIN), deponent, THOMAS E. R. HARRIS and ARABELLA R. HARRIS (afterwards the wife of BENJAMIN F. HARDEMAN). ARABELLA is since deceased. Signed: BENJ. F. HARDEMAN & THOS. E. R. HARRIS before GEORGE F. PLATT, J.P. 21 December 1843.

CHATHAM COUNTY: Lot 24-14-2 Cherokee. Personally appeared
MATTHIAS AMORES to claim lot 24-14-2 drawn by SARAH ANN McCALL, orphan. Includes app't. of WILLIAM H. PRITCHARD of Baldwin County as attorney. Signed: MATHIAS AMOROS bef. JAMES S. WILKINS & R. RAIFORD, J.P. 5 April 1843.

TALBOT COUNTY: Lot 14-14-2 Cherokee. Personally app'd.
ALLEN C. RAMSAY to claim lot 14-14-2 that he drew and, as Adm'r. of his father, JAMES RAMSAY, lot 583-2-2. Includes app't. of RANDOLPH H. RAMSAY of Baldwin County as att'y. Signed: ALLEN C. RAMSAY before J. J. JAMESON & JOSEPH JACKSON, J.P. 26 June 1843.

MACON COUNTY: Lot 1270-15-2 Cherokee. Personally app'd.
WILLIAM McDOWEL & JEPTHA McGLAMMARY, legatees of JOHN McGLAMMARY, to claim lot 1270=15-2. Includes app't. of McKENNETH PAGE as att'y. Signed: WILLIAM McDOWELLE & JEPTHA McGLAMMARY (by mark) before GIDEON SMITH, J.P. 24 June 1843.

RICHMOND COUNTY: Lot 189-27-2 Cherokee. Personally app'd.
                        WILLIAM H. SIKES to claim lot 189-27-2 in
Gilmer County as heir of HENRY SIKES, dec'd. Includes app't. of
PORTER FLEMING as att'y. Signed: WM. H. SIKES before J. C. GREEN,
J. P. and JOHN F. HUNT. 8 June 1843.

WARREN COUNTY: Lot 104-27-2 Cherokee. Personally app'd.
                        JOHN MOORE, Ex'r. of the estate of MONT-
CLAIBORN ANDREWS, dec'd., toclaim lot 104-27-2. Includes app't.
of CHARLES E. RYAN of Baldwin County as att'y. Signed: JOHN MOORE
before G. W. DICKSON & HENRY HINTON, J.P. 13 June 1843.

JACKSON COUNTY: Lot 47-27-2 Cherokee. Personally app'd.
                        EPHRAIM JACKSON who says that he is a
judgement creditor against WILLIAM LEACHMAN who married one of
the orphans of THOS. JACKSON and claims lot 47-27-2 and lot 903-
2-4. Includes app't. of N. C. JARR as att'y. Signed: EPHRAIM
JACKSON before SYLVANIUS E. PARKES & THOMAS L. STAPLER, J.P.
31 May 1843.

PUTNAM COUNTY: Lot 103-27-2 Cherokee. Personally app'd.
                        MARY ANN COPELAND, formerly MARY ANN
WENGET, widow of AMOS WENGET of Pulaski County, to claim lot No.
103-27-2 and Lot No. 910-3-4, Lot No. 92-3-2 and Lot 49-6-3.
Signed: MARY ANN COPELAND (by mark) before LEWIS H. LURCH, J.P.
14 June 1843.

TROUP COUNTY: Lot 19-26-2 Cherokee. JAMES CULBERSON,
                        heir of MARGARET WILKINSON, dec'd., ap-
points MICKLEBURY FERREL attorney for receiving the grant for lot
19-26-2. Signed: JAMES CULBERSON before THOS. F. MITCHELL & R. D.
McGEHEE, J.P. 14 June 1843.

FRANKLIN COUNTY: Lot 27-26-2 Cherokee. Personally app'd.
                        SARAH MESLEY, widow of GARLAND MESLEY,
to claim lot 27-26-2 in original Cherokee now Gilmer County. Includes app't. of ALFRED M. HORTON of Milledgeville as att'y.
Signed: SARAH MESLEY (by mark) before JACOB WISUNANT (by mark)
and WM. E. SMITH, J.P. 20 April 1843.

PUTNAM COUNTY: Lot 269-23-2 Cherokee. Personally app'd.
                        JOHN C. BEARDIN, Adm'r. of the estate of

AUGUSTUS C. HARTON, dec'd. to claim lot 269-23-2 as part of that estate, having been drawn by CHARLOTTE A. HARTON earlier as the widow of JOHN WRIGHT, dec'd. Signed: JOHN C. BEARDIN before B. W. SANFORD, J.I.C. 23 June 1843.

TROUP COUNTY: Lot 205-26-2 Cherokee. Personally app'd. THOMAS M. FOSTER, legal heir in right of his wife, to claim the lot drawn by JOHN DARLEY's orphans of Monroe county. Signed: THOMAS M. FOSTER (by mark) before THOMAS W. WYATT, J.P. 18 March 1845.

Personally appeared PAINTAN S. FOSTER, legal heir in right of his wife, to claim the lot drawn by the orphans of JAMES DARLEY, dec'd. Signed:PAINTAN S. FOSTER before THOMAS W. WYATT, J.P. 18 March 1845. Includes app't. of DANIEL GODARD & WILLIAM H. GUNN of Monroe County as att'ys. to take out this grant, for the legal heirs in right of the Fosters' wives, witnessed by LOVENA WYATT (by mark) and THOMAS W. WYATT, J.P.

MONROE COUNTY: Lot 113-6-2 Cherokee. Personally app'd. GEORGE A. WINN, Adm'r. of the estate of SARAH STALLINGS, dec'd., claims lot 113-6-2. Includes app't. of SAMUEL B. HUNTER of Bibb County as att'y. Signed: GEO. A. WINN before JAMES NORRIS, J.P. 3 June 1843.

MUSCOGEE COUNTY: Lot 114-6-2 Cherokee. Personally app'd. HENRY KENDALL, agent of ELIZABETH KENDALL, to claim lot 114-6-2. Includes app't. of ALFRED M. HORTON of Baldwin co. as att'y. Signed: HENRY KIMBALL, agt. before R. W. CARNES N.P. 26 June 1843.

CRAWFORD COUNTY: Lot 197-6-2 Cherokee. Personally app'd. SUSANNAH MILLS, guardian of NANCY, GREEN, MOSES, MARTHA, NELLY & ALEXANDER MILLS, orphans of JESSE MILLS, dec'd., to claim lot 197-6-2 and lot 156-1-2. Includes app't. of GEORGE R. HUNTIN as att'y. Signed: SUSANNAH MILLS (by mark) bef. ELISHA MILLS & W. H. BROOKS, J.P. 31 May 1843.

UPSON COUNTY: Lot 37-5-2 Cherokee. EDWARD HOLLOWAY,gdn. of FRANCIS HENRY WHEAT, orphan of FRANCIS ASBURY WHEAT, dec'd., and WILLIAM TRYLOR, husband of the widow of FRANCIS ASBURY WHEAT, app't. WILLIAM G. ANDREWS of Upson Co. att'y. for taking out a grant for lot 37-5-2. Signed: EDWD. HOL-

LOWAY and WILLIAM TRAYLOR before WILLIAM GAW(TAW?) and L. M. ANSLEY, 18 March 1843.

RICHMOND COUNTY: Lot 292-5-2 Cherokee. Personally appeared WILLIAM T. BRANHAM, representative of the orphans of widow HARRIET GARNER of Morgan County claims lot 292-5-2. Includes app't. of ELI O. KINRICK of Columbia County as the att'y. Signed: WM. T. BRANHAM before JOHN NELSON & ALEXR. PHILIP, M.C.C.A. 24 June 1843.

BIBB COUNTY: Lot 186-4-2 Cherokee. Personally app'd. ROBERT M. BROACH, guardian of FRANCIS WHITSETT, one of the orphans of JOHN WHITSETT, to claim Lot 186-4-2. Includes app't. of JAMES M. ELLIS as att'y. Signed: R. M. BROACH before JESSE L. OWEN, J.P. 14 June 1843.

HENRY COUNTY: Lot 179-4-2 Cherokee. Personally app'd. MARY CROWLEY, guardian of SPENCER CROWLEY's orphans, to claim lot 179-4-2 ...Signed: MARY CROWLEY (by mark) before SEABORN JONES, J.P. 8 June 1843. Includes app't. of WILLIAM KIMBELL as att'y.

MUSCOGEE COUNTY: Lot 176-4-2 Cherokee. Personally app'd. TURNER MORELAND, Ex'r. of the estate of HARTWELL BASS, dec'd. to claim lot 176-4-2. Includes app't. of ISAM BROOKS of Baldwin County as attorney. Signed: TURNER MORELAND before AUG. S. GRANT & JOHN J. McKENDREE, J.P.

TROUP COUNTY: Lot 318-4-2 Cherokee. I am the owner of Lot 49-4- of Troup Co., drawn by ISAAC CALLAWAY's orphans of Wilkes County by purchasing one half of the lot from FELIX CALLAWAY, one of the orphans, on 14 May 1833 and the rest of the lot from HENRY POPE, the guardian for the rest of the orphans, in 1834. I also hold power of attorney from THOMAS VALENTINE, the drawer of lot 318-4-2, Cherokee County. VALENTINE has since moved to Mississippi. I am also the owner of lot 103-2 of Cherokee County. The drawee is not known but the lot was purchased from WILLIAM POE on 13 January 1834. Signed: P. E. MORGAN before JAS. M. BEALL, J.I.C, 27 April 1843.

JASPER COUNTY: Lot 747-3-2 Cherokee. Personally app'd. EDMUND DOSSEY to claim the lot drawn by

him and the lot drawn by MARTHA HOOD, orphan, subsequently MARTHA
DOSSEY. Both lots were drawn in Newton County. Includes app't. of
MATTHEW WHITFIELD as att'y. Signed: EDMUND DOSSEY (by mark) bef.
LEROY M. WILLSON, J.P. 12 June 1843.

WALKER COUNTY: Lot 895-18-2 Cherokee. Whereas I, AUGUSTUS
                       HARRIS am possessed in my own right of the
following described lot of land: lot 895-18-1; lot 966-2-3; lot
385-17-3; lot 6-16-3 and also the lot drawn by GILES HARRIS while
living in Madison County but now living in Paulding County, as
his agent. Includes app't. of STEPHEN SMITH as att'y. Signed:
AUGUSTUS HARRIS before JAS. E. BURROWS, and JOHN M. CICKER, J.I.C.
25 May 1843.

ELBERT COUNTY: Lot 95-5-2 Cherokee. Personally appeared
                       SARAH CAVENESS, widow of HENRY CAVENESS
and mother of DeMARCUS A. LAFAYETTE CAVENESS and NAPOLEON BONA-
PART CAVENESS to claim lot 95-5-2 and lot 116-19-3. Includes appointment of JEREMIAH S. WARREN as attorney. Signed: SARAH CAVE-
NESS before WM. BURRIS & JAS. H. REYNOLDS, J.P. 12 June 1843.

WASHINGTON COUNTY: Lot 1123-21-2 Cherokee. Personally app'd.
                       MICAJAH BLAND, Adm'r. of the estate of
FOREMAN HODGES dec'd. of Pulaski County, to claim lot 1123-21-2.
Includes app't. of JOHN HODGES as att'y. Signed: MICAJAH BLAND
before WM. G. McBRIDE and JOHN R. TUCKER, J.I.C. 27 June 1843.

CASS COUNTY: Lot 1127-21-2 Cherokee. Personally app'd.
                       JAMES S. ELLIOT, temporary administrator
of the estate of MORE GRAVES, dec'd. to claim lot 1127 and lot
1106 in the 21st Dist., 2nd Section. Signed: JAS. S. ELLIOT bef.
JAMES J. TEAT, acting J. P. 15 June 1843.

MUSCOGEE COUNTY: Lot 144-20-2 Cherokee. Personally app'd.
                       SAML. A. BAILEY, guardian of Bibb county,
surviving orphan of SAMUEL GELLESBEE of Bibb Co. to claim lot
144-20-2 and lot 218-21-2. Includes app't. of KENNETH McKENZIE
as att'y. Signed: SAML. A. BAILEY before W. W. MURRAY, J.I.C.
12 June 1843.

RICHMOND COUNTY: Lot 292-21-2 Cherokee. Personally app'd.
                       JAMES McLAWS, temporary adm'r. of the es-

tate of the late JAMES W. E. REID of the United States Navy, to claim lot 292-21-2. Includes app't. of WILLIAM R. McLAWS as attorney. Signed: JAMES McLAWS before BENJAMIN B. RUSSELL, J.P.R.C. 3 June 1843.

NEWTON COUNTY: Lot 301-21-2 Cherokee. Personally app'd. ELIZABETH LARD, widow of SAMUEL LARD, to claim lot 301-21-2. Signed: ELIZABETH LARD (by mark) before G. W. BLAKE, 18 May 1843. Includes app't. of JAMES R. McCALLA as attorney.

HANCOCK COUNTY: Lot 536-21-2 Cherokee. TUTTLE H. ANDAS, one of the executors of the estate of PHILIP TURNER, dec'd., appoints RICHARD PHILIP SASNETT as att'y. for the ex'rs., JOSEPH R. SASNETT, RICHARD FRARS & TUTTLE H. ANDAS, to apply for grant to lot 536-21-2. Signed: TUTTLE H. ANDAS before BANJAMIN T. HARRIS & THOMAS COLEMAN, J.P. 3 June 1843.

DADE COUNTY: Lot 196-11-2 Cherokee. Personally appeared JOHN A. STEVENS & GALLATIN STEVENS to claim lot 196-11-2 in Gilmer Co., and lot 619-17-2 in Cobb Co. Includes app't. of JOHN W. A. SANFORD and JOHN G. PARK of Baldwin Co. as att'ys. Signed: JOHN A. STEVENS & GALLATIN STEVENS bef. MARK A. HALE, J.P. 1 May 1843.

HARRIS COUNTY: Lot 960-17-2 Cherokee. Personally app'd. THOMAS CLOWER, to claim the lot belonging to his ward, WILLIAM DAVIS, minor of THOMAS DAVIS of Putnam Co. Includes app't. of Gen. CHARLES H. NELSON of Baldwin Co. as atty. Signed: THOMAS CLOWER before A. W. REDDING and JAMES COX, J.P. 4 June 1843.

COBB COUNTY: Lot 604-17-2 Cherokee. ELIZABETH ROMANS of DeKalb County appoints Gen. CHARLES H. NELSON of Milledgeville as att'y. to receive the grant for lot 604-17-2 drawn by her husband, ALEXANDER ROMANS, who is absent. Signed: ELIZABETH ROMANS (by mark) bef. THOS. HOOPER, J.P. 19 June 1843.

WILKES COUNTY: Lot 456-17-2 Cherokee. Personally app'd. MARTHA COLLY, mother and gdn. of the orphans of JAMES COLLY, to claim lot 456-17-2. Includes app't. of

ROBERT A. TOOMBS as attorney. Signed: MARTHA COLLY (by mark) bef. LUKE TURNER & O. S. BATTLE, J.P. 9 June 1843.

BUTTS COUNTY: Lot 312-17-2 Cherokee. Personally app'd. STERLING T. HIGGINS, gdn. for SILAS N. BEAVERS' orphans, to claim lot 312-17-2. ANDERSON C. SCOTT is appointed att'y. Signed: STERLING T. HIGGINS before S. H. SANDERS, J. I. C. 10 June 1843.

PUTNAM COUNTY: Lot 159-17-2 Cherokee. Personally app'd. JOHN M. ASHURST, legal representative of the orphans of ANDREW PARK, dec'd. to claim lot 159-17-2. IVY HUDSON (?) app'td. att'y. Signed: JNO. M. ASHURST before T. B. HARWELL, J.P. 3 June 1843.

CHATHAM COUNTY: Lot 108-17-2 Cherokee. Personally app'd. SARAH ASH (formerly SARAH BURTON, widow of HENRY A. BURTON of Effingham Co.) to claim lot 108-17-2 of Cobb Co. that was drawn by HENRY BURTON's orphans and lot ___-19-2 and lot 47-9-3 in Murray Co. Signed: SARAH ASH before R. RIAFORD, J. P. JOHN W. EXLEY app'td. att'y. Signed: GEO. A. ASH before R. RAIFORD, J.P. 30 May 1843.

MORGAN COUNTY: Lot 564-15-2 Cherokee. Personally app'd. THOS. NOLAN to claim lot 564-15-2 that he received from the estate of ISAAC THRASHER's orphan; and lot 28-4- of Muscogee county that he owns as a judgement creditor of the orphans of WILLIAM WILLIAMS; and lot 288-23-3 of Cherokee as a mortgage creditor of one of the orphans of STEPHEN COX. Signed: THOS. NOLAN before A. B. BOSTWICK, J.P. 12 June 1843.

CHATTOOGA COUNTY: Lot 533-15-2 Cherokee. Personally app'd. JOSEPH I. EASLY to claim lot 533-15-2 also, as heir of ELIZABETH GARRISON, widow, lot 1039-2-3, and lot 916-2-1, as orphan of DAVID GARRISON of Crawford County. Includes app't. of CHARLES H. NELSON of Baldwin County as att'y. Signed: J. I. EASLY before W. P. HINTON and JOHN F. BEAVENS,J.I.C 17 June 1843.

MARION COUNTY: Lot 234-15-2 Cherokee. Personally app'd. BENJAMIN A. STORY to claim lot drawn by BENJAMIN A. STORY of Harris Co. and a lot drawn by LETTLETON B.

STORY of Columbia County. JOHN CAMPBELL appointed attorney. sgn: B. A. STORY before BURTON W. DOWN & R. W. MASTON, J.P. 16 June 1843.

BALDWIN COUNTY: Lot 207-12-2 Cherokee. Personally app'd. THOMAS KING to claim lot 207-12-2 in Gilmer Co. and also, as the adm'r. of JAMES KING, dec'd., to claim 16-24-2. Signed: THOS. KING before JAS. MORRIS, J.I.C. 5 June 1843.

GILMER COUNTY: Lot 57-23-2 Cherokee. Personally appeared GEORGE P. BEDFORD to claim lot 57-23-2 that he purchased from WILLIAM PICKET, one of the orphans who drew the lot. Signed: G. P. BEDFORD before BENJN. JOHNSTON,J.I.C., 21 August 1853.

GILMER COUNTY: Lot 188-11-2 Cherokee. Personally app'd. WILLIAM GUDGER to claim lot 188-11-2..... drawn by JOSHUA DRAKE's orphans. Signed: WM. GUDGER before WM. MAY, J.P., 23 November 1853. At the top of the document is written: "Mrs. PICKETT".

CHATHAM COUNTY: Lot 1244-3-2 Cherokee. Personally app'd. WILLIAM H. KELLY to claim lot 1244-3-2 & lot 408-2-4 for himself and lot 87-27-2 and lot 983-4-1 as the agent of MARY A. KELLY, widow. ISAAC NEWELL of Baldwin Co. is app'td. Att'y. Signed: W. H. KELLY before R. RAIFORD, J. P. 6 June 1843.

COBB COUNTY: Lot 981-16-2 Cherokee.
"georgia cobb county March the 8th 1835 Mr. WILSON LUMPKINS govenor of georgia to your exelency in office sir I write these few lins to inform you of the trobel an destress I am in concerning my improvement in the 16 and 2 cobb co. I went thare eight years ago in the woods bilt my hous an cleard my ground an has impoved it a litle every year since an never has bin off it sense JACOB R. BROOKS of the guard was sent to take down all wust an amegrated plases to rent an come to my house and staid 2 or 3 ours an eat his dinner and then went and put down my plase evacuated and rented it an made me pay forty one dollars Mr. COFFERY the next year did not rent and said that BROOKS had know authorety to rent my plase then BROOKS told COFFERY that he rented my palse threw a mistake that he suposed it was south of Cofes line but he had found sense that it was noth of Mr. coffey said he had know right to rent my plase whare a indian was living only whare was left or emegrated mister clevelin when he survaid the district mistoke the number and put down 863 in stead of 963 know one grant is come by mistake of the

number and the other becaws it was rented I cannot help these mistakes and if any such mistakes could be rectifide I would be very glad so that I could stay on my plase this year until I can by me a peace of land I fermly bout one of my lots by leter mr. gober my inveous naber went an bought if my little children has made all the improve ments with thare hands an know to loose it this time of yeare an go in the woods they cant make nothing to live on my children has not bin raised with the indians nor dent spek the indian tongue I do not woush to raise them among the indians I do not ever in ten taken them to the arkensaw if you can do me any faver please to stop the agent from turning my children out of dors it is hard to take my childrens laber and giveit to them that has plenty I have know plase to go to with out going to tennese or alabam side which will be a hundred miles and I shall loose every thing that I have got to live on my cows is pore my corn an fodder I cant sell and every thing will be lost if thare can be any mistakes rectified please to write on the subject you kneed not hisetate to write to the agent for if it will do I can send the affedaveds of 5 or 6 good men to certfy every thing that I have stated to you and if we are turned out my children will perish nothing more but remain your umble servent..
signed: NANCY SLILL
the No of my lots is 981-982-983-963 16 and 2"

Lot 564-1-2 Cherokee:
"Senate Chamber Milledgeville
I do certify that Lot number Five hundred & sixty four (564) 1st District second section. Returned by the surveyor of sd. Dist. as having an Indian Improvement on it. Is an Emigrated Place. Valued as CHARLES WOFFORD's Improvement, and has been Routed Two years by the States Agents, & is not at This time in possesion of an Indian or the descendant of an Indian at this Time.
    Given under my hand this
    18th December 1833.
    JACOB R. BROOKS
    C. Agent Cobb County
I certify that the above statement is true---ELISHA WINN"

Lot 108-3-2 Cherokee. Certification that JOHN DUNCAN, a native Cherokee, has relinguished his claim to the improvement on lot 108-3-2. Signed: WM. HURDIN, Enrolling Agent, 14 Nov. 1833.

CHEROKEE COUNTY: Lot 87-14-2 Cherokee. Certification that BLANKETT, an Indian who lived on lot 87-14-2 has left this lot and has not returned to claim it. Signed: WM. DANIEL, Indian Agent for Cherokee County, 28 August 1833.

Lot 44-25-2 Cherokee: Lots 44,43,30,29,28, 25th District, 2nd. Section are covered by the improvements of JNO. WILLIAM but by the law of 1830 no Indian has a right to such a claim except to the State of Georgia or the general government. These lots were occupied by Mrs. MONROE until the spring of 1832 when JNO. WILLIAMS, a white man of bad characrer took over these lots claiming to have purchased them. This land should be considered abandoned and subject to being granted to fortunate drawers. Signed: BEN. F. CURRCY, Murray County, 8 October 1833.

MONROE COUNTY: Lot 677-19-2 Cherokee. Personally app'd.

THOMAS BULLOCK and JOSEPH GRANT who sworn that no one named JAMES STINSON has resided in Phillips District of Monroe County in the last four years but that a GEORGE STINSON has. Signed: THOMAS BULLOCK & JOSEPH GRANT bef. W. L. CLEMANTS, J.P. 30 Nov. 1833.
        Personally app'd. WILEY G. HIGGINS who deposeth that he was a captain in Phillips District from 1825 to 1830 and that he believed the man in question should be GEORGE STINSON. Signed: WILEY G. HIGGINS bef. BENJAMIN KING, J.P., 14 December 1833.

Lot 703-3-2 Cherokee: "Apalachicola Florida March 2d. 1833.
Sir   My object in this communication is to request your Excellency to perform a small service for me in relation to the Gold Lottery. The circumstances of the case are these ...Having some precuming(?) matters to transact with BENJ. BROWN a Receiver for draws for the Land and Gold Lotteries for the co. of Morgan he informed me that as I was a widower with a family of children I was entitled to two draws in the Gold Lottery and that the Inferior Court had formed an Oath in accordance with the incaning? and intent of the statute which such persons might consciously take. I accordingly gave my name for two draws swearing according to the Oath which he administered that I was the Head of a family. In this way I gave my name in Morgan although an inhabitant of Jasper County. In the recent act of the Legislature of Ga. on this subject I was in doubt whether I was required to give in acquire or to take another Oath or not.I how ever at last came to the conclusion that it was not required. I had come to Florida for my health being threatened with a pulmonary disease, and could not think of returneing to Georgia to be qualified again; especially as the late act seems to refer to them who had not given in; and this was not my case. I wrote to Gen. SHORTER, Senator from Jasper on the subject. But as there was no Mail at that time between this place and Columbus and as I have not heard from him, If you Excellency would please to have the Books examined to ascertain whether my name was returned by McGUIRE (I think this is his name) the Colleague of BROWN & whether my name was put in the Lottery for two draws; and if not to have it put in for two, you will confer on me a distinguished favor. I was a widower with three children and had lived in Georgia from the year 1820 at the time of giving in my name. I had previously drawn in a Land Lottery. I am personally acquainted with Mr.JOHN A. CUTHBERT to whom your Excellency can apply for information as to character &c if any such information is necessary. Having long enjoyed the friendship of almost all the brothers of your Excellency, accept the assurances of my respect, and of my desire that Grace, Mercy, Peace and Long Life may be the happy Lot of your Excellency. Signed: WILLIAM B. RICHARDS
His. Excell. WILSON LUMPKIN
Gov. of Ga.
P. S. Please to pardon inperfections as this has been written in momentary expectation of the Departure of the Mail. W.B.R."

BALDWIN COUNTY: Lot 289-8-2 Cherokee. Personally appeared
         P. M. COMPTON to take out a grant for lot 289-8-2 Cherokee as a friend of the drawer. Signed: P. M. COMPTON before W. U. MITCHELL, N.P. 9 March 1854.

COLUMBIA COUNTY: Lot 1260-3-2 Cherokee. Personally app'd.
                        FELIX PRYOR, agent for the orphans of OWEN
BALDWIN, to claim their lot. Includes app't. of WM. H. PRITCHARD
as attorney. Signed: FELIX PRYOR before H. W. MASSENGALE, J.I.C.
25 June 1843.

JEFFERSON COUNTY: Lot 1273-3-2 Cherokee. Personally app'd.
                        DAVID F. BAILEY, husband of ELIZABETH W.
BEAL (the orphan of JACOB BEAL, dec'd.) to claim lot 1273-3-2.
Signed: DAVID F. BAILEY before HENRY B. TODD, J.I.C. 3 Jan.1853

BALDWIN COUNTY: Lot 1048-3-2 Cherokee. Personally app'd.
                        JOHN T. BARNES to claim lot 1048-3-2 for
his brother RICHARD G. BARNES of Alabama. Signed: JOHN THOMAS
BARNES before R. MICKLJOHN, J.P. 26 June 1843.

MUSCOGEE COUNTY: Lot 904-3-2 Cherokee. Personally app'd.
                        JAMES COOPER lawful agent of SAMUEL COOP-
ER, dec'd., to claim lot 904-3-2. JONATHAN ENGLISH is appointed
attorney. Signed: JAMES COOPER before JOHN C. CORLEY & JONATHAN
ENGLISH, J.P. 24 June 1843.

BALDWIN COUNTY: Lot 260-12-2 Cherokee. Personally appeared
                        MORGAN BROWN, appointed in Washington Co.
as Ex'r. of the estate of SYLVA COKER, dec'd. and Adm'r. of the
estate of JOHN WILSON by HAYWOOD BROOKINS, Clk., to claim lot No.
260-12-2. Signed: MORGAN BROWN 1843.

MORGAN COUNTY: Lot 1206-3-2 Cherokee. CHARLES ROBERTSON,
                        Adm'r. of HENRY ROBERTSON, dec'd., appt's.
A. B. BOSTWICK attorney for taking out a grant for lot 1206-3-2
drawn by the orphans of HENRY ROBERTSON, dec'd. Signed: CHARLES
ROBERTSON before R. A. PRIOR, J.P. 22 May 1843.

RICHMOND COUNTY: Lot 957-3-2 Cherokee. Personally appeared
                        ROBERT A. REID, Adm'r. of DAVID REID, de-
ceased, to claim lot 957-3-2. Signed: ROBERT REID before RICH-
ARD ALLEN, J.P. 17 June 1843.

CHEROKEE COUNTY: Lot 132-3-2 Cherokee. Personally appeared
                        WILLIAM & RICHARD TAYLOR to claim lots 132
and 227, 3rd Dist., 2nd Sect. CHARLES H. NELSON of Baldwin Co. is

appointed attorney. Signed: WILLIAM TAYLOR and RICHARD TAYLOR before MARTIN R. PHATON and JOHN H. BIBB, J.P. 14 June 1843.

GILMER COUNTY: Lot 259-6-2 Cherokee. Personally appeared JEREMIAH McBEE, guardian of JOHN A. SMITH orphan, to claim lot 259-6-2. Signed: JEREMIAH McBEE (by mark) before D. QUILLIAN, J.P. 29 January 1849.

CASS COUNTY: Lot 69-8-2 Cherokee. Personally appeared SAM M. SHEET of Darien, McIntosh County, who deposeth that JAMES UNDERWOOD of Tatnall County, sold lot 69-8-2 to the late ANSON KIMBERLY of Darien 1 February 1836. Sheet authorizes A. M. HORTON to take out the grant for the lot. Signed: SAM M. SHEET before WM. LATIMOR, J.P. (no date)

CASS COUNTY: Lot 119-7-2 Cherokee. Personally appeared OLIVER C. WYLLY, Adm'r. of the estate of WILLIAM A. DAWSON, dec'd. to claim lot 119-7-2 in Gilmer County and lot 226-6-3 of Cass County. Signed: OLIVER C. WYLY before O. WILLIAM LYLAR, J.P. 6 June 1843.

COWETA COUNTY: Lot 284-4-2 Cherokee. Personally appeared BRIGGS W. HOPSON to claim lot 284-4-2 he purchased from JAMES MERRILL's orphans of Monroe County. Signed: BRIGGS W. HOPSON before PETER HERREN, J.P. 11 Oct. 1848.

WASHINGTON COUNTY: Lot 273-4-2 Cherokee. Personally appeared MILES SCARBOROUGH, guardian of the property and person of EDWARD CAMPBELL, orphan of JOHN S. CAMPBELL, to claim lot 273-4-2. Signed: MILES SCARBOROUGH before SAMUEL ROBISON, J.I.C. 6 June 1843.

CHATHAM COUNTY: Lot 210-4-2 Cherokee. Personally appeared JOHN NOCK, one of the owners and agent for the other owners of lot 210-4-2 drawn by JAMES NOCK's orphans. to claim sd. lot. JOHN M. CLARK is appointed attorney. Signed: JNO. NOCK before R. RAIFORD, J.P. 13 June 1843.

CHATHAM COUNTY: Lot 543-17-2 Cherokee. Personally appeared JAMES B. HANKS to claim lot 543-17-2 and lot 27-4-2 drawn by the orphans of JOHN WOLFE of Effingham Co. HANKS married MARY A. WOLFE, one of the orphans, and is the agent for the other heirs. Signed: JAMES B. HANKS before ISAAC RUSSELL, J.P.   15 July 1844.

HARRIS COUNTY: Lot 159-5-2 Cherokee. Personally appeared THOMAS CUMMINGS, SETH HAMER & ALAHALA CUMMINGS, legal heirs of GIDEON CUMMINGS, dec'd. to claim lot 159-5-2 in Gilmer County and to appoint ANDREW J. GLENN to take out the grant for the said lot. Signed: THOMAS CUMMINGS, SETH HAMER & ALAHALA CUMMINGS (by mark) before FLYNN HARGETT, J.P. 15 May 1847.

HENRY COUNTY: Lot 16-5-2 Cherokee. Personally appeared DREDSIL WARREN to claim lot 16-5-2 and lot 521-4-1 as one of the orphans of BRAY WARREN, dec'd. and having reached the age of 21. Signed: DREDSIL WARREN (by mark) before HENRY BANKS, J.P.   3 October 1843.

MADISON COUNTY: Lot 768-19-2 Cherokee. Personally appeared AUGUSTUS G. CARRINGTON, Adm'r. of the estate of HENSON CARRINGTON, dec'd. to claim lot 768-19-2 and lot 712-11-1. TULLEY HOWLKELD appointed agent. Signed: AUGUSTUS G. CARRINGTON before JAMES McCURDY, J.P.   3 June 1843.

ELBERT COUNTY: Lot 264-9-2 Cherokee. Personally appeared MADISON HUDSON, agent for the orphans of WILLIAM HUDSON, dec'd. to claim lot 264-9-2. Signed: MADISON HUDSON before DAVID BELL, J.P., 17 October 1853.
    DAVID N. HUDSON, in right of himself and his sister ELIZABETH A. EDWARDS (?) and her husband DAVID R. EDWARDS (?), the only surviving heirs of WILLIAM HUDSON; in consideration of his moving, appoints MADISON HUDSON his att'y. to take out the grant for the lot drawn by the orphans of WILLIAM HUDSON. Signed. DAVID N. HUDSON bef. JOHN M. JACKSON & DAVID BELL, J.P., 1 November 1853. "we the undersigned are hereby that DAVID N. HUDSON and Mrs. ELIZABETH A. EDWARDS and her husband is the only heirs of WILLIAM HUDSON." Signed: JOHN M. JACKSON, DAVID BELL, JOHN SNELLINGS & THOMAS BELL.

WASHINGTON COUNTY: Lot 45-5-2 Cherokee. JOHN WILLIAMS, for the orphans of ISAAC JOHNSON, to claim lot 45-5-2 and lot 142-5-4. The orphans are LAND JOHNSON, MARY JOHNSON, ISAAC DANIEL JOHNSON & ELIZABETH JOHNSON. WILLIAMS is the husband of MARY JOHNSON. He appoints JEPTHA BRANTLEY attorney. Signed: JOHN WILLIAMS before A. P. PEACOCK, J.I.C. 12 June 1843.

UPSON COUNTY: Lot 725-1-2 Cherokee. NANCY M. GRIFFITH, widow of HENRY W. GRIFFITH, to claim lot 725-1-2 and lot 259-11-2. HENRY BUTTS is appointed attorney. Signed: NANCY M. GRIFFITH before L. M. GATLIN, J.P. 14 June 1843.

RICHMOND COUNTY: Lot 118-4-2 Cherokee. Personally appeared JOHN NELSON, Ex'r. of the estate of MATTHEW NELSON, dec'd. to claim lot 118-4-2 and lot 1198-2-4. EDWARD W. COLLIER is appointed att'y. Signed: JOHN NELSON before WM. K. KITCHEN and ALEX"R. PHILIPS, M.C.C.A. 23 June 1843.

RICHMOND COUNTY: Lot 118-   JAMES HARPER & JOHN NELSON are appointed executors of the estate of MATHEW NELSON. Signed: P. DUGAS, Clerk of Ordinary. 20 June 1843.

MUSCOGEE COUNTY: Lot 395-17-2 Cherokee. Personally app'd. MILTON J. TARVER, representative of the estate of BENJAMIN P. TARVER, dec'd., to claim lot 895-17-2; lot 571-2-4; lot 195-12-4; and lot 229-16(Lee County). He is also the representative of the orphans of ELIJAH TARVER to receive lot 170-6-2 and wishes to claim the lot that he drew, lot 127-18-2. Includes app't. of ALFRED M. HORTON as att'y. Signed: MILTON J. TARVER before AUGUSTUS J. ABBOTT, J.P. 2 June 1843.

WARREN COUNTY: Lot 105-17-1 Cherokee. Personally app'd. MICHAEL SWEADEMAN to claim to be lawful agent for lot 105-17-1. Includes app't. of JOHN W. A. LANFORD of Baldwin Co. as att'y. Signed: MICHAEL SWEADEMAN before JOHN E. TORRENCE and SEPTEMUS TORRENCE, J.P. 13 May 1843.

Lot 105-17-1 Cherokee
"Georgia Warren Cty.   May 15th 1843
    Dear Sir
The within named lot of land was drawn by the orphans of Mr. FRANK of Taliaferro County. Mr. SWINNAMON who applies for the grant making you his attorney to take out the said grant, married one of the drawers, there being two others only, for which he is now acting, there is no other mode that he knows of whereby he can obtain said grant, Mr. SWENNAMON has also purchased one of the childrens interest in sd. lot, he therefore owns two thirds himself. there being only three of the heirs living. Mr. SWINNAMON is not acquainted with you I therefore write to you in

his behalf. Yours respectfully &c. Signed: JETHRO DARDEN(?)".

MONROE COUNTY: Lot 378-3-2 Cherokee. Personally appeared HAMILTON DELL MADDOX says he is the proper owner, as are FREDERICK R. STOKES, WILLIAM S. MADDOX and NANCY J. MADDOX, as legatees, of lot 378-3-2 drawn by TABITHA MADDOX. Signed: H. D. MADDOX bef. B. PETERS, J.P. 17 June 1843. HAMILTON D. MADDOX appt'd. att'y. Signed: F. R. STOKES, WILLIAM MADDOX (by mark), NANCY MADDOX (by mark), before J. JOHNSTON, J.P. 17 June 1843.

ELBERT COUNTY: Lot 556-3-2 Cherokee. Personally appeared THOMAS W. JONES, one of the orphans of WILEY W. JONES, dec'd., to claim the lot drawn by sd. orphans. Includes app't. of Dr. WILLIAM G. ALLEN as att'y. Signed: THOMAS W. JONES, before JOHN A. DENARD & LINDSAY H. SMITH, J.P. 30 May 1843.

WILKES COUNTY: Lot 682-3-2 Cherokee. Personally appeared JOHN H. DYSON, Adm'r. of the estate of ANDREW G. SEMMES, dec'd., to claim lot 682-3-2. Includes appointment of JOHN R. ANDERSON of Baldwin County as attorney. JOHN DYSON signed before LEWSI S. BROWN, J.I.C., 19 June 1843.

CHATHAM COUNTY: Lot 1191-3-2 Cherokee. Personally appeared ISAAC RUSSELL to claim lot 1191-3-2, drawn by MARGARET McGOWEN. Signed: ISAAC RUSSELL bef. LEVI S. RUSSELL, J.P., 6 June 1843. Includes app't. of JOHN W. ESLEY of Effingham County as attorney.

CHATHAM COUNTY: Lot 1239-3-2 Cherokee. Personally appeared M. MAUPUS, widow of L. N. MAUPUS, to claim lot 1239-3-2 for herself and her children. Includes app't. of SOLOMON COHEN as att'y. Signed: M. MAUPAS bef. RICHARD D. ARNOLD, Mayor of Savannah. 1 June 1843.

HABERSHAM COUNTY: Lot 1081-3-2 Cherokee. Personally appeared HEZEKIAH DYER, husband of the former SARAH D. ALSTON, widow, to claim lot 1081-3-2. Includes app't. of E. S. BARNLAY(?) as att'y. Signed: H. DYER before BOLEVRE J. VESTER & LOVEN J. KEEL, J.P. 30 May 1843.

WASHINGTON COUNTY: Lot 542-21-2 Cherokee. Personally appeared

ELDRIDGE PERKINS, one of the heirs of JOSEPH PERKINS, to claim lot 542-21-2 and lot 1190-4-1. Includes app't. of JOHN H. WALKER as att'y. Signed: ELDRIDGE PERKINS (by mark) before SAMUEL HOWARD & T. H. BAKER, J.P., 14 June 1843.

GWINNETT COUNTY: Lot 255-9-2 Cherokee.
"june the 3rd 1843
Mr. CHARLES H. NELSON Dear Sir we have inclosed twelve dollars and 50 cents we wish you to apply for and take out the grants of four lots of land which numbers will be seen by Reference to the powers of attorneys here inclosed we wish you to detain the grants in your hands untill the 3rd monday of this Instant and if Dr. ALEXANDER of this County is there hand them to him or to any safe hand that will Deposit them in Lawrence Ville, if you do not have a chance to Send them by that time by hand pleas Send them by Mail to Lawrence Ville all four dun up in one package directed to D. SANFORD & JOHNSON, we take this liberty of writing to you by noticing your avertise ment & will take it as a great favor of yours, yours truly,
Signed: DANIEL SANFORD   JOEL JOHNSON"

GWINNETT COUNTY: Lot 255-9-2 Cherokee. Personally appeared WINNEY D. LANGSTON, the natural guardian of DAWSON DAVIS' orphans, to claim lot 255-9-2 and lot 885-4-1. Includes app't. of CHARLES H. NELSON of Baldwin County as att'y. Signed: WINNEY D. LANGSTON before ROBERT H. CATES (by mark) and DANIEL SANFORD, J.P. 2 June 1843.

GWINNETT COUNTY: Lot 205-9-2 Cherokee. Personally appeared DAVID PHILIPS to claim lot 205-9-2 drawn by DAVID PHILIPS, having a legal interest in the estate of DAVID PHILIPS. Includes app't. of JAMES McGINNES as att'y. Signed: DAVID PHILIPS before WILLIAM McGINNES & JAMES McGINNES, J.P. 24 May 1843.

WALKER COUNTY: Lot 177-9-2 Cherokee. Personally appeared JAMES HALL, Ex'r. of the estate of NANCY WADKINS, dec'd., to appoint RICHARD A. LANE att'y. for receiving the grant to lot 177-9-2 of now Gilmer Co., drawn by NANCY WADKINS in Dekalb Co. Signed: JAMES HALL bef. ELISHA CRAWFORD, J.P. and GEORGE CLEMENTS. 6 June 1843.

BALDWIN COUNTY: Lot 382-1-2 Georgia. Personally appeared JOHN G. SAPP, Adm'r. of the estate of DELANY SAPP, to claim lots 382-1-2 and 468-15-2. Signed: JOHN G. SAPP bef. A. M. HORTON, N.P. 23 December 1843.

BIBB COUNTY: Lot 755-15-2 Cherokee. Personally appeared CHARLES W. BROWN, one of the orphans of CHARLES BROWN late of Harris County, dec'd., to claim lot 755-15-2. SPENCER RILEY is appointed att'y. Signed: C. W. BROWN before KEELIN COOK, J.I.C. April 1848.

MUSCOGEE COUNTY: Lot 299-15-2 Cherokee. Personally appeared CARNOT WOODRUFF, agent of PHILP D. WOODRUFF, to claim lot 299-15-2. Signed: CARNOT WOODRUFF before JOHN J. McKENDEN, J.P. 22 June 1843.

JEFFERSON COUNTY: Lot 861-15-2 Cherokee. Personally appeared JAMES ANDERSON, JR., agent for ABRAHAM BEESLEY & JAMES ANDERSON, to claim lot 861-13-2 drawn by ABRAHAM BEASLEY and lot 868-2-3 drawn by VINEY PHILLIPS, widow, now the wife of JAMES ANDERSON, JR. Signed: James Anderson before ALFRED M. HORTON, N.P. 15 March 1843.

UPSON COUNTY: Lot 296-12-2 Cherokee. Personally appeared DRAKEFORD L. TRAMMELL, agent of LEROY McCOY who is Adm'r. of the estate of SUSAN HICKS, widow, (the name DANIEL HICKS is crossed out), to claim lot 296-12-2. Signed: D. L. Trammell before JAS. H. BLACK, J.P. 29 May 1843.
    Personally appeared DRAKEFORD L. TRAMMELL to claim lots 244-246-267-231-235 and 248, 10th Dist. in Monroe, now Upson Co. Signed: D. L. Trammell bef. Jas. H. Black, J.P. 29 May 1843.

TATNALL COUNTY: Lot 874-3-3 Cherokee. Personally appeared SIMON SMITH, adm'r. of the estate of WILLIMINGTON SMITH of Bulloch Co., dec'd., to claim lot 874-3-3 and lot 305-5-1. Signed: SIMON SMITH bef. JOHN A. ROGERS, J.P. 9 June 1843.

GREENE COUNTY: Lot 321-12-2 Cherokee. Personally appeared SAMUEL M. FINDLEY, Adm'r. of the estate of ROLEET FINDLEY, dec'd., to claim lot 321-12-2. Signed: SAMUEL FINDLEY before J. R. HALL, J.P. 6 June 1843.

RICHMOND COUNTY: Lot 58-23-2 Cherokee. Personally appeared ROBERT S. DILL, Adm'r. of the estate of WM. H. DILL, dec'd., to claim lot 58-23-2. Includes app't. of

WILLIAM R. McLAWS as attorney. Signed: ROBERT S. DILL before WiILIAM R. McLAWS. N. P. 1 June 1843.

GWINNETT COUNTY: Lot 173-19-2 Cherokee. Personally appeared DAVID W. SPENCE who saith that AMANDA TURNER, who married LADAWICK M. CATES; SOPHIA TURNER, who married DAVID W. SPENCE; SARAH TURNER, who married THOMAS W. CUNNINGHAM; and MARGARET TURNER, who married WILLIAM H. GIRIAM(?), are the only orphans of JOHN W. TURNER and for them he claims lot 173-19-2. Signed: D. W. SPENCE before JESSE MURPHEY, J.P. 4 Apr. 1850.

JONES COUNTY: Lot 18-26-2 Cherokee. Personally appeared ANN CHESTNUT, widow of DANIEL CHESTNUT, dec'd. of Putnam County and mother of ISAAC CHESTNUT, orphan,deceased, to claim lot 18-26-2. Includes app't. of JOHN WILLIAMS as att'y. Signed: ANN CHESTNUT (by mark) bef. JOHN WILLIAMS,J.P. 17 June 1843.

DEKALB COUNTY: Lot 78-27-2 Cherokee.
"Jesse C. farrar...is authorized to take out the Grant of 78-27-2 Gilmer County for the heirs of PRESLEY HOLLEY formerly of Laurens County Georgia, but now of Henry Co. Alabama. Agreeably to the authority of the within to me. 31st Oct. 1853.
Signed: H. W. McDANIEL
Atlanta, Ga."
Includes claim by JESSE C. FARRAR for lot 78-27-2 in Gilmer Co., as owner in part. It includes a note of consent by GEORGE WALKER, his wife MARY M. WALKER, and JOHN HOLLEY, orphans of PRESLEY HOLLEY for HENRY McDANIEL to take out the grant for their lot, Barler(?) Co., Alabama.

RICHMOND COUNTY: Lot 1002-3-2 Cherokee. ISAAC A. HIBLER, in right of his wife JUDITH S. HIBLER, (formerly JUDITH S. KRATH) and with HARRIET KRATH (now HARRIET VANCE) and TARLTON F. KRATH, the orphans of TARLTON F. KRATH,deceased, appoints WILLIAM A. MOTE of Baldwin Co. att'y. to take out the grant for the lot. Signed: I. A. HIBLER before T. W. MILLER, N.P. 23 January 1843.

CARROLL COUNTY: Lot 236-24-2 Cherokee. Personally appeared PEYTON BAUGHN to claim lot 236-24-2 as a legatee and also lot 443-13-1. Includes app't. of S. C. CANDLER as att'y. Signed: PEYTON BAUGHN bef. W. S. CANDLER and R. V. C. RUFFIN, J.P. 20 May 1843.

CASS COUNTY: Lot 149-24-2 Cherokee. Personally appeared SARAH HAMILTON to claim lot 149-24-2 drawn by the orphans of DAVID CROMPTON of Twiggs County. Signed: SARAH HAMILTON (by mark) before NATHANIEL GRANT, acting J.P. 27 March 1843.

DEKALB COUNTY: Lot 289-13-2 Cherokee. Personally appeared WALTER WADSWORTH to claim as Adm'r. Lot 289-13-2 and lot 122-4-1. Signed: WALTER WADSWORTH before J. B. WILSON, J.P. 23 June 1843.

TROUP COUNTY: Lot 217-12-2 Cherokee. Personally appeared NATHAN LIPSCOMB to claim lot 217-12-1, applied for by his agents PARK & ANDERSON, as a judgement creditor of JOHN W. D. BOWLING dec'd. Signed: NATHAN LIPSCOMB before JAS. M. BEALL, J.I.C. 23 June 1843.

TWIGGS COUNTY: Lot 17-13-2 Cherokee. Personally appeared JAMES WICKER, one of the orphans of ALLEN WICKER, to claim lot 17-13-2 Cherokee. Signed: James Wicker bef. ALLEN EDWARDS, J.P. 15 May 1843.

MERIWETHER COUNTY: Lot 278-6-2 Cherokee. Personally appeared FREEMAN W. BLOUNT, guardian of JOHN BLOUNT orphans, to claim lot 278-6-2. Signed: F. W. BLOUNT bef. ADAM RAGLAND, J.P. 14 June 1843.

MUSCOGEE COUNTY: Lot 99-12-2 Cherokee. Personally appeared ABNER H. FLEWELLEN, guardian of the minors of WILLIAM FLEWELLEN, dec'd., to claim lot 99-12-2. Includes appointment of ALFRED M. HORTON of Baldwin Co. as att'y. Signed: ABNER H. FLEWELLEN bef. TOMPKINS ECHOLS, J.I.C., 28 June 1843.

WASHINGTON COUNTY: Lot 273-4-2 Cherokee. Certification that MILES SCARBOROUGH is guardian of EDWARD H. CAMPBELL, minor of JOHN S. CAMPBELL, dec'd. Signed: HAYWOOD BROOKIN, Clk. 17 June 1843.

JEFFERSON COUNTY: Lot 200-8-2 Cherokee. Personally appeared SEABORN SAMMONS to claim lot 200-8-2.... drawn by NANCY SAMMONS, widow, and lot 1152-2-4. Signed: SEABORN SAMMONS bef. PLEASANT WALDEN, J.P. 2 June 1843.

TROUP COUNTY: Lot 285-8-2 Cherokee. Personally appeared ELIJAH W. CHRISTIAN Jr. to claim lot 285-8-2 as agent of WILLIAM CHRISTIAN, through his agent JOHN HARDEN. Signed: ELIJAH W. CHRISTIAN before IRWIN WILKERSON, J.P. 29 May 1843.

"Meml. of Granted or imgrated Lands belonging to the Estate of SOLOMON GROCE of Bibb County, deceased.
Grantor: FRANCIS L. BEUTON - No. 468/Dist.Gr./Co.-Cherokee Pur. Acres- 40 more or less.
" ELIZABETH HOOD: No. 1098/Dist. 21/ Sect. 2/ Co.-Cass/ Acres- 40 not gr. JOEL JONES
" ISAAC JONES: No. 256/ Dist. 23/ Sect. 3/ Co.-Cherokee Pur./ Acres-160 JAMES JONES GROSS BIBB
" MARY GLOVER & Gr. drawn by H. GLOVER
" SABETHA F. GLOVER: No. 1146/ Dist. 16/ Sect. 2/ Co.-Cobb/ Acres-40 more or less
" JOHN P. HARVEY: No. 761/ Dist. 18/ Sect. 3/ Co.-Cherokee pur./ Acres-not grn. JAMES COB PUTNAM
" G. C. BRASSWELL: No. 74/ Dist. 6/ Sect. 3/ Co.-Cass gr. Acres-160 more or less
" G. C. BRASSWELL: No. 74-Dist. 3/ Sect. 4/ Co. Cherokee pur./ BENJ. COONCE Twiggs
" DANL. ADAMS &   Drawn by M. T. JONES
" BENJ. B. SMITH: No. 752/ Dist. 21/ Sect. 2/ Co.- Cherokee pur./ Acres-40 more or less
" CHAS. Y. BROOKS: No. 793/ Dist 16/ Sect. 2/ Co.-Cobb/ Acres-40 gr.
" ANDREW OWENS: No. 1024/ Dist. 4/ Sect. 1/ Co.-Cherokee pur./ Acres- 40 not gr.
" WILLIAM BROWN: No. 160/ Dist. 26/ Sect. 2/ Co.-not gr./ Acres- Wilkerson co.
" GEORGE NORTHERN: No. 114/Dist. 5/ Sect.2/ Acres-160 gr.
" RICHD. DRAWHORN: No. 8-Dist. 26-Sect. 3/ Co.-Walker/ acres-160 Baismore Dist. Jones
" RICHD. DRAWHORN: No. 392-Dist.21-Sect.2/ Co. Cherokee/ acres-40
" PHILIP H. BROOKS: No. 573-Dist. 21-Sect. 2/ Co.-Cass/ Acres- 40
" JAMES HIGHTOWER: No. 1159-Dist.2-Sect.4/ Co.-Cherokee pur./ Acres-40
" ALEX JOHNSON: No. 106-Dist. 6-Sect. 2

Grantor: BARNETT HARRIS: No. 76-Dist. 11-Sect. 2
No. 37-Dist. 13-Sect. 3
SOLM. GROCE drawer lived in Permuchs. Dist. Jones County 252 3rd Dist. Dooly not gr"

BIBB COUNTY: Lot 1098-21-2 Cherokee. Personally app'd. THOMAS A. BROWN, Adm'r. of the estate of GROCE, dec'd. to claim the lots on the above list. Signed: THOMAS A. BROWN before PHILP P. ALWELL, J.O. 1843

PULASKI COUNTY: Lot 1176-21-2 Cherokee. Personally app'd. SARAH PHELPS, widow of JAMES PHELPS, dec'd. to claim lot 1176-21-2. Signed: Sarah Phelps before H. L. DAVIS, J.I.C., 13 May 1843.

RICHMOND COUNTY: Lot 33-20-2 Cherokee. Personally appeared JOHN P. KING, guardian of MARY M. KNIGHT, WOODWARD KNIGHT, WILLIAM KNIGHT, & SUSAN KNIGHT (orphans of ENOCH KNIGHT), to claim lot 33-20-2. Signed: John P. King before MICH. F. BOIRDAIN, N.P. 10 June 1843.

JONES COUNTY: Lot 627-21-2 Cherokee. Personally app'd. STERLING W. SMITH, Ex'r. of HAMSON SMITH of Talbot County, dec'd., to claim lot 627-21-2. Signed: STERLING W. SMITH, SENR. before WILLIAM MORELAND, J.P. 10 June 1843.

COOSA COUNTY: Lot 235-21-2 Cherokee. Personally appeared JAMES TRIMBLE to claim lot 235-21-2 and, for his wife the former SARAH AMANDA WHATLEY, orphan of MICHAEL WHATLEY, dec'd., he claims lot 216-3-13. Signed: JAMES TRIMBLE before SETH P. STORRS, 8 June 1843.

MORGAN COUNTY: Lot 77-14-2 Cherokee. Personally appeared LOVICK L. WITTICH to claim the lot 77-14-2, having bought the interest of one of the orphans of sd. lot. Signed: Lovick L. Wittich before JOHN ROBSON, J.I.C. 24 Mar.1847.

GREENE COUNTY: Lot 239-20-2 Cherokee. Personally appeared EDWARD CROSSLEY and MARY BREWER, brother and sister of JOHN CROSSLEY, to claim lot 239-20-2, as two fifths owner of this lot drawn by JOHN CROSSLEY, dec'd. They appoint LEMUEL P. CROSSLEY as their att'y. Signed: MARY BREWER (by mark) and EDWARD CROSSLEY bef. ROBT F. GRIFFIN, J.P. 20 June 1843.

ELBERT COUNTY: Lot 518-3-2 Cherokee. Personally appeared JOHN M. CARLETON, Ex'r. of the estate of STEPHEN CARLETON, dec'd., to claim lot 518-3-2. Signed: John M. Carleton before P. B. ROBERTS, J.P. 1 May 1843.

ELBERT COUNTY: Lot 17-3-2 Cherokee. Personally appeared BENJAMIN THORNTON, Adm'r. of the estate of JOHN THORNTON, dec'd. to claim lot 17-3-2. Signed: Benjamin Thornton before WILLIAM EAVES, 2 May 1843.

JACKSON COUNTY: Lot 133-6-2 Cherokee. Personally appeared EVAN POLK, guardian of T. A. POLK, an idiot, to claim lot 133-6-2 in present Gilmer Co. Signed: Evan Polk before POLLY LOWEREY and J. B. LOWEREY, J.P. 25 May 1843. Includes appointment of R. SANFORD of Hall Co. as att'y.

BALDWIN COUNTY: Lot 382-3-2 Cherokee. Personally appeared BENJAMIN R. DAVIDSON, legal heir of JOHN H. DAVIDSON, to claim lot 382-3-2. Signed: Benjamin R. Davidson (by mark) before ROBERT ROBINSON, J.I.C. 19 June 1843.

WASHINGTON COUNTY: Lot 86-7-2 Cherokee. Personally appeared LEWIS PARKER to claim lot 86-7-2 drawn by SARAH PARKER, widow, dec'd., of Hancock Co. Lewis Parker is part owner (one half) of the lot. RICHARD BLOUNT is authorized to take out grant. Signed: Lewis Parker before JOHN T. NEAL, J.P. 23 June 1843.

GREENE COUNTY: Lot 72-4-2 Cherokee. Personally appeared CROSBY S. SKIDMORE, for himself and his brothers and sisters, to claim lot 72-4-2 drawn by his brother, SAMUEL W. SKIDMORE. Signed: Crosby S. Skidmore before J. R. HALL, J.I.C. 17 June 1843.

TROUP COUNTY: Lot 146-10-2 Cherokee. Personally appeared WILLIAM DOUGHTERY, an ex'r. of the estate of HENRY ROGERS, dec'd., to claim lot 146-10-2 through his agent O. K. BULL. Signed: WM. DOUGHERTY before R. F. McGEHEE, J.P. 29 May 1843.

MORGAN COUNTY: Lot 51-8-2 Cherokee. Personally appeared JOHN R. HUDSON, one of the orphans of

CHARLES HUDSON, to claim lot 51-8-2 drawn while he lived in Newton county. Signed: JOHN R. HUDSON bef. WM.F. STOKES, J.I.C. 24 May 1843.

PIKE COUNTY: Lot 40-7-2 Cherokee. Personally appeared THOMAS G. HUNT to claim lot 40-7-2 of Cherokee, now Gilmer County and lot 113-3-1 as a legatee of JUDKINS HUNT, dec'd. Signed: THOMAS G. HUNT before THOS. E. DANIEL, J.P. 16 June 1843.

TWIGGS COUNTY: Lot 281-12-2 Cherokee. Personally appeared HENRY ANGLIN, JR., one of the heirs of ABNER ANGLIN, dec'd., to claim lot 281-12-2 and lot 494-11-1. Signed: HENRY ANGLIN, JR. bef. JOSIAH MURPHY, J.P. 17 June 1843.

TROUP COUNTY: Lot 138-12-2 Cherokee. Personally appeared JAMES M. FLOWERS, guardian of ELIZABETH EVANS, idiot, to claim lot 138-12-2 through his agent ORVILLE H. BULL. Signed: JAMES M. FLOWS before JAS. M. BEALL, J.I.C. 31 May 1843.

TALBOT COUNTY: Lot 152-13-2 Cherokee. ALLEN F. OWEN, attorney for MARMADUKE F. MENDENHALL of Charleston, South Carolina, to apply for grants to lot 152-13-2; lot 3-10-4; lot 1158-5-1; lot 727-21-3; lot 58-12-Lee Co.; and lot 233-10-Muscogee Co. He appoints MANAR BUTRUME att'y. Signed: ALLEN F. OWEN before C. R. WYNN and JOSEPH JACKSON, J.P. 24 June 1843.

STEWART COUNTY: Lot 130-13-2 Cherokee. Personally appeared CHRISTOPHER S. BALDWIN, Adm'r. of the estate of WILLIAM D. BALDWIN, to claim lot 130-13-2. Includes appointment of WILLIAM BOYNTON as att'y. Signed: Christopher Baldwin before FREEMAN WALKER & ISAAC L. STREETMAN, J.P. 6 June 1843.

BALDWIN COUNTY: Lot 1190-16-2 Cherokee. Personally app'd. SANFORD KINGSLEY, agent of the owner of lot 1190-16-2 and lot 873-20-3. Signed: Sanford Kingsley before ALFRED M. HORTON, N.P. 5 June 1843.

CARROLL COUNTY: Lot 1190-16-2 Cherokee. Personally app'd. JOHN CARMICHAEL and JOHN ROBINSON to appoint SANFORD KINGSBURY their att'y. to take out grants for lots 1190-16-2 and lot 873-20-3. Signed: JOHN CARMICHAEL & JOHN ROBINSON before JOHN LONG, J.P. 30 May 1843.

CASS COUNTY: Lot 685-16-2 Cherokee. Personally appeared EDMUND S. HART (HUNT?), husband of ELIZABETH W. BEARD, orphan of WILLIAM BEARD of Walton County, to claim lot 685-16-2. Signed: EDMUND S. HUNT? before JONATHAN McDOW, 7 October 1850.

BURKE COUNTY: Lot 309-2-2 Cherokee. Personally appeared SARAH REDDICK, guardian for the orphans of JACOB REDDICK, to claim lot 309-2-2. Signed: Sarah Reddick before HOMER MULKEY, J.P. 12 May 1843.

BALDWIN COUNTY: Lot 129-1-2 Cherokee. Personally appeared JAMES SMITH, Adm'r. of the estate of JOHN MERAN, to claim lot 129-1-2 and lot 672-11-1. Signed: James Smith before JAMES H. R. WASHINGTON, J.I.C. (no date).

BALDWIN COUNTY: Lot 192-16-2 Cherokee. Personally app'd. WILLIAM A. JARRATT, Adm'r. of the estate of WILLIAM D. JARRATT, dec'd., to claim lot 192-16-2. Signed: William A. Jarratt before R. MICKLEJOHN, J.P. 24 June 1843.

BALDWIN COUNTY: Lot 823-16-2 Cherokee. Personally appeared WILLIAM B. TINSLEY to claim lot 823-16-2 for the mother of the drawers. Signed: Wm. B. Tinsley before P. M. COMPTON, N.P. 14 Feb. 1851.

ELBERT COUNTY: Lot 765-3-2 Cherokee. Personally appeared WILLIAM D. CAMPBELL, Ex'r. of the estate of JAMES DILLARD, dec'd. to claim lot 765-3-2 and lot 1023-14-1/ Signed: William D. Campbell before Z. SMITH, J.P. 15 May 1843

BIBB COUNTY: Lot 247-2-2 Cherokee. Pers. app'd. ROBERT JOHNSON, guardian of WILLIAM JOHNSON, one of the owners of the lot he claims, lot 247-2-2. Signed: Robert Johnson before WM. H. CALHOUN, J.I.C. 28 June 1843.

WARREN COUNTY: Lot 210-14-2 Cherokee. Pers. app'd.WASHINGTON CULPEPPER to claim lot 210-14-2 and lot 652-21-2 drawn by NANCY McCULLARS, widow. Signed: WASHINGTON CULPEPPER (by mark) before STODDARD W. SMITH, J.P. 26 June 1843. Includes app't. of WILLIAM LITTLETON as att'y.

JEFFERSON COUNTY: Lot 188-16-2 Cherokee. Prs. app'd. NANCY STEPHENS, widow of NATHAN STEPHENS, dec'd. and one of the heirs of his estate, to claim lot 188-16-2. Includes appt. of Dr. PHILIP S. LEMLE as att'y. Signed: Nancy Stephens before SUSAN CASON (by mark) and WYRIOTT CASON, J.P. 17 June 1843.

JASPER COUNTY: Lot 953-16-2 Cherokee. Pers. app'd. ABEL S. WILSON, one of the Ex'rs. of the estate of JOSEPH A. WILSON, dec'd. to claim lot 953-16-2. Signed: Abel P. Wilson before CHAS. S. INDAN, J.I.C. 29 June 1843.

CHATHAM COUNTY: Lot 84-2-2 Cherokee. Pers. app'd. JOHN D. DELANNEY, lawful heir of the owner of lot 84-2-2. Includes app't. of ASA HOLT as att'y. Signed. J. D. DeOlanney before ELISHA WYLLY, N.P. 10 June 1843.

CHATHAM COUNTY: Lot 684-2-2 Cherokee. Pers. app'd. WILLIAM RENISHART of the late firm of GEORGE NEWHALL & Co., judgement creditors of JOSEPH LAW of Liberty county, to claim lot 684-2-2. Signed: W. Renishart before LEONIDAS WYLLY, J.P., 9 June 1843.

CHATHAM COUNTY: Lot 114-2-2 Cherokee. Pers. app'd. ESTHER STEWART, daughter of SOPHIA RISE, dec'd. to claim lot 114-2-2. Signed: Esther Stewart before Leonidas Wylly, J.P., 30 May 1843.

CHATHAM COUNTY: Lot 1010-16-2 Cherokee. Pers. app'd. ALEXR. W. ELANDS, son of WILLIAM ELANDS of McIntosh county, to claim lot 101-16-2. Includes app't. of JOHN W. ELEG of Effingham co. as att'y. Signed: Alex. W. Elands bef. LIN T. STINSELL, J.P. 30 May 1843.

CHATHAM COUNTY: Lot 243-18-2 Cherokee. Pers. app'd. FREDERICK G. TEBEAU, trustee of ELIZA T. BOYD, and children, to claim lot 243-18-2 that was drawn by JANE JARVIS, dec'd., mother of ELIZA BOYD. Includes app't. of JOHN W. EX-

LEY of Effingham as attorney. Signed: F. G. TEBEAU before LEONIDAS WYLLY, J.P. 30 May 1843.

COBB COUNTY: Lot 269-5-2 Cherokee. Pers. app'd. CHARLES W. STONE one of the orphans of JOSHUA STONE, to claim lot 269-5-2 and lot 24-13-3. Signed· CHAS. W. STONE before N. B. GREEN, J.I.C., 18 March 1848.
"Marietta March 17th 1848
P. M. COMPTON Esq.
Surveyor Genl. State Geo.
                Dear Sir
                      Enclosed I hand you Five dollars and affidavit as per form which you furnished you will please forward by return mail the Grants to me at this place
            yrs very respectfully
            M. MYERS
                for HENRY MYERS"

BURKE COUNTY: Lot 154-7-2 Cherokee. Pers. app'd. EDWARD GARLICK, for himself and EDWARD GARLICK of Alabama, the heirs of JUDAH GARLICK, dec'd., to claim lot 154-7-2. Includes app't. of WILLIAM J. LAWTON of Burke Co. as att'y. Signed: JOHN GARLICK before JOHN A. ROBERTS, J.P. 29 May 1843. (Note: the first EDWARD obviously should be JOHN..Ed.)

CAMDEN COUNTY: Lot 953-19-2 Cherokee. Pers. app'd. PETER CORB, guardian of MARGARET BANARDY, orphan to claim lot 953-19-2.
                Pers. app'd. PETER CORB, trustee for Mrs. CATHERINE LAEN, formerly the widow of BANARDY, to claim lot 600-1-2. Includes app't. of CHAS. J. McDONALD of Baldwin Co. as attorney. Signed: Peter Corb bef. ARCH. P. LARK(?), J.I.C and bef. ALEX D. ATKINSON, 9 June 1843.

CHATHAM COUNTY: Lot 260-2-2 Cherokee. Pers. app'd. MULFORD MARSH of Savannah, Adm'r. of the estate of and husband of the widow of JOHN WATTS, dec'd., of Burke County, to claim lot 240-2-2 and lot 185-12-1. Signed: Mulford Marsh before M. MYERS, J.I.C. 13 June 1843.

WILKES COUNTY: Lot 140-3 Baldwin. "Superior Court Office I do Certify that I have examined the Book containing the names of persons entitled to draws in the late land lottery, and the name of GEORGE PETERMAN does not appear on sd. Book, but that the name of JOHN PETERMAN does appear with the Name of JAMES FINNEY and orphans of ABRAHAM POTTER, preseeding and the names of CHRISTOPHER POSS and BAPTIST McDOWELE immediately after. Given under my hand this 10th day of February 1806. Signed: DD. TERRELL, Clk."

WILKES COUNTY: Lot 174-3 Baldwin. I do certify that I have examined the book of persons who drew names in the land lottery and the name of JONAS RAY is preseeded by JAMES HULING, JACOB RAY & CHRISTIANA RAY and immediately after it are the names of BENJAMIN PHULIPS, JOHN McKINSEY, & WILLIAM WEST. JONAS RAY is entitled to two draws. Signed: NATHL. WILLIS before Dd. TERRELL, C.S.C. 5 June 1806.

Lot 210-10 Baldwin
Augusta July 30th 1807
"Sir
I received your letter of the 2nd instant, the last evening, by Mr. CLAYTON and suffer me to assure you sir, that the Orphans returned by AUGUSTUS G. WALTON in Wilkes County, are the same family of Orphans, as returned in Richmond, say, ELIZABETH, ROBERT & THOMAS WALTON. I had no knowledge that AUGUSTUS G. WALTON had returned the above Orphans in Wilkes, until I received your letter. I am sir...very respectfully
yr. most obt. servt.
THOMAS GLASCOCK"

Lot 253-15 Baldwin
"Whereas I have filed in the Clerks office of the Superior Court of Washington County a complaint that SAMUEL BOLTON of that County did fraudenlly and Contrary to the true intent and meaning of the law for making distribution of the late Cession of land from the Creek nation, enter his name for a draw or draws in the lottery authorized by the aforesaid act. and... whereas the said SAMUEL BOLTON did draw a lot of land..to wit.. No. 253-15 Baldwin County, Now the said SAMUEL BOLTON or his legal Representatives are therefore hereby required to be and appear at a Superior Court to be held in and for the County of Washington on Monday the   of March next, to support the legality of his or their claim to the lot of land aforesaid. 28 June 1808. (not signed).

Lot 46-20 Baldwin
"Sir   Wilkes Sepr. 14th 1807
I observe by the papers, that HENRY BURLONG has drew a tract of land in the present lottery.
I dont know how he could take the oath to entitle him to a draw or how the receiver Could administer it as one of them in my hearing observed he had no right to the land. he is a French man by birth, deserted from the french Leagon at Charlotte Court house in Virginia in the year 1782.
got wounded but made his escape in trying to take him....this is a fact tho I dont know it Can be proved.. but every one of his acquaintance has heard him acknowlege it.
BARNABA KELLEY a fortunate drawer as Irish man by birth served in the British Armey in the time of the revolutionary War (tho not in America) came to America Since the peace of 1783. neither of the above men naturalized. ...neither was LOUIS PRUDHOMME a french man who drew lot of land in the former Lottery and has got his grant.
I have heard it observ'd by Several that some of the STANTON family has drew Land in the present lottery that had no right to draws....that between the time of there first comeing to Georgia that entitled them to a draw...they left georgia and lived some months in South Carolina and then returned

to georgia again. with Respect ...yr. excellence's
obedent servt. (not signed)"

PULASKI COUNTY: Lot 29-13 Appling. Pers. app'd. MARY A.
WHITFIELD Extrx. of the estate of WILLIAM
S. WHITFIELD, dec'd. to claim lots 29 and 30, 13th district of
Ware County for herself and her orphans. Signed: M. A. WHITFIELD
before P. F. SCARBOROUGH, N.P. 25 Sept. 1850.

BALDWIN COUNTY: Lot 548-12 Appling. Pers. app'd. JOHN W.
S. DANIEL, for his wife, the widow of AN-
DREW CUMMING, to claim the lots purchased by ANDREW CUMMING in
his life, lots 548,549,550,603,604 and 605 in the 12th District
of Appling County and lot 98-13 in Appling County. Signed: JNO.
W. S. DANIEL bef. LUTHER SWANK, J.P. 30 Sept. 1850.

Lot 180-9 Appling
"I do herby certify that I have lived more than thirty years in
the District known as Mecons Dist. in Greene County at the time
of the land lottery of 1818 and that I know HUGH HALL SENR. of
said District and that he the said HUGH HALL died before said
lottery and left sons under the age of twenty one years and that
I never knew any man of the name HENRY HALL nor the orphants of
HENRY HALL.   17 Decr. 1820 Signed: ROBERT RAE"

BIBB COUNTY: Lot 367-8 Appling. LUCINDA STUBBS, widow
of THOMAS STUBBS, dec'd., appointes JAMES
W. STUBBS att'y. for taking out a grant for lot 367-8-Appling Co.
Signed: Lucinda Stubbs before F. P. STUBBS (?) and JAMES A.STUBBS
dated: 5 August 1840.

COWETA COUNTY: Lot 110-8 Appling. Pers. app'd. HUGH BREW-
STER, Adm'r. of the estate of JOHN THUR-
MOND, dec'd. of Morgan County to claim lot 110-8 Appling County.
Signed: Hugh Brewster bef. WM. B. BROWN, J.P. 21 Aug. 1841.

MACON COUNTY: Lot 12-1 Appling. Pers. app'd. NANCY MUS-
LEWHITE to claim lot drawn by WM. MUSLE-
WHITE, dec'd. of Baldwin Co. Signed: Nancy Muslewhite (by mark)
bef. WM. SOWDEN, J.P. 15 June 1843. Mr. FELTON is att'y.

RANDOLPH COUNTY: Lot 82-9-4 Cherokee. BEVERLY R. BARKSDALE
and JOSEPH C. BARKSDALE of Burbon County,
Alabama app't. C. H. NELSON att'y. for obtaining land grants for
them at the land office in Milledgeville. Signed: Joseph C.Barks-
dale & Beverly R. Barksdale bef. JOHN MALFOON & AUSTIN FEDRICK,

Justice of the Peace. 16 June 1843.

Pers. app'd. JOSEPH C. BARKSDALE to claim lot 82-9-4 and lot 1225-19-2. Signed: Joseph C. Barksdale before AUSTIN FEDERICK, J.P. 16 June 1843.

Pers. app'd. BEVERLY R. BARKSDALE to claim lot (not given) as the only surviving legal representative. The lot was drawn by the orphans of WILLIAM BARKSDALE or "B. R. & HENRY BARKSDALE". Signed: Beverly R. Barksdale bef. Austin Fedrick, J. P. 16 June 1843.

FRANKLIN COUNTY: Lot 343-3-4 Cherokee. Pers. app'd. JOHN B. HARRISON, Adm'r. of the estate of ORVILLE CAWTHORN, dec'd. to claim lot 343-3-4. Includes app't. of TEMPLE F. COOPER as att'y. Signed: John B. Harrison bef. THOS. MORRIS & R. A. P. NEAL J.I.C. 28 May 1843.

TATTNALL COUNTY: Lot 1146-3-4 Cherokee. JOSEPH TILLMAN appoints CHARLES H. NELSON of Baldwin Co., att'y. for taking out a grant to lot 1146-3-4 drawn by SARAH TILLMAN of Bulloch Co. Signed: Joseph Tillman bef. JAMES P. DANIEL, J.P., 17 June 1843.

TROUP COUNTY: Lot 151-16-4 Cherokee. Pers. came ANTHONY HOLLOWAY, Adm'r. of the estate of JOHN G. WILLIAMSON, dec'd., to authorize JOHN HARDEN of Troup County to take out grants for lot 151-16-4 now in Floyd Co. Signed: Anthony Holloway before JAS. M. BEALL, J.I.C. 30 May 1843.

GREENE COUNTY: Lot 18-19-4 Cherokee. Pers. app'd. OSBORN S. FURLOW, Ex'r. of the estate of JETT T. SKIDMORE, dec'd. to claim lot 18-19-4 and lot 241-12-2. Signed: O. S. Furlow bef. JAMES MOORE, J.P. 12 June 1843.

BALDWIN COUNTY: Lot 153-4-4 Cherokee. Pers. appd. PURNEL W. OWENS, one of the heirs of the owner of lot 153-4-4 to claim sd. lot. Signed: Purnel W. Owens before ALFRED M. HORTON, N.P. 20 June 1843. Also includes claim for lot 86-16-4.

RANDOLPH COUNTY: Lot 36-12-4 Cherokee. Pers. app'd. STEPHEN THOMAS to claim lot 36-12-4 as part owner. Signed: Stephen Thomas before BARZELLAI (?) GRAVES,JIC 19 Jun.1848

MORGAN COUNTY: Lot 18-19-4 Cherokee. Pers. app'd. WILLIAM BALLARD, guardian of the minor children of JETT T. SKIDMORE, (SKIDMON?), dec'd., to claim lot 18-19-4 and lot 241-12-2. Signed: William Ballard bef. WM. S. STOKES, J.I.C. 15 June 1843.

MONROE COUNTY: Lot 1090-3-4 Cherokee. Pers. app'd. LARKIN ROSS, agent of DAVID ROSS, to claim lot 1090-3-4 and lot 708-5-1 and lot 608-21-3. Signed: Larkin Ross before CAMPBELL RAIFORD, J.P. 27 June 1843.

BALDWIN COUNTY: Lot 1147-3-4 Cherokee. Pers. came JAMES GATES, Adm'r. of the estate of THOS. GATES dec'd, to claim lot 1147-3-4. Signed: Jas. Gates before J. R. ANDERSON, J.I.C. 19 June 1843.

BALDWIN COUNTY: Lot 33-4-4 Cherokee. Pers. app'd. O. F. ADAMS to claim lot 33-4-4 as part owner. Signed: O. F. Adams before P. M. COMPTON, N.P. 13 Sept. 1853

BALDWIN COUNTY: Lot 89-27-3 Cherokee. Pers. app'd. SEABORN SOUTHALL to claim lot 89-27-3 as owner in part. Signed: Seaborn Southall bef. P. M. Compton, N.P. 22 Apr. 1848.

BALDWIN COUNTY: Lot 364-3-4 Cherokee. Pers. app'd. D. SOLOMON to claim lot 364-3-4 as Adm'r. Signed by D. Solomon bef. Alfred M. Horton, N.P. 23 June 1843. The name DANIEL COKER of Washington county is written in pencil at the bottom of the page.

BALDWIN COUNTY: Lot 22-7-4 Cherokee. Pers. app'd. H. J. SPRAYBURY to claim lot 22-7-4 as owner in part. Signed: H. J. Spraybury bef. P. M. Compton, N.P. 17 May 1853.

BALDWIN COUNTY: Lot 548-3-4 Cherokee. Pers. app'd. NATHANIEL J. HOLTON to claim lot 548-3-4 as owner in part. Signed: Nathaniel J. Holton bef. Alfred M. Horton, N.P. 14 January 1843.

BALDWIN COUNTY: Lot 202-2-4 Cherokee. Pers. app'd. WILLIAM G. HARRIS, to claim lot 202-2-4 as owner in part. Signed: WM. G. HARRIS before P. M. COMPTON, N.P. 18 September 1852.

BALDWIN COUNTY: Lot 172-4-4 Cherokee. Pers. app'd. Z. TALIAFERRO to claim lot 172-4-4 as only heir of the owner. Signed: 22 June 1843. (the rest of the document is obscured.)

MACON COUNTY: Lot 1052-3-4 Cherokee. Pers. app'd. JANE B. WENDERWEEDLE to claim lot 1052-3-4 as Admtrx. Signed: Jane B. WINDERWEDLE bef. SILAS A. STOKES, J.P. 4 April 1843.

BALDWIN COUNTY: Lot 288-17-4 Cherokee. Pers. app'd. THOMAS E. HARDAWAY to claim lot 288-17-4 as one of the heirs of the owner. Signed: Thos. E. CALLAWAY before Alfred M. Horton, N.P. 3 May 1843.

BALDWIN COUNTY: Lot 819-2-4 Cherokee. Pers. app'd. THOMAS G. JAMES to claim lot 819-2-4 as owner in part. Signed: Thos. G. James before Alfred M. Horton, N.P. 25 April 1843.

BALDWIN COUNTY: Lot 116-8-4 Cherokee. Pers. app'd. IVERSON L. HARRIS to claim lot 116-8-4 as Exr. of the owner. Signed: Iverson L. Harris before J. R. ANDERSON, J.I.C. 26 Decmr. 1844.

BALDWIN COUNTY: Lot 237-12-4 Cherokee. Pers. app'd. HENRY SANFORD to claim lot 237-12-4 as Adm'r.of the drawer. Signed: Henry Sanford before Alfred M. Horton, N.P. 29 March 1843.

TWIGGS COUNTY: Lot 635-1-4 Cherokee. Pers. app'd. JAMES G. FAULK to claim lot 635-1-4 as Adm'r. Signed: James G. Faulk before PEYTON REYNOLDS, J.I.C.14 Apr.1843.

MURRAY COUNTY: Lot 59-27-3 Cherokee. Pers. app'd. ISRAEL NATIONS to claim lot 59-27-3 in Walker co. as five sixths owner. Signed: Israel Nations (by mark) before C. B. TUCKER, J.P. 1 January 1850.

BUTTS COUNTY: Lot 392-3-4 Cherokee. Pers. app'd. SARAH

WYNN to claim lot 392-3-4 as owner in part. Signed: SARAH WYNN before CHARLES BAILEY, J.P. 17 June 1843.

HENRY COUNTY: Lot 266-5-4 Cherokee. Pers. app'd. GEORGE W. WIGGINS to claim lot 266-5-4 as part owner. Signed: George W. Wiggins (by mark) before JESSE HIGHTOWER, J.P. 16 December 1848.

HABERSHAM COUNTY: Lot 149-17-4. Pers. app'd. NATHANIEL G. TILLEY to claim lot 149-17-4 as one of the drawers. Signed: N. G. TILLY before C. H. LUTTON, N.P. 19 November 1851.

GWINNETT COUNTY: Lot 95-16-4 Cherokee. Pers. app'd. GEORGE LEE to claim lot 95-16-4 as owner in part. Signed: George (by mark) Lee before DAVID R. PHILLIPS, J.P. 26 December 1851.

OGLETHORPE COUNTY: Lot 148-11-4 Cherokee. Pers. app'd. JAMES JARVIS and LANY McKANNON to claim lot 148-11-4. Signed: James (by mark) Jarvis and LANEY (by mark) McKannon before WM. GOOLSBY, J.P. 24 April 1849.

BALDWIN COUNTY: Lot 1291-2-4 Cherokee. Pers. app'd. D. M. McDONALD, Adm'r. of the estate of D. B. MITCHELL, to claim lot 1291-2-4. Signed: D. M. McDonald before J. R. Anderson, 20 June 1843.

RICHMOND COUNTY: Lot 130-10-4 Cherokee. Pers. app'd. MARCUS C. M. HAMMOND to claim lot 130-10-4 as a part owner. Signed: M. C. M. Hammond before JNO. CRAIG, N.P. 12 June 1849.

DEKALB COUNTY: Lot 187-11-4 Cherokee. Pers. app'd. ANDREW NEESE to claim lot 187-11-4 as owner in part. Signed: Andrew Neese bef. Y. L. THOMAS, J.P. 25 Aug. 1853.

EARLY COUNTY: Lot 269-10-4 Cherokee. Pers. app'd. WM. G. GILMER, THOS. MILLER, HENRY MILLER, & WM. S. GRAY to claim lot 269-10-4. Signed: Henry Miller, William S. (by mark) Gray, William G. (by mark) Gilmer and Thomas (by mark) Miller before D. G. KILLINGSWORTH, J.P. 14 Jan. 1854.

BALDWIN COUNTY: Lot 96-12-4 Cherokee. Pers. app'd. JAMES TURNER JR. to claim lot 96-12-4 as Adm'r. of the owner. Signed: James Turner, Jr. before Alfred M. Horton, N.P., 9 March 1843.

BALDWIN COUNTY: Lot 36-14-4 Cherokee. Pers. app'd. ELI H. BAXTER to claim lot 36-14-4 as Adm'r. of the owner. Signed: Eli H. Baxter before Alfred M. Horton, N.P. 7 March 1843.

MC INTOSH COUNTY: Lot 789-1-4 Cherokee. Pers. app'd. ALEXANDER MILCHELL, general agent of HUGH W. PROUDFOOT (the guardian of ELIZABETH E. & LUCY ANN SPIERS,minors) to claim lot 789-1-4; lot 281-12-4; and lot 323-10-2. Signed: Alexander Mitchell before ARMOUND LESILS, J.P. 10 June 1843.

MC INTOSH COUNTY: Lot 271-5-4 Cherokee. Pers. app'd. JACOB DREGORS, lawful heir of MARY ROZAR (one of the drawers of lot 271-5-4) being the husband of MARY ROZAR, to claim sd. lot and to app't. J. E. TOWNSEND, att'y. Signed: Jacob Dregors bef. WILLIAM BAGGS, J.P. 13 June 1843.

MC INTOSH COUNTY: Lot 1265-2-4 Cherokee. Pers. app'd. MARY McDONALD, lawful heir of GEORGE McDONALD, JR. to claim lot 1265-2-4. Signed: Mary (by mark) BAKER before W. W. CARPENTER, J.P. 15 June 1843.

MC INTOSH COUNTY: Lot 202-16-4 Cherokee. Pers. app'd. JAMES HAMILTON, one of the owners and agent for the other owners of lot 202-16-4, to claim sd. lot. I. E. TOWNSEND is appointed att'y. Signed: Jas. Hamilton before C. I. W. THORP, J.P. 19 June 1843.

Lot 243-14-4 Cherokee.
"Executive Department Ga.
Milledgeville 27 July 1835
  It satisfactorily appeareing to the Governor from the affidavit of THOMAS GLASCOCK that the Lot of Land No. 243-14-4 drawn by the names of RACHAEL & PRISCEY HILL, orphans of the 123rd Dis. Richmond County should be RACHAEL AND PRESSLEY HILL orphans of sd. Dist. instead of PRISCEY HILL. It is therefore, ..ordered, that the books be corrected, and the plat and grant issued to the sd. Rachael and Pressley Hill, orphs. on the payment of the usual fees. Attest...JOHN W. LUMPKIN, Sec. E.D."

FLOYD COUNTY: Lot 944-3-4 Cherokee. Pers. app'd. JOHN W.

EDY(?), Adm'r. of the estate of JOHN EDY, dec'd. to appoint H. V. M. MILLER att'y. for taking out grants to lots 944-3-4 in present Floyd County, and lot 638-3-4. Signed: John M. Edv(?) before WM. BERRYHILL, J.P. 5 June 1843.

BALDWIN COUNTY: Lot 27-1-4 Cherokee. Pers. app'd. JAMES W. TINSLEY, Adm'r. of the estate of JAMES W. TINSLEY, dec'd. (who was the Adm'r. of the estate of EDWARD SWEARINGIN and Ex'r. of the estate of ABRAHAM GOGGINS), to claim lots 27-1-4; 223-3-3; and 285-21-3. Signed: J. W. Tinsley before R. MICKLEJOHN, J.P. 27 June 1843.

BIBB COUNTY: Lot 392-2-4 Cherokee. Pers. came EUGENUS A. NISHT, guardian of MILES C. NISHT (orphan of MILES NISHT, dec'd.), to claim lot 392-2-4 in Paulding County and lot 54-7-3 in Murray County. Signed: EUGENIUS A. NISHT before JESSE L. OWEN, J.P. 26 June 1843.

PIKE COUNTY: Lot 213-11-4 Cherokee. Pers. app'd. MARTHA ALEXANDER, guardian of the property of the orphans of ADAM(?) ALEXANDER, dec'd., to claim lot 213-11-4 of Walker Co. Includes app't. of JOHN W. COPPEDGE as att'y. Signed: Martha Alexander before JAS. H. ALEXANDER, J.P. 17 June 1843.

BALDWIN COUNTY: Lot 533-3-4 Cherokee. Pers. app'd. SOLOMON D. BETTAR, to claim he is one of the heirs of SOLOMON D. BETTAR, who drew lot 533-3-4. Signed: Solomon D. Bettar before J. R. ANDERSON, J.I.C. 9 June 1843.

NEWTON COUNTY: Lot 603-3-4 Cherokee. Pers. app'd. JESSE L. BAKER, att'y. for the legatees of ELIZABETH HARPER, dec'd., to claim lot 603-3-4. Includes app't. of JAS. R. McCALLA as agent for taking out the grant for sd. lot. Signed: Jesse L. Baker before (..?..), 20 May 1843.

CAMDEN COUNTY: Lot 1068-3-4 Cherokee. Pers. app'd. JAMES THOMPSON, Ex'r. of JAMES C. SCOTT, dec'd. to claim lot 1068-3-4. Includes app't. of ALFRED M. HORTON of Baldwin Co. as att'y. Signed: James Thompson bef. JOHN MIZELL, J.P., 19 June 1843.

FORSYTH COUNTY: Lot 205-6-4 Cherokee. Pers. app'd. MADISON

C. CHASTAIN, guardian of BENJAMIN T. CHASTAIN, lunatic, of Hall County, to claim lot 205-6-4. Signed: Madison C. Chastain before CURTIS GREEN, J.P. 2 July 1850.

CHATHAM COUNTY: Lot 103-4-4 Cherokee. Pers. app'd. Mrs. ELLEN BARTON of Savannah, the widow of JOHN B. BARTON, dec'd.,..they were married in Charleston, S. C. and he died in Liberia as a minister of the Methodist Episcopal Church sent to Africa by the American Colonization Society. She claims lot 103-4-4 in Cherokee now Floyd County. Signed: Ellen Barton before L. W. SMITH, J.P. 12 May 1843.

RICHMOND COUNTY: Lot 1238-3-4 Cherokee. Pers. app'd. WILLIAM SCHLY, Ex'r. of the estate of MICHAEL FLECK, to claim lot 1238-3-4 in Floyd Co. Signed: William Schly bef. RICHARD ALLEN, J.P. 5 June 1843.

MONROE COUNTY: Lot 1216-3-4 Cherokee. Pers. app;d. S. A. MANN, formerly of Elbert Co., to claim lot 1216-3-4. Signed: S. A. Mann before WILLIAM McMICKLE, J.P. 27 June 1843.

MERIWETHER COUNTY: Lot 533-3-4 Cherokee. Pers. app'd. BAKER MANN to claim lot 533-2-4 as part owner. The other owner is LEROY McCOY of Alabama. Signed: Baker Mann before JAMES M. MADDEN, J.P. 9 Sept. 1844. Includes app't. of EZEKIEL TRICE as att'y.

DOOLY COUNTY: Lot 6-3-4 Cherokee. Pers. app'd. MILLS ROUNTREE, legal heir of ARTHUR ROUNTREE, to claim lot 6-3-4. Includes app't. of ALFRED M. HORTON as att'y. Signed: Mills Rountree (by mark) before THOS. H. KEG and WILLIAM C. GREER, J.P. 14 June 1843.

LINCOLN COUNTY: Lot 791-2-4 Cherokee. Pers. app'd. WM. HARPER, JR. one of the legatees of WILLIAM HARPER, SR., dec'd., to claim lot 791-2-4. Signed: GEORGE HARPER before THOMAS PSALMONDS, J.P. 24 June 1843.

CHATTOOGA COUNTY: Lot 79-15-4 Cherokee. Pers. app'd. JEREMIAH W. HENDERSON to claim lot 79-15-4 for himself and ROBERT S. T. HENDERSON and their sister H. A. T.
Chattoogaville

E. J. BELLE, the orphans of DAVID HENDERSON, dec'd. Signed: J. H. HENDERSON before A. K. RINEHART, J.P. 13 September 1850.

MORGAN COUNTY: Lot 336-16-4 Cherokee. Pers. came FRANCIS A. CHEANY, Adm'r. of the estate of RICHEN L. McGUINE, dec'd. (Adm'r. of LEA RICHEAN L. McGUINE), to claim lot 336-16-4. Signed: F. A. CHE<u>NY</u> before CANTON SHEPTAN, J.P. 13 June 1843.

DECATUR COUNTY: Lot 333-16-4 Cherokee. Pers. app'd. AUGUSTUS J. BELL, Adm'r. of the estate of MARGARET BELL, dec'd. to claim lot 333-16-4. Signed: Augustus J. Bell before CANNETH W. T. SWAIN, J.P. 23 June 1843.

RICHMOND COUNTY: Lot 291-17-4 Cherokee. Pers. app'd. HENRY GABLE, for the benefit of JAMES FARMAN (the only surviving heir of JOEL C. FARMAN), to claim lot 291-17-4. JAMES FARMAN is about age 14 and has resided in Gable's family since the death of Gable's mother in 1840. Signed: Henry Gable before J. W. MEREDETH, J.P. 18 January 1853.

BALDWIN COUNTY: Lot 217-10-4 Cherokee. Pers. app'd. JOHN H. BROWN, surviving Ex'r. of GEORGE A. BROWN, dec'd. to claim lots 217-10-4 and 604-19-3. Signed: John H. Brown bef. R. MICKLEJOHN, J.P. 23 June 1843.

MONROE COUNTY: Lot 42-5-4 Cherokee. Pers. came THOMAS BANKS (for his wife the former ESTHER ANN WILMOT of Elbert Co. -an orphan of ISAAC WILMOT), to claim lot 42-5-4. Signed: Thomas Banks before J. A. BANKS, J.I.C. 16 Feb. 1843. Includes app't. of WILLIAM L. COOK as att'y.

TALIAFERRO COUNTY: Lot 249-11-4 Cherokee. Pers. app'd. JOSEPH R. PARKER, agent for the orphans of T. R. WILSON, to claim lot 249-11-4. Includes app't. of WILLIAM M. HARRISON as att;y. Signed: Joseph R. Parker before JESSE WOODALL, J.P. 9 July 1844.

DOOLY COUNTY: Lot 142-2-4 Cherokee. Pers. app'd. OLIVER H. ROWELL, legal heir of JOAB T. ROWELL (orphans of Joab T. Rowell of Burke Co.) and RICHARD ROWELL. Signed: Oliver H. Rowell bef. William C. Greer, J.P. 14 June 1843.

BALDWIN COUNTY: Lot 248-2-4 Cherokee. Pers. app'd. JAMES
                       M. BULLARD, Adm'r. of the estate of ANDREW
JOHNSON, dec'd. to claim lot 248-2-4 and lot 323-17-2. Signed:
James M. BALLARD before R. MICKLEJOHN, J.P. 26 June 1843.

PULASKI COUNTY: Lot 101-3-4 Cherokee. Pers. app'd. J. B.
                       TROY JOHNSON, in right of his wife, to
claim lot 101-3-4 drawn by the orphans of AMOS WINGATE. Signed:
J. B. Troy Johnson (by mark) before MATTHEW GRACE, J.P. (no date)

JEFFERSON COUNTY: Lot 91--3-4 Cherokee. Pers. app'd. LEMON
                       RUFF, "distributee" of the estate of WIL-
LIAM ROLLINS, dec'd. of Burke County, to claim lot 91-3-4 and
lot 186-17-4. Includes app't. of BENNETT CROFTON as att'y.
Signed: Lemon Ruff before THOMAS W. BATLEY, J.I.C. 26 June 1843.

GWINNETT COUNTY: Lot 267-16-4 Cherokee. Pers. app'd. DAVID
                       ROLLINS to claim lot 267-16-4 and as Admr.
of the estate of his father, NICHOLAS ROLLINS, dec'd., to claim
lot 735-20-3. Includes app't. of CHARLES H. NELSON of Milledgeville as att'y. Signed: David ROWLINS before EZEKIEL THACKER &
JESSE MURPHEY, J.P. 16 June 1843.

PIKE COUNTY: Lot 193-9-4 Cherokee. Pers. app'd. SUSAN-
                       NAH WOOD, agent for the minors of ROBERT
WOOD, dec'd., to claim lot 193-9-4. Includes app't. of CHARLES
WOOD as att'y. Signed: Susannah Wood before THOS. D. JONES &
J. N. MAUGHUM, J.P. 10 June 1843.

COWETA COUNTY: Lot 163-4-4 Cherokee. Pers. appd. ELIZA-
                       BETH CORLEY to claim lot 163-4-4 and lot
210-11-2 drawn by her late husband DAVENPORT CORLEY. Includes
app't. of HILLSBERRY R. HARRISON as att'y. Signed: Elizabeth (by
mark) Corley before JEREMIAH CORLEY & WILLIAM B. BROWN, J.P.
7 June 1843.

FAYETTE COUNTY: Lot 244-10-4 Cherokee. Pers. came JEPTHA
                       LANDRUM, legatee of EDA FOWLER, dec'd.,
to claim lot 244-10-4. Signed: Jeptha Landrum bef. EDWARD CONNER,
J.I.C. 23 June 1843.

BALDWIN COUNTY: Lot 270-2-4 Cherokee. Pers. app'd. JOHN

BLEWETT to claim lot 270-2-4 as Adm'r. of the owner. Signed: John Blewett before ALFRED M. HORTON, N.P. 30 May 1843.

GREENE COUNTY: Lot 758-2-4 Cherokee. Pers. app'd. JOHN COLEBY to claim lot 758-2-4 as Adm'r. of the owner. Signed: John Coleby before J. R. HALL, J.I.C. 24 June 1843.

HANCOCK COUNTY: Lot 127-17-4 Cherokee. Pers. app'd. PARHAM ALLEN, Adm'r. of the estate of WILEY MEADOWS, to claim lot 127-17-4. Signed: Parham Allen before JAMES McC. CASON, J. P. 17 June 1843.

BALDWIN COUNTY: Lot 273-13-4 Cherokee. Pers. came D. SOLOMON, legal representative of the orphans of WILLIAM Mc. CANDLER, to claim lot 273-13-4. Signed: D. Solomon before Alfred M. Horton, N.P. 23 June 1843.

WARREN COUNTY: Lot 1204-2-4 Cherokee. Pers. came TAMSY MARTIN, widow of JOHN L. MARTIN, dec'd., to claim lot 1204-2-4. Signed: TAMSA (by mark) MARTIN before JAMES BRADY, J.P. 15 June 1843.

PAULDING COUNTY: Lot 72-8-4 Cherokee. Pers. appd. JOSHUA R. JORDON, one of the orphans of JAMES JORDON of Elbert Co., dec'd., to appoint EDWARD D. CHISOLM as att'y. for taking out a grant to lot 72-8-4. Signed: Joshua R. Jordon before JOSEPH G. BLANCE, J.I.C. 8 January 1850.

MURRAY COUNTY: Lot 312-8-4 Cherokee. Pers. app'd. ALEXANDER STEWART, agent of the heirs of DAVID M. STEWART, dec'd. of Henry Co., to claim lot 312-8-4. Signed: A. Stewart before FRANKLIN GLENN, J.P. 24 January 1846.

HARRIS COUNTY: Lot 84-5-4 Cherokee. Pers. app'd. STEPHEN BRINSON, legatee and agent for the other heirs of BELIEA STRINGER, dec'd., to app't. TALLAVER JONES agent for taking out a grant for lot 84-5-4. Signed: Stephen Brinson before WILLIAM WILLIAMSON, J.P. 14 June 1847.

HANCOCK COUNTY: Lot 269-9-4 Cherokee. Pers. app'd. JESSE

M. PINKSTON, one of the heirs of EVANS W. PINKSTON (bachelor), dec'd., to claim lot 269-9-4. Signed: Jesse M. Pinkston before THOMAS COLEMAN, J.P., 15 June 1843.

ELBERT COUNTY: Lot 50-18-4 Cherokee. Pers. app'd. FRANCIS G. STOWERS, for his wife MARY E. GAINES (the only surviving orphan of LIVESTON P. GAINES, dec'd.) to claim lot 50-18-4. Signed: Francis G. Stowers before ELSEY B. THORNTON, J.P. 16 February 1847.

FRANKLIN COUNTY: Lot 139-19-4 Cherokee. Pers. app'd. THOMAS MORRIS, to claim lot 139-19-4 as half owner and as agent for JOHN W. BUSH, the other half owner. The lot was drawn by SARAH ENGLISH. Signed: Thos. Morris before R. A. R. NEAL, J.I.C. 17 June 1843.

MORGAN COUNTY: Lot 172-17-4 Cherokee. Pers. app'd. THOMAS G. COCHRAN, husband of one of the orphans of JOHN LUNSDEN, to claim lot 172-17-4. Signed: Thomas G. Cochran before JOHN R. COKRAN(?) J.I.C. 13 June 1843.

JEFFERSON COUNTY: Lot 18-13-4 Cherokee. Pers. app'd. MARTHA SAMMONS to claim lot 18-13-4 (the lot citation for this file appears to be incorrect viz. Lot 13-18th Dist.-4th Sect.) drawn by WILEY SAMMONS. Signed: Martha Sammons (by mark) before LEWIS LAMPP, J.P. 24 June 1843.

HOUSTON COUNTY: Lot 768-2-4 Cherokee. Pers. app'd. NELSON RAFIELD, husband of MARY CHESNUT, to claim lot 768-2-4. Signed: Nelson Rafield (by mark) before WILLIAM M. BATEMAN, J.P. 9 October 1845.

STEWART COUNTY: Lot 719-2-4 Cherokee. Pers. app'd. RICHARD L. SATTER, owner with EMILY HADDOCK & SARAH HADDOCK, to claim lot 719-2-4. Signed: R. L. Satter 13 May 1853.

TALBOT COUNTY: Lot 37-10-4 Cherokee. Pers. app'd. WILLIAM L. BISHOP, Adm'r. of the estate of JOHN O. GRANT, to claim lot 37-10-4. Includes app't. of WM. F. BROOKS as att'y. Signed: Wm. S. Bishop before A. C. McCOY & DICKSON CARETON, J.P. 14 June 1843.

MORGAN COUNTY: Lot 5-4-4 Cherokee. Pers. came JOHN C.
MOORE, guardian for the orphans of JOSEPH
MOORE, dec'd. to claim lot 5-4-4. Signed: John C. Moore before
ELIJAH E. JONES, J.I.C. 11 June 1843.

UPSON COUNTY: Lot 307-8-4 Cherokee. Pers. app'd. THOMAS
B. GREENE, Adm'r. of the estate of JAMES
W. GREENE, dec'd., to claim lot 307-8-4. Includes app't. of JAMES
W. GREENE as att'y. Signed: Thos. B. Greene before JAS. H. BLACK,
J.P., 17 June 1843.

WHITFIELD COUNTY: Lot 297-13-4 Cherokee. MOSES C. SMITH of
Thomas County appt's. SPENCER RILEY atty.
to take out the grant to lot 297-13-4 in Chattooga Co. for the
minors of WILLIAM PHILLIPS, dec'd. of Thomas Co. Signed: Moses C.
Smith before J. C. SMITH and WILLIAM WHITTEN, J.P. 3 Sept. 1853.

UPSON COUNTY: Lot 90-15-4 Cherokee. Pers. app'd. MARY
HAMMOC to claim lot 90-15-4 for the heirs
of LEROY POLLARD of Pike Co. Includes app't. of JAMES HOLLEY as
att'y. Signed: Mary Hammoc (by mark) before L. M. GATLIN, J.P.
15 April 1843.

RANDOLPH COUNTY: Lot 106-15-4 Cherokee. Pers. app'd. WIL-
LIAM R. CARAWAY, for himself, JAMES CARA-
WAY & SARAH ANN CARAWAY (the only surviving orphans of THOMAS
CARAWAY, dec'd.) to claim lot 106-15-4. Signed: William R. Cara-
way before S. THOS. ANDREWS, J.P. 19 July 1848.

PUTNAM COUNTY: Lot 273-16-4 Cherokee. MARGERET AOREA appoints ABRAHAM COTTON att'y. to take out
a grant for lot 273-16-4 drawn by BRADLEY AOREA. Signed: Margerett (by mark) Aorea before JOHN A. COGBURN, J.P. 27 Apr. 1843.

PIKE COUNTY: Lot 917-1-4 Cherokee. Pers. app'd. ABRAM
PEEBLES to claim lot 917-1-4 and lot 1212-
18-3 and lot 239-10-Muscogee County owned by himself and ALBERT
PEEBLES, dec'd. Includes app't. of JOHN W. COPPEDGE as att'y.
Signed: ABRAM PEEBLES before THOS. J. LERVIS and A. A. GAULDING,
J. P., 10 June 1843.

FORSYTH COUNTY: Lot 1170-2-4 Cherokee. JOHN BORING appoints

ISAAC BORING of Baldwin County his att'y. to claim lot 1170-2-4. Signed: JOHN BORING before CORNELIUS CAWLEY, J.P. 21 Feb. 1843.

HENRY COUNTY: Lot 247-2-4 Cherokee. CAMP UPCHURCH appts. ALFORD M. WARTON of Milledgeville att'y. to take out the grant for lot 247-2-4 drawn by JOHN GRANT's orphans. Signed: Camp Upchurch before A. STEWART, J.P. 6 Jan. 1849.

PUTNAM COUNTY: Lot 240-3-4 Cherokee. Pers. app'd. NANCY MIDDLETON, widow of WILLIAM MIDDLETON, deceased, to claim lot 240-3-4. Includes app't. of JOHN G. LUNSDEN as att'y. Signed: Nancy (by mark) Middleton before B. W. SANFORD, J.I.C., 21 June 1843.

FLOYD COUNTY: Lot 54-4-4 Cherokee. Pers. app'd. THOMAS L. MALONE, one of the heirs and legatees of the estate of THOMAS MALONE, dec'd., to claim lot 54-4-4 and lot 36-1-3. Includes app't. of JOHN W. HOOPER as att'y. Signed: T. L. Malone before THOMAS J. VERDERY & N. YARBROUGH, J.I.C. 31 May 1843.

WARREN COUNTY: Lot 1011-3-4 Cherokee. Pers. app'd. GEORGE W. COOPER to claim lot 1011-3-4 drawn by MARTHY COOPER, widow. Because he is moving, COOPER appoints JAMES BAREFIELD att'y. for taking up his grant. Signed: George W. Cooper (by mark) before THOMAS DOWNE (by mark) and JAMES BOADDY, J.P. 26 June 1843.

BIBB COUNTY: Lot 993-3-4 Cherokee. Pers. app'd. PETER SOLOMON, husband of MARIA LOUISE MALONE, orphan, to claim lot 993-3-4 in Floyd County. Includes app't. of JOSHUA G. MOORE as att'y. Signed: Peter Solomon before EDWD. C. WADLY(?), J.S.C., 26 May 1843.

OGLETHORPE COUNTY: Lot 133-6-4 Cherokee. Pers. app'd. WILLIAM W. BUSH, Adm'r. of the estate of WILLIAM G. JENNINGS, dec'd., to claim lot 133-6-4. Includes app't. of JOSEPH H. ECHOLS as att'y. Signed: Wm. W. Bush before J. B. JACKSON, J.P., 30 May 1843.

GWINNETT COUNTY: Lot 106-6-4 Cherokee. Pers. app'd. MARTHA

JONES, widow of THOMAS JONES, dec'd., to claim lot 106-6-4 Chattooga County, and lot 350-3-4 Cobb County. Signed: MARTHA JONES (by mark) before G. W. JONES & LOT BOWDEN, J.P., 8 June 1843.

HEARD COUNTY: Lot 127-16-4 Cherokee. Pers. app'd. LUCY WARD, extrx. of the estate of JOHN M. WARD, dec'd., to claim lot 127-16-4. Includes app't. of GILES S. TOMPKINS as att'y. Signed: Lucy (by mark) Ward before Z. T. TIMMONS and SAML. LANE, J.P., 31 May 1843.

BUTTS COUNTY: Lot 38-16-4 Cherokee. Pers. app'd. LUCY BOND, heir of JOHN M. D. BOND, dec'd., to claim lot 38-16-4. Includes app't. of AUGUSTUS CARGILL as att'y. Signed: Lucy Bond before W. G. McMICHAEL, J.P., 3 June 1843.

HARRIS COUNTY: Lot 280-11-4 Cherokee. Pers. app'd. WILLIAM B. COX to claim lot 280-11-4 drawn by SARAH BLAKE's orphans. Signed: Wm. B. Cox before FLYNN HARGETT, J.P., 19 June 1843. Includes app't. of JOHN LIGHTFOOT as attorney.

WARREN COUNTY: Lot 44-15-4 Cherokee. Pers. app'd. ADAM & STEPHEN JONES to claim lot 44-15-4 drawn by WILLIAM BALES, JR. of Warren Co.; lot 130-21-3 drawn by JABEL ARNETT of Warren Co.; lot 187-21-3 drawn by JABEL ARNETT of Warren Co.; lot 146-25-2 drawn by ALLEN GLOVER of Harris co., lot 99-5-1 drawn by ADAM JONES; and lot 693-19-2 drawn by STEPHEN JONES. Signed: Adam Jones and Stephen Jones before WILLIAM FOWLER, J.P. 16 June 1843.

STEWART COUNTY: Lot 15-15-4 Cherokee. Pers. came DANIEL TERRY, JOHN W. BOWDOIN, SILAS GILMER & WILLIAM KING, "friends" of the drawers of lot 15-15-4 and lot 28-2-1. The drawers were the orphans of NELSON GUNN of Twiggs Co.: ELIZABETH GUNN, now wife of DAVID TERRY: MARY GUNN now wife of JOHN W. BOWDOIN: PAMILIA GUNN, now wife of SILAS GILMORE: and JANE GUNN, now wife of WILLIAM KING. Signed: David Terry, John W. Bowdoin, Silas Gilmer, and William King before JAMES A. HARRIS, J.P. 1 Oct. 1842.

DEKALB COUNTY: Lot 111-17-4 Cherokee. Pers. app'd. JOSEPH

WALKER, one of the legatees of JOHN MURPHEY, dec'd., of Dekalb Co., to claim lot 111-17-4. Includes appt. of W. S. ROGERS of Baldwin Co. as att'y. Signed: Joseph Walker before E. N. CALHOUN & J. B. WILSON, J.P., 21 March 1843.

WILKES COUNTY: Lot 157-17-4 Cherokee. Pers. app'd. NANCY HOLLIDAY, Ex'r. of the estate of ALLEN HOLLIDAY, dec'd. to claim lot 157-17-4 Paulding County. Includes app't. of ALFRED M. HORTON as att'y. Signed: Nancy Holliday bef. WILLIAM D. HOLLIDAY & RICHD. F. HOLLIDAY, J.P., 21 June 1843.

BULLOCH COUNTY: Lot 38-17-4 Cherokee. Pers. app'd. PATRICK LANIER to claim lot 38-17-4 as owner by marriage. Signed: Patrick Lanier before PETER STRICKLAND, J.P. 29 May 1843. Includes app't. of MALACHI DENMARK, as att'y.

PUTNAM COUNTY: Lot 2-17-4 Cherokee. Pers. app'd. MARY A. HARRIS and ELLEN JOHNSON, formerly ELLEN HARRIS, (orphans of MICHAEL HARRIS, dec'd.), to claim lot 2-17-4. Includes app't. of WM. J. DAVIS(?), as att'y. Signed: Mary ANN Harris and Ellen B. Johnson before T. B. HARWELL, J.P. 22 April 1843.

WILKES COUNTY: Lot 32-19-4 Cherokee. Pers. app'd. JAMES ARNOLD, Adm'r. of the estate of WYLIE MAXWELL, dec'd., to claim lot 32-19-4. Includes app't. of ROBERT TOOMBS as att'y. Signed: James Arnold before LEWIS S. BROWN, J.P. 16 June 1843.

RICHMOND COUNTY: Lot 75-19-4 Cherokee. Pers. app'd. THOMAS DUFFY, Adm'r. of the estate of JOHN PHALAN, to claim lot 75-19-4. Includes app't. of JOHN R. ANDERSON as att'y. Signed: Thos. Duffy bef. JAMES HARPER, J.I.C. and JOHN REILLY, 24 June 1843.

MERIWETHER COUNTY: Lot 168-10-4 Cherokee. Pers. app'd. JOSIAH RAINS, to claim lot 168-10-4. Includes appointment of THOS. W. COOK of Baldwin Co. Signed: Josiah Rains bef. DAVIS C. GRESHAM and A. L. ANTHONY, J.P. 23 June 1843.

MERIWETHER COUNTY: Lot 312-11-3 Cherokee. Pers. app'd. JESSE M. DOWNS to claim lot 312-11-3 drawn by

ELIZABETH PACE, minor, of Elbert County. Includes app't. of THOS. M. COOK of Baldwin Co. as att'y. Signed: JESSE M. DOWNS (by mark) before ADAM RAGLAND, J.P., 17 Feb. 1843.

GWINNETT COUNTY: Lot 187-11-3 Cherokee. Pers. app'd. ASA GOBER, Ex'r. of the estate of WILLIAM Y. GOBER, dec'd., to claim lot 187-11-3. Includes app't. of SAMUEL MARTIN as att'y. Signed: Asa Gober before WM. CROWD & LOT ROWDEN, J.P., 10 June 1843.

PUTNAM COUNTY: Lot 129-11-3 Cherokee. Pers. app'd. ROBBERT S. DENHAM and WILLIAM D. BEVIL to claim lot 129-11-3 now Murray County, drawn by JOSEPH BARNES orphans of Putnam County. Signed: R. S. Denham and W. D. Bevil (by mark) before JAMES WRIGHT, J.I.C., 25 Nov. 1845.

JACKSON COUNTY: Lot 166-10-3 Cherokee. Pers. app'd. JOHN VENABLE, one of the heirs (formerly minors) of NATHANIEL VENABLE, of Jackson Co., dec'd., to claim lot 166-10-3. Signed: John Venable before N. H. PENDERGRASS, J.P. 23 July 1850.

COWETA COUNTY: Lot 120-10-3 Cherokee. Pers. came LITTLEBERRY HUDGINS, one of the legatees of SAMUEL WRIGHT of Troup Co., to claim lot 120-10-3. Signed: Littleberry Hudgins (by mark) bef. A. BOWEN, J.P. (no date).

PIKE COUNTY: Lot 126-27-3 Cherokee. Pers. app'd. LANIER BANKSTON to claim lot 126-27-3 drawn by the orphan of JOHN FLING. Signed: L. Bankston bef. ALLISON SPEIR, J.I.C., 30 Nov. 1847.

COBB COUNTY: Lot 124-13-3 Cherokee. Pers. app'd. DAVID W. LINDSAY, one of the heirs of JOHN LINDSEY, dec'd. of Irwin County, to claim lot 124-13-3, now in Murray County. Signed: David W. Lindsey bef. JAMES W. GROVES, J.P. 28 January 1850.

BIBB COUNTY: Lot 1-14-3 Cherokee. GEORGE WALKER, Ex'r. of the estate of JOHN MARTIN, dec'd., to claim lot 1-14-3, now in Murray County. Signed: George Walker before JAMES DENTON, J.P. 2 June 1843.

OGLETHORPE COUNTY: Lot 133-16-3 Cherokee. Pers. app'd. FRAN-
                       CIS BROWN, Adm'trx. of the estate of THOM-
AS R. BROWN, dec'd., to claim lot 133-16-3. Includes app't. of
JOSEPH ECHOLS as att'y. Signed: Francis Brown (by mark) before
SAML. LUMPKIN, J.I.C., and BURDIT FINCH, 14 June 1843.

FLOYD COUNTY: Lot 42-15-3 Cherokee. Pers. app'd. JAMES
                       L. LOGAN to claim lot 42-15-3 drawn by
RANSOM POWELL's orphans of Habersham County, Logan is two thirds
owner. Signed: James L. Logan before WILL A. MOORE, J.P. 30 December 1852.

COBB COUNTY: Lot 68-15-3 Cherokee. Pers. app'd. M. MY-
                       ERS, for the orphans of JOHN M. RUSSELL,
dec'd., of Chat(?) Co., to claim lot 68-15-3. The orphans are now
living in Maryland and in the District of Columbia. Signed: M.
MYERS before SAMUEL C. HOUSE, N.P., 31 March 1853.

                       Lot 209-15-3 Cherokee.
                       "Executive Department Georgia
                       Milledgeville 25th Sept. 1833.

                       It appearing to the Executive from the
Statement BENJAMIN F. CURREY U. States enrolling agent, that the
granting of lot No. 209-15-3 Cherokee, having thereon improvements claimed by WM. HICKS, will not interfere with said claim...
sd. Hicks having enrolled for emigration...Ordered that the Surveyor General issue the plat of said lot in the name of the
drawer and that a grant issue accordingly. Attest. R. A. GREENE,
Secretary."

BIBB COUNTY: Lot 176-16-3 Cherokee. Pers. app'd. SCOTT
                       CRAY, by marriage in right of the heir of
EVELINE HOLZERDORF, an orphan, to claim lot 176-16-3. Signed:
Scott Cray bef. ISAAC HOLMS, N.P., 28 June 1843.

COWETA COUNTY: Lot 278-11-3 Cherokee. Pers. came BRIGGS
                       W. HOPSON to claim lot 278-11-3 drawn by
JAMES MERRILL's orphans of Monroe County, for himself and said
orphans. Signed: Briggs W. Hopson before PEETER HERVIN, J. P.
11 October 1848.

BALDWIN COUNTY: Lot 134-16-3 Cherokee. Pers. app'd. JOHN
                       W. COPPEDGE, one of the administrators of
the estate of CHARLES R. COPPEDGE, dec'd., to claim lot 134-16-3. Signed: John W. Coppedge bef. R. MICKLEJOHN,J.P. 23 June 1843.

TROUP COUNTY: Lot 574-3-3 Cherokee. Pers. app'd. JOHN M.
                        FORBES to claim lot 574-3-3 and, in the
name of CATHARINE FORBES, lot 91-3-2, and, in the name of RICH-
ARD DAVENPORT, lot 1068-3-2. WILLIAM B. SMITH is app'td. agent
for Forbes. Signed: John M. Forbes before GILLUM SCOGIN, J.P.
29 May 1843.

PULASKI COUNTY: Lot 975-3-3 Cherokee. Pers. app'd. JAMES
                        HOLLAND, agent for his mother, CHARITY
BREWER, to claim lot 975-3-3 drawn by her husband, SOLOMON BREW-
ER, dec'd. Signed: James (by mark) Holland bef. D. C. PHAIL,J.P.
27 May 1843.

TALBOT COUNTY: Lot 944-3-3 Cherokee. Pers. app'd. ELIJAH
                        M. LAWRENCE to claim lot 944-3-3 and, for
his wife the former JULIA ANN SHERRARD of Twiggs County, to claim
lot 215-4-of Dooly Co. Signed: E. M. Lawrence bef. WM. HOLT,J.I.C.
25 January 1843.

CARROLL COUNTY: (Lot not given) The Inferior Court, their
                        Honors JAMES H. RODGERS, DANIEL W. PARR,
HINCHEY P. MABRY, WM. G. SPRINGER, & A. M. McWHORTER, order SAN-
DERS W. GRAY, Adm'r. of the estate of ISAAC S. WOOD, dec'd., to
be able to sell the property of the deceased for the heirs. Order
is dated: 5 March 1832. Signed: Wm. S. Parr, Clerk, 14 Jan. 1837.

                        (Lot not given) "I BENJAMIN H. CAMERON do
hereby certify that BENJAMIN P. ROBINSON is the Ex'r. and JANE
WORTHY is the Ext'rx. of THOMAS WORTHY, dec'd. of Troup & that
the will of the sd. dec'd. to be the best of my recollection di-
rects the sale of all the property of sd. Worthy's estate
Milledgeville   11 Nov. 1842. B. H. Cameron, J.I.C."

EFFINGHAM COUNTY: (Lot not given) PAUL MARLOW & BEAL EDWARDS
                        are Ex'rs. of the estate of JOHN DUGGER,
JR., dec'd. March Term 1837. Copy signed by JNO. CHARLSTON,Clk.
Ordy. 7 August 1843.

CHATHAM COUNTY: (Lot not given) Copy of appointment by
                        PETER WORTHINGTON of the City of Savannah
of his wife, MARGARET C. WORTHINGTON, as att'y. Signed: Peter
Worthington bef. R. RAIFORD, J.P. 14 June 1843.

BIBB COUNTY: Lot 88-3-3 Cherokee. SANBURN HARRIS app'ts.
                      SPENCER RILEY att'y. for taking out a
grant for lot 88-3-3 drawn by the orphans of ELIAS HARRIS. Signed: Sanburn Harris bef. WM. BONE, J.P., 16 April 1853, and bef.
NANCY DOYLE (by mark).
                      Pers. app'd. SPENCER RILEY to claim lot
88-3-3 Cherokee which he purchased from SANBURN HARRIS. Signed:
Spencer Riley bef. Wm. Bone, J. P. 16 April 1853.

CHATHAM COUNTY: Lot 161-3-3 Cherokee. Pers. app'd. MARY
                      AUSTON (late MARY KENNEDY) to claim lot
161-3-3. Signed: MARY AUSTIN bef. R. RAIFORD, J.P. 19 June 1843.
Includes app't. of WILLIAM H. PRITCHARD of Baldwin Co. as att'y.

FORSYTH COUNTY: Lot 357-3-3 Cherokee. Pers. app'd. CURTIS
                      GREEN, Adm'r. of JACOB LINDSAY, dec'd.,
to claim lot 357-3-3. Signed: Curtis Green bef. JOHN DICKSON,J.P.
27 May 1843. Includes app't. of JAMES A. GREEN as att'y. before
I. J. MULKEY & JOHN DICKSON, J.P. 27 May 1843.

UPSON COUNTY: Lot 284-3-3 Cherokee. WILLIAM MURCHISON
                      appoints his brother COLEN MURCHISON of
Crawford Co. his att'y. for taking out a grant for lot 284-3-3.
Signed: William MURCHESON bef. EDMUND STEWART, J.P. 2 May 1843.

JEFFERSON COUNTY: Lot 1096-3-3 Cherokee. Pers. app'd. PHILIP
                      S. LEMH, one of the "distributees" of the
estate of DANIEL LEMH, to claim lot 1096-3-3. Includes app't. of
ROGER K. DIXON as att'y. Signed: PHILIP S. LEMH bef. G. J. MILLER,
and WYNETT EASON, J.P. 26 June 1843.

SCREVEN COUNTY: Lot 1406-14-1 Cherokee. Pers. came JAMES
                      LEE, gdn. of orphan MARY LEE, to claim lot
1406-14-1. Signed: James Lee bef. HENRY R. R.(ROBBARDES) J.I.C.
5 June 1843.

MORGAN COUNTY: Lot 1028-2-3 Cherokee. Pers. app'd. HIRAM
                      THOMPSON, husband of one of the orphans of
WILLIAM EVANS of Stewart Co., to claim lot 1028-2-3. Signed: Hiram Thompson bef. JOHN F. WALKER, J.P. 15 June 1843.

                      Lot 1261-4-3 Cherokee;"Macon June 28,1843

                    To the Postmaster at Milledgville haveing
found out tommror being the Last day for taking out grants for
fortunate drawers my husband beeing one and having died without
taking out the grant I hereby make a requst on you not being ac-
quanted with any person in melledgville to be so good as confer
the favour on a poor widow to take out the grant for Lot of Land
drawn by JAMES McGRAW who give in, in Henry County the Capts.
Dist. I am not at this time able to ascertain therefore you will
Confer a favour on a poor widow who has no one to help her by
getting the grant for lot No. 1261 in the 4th Dist. & 3 Section
which if you will take the trouble To Look I think you will find
drawn by Jas. McGraw of Henry Co.
                    Enclosed you will find the money to pay
for the Land In doeing this you will doe a poor widow a favour
that Shall be Remembered
your with due Respect
                    Signed: MELLEY McGRAW"

BIBB COUNTY: Lot 352-17-3 Cherokee. Pers. app'd. MARTHA
                        JONES to claim 2 gold lots drawn by her
husband and which she and her children are now the owners. The
lots are No. 352-17-3 and No. 1219-4-3. Includes app't. of JOS-
EPH B. ANDREWS (ANDRUS?) as att'y. Signed: Martha (by mark) Jones
before LEWIS J. GROCE & JAMES DURTON, J.P.   28 June 1843.

BALDWIN COUNTY: Lot 1197-4-3 Cherokee. Pers. app'd. JAMES
                        C. LOUGHRIDGE, brother of WILFORD R. LOUGH-
RIDGE, a deaf and dumb person, to claim lot 1197-4-3. Signed: J.
C. Loughridge before R. MICKLEJOHN, J.P.   21 June 1843.

JASPER COUNTY: Lot 45-4-3 Cherokee. OBADIAH R. BELCHER
                        appoints AMOS WARD of Morgan Co. as att'y.
to take out the grant to lot 45-4-3 drawn by OBADIAH BELCHER, deceased, of which OBADIAH R. BELCHER is Ex'r. of his estate.
Signed: Obadiah R. Belcher bef. JAMES H. SHI, A. A. MADDOX, and
JOHN D. WELLS, J.P.   12 June 1843.

JASPER COUNTY: Lot 946-2-3 Cherokee. Pers. app'd. THOMAS
                        K. SLAUGHTER to claim lot 946-2-3 drawn by
HENRY SLAUGHTER's orphans. The orphans are WILLIAM A. SLAUGHTER,
THOMAS K. SLAUGHTER, & ISAAC SLAUGHTER. Includes app't. of EDWARD
A. BRODDUS as att'y. Signed: Thos. K. Slaughter bef. WILLIAM W.
BARNETT & THOS. J. SMITH, J.I.C., 5 June 1843.

MONROE COUNTY: Lot 318-9-3 Cherokee. MARY HAMILTON, CAR-
                        OLINE HAMILTON & T. T. HAMILTON, because
we are moving, app't. DANIEL GODARD att'y. to claim lot 318-9-3
drawn by DAVID HAMILTON's orphans of Meriwether County. Signed:

THOMAS J. OLIVER, T. T. HAMILTON and CAROLINE HAMILTON before HENRY McCOY and W. D. DUNCAN, J.P., 4 March 1848.

NEWTON COUNTY: Lot 315-8-3 Cherokee. Pers. app'd. the orphans of ELIJAH CRAWFORD of Dekalb County to appoint PUOMEDUS REYNOLDS att'y. to claim lot 315-8-3. Signed: JEFFERSON (by mark) CRAWFORD, JABOC N. WIPPER & JAMES (by mark) CRAWFORD before THOS. S. BAKER, October 1853.

GORDON COUNTY: Lot 121-8-3 Cherokee. Pers. app'd. FRANCIS M. REESE, one of the orphans of REDMAN REESE, dec'd. of Warren County, to claim lot 121-8-3 for himself and his brothers and sisters. Signed: F. M. Reese before G. W. RANSOM, J.P., 12 February 1853.

COWETA COUNTY: Lot 121-9-3 Cherokee. Pers. app'd. ALEXANDER FLOYD, gdn. of DOCTOR W. DIAL, to claim lot 121-9-3, now in Murray County. Includes app't. of LEVI NEWTON as att'y. Signed: Alexander Floyd before A. (ALANSON) BOEN, J.P., 27 March 1843.

RICHMOND COUNTY: Lot 495-2-3 Cherokee. Pers. app'd. JAMES W. DAVIES, legal representative of the estate of ELEANOR L. NESBITT, dec'd., to claim lot 495-2-3. WILLIAM H. PRITCHARD is app'td. att'y. Signed: James W. Davies before BENJ. HALL, J.P. 29 June 1843.

GREENE COUNTY: Lot 1248-2-3 Cherokee. Pers. app'd. JOSHUA BARNES, legal Adm'r. for the estate of his father (NATHAN BARNES), to claim lot 1248-2-3 and, for NOAH BARNES, dec'd., lot 73-9-4. Signed: Joshua Barnes before JOHN J. HOWELL, J.I.C. 24 June 1843.

BURKE COUNTY: Lot 1142-2-3 Cherokee. Pers. app'd. WILLIAM P. TAYLOR, lawful gdn. of the heirs of ABSALOM TAYLOR, dec'd., to claim lot 1142-2-3. Includes app't. of WM. H. PRITCHARD of Baldwin Co. as att'y. Signed: William P. Taylor before N. W. TAYLOR & ELBERT D. TAYLOR, J.P. 12 June 1843.

CHATHAM COUNTY: Lot Lot 798-2-3 Cherokee. Pers. came Mrs. MARIA R. DAVIS, Adm'trx. of the estate of JOHN SPEAKMAN and mother and gdn. of his orphans, to claim lot

798-2-3 and lot 289-7-1. Includes app't. of JOHN W. EXLEY of Effingham County as att'y. Signed: MARIA R. DAVIS before JOSEPH FELT, J.P., 2 June 1843.

BALDWIN COUNTY: Lot 178-19-3 Cherokee. Pers. app'd. JOHN BUCHAN to claim lot 178-19-3 and lot 1206-5-1 as owner in part. Signed: John Buchan before ALFRED M. HORTON, N.P., 26 June 1843.

TALBOT COUNTY: Lot 69-19-3 Cherokee. Pers. came JEREMIAH C. McCANTZ to claim lot 69-19-3 drawn by the orphans of WILLIAM McCRARY. McCANTZ's wife is one of the orphans. His att'y. is JAMES STALLINGS. Signed: J. C. McCantz before RICHD. HATT, J.P. 29 March 1843.

GWINNETT COUNTY: Lot 545-21-3 Cherokee. NATHAN L. HUTCHINS claims lot 545-21-3 for the orphans of JOHN PEAVY as their friend and in good faith and without interest in said grant. Signed: N. L. Hutchins before JESSE MURPHEY, J.P. 17 August 1852.

JACKSON COUNTY: Lot 292-21-3 Cherokee. Pers. app'd. MATTHEW ELLISON, Adm'r. of the owner of lot 292-21-3 to claim sd. lot. Includes app't. of WM. J. PARKS of Franklin Co. as att'y. Signed: Matthew Ellison before A. H. HENDERSON, J.P. and JAS. W. SHANKLE, 16 March 1843.

BALDWIN COUNTY: Lot 322-12-3 Cherokee. Pers. app'd. BURCH M. ROBERTS, Ex'r. of the owner of lot 322-12-3 to claim sd. lot. Signed: B. M. Roberts before Alfred M. Horton, N.P., 2 May 1843.

BALDWIN COUNTY: Lot 765-20-3 Cherokee. Pers. app'd. WOODSON HUBBARD, Adm'r. of the estate of CLARBORN KEMP, to claim lot 765-20-3. Signed: Woodson Hubbard before Alfred M. Horton, N.P., (no date).

BALDWIN COUNTY: Lot 364-19-3 Cherokee. Pers. app'd. ROBERT M. THOMPSON, Adm'r. of the estate of the owner of lot 364-19-3 and lot 1237-2-1. Signed: Robt. M. Thompson before A. M. Horton, N.P., 30 June 1843.

BALDWIN COUNTY: Lot 684-3-3 Cherokee. Pers. app'd. JOHN B. PARKER, Adm'r. of the estate of the owner of lot 684-3-3 to claim sd. lot. Signed: John B. Parker before Alfred M. Horton, N.P., 13 April 1843.

BALDWIN COUNTY: Lot 681-3-3 Cherokee. Pers. app'd. FRANCIS C. TAYLOR to claim lot 681-3-3 as Ex'r. of the estate of the drawer. Signed: FRANCIS CORBETT TAYLOR before Alfred M. Horton, N.P., 19 June 1843.

BALDWIN COUNTY: Lot 649-20-3 Cherokee. Pers. app'd. EVIRARD HAMILTON, the Adm'r. of the estate of DUKE HAMILTON, to claim lot 649-20-3. Signed: E. Hamilton before Alfred M. Horton, N.P., 19 June 1843.

HEARD COUNTY: Lot 1096-21-3 Cherokee. Pers. app'd. DEMPSEY PITMAN, one of the Ex'rs. of I. PITMAN, to claim lot 1096-21-3 as one of the owners. Signed: Dempsey Pitman before SAMUEL M. COLE, J.P., 6 April 1850.

PUTNAM COUNTY: Lot 900-20-3 Cherokee. Pers. app'd. STEPHEN COPELAND, husband of LUCY STEWART and agent of JESSE STEWART, orphan of JESSE STEWART, dec'd., to claim lot 900-20-3. Signed: Stephen Copeland (by mark) before WM. TURNER, J.P., 23 June 1843.

BALDWIN COUNTY: Lot 1244-21-3 Cherokee. Pers. app'd. THOMAS H. WYNN to claim lot 1244-21-3 as owner in part. Signed: Thomas H. Wynn before Alfred M. Horton, N.P. 7 April 1843.

BALDWIN COUNTY: Lot 789-19-3 Cherokee. Pers. app'd. JAMES BALKCOM to claim lot 789-19-3 as Adm'r. of the owner. Signed: James Balkcom before Alfred M. Horton, N.P. 28 June 1843.

BALDWIN COUNTY: Lot 769-20-3 Cherokee. Pers. app'd. J. A. R. KENNEDY to claim lot 769-2-3 as Ex'r. of the drawer. Signed: James A. R. Kennedy before A. M. Horton, N.P., 30 June 1843.

JEFFERSON COUNTY: Lot 32-21-3 Cherokee. Pers. app'd. FERRIBE

COOKSY, the only surviving heir of CALEB COOKSY, minor, to claim lot 32-21-3 in Cass County. Signed: FERRIBE COOKSY (by mark) before FR. A. HAYLES, J.P., 5 Jan. 1844.

JEFFERSON COUNTY: Lot 997-20-3 Cherokee. Pers. app'd. W. M. WOODS, husband of ELIZABETH SLONE, to claim lot 997-20-3. Signed. W. M. Woods before (illegible), N.P. 13 February 1854.

WARREN COUNTY: Lot 284-20-3 Cherokee. Pers. app'd. ROBERT RONEY, for FRANSEY WATSON (now his wife), URIAH WATSON & LURENIA WATSON (now LAURENA BROOKS) to claim lot 284-20-3. Signed: Robert Roney (by mark) before ELISHA PURYMAN, J.P., 24 January 1850.

BALDWIN COUNTY: Lot 136-23-3 Cherokee. Pers. app'd. HIRAM DUNBAR to claim lot 136-23-3 as Adm'r. of ASOPH HALL, dec'd. Signed: Hiram Dunbar before Alfred M. Horton, N.P., 10 May 1843.

BALDWIN COUNTY: Lot 854-4-3 Cherokee. Pers. app'd. M. B. JOHNSON to claim lot 854-4-3 now in Cass County, being owner in part. Signed: MELANDOR B. JOHNSON before P. M. COMPTON, N.P., 8 December 1851.

BALDWIN COUNTY: Lot 59-13-3 Cherokee. Pers. app'd. SEABORN HALL to claim lot 59-13-3. Signed: Seaborn Hall before Aldred M. Horton, N.P., 1 March 1844.

BALDWIN COUNTY: Lot 106-4-3 Cherokee. Pers. app'd. WILLIAM HEFLEN to claim lot 106-4-3. Signed: William Heflen before Alfred M. Horton, N.P., 22 March 1843.

BALDWIN COUNTY: Lot 1267-20-3 Cherokee. Pers. app'd. WILLIAM BRICE to claim lot 1267-20-3 as Ex'r. of the estate of the owner. Signed: William BRYCE, N.P. 1 June 1843.

BALDWIN COUNTY: Lot 1052-21-3 Cherokee. Pers. app'd. ZADOCK RACHEL to claim lot 1052-21-3 as Adm'r. of the estate of the owner. Signed: Zadock Rachel before Alfred M. Horton, N.P. 27 January 1843.

Lot 19-15-3 Cherokee. Pers. app'd. JAMES GAMBLE, Ex'r. of the estate of JAMES RUSSELL, SR. of Henry County, to claim lots 19-15-3; 264-20-2 and 203-1-1. Signed: James Gamble before MIDDLETON HILL, J.P. 19th April 1843.

JACKSON COUNTY: Lot 177-5-3 Cherokee. Pers. app'd. FRANCIS T. COOK to claim lot 177-5-3 and, also, lot 726-18-2 drawn by JOSHUA JUMON's orphans, of Clark County. Signed: F. T. Cook before J. B. NABUS, J.P., 1 September 1846.

HARRIS COUNTY: Lot 43-19-1 Cherokee. Pers. app'd. JOHN SHOLARS, agent for MARSHALL's orphans of Jasper County, to claim lot 122, 13th Dist. of Muscogee. Signed: John Sholars before DENNIS MILLER, J.P. 12 June 1843. (Written at the bottom of the page is "43-19-1 and 291-4-4", which is apparently reference to other lots drawn in the Cherokee and Gold Lotteries of 1832.)

WALKER COUNTY: Lot 114-19-1 Cherokee. Pers. app'd. JOSEPH M. WARDLAW to claim lot 114-19-1 having married one of the orphans who drew the sd. lot. Signed: Joseph M. Wardlaw before JOHN CALDWELL, J.I.C., 10 February 1854.

MORGAN COUNTY: Lot 54-18-1 Cherokee. Pers. app'd. CHARLES THOMPSON to claim lot 54-18-1, purchased by ALEXANDER STEWART; lot 506-4-1, drawn by himself; lot 76-2-2 purchased from the orphans of ROBERT C. RAWKINS, who are of age; lot 235-4-of Muscogee, now Marion, also drawn by sd. orphans; & lot 697-3-3, drawn by JAMES STUDDARD. Signed: Charles Thompson before A. B. BOSTWICK, J.P., 17 June 1843.

MORGAN COUNTY: Lot 47-18-1 Cherokee. Pers. app'd. JOHN P. EVANS, one of the orphans of ARDEW EVANS, dec'd. and gdn. of the legatees of sd. Evans, to claim lot 47-18-1 now in Union County and lot 60-14-1 now in Lumpkin Co. Includes app't. of DAVID DEMOREST as att'y. Signed: John P. Evans before JOHN RABUN, J.I.C., 3 June 1843.

WALTON COUNTY: Lot 204-18-1 Cherokee. Pers. app'd. CHARLES W. BUCHANAN, one of the legal heirs of JOHN D. BUCHANAN, dec'd., to claim lot 204-18-1. Signed: C.W.

BUCHANAN before GEORGE J. HEWET (?), J.P., 1 June 1843.

PIKE COUNTY: Lot 214-18-1 Cherokee. Pers. app'd. THOMAS A. TRICE, agent for ZACHARIAH TRICE,to claim lot 214-18-1. Includes app't. of EZEKIEL TRICE of Baldwin Co. as att'y. Signed: Thos. C. Trice before JOSEPH SCOTT, JR., and A. A. GAULDING, J.P., 16 June 1843.

MC INTOSH COUNTY: Lot 251-18-1 Cherokee. Pers. app'd. SELINA BLOUNT, formerly SELINA SMITH, sister of SHADDRACK SMITH, dec'd., to claim lot 251-18-1. She appoints JOS. E. TOWNSEND as her agent. Signed: Selina Blount before ARMOUND LEFILS, J.P., 15 June 1843.

RICHMOND COUNTY: Lot 258-17-1 Cherokee. Pers. app'd. JOSEPH JAMES, gdn. of JOHN M. JAMES, an idiot and infant son, to claim lot 258-17-1. Signed: Joseph (by mark) James before A. J. MILLER, N.P., 30 June 1843.

WASHINGTON COUNTY: Lot 182-17-1 Cherokee. Pers. app'd. JOHN B. MASSEY, gdn. of the orphans of CALVIN HAMELTON (to wit SARAH ANN HAMELTON, ADEIR HAMELTON, IRWIN HAMELTON & JOSEPH HAMELTON) to claim lot 182-17-1. Signed: John B. Massey before A. P. PEACOCK, J.I.C., 21 June 1843.

TALBOT COUNTY: Lot 143-17-1 Cherokee. Pers. app'd. EDWARD GIDDENS, Adm'r. of the estate of WALTER STONE, dec'd., to claim lot 143-17-1. Includes app't. of CHARLES STILLWELL & MARION BETHUME as att'ys. Signed: Edward Giddens bef. J. C. GOODWIN & G. B. CLAY, J.P., 19 May 1843.

WARREN COUNTY: Lot 84-17-1 Cherokee. Pers. app'd. STODDARD W. SMITH to claim lot 84-17-1, now in Union Co., drawn by JOHN S. HIGDON's orphans, for himself, MATHEW SHIELDS, and,JOHN B. HIGDON. Includes app't. of JAMES A. CHAPMAN as att'y. Signed: Stoddard W. Smith bef. THOS. W. SHIVERS and PETER CODY, J.P., 15 June 1843.

WILKINSON COUNTY: Lot 247-17-1 Cherokee. Pers. came ALAN EVANSON, husband of VIENNA MURRY, an orphan and owner of half of the lot drawn by HARTWELL MURRY, dec'd. to claim lot 247-17-1. Signed: ALLEN EAVERSON before WILLIAM GAR-

RATT, J.P., 24 June 1843.

CHATHAM COUNTY: Lot 71-17-1 Cherokee. Pers. app'd. JOHN MURPHY of Savannah, husband of the widow of PHILIP KENNEDY of McIntosh County. Signed: John Murphy before (illegible) WILLIAM, J.I.C.C.C., 25 May 1843.

TALBOT COUNTY: Lot 80-17-1 Cherokee. Pers. app'd. DEXTER G. KILLUM who saith that he was a militia captain at the time of the drawing of the land Lottery and that no one named PETER CASTER was living there but that there was a PETER EASTER. Signed: Dexter KELLUM before WM. STALLING, J.I.C. 22 January 1839.

FAYETTE COUNTY: Lot 255-16-1 Cherokee. Pers. came WILLIAM MILES, Ex'r. of the estate of AARON TILMAN, dec'd., to claim lot 255-16-1 and lot 808-2-3. Signed: Wm Miles before G. C. KING, J.P., 21 June 1843.

EARLY COUNTY: Lot 141-16-1 Cherokee. Pers. app'd. LUCRETIA MILLER, mother of THOMAS MILLER, HENRY MILLER, FRANCIS MILLER (now the wife of WILLIAM S. GAY), and LUCINDA MILLER (wife of WILLIAM G. GILMON), to claim lot 141-16-1, now in Union County, and lot 269-10-4, now in Dade County. She claims this land for sd. orphans of LEWIS MILLER of Early Co. Signed: Lucretia Miller (by mark) bef. D. G. HOLLINGSWORTH, J.P. 14 January 1854.

NEWTON COUNTY: Lot 105-16-1 Cherokee. Pers. app'd. MARY ESTES, widow of JAMES ESTES, dec'd., natural guardian of the minors of JAMES ESTES to claim lot 105-16-1 and lot 153-7-4; lot 148-17-1; lot 262-26-2; lot 889-21-3; lot 1115-11-1 and lot 87-6-2. Includes app't. of SIMEON ESTES as attorney. Signed: Mary (by mark) Estes bef. GEORGE HAYS, J.P. 13 June 1843.

EARLY COUNTY: Lot 151-16-1 Cherokee. Pers. app'd. RICHARD GIST, gdn. of the orphans of JOSEPH BRYAN (to wit JAMES E., SUSAN P. & MARY G. BRYAN) to claim lot 151-16-1. Includes app't. of BOLLING H. ROBINSON as att'y. Sgn: Richd. GRIST bef. JNO. H. JONES & WILLIAM CASTLEBERRY, J.I.C. 22 March 1843.

MADISON COUNTY: Lot 64-16-1 Cherokee. Pers. app'd. ROBERT
                       WILLIAMS to claim lot 64-16-1 as owner of
one share. Included app't. of JAMES POLBE as att'y. Signed: Robert Williams, SR (by mark) bef. ISHAM WILLIAMS, J.P. 10 Apr. 1843.

TATTNALL COUNTY: Lot 261-15-1 Cherokee. Pers. app'd. REBECCA E. GRAY to claim lot 261-15-1 drawn by
DANIEL GRAY's orphans. Signed: Rebecca Gray bef. JOHN J. GRAY, J.P., 10 June 1843.

BURKE COUNTY: Lot 240-15-1 Cherokee. Pers. came ELISHA
                       HAYMAN, Ex'r. of the estate of STEPHEN
HAYMAN, dec'd., to claim lot 240-15-1. Signed: Elisha Hayman bef. HOMER V. MULKY, J.P. 30 May 1843.

BAKER COUNTY: Lot 245-15-1 Cherokee. Pers. app'd. EXEKIEL PIERCE, Adm'r. of the estate of WILLIAM PIERCE, dec'd., to claim lot 245-15-1 and lot 271-4-3. Signed: Ezekiel PIERCE before JOHN COLLEY, J.P., 13 May 1843.

MORGAN COUNTY: Lot 150-15-1 Cherokee. Pers. app'd. JAMES
                       FARELL, legal representative of EDY FERRILL, dec'd., his mother, to claim lot 149-1-4 (no.'s don't agree with above...ED.) Includes app't. of DENNIS DEMERS as att'y. Signed: JAMES FARRELL before ELIJAH E. JONES, J.I.C., 3 June 1843.

APPLING COUNTY: Lot 415-15-1 Cherokee. Pers. app'd. JESSE
                       SUMMERALL, Adm'r. of the estate of NEEL W.
SUMERALL, dec'd., to claim lot 415-15-1 drawn by ELKANAN McCALL and lot 346-16-4 drawn by JOHN BRACK. Signed: Jesse Summerall before WILLIAM WILLIAMS, J.I.C., 10 June 1843.

TWIGGS COUNTY: Lot 155-15-1 Cherokee. Pers. app'd. SARAH
                       CLARK, widow of JAMES CLARK, dec'd., to
claim lot 170-13-4 and lot 155-15-1, for herself and five minor children. Signed: Sarah (by mark) Clark bef. WM. S. KELLY, J.P. 2 June 1843.

UPSON COUNTY: Lot 323-15-1 Cherokee. Pers. app'd. JOHN
                       C. DRAKE, husband of MARY ANN FLEWELLEN,
an orphan, to claim lot 323-15-1. Includes app't. of WILLIAM G. ANDREWS as att'y. Signed: John C. Drake before WM. D. JOHNSTON

and WM. A. COBB, J.P., 29 March 1843.

JONES COUNTY: Lot 368-15-1 Cherokee. Pers. app'd. JOHN WILLIAMSON, one of the distributees of estate of GREEN WILLIAMSON, dec'd., to claim lot drawn by Green Williamson. Includes app't. of JOHN WILLIAMSON as att'y. Signed: John Williamson before LEWIS DAVIS & GREEN B. WILLIAMSON, J.P. 26 June 1843.

HOUSTON COUNTY: Lot 130-15-1 Cherokee. WASHINGTON SANGESTER, ELIZABETH J. SANGESTER, ALLEN HOWARD and ROBERT SANGESTER, app't. JOHN SANGESTER att'y. to take out the grants to the lots that they won as the orphans of PETER SANGESTER. Signed: Washington Sangester (by mark), Elizabeth Sangester (by mark), Allen Howard (by mark), and Robert Sangester (by mark), before MICHAEL HOWARD, J.P., 1 May 1843.

PULASKI COUNTY: Lot 45-15-1 Cherokee. Pers. app'd. MARTHA ROEBUCK, one of the orphans of JAMES ROEBUCK, dec'd., to claim lot 45-15-1 and lot 27-15-2. Includes appointment of LUALLIN ROEBUCK as att'y. Signed: MARTHA N. ROEBUCK before THOMAS B. HOWELL and JOHN B. BUSH, J.P., 26 June 1843.

MORGAN COUNTY: Lot 221-15-1 Cherokee. Pers. app'd. JOEL W. BUTTS, one of the legatees of his mother, CELIA WILKERSON, to claim lot 221-15-1. Signed: Joel W. Butts before JOHN ROBSEN, J.I.C. (no date).

BALDWIN COUNTY: Lot 138-15-1 Cherokee. Pers. came THOMAS F. GREEN, Ex'r. of THOMAS CROWDER, dec'd. of Hancock County, to claim lot 138-15-1. Signed: Thomas F. Green before J. R. ANDERSON, J.I.C., 29 June 1843.

NEWTON COUNTY: Lot 32-15-1 Cherokee. Pers. app'd. CHARLES H. SANDERS to claim lot 32-15-1 drawn by himself. Also lot 342-3-4 drawn by ELISHA BURKS. Also for lot No. 272-13-of Dooly Co. (latter lot was crossed out) that was drawn by his father, RICHARD SANDERS. Also lot 845-21-2 drawn by his mother, RACHEL SANDERS, widow, since dec'd. The latter lots belong to the legal representative of sd. estate: LOVERD MOORE, ZECHARIAH COLLEY, JAMES SANDERS, BRIDGER SANDERS, SEABORN SANDERS, MOSES WATSON & CHARLES H. SANDERS. Signed: Chs. H. Sanders before COLUMBUS D. PACE, J.I.C. 2 June 1843.

MUSCOGEE COUNTY: Lot 1411-14-1 Cherokee. Pers. app'd. WILLIAM T. DINSON (DIMON?), to claim lot 1411-14-1 drawn by himself in Talbot Co. and lot 50-15-2 drawn by his father, ABEL DIMON. Includes app't. of KENNETH McKENZIE as attorney. Signed: William T. Dimon before GEON(?) TERRENTIN, J.P. 15 June 1843.

WAYNE COUNTY: Lot 1266-14-1 Cherokee. Pers. app'd. WILLIAM H. PARRISH, husband of ELIZA WELLS of Camden County, to claim lot 1266-14-1. Signed: Wm. H. Parrish before JAMES HIGHSMITH, J.I.C., 31 January 1854.

MC INTOSH COUNTY: Lot 1018-14-1 Cherokee. JOHN A. ODENA, administrator of the estate of JOSEPH DALONVILLE, to claim lot 1018-14-1 and to app't. E. A. TENNSEND as att'y. Signed: John A. Odena before ARMOND LEFITZ, J.P., 15 June 1843.

BALDWIN COUNTY: Lot 964-14-1 Cherokee. Pers. app'd. JOHN ADKINS to claim lot 964-14-1 as agent of the owner; lot 1213-19-2 as representative of the heirs of JOSEPH AKINS, dec'd.; lot 226-10-4 for himself; and lot 266-10-2 by special power of att'y. by the owner. Signed: John Adkins before ALFRED M. HORTON, N.P., 28 June 1843.

BALDWIN COUNTY: Lot 642-14-1 Cherokee. Pers. app'd. JAMES EPPINGER who claims that he had a certificate that revealed that JOHN LANGLY emigrated from lot 642-14-1 and that he has received rent from two white men who cultivated a part of the lot. Signed: Jas. Eppinger before GEO. W. MURRAY, N.P., 26 Sept. 1833.

TROUP COUNTY: Lot 491-14-1 Cherokee. EDMUND JACKSON appoints HENRY T. SMART of Chambers Co., Alabama his att'y. for taking out a grant to lot 491-14-1. Signed: Edmond Jackson before RILEY G. INGRAHAM (?) & THOMAS M. WYATT, J.P., 24 June 1843.

PUTNAM COUNTY: Lot 407-14-1 Cherokee. Pers. app'd. ADOLPHUS A. UNDERWOOD, Ex'r. of the estate of ISAAC UNDERWOOD, dec'd., to claim lot 407-14-1, now in Forsyth Co. Signed: A. A. Underwood bef. LEWIS H. LINCH, J.P. 19 June 1843.

JASPER COUNTY: Lot 283-14-1 Cherokee. Pers. app'd. FRAN-
                       CIS, one of the orphans of FRANCIS JINKINS
dec'd., to claim lot 283-14-1 as one of the owners. Includes appointment of ROBERT _ELLUM as att'y. Signed: Francis Jenkins bef.
JOSEPH C. LITTLE & HUGH P. KILPATRICK, J.P. 2 June 1843.

JACKSON COUNTY: Lot 281-14-1 Cherokee. Pers. app'd. BAIL-
                       EY CHANDLER to claim lot 281-14-1 as a
judgement creditor. Includes app't. of ROBERT MOORE as att'y.
Signed: Bailey Chandler before G. WITHORS & B. F. BURSON, J.P.
2 June 1843.

HABERSHAM COUNTY: Lot 273-14-1 Cherokee. Pers. app'd. DAVID
                       MULKEY, one of the lawful heirs of ELIZA-
BETH MULKEY, dec'd., widow, to claim lot 273-14-1. Signed: David
Mulkey before J. TAYLOR, J.P., 6 May 1843.

NEWTON COUNTY: Lot 266-14-1 Cherokee. Pers. app'd. DANIEL
                       MOORE & THOMAS KITCHENS to claim lot 266-
14-1 drawn by JOHNSON SAWYER of Putnam Co. Includes app't. of
JOHN WELB as att'y. Signed: Thomas Kitchens and Daniel Q.(?)
Moore before JOHN L. SAWYER, J.P., 16 June 1843.

SCREVEN COUNTY: Lot 22-14-1 Cherokee. Pers. app'd. ROBERT
                       LUNDAY, Adm'r. of the estate of McLIN LUN-
DAY, dec'd., to claim lot 22-14-1. Signed: Robert Lunday before
JAMES LEE, J.P., 27 April 1843.

BURKE COUNTY:
Birdsville   Lot 240-14-1 Cherokee. "Personally appear-
                       ed before me H. P. JONES who declars on
oath...that, HENRY HANBERRY one of the heirs of MOSES HANBERRY,
dec'd., 74 Dist., Burke Co., Ga., who drew lot No. 240-14-1 request Him, for the benefit, of himself, and the ballance of the
Heirs, consisting of his Mother and two other Brothers...to take
out said lot, HENRY HANBERRY is now living with sd. Lot, Henry
Hanberry is now living with sd. Jones sworn to and subscribed.
this 27th May 1843. Signed: Henry P. Jones bef. N. BULLARD, J.P."

LUMPKIN COUNTY: Lot 530-13N-1 Cherokee. Pers. app'd. SILAS
                       B. PALMOUR to claim the undivided half of
lot 530-13-1, north half, drawn by WM. ROBERTS orphans of Coweta

County. Signed: T. B. PALMOUR before W. M. VARNUM, N.P. 13 May 1849.

COBB COUNTY: Lot 22-1-1 Cherokee. Pers. app'd. DAVID W. LINDSAY, one of the orphans of JOHN LINDSAY, dec'd., of Irwin County, to claim lot 22-1-1 now in Forsyth County. Signed: David W. Lindsay before JAMES W. GROVES, J.P. 15 June 1849.

TALBOT COUNTY: Lot 480-13N-1 Cherokee. Pers. app'd. JOHN B. ARNOLD, one of the orphans of WILLIAM W. ARNOLD, to claim lot 480-13-1. Signed: Jno. B. Arnold before JOSEPH JACKSON, J.P., 16 June 1843.

CHATHAM COUNTY: Lot 463-13S-1 Cherokee. Pers. app'd. FREDERICK E. TEBEAU, the only surviving ex'r. of the estate of GEORGE HERB, to claim lot 463-13-1-S½ drawn by HERB's orphans. Includes app't. of JOHN W. EXLEY of Effingham co. Signed: F. E. Tebeau before JOSEPH PELT, J.P., 30 May 1843.

BALDWIN COUNTY: Lot 436-13N-1 Cherokee. Pers. app'd. EZEKIEL GARDNER to claim lot 436-13-1-N½ as owner in part. Signed: Ezekiel Gardner before Alfren M. Horton, N.P., 20 June 1843.

BALDWIN COUNTY: Lot 459-13N-1 Cherokee. Pers. app'd. A. W. SMITH to claim lot 459-13-1-N½ as owner in part. Signed: A. W. Smith before ALLEN EDWARDS, J.P., of Twiggs Co., 17 May 1843.

JASPER COUNTY: Lot 432-13-1 Cherokee. Pers. came WILLIAM P. HARDY, agent of LEE SWANN of Alabama, to claim lot 432-13-1 and lot 189-27-3. Signed: Wm. P. Hardy bef. JOHN M. KING, J.P., 28 June 1843.

FAYETTE COUNTY: Lot 421-13N-1 Cherokee. Pers. came FANNY SCALES, wife and Ext'rx. of JOEL SCALES, dec'd., to claim lot 421-13-1. T. BYRON is app'td. agent Signed: Fanny Scales(by mark) bef. JOHN S. DODD, J.P., 15 June 1843.

FRANKLIN COUNTY: Lot 367-13N-1 Cherokee. Pers. app'd. JAMES McDONALD, ALEXANDRIA P. McDONALD, AARON

SANDERS & WESTLEY WILEY to claim certain lots:
Lot 367-13-1-N½ owned by JAMES McDONALD
Lot 398-17-2 owned by ALEXANDRIA McDONALD
Lot 503-13 ___ owned by AARON SANDERS
Lot 214-6-1 owned by WESTLEY WILEY (drawn by JOHNSON WILEY) Includes app't. of JOSEPH CUNNINGHAM of Jackson County as att'y. Signed: James McDonald, Alexander McDonald (note: in the text, the name is spelled "Alexandria"), Aaron Sanders, and Wesley Wiley before MENYARD SANDERS, J.P., 13 June 1843.

JACKSON COUNTY: Lot 357-13S-1 Cherokee. Pers. app'd. AUGUSTIN NIBLOCK, Adm'r. of the estate of THOMAS NIBLOCK, dec'd., to claim lot 357-13-1. Signed: Augustin Niblock before S. J. NIBLOCK, J.P., 22 May 1843.

CHATHAM COUNTY: Lot 348-13S-1 Cherokee. Pers. app'd. SOPHIA M. MEGAN, Ext'rx. of the estate of SAMUEL DIBBLE, dec'd., to claim lot 348-13-1-S½. Includes app't. of WILLIAM H. PRITCHARD of Baldwin Co. as att'y. Signed: Sophia E. Megan (by mark) before R. RAIFORD, J.P., 22 June 1843.

LUMPKIN COUNTY: Lot 337-13S-1 Cherokee. "I JAMES DONOHAO, Indian Agent for said County do certify that Lot 337 and 400 in the 13th Dist. of the 1st section south was Emigrated by RIAL HUBARD and there is no other Native living here on given under My hand this 19th of December 1833.
Signed: James Donohao
Indian Agent for Lumpkin Co.
Do also certify that there is no Native Claiming said Lots."

TALIAFERRO COUNTY: Lot 281-13S-1 Cherokee. Pers. app'd. JAMES WILKINSON, agent for the minors of CALN(?) WILKINSON, dec'd., to claim lot 281-13-1. Includes app't. of ALEXANDER H. STEPHENS as att'y. Signed: J. F. WILKINSON bef. JAMES FRAEME & JESSE WOODALL, J.P., 5 June 1843.

WASHINGTON COUNTY: Lot 231-13-1 Cherokee. Pers. app'd. NANCY PRICE, widow of JOSHUA PRICE, to claim lot 231-13-1. JOSHUA PRICE had four minor children: NANCY ANN, ARRIAIA, DAVID SOLOMON, & GEORGE WASHINGTON PRICE. He also had SARAH PRICE, who has married PHINIAS SMITH: BETSY JANE PRICE, who married ROBERT CAULLY; MARY ELKINS PRICE, who married GODFREY WILLIAMS: & JAMES PRICE, who left the State of Georgia several years ago. All of the above are the heirs of JOSHUA PRICE. Signed: Nancy Price bef. GREEN WIDDON, J.P., 27 June 1843.

WALTON COUNTY: Lot 210-13N-1 Cherokee. Pers. app'd. PETER
                        W. KILGORE to claim lot 210-13-1, now in
Lumpkin County, drawn by ROBERT MATHIS orphans. Includes app't.
of JAMES V. LECKLIN as att'y. Signed: Peter W. Kilgore before
WM. L. LACKLIN & WARREN J. HILL, J.I.C., 13 June 1843.

WALTON COUNTY: Lot 203-13-1 Cherokee. Pers. app'd. B. B.
                        RANSOM, agent for WILLIAM McMICHAEL of
Alabama to claim lot 203-13-1 and lot 195-1-1. Includes app't. of
JAMES JACKSON as att'y. Signed: BEVERLY B. RANSOM before BENJAMIN
J. HILL & NEH JOHNSON, J.I.C., 2 June 1843.

LUMPKIN COUNTY: Lot 179-13S-1 Cherokee. JAMES DONOHAO, In-
                        dian Agent for Lumpkin County, certifies
that lot 179-13-1 South was "emigrated" by JOHN DOWNING, a native
who has removed to Arkansas. Signed: James Donohoa, Indian Agent
23 November 1833.

HENRY COUNTY: Lot 166-13S-1 Cherokee. Pers. app'd. JACK-
                        SON J. MOORE, one of the orphans of ALEX-
ANDER MOORE, dec'd., to claim lot 166-13-1, south half. The other
orphans are ELIZABETH THOMAS, formerly ELIZABETH MOORE: ZACHARIAH
MIDDLEBROOKS, in right of his wife MARY MIDDLEBROOK_ (formerly
MARY MOORE): THOMAS J. MOORE & WILLIAM J. MOORE. Signed: Jackson
J. Moore bef. B. MORRIS, J.P., 1 March 1851.

WILKES COUNTY: Lot 27-13S-1 Cherokee. Pers. app'd. SARAH
                        BENSON, Ex'trx. of the estate of WILLIAM
BENSON, SR., to claim lot 27-13-1. Includes app't. of WM. H. PRI-
TCHARD of Baldwin Co. Signed: Sarah (by mark) Benson before IS-
AAC A. McLENDON, J.P. & J. A. BENSON, 3 June 1843.

CRAWFORD COUNTY: Lot 6-13N-1 Cherokee. Pers. came ABRAHAM
                        DAVIS, son-in-law, Adm'r. of the estate
of and one of the heirs of ELIZABETH GANIER, dec'd. to claim lot
6-13-1. Includes app't. of ISAIAH DAVIS as att'y. Signed: A. Davis
before JAMES C. LOYD and W. H. BROOKS, J.P., 28 June 1843.

TALBOT COUNTY: Lot 1211-12-1 Cherokee. WILLIAM TOWNS is
                        the Adm'r. of the estate of JOHN P. BLACK-
MON. Signed: WILLIAM S. GOSS, C.C.O., 20 March 1840.

MUSCOGEE COUNTY: Lot 1178-12-1 Cherokee. EDMUND O'NEAL, Administrator of the estate of BENJAMIN O'
NEAL of Newton County, appoints SPENCER RILEY of Bibb Co. to take
out the grant to lot 1178-12-1 now in Lumpkin Co. Signed: Edmund
Oneal (not witnessed), 17 April 1843.

HALL COUNTY: Lot 1157-12-1 Cherokee. Pers. app'd. ISAAC
GREEN, Ex'r. of the estate of THOMAS JACKSON, dec'd., to claim lot 1157-12-1, now in Lumpkin Co.; lot 31-10-3, now in Murray Co.; and, for himself, lot 241-1-1, now in
Forsythe Co. Includes app't. of JOSEPH DUNAGANE of Hall Co. as
att;y. Signed: Isaac Green before THOMAS GREEN and JOHN WHELCHEL,
J.P., 26 May 1843.

BALDWIN COUNTY: Lot 1119-12-1 Cherokee. Pers. app'd. N. J.
WAY, one of the orphans of JOHN WAY, SR.,
to claim lot 1119-12-1. Signed: N. J. Way before S. B. BROWN, J.P.
8 November 1851.

MADISON(?) COUNTY: Lot 1047-12-1 Cherokee. Pers. app'd. JOHN
HARRELL, one of the orphans of SIMEON HARRELL, to claim lot 1047-12-1. Signed: John (by mark) Harrell before ALLEN EDWARD, J.P., for Twiggs Co., 8 June 1843.

WARREN COUNTY: Lot 1021-12-1 Cherokee. Pers. app'd. HENRY
LOCKHART, Adm'r. of the estate of ELI G.
SHERMAN, dec'd., to claim lot 1021-12-1. Includes app't. of JOHN
J. PILCHER as att'y. Signed: Henry Lockhart bef. PETER CODY, J.P.
16 June 1843.

CHATHAM COUNTY: Lot 827-12-1 Cherokee. Pers. app'd. JAMES
M. RUSSELL, orphan of PHILIP RUSSELL, to
claim lot 827-13-1. Signed: James M. Russell before JAMES H. WADE
J.P., 10 February 1843.

SCREVEN COUNTY: Lot 753-12-1 Cherokee. ELIJAH ROBERTS, Administrator of the estate of BENJN. FERRILL, dec'd., appoints JOHN ROBERTS as att'y. for taking out the
grant to lot 753-12-1. Signed: Elijah Roberts before JEFFERSON
ROBERTS, ALFRED ROATH & W. J. LAWSON, N.P., 1 June 1843.

OGLETHORPE COUNTY: Lot 743-12-1 Cherokee. Pers. app'd. SUSAN

ARNOLD, THOS. R. ARNOLD, JOHN T. ARNOLD, & MOSES ARNOLD to claim lot 743-12-1. Includes app't. of JOSEPH H. ECHOLS as att'y. Signed: Susan Arnold (by mark), Thomas R. Arnold (by mark), John T. Arnold (by mark) and Moses Arnold (by mark) before LUES. COBB & MOSES WRIGHT, J.P., 12 June 1843.

ELBERT COUNTY: Lot 690-12-1 Cherokee. Pers. app'd. HOLMAN CHILDRESS, Ex'r. of the estate of THOMAS COLBERT, dec'd., to claim lot 690-12-1. Signed: Holman Childress before WILLIAM D. THORNTON, J.P., 20 February 1843.

BURKE COUNTY: Lot 688-12-1 Cherokee. Pers. app'd. REBECCA ATTAWAY, one of the heirs of EVAN LEWIS dec'd. to claim lot 688-12-1. Includes app't. of WILLIAM H. PRITCHARD of Baldwin Co. as att'y. Signed: Rebecca Attaway before JOHN A. ROBERTS, J.P., 23 June 1843.

WILKES COUNTY: Lot 648-12-1 Cherokee. Pers. app'd. DWATIES McJUNKIN, Adm'r. of CUNNINGHAM DANIEL, dec'd.,to claim lot 648-12-1, now in Lumpkin Co. Includes app.t. of WM. H. PRITCHARD of Baldwin Co. Signed: DWATIES McJUNKIN before JOHN HARRISON, J.P., 20 Juje 1843.

COLUMBIA COUNTY: Lot 575-12-1 Cherokee. ISAAC W. JONES, Executor of the estate of WALTON JONES, deceased, appoints SHADRACK A. GIBSON att'y. to apply for the grant to lot 575-12-1 Cherokee. Signed: Isaac W. Jones before H. W. GERALD & E. M. BALLARD, J.I.C., 7 June 1843.

MORGAN COUNTY: Lot 568-12-1 Cherokee. ADAM G. SAFFOLD appoints WILLIAM OLIVER SAFFOLD as att'y. to take out grants to lot 568-12-1, drawn by DANIEL T. COLEMAN and lot 688-1-3 drawn by WILLIAM KENT. Signed: Adam G. Saffold bef. J. M. HILLS & WM. Y. STOKES, J.I.C., 15 June 1843.

DEKALB COUNTY: Lot 522-12-1 Cherokee. Pers. app'd. J. B. WILSON to claim lot 522-12-1, drawn by JAS. W. P. JOHNSON. Signed: Jas. B. Wilson before ROBERT JONES, J.I.C. 15 June 1843.

PULASKI COUNTY: Lot 501-12-1 Cherokee. Pers. app'd. GEORGE MARTIN, gdn. for MARY JANE HASKINS, to claim lot 501-12-1 and, for himself, lot 219-27-2. Includes appointment of JOSEPH CARN as att'y. Signed: GEORGE MARTIN before JOHN J. ANDERSON, J.P., 24 June 1843.

BIBB COUNTY: Lot 482-12-1 Cherokee. Pers. app'd. ANN G. SANDERS, widow of DENIS D. SANDERS, to claim lot 482-12-1. Signed: Ann G. Sanders before JNO. H. BRANTLEY, J.I.C., 29 June 1843.

BALDWIN COUNTY: Lot 434-12-1 Cherokee. Pers. app'd. ZADOCK RACHEL to claim lot 434-12-1 as Adm'r. of the estate of the owner. Signed: Zadock Rachel before Alfred M. Horton, N.P., 27 January 1843.

ELBERT COUNTY: Lot 383-12-1 Cherokee. Pers. app'd. JOHN A. TEASBY, Ex'r. of the estate of ISHAM TEASBY, to claim lot 383-12-1. Signed: John A. Teasby and JEREMIAH S. WARREN, J.I.C., 14 June 1843.

BALDWIN COUNTY: Lot 201-12-1 Cherokee. Pers. app'd. JOHN THOMPSON, one of heirs of SAMUEL THOMPSON to claim lot 201-12-1. Signed: John Thompson before J. R. ANDERSON, J.I.C., 12 June 1843.

FRANKLIN COUNTY: Lot 18-12-1 Cherokee. Pers. came CATHERINE W. TERRELL, Adm'trx. of the estate of JAMES C. TERRELL, dec'd., to claim lot 81-12-1. Signed: Catherine W. Terrell before THOS. MORRIS & R. A. R. NEAL, J.I.C., 29 May 1843.

BALDWIN COUNTY: Lot 1288-11-1 Cherokee. Pers. app'd. JAMES W. TINSLEY, Adm'r. of the estate of JAMES W. TINSLEY, dec'd. to claim lot 1288-11-1. Signed: T. W. Tinsley before R. MICKLEJOHN, J.P., 27 June 1843.

RICHMOND COUNTY: Lot 1132-11-1 Cherokee. JAMES GARDNER, JR. Adm'r. of the estate of JAMES GARDNER, deceased, to claim lot 1132-11-1. Signed: JAMES GARDNER, JR. bef. JOHN SHLY, Judge of the Middle District of Georgia, 16 Jan. 1844.

LEE COUNTY: Lot 1117-11-1 Cherokee. Pers. came ELIZABETH GILBERT, Ex'trx. of the estate of ALLEN GILBERT, dec'd., to claim lots 1117-11-1 and 894-21-3. Includes app't. of ALPHEOUS DICKERSON of Hancock County as att'y. Signed: ELIZABETH J. GILBERT, now ELIZABETH T. DAVIS, before AMBROSE H. GRANT, J.I.C., and CHAS. RANDALL, 27 June 1843.

MERIWETHER COUNTY: Lot 1105-11-1 Cherokee. Pers. app'd. ABRAHAM M. MATTHEWS, one of the heirs of REBECCA MATTHEWS, dec'd., to claim lot 1105-11-1. Includes appointment of JOHN R. ADERSON of Baldwin Co. as att'y. Signed: A. M. Matthews before EDWY. L. VARDAMAN, J.P., 23 June 1843.

CHATHAM COUNTY: Lot 1060-11-1 Cherokee. Pers. app'd. PAMELLA WINGATE, representative of the orphans of CYNTHIA LADSON, widow, to claim lot 1160-11-1, now in Lumpkin Co.; lot 34-26-2, now in Gilmer Co.; and lot 729-11-1. Includes app't. of L. B. MORISON as att'y. Signed: P. A. Wingate before ISAAC RUSSELL, J.P., 24 June 1843.

CAMDEN COUNTY: Lot 990-11-1 Cherokee. Pers. app'd. GEORGE LANG, agent of RICHARD LANG, to claim lot 990-11-1. Includes app't. of CHARLES H. NELSON of Milledgeville as att'y. Signed: George Lang before JAS. M. SMITH, J.I.C., 27 June 1843.

ELBERT COUNTY: Lot 868-11-1 Cherokee. Pers. app'd. LINDSAY H. SMITH, one of the legatees of the estate of SINGLETON W. SMITH, to lot 868-11-1. Signed: Lindsay H. Smith bef. ENOCK BELL, J.P., 25 May 1843.

MC INTOSH COUNTY: Lot 859-11-1 Cherokee. Pers. app'd. EDWARD W. DE LE GAL, as agent of EDWARD J. DELEGAL, to claim lot 859-11-1; as agent of THOMAS DELEGAL, lot 456-13-1 and lot 181-10-1; as agent of EMBRIE, EDWARD W., THOMAS and HENRY DELEGAL, orphans, lot 82-6-of Carroll County. Signed: E. W. De Le Gal before ARNOUND LEFILS, J.P., 17 June 1843.

OGLETHORPE COUNTY: Lot 737-11-1 Cherokee. Pers. app'd. DANIEL MC CARTY, orphan of SHEROD MC CARTY, decd. to claim lot 737-11-1. Includes app't. of JOSEPH H. ECHOLS of Oglethorpe Co. as att'y. Signed: Daniel McCarty bef. SHEROD McCARTY and RICHARD O'KELLY, J.P., 14 June 1843.

WILKES COUNTY: Lot 718-11-1 Cherokee. Pers. app'd. FELIX

WELLMAKER to claim lot 718-11-1 and, as legal guardian of the owner, lot 386-3-4, drawn by the orphans of JOHN WELLMAKER. Includes app't. of LEWIS S. BROWN as att'y. Signed: Felix Wellmaker (by mark) before LEWIS S. BROWN, J.I.C. and A. J. WINGFIELD, J.I.C. 2 May 1842.

OGLETHORPE COUNTY: Lot 699-11-1 Cherokee. Pers. app'd. MOSES ARNOLD to claim lot 699-11-1 drawn by the orphans of HENRY ASHTON. Includes app't. of JOSEPH ECHOLS as attorney. Signed: Moses Arnold (by mark) bef. LEWIS COBB & MOSES WRIGHT, J.P., 12 June 1843.

MUSCOGEE COUNTY: Lot 692-11-2 Cherokee. Pers. came ELIZABETH TILLY to claim lot 692-11-1 and, as guardian of her children, lot 781-21-3. Signed: Elizabeth Tilly before AUGUSTUS J. ABBOTT, J.P., 14 June 1843.

FRANKLIN COUNTY: Lot 648-11-1 Cherokee. CYNTHIA A. MAYES, appoints PLENEY A. TURK of Jackson County as att'y. to take out the grant for her part of lot 648-11-1, drawn by the orphans of JOHN MAYES, dec'd. Signed: CYNTHA A. MAYES and PLINEY A. TURK before CYNTHA J. TURK & WILLIAM TURK, J.I.C., 22 February 1843.

TALBOT COUNTY: Lot 628-11-1 Cherokee. Pers. app'd. THOMAS K. MC CRARY to claim lot 628-11-1 for his wife one of the legatees of BENJAMIN CULPEPPER. Includes app't. of JAMES S. PARK as att'y. Signed: T. K. MC CRARY before H. H. HANNCOCK, J.P., 26 June 1843.

CHATHAM COUNTY: Lot 614-11-1 Cherokee. Pers. app'd. JOSEPH CUMMINS, Adm'r. of the estate of JOHN C. STARR, dec'd., to claim lot 614-11-1. Includes app't. of JOHN R. ANDERSON of Baldwin Co. as att'y. Signed: Jos. Cummins before I. K. TEFFT, N.P., 28 April 1843.

CLARKE COUNTY: Lot 561-11-1 Cherokee. Pers. app'd. ANN CROW, wife of ELI CROW, dec'd., to claim lot 561-11-1. Includes app't. of THOMAS A. TUCK as att'y. Signed: Ann Crow before FRANCIS JACKSON & WILLIAM JACKSON, J.P. 27 May 1843.

JONES COUNTY: Lot 558-11-1 Cherokee. HOSEA JOHNSON of

Jones County and AHAB JOHNSON of Monroe co., because of their moving, app't. HENRY CHILDS & BENNETT BRIDGES as attornies to take out the grants to lots 558-11-1 and lot 744-1-2. Signed: Ahab Johnson and Hosea Johnson before LEWIS DAVIS & GREEN B. WILLIAMSON, J.P., 9 June 1843.

MORGAN COUNTY: Lot 552-11-1 Cherokee. ARCHIBALD PRESTON, agent for the orphans of THOMAS PRESTON, dec'd., of Walton Co., appoints ARCHIBALD B. BOSTWICK as att'y. for taking out the grant to lot 552-11-1. Signed: Archibald Preston before A. B. Bostwick, and R. A. PRIOR, J.P., 9 June 1843.

MUSCOGEE COUNTY: Lot 530-11-1 Cherokee. Pers. came REESE H. MOSS, for himself and his brothers and sister, to claim lot 93-6-1 and lot 530-11-1. Includes appointment of THOS. A. BRANNON as att'y. Signed: Reese H. Moss (by mark) before F. P. ABBOTT & AUGUSTUS ABBOTT, J.P., 2 June 1843.

PULASKI COUNTY: Lot 459-11-1 Cherokee. Pers. app'd. THOMAS HOWELL, gdn. of the heirs of N. STEVENS, R. HOWELL & B. HOWELL, to claim lot 459-11-1 and lot 259-20-2, drawn by NEEDHAM STEVENS, dec'd.; lot 946-19-3, drawn by ROBERT HOWELL, dec'd.; and lot 1252-3-2 drawn by BENJAMIN HOWELL, dec'd. Includes app't. of LUALLIN ROEBUCK as att'y. Signed: Thomas B. Howell before BURWELL B. DYKES & JOHN B. BUSH, J.P., 26 June 1843.

PUTNAM COUNTY: Lot 450-11-1 Cherokee. Pers. came WILLIAM WHITFIELD, Adm'r. of the est. of ASA MARTIN, dec'd. of Morgan Co., to claim lot 450-11-1. Includes app't. of CARTER SHEPPARD as att'y. Signed: WM. WHITFIELD bef. J. ADAMS and IRBY (?) HUDSON, J.I.C., 2 June 1847.

BALDWIN COUNTY: Lot 397-11-1 Cherokee. Pers. app'd. EDWARD A. MORGAN, gdn. of the orphans of ANDREW VALENTINE, dec'd., to claim lot 397-11-1 and lot 791-2-2. Signed: A. Morgan (by mark) before R. MICKLEJOHN, J.P., 30 June 1843.

MUSCOGEE COUNTY: Lot 316-11-1 Cherokee. Pers. app'd. LORENZO D. MONROE, Gdn. of the orphans of JACKSON A. MONROE, dec'd. of Gwinnett Co., to claim lot 304-27-2 and lot 316-11-1. Includes app't. of JOSEPH STURGES as att'y. Signed: L. D. MONROE bef. THOMAS R. HERINGDINE & AUGUSTUS J. ABBOTT, J.P.

2 June 1843.

RANDOLPH COUNTY: Lot 294-11-1 Cherokee. Pers. app'd. JOHN MC INNIS, Gdn. of DANIEL, LASLIE, MARY JEAN LASLIE & RACHEL LASLIE (orphans of CHARLES LASLIE, dec'd. of Telfair County), to claim lot 294-11-1. Signed: John McInnis bef. WM. H. BARTON, J.P. and JAMES BUCHANAN, C.C.O., 26 Jan. 1843.

THOMAS COUNTY: Lot 278-11-1 Cherokee. Pers. app'd. THOMAS C. WYCHE and HENRY WYCHE, Adm'r. of LITTLETON WYCHE, to claim lot 278-11-1 and lot 655-21-3. Signed: THOMAS C. WYCHE & HENRY WYCHE bef. THOMAS M. GATLIN, J.I.C. 13 May 1843.

RANDOLPH COUNTY: Lot 257-11-1 Cherokee. Pers. app'd. JONATHAN HARRISON, Gdn. of ELIZABETH HOBBS, to claim lot 257-11-1. Includes app't. of JOSEPH SESSIONS as attorney. Signed: J. Harrison bef. J. B. ELLIS, J.P. 16 June 1843.

WARREN COUNTY: Lot 235-11-1 Cherokee. Pers. app'd. HARDY PITTS, one of the justices of the inferior court, that DICKERSON CULPEPPER, a militiaman, was registered in the lottery and not DAVID CULPEPPER. Signed: Hardy Pitts bef. JOHN BUTT, J.P. & THOMAS GIBSON, Clk., 16 Jan. 1832.

SUMPTER COUNTY: Lot 204-11-1 Cherokee. Pers. app'd. WILLIAM DELOUCH to claim lot in the 11th District, 1 section, now in Union Co., drawn by FREDERICK SIMS and SUSAN SIMS, widow. Signed: WILLIAM DELOUCH bef. PHILIP WALKER, J.P., 9 June 1843.

WASHINGTON COUNTY: Lot 139-11-1 Cherokee. Pers. app'd. JAMES ARNSWORTH to claim lot 139-11-1 and lot 348-3, as Adm'r. of the estate of the owner. Signed: James Arnsworth bef. WM. HUST, J.P., 26 Sept. 1844.

RICHMOND COUNTY: Lot 121-11-1 Cherokee. Pers. app'd. SAML. DOWSE to claim lot 121-11-1; for his wife, the former ELIZABETH M. WHITHEAD, lot 50-3-2 and lot 60-9-1; and as Adm'r. of the estate of AMOS P. WHITEHEAD, lot 369-18 in Henry Co., EDWARD GRESHAM is app'td. agent. Signed: Saml. Dowse before JAMES BRANDON, JR., J.P., 14 June 1843. (Includes app't. of att'y. for Edward Gresham, also signed bef. James Brandon, Jr., but filed in Burke County.)

CHATTOOGA COUNTY: Lot 75-11-1 Cherokee. Pers. came JAMES G. STURDIVANT, one of the heirs of EDWARD STURDIVANT, dec'd., to claim lot 75-11-1. Includes app't. of CHARLES H. NELSON of Baldwin Co. as att'y. Signed: James G. Sturdivant bef. J. I. EASTY and JOHN F. BEAVERS, J.I.C., 17 June 1843.

MACON COUNTY: Lot 247-10-1 Cherokee. Pers. app'd. JOSEPH J. MIERS, Adm'r. of the est. of WILLIAM WILD, dec'd., to claim lot 247-10-1 and lot 68-18 of Lee County, for the legatees. Signed: Joseph J. Miers bef. T. C. PREER, and WILLIAM ALEXANDER, J.P., 16 June 1843.

Lot 22-10-1 Cherokee.
"Sir
    My father BENJAMIN COXWELL drew Lot number twenty two, in the tenth District, and first section, he sold it to JOHN COXWELL and both himself and John Coxwell have departed this life, and there is no administration on either estate, & not being willing to see the children of John Coxwell lose it I have paid to the Treasurer five dollars for the grant fee, and if the grant cannot issue upon this state of facts I wish the matter to remain, so that I may apply to the Legislature for relief 27 June 1843.
ALFORD M. HORTON, Esq.   Signed: MITCHELL COXWELL"

MARION COUNTY: Lot 170-9-1 Cherokee. D. N. BURKHALTER appoints THOMAS BEVIN as his att'y. to claim lot he drew in the Cherokee and Gold Lotteries and the lot, in the 12th Dist. of Dooly Co., drawn by THOMAS SHVITS' orphans of Columbia Co., his wife being the youngest of the orphans. Signed: D. N. Burkhalter bef. R. W. MASTON, J.P., 5 May 1843.

STEWART COUNTY: Lot 162-9-1 Cherokee. BENJAMIN WALKER appoints SPENCER RILEY as att'y. to take out a grant for lot 162-9-1, drawn by WILLIAM WALKER's orphans. Signed: Benj. Walker bef. EDMUND C. BEARD & SAMPSON BELL, J.I.C. 14 April 1853.

BALDWIN COUNTY: Lot 147-9-1 Cherokee. "December the 21 day 1833..I do hear by certify that there is no Indian Claim on No 147 in the 9th dist of the first Section and I do further certify that it is Inroled by EBENESAR WILL COX* who has gaune to Arkin Saw given under my hand the year above written
(*Willcox)   Signed: JOHN B. CHASTAIN"

LOWNDES COUNTY: Lot 146-9-1 Cherokee. Pers. came HAMILTON
                        W. SHARPE, Adm'r. of the est. of PENSEVILLE
FOLSOM, dec'd, to claim:
                        Lot 200-9- Lee County
                        Lot 1033-15-2
                        Lot 578-2-4
                        Lot 285-9-4
                        Lot 146-9-1
                        Lot 290-2-2
                        Lot 265-17-1
Signed: Hamilton W. Sharpe before M. MORRISON, J.P.,21 June 1843.

MONROE COUNTY: Lot 142-9-1 Cherokee. Pers. app'd. J. A.
                        J. MYERS, one of the heirs at law of JOHN
MYERS orphans, to claim lot 142-9-1. Signed: JOHN A. J. MYERS before WM. H. SHARP, J.P., 6 March 1849.

WASHINGTON COUNTY: Lot 127-9-1 Cherokee. Pers. app'd. MILES
                        SCARBOROUGH to claim lot 127-9-1, drawn
by AGNES SCARBOROUGH, for himself, ABSLEY SCARBOROUGH, DAVID SCARBOROUGH & IVEY SCARBOROUGH. Signed: Miles Scarborough before SAMUEL ROBISON, J.I.C., 6 June 1843.

MADISON COUNTY: Lot 90-9-1 Cherokee. Pers. app'd. JAMES R.
                        ANDERSON to claim lots 90-9-1 and 487-5-1,
for himself and SARAH ANN ANDERSON. Signed: James B. Anderson before R. H. BULLOCK, J.I.C., 28 October 1847.

LOWNDES COUNTY: Lot 87-9-1 Cherokee. Pers. came JAMES M.
                        SMART, husband of the only living heir of
JOHN HICHCOCK,dec'd., of Screven Co., to claim the lot drawn by John Hichcock. Signed: James M. Smart bef. WILLIAM HINES, J.I.C. 6 July 1844.

FRANKLIN COUNTY: Lot 65-9-1 Cherokee. Pers. app'd. JOHN B.
                        HARRISON & DAVID DUMASS, Ex'ts. of the estate of BENJAMIN HARRISON, dec'd., to claim lot 65-9-1, now in Union Co., and lot 716-21-3. Includes app't. of TEMPLE F. COOPER as att'y. Signed: D. Dumass and John B. Harrison bef. THOS MORRIS & R. A. R. NEAL, J.I.C., 29 May 1843.

CHATTOOGA COUNTY: Lot 20-9-1 Cherokee. Pers. app'd. JAMES
                        HERNDON, husband of MARY BURNS, to claim
lot 20-9-1 for MARY BURNS, JAMES BURNS, & ROBERT L. BURNS, orphans of LARD BURNS, dec'd. of Gwinnett County. Signed: James Herndon

before OSCAR F. PERRY, justice of the Peace, 8 June 1843.
FLOYD COUNTY: JAMES HERNDON appoints J. W. M. BERREN as his att'y. signed..James Herndon bef. JOHN J. DODD, J.P. 10 June 1843.

BIBB COUNTY: Lot 16-9-1 Cherokee. Pers. app'd. JOHN MC DONALD, JR., heir at law of the orphans of ANDREW EDWARDS, dec'd., to claim lot 16-9-1. Signed: John McDonald bef. KEELIN COOK, J.I.C., 1 April 1853.

APPLING COUNTY: Lot 324-8-1 Cherokee. Pers. came BENAJAH SMITH, Gdn. of CALVIN HAGAN's orphans, to claim lot 324-8-1. Signed: B. SMITH bef. EZEKIEL P. TUTEND, J.P. 2 November 1852.

BALDWIN COUNTY: Lot 299-8-1 Cherokee. N. N. (W.?) HOWELL claims lot 299-8-1, as Adm'r. of the estate of SAMUEL JOHNSON. Signed: N. W. Howell bef. W. S. MOORE, J.P., Irwin Co., 19 June 1843.

MONROE COUNTY: Lot 239-8-1 Cherokee. Pers. app'd. ALBERT T. WHITE, one of the orphans of WILLIAM WHITE, dec'd., to claim lot 239-8-1. Includes app't. of JAMES TURNER as att'y. Signed: Albert T. White before JAMES TURNER, J. P., 20 May 1843.

WALTON COUNTY: Lot 218-8-1 Cherokee. Pers. app'd. WILLIAM HARRIS, one of the orphans of JOHN HARRIS of Oglethorpe County, to claim lot 218-8-1. Includes app't. of JAMES THOMPSON as att'y. Signed: William Harris bef. JESSE C. MC CORD, J.P., 11 March 1844.

TALIAFERRO COUNTY: Lot 71-8-1 Cherokee. Pers. came WILLIAM T. FLUKER, husband of the former CAROLINE HARRIS, orphan of ROBERT HARRIS of Wilkes Co., to claim lot 71-8-1. Signed: William T. Fluker bef. S. P. CRENSHAW, J.I.C., 12 June 1843.

BALDWIN COUNTY: Lot 20-8-1 Cherokee. Pers. app'd. JOSEPH J. CHURCHILL to claim lot 20-8-1 as one of the orphans who drew sd. lot. Signed: Joseph J. Churchill before P. M. COMPTON, N.P., 26 Dec. 1851.

JASPER COUNTY: Lot 10-8-1 Cherokee. Pers. app'd. THOMAS J. SMITH, to claim lot 10-8-1, drawn by JAMES HALLAWAY. Smith is part owner. Includes app't. of LUKE WILLIAMS as att'y. Signed: Thos. J. Smith before JOHN M. KING, J.P., 28 June 1843.

CHATTOOGA COUNTY: Lot 278-7-1 Cherokee. Pers. app'd. SAMUEL FINLEY to claim lot 278-7-1, now in Union Co.; lot 45-8-3, now in Murray Co.; and lot 272-11-3, now in Murray Co. Also, as Adm'r. of the estate of ROBERT ROUNSAVILLE, deceased, to claim lot 308-12-3. Signed: Saml. Finley before WM. M. AYCOCK, J.P., 13 May 1843.

DEKALB COUNTY: Lot 178-7-1 Cherokee. Pers. app'd. EDMUND R. HERREN, one of the three orphans of ELBERT HERREN, dec'd. of Dekalb Co., to claim lot 178-7-1. Signed by Edmund R. Herren bef. N. L. ANGIER, J.P., 22 August 1853.

GREENE COUNTY: Lot 165-7-1 Cherokee. Pers. app'd. JAMES H. HALL, one of the orphans of THOMAS HALL of Oglethorpe Co., to claim lot 165-7-1. Signed: James H. Hall before PAS. W. GODKIN, J.I.C., 20 May 1843.

UPSON COUNTY: Lot 227-6-1 Cherokee. Pers. came JAMES L. LOYD, agent of WILLIAM H. LOYD and MARTHA S. LOYD, to claim lot 227-6-1. Includes app't. of M. H. SANDWICH as att'y. Signed by James L. Loyd (by mark) bef. JAS. H. BLACK, J.P., 27 June 1843.

FRANKLIN COUNTY: Lot 203-6-1 Cherokee. Pers. app'd. JOHN HEMPHILL, one of the heirs of ROBERT HEMPHILL, lot 203-6-1 and lot 532-11-1. Includes app't. of THOMAS KING as att'y. Signed by John Hemphill (by mark) before JOHN SMITH & R. A. R. NEAL, J.I.C., 2 June 1843.

BALDWIN COUNTY: Lot 73-6-1 Cherokee. Pers. app'd. FARISH CARTER, Ex'r. of the est. of GEORGE W. MURRAY, dec'd., to claim lot 866-5-1 and lot 272-9-4. Signed: Signed: Farish Carter bef. J. U. HORNE, N.P., 12 May 1843.

CASS COUNTY: Lot 45-6-1 Cherokee. Pers. app'd. JOHN A. WILLIS, legal representative of JANE WILLIS to claim lot 45-6-1. Signed: JOHN A. WILLIS before JAMES STOVALL, J.P., 27 May 1843.

RICHMOND COUNTY: Lot 28-6-1 Cherokee. Pers. app'd. CATHERINE BELL, Gdn. of ELIZABETH BELL, HARRIET BELL, WILLIAM BELL, & GEORGE BELL (heirs of JAMES BELL, dec'd.) to claim lot 28-6-1. Signed: Catherine Bell before WILLIAM R. MC LAWS, N.P., 29 June 1843.

RICHMOND COUNTY: Lot 1154-5-1 Cherokee. Pers. app'd. ALLEN C. YOUNG, husband of the former ELIZABETH DYE, daughter of and one of the orphans of BENJAMIN DYE, to claim lot 1154-5-1. Signed: Allen C. Young before RICHARD ALLEN, J.P., 7 December 1852.

NEWTON COUNTY: Lot 1141-5-1 Cherokee. Pers. app'd. LEVI MERCER, one of the Adm'rs. of the estate of THOMAS SIMS, to claim lot 1141-5-1. Includes app't. of JOHN BASS as att'y. Signed: Levi Mercer before CHARLES JONES, HENRY B. SMITH & JAMES B. WEAVER, J.P., 14 April 1843.

FRANKLIN COUNTY: Lot 1045-5-1 Cherokee. Pers. came SIGNAL A. WILKINSON, Adm'r. of the estate of ELISHA WILKINSON, dec'd., to claim lot 1045-5-1. Includes app't. of JAMES RICE as att'y. Signed: Signal A. Wilkinson before OSBORN GARNER, J.P., 22 June 1843.

WILKES COUNTY: Lot 977-5-1 Cherokee. Pers. app'd. ANN SMITH, agent of WILLIAM E. SMITH (orphan of JOHN W. SMITH), to claim lot 977-5-1. Includes app't. of ROBERT A. TOOMBS as att'y. Signed: Ann Smith before CALEB SAPPINGTON, J.P., 1 June 1843.

MUSCOGEE COUNTY: Lot 948-5-1 Cherokee. Pers. app'd. THOMAS MORRIS of Muscogee Co., Georgia and BENJAMIN RUNNELS of Russell Co., Alabama, to claim lot 948-5-1 and lot 122-4-3. Signed: Thomas Morris before GEON(?) TURENTIN, J.P. 13 May 1843.

WILKES COUNTY: Lot 896-5-1 Cherokee. Pers. app'd. FRANCIS W. DERRYCOAT, one of the orphans of GARLAND W. DERRYCOAT, to claim lot 896-5-1. Includes app't. of JOHN

R. ANDERSON of Baldwin County as att'y. Signed: F. W. DARRACOTT before J. A. TRUSTON & SAMUEL DANFORTH, J.P., 28 June 1843.

STEWART COUNTY: Lot 825-5-1 Cherokee. Pers. app'd. SARAH BRIDGES, Adm'r. of the estate of RUEBEN BRIDGES, dec'd., to claim lot 825-5-1. Includes app't. of JOHN WILLIAMS as att'y. Signed: Sarah Bridges before John Williams, J.P., __ May 1843.

JONES COUNTY: Lot 807-5-1 Cherokee. Pers. app'd. ORREN W. MOSSEY, Adm'r. of the estate of DENNIS D. WIMBERLY, dec'd., to claim lot 807-5-1. Signed: O. W. Mossey before J. WINSHIP, J.P., 30 June 1843.

DEKALB COUNTY: Lot 649-5-1 Cherokee. Pers. came ABNER CROW to claim lot 649-5-1 and lot 287-9-1, drawn by MARTIN CROW. Signed: Abner Crow before T. J. PARKERSON, J.P., 25 June 1843.

COLUMBIA COUNTY: Lot 439-5-1 Cherokee. Pers. came SAMUEL B. HOLLIMAN, agent of the orphans of JAMES HOLLIMAN, to claim lot 439-5-1. Includes app't. of WILLIAM H. PRITCHARD of Baldwin Co. as att'y. Signed: Samuel B. Holliman before H. W. MASSENGALE, J.I.C., 29 May 1843.

TALIAFERRO COUNTY: Lot 433-5-1 Cherokee. Pers. app'd. THOMAS R. SIMMONS, agent for LAZARUS SIMMONS who moved from Georgia six years ago, to claim lot 433-5-1. Includes app't. of ALEXANDER H. STEPHENS as att'y. Signed: Thomas R. Simmons before JOSEPH CAMPBELL & JESSE WOODALL, J.P., 14 June 1843.

MERIWETHER COUNTY: Lot 413-5-1 Cherokee. Pers. app'd. JNO. THO. OWENS and JACKSON TYNER, JR., Adm'rs. of the estate of JACKSON TYNER, SR., to claim lot 415-5-1. Signed by Jno. Tho. Owens and Jackson Tyner before EDWARD GRESHAM and FRANKLIN H. GLAZIER, J.I.C., 25 May 1843.

BUTTS COUNTY: Lot 348-5-1 Cherokee. In person came JAMES R. MC CORD, Gdn. of the orphans of JUBAL WATTS, dec'd., of Greene Co., to claim lot 348-5-1. Includes appointment of AUGUSTUS CARGILE as att'y. Signed: J. R. McCord bef. JOHN VANDEGRAFT, J.P., 3 June 1843.

BUTTS COUNTY: Lot 340-5-1 Cherokee. In person appeared
                       LARKIN D. LEE to claim lot 340-5-1, drawn
by JOHN W. MC CURDY, orphan. Signed: Larkin D. Lee before W. G.
MC MICHAEL, J.P., 21 September 1844.

CLARKE COUNTY: Lot 200-5-1 Cherokee. Pers. app'd. RANSOM
                       NICHOLS, Ex'r. of the estate of JULIUS
NICHOLS of Franklin County, to claim lot 200-5-1. Includes app't.
of WILLIAM L. MITCHELL as att'y. Signed: Ransom Nichols before
SAML. FROST, J.P., 25 May 1843.

MONROE COUNTY: Lot 174-5-1 Cherokee. Pers. app'd. LAWSON
                       G. CHAMBLISS, Ex'r. of HENRY CHAMBLISS,
to claim lot 174-5-1. Includes app't. of WILLIAM S. NORMAN as
att'y. Signed: L. G. Chambliss before DOLPHIN FLOYCE & JONA JOHN-
STON, J.P., 15 June 1843.

HENRY COUNTY: Lot 140-5-1 Cherokee. Pers. app'd. AZARIAH
                       DOSS to claim lot 140-5-<u>4</u>. Includes ap-
pointment of JOHN HAIL as att'y. Signed: Azariah Doss before
WM. C. ADAMSON, J.P., 2 May 1843.

CAMPBELL COUNTY: Lot 114-5-1 Cherokee. HIRAM STRAWN app'ts.
                       JOHN H. JOHNSON as att'y. to take out a
grant for lot 114-5-1, drawn by MARGARET LYNCH. Signed: Hiram
Strawn before W. H. YATES & JAMES GATES, J.P., 14 June 1843.

RICHMOND COUNTY: Lot 17-5-1 Cherokee. Pers. app'd. THOMAS
                       TANT, one of the surviving children of
ELIZABETH TANT, dec'd., to claim lot 17-5-1. Includes app't. of
WILLIAM H. PRITCHARD of Baldwin Co. as att'y. Signed: Thomas
Tant (by mark) before BENJAMIN B. RUSSELL, N.P., 29 June 1843.

BALDWIN COUNTY: Lot 16-5-1 Cherokee. Pers. app'd. ROBERT
                       F. MITCHELL to claim lot 16-5-1 as Adm'r.
of the owner. Signed: Robert F. Mitchell before ALFRED M. HORTON,
N.P., 28 June 1843.

PUTNAM COUNTY: Lot 1117-4-1 Cherokee. Pers. app'd. VIR-
                       GINIA CAMPBELL, widow of GRIFFITH CAMPBELL
to claim lot lot 1117-4-1, now in Lumpkin Co. and lot 292-28-3.
Includes app't. of THOMAS D. SPEER as att'y. Signed: Virginia

Campbell before BRANSON TROTHER and FRANCIS S. HEARN, J.P. 17 June 1843.

RICHMOND COUNTY: Lot 1067-4-1 Cherokee. Pers. app'd. JOS. LAW, Ex'r. of the estate of JAMES LAW, deceased, to claim lot 1047-4-1. Signed: Jos. Law before F. W. QUARTERMAN, J.P., 26 June 1843.

"Riceborough June 26 1843
Genl. C. H. NELSON
   Dr. Sir
   Having Seen an advertisement of yours kindly proposing to forward grants to those who might trouble you, I have taken the liberty to enclose you three dollars & the necessary papers to request the favour of you to take out and forward to me Gold Lot no. 1067-4 dist. 1st Section cherokee County, drawn by JAMES LAW of Liberty County your timely attention to the above will greatly oblige
   Very respectfully
   your Obt St
   JOS. LAW
P. S. Fifty cent enclosed for the postage J.L."

PULASKI COUNTY: Lot 889-4-1 Cherokee. Pers. app'd. JOSEPH HASKINS to claim lots: 889-4-1 drawn by MARIA HASKINS; 82-17-4 drawn by SELVINUS HASKINS; 157-1-Lee Co. drawn by SELVINUS HASKINS. JOSEPH HASKINS is one of the heirs of the estate holding the above. Includes app't. of JOSEPH CARRUTHERS as att'y. Signed: JOSEPH HASKINS before JOSEPH J. ANDERSON, J.P., 24 June 1843.

CRAWFORD COUNTY: Lot 887-4-1 Cherokee. Pers. came RAYMOND BOWMAN, Adm'r. of the estate of ROBERT BOWMAN, to claim lot 887-4-1. Signed: Raymond Bowman before W.H. BROOKS, J.P., 26 June 1843.

"Knoxville, June 27th 1843
Dear Sir
   Enclosed I hand you two Dollars & fifty cents it being the grant fee for a Gold lot as per No in the above affidavit which you will please send a receipt for the money for said Grant on receipt of this the Grant he will send for at some convenient time please attend to the above and much oblige yours &c
   E. W. DENNIS for RAYMON BOWMAN"

DOOLY COUNTY: Lot 749-4-1 Cherokee. Pers. app'd. WILLIAM C. GREER to claim lot 749-4-1 and lot 124-15-2 as heir and owner in part. Includes app't. of ALFRED M. HORTON of Baldwin Co. as att'y. Signed: William C. Greer before THOS. H. KEY & WM. MC DANIEL, J.P., 24 June 1843.

PIKE COUNTY: Lot 736-4-1 Cherokee. JAMES POWELL app'ts. JAMES MC KENZIE as att'y. to take out the grant 736-4-1 drawn by LUCY & AMANDA JACKSON, orphans of JOHN JACKSON, dec'd. Signed: JAMES POWELL (by mark) before JAMES L. WINGFIELD, J.P., 23 February 1843.

JEFFERSON COUNTY: Lot 709-4-1 Cherokee. Pers. app'd. SARAH MC COULLOUGH, widow, and HANNAH GRUBBS, widow, to claim lot 709-4-1, drawn by SARAH MC CALLOUGH and lot 367-21-3 drawn by HANNAH GRUBBS. Includes app't. of ALFRED M. HORTON as att'y. Signed: SARAH MC COLLOUGH (by mark) and HANNAH GRUBBS before EBENEZER BOTHWELL & HENRY B. TODD, J.I.C., 7 June 1843.

MC INTOSH COUNTY: Lot 644-4-1 Cherokee. Pers. app'd. JAMES BLUE, one of the heirs of DANIEL BLUE, SR. of Glynn county, to claim lot 644-4-1 and lot 145-11-2. Includes app't. of JOHN R. ANDERSON as att'y. Signed: James Blue before W. M. BRY, N.P., 24 June 1843.

CHATHAM COUNTY: Lot 567-4-1 Cherokee. Pers. app'd. JAMES Y. WATERS, orphan, to claim lot 567-4-1. Signed: James Y. Waters before F. H. BLOIS, N.P., 8 April 1853.

MORGAN COUNTY: Lot 555-4-1 Cherokee. Pers. came SARAH W. COCKRAN, formerly SARAH W. BAILEY, to claim lot 555-4-1, and as guardian of the orphans of JOEL BAILEY lot 57-5-1. Signed: Sarah W. Cockran before GEORGE R. EDWARDS, J.P., 27 June 1843. Lot was drawn in Jasper County by Sarah W. BAILEY, widow of JOEL BAILEY.

JONES COUNTY: Lot 530-4-1 Cherokee. JOHN T. PEARSON of Talbot County app'ts. JOSEPH DAY as att'y. for taking out a grant to lot 530-4-1, drawn by JOHN PEARSON's orphans. Signed: John T. Pearson before J. G. MARTIN, J.P. 27 March 1843.

HALL COUNTY: Lot 373-4-1 Cherokee. Pers. came JOHN BELL to claim lot 373-4-1 and lot 88-10-3, both drawn by THOMAS BELL. Signed: John Bell bef. JORDAN REESE, J.I.C. 26 May 1843.

STEWART COUNTY: Lot 286-4-1 Cherokee. Pers. came JOSEPH J. TALLY, son of RUSSEL TALLY, to claim lot

286-4-1. Signed: JOSEPH T. TALLY before JOHN TALBOT, J.I.C. 26 April 1844.

WILKINSON COUNTY: Lot 209-4-1 Cherokee. Pers. came SILPHA MIXON, widow of MICHAEL MIXON and guardian of his orphans, to claim lot 209-4-1. Includes app't. of LARKIN BEAREFIELD as att'y. Signed: Silpha (by mark) Mixon before DANIEL BREWER, J.P., 26 June 1843.

SCREVEN COUNTY: Lot 191-4-1 Cherokee. Pers. app'd. JAMES M. ROBBINS, Adm'r. of the estate of GEORGE ROBBINS, dec'd., to claim lots not recollected and lot 191-4-1. Signed: James M. Robbins before WILLIAM IVEY, J.P. 27 June 1843.

CHATHAM COUNTY: Lot 1164-3-1 Cherokee. Pers. app'd. ANN B. BOURKE, guardian of Mrs. CATHERINE ODELL, to claim lot 1164-3-1. Includes app't. of Col. A. H. KENAN of Baldwin County as att'y. Signed: Ann M. Bourke before R. RAIFORD, J.P. 10 May 1843.

BALDWIN COUNTY: Lot 1054-3-1 Cherokee. Pers. app'd. THOMAS M. MANN, Adm'r. of the estate of ISHAM WEST, dec'd., to claim lot 1054-3-1; lot 475-13-1 N½; and lot 43-10-2. Signed: Thomas M. Mann before ALFRED M. HORTON, N.P. 20 June 1843.

TALBOT COUNTY: Lot 652-3-1 Cherokee. ISAIAH C. FITTEN of Chambers Co., Alabama, appoints JOHN C. FITTEN of Baldwin Co., Georgia to claim lot 652-3-1. Signed: Isaiah C. Fitten before R. B. RUCKER, J.P., 18 January 1843.

COBB COUNTY: Lot 265-3-1 Cherokee. Pers. app'd. WILLIAM DUNN & ELIZABETH CHAMBERS to claim lot No. 265-3-1, now in Forsyth Co., drawn by Chambers orphans of Dekalb Co. Includes app't. of N. B. KNIGHT as att'y. Signed: William Dunn & Elizabeth Chambers (by mark) before JOEL B. RUE & PARKS HARDMAN, J.P. 7 June 1843.

JACKSON COUNTY: Lot 116-3-1 Cherokee. Pers. app'd. GEORGE F. ADAMS, to claim lot 116-3-1. Includes app't. of JAMES B. NABERS of Jackson Co. as att'y. Signed: Geo. F. Adams before G. W. THOMPSON and J. H. RANDOLPH, 15 May 1843.

MUSCOGEE COUNTY: Lot 1201-2-1 Cherokee. Pers. app'd. HENRY
                         PRUETT, Ex'r. of JACOB PRUETT, dec'd., to
claim lot 1201-2-1. Includes app't. of KENNETH MACKENZIE as at-
tyorney. Signed: Henry Pruett before THOS. J. SHIVENER, N.P. and
A. L. WATKINS, 14 June 1843.

                         Lot 1077-2-1 Cherokee. "Greensborough
                                                 18 January 1834
Dr Sir
     The bearer of this will apply for the grants to Fractions
Number 1077 & 1078 in the second district & first section Cherokee. Under the existing regulations in relation to Indian improvements no grant can issue for a lot returned by the Surveyor as
improved until satisfactory evidence is had that there is no Indian occupant Claiming the land. The difficulty in obtaining the
Certificate of the agent of this fact in regard to the fractions
mentioned arises alone from the want of an opportunity of seeing
him. But if your Excellency can grant the lots relying upon my
statement, I assure you upon honor that there is no Indian claiming these fractions or either of them, nor is there any Indian
or descendant; residing within a mile & ½ of them. I am now in
possession of the fractions, and they have been for the last 3
years rented & occupied by R. HAYS. They were rented by the agent
of the state, and are part of the land enrolled by JOHN MOSEBY
who emigrated 3 years since. There is not now, nor has there been
any Indian or other person the state or drawer, for 3 years past
who has or can have any claim upon them. If the grants can be
had upon this statement made with the strictest regard to its
correctness, and the knowledge of the situation it would place
you in if not then it will enable me to procure a title with less
expence and relieve the trouble of going after the agent to procure his certificate which I promise to obtain if you still think
necessary.   yours Respefly
                              JOHN G. PARK'"

CRAWFORD COUNTY: Lot 1063-2-1 Cherokee. Pers. app'd. DAVID
                         AVERA, Ex'r. of the estate of ELI RUSHING,
dec'd, to claim lot 1063-2-1 Cherokee. Includes app't. of MATTHEW
J. JORDAN as att'y. Signed: David Avera before WILLIS TAYLOR &
C. JOYNER, J.P., 11 April 1843.

NEWTON COUNTY: Lot 1033-2-1 Cherokee. Pers. came SARAH
                         CHURCHILL, widow of SIMON CHURCHILL, to
claim lot 1033-2-1. Includes app't. of General JOHN N. WILLIAM-
SON as att'y. Signed: Sarah Churchill (by mark) before R. A.
BLAKE, J.P. 10 June 1843.

THOMAS COUNTY: Lot 1002-2-1 Cherokee. JOHN L. MAC INTYRE,
                         Ex'r. de son of the estate of HANNAH MAC-
INTYRE, appoints CHARLES A. NELSON of Baldwin Co. as att'y. to
claim lot 1002-2-1 and lot 266-3-4. Signed: John L. MacIntyre before JOHN SMITH, J.I.C., 10 June 1843.

WARREN COUNTY: Lot 897-2-1 Cherokee. Pers. app'd. WILLIAM LITTLETON, with CASSANDRA WRIGHT, Adm'r. of the estate of JAMES WRIGHT, dec'd., to claim lot 897-2-1. Signed: William Littleton before SEPTIMUS TORRENCE, J.P. 27 June 1843.

RICHMOND COUNTY: Lot 835-2-1 Cherokee. Pers. app'd. MARY ANN VEITCH, widow and sole heir of WALKER VEITCH, dec'd.,to claim lot 835-2-1. Includes app't. of CHARLES H. NELSON as att'y. Signed: Mary Ann Veitch before J. S. GRIFFIN, N.P., 17 June 1843.

HARRIS COUNTY: Lot 816-2-1 Cherokee. Pers. came MARY POWELL, widow of MILLINGTON POWELL, to claim lot 816-2-1. Signed: Mary (by mark) Powell before G. B. ELLIS, J.P., 3 June 1843.

COWETA COUNTY: Lot 809-2-1 Cherokee. Pers. app'd. GILBERT D. GREER, Ex'r. of the estate of JOHN GREER, dec'd., to claim lot 809-2-1. Includes app't. of WILLIAM V. ANDERSON as att'y. Signed: Gilbert D. Greer before H. ELDER and WILLIAM B. BROWN, J.P., 1 June 1843.

JACKSON COUNTY: Lot 782-2-1 Cherokee. Pers. app'd. HARRIET PHELPS, Adm'trx. of GLENN PHELPS, dec'd., to claim lot 782-2-1. Includes app"t. of THOMAS C. CLARK as att'y. Signed: Harriet Phelps before GEORGE SHAW & J. B. NABUS, J.P. 1 March 1843.

TROUP COUNTY: Lot 718-2-1 Cherokee. Pers. app'd. BENJAMIN H. CAMERON to claim:
Lot 718-2-1, drawn by BENJAMIN RAY
Lot 103-11-4, drawn by BENJAMIN RAY
Lot 180-3-3, drawn by ROBERT FELTON of Monroe County. He also claims, but as Ex'r. of the estate of JAMES CAMERON, dec'd., lot 150-11-5(?), now in Carroll Co., and lot 194-15-2, now in Muscogee Co. Also, as lawful agent of ROBERT LYONS of Tallapoosa County, Alabama, to claim lot 173-14-3. Also, as agent of RUFFIN LAWSON of Tallapoosa County, Alabama, to claim lot 292-14-2, drawn by DAVID LAWSON of Jasper County. Signed: B. H. Cameron before (illegible) BEALL, J.I.C., 15 June 1843.

WILKES COUNTY: Lot 690-2-1 Cherokee. Pers. app'd. FRANCIS B. BILLINGSLEA, Adm'r. of the estate of DANIEL S. WATTS, to claim lot 690-2-1 and lot 197-7-1. Includes app't. of ROBERT TOOMBS as att'y. Signed: Frs. B. Billingslea before LEWIS S. BROWN, J.I.C., 16 June 1843.

BURKE COUNTY: Lot 679-2-1 Cherokee. Pers. app'd. KENNY WHITE to claim a lot drawn by JOSEPH GOLDEN's orphans of Burke County. The lot is no. 679-2-1. Includes app't. of WILLIAM PRITCHARD as att'y. Signed: Henry White before J. GRUBBS & JOHN A. ROSIER, J.P., 24 (month not given) 1843.

STEWART COUNTY: Lot 665-2-1 Cherokee. Pers. came MARY DOSTER, Ex'trx. of the estate of BENJAMIN DOSTER, dec'd. (he was the Adm'r. of the estate of REBECCA ALLEN, deceased), to claim lot 665-2-1. Signed: Mary Doster before SAMUEL PURDY, J.P., 26 March 1844.

GWINNETT COUNTY: Lot 548-2-1 Cherokee. Pers. came JAMES HARDIN, in right of his wife, to claim lot 548-2-1. Signed: James Harden (by mark) before W. S. IVIE, J.P. 24 March 1843.

FORSYTH COUNTY: Lot 478-2-1 Cherokee. Pers. came WILLIAM M. CASTLEBERRY, one of the heirs of MARK CASTLEBERRY, dec'd., to claim lot 478-2-1. Signed: Wm. S. Castleberry bef. RICHARD HAYS, J.P., 5 April 1843.

JASPER COUNTY: Lot 461-2-1 Cherokee. Pers. came ALFRED JOHNSON, Adm'r. of the estate of SNELLIN JOHNSON, dec'd., to claim lot 461-2-1. Signed: Alfred Johnson before ELISHA T. WYNEN, J.P., 20 May 1843.

TALBOT COUNTY: Lot 401-2-1 Cherokee. DAVID BRYAN app'ts. C. H. NELSON of Milledgeville as att'y. to take out a grant for lot 401-2-1. Signed: David Bryan before ROBERT HOLMES & DICKSON CURETON, J.P., 5 April 1843.

BIBB COUNTY: Lot 213-8-1 Cherokee. This day came and app'd. MARCUS AURELIUS FRANKLIN to claim lot 213-8-1, that he drew while in Clarke County and lot 506-17-3, drawn by ANN EDWARDS. Signed: Marcus A. Franklin bef. ELIPHALET E. BROWN, J.P., 8 June 1843.

BALDWIN COUNTY: Lot 200-2-1 Cherokee. Pers. app'd. GILES M. CHAPMAN, to claim lot 200-2-1 and lot 70-11-1 and, as agent of SAMUEL CHAPMAN, claims lot 50-8-Carroll

County. Signed: G. M. CHAPMAN before R. MICKLEJOHN, J.P., 30 June 1843.

MUSCOGEE COUNTY: Lot 420-1-1 Cherokee. Pers. came HENRIETTA STRATTON, formerly HENRIETTA WHITE and Adm'rrx. of the estate of P. S. W. WHITE, dec'd., of Troup Co., to claim lot 420-1-1, now in Forsyth Co. Includes app't. of PETER FAIR of Milledgeville as att'y. Signed: Henrietta Stratton bef. AUGUSTUS J. ABBOTT, J.P., 16 June 1843.

CHATHAM COUNTY: Lot 305-1-1 Cherokee. Pers. app'd. GEORGE TITCOMBE, only heir of his father SAMUEL TITCOMBE, dec'd., to claim lot 305-1-1. Includes app't. of JOHN W. EXLEY of Effingham Co. as att'y. Signed: George Titcombe bef. ISAAC RUSSELL, J.P., 6 June 1843.

Lot 282-1-1 Cherokee. "Executive Depar't. Georgia Milledgeville 19 August 1833.

It appearing to the Executive from the certificate of CURTIS GREEN Esquire Agent of the Indians in the county of Forsyth, that lot No. 282-in the first district of the first section is not in the occupancy of an Indian or descendant of an Indian. Ordered therefore that the surveyor General do issue the plat for said lot to the drawer & that he receive a grant for the same upon payment of grant fees. Attest.

R. A. GREENE, S.E.D."

BALDWIN COUNTY: Lot 199-1-1 Cherokee. Pers. came FRANCES M. JONES, widow of EZRA B. JONES of Baldwin co., to claim lot 199-1-1. Signed: F. M. Jones before A. M. HORTON, N.P., 30 June 1843.

MORGAN COUNTY: Lot 93-1-1 Cherokee. Pers. app'd. ALLEN WEATHERS, husband of one of the orphans of DANIEL TAYLOR, dec'd., to claim lot 93-1-1. Signed: Allen Weathers before JOHN J. WALKER, J.P., 27 June 1843.

CASS COUNTY: Lot 30-1-1 Cherokee. Certification that fractions 30 and 31 and lot 335, 1st Dis. 1 Sect. may be granted, having been occupied by GEORGE M. WATER, who drew a lot of land in a lottery. Signed: WM. G. SPRINGER, agent for the Cherokees In Georgia, 9 February 1834.

TROUP COUNTY: (VANON) Lot 10-16 Carroll. "Feb. 14th 1833
Dear Sir
I wish you to send me the plat and grant for Lot Number ten (10) in the sixteenth district formerly

Carrol County now Troup County drawn by HARRIET L., MARY A. and SHEPHERD W. RILEY orphans, enclosed is eight dollars for the payment of the same. I wish you to direct the letter to Shepherd W. Riley, Vernon Post Office Troup County by the first mail.
Respectfully, SHEPHERD W. RILEY
Granted and grant deposited in Post office directed to S. W. Riley Vernon Troup Co.
Feby. 22d 1833   P. FAIR"

TROUP COUNTY: Lot F124-14 Carroll. Pers. app'd. WILLIAM WOOD, brother of ISAAC S. WOOD, dec'd.,to claim lot 124-14 of Carroll County, a fraction. ISAAC S. WOOD never married. SAUNDERS H. RAY is Adm'r. of his estate. Signed: WM. WOOD before WM. B. HESTER, J.P., 5 May 1837.

COWETA COUNTY: Lot 14-14 Carroll. Pers. app'd. WILLIAM MC GEE, agent for the orphans of MC GEE of Elbert county, to claim lot 14-14 Carroll and lot 206-8 Carroll. Signed: William McGee before SION P. STEED, J.P. 20 June 1843.

HEARD COUNTY: Lot 131-13 Carroll. Pers. app'd. STEWART BRIMER, husband of one of the orphans of JAMES COLLIERS, dec'd., to claim lot 131-13 of Carroll County. Includes app't. of WILEY KIRD as att'y. Signed: STUEART BREMER (by mark) bef. THOS. P. RIDGWAY & SAMUEL BLANDRUM, J.P. 6 June 1843.

PULASKI COUNTY: Lot 114-13 Carroll. Pers. app'd. MARY MANNING, illegitimate child of MARY MANNING, to claim lot 114-13 of Carroll County. Signed: Mary Manning (by mark) before WILLIS ALLEN, J.P., 1 June 1848.

TROUP COUNTY: Lot 131-12 Carroll. Pers. app'd. ROBERT F. MC GEHN, agent of his wife MARY GWINN, orphan, to claim lot 131-12=5, now Carroll Co. Includes app't. of PARK & ANDERSON of Baldwin Co. as att'y. Signed: R. F. McGehn before ROBERT A. Y. RIDLEY, J.I.C., 21 June 1843.

GWINNETT COUNTY: Lot 99-12 Carroll. Pers. came JOHN EVANS to claim lot 99-12 of Carroll Co., now Heard Co., drawn by the orphans of EDGAR. Signed: John Evans bef. JESSE MURPHEY, J.P., 28 April 1843.

TWIGGS COUNTY: Lot 86-12 Carroll. In person app'd. GREEN

ALLEN to claim lot 86-12-5, now Carroll Co. drawn by the orphans of WILLIAM ALLEN. He is the owner of the undivided half of the lot and he is the only surviving heir and is now over 21 years old. Includes app't. of ELIJAH E. CROCKER as att'y. Signed: GREEN ALLEN (by mark) before PEYTON REYNOLDS, J.I.C., 7 June 1843.

FAYETTE COUNTY: Lot 35-12 Carroll. Pers. came MARTHA COWEN widow of JAMES COWEN, dec'd., to claim lot 35-12 of Carroll Co., now Heard Co. Signed: Martha Cowen (by mark) before EDWARD CONNOR, J.I.C., 14 June 1843.

TELFAIR COUNTY: Lot 241-11 Carroll. Pers. app'd. STEPHEN HUBBARD, one of the heirs and judgement creditor of ELIJAH HUBBARD, dec'd., to claim lot 241-11 of Carroll County. Signed: Stephen Hubbard bef. JOHN STULL, J.P. 15 January 1844.

JASPER COUNTY: Lot 221-11 Carroll. Pers. app'd. JAMES W. MORGAN, one of the orphans of ELIZABETH MORGAN, widow of Revolutionary Soldier of Jasper County dec'd., to claim lot 221-11-5, now in Carroll Co. Includes app't. of EDWARD Y. HILL as att'y. Signed: James W. Morgan before TH. C. BRODDUS and CHS. JUDAN, J.I.C., 13 June 1843.

HEARD COUNTY: Lot 212-11 Carroll. Pers. came JOHN A. WALLS to claim lot 212-11 of Carroll Co., now in Heard Co., drawn by NANCY COPELAND's illegitamates of Hancock Co. Includes app't. of GILES L. TOMPKINS as att'y. Signed: John A. Walls before WILLIAM S. HEARN & ELIJAH MOORE, J.P. 27 May 1843.

ELBERT COUNTY: Lot 188-11 Carroll. Pers. app'd. BENNETT W. BROWN to claim lot 188-11-5, now Carrol Co. drawn by SUSAN A. DEPRIEST, illegitimate. Signed: Bennett W. Brown before JOHN G. DEADWYLER, J.P., 13 March 1843.

WALTON COUNTY: Lot 145-11 Carroll. Pers. app'd. JNO. I. MC CULLOCH to claim lot 145-11-Carroll Co. drawn by REUBEN GREGORY, illegitimate. Signed: John L. McCulloch before CHARLES HUFF, J.P., 17 June 1843.

DEKALB COUNTY: Lot 105-11 Carroll. Pers. app'd. SAMUEL

POTTS, agent of FRANCIS M. POTTS, illegitimate, now living in Alabama, to claim lot 105-11 of Carroll Co. Signed: SAMUEL POTTS bef. J. B. WILSON, J.P., 2 May 1848.

CLARKE COUNTY: Lot 75-11 Carroll. Pers. app'd. BENJAMIN TOWNS, Ex'r. of JAMES TOWNS, dec'd., of Madison County, to claim lot 75-11-Carroll Co., drawn by JAMES TOWNS as a Revolutionary War soldier, and lot 912-3-2. Includes app't. of WM. H. PRITCHARD of Baldwin Co. as att'y. Signed: Benjamin Towns bef. SAML. FROST, J.P., 26 June 1843.

JASPER COUNTY: Lot 249-10 Carroll. JEMIMA ROBERTSON, widow and Adm'r. of WILLIAM ROBERTSON, decd. appoints JOHN WEBB of Newton Co. as att'y. to take out grants for lot 249-10 of Carroll. Signed: Jemima Robertson (by mark) before WM. CONNAWAY, J.P., 10 June 1843.

MERIWETHER COUNTY: Lot 234-10 Carroll. Pers. app'd. JAMES GRANT, one of the orphans who drew lot 234-10 of Carroll Co., to claim said lot. Includes app't. of ABSALOM THORNTON of Forsyth Co. as att'y. Signed: James Grant before MOSES ALMAN, J.P., 15 April 1848.

JACKSON COUNTY: Lot 43-10 Carroll. Pers. app'd. J. B. NABUS to claim lot 43-10-Carroll Co., drawn by ELISABETH GOOLSBY, widow, of Jackson Co. Includes app't. of N. C. BARRNETT as att'y. Signed: J. B. Nabus before MIDDLETON WITT, J.I.C., 15 August 1844.

MARION COUNTY: Lot 20-10 Carroll. JAMES JORDEN, husband of JUDY COOK, the daughter of JAMES COOK, dec'd., to claim lot 20-10 of Carroll Co. Includes appt. of Col. THOMAS BERINS as att'y. Signed: James Jorden (by mark) before CULLIN L. BATTLE, J.P., 27 March 1843.

PULASKI COUNTY: Lot 212-9 Carroll. Pers. app'd. JESSE WADE one of the orphans of MOSES WADE of Columbia Co., to claim lot 212-9 of Carroll Co. Signed: Jesse Wade (by mark) before WILLIS ALLEN, J.P., 16 May 1848.

MONTGOMERY COUNTY: Lot 175-9 Carroll. ALFRED P. KING appoints ALFRED M. HOUGHTON as att'y to take out grants to lot 175-9-of Carroll Co.; lot 1228-19-3, now in Cobb Co., "that I the sd. ALFRED P. gave in to JOHN BETHUNE in Greensborough in the County of Green at one time". Signed: ALFRED P. KING, 19 June 1843.

WILKES COUNTY: Lot 73-9 Carroll. Pers. app'd. BENJAMIN SMITH & ALEXANDER SMITH, agents of WILLIAM SMITH, to claim lot 73-9-5, now Carroll Co. Includes app't. of WILLIAM H. PRITCHARD as att'y. Signed: Benjamin Smith and Alexander Smith bef. JOSEPH M. WILLIAMS and SAML. DANFORTH, J.P. 12 June 1843.

MUSCOGEE COUNTY: Lot 30-9 Carroll. Pers. app'd. JULIUS R. CLAPP & SAMUEL W. FLOURNOY, owners with the heirs of BENJ. WALKER, dec'd., to claim lot 30-9 Carroll Co. drawn by the orphans of NEHEMIAH M. HOWARD. The deponents and BENJAMIN WALKER married said orphans. Signed: J. P. Clapp and Saml. W. Flournoy before JNO. W. BETHUNE, J.I.C., 27 June 1843.

CARROLL COUNTY: Lot 22-9 Carroll. Pers. came ABNER R. WALTON, Adm'r. of the estate of WILLIAM WOOD, to claim the fractions bought from SANDERS W. RAY, Adm'r. of the estate of ISAAC S. WOOD. These are fractions 22,44,23,66,838,147, 9th District of Carroll Co. and lots 17,3,13,12th District of Carroll Co. Signed: Abner R. Walton bef. B. S. MERRELL, J.P. 13 October 1848.

WALTON COUNTY: Lot 279-8 Carroll. Pers. app'd. ROBERT STEWART, Ex'r. of the estate of JAMES GREER, dec'd., toclaim lot 279-8 of Carroll Co. Includes app't. of WARREN J. HILL as att'y. Signed. Robert STUART bef. JAMES LINDLY, J.P. and CORNELIUS HELST, 3 June 1843.

Lot 281-7 Carroll.
"May 21st 1843
General C. H. NILSEN I have taken it on my self to get you to Do me the favor of attending to some business for me and hope it will not trouble you much I have in closed you ten Dollars for of central Bank money to get you to take out a plat and grant for me in the name of JAMES DAVIS it was Drawn by him in the county of Carol Number two hundred and Eighty one as I am the rightfull owner if it is not taken out and your Doing you much oblige me Direct your letter to Ferte(?) Henderson Macon co Alibama I have had the miss fertun to slip thruw what I had and have to work for my bred now but I must Do the best I can I hope (the bottom of the page is missing; Ferte may be Fort) I also

wish to take out one more plot and grant for 1265 in the 3 district and seckand section in the name of JOHN WRIGHT if they have not been taken out and send that plot and grant on and you will much oblige me
     JOHN G. ROBERTS"

CHATHAM COUNTY: Lot 269-7 Carroll. Pers. app'd. MARY SCRANTON, orphan of DANIEL BAKER and now the wife of DANIEL T. SCRANTON, to claim lot 269-7 of Carroll County. Includes app't. of A. G. LA TARTE of Baldwin Co. as att'y. Signed by MARY SCRANTON and D. T. SCRANTON bef. R. RAIFORD, J.P. 24 May 1843.

BUTTS COUNTY: Lot 221-7 Carroll. Pers. came ELISHA T. PRESTON, Adm'r. of the estate of GILLUM PRESTON, dec'd., to claim lot 221-7-Carroll Co. Includes app't. of AUGUSTUS CARGILE as att'y. Signed: Elisha J. Preston before WILLIAM ANDREWS and STEPHEN BAILEY, J.P., 20 May 1843.

COLUMBIA COUNTY: Lot 188-7 Carroll. Came pers. ELISHA ROBERTS of Warren County to claim lot 188-7 of Carroll Co; lot 156-15-2, Cherokee; as agent of MARY ROBERTS of Warren County, lot 237-2-2, Cherokee; and, as agent of the orphans of ELISHA ROBERTS, lot 132-6 Dooly County. Includes appt. of CHARLES EATON RYAN of Baldwin Co. Signed: Elisha Roberts bef. H. W. MASSENGALE, J.I.C., 22 June 1843.

WASHINGTON COUNTY: Lot 210-6 Carroll. Pers. app'd. CAROLINE ELIZA HOWARD to claim lot 210-6 Carroll co. Includes app't. of JOHN H. WALKER as att'y. Signed: ELIZA HOWARD (by mark) bef. GREEN WHIDDEN, J.P. and JOHN SHEPPARD. 10 June 1843.

       Lot 226-5 Carroll. "Jacksonboro 6th Sept. 1827.
His Excellency GEORGE M. TROUP
    Sir Permit me to enquire of you, on behalf of an honest but poor man whether the Returns of the Militia and Volunteers of this state during the late war was made to your office or to the War Department at Washington and if made to your office to be good enough to inform me whether HUMPHREY BAZEMON a private in a volunteer Rifle Company commanded by Capt. HENRY BUFORD of Screven Countyit was not returned as a regular soldier of said company.
    The object of Inquiry is to save two tracts of land that he drew in the late Lottery they are returned on the ground of his deserting from the said company. The individual has a large family and is only in low circumstances; your attention to the above will confer a favor on him.

                        Please state the fees for obtaining a cer-
tificate of the return (if in your office) under the seal of your
department and I will foreward the same for it
                        I am with great respect your most
                        obedient Servant,MALFORD MARSH"

HEARD COUNTY: Lot 127-5 Carroll. Pers. app'd. LEWIS P.
                        STRONG, to claim lot 127-5 of Carroll Co.
and, as one of the orphans of SHERROD STRONG, dec'd., claims lot
66-2 of Lee Co. Includes app't. of JOHN G. PARK of Baldwin Co.,
as att'y. Signed: Lewis P. Strong before WM. B. W. DENT, J.P.
and G. TOMPKINS, 15 June 1843.

RICHMOND COUNTY: Lot 11-4 Carroll. Pers. app'd. SAMPSON
                        MC CARTY, one of the orphans of MICHAEL
MC CARTY, formerly of Jefferson County, one of the orphans of
MICHAEL J. MC CARTY, to claim lot 11-4-5 Carroll Co. and lot 119-
21-2 Cherokee. Signed: Sampson McCarty before JOHN SHLY, Judge of
the Superior Court, Middle District, 10 June 1843.

MONTGOMERY COUNTY: Lot 82-3 Carroll. Pers. came THOMAS ALL-
                        MAN to claim lot 82-3 Carroll Co., as one
of the owners in part. Includes app't. of A. M. SCOTT as att'y.
Signed: Thomas Allman (by mark) before NORMAN GILLIS, J.P.
25 November 1847.

WALTON COUNTY: Lot 36-3 Carroll. GREENBERRY MC MAHAN ap-
                        points JAMES LOCKLAR to claim lot 36-3 of
Carroll Co. drawn by SUSAN MC MAHAN. Signed: Greenberry McMahan
(by mark) bef. W. H. BRIMBERRY, J.P., 27 May 1843.

WALTON COUNTY: Lot 36-3 Carroll. Pers. app'd. CREENBERRY
                        MC MAHAN to claim lot 36-3 of Carroll Co.
as owner in part in right of his wife. Signed: Greenberry McMahan
(by mark) bef. WM. L. LACKLIN & JAMES B. LACKLIN, J.P. 13 June
1843.

ELBERT COUNTY: Lot 52-2 Carroll. Pers. app'd. HERATIO G.
                        TATE, one of the orphans of ZIMM TATE of
Elbert Co., dec'd., to claim lot 52-2 Carroll. Includes app't. of
WILLIAM G. ALLEN as att'y. Signed: H. G. Tate bef. THOMAS BELL &
LINDSAY H. SMITH, J.P., 31 May 1843.

COLUMBIA COUNTY: Lot 21-2 Carroll. Pers. app'd. HENRY SCOTT,

Ex'r. of the estate of HUGH REESE, to claim lot 21-2- of Carroll Co. Includes app't. of JAMES A. CHAPMAN of Warren Co. as att'y. Signed: HENRY SCOTT bef. H. W. MASSENGALE, J.I.C., 15 May 1843.

CLARKE COUNTY: Lot 149-1 Carroll. Pers. app'd. JAMES HANSON, Ex'r. of the est. of JAMES HANSON, dec'd., to claim lot 149-1 of Carroll Co. Includes app't. of JOHN H. SOUR, SR. as att'y. Signed: James Hanson bef. GEO. M.LANIER & THOMAS FERNANDO LOWE, N.P. 30 May 1843.

CLARKE COUNTY: Lot 184-1 Baldwin. WILLIAM STRONG & ABR. RAMEY certify that MOSES MELTON was entitled to two draws in the late purchase of land from the Creek Indians, having one day been entered by his father and the next day by his father-in-law. This was not discovered until the books were sent in. Signed: Wm. Strong and Abr. Ramey, Justices of the Inferior Court, 12 January 1806.

CLARKE COUNTY: Lot 184-1 Baldwin. Pers. came ISAAC CROW, commissioner for the county, who certifys that he placed the name of his son-in-law MOSES MELTON on the list of the land lottery and that he is the only the man by that name in this county that he knows of. Signed: Isaac Crow (by his mark) bef. WM. DYSON, J.P., 14 December 1805.

Lot 66-2 Baldwin.
"Sir
   Having been informed that it is represented to your Excellency that HARLEY ATTAWAY Jr. is not a citizen of this state & therefore not entitled to the land which was drawn opposite his name in the late land lottery, we think proper to state to you that at the time said ATTAWAY entered his name for a draw in said Lottery he resided in Burke County and had so done for more than a year previous thereto to the best of our knowledge. We are respectfully yr. Excys. obt. servts.
                    WILLIAM BYRE and GEO. POYTHES.
His Excy. JOHN MILLEDGE Govr. &C &C"

BURKE COUNTY: Lot 66-2 Baldwin. "Pers. app'd. THOS. STEPTOE who being duly sworn maketh oath and Saith that he was present at the making of a Contract between HARLEY ATTAWAY SENR. and a certain THREEWISS WYNN for a chance in the Land Lottery which as follows. To wit. that the said HARLEY woud vouch for or guarentee to the said WYNN that his nephew HARLEY JUNR. shou'd sell unto the said Wynn his draw or Chance in the Land Lottery/ or in failure thereof/ that the said ATTAWAY, Senr. wou'd refund the money rec'd. from said Wynn, say two Dolars & fifty Cents, with double Interest.
                              THOS. STEPTOE

Sworn to before me this 5th of Novr. 1805. Signed: D. R. CINSON, J. I..C., 5 Nov. 1805"

CHATHAM COUNTY: Lot 172-5-4 Cherokee. Pers. app'd. CATHERINE GROVES & ELIZA GROVES to claim lot 172-5-4 that they and their brother CHARLES GROVES drew. Charles is not in the county of Chatham. Includes app't. of JOHN W. EXLEY of Effingham Co. as att'y. Signed: Catherine Groves and Eliza Groves before LIN T. STRESSELL(?), J.P., 31 May 1843.

WASHINGTON COUNTY: Lot 16-9-4 Cherokee. BENJAMIN HARRIS and WILEY HARRIS, orphans of CHRUCHILL HARRIS, appoint SOLOMON D. BRANTTEY as att'y. to claim lots they drew in the land lottery. Signed: Benj. Harris and Wiley Harris before WM. SNEED, J.P., 19 June 1843.

Lot 116-16-4 Cherokee.
"I BROCKMAN W. HENDERSON the Surveyor of the 16th Dist. of the 4th Sect. of the Territory of Georgia which is in the Occupancy of the Cherokee Indians do hereby certify that Lots Numbers 116 and 246 in sd. district which was returned by me as improved lots was not at the Time of the Survey in the Occupancy of any Indians but in the possession of a Mr. DEMPSY and a Mr. WRIGHT two whitemen who stated to me that they rented said improvements from the state of Georgia. I further certify that at the time of the survey no Indian resided in said district given under my hand this 8th day of May 1833. Brockman W. Henderson"

Lot 177-4-4 Cherokee. "Georgia Cassville, Cass County February 8th 1834 I WILLIAM G. SPRINGER Agent do hereby certify that lot no. 177 in the 4th District 4 Section now occupied by BABIN SMITH a Cherokee Indian is subject to be granted as said SMITH received a Reservation in fee simple in the treaty the United States with the Cherokee Indians on the 27th Feby. 1819 Given under my hand the day and date above written
Wm. Springer Agent for the Cherokees in Georgia"

NEWTON COUNTY: Lot 315-9-4 Cherokee. "We the under signed do certify that we have Lived ten years in the aforesaid district and have known WILLIAM FULLER as a Citizen in said dist ever since and have never known a man by the name of WILLIAM FIELDER in the district under our hands this the 29th of November 1833
THOMAS W. PIERCE
B. S. STANTON, J.P.
G. A. GUNN"

FLOYD COUNTY. Lot 338-3-4 Cherokee. "I do Certify that Lot No. 338-3-4 is not Claimed by an Indian nor the descendant of an Indian...this December 9th 1833. Signed: WILLIAM H. CLEGHORN agent for the Cherokees in the aforementioned County."

Lot 4-7-4 Cherokee. "Surveyor Generals Office Milledgeville Decr. 12, 1834. It appears from the return of the Surveyors of the Seventh District, fourth Section, that No. 4 in said district has an Indian improvement upon it. Signed: JOHN BETHUNE, Sur. Genl. Drawn by DAVID ELMORE Herndon's Hall".

FLOYD COUNTY: Lot 181-4-4 Cherokee. "I do certify that B. F. CURRY the in Rolling Agent told me that CHARLES FIELDS a Cherokee Indian had inrolled his name for Imegration and that he had Relinquished all his Claim and title to his Improvement in the Cherokee nation to the governmant and in the Survey of the Country it Seems that No. 181, in the 4th Dist of the fourth Section takes part of the said FIELDS improvement the part where on Dr. BUTLER the Missionary now lives and the owner of the sd. lot of land no. 181, in the 4th Dist. if the 4th Sect. has come on and has Demanded possession and the said Butler will not give up possession Oct. 18th 1833."
WILLIAM H. CLEGHORD, Agent for the Cherokee Indians in Floyd Co."

OGLETHORPE COUNTY: Lot 30-3 Baldwin. Whereas the Inferior court put down the name JAMES FREEMAN on the list of persons entitled to draws in the land lottery without making a distinction between JAMES FREEMAN SR. and JAMES FREEMAN JR. and whereas JAMES FREEMAN won a lot in sd. lottery, James Freeman Sr. allows James Freeman, Jr. to claim sd. lot, for the sum of $200. Signed: James Freeman, Sr. bef. THOMAS DUNN, T. W. COBB & HUGH FREEMAN, Jr., 2 Dec. 1805.

    Lot 181-4-4 Cherokee. "Floyd Co. Septr. 21st. 1833. Head of Coosa.
My Dear Uncle
    The enclosed certificate of WM. H. CLEGHORN, relates to a relinquished improvement on Lot No. 181 in the 4th Dist. and 4th Sect. I have thought it necessary farther to state to you that several of the Judges of the Inferior Court of this county have all confirmed the statement of the County Agent. and Seem anxious that the owner of the Lot should have a grant to issue in his favor..their anxiety originates in the fact, that the lot is now in the possession of Dr. BUTLER, and he is using all his influence to retard a correct administration of the Laws, and to injure the owner of sd. lot, who is and ever has been your warm supporter..you will please have this lot granted, and direct it to JACOB C. PUTNAM of Vanns Valley...Floyd Co. and you will oblige
    yr Nephew &c
        JNO. H. LUMPKIN
I enclose $8.00 for the grant fee.
N.B. your friends have together with yr. nephew are much elated at your success. I shall be in Milledgeville on the first Monday in Novr.
/To His Excellency WILSON LUMPKIN Milledgeville Georgia."

MUSCOGEE COUNTY: Lot 59-9-2 Cherokee. HUDSON A. THOMSON, trustee of JEREMIAH C. JETER & FRANCIS M. JETER (minors and orphans of WILLIAM JETER, dec'd.), appoints KENNETH MC KENZIE as att'y. to claim lot 59-9-2 of Cherokee and

lot 75-3-2 of Cherokee. Also lot 124-11 of Muscogee Co. and lot
84-1 of Lee Co. Signed: HUDSON A. THOMSON bef. WILLIAM L. GILES
and JENKINS ECHOLS, J.I.C., 13 June 1843.

CHATHAM COUNTY: Lot 125-8-2 Cherokee. Pers. app'd. GEORGE
MILLEN to claim lot 125-8-2 and also alot
322-4-2 drawn by JAMES BRYAN. Also, through his agent Sheriff
FITTES, lot 322-4-2 drawn by WILLIAM W. OATES; lot 1026-3-2 drawn
by HENRY G. VALBEAU; lot 24-18-2 drawn by THOS. ASKEW; lots 595-
2-1, 273-12-3, and 1130-15-2 drawn by JNO. F. HERB; lot 221-24-3
drawn by JOHN C. AUSTIN; lots 9-24-3 and 589-2-4 drawn by BENJA-
MIN W. SRACH; and lot 238-5-2 drawn by R. K. TRUBROOK. Signed:
George Millen before TUROIDAS WYLLY, J.P., 19 April 1843. Includes appt. of MC PHERSON BERRIEN MILLEN as att'y.

RICHMOND COUNTY: Lot 440-2-2 Cherokee. Pers. app'd. ANN MC-
KINNE, Adm'trx. of the est. of her deceas-
ed. husband BARNA MC KINNIE, to claim lot 440-2-2 and lot 356-
21-2. Signed: Ann McKinne bef. WILLIAM R. MC LAWS, N.P.,
28 June 1843.
"Mr. WM. H. PRITCHARD   Dr Sir
                            I send you the application of my Mother
as Administratrix of the Estate of BARNA MC KINNE for Grants on
two lots of land as described above Also and on the opposite page
drawn by my Brother & myself of which I am sole owner, you will
confer a very great favor for me by Granting viz them & Holding
the Plats untill I visit Milledgeville next week, When I will take
them up & pay you any currency issue you may order. A Mr. PARK of
your place wishes to purchase No. 444-2-2 drawn by B. MC KINNE &
if I should not possibly see you in the course of next week or
you should not hear from me. Of course you can make the money out
of the order. Indoing this you will confer a great favour on yr.
Obt. sevt.
        JNO. MC KINNE JR.
In great Haste I would enclose the money but the postage would be
considerable and (illegible) next week I will answer your purposes
when you shall see or hear from me."

                    Lot 522-1-2 Cherokee. "January 21st 1834
Respected & dear Brother
                        Inclosed I send you ten dollars & ask the
favor of you to send by mail to my Brother SIMPSON C. DYER two
plats & grants, send but one at atime, one by one mail & the other
by the next. First send the plat & grant for No. 522 in 1 Dist.
and 2 Sect. drawn by WILLIAM MCNEAL who give in Franklin County
Willis Dist. The other is lot No. 547-21-2 drawn by JOHN FARLEY
Pike Co. Bustins Dist. for the last No. 549 there has been an application for the grant, but in consequence of its having been
returned Indian Improvement Farley failed to get the grant, but
there is not any Indian improvement on it either old or new, but
if you cannot send the grant for it now, retain five dollars of
the money in your own hands & my Brother Simpson C. Dyer will get
& send you a certificate showing that there is no improvement on

it. The above business belongs intirely to my Brother but in consequence of my acquaintance with you he got me to write, I have nothing special or interesting to write you only the Missionary Cause is gaining ground in the up country.
N.B. Direct the grant to Lebanon Post Office Cobb County Ga. my Brother is Post Master of that office Direct them to him as post master nothing more at present but remains yours truely in the bonds of Love.
      EDWIN DYER"

ATTALA COUNTY: Lot 64-27-3 Cherokee. SHELMAN DURHAM, gdn. of the heirs of ELIJAH CURRS, formerly of Monroe County, Georgia, appoints SANDERS W. DURHAM of Talbot Co. as att'y. to claim lot 64-27-3 drawn by himself, and lot 135-29- of Lee County. Signed: Shelman Durham bef. JOSHUA BROOKS, J.P. 3 April 1843.

MERITHER/MERIWETHER? COUNTY:
  Lot 862-20-3 Cherokee. GREEN REEVES appts JOHN BAYNES of Jasper Co. as att'y. to claim lot drawn by GREEN REEVES and the lot drawn by POLLY GIBSON, now the wife of GREEN REEVES, both formerly of Jasper co. Signed: Green Reeves (by mark) bef. WM. C. ROPER, J.P., 1 Feb. 1843. No. 1168-2-3 Green Reeves 364 Jasper; No. 862-20-3 Polly Gibson, wid., Phillips,Jasper.

EARLY COUNTY Lot 5-19-3 Cherokee. Pers. app'd. JOSEPH IRWIN, Adm'r. of the est. of JOHN RICKS, dec'd., of Jackson Co., Territory of Florida, to claim lot 5-19-3. Signed: Joseph Irwin bef. JOEL L. POERTER, J.P., 19 June 1843.

JACKSON COUNTY: Lot 101-13-3 Cherokee. SAMUEL KNOX of Chattooga Co. appoints PLEYNEY A. TURK of Jackson Co. as att'y. for taking out grants to lot 101-13-3 drwn by him, Samuel Knox, Jr., and lot 34-8-3, drawn by Samuel Knox, Sr., dec'd., of whom Samuel Knox Jr. is one of the Ex'r.s Signed: Samuel Knox bef. ROBERT TRUITT, J.B. NABUS, J.P. & PHINEY A. TURK, 27 Feb. 1843.

     Lot 621-4-3 Cherokee. "Cass Co. Apr. 15th 1833
His Excellency WILSON H. LUMPKIN
    Dear Sir
       In the performance of my duty as Indian Agent for this county I have met with some cases which have rather puzzled me. One is, where a Lot has, (a large portion of it) been Enrolled, and is now, and has been all last year in the possession of the Individual who rented it last year; and on

a part of the Same lot, there is an Indian improvement in the occupation of Indian. Another case is an Improvement that has been made by a white man, that falls on the same Lot where there is an Indian Occupant. And another is, where in addition to either of the above stated cases, the lot has (for some cause or other) been granted. If you should feel at liberty to do so, I would be glad it you would write me, and give me your opinion relative to these cases.

I have been informed that you have granted Lot 621 in the 4th Dist. and 3rd Sect. to some individual on account of a Certificate from Genr. COFFEE that the Improvement on it was made by a Mr. DAWSON, instead of an Indian. This is an error; I have examined the lines and find that no part of Dawsons improvement is made by an Indian who lives on the lot, and has lived there (it is said) for twenty or thirty years Dawson's improvement is on lot No. 676-in the same Dist., and a part of the same Indian's Improvement falls on a part of that lot, and I ought I think by no means be granted, if I understand the Law right on the subject. Dawson's ferry is on Lot no 677 in the same district; this is also on a Lot, in Indian Occupancy, There will (I am informed) be an effort made to get the grant for that, but I cant believe it will be Granted, unless its done under incorrect information.

Being settled in this Cherokee Country and having resumed the Practise of the Law, I would be glad to get the collection of the notes due the State for rent in this Circuit, that will be sent out tor Collection. If they are forwarded to me by the bearer Mr. MAXEY. I will send a receipt for them by mail, or if it would be thought necessary, I would go down to Milledgeville after them. Pleas to write to me by the bearer and much oblige your most obedient Servt.
C. D. TERHUNE"

TROUP COUNTY: Lot 467-1-3 Cherokee. REBECCA RHODES appoints JOHN Y. RHODES of Chambers Co., Alabama, as her att'y. to take out the grant to lot 467-1-3 drawn by her in Jones Co., Ga. Signed: Rebecca Rhodes (by mark) before MARY P. ANDERSON & J. M. HARRINGTON, J.P., 27 June 1843.

NEWTON COUNTY: Lot 227-13-4 Cherokee. Pers. app'd. OLIVER P. HILL to claim lot 227-13-4 of Henry now in Newton Co., "in connection" with ELIZABETH HILL, SUSAN HILL, & SARAH A. HILL (the orphans of BENJAMIN HILL.) Includes app't of JOHN BASS of Newton Co. as att'y. Signed: Oliver P.Hill bef. WILLIAM H. C. PACE & COLUMBUS D. PACE, J.I.C., 21 Apr.1843.

COLUMBIA COUNTY: Lot 241-13-4 Cherokee. Pers. came WILLIAM SCOTT to claim lot 241-13-4, drawn by JAMES J COOLY, since deceased, as guardian of the owner. Includes app't. of JAMES M. JENNINGS as att'y. Signed. William Scott bef. STEPHEN DRANE, J.P., 27 June 1843.

CHATTOOGA COUNTY: Lot 309-7-4 Cherokee. Pers. app'd. ABRAHAM

GREATHOUSE to claim lot 309-7-4, drawn by ROBT. C. LANE. Includes appt. of R. W. JONES as att'y. Signed: A. Greathouse before JOHN J. STOREY and SAML. JACKSON, J.P. 6 June 1843.

TELFAIR COUNTY: Lot 117-8-4 Cherokee. ARCHIBALD MC KINON appoints WM. W. PAIN as att'y. to take out the grants to lots 117-8-4 drawn by the orphans of DANIEL FURLASON. McKinon is legal representative for the orphans. Signed. Archibald McKinon bef. F. S. MC CALL, J.I.C., 2 June 1843.

CHATTOGA COUNTY: Lot 249-9-4 Cherokee. Pers. app'd. SAM'L. MC WHORTER, Ex'r. of the estate of JAMES MC WHORTER, dec'd.,to claim lot 249-9-4. Includes app't. of WILEY DYER of Walker Co. as att'y. Signed. Saml. McWhorter bef. JOHN B. LANSFORD, J.P. & ROBERT A. HENRY, 8 March 1843.

GREENE COUNTY: Lot 170-26-3 Cherokee. Pers. came DAVID ALLISON, legatee of MARTHA ALLISON, dec'd. to claim lot 170-26-3. Signed: David Allison bef. PAS. W. GODKIN, J.I.C., 18 April 1843.

WARREN COUNTY: Lot 106-14-3 Cherokee. Pers. app'd. EZRA MC CRARY to claim lot 106-14-3 and lot 283-22-3. Includes app't. of ADAM JONES of Warren Co. as att'y. Signed: Ezra McCrary bef. WILLIAM FOWLER, J.P., 13 June 1843.

OGLETHORPE COUNTY: Lot 51-15-3 Cherokee. Pers. came THOMAS HOWARD to claim lot 51-15-3 as owner of one half of the lot. The other half is owned by F. M. SMITH. Includes app't. of FERDINAND PHINIZY as att'y. Signed: Thomas Howard bef. WILLIAM CALDWELL & ELISHA CRAMER, J.P., 31 May 1843.

Lot 59-5-3 Cherokee. "Cass County Sept. 10th 1833.
To His Excellency WILSON LUMPKIN
           I do hereby certify that I have examined lot no. 59-5-3 of formerly Cherokee, now Cass Co. and that I find on it, no other improvement, than a Cabbin, which (as the Claimant WALTER ADAIR admits) was built by himself and others but principally by himself for the purpose of a school house and probably also a meeting house and I am also told by the neighbours that said house was built between the first of January 1830 and the time that the country was surveyed off into lots said Adair,.... claims it as his own improvement however and therefore Claims the lot on which it is situated These facts I have certified in order

that the governor might know them and could use his own discretion in issueing the grant for the same.
very respectfully
C. D. TERHUNE
Indian Agent for Cass County"

CASS COUNTY: Lot 244-23-3 Cherokee. Certification that lot 244-3-3 occupied by JOHN ROSS, is subject to being granted having received a fee simple reservation under the treaty of 1819. Signed: WM. G. SPRINGER, Agent for the Cherokees in Georgia, 7 February 1834.

Lot 209-15-3 Cherokee. "Adairsville Cass Co., Ga. Aug. 11th 1833

Dear Sir
Agreeably to request, I enclose you the desired certificate from Majr. CURNEY concerning lot no. 209-15-3. I luckily met with him at ELI HICK's next day after I met with you on the Flint hill. You will have no difficulty I presume, in obtaining a grant for said lot.
Your son's health is improving I think. In haste yours &c
Capt. Stephens   B. S. HARDMAN"

MURRAY COUNTY:
New Echota: Lot 172-9-3 Cherokee. Certification that lot 172-9-3 late emigrated by POLLY, one of the wives of JOSEPH VANN, may be granted. Signed: WM. G. SPRINGER, Agent of the Cherokees in Georgia, 14 Feb. 1834.

Lot 106-7-3 Cherokee. "Clinton. April 16, 1834.
Governor Lumpkin
Dear Sir
Mr. WILEY GLOVER a citizen of this County, called on me today and requested me to write your Excellency and ascertain from you, if your had ordered a grant for a lot drawn by him, number 106 in the 7th District and 3rd Section of originally Cherokee County. During the last term of the Superior Court for Baldwin County, Mr. Glover put into the hands of Major HARDIMAN of this county, a certificate of Mr. Hardin one of the agents for the state, before the last act of the Legislature, appointing one general agent, certifying that the Indians who had made improvements on the lot had emigrated and that the lot was not incumbered with the residence of a native or Indian. Major Hardiman put the certificate into the hands of one of your secretaries, I think Mr. WELLBOURNE. Will your Excellence do Mr. Glover the kindness to cause the matter to be examined into, and write to me whether you will order the grant to issue, and he will forward the fee for the grant to the proper department. The above is in complience with his request he adds this, with my best wishes for your happiness, Respectfully your obt sert
JOHN L. LEWIS"

CASS COUNTY: Lot 15-5-3 Cheroee. WLATER ADAIR claims to be Cherokee Indian and resides upon lot 15-5-3. He also claims lots 16 and 22 in the same district and section. But as he had a reservation for life attached to him under the treaty with the Cherokee Indians and he is not entitled to said lots. Signed: WM. G. SPRINGER, Agent for the Cherokees in Georgia, 6 Feb. 1834.

CASS COUNTY: Lot 845-4-3 Cherokee. Certification that the Cherokee Indian named OLD FIELD and his family have abandoned lot 845-4-3 and left Georgia, for upwards of a year. The lot should be granted. Signed: C. D. TERHUNE Indian Agent for Cass County, 17 August 1833.

JONES COUNTY: Lot 150-12-3 Cherokee. Pers. came JOHN MARSH who testifys that he has known WILLIAM GUNN from a boy and that the "WILLIAM C. GUNN" on the lottery list was a mistake and should have been "WILLIAM GUNN". Personally came EPHRAIM SANDERS, who says that he has known William Gunn for twenty years and that he has always signed his name without a "C.". WILLIAM A. INGRAM certifys that he was at the school at the time of the registration of the lottery and that William Gunn did not sign his name as "William C. Gunn". and that there is no such person in the district. Signed: JOHN MARSH, EPHRAIM SANDERS & WILLIAM A. INGRAM, J.P., 10 May 1837. John Marsh had been one of the commissioners for the land lottery for Jones County.

CHATHAM COUNTY: Lot 1008-4-3 Cherokee. Pers. app'd. JAMES F. BLOIS, eldest orphan of PETER BLOIS, to claim lot 244-9-2 and lot 1008-4-3. Blois appoints JOHN EXLEY as att'y. for himself and his brothers. Signed: James F. Blois bef. JOSEPH FELT, J.P., 31 May 1843.

WARE COUNTY: Lot 58-21-3 Cherokee. Pers. app'd. JUNIPHER GRIFFIS and WINNEFRIED DYESS to claim lot 58-21-3 and lot 1205-3-2. Signed: JUNNIPER GRIFFIS and WINAFRED DYESS bef. JAMES FELWOOD, J.I.C., 16 March 1843.

CHATHAM COUNTY: Lot 276-25-3 Cherokee. Pers. app'd. JOHN HENRY STIBBS, agent for the widow and orphan of THOMAS WILLIAMS, to claim lot 276-7-3 and lot 318-7-4. Signed: John Henry Stibbs bef. R. RAIFORD, J.P., 29 May 1843.

HALL COUNTY: Lot 175-28-3 Cherokee. Pers. app'd. JOHN DEAVOURS to claim lot 175-8-3; lot 562-1-4; lot 272-7-2; and as heir of ROBERT WOOD, SR., dec'd., to lot

322-1-4 and lot 318-11-4. Includes app't. of BENJAMIN B. SMITH of Baldwin Co. as att'y. Signed: JOHN DEAVOURS before GALATHILL HULSEY & ROBERT LAWRENCE, J.P., 20 June 1843.

CLARKE COUNTY: Lot 54-28-3 Cherokee. Pers. came JAMES FULTON, guardian of the minors of JAMES ESPY, to claim lot 54-28-3. Includes app't. of DILLION D. FULTON as attorney. Signed: James Fulton bef. CHARLES NEWTON & E. L. NEWTON, J.P., 2 June 1843.

CHAMBERS COUNTY: Lot 109-27-3 Cherokee. Pers. came EZEKIEL RATCHFORD to claim lot 109-27-3; lot 508-20-3; lot 2-5-2; and lot 270-8-3. The latter two were purchased from JOSIAH MEEKS who owns half of both lots. Signed: Ezekiel Ratchford bef. JOHN J. KEMPSEY, J.P., 5 June 1843.

TROUP COUNTY: Lot 305-27-3 Cherokee. Pers. app'd. JUDITH BRIDGEMAN, Adm'trx. of the est. of FRANCIS BRIDGEMAN, to claim lot 305-27-3. Includes app't. of WILLIAM E. MARCUS as att'y. Signed: Judith Bridgeman before THOMAS WOOD & ROBERT H. SLEDGE, J.P., 1 May 1843.

WALKER COUNTY: Lot 197-25-3 Cherokee. Pers. app'd. HUGH BEATY, Adm'r. of the estate of TIMOTHY C. WOODS, dec'd., to claim lot 197-25-3. Includes app't. of TIMOTHY C. WOODS as att'y. Signed: Hugh Beaty bef. JAMES M. SIMS & JAMES HARBUCK, J.P., 11 May 1843.

HABERSHAM COUNTY: Lot 306-28-3 Cherokee. Pers. app'd. JOEL PAINTER, one of the heirs of EZEKIEL PAINTER of Hall Co., to claim lot 306-28-3, as part owner. Includes app't. of BENJAMIN CLEVELAND as att'y. Signed: Joel Painter bef. THOMAS DOOLY & LOVEN J. KEEL, J.P., 15 June 1843.

WALKER COUNTY: Lot 261-28-3 Cherokee. SUSANNAH SPENCE, for her absent father BARRY SPENCE, to claim lot 261-28-3, app'ts. CHARLES H. NELSON of Baldwin County as att'y. Signed: Susannah Spence bef. A. SHAMBLIN, J.P. 16 June 1843.

TALBOT COUNTY: Lot 218-20-3 Cherokee. Pers. app'd. ARCHIBALD GRAY, Ex'r. of the est. of JAMES GRAY, deceased of Pike County, to claim lot 218-20-3 and lot 204-17-1. Includes app't of GREGORY J. TURNER as att'y. Signed: A. GRAY before PETER T. MONTFORT & RICHD. HOTT, J.P., 25 June 1843.

HANCOCK COUNTY: Lot 9-21-3 Cherokee. Pers. app'd. ALBERT A. SIMONTON, Ex'r. of the est. of NANCY VINCENT of Greene Co., to claim lot 9-21-3. Nancy Vincent was the widow of WILLIAM VINCENT. Includes app't. of WILLIAM ASKEW as attorney. Signed: A. S. Simonton before WILLIAM ASKEW, J.P. 9 June 1843.

MUSCOGEE COUNTY: Lot 463-21-3 Cherokee. Pers. app'd. JOHN A. RAY, Adm'r. of the est. of SANDERS W. RAY, to claim lot 463-21-3 and lot 224-21-2. Includes app't. of JOHN W. A. SANFORD of Baldwin Co. as att'y. Signed: John A. Ray bef. ALEXANDER MOSS & P. M. THOMAS, J.P., 17 June 1843.

MONROE COUNTY: Lot 822-21-3 Cherokee. GEORGE DOUGLAS, agent for NANCY C. STRONG (widow of ALLEN B. STRONG, dec'd.) of Bibb County, appoints SAMUEL B. HUNTER of Bibb Co. as att'y. to take out a grant for lot 822-21-3. Signed: George Douglas before JAMES NORRIS, J.P., 3 June 1843.

WILKES COUNTY: Lot 836-21-3 Cherokee. Pers. app'd. JACOB HUBBARD, guardian of JOHN B. MILNER's orphans to claim lot 836-21-3. Includes app't. of THOMAS W. THOMAS as att'y. Signed: Jacob Hubbard before BRADFORD MERRY, J.P. 15 May 1843.

WALKER COUNTY: Lot 333-4-3 Cherokee. JOHN M. HOOPER of Leak County, Mississippi, appoints CHARLES G. HOOPER of Walker County, Georgia, as att'y. to take out grant to lot 333-4-2; lot 645-19-3; and lot 288-11-4. Signed: JOHNSON M. Hooper bef. John M. Hooper, E.M. CHATHAM, and R. MICKLEJOHN, J.P., 23 January 1843.

JONES COUNTY: Lot 793-19-3 Cherokee. Pers. came WILEY LITTLE, distributee of the est. of NAHUME LITTLE, dec'd., to claim lot 793-19-3. Includes app't. of CULLEN WHITMAN as att'y. Signed: Wiley Little (by mark) before JOHN WILLIAMSON & GREEN B. WILLIAMSON, J.P., 26 June 1843.

JEFFERSON COUNTY: Lot 847-19-3 Cherokee. Pers. app'd. WIL-
LIAM U. YOUNG, guardian of the estate of
RUFUS G. WEEKS (minor and only heir of JESSE WEEKS), to claim
lot 847-19-3 and lot 191-9-4. App't. of LEVAN C. MATTHEWS as at-
t'y. Signed: Wm. U. Young bef. WM. P. DAVIS & STERLING G. JORDAN,
J.P., 6 June 1843.

MORGAN COUNTY: Lot 156-12-3 Cherokee. Pers. came JAMES W.
JOHNSON, one of the orphans of RICHARD
JOHNSON of Walton co., to claim lot 156-12-3. App't. of ARAVIAH
B. BOSTWICK as att'y. Signed: J. W. Johnson bef. SHERROD W. TURN-
ER & AB. BOSTWICK, J.P., 13 June 1843.

JACKSON COUNTY: Lot 139-12-3 Cherokee. Pers. came THOMAS
BROOKS to claim lot 139-12-3 as three
fifths owner. He purchased the parts from MOSES DILLARD (husband
of NANCY BLANCHARD), ZACHARIAH BLANCHARD, & JEREMIAH BLANCHARD
(orphans of PHILIP BLANCHARD) and he claims the lot for himself
and as agent for the other two orphans. Signed: Thomas Brooks
before N. A. PENDERGRASS, J.P., 9 Feb. 1849.

HALL COUNTY: Lot 1040-19-3 Cherokee. Pers. app'd. JAMES
RYLIN, Ex'r. of the est. of JAMES RYLIN,
dec'd., to claim lot 1040-19-3 and lot 181-7-1. App't. of CINCI-
NNATUS HALL as att'y. Signed: James Rylin bef. ALLEN LANGFORD &
MARTIN GRAHAM, J.P., 6 June 1843.

TALBOT COUNTY: Lot 1106-19-3 Cherokee. Pers. app'd. JON-
ATHAN B. MC CRARY, Adm'r. of the estate
of WILLIAM DURDEN, to claim lot 1106-19-3 and lot 105-5 of Muscogee Co. App't. of MATTHEW MC CRARY as att'y. Signed: Jonathan
B. McCrary bef. MILTON B. ROSE & HOPE H. HAMMOCK, J.P., 13 June
1843.

PAULDING COUNTY: Lot 1179-19-3 Cherokee. Pers. app'd. THOM-
AS JOHNSTON, Adm'r. of the est. of JOHN
GHOLSON, dec'd., to claim lot 1179-19-3. App't. of WILLIAM C.
JOHNSTON as att'y. Signed: T. Johnston bef. BUSHROD W. JOHNSTON,
J.P., 26 June 1843.

NEWTON COUNTY: Lot 1212-19-3 Cherokee. Pers. app'd. ROB-
ERT PATRICK, agent for SINTHA PATRICK (or-

phan of JOSHUA PATRICK, dec'd.) to claim lot 513-7 of Appling Co. and lot 1212-19-3. App't. of JOHN A. BROUGHTON as att'y. Signed: ROBERT PATRICK bef. SIMEON ESTES & GEORGE HAYS, J.P., 13 June 1843

MACON COUNTY: Lot 1249-19-3 Cherokee. Pers. app'd. JOHN M. CLOUD, one of the orphans of WILLIAM CLOUD, dec'd., to claim lot 1249-19-3. Signed: J. M. Cloud bef. JOSEPH MOTT, J.I.C., 3 Jan. 1853.

GWINNETT COUNTY: Lot 116-22-3 Cherokee. Pers. came BUCKNER HARRIS, son of EUNICE HARRIS, dec'd., to claim lot 116-22-3. App't. of ROBERT W. CLEVELAND as att'y. Signed: Buckner Harris bef. MADISON L. ADAIR & JESSE MURPHEY,J.P. 15 June 1843.

WILKES COUNTY: Lot 147-22-3 Cherokee. Pers. app'd. WILLIAM POOL, judgement creditor of LEWIS S. BROWN, dec'd., to claim lot 147-22-3. App't. of JOHN R. ANDERSON of Baldwin Co. as att'y. Signed: William Pool bef. Lewis S. Brown J.I.C., 20 June 1843.

BIBB COUNTY: Lot 430-20-3 Cherokee. Pers. app'd. ANDREW J. WHITE and REUBEN H. WHITE, Adm'rs. of the est. of MAXFIELD H. WILLIFORD, to claim lot 430-20-3. Appointment of G. G. STUBBLEFIELD as Att'y. Signed: A. J. White & Reuben H. White bef. BENJ. F. ROSS, N.P., 27 June 1843.

RANDOLPH COUNTY: Lot 335-20-3 Cherokee. Pers. app'd. ROBERT T. DUKE, to claim lot 335-20-3 and 614-18-2, drawn by SAMUEL P. DUKE & JAMES DUKE's orphans, as an agent for the other legatees. App't. of DAVID L. RICE as att'y. Signed: R. T. Duke bef. BENJAMIN H. RICE, J.P., 23 June 1843.

ELBERT COUNTY: Lot 234-20-3 Cherokee. Pers. app'd. HORATIO G. TATE, one of the orphans of ZIMM TATE, dec'd., to claim lot 234-20-3. App't. of Doctor WILLIAM G. ALLEN. Signed: H. G. Tate bef. THOMAS BELL & LINDSAY H. SMITH, J.P., 31 May 1843.

CHATTOOGA COUNTY: Lot 1054-21-3 Cherokee. Pers. app'd. ROBERT W. SMITH, as one of the proper owners and agent for the other, to claim lot 822-5-1. App't. of RICHARD

M. JONES as att'y. Signed: ROBT. W. SMITH bef. ROBT. CAMSON JOHN HORN, J.P., 17 May 1843.

CAMPBELL COUNTY: Lot 108-20-3 Cherokee. Pers. app'd. SAMUEL LEWIS, W. F. DWINE & MARY DWINE, heirs of JOHN J. DWINE, dec'd., of Pike County, to claim lot 108-20-3. App't. of JOHN CARLTON as att'y. Signed: Sml. Lewis, W. D. Dwine and Mary Dwine bef. JOHN W. PALMAR & E. L. JACKSON, J.P. 19 May 1843.

DOOLY COUNTY: Lot 77-20-3 Cherokee. Pers. app'd. NANCY HILLIARD, mother and agent of TILLETHA, QUINTINE, WILLIAM, ROBERT & MANIY, the orphans of LEVI HILLIARD, dec'd., to claim lot 77-20-3. App't. of ECHOLS HIGHTOWER as atty. Signed: Nancy Hilliard (by mark) bef. THOS. H. KEY & WM. C. GREEN, J.P., 20 May 1843.

MURRAY COUNTY: Lot 121-20-3 Cherokee. Pers. app'd. WILLIAM P. CHESTER & A. N. HARGRAVE, to claim lot 121-20-3 and lot 687-21-3. App't. of JAMES MORRIS as att'y. Signed: William P. Chester and A. N. Hargrave bef. A. J. HOLDEN & JAMES BUCKANNON, J.P., 25 May 1843.

MUSCOGEE COUNTY: Lot 82-20-3 Cherokee. Pers. app'd. JOHN ROLAND, agent of JAMES GARVIN & WILLIAM ROLAND, to claim lot 82-20-3 and lot 1184-2-3. App't. of BENJAMIN Y. BETHUNE of Baldwin Co. as att'y. Signed: John Roland bef. RICHARD BISSELL and JOHN J. MC KENDUE, J.P., 10 June 1843.

BUTTS COUNTY: Lot 60-19-3 Cherokee. In person came JAMES CARTER, Adm'r. and Gdn. for two of the orphans of REDMAN, dec'd. of Butts Co., to claim lot 60-19-3. Appt. of AUGUSTUS CARGILL as att'y. Signed: James Carter bef. J. H. MACK (MARK?) and STEPHEN BAILEY, J.P., 30 May 1843.

MARION COUNTY: Lot 434-19-3 Cherokee. JOHN M. GODLEY, Adm'r. of the est. of JAMES M. GODLEY, appoints THOMAS BENNES(?), as att'y. to take out grant to lot 434-19-3. Signed: John M. Gogley bef. CULLIN L. BATTLE, J.P. 19 May 1843.

MUSCOGEE COUNTY: Lot 6-2-3 Cherokee. Pers. app'd. THEOPHE-

LUS BRYAN, Adm'r. of the estate of THOMAS P. BRYAN, dec'd., to claim lot 6-2-3, drawn by SIMON GASLIN; lot 420-19-3 drawn by WILLIS RODES; lot 859-15-2, drawn by WILLIAM WETHERS; lot 218-18-2, drawn by THOS. P. BRYAN; lot 50-5 of Muscogee Co.; fractional lot on the Chattahoochee in the 33rd Dist. of Lee County, bought from SOWEL WOLFOLK; lot 80-9 of Muscogee County; and lot 118-12-Muscogee County. Signed: THEOPHILUS BRYAN bef. COEDY MASSEY, J.P., 28 May 1843.

HABERSHAM COUNTY: Lot 644-1-3 Cherokee. Pers. app'd. NELSON CASH, one of the heirs of HOWARD CASH, deceased, to claim lot 644-1-3. App't. of E. S. BARCLAY as att'y. Signed: Nelson Cash bef. LOVEN J. KEEL, J.P., 30 May 1843.

WALTON COUNTY: Lot 440-1-3 Cherokee. Pers. app'd. BURTON TREADWELL, one of the heirs of ISAAC TREADWELL, dec'd., to claim lot 440-1-3. App't. of CHARLES H. NELSON as att'y. Signed: Burton Treadwell bef. H. H. CAMP & R. A. JOHNSTON, J.P., 16 June 1843.

IRWIN COUNTY: Lot 183-1-3 Cherokee. JOHN FITZGERALD, father of JOSHUA FITZGERALD, dec'd., appoints JOSEPH N. MILLER as att'y. to take out grant to lot 183-1-3 and lot 319-18-2. (The rest of the document cannot be read).

BALDWIN COUNTY: Lot 940-20-3 Cherokee. Pers. app'd. BENJAMIN ROBERTS, Ex'r. of the est. of LEVI SPRIGHTS, dec'd., to claim lot 940-20-3. Signed: Benjamin Roberts bef. ALFRED M. HORTON, N.P., 27 June 1843.

BALDWIN COUNTY: Lot 1270-20-3 Cherokee. Pers. app'd. ROBT. S. PILES, Adm'r. of the est. of SARAH A. BROWN, dec'd., to claim lot 1270-20-3. Signed: Robt. S. Piles before ALEXANDER HALL, J.P., 20 December 1843.

HARRIS COUNTY: Lot 750-20-3 Cherokee. Pers. came L. B. BOLES, to claim lot 750-20-3. having married the orphan who drew it. Signed: L. B. Boles bef. A. H. LUTT, J.P., 26 June 1843.

ELBERT COUNTY: Lot 54-19-3 Cherokee. Pers. app'd. Z. H. CLARK, Adm'r. of the est. of LEWIS J. JONES dec'd. to claim lot 54-19-3 and lot 1283-17-3. Signed. Z. H.Clark before LINDSAY H. SMITH, J.P., 27 Feb. 1843.

BIBB COUNTY: Lot 142-20-3 Cherokee. Pers. came NATHAN B. JOHNSON, to claim a certain lot for JOHN BUCKHANNON's orphans and to app't. SPENCER RILEY as his agent for taking out grant to same. Signed: N. B. Johnston bef. KEELIN COOK, J.I.C., 22 July 1853.

CHATHAM COUNTY: Lot 1157-20-3 Cherokee. Pers. app'd. Dr. SAMUEL A. F. LAWRENCE, agent of MARY H. BROWNE, widow, to claim lot 1157-20-3. Signed: S. A. F. Lawrence before LEONIDAS WYLLY, J.P., 2 June 1843.

LINCOLN COUNTY: Lot 292-24-3 Cherokee. ELIZABETH DENNIS, widow, the mother of the orphans of ALLEN DENNIS, appoints PETER LAMAR as att'y. to claim lot 292-24-3. (The rest of this document cannot be read.)

UPSON COUNTY: Lot 109-22-3 Cherokee. Pers. came JAMES GARRETT, Gdn. of WILLIAM LOFLIN, one of the orphans of JOHN LOFLIN, to claim lot 109-22-3. Signed: James Garrett bef. LEMUEL JACOBS, J.P., 2 December 1847.

HENRY COUNTY: Lot 593-20-3 Cherokee. Pers. app'd. ELISHA S. CROWELL to claim lot 593-20-3. Signed: E. S. Crowell before JOHN HAIL, J.P., 3 June 1843.

FRANKLIN COUNTY: Lot 951-3-3 Cherokee. Pers. came THOMAS MORRIS, agent for ALVAN E. WHITTEN of Holmes Co., Mississippi, to claim lots 51-3-3; 911-4-3; 32-10-1 and 239-_2-4. Signed: Thos. Morris bef. R. A. R. NEAL, J.I.C. 17 June 1843.

MORGAN COUNTY: Lot 277-28-3 Cherokee. Pers. came ELIZA-BETH RAINEY, widow of JOHN RAINEY, dec'd. to claim lott 277-28-3. Signed: Elizabeth Rainey bef. LUMPKIN J. GARRETT, J.P., 24 May 1843.

HARRIS COUNTY: Lot 106-28-3 Cherokee. Pers. came THOMAS J. HAMBY, one of the orphans of THOMAS HAMBY, dec'd., of Newton Co., to claim lot 106-28-3, as the orphans are now of age and wish to make a division. Signed: THOMAS J. HAMBY before A. H. SCOTT, J.P., 5 May 1843.

WILKINSON COUNTY: Lot 128-26-3 Cherokee. Pers. app'd. WILLIAM E. CARSWELL, Ex'r. of the estate of SARAH CARSWELL, to claim lot 128-26-3. Signed: W. E. Carswell before S. J. BUSH, J.P., 17 June 1843.

BALDWIN COUNTY: Lot 151-26-3 Cherokee. Pers. app'd. A. H. STEPHENS to claim lot 151-26-3, as having an interest in it. Signed: A. H. Stephens bef. ALFRED M. HORTON, N.P., 17 June 1843.

HANCOCK COUNTY: Lot 306-26-3 Cherokee. Pers. app'd. MOSES BROOM, Adm'r. of the estate of SOLOMON BROOM, dec'd., to claim lot 306-26-3. Signed: Moses Broom (by mark) before SEABORN LAURENCE, J.P., 26 June 1843.

WAYNE COUNTY: Lot 190-27-3 Cherokee. Pers. app'd. JAMES HIGHSMITH, JACOB HIGHSMITH, HENRY HIGHSMITH, JOHN HIGHSMITH, & WALTER YONELLS, (the heirs of SARAH HIGHSMITH), to claim lot 190-27-3. Signed: James Highsmith, Jacob Highsmith (by mark), Henry Highsmith (by mark), John Highsmith and Walter Yonell, before ELIAS F. STEWART, J.P. 6 Apr. 1843.

GREENE COUNTY: Lot 69-27-3 Cherokee. Pers. app'd. STERLING H. R. GRESHAM, Adm'r. of the estate of POLLY JENKINS, dec'd., to claim lot 69-27-3. Signed: S. H. R. Gresham before J. R. HALL, J.I.C., 5 June 1843.

BIBB COUNTY: Lot 65-21-3 Cherokee. Pers. app'd. SARAH Q. FLUKER, for herself and as guardian of the orphans of B. F. FLUKER, to claim lot 65-21-2 and lot 172-17-3. App't. of JAMES M. ELLIS as att'y. Signed: S. Q. Fluker bef. EDW. D. MC KEY(?), Judge Superior Crt., 14 June 1843.

BALDWIN COUNTY: Lot 50-28-3 Cherokee. Pers. app'd. JOHN HODGES to claim lot 50-28-3 as Adm'r. of the estate of the owner. Signed: John Hodges bef. Alfred M. Horton, N.P., 28 June 1843.

BALDWIN COUNTY: Lot 116-28-3 Cherokee. Personally app'd.

McKENNETH PAGE to claim lot 116-28-3, as one of the heirs of the owner. Signed: McKenneth Page before Alfred M. Horton, N.P., 26 June 1843.

BALDWIN COUNTY: Lot 143-4-3 Cherokee. Pers. app'd. EDWIN R. BROWN, to claim lot 143-4-3 as owner of one half and as guardian for MARY (?) HALL, owner of the other half. Signed: Edwin R. Brown bef. Alfred M. Horton, N.P., 7 January 1843.

BALDWIN COUNTY: Lot 31-25-3 Cherokee. Pers. app'd. JOSEPH M. EVANS to claim lot 31-25-3, as guardian of the owners. Signed: Jos. M. Evans before Alfred M. Horton, N.P., 5 June 1843.

BALDWIN COUNTY: Lot 146-25-3 Cherokee. Pers. app'd. SIMEON FULLER JR., to claim lot 146-25-3 in part as one of the heirs of the drawer. Signed: Simeon Fuller,Jr. before Alfred M. Horton, N.P., 25 May 1843.

BALDWIN COUNTY: Lot 290-25-3 Cherokee. Pers. app'd. ROBERTSON PARKER to claim lot 290-25-3. Signed: Robertson Parker (by mark) before Alfred M. Horton, N.P. 26 June 1843.

FAYETTE COUNTY: (Designation illegible) Pers. came JAMES HANES, SR., to claim the lot he drew in the lottery. Signed: James Hanes, Sr. before THOS. P. JONES, J.P. 1 June 1843.

Pers. came JOSHUA HANES, Adm'r. of the estate of RABY ROUNTREE, to claim lot 499-4-3 and 61-8-1. Signed: Joshua Hanes bef. Thos. P. Jones, J.P. 1 June 1843.

SPALDING COUNTY: Lot 109-26-3 Cherokee. Pers. app'd. EVELINE A. MC KEE to claim lot 109-26-3, as owner in part. Signed: Eveline A. McKee before A. MERRITT, N.P. 12 October 1853.

DECATUR COUNTY: Lot 187-4-3 Cherokee. Pers. app'd. WILLIAM M. C. NEEL to claim lot 187-4-3, drawn by JAMES WILLIS orphans of Twiggs County. Signed: Wm. M.C. Neel before DAVID C. SMITH, J.P., 14 June 1843.

GREENE COUNTY: Lot 220-4-3 Cherokee. Pers. came ROBERT NEWSOM, agent for JESSE ASBURY of Alabama to claim lot 220-4-3. Signed: Robert Newsom bef. SPARKS STUNTER, J.P., 23 June 1843.

BALDWIN COUNTY: Lot 983-2-3 Cherokee. Pers. app'd. G. B. POWELL, Adm'r. of the estate of EMILY E. FEW, dec'd., widow, to claim lot 983-2-3. Signed: Green B. Powell before Alfred M. Horton, N.P., 19 June 1843.

TROUP COUNTY: Lot 910-2-3 Cherokee. Pers. app'd. ELIZABETH SMITH, widow of DAVID SMITH, to claim lot 910-2-3. Dr. N. N. HOWELL is appointed as her agent. Signed: Elizabeth Smith (by mark) before DANIEL W. HOWELL, J.P. June 1843.

ELBERT COUNTY: Lot 29-4-3 Cherokee. Pers. came JEREMIAH S. WARREN, Adm'r. of the estate of JAMES BANKS, dec'd., to claim lot 29-4-3. Signed: Jeremiah S. Warren before Z. SMITH, J.P., 16 June 1843.

GWINNETT COUNTY: Lot 279-6-3 Cherokee. Pers. app'd. JOSEPH W. BAXTER, one of the legatees of MARTHA BAXTER, to claim lot 279-6-3. Signed: Joseph W. Baxter before JESSE MURPHEY, J.P., 5 January 1844.

CASS COUNTY: Lot 317-12-3 Cherokee. Pers. came COOPER L. BENNETT, guardian of MITCHELL and D. BENNETT, orphans, to claim lot 317-12-3. Signed: Cooper L. Bennett before NATHAN HOWARD, J.P., 15 April 1847.

BALDWIN COUNTY: Lot 66-5-3 Cherokee. Pers. app'd. WILLIAM CHAPMAN to claim lot 66-5-3, as owner in part. Signed: William Chapman before P. M. COMPTON, N.P. 21 May 1849.

WILKINSON COUNTY: Lot 179-1-3 Cherokee. Pers. app'd. ALLEN CANNON, guardian of the orphans of JONATHAN RIGBY, dec'd. Signed: Allen Cannon bef. Allen Cannon(?),J. P., June 1843.

UPSON COUNTY: Lot 589-1-3 Cherokee. Pers. app'd. SARAH WELBORN widow of JAMES WELBORN, to claim lot 589-1-3. She cannot remember if she was living in Jones or Upson County when he gave in for the lottery. Signed: Sarah Welborn (by mark) before L. M. GATLIN, J.P., 24 May 1843.

BALDWIN COUNTY: Lot 318-27-3 Cherokee. Pers. app'd. J. C. RUMSNIA (?), Adm'r. of the estate of ISAAC FITHEAN, to claim lot 318-27-3 and lot 1244-19-2. Signed: H.(?) C. Remsnia(?) before Alfred M. Horton, N.P., 21 June 1843.

BALDWIN COUNTY: Lot 404-1-3 Cherokee. Pers. app'd. MOSES S. WEST to claim lot 404-1-3 as Ex'r. of the estate of JOS. WEST. Signed: Moses West before J. R. ANDERSON, J.I.C., 27 June 1843.

NEWTON COUNTY: Lot 438-2-3 Cherokee. Pers. app'd. JAMES R. MC CALLA, Ex'r. of the estate of DAVID STOVALL of Franklin County (when he drew sd. lot), to claim lot 438-2-3. Signed: James R. McCalla before K. H. BLAKE, J.P. 20 May 1843.

BALDWIN COUNTY: Lot 501-19-2 Cherokee. Pers. app'd. MARSHAL D. WALKER to claim lot 501-19-2 as owner in part, being a legatee of the drawer. Signed: Marshal Walker before Alfred M. Horton, N.P., 6 May 1843.

HANCOCK COUNTY: Lot 133-2-3 Cherokee. Pers. came BENJAMIN RUSSELL to claim lot 133-2-3 drawn by the orphans of HARDIN CHAMBERS, as owner in part. Signed: Benjamin Russell (by mark) bef. M. H. SPERGHTS, J.P. September 1844.

BIBB COUNTY: Lot 546-2-3 Cherokee. Pers. came HENRY E. ROSS, Adm'r. of the estate of EDWARD GRIFFIN, dec'd., to claim lot 546=2=3. Signed: Henry G. Ross. before J. L. OWEN, J.P., 26 June 1843.

BURKE COUNTY: Lot 138-14-3 Cherokee. Pers. came FERLEY (HERELY?) LEVERETTE, guardian for JAMES, AMANDA & WILLIAM LEVERETTE, orphans, to claim lot 138-14-3. Signed: Pherely(?) Leverett bef. WM. SAPP, J.P. 26 Apr. 1843.

BALDWIN COUNTY: Lot 77-16-3 Cherokee. Pers. came FREDERICK FARMER to claim lot 77=16=3 as owner in part. Signed: F. Farmer before Alfred M. Horton, N.P. 27 May 1843.

BALDWIN COUNTY: Lot 181-2-3 Cherokee. Pers. came SAMUEL PATE to claim lot 181-2-3 as Ex'r. of the estate of STEPHEN DAY, dec'd. Signed: Samuel Pate before Alfred M. Horton, N.P., 16 January 1843.

CARROLL COUNTY: Lot 223-8-3 Cherokee. Pers. came JOHN WHISENHUNT, agent for HESTER BELL, deaf and dumb woman, to claim lot 223-8-3. Signed: John Wisenhunt before A. M. MC WHORTER, J.P., 5 June 1843.

BALDWIN COUNTY: Lot 277-13-3 Cherokee. Pers. came REUBEN H. LUCKEY to claim lot 277-13-3. Signed: R. H. Luckey before Alfred M. Horton, N.P., 17 January 1843. Luckey is owner in part.

CHEROKEE COUNTY: Lot 98-8-3 Cherokee. Pers. came ELIJAH DEAN and MARY DEAN, the only surviving children of ARCHIBALD DEAN, dec'd., of Gwinnett County, to claim lot 98-8-3. Signed: Elijah Dean and Mary Dean (by mark) before RUSSELL JONES, J.P., 18 March 1843.

JASPER COUNTY: Lot 32-5-3 Cherokee. Pers. came WILLIAM Y. HARRIS, who says that he, JOEL N. HARRIS, MARY H. HARRIS & JAMES J. HARRIS are the orphans of ISOM HARRIS, dec'd. and are the owners of lot 32-5-3. Signed: Wm. Y. Harris before DAVID HARRIS, J.P., 24 June 1843.

TROUP COUNTY: Lot 452-17-3 Cherokee. Pers. came GEORGE N. HAMILTON, Adm'r. of the estate of THOMAS P. HAMILTON, to claim lot 452-17-3. Signed: George N. Hamilton before ROBERT H. SLEDGE, J.P., 2 June 1843.

BALDWIN COUNTY: Lot 289-17-3 Cherokee. Pers. came JOHN DAVENPORT to claim lot 289-17-3, as gdn. of the owner. Signed: John Davenport bef. Alfred M. Horton, N.P. 27 May 1843.

BALDWIN COUNTY: Lot 1225-18-3 Cherokee. Pers. app'd. WILEY BARRON to claim lot 1225-18-3 as Adm'r. of the estate of the owner. Signed: Wiley Barron bef. Alfred M. Horton, N.P. 30 May 1843.

BALDWIN COUNTY: Lot 879-17-3 Cherokee. Pers, app'd. LEVI KINSLOW to claim lot 879-17-3, as owner in part. Signed: Levi Kinslow bef. P. M. COMPTON, N.P. 3 November 1849.

HENRY COUNTY: Lot 1169-18-3 Cherokee. Pers. app'd. JOAB COOK, Ex'r. of the estate of ISAKEN(?) COOK, dec'd. of Paulding County, to claim lot 1169-18-3. Signed: Joab Cook before ISAIAH HANA, J.P., 6 June 1843.

JASPER COUNTY: Lot 1162-18-3 Cherokee. GEORGE CLARK appoints JOSEPH L. HOLLAND of Jones Co. as att'y. to claim lot 1162-18-3, drawn by THOMAS R. CLARK, idiot. Signed: George Clark bef. JAS. H. JOHNSON, J.P., 20 June 1843.

Lot 143-5-3 Cherokee. "Louisville 20th Feb. 1833
His Execellenty W. LUMPKIN
Sir
Mrs. ELIZA MILTON of this County has desired me to inform you of an error that she committed by improper advice in fiving in for a draw both in the Gold & Land Lotterys for a Grand child of hers an orphan of JOSIAH STEPHENS. the mistake occured in this way. Josiah Stephens married the daughrer of Mrs. Milton and had a child by her, the mother died Mrs. Milton took the child and has had it ever since its mothers death, when she made the return it did not occur to her that Josiah Stephens again married in this County and had some three or four children ....by his last wife and died the last wife has returned for the orphans and Mrs. Milton has returned for her grand child as an individual orphan when the whole number of children make but one family of orphans and of course as such should be returned for Mrs. Milton returned in one Dist and the Widow of Josiah Stephens in another both in Jefferson County Mrs. Milton returned in Alexanders district and Mrs. Stephens in Christees dist. the name of the orphan of Josiah Stephens for Alexanders dist should be of course withdrawn. this information is given by express request of Mrs. Milton and she is very desirous that the error should be corrected ye will do what is right should be done uner the circumstances very respectfully your obdt. servt.
R. L. GAMBLE"

BURKE COUNTY: Lot 333-2-3 Cherokee. Pers. came ZILPHAY OLIVER widow and guardian of a minor of BENJAMIN OLIVER, to claim the lot drawn by BENJAMIN OLIVER and a part of any lands drawn by CHARLES OLIVER dec'd. (the father of Benjamin Oliver, dec'd.) Signed: Zilpheha Oliver before B. S. KIRKLAND, J.P., 9 June 1843.

HABERSHAM COUNTY: Lot 691-12-3 Cherokee Pers. app'd. FREDERICK WEAVER to claim lot 691-20-3 and lot

134-18-1, drawn by himself and, in right of his wife the former MARTHY NICHOLS, lot 606-3-4. Signed: FREDERICK WEAVER (by mark) before THOS. B. WEAVER, J.P., 23 May 1843.

DEKALB COUNTY: Lot 278-24-3 Cherokee. Pers. came JAMES W. REEVE to claim lot 278-24-3, drawn by HEATH's children, for sd. children. Signed: Jas. W. Reeve before JOHN N. BELLINGER, J.I.C., 31 October 1849.

GWINNETT COUNTY: Lot 35-12-3 Cherokee. Pers. app'd. NEWTON MC DILL to claim lot 35-12-3, drawn by McDill's orphans. Signed: Newton McDill before JAMES MC GINNES, J.P., 24 June 1843.

APPLING COUNTY: Lot 682-21-3 Cherokee. Pers. app'd. WILLIAM ROBINSON, Adm'r. of the estate of JOHN ROBERTSON, dec'd., to claim lot 686-21-3; lot 216-20-3; lot 552-19-3; lot 496-17-3; lot 222-6-1; lot 259-7-2; and lot 167-10-1. App't. of C. B. COLE as att'y. Signed: William Robinson before C. B. Cole, J.I.C., 9 June 1843.

BALDWIN COUNTY: Lot 96-17-3 Cherokee. Pers. app'd. GEORGE W. FISH, Ex'r. of the estate of WILLIAM FISH, dec'd., to claim lot 96-17-3; lot 71-14-1; lot 12-18-4; & lot 563-4-3. Signed: Geo. W. Fish before R. MICKLEJOHN, J.P. 28 June 1843.

DOOLY COUNTY: Lot 240-17-3 Cherokee. JOHN W. COPPEDGE to appoint ELISHA COLLIERS as att'y. for taking out a grant to lot 240-17-3. Signed: John W. Coppedge bef. BENNETT PERVIS, J.P., 15 Feb. 1843.
Pers. app'd. LEWIS COPPEDGE who says that he drew lot 240-17-3, and that he sold the same to John W. Coppedge. Signed: Lewis Coppedge bef. Bennett Purvis, J.P. 15 Feb. 1843.

RICHMOND COUNTY: Lot 497-17-3 Cherokee. Pers. app'd. GEORGE THOMAS, husband of ROSE HEARY, orphan, to claim lot 497-17-3. Signed: George Thomas bef. BENJAMIN B. RUSSELL, N.P., 31 May 1843.

CRAWFORD COUNTY: Lot 293-5-3 Cherokee. Pers. app'd. VAN

HOLTON, being of age, to claim lot 293-5-3 and lot 238-5-3,drawn by the orphans of STEPHEN HOLTON of Washington County, as owner in part. App't. of WILLIAM J. JORDAN as att'y. Signed: Van Holton before WILLIS TAYLOR & E. JOYNER, J.P., 11 April 1843.

TELFAIR COUNTY: Lot 151-7-3 Cherokee. Pers. came BENJAMIN MC LENDON, friend of MARY CRADDICK now MARY MC LENDON, to claim lot 151-7-3. Signed: Benjamin McLendon (by mark) before WM. R. MANNING, J.P., 27 September 1844.

FORSYTH COUNTY: Lot 333-20-3 Cherokee. Pers. app'd. JOHN HENDERSON, Ex'r. of the estate of ROBERT HENDERSON, JR., dec'd., to claim lot 533-20-3. App't. of JAMES A. GREEN as att'y. Signed: John Henderson bef. LEWIS STOVALL & WILLIAM STOVALL, J.P., 1 June 1843.

HEARD COUNTY: Lot 57-22-3 Cherokee. Pers. came MENORAH D. ROBINSON to claim lot 175-12-of Lee Co. drawn by HEZEKIAH SALMON of Richmond Co. and, as Ex'r. of the estate of JOHN ROBINSON, dec'd. to claim lot 57-22-3. Signed: M.D. Robinson before WILLIAM B. W. DENT, J.P., 27 June 1843.

OGLETHORPE COUNTY: Lot 218-23-3 Cherokee. Pers. app'd. WHITFIELD LANDRUM to claim lot 218-23-3, drawn by the orphans of RICHARD DERBY, as a friend and/of the orphans. Signed: Whitefield Landrum bef. G. F. PLATT, J.I.C.,2 May 1848.

CAMPBELL COUNTY: Lot 60-22-3 Cherokee. Pers. came MARGARET COLDWELL, agent for SARAH & ANN COLDWELL (orphans of WILLIAM COLDWELL, dec'd.), and Ex'trx. of the estate of William Coldwell, Dec'd., to claim lot 60-22-3. Signed: Margaret Coldwell before FREDK. BEALL, J.P., 7 June 1843. App't. of BENJAMIN MESENCY(?), as att'y.

CLARKE COUNTY: Lot 259-23-3 Cherokee. Pers. app'd. THOMAS E. WILLIAMSON, Adm'r. of the estate of ANNE E. WILLIAMSON, dec'd., to claim lot 259-23-3. App't. of JOHN H. LOW as att'y. Signed: Thos. E. Williamson bef. WILLIAM HOLLANDS and THOMAS F. SOUR, N.P., 31 May 1843.

HARRIS COUNTY: Lot 134-23-3 Cherokee. Pers. came ISAAC ALMAND, one of the heirs of ANN ALMAND, dec'd., to claim lot 134-23-3, drawn by ANN ALMAND, widow. Signed: Isaac Almand before A. H. SCOTT, J.P. 3 May 1843.

WALTON COUNTY: Lot 194-24-3 Cherokee. Pers. app'd. BENJAMIN STEVENS, guardian of the orphans of WM. H. DAVIS, to claim lot 194-24-3 and lot 157-3-4. App't. of WARREN H. HILL as att'y. Signed: Benjamin Stephens (by mark) before W. H. BRIMBERRY, J.P., 2 May 1843.

THOMAS COUNTY: Lot 1011-19-3 Cherokee. Pers. came JOHN JONES, JR., for himself and his sister, ANN JONES (now ANN MILLER, wife of JAMES MILLER), to claim lot 1011-19-3 and lot 205-7-2. Signed: John Jones, Jr., before JOHN NUTT, J.I.C., 20 March 1843.

CASS COUNTY: Lot 297-12-3 Cherokee. Pers. app'd. HENRY A. GODWIN and JONATHAN H. GODWIN, two of the heirs of BARNABAS GODWIN, dec'd., to claim lot 297-12-3. Signed: J. H. Godwin bef. HENRY F. GODWIN before JAMES STOVALL, J.P., 30 May 1843.

SUMTER COUNTY: Lot 690-19-3 Cherokee. GEORGE DYKES, Admr. of the estate of HENRY DYKES, dec'd., appoints WILLIAM MIMS as att'y. to apply for lot 690-19-3. Signed: George Dykes bef. IRWIN D. HEATH & ROBERT N. MC LIN, 31 May 1843.

STEWART COUNTY: Lot 733-19-3 Cherokee. Certification that DELATHA NIX has been appointed guardian of MARTHA F. MC CANT. Signed: YOUNG H. GRESHAM, Deputy Clerk of the Court of Ordinary, 10 September 1847.

MORGAN COUNTY: Lot 533-19-3 Cherokee. Pers. came STERLING ATAWAY, one of the legatees of JAMES JONES dec'd., of Putnam Co., to claim lot 533-19-3. Signed: Sterling Ataway (by mark) bef. JOHN D. WELLS, J.P. 15 June 1843.

MONROE COUNTY: Lot 822-21-3 Cherokee. Pers. came GEORGE DOUGLAS, agent for NANCY C. STRONG (widow of ALLEN B. STRONG, dec'd. of Bibb County), to claim lot 822-21-3. Signed: George Douglas bef. JAMES NORRIS, J.P., 2 June 1843.

FAYETTE COUNTY: Lot 691-21-3 Cherokee. Pers. came JOSIAH

F. REAVES, guardian of THOMAS WILSON, JOSEPH WILSON & NANCY WILSON (orphans of WILLIAM P. WILSON, dec'd.) to claim lot 691-21-2 and lot 378-13-1. Signed: J. F. Reaves before G. C. KING, J.P., 23 June 1843.

MADISON COUNTY: Lot 1160-20-3 Cherokee. Pers. came SIBBY A. SMITH, Adm'trx. of the estate of BENJAMIN SMITH, dec'd., to claim lot 1160-20-3. Signed: Sibby A. Smith before JAMES MC CURDY, J.P., 29 May 1843.

PUTNAM COUNTY: Lot 1164-20-3 Cherokee. Pers. app'd. BYRD WHITLEY, Adm'r. of the estate of NATHAN MARCHMAN, to claim lot 1164-20-3. Signed: BIRD WHITLY before V. O. W. SANFORD, J.I.C., 28 June 1843.

TROUP COUNTY: Lot 1223-20-3 Cherokee. JAMES EBERHART appoints HENRY T. SMART of Chambers County, Alabama, as att'y. to take out a grant to lot 1223-20-3. Signed: James Eberhart before LORANA WYATT (by mark) and THOMAS M. WYATT, J.P., 23 June 1843.

COWETA COUNTY: Lot 1233-20-3 Cherokee. SARAH BACKUS, widow and representative of the heirs of WILLIAM BACKUS, dec'd., appoints SAMUEL HOUSTON as att'y. to claim lot 1233-20-3 and lot 558-4-1. Signed: Sarah Bachus (by mark) bef. WESTERN BACKUS & WM. A. SPEER, J.P., 24 May 1843.

PIKE COUNTY: Lot 1055-21-3 Cherokee. Pers. came JAMES MAXWELL, husband of SARAH A. W. MAXWELL (formerly SARAH A. W. KIRK, the only surviving orphan of THOMAS KIRK, dec'd., all other orphans having died without issue), to appoint JOHN Y. THERCOTT as att'y. to take out the grant to the lot drawn by sd. orphans. Signed: James Maxwell bef. JASON BURR, J. P., 9 November 1850.

MONROE COUNTY: Lot 981-21-3 Cherokee. Pers. came CARY COX heir of REBECCA BURGE, dec'd., to claim lot 981-21-3 and lot 1179-3-2. App't. of LEONARD Y. DOYAL as attorney. Signed: Cary Cox before J. D. CALLAWAY, J.P. 12 June 1843.

JONES COUNTY: Lot 460-20-3 Cherokee. Pers. came WILLIAM MORELAND, Adm'r. of the estate of LUCY AD-

KINSON, dec'd., to claim lot 460-20-3. Signed: WILLIAM MORELAND before JAMES GRAY, J.I.C., 16 June 1843.

CLARKE COUNTY: Lot 528-20-3 Cherokee. Pers. app'd. JOANNAH SIMS, widow and Ex'trx. of the estate of ROBERT SIMS, de'cd., to claim lot 528-20-3 and lot 331-2-4. App't. of THOMAS A. TURK as att'y. Signed: Joannah Sims (by mark) before GEO. M. LUNIES & BEDFORD LANGFORD, J.I.C. 29 May 1843.

RICHMOND COUNTY: Lot 592-20-3 Cherokee. FRANCIS C. V. HILL, widow and sole heiress, and Adm'trx. of the estate of CHARLES M. HILL, dec'd. of Columbia County, appoints ISAAC A. HIBLER & JAMES W. HONES as her lawful attornies to take out a grant to lot 592-20-3 and lot 663-1-4, drawn by sd. CHAS. M. HILL while he was living in Burke Co. Signed: FRANCES C. V. HILL before LEON G. DUFUS, (no date).

FAYETTE COUNTY: Lot 537-21-3 Cherokee. Pers. came MARTHA CORDEMON, widow of FREDERICK CORDEMON, dec'd., to claim lot 537-21-3. Signed: Martha Cordemon (by mark) before G. C. KING, J.P., 1 June 1843.

MUSCOGEE COUNTY: Lot 23-20-3 Cherokee. Pers. app'd. PRUDENCE RUNNELLS, widow of RICHARD RUNNELLS dec'd. of Upson County, to claim lot 23-20-3 for herself and her children. One of her children, WILLAIM RUNNELLS, has died but without having married and so she and his brothers and sisters are the only heirs. Signed: Prudence Runnells (by mark) before JNO. W. BETHUNE, J.I.C., 21 June 1843.

COWETA COUNTY: Lot 325-3-3 Cherokee. Certification of WOOTSEN RAINEY as executor of the estate of MATTHEW RAINEY dec'd. of Oglethorpe County. Signed: HILLSBERRY R. HARRISON, C.C.O., 22 April 1843.

ELBERT COUNTY: Lot 758-20-3 Cherokee. Pers. app'd. THOMAS J. TURMAN, Adm'r. of the estate of WILLIAM PULLIAM, dec'd., to claim lot 758-20-3 and lot 767-15-2. Signed: Thomas J. Turman bef. Z. SMITH, J.P., 26 May 1843.

FAYETTE COUNTY: Lot 58-1-3 Cherokee. Pers. came TABITHA STEEN, widow of JAMES STEEN, to claim lot

58-1-3. Signed: TEBITHA STEEN (by mark) before G. C. KING, J.P., 14 June 1843.

RANDOLPH COUNTY: Lot 304-7-5 Cherokee. Pers. app'd. JOHN WOOD, one of the surviving orphans of JOSEPH WOOD, to claim lot 304-7-5 for himself and for his sister LAICA WOOD. Their sister ELIZABETH WOOD is dead and they are the children of Joseph Wood, dec'd. of Houston County. Signed: John Wood before GREEN B. WOOD, J.P., 20 April 1843. App't. of SOLOMON D. BETTER as att'y.

TATTNALL COUNTY: Lot 6-8-3 Cherokee. Pers. app'd. THOMAS BURKE, heir of THOMAS (?) J. BURKE, dec'd. to claim lot 6-8-3 and lot 63-2-3; and lot 415-18-2. Signed: Thomas Burke before JOHN J. GRAY, J.P., 10 June 1843.

HOUSTON COUNTY: Lot 90-8-3 Cherokee. CHARLES H. RICE, Admr' of the estate of FAUNTLEROY F. CHAIN, decd. appoints EZRA DAGGETT of Baldwin Co. as att'y. for taking out a grant to lot 90-8-3. Signed: Charles S. Rice before EPHR. RENDRICK & E. MOUNGER, J.I.C., 15 May 1843.

DOUGLAS COUNTY: Lot 633-1-3 Cherokee. Received of NANCY STEWART, guardian of my wife, EMELY SAVANNAH STEWART (and my guardian), lots 633, 640, 639 and 701, 1st Dist., 3rd Sect. of Cherokee then Campbell and now Douglas Co. Signed: L. W. MC LARTY & EMILY S. MC LARTY bef. W. S. HUDSON, J.P. and JOHN M. HUEY, 21 October 1870.

Lot 251-8-3 Cherokee. "Centrevillage Ga. July 11, 1850
Mr. JAMES R. BUTTS
    Dear Sir.
                    Yours under date 20th ult. was duly received and in reply have to say that lot 251-8-3 drawn by SIMPSON's orphans cannot be bought for $50. a Gentleman in Murray County has requested me to offer seventy five Dolls for the lot, but the owner will not take it, in fact 100 Dollars, was sometime back offered for the lot by a man by the name of DENTON but where he is now I cannot say, I presume that $100 may buy it, but do not know that it will any thing I can do for you in the matter will afford me pleasure
                    Yours very truly
                    JNO. S. DILLATONYN(?)"

JASPER COUNTY: Lot 37-7-3 Cherokee. "I do certify that I enrolled JOHN ROGERS, head of a Cherokee family in the Cherokee nation (then living near New Echota) whlst

I was duly authorized agent for enrolling Cherokees for Arkansas in conformity with the instructions of the U.S. government Given under my hand this fourth day of may 1833. Signed: D. A. REECE.

Millidgeville 5th May 1833
I have precused satisfactory information that the Indian improvement on lot No 37-7th Dist. 3rd Section was made by JOHN ROGERS and that the same has been relinguished to the United States for the use of Georgia agreeable to the Treaty stepulations of the 6th of May 1828
                        WM. HARDIN U.S. enrolling Agent
It comes within my personal knowledge that the statements of the above gentlemen are correct. Given under my hand this 6th of May 1833. WM. J. TARVIN

Lot 182-15-3 Cherokee. "Certification that WILLIAM HICKS, a Cherokee, has enrolled for Arkansas and will give up lot 182, 15th District, 3rd Section early this winter. WM. HARDIN, enrolling agent, 17 October 1833."

Lot 244-23-3 Cherokee. Order that lot 244, 23rd District, 3rd Section be granted as the occupant, JOHN ROSS, a Indian, had a fee simple reservation allowed him under the treaty of 1819.

Ordered that lot 15, 5th District, 3rd Section be granted as well as lots 16 and 20 with their improvements, as WALTER ADAIR, the occupant and a Cherokee Indian has been granted a reservation for life. R. A. GREEN, secretary, Executive Department, Milledgeville, 14 February 1834.

MERIWETHER COUNTY: Lot 47-27-3 Cherokee. ALEXANDER SMITH ...
                       binds himself to SAMUEL WELLS for the sale of lot 47-27-3. Signed: Alexander Smith before JOHN SCOTT and THOS. G. W. MC LIN, 14 October 1835.

TELFAIR COUNTY: Lot 534-1-3 Cherokee. WILLIAM PARKER, gdn.
                       of the heirs of HUGH COOK, appoints JAMES A. ROGERS as att'y. to take out grant to lot drawn by sd. orphans. Signed: William Parker bef. SUSAN A. COFFIE and PETER H. COFFIE, J.I.C., 30 May 1843.

Lot 936-4-3 Cherokee. "Vernon Troup Co.
Feb. 24th 1834
Dear Sir
     Enclosed I send you two dollars and wish you to enclose the plat and grant for lot No. 936-4-3 Cherokee Teritory the balance of the money after paying for the grant. I wish you to hand to the editors of the Georgia Journal in payment for my subscription to that paper for the year 1833 you will enclose the grant in a leter immediately on the receipt of this and direct it to me at Vernon Troup to Sir
                    Very Respectfully Yours
                    JOSIAH M. BONNER"

MC INTOSH COUNTY: Lot 739-21-3 Cherokee. Personally app'd.

JOHN BUCKLEY, husband of ELIZABETH HORNSBY, to claim lot 739-21-3 and lot 605-18-2, for ELIZABETH HORNSBY "one of the Drawees of sd. Lots, JOHN HORNSBY being dead." J. E. TOWNSEND is app'td. att'y. Signed: John Buckley (by mark) bef. CHARLES A. HARDIN, J.P., 14 June 1843.

BURKE COUNTY: Lot 799-2-3 Cherokee. Pers. app'd. JOHN APPLEWHITE, Adm'r. of the est. of PETER APPLEWHITE, dec'd., to claim lot 799-2-3. Signed: John Applewhite before JOHN A. ROBERTS, J.P. and EDWARD GARLICK, D.Clk., C.O.B.C. 14 June 1843.

BURKE COUNTY: Lot 1125-20-3 Cherokee. Pers. app'd. REUBEN BASTER who saith that himself, MARY JEFFERS (formerly MARY BAXTER), DACEY BAXTER, ELIZABETH BAXTER, & FELIX BAXTER claim lot 303-13-1; lot 1125-20-3, drawn by CHARLES BAXTER, dec'd. of Burke Co.; and lot 812-19-3, drawn by LETHE BAXTER, widow, of Burke Co. Himself and JOHN JEFFERS, husband of MARY JEFFERS, are the only heirs of age and that CANDACEY BAXTER, ELIZABETH BAXTER & FELIX BAXTER have no legal guardian. Signed: REUBEN BAXTER before ELBERT D. TAYLOR, J.P., 12 June 1843.

MONROE COUNTY: Lot 7-21-3 Cherokee. Pers. app'd. JOHN JAMES, husband of MARY JAMES, formerly MARY JACKSON, widow, to claim lot 7-21-3; lot 10-11-4; and lot 22-16-of Dooly County. Signed: John James (by mark) before ZACH. HARMAN, J.P., 13 May 1843.

CASS COUNTY: Lot 97-2-3 Cherokee. THOMAS J. NAYLOR, one of the orphans of JOHN NAYLOR, appoints ALFRED M. HORTON of Milledgeville as his att'y. for taking out a grant to lot 97-2-3. 18 June 1843. (not signed)

CHATHAM COUNTY: Lot 141-2-3 Cherokee. Pers. app'd. JOHN WILLIAMSON, Ex'r. of (illegible) J. WILLIAMSON and property creditor of PETER MITCHELL, to claim lot No. 141-2-3. Signed: Jno. Williamson before R. RAIFORD, J.P. 13 June 1843.

MUSCOGEE COUNTY: Lot 721-20-3 Cherokee. Pers. app'd. JOHN R. DAWSON to claim lots drawn by DRURY TOWNS orphans as part owner. Signed: Jno. R. Dawson bef. AUGUSTUS

J. ABBOTT, J.P. 15 May 1843.

"Columbus 15 May 1843

Dear Sir   I perused this morning in the Chronicle & Sentinel of Augusta, that DRURY TOWNS orphans land was still ungranted. as I am ½ owner, having married one of the orphans, I send you $7.50 which will grant the two lots I see published.and will thank you to get the grants and send them to me by first opportunity. I will send Dr. SANKEY (?) the affidavit So soon as it can be procured.

Very Resply. JNO. R. DAWSON"

CAM(?) COUNTY: Lot 548-2-3 Cherokee. In person came LITTLEBERRY JAMES, one of the orphans of MICAEL JAMES, to claim lot 548-2-3. Signed: Littleberry James bef. WILLIAM LATIMER, J.P., 21 April 1848.

WALKER COUNTY: Lot 187-27-3 Cherokee. Pers. app'd. JOHN C. MURPHY, husband of the former ELIZABETH HAILE, orphan, to claim lot 187-27-3. Signed: John C. Murphy bef. MICHAEL DICKSON, J.P., 20 October 1846.

Lot 256-7-3 Cherokee. "Salem Ga Septr 12th 1832

Dear Sir
         At the particular request of a friend of mine. I am induced to address you a few lines, on a subject of some importance to my friend...Mr. BARTON THRASHER of this County a very respectable Citizen and a man of wealth and influence in the County was during the last Indian War (It appears) illegally drafted and in consequence of the Draft having been illegally made he refused to serve and was at the time the men were ordered out on service out of the state on business and consequently did not perform his tour of duty agreeably to the draft in consequence of his having been illegally made which circumstances will appear by refference to certain certificates exhibited to the legislature at its session in 1825 and the Legislature having taken the subject into consideration and being satisfied with regard to the facts set forth in these certificates passed a special act for the particular benefit of said Thrasher entitling him to two chances in the contemplated Land Lottery this act you will find by turning to the acts of the Legislature in 1825 and Page 113. Mr. Thrasher it appears never has drawn land as a citizen or in any other capacity and in consequence of the manner in which the Oath is worded that is to be administered to the person (said to be entitled) to Draws in the present contemplated land & gold Lotteries he considers himself excluded from the right to a draw or draws by the wording of the oath as he refused to serve as a soldier when Drafted in consequence of the draft having been illegally made. now it would appear that the Legislature of 1825 considered him entitled and therefore passed an act for his benefit. Now the subject of this letter is to know of your Excellency your opinion with regard to this matter and also to know if

its in your Excellency's power to afford any relief to Mr. Thrasher in this case, or not. or is he to be deprived of his right to a draw in the present contemplated lottery for the land and gold in consequence of his having refused to serve when illegally drafted. If your Excellency will have the goodness to give Mr. Thrasher (through me) your views on this subject at as early a period as possible. you will confer a lasting favour on your friend and also upon Mr. Thrasher.
>Sincerely & Respectfully
>Yours A. H. SCOTT"

His Excellency W. LUMPKIN

Lot 280-13-3 Cherokee. "Covington March 6th 1851

JAMES R. BUTTS, /esq.

Dear Sir yours of 3rd Inst. came duly to hand and contents noticed I have called on Mr. NATHAN TURNER of this county to see if I could purchase No. 250 in 13 of 3. But he has recently been up in Murry and states he was offered 300 Dollars for the lot and would not take less than $500.00 so there is no chance to purchase at the full value Mr. Turner is a land trader and has plenty of means...no chance to purchase of him was to make money
>Respectfully yours
>PUDMEDUS REYNOLDS"

J. B. Butts, Esq./Milledgeville Ga.

CHATHAM COUNTY: Lot 10-16 Dooly. Pers. app'd. STEPHEN L. W. HARRIS to claim lot 10-6 of Dooly Co. drawn by STEPHEN HARRIS. Signed: S. L. W. Harris bef. R. RAIFORD, J.P., 1 June 1843. App't. of JOHN W. EXLEY of Effingham County as att'y.

CAMPBELL COUNTY: Lot 43-9 Coweta. Pers. app'd. ALSTON A. ARNOLD and THOMAS A. LATHAM who saith that fraction 43-9 of Coweta, being part of the plantation of JAMES MCKOY at the mouth of Deep Creek, has been in the possession of JAMES MCKOY and since his death, about 10 years ago, in the ownership of his representatives. The fraction was owned by THOMAS HILL and transfered to his son WILLIAM M. HILL, who sold the same to JAMES MCKOY. Signed: Alston A. Arnold & Thomas A. Latham bef. W. M. BUTT, J.I.C., 16 Sept. 1848.

CAMPBELL COUNTY: Lot 27-9 Coweta. SARAH M. BROWN, widow of EVAN BROWN (who died in October, 1839),.. saith that EVAN BROWN purchased in 1830 or 1831 fraction no. 27 and no. 40, 9th District of Coweta, now Campbell County, from

THOMAS SMITH. She and their children still hold said fractions. Signed: SARAH M. BROWN (by mark) before W. M. BUTT, J.I.C. 16 June 1848.

CAMPBELL COUNTY: Lot F24-9 Coweta. Pers. came BENNETT LEE who saith that TARLTON SHEETS of Campbell County owned fraction no. 24-9th Dist. of Coweta. Upon his death it was sold by his Adm'rs. to JOEL FOSTER, who sold it to BENNETT LEE. The fraction was sold by the sheriff, as the property of Lee to ALFRED AUSTELL in February of 1844. SHEETS had died in 1839. signed: B. B. LEE before W. M. BUTT, J.I.C, 19 May 1848.

COWETA COUNTY: Lot 140-6 Coweta. Pers. came JAMES BELL, one of the Adm'rs. of the estate of S.BELL dec'd, to claim fraction 140 and fraction 141, 6th Dist. of Coweta. Signed: James Bell bef. WM. HEARN, J.P., 17 Oct. 1848.

COWETA COUNTY: Lot 244-5 Coweta. WESTERN BACKUS, agent for SARAH BACKUS (representative of the heirs of WILLIAM BACKUS, dec'd.) appoints JOHN H. JOHNSON as attorney for taking out a grant to lot 244-5 of Coweta. Signed: Western Backus before M. Y SLAUGHTER & WM. A. SPEAR, J.P. 15 June 1843.

WARREN COUNTY: Lot 147-4 Coweta. Pers. app'd. JEREMIAH WELCHER and LARKIN WELCHER of the 151 District, Captain DOWNS, of Coweta, who saith that they know of no one named SOPHRANY KITCHENS, widow, but they do know SOPHRANY KITCHENS, illegitimate of SALLY KITCHENS. JEREMIAH WELCHER has been a justice of the peace in sd. dist. for upwards of twenty years and LARKEN WELCHER has been a constable for sd. district for upwards of eight years. Signed: Jeremiah Welcher and Larkin Welcher bef. THOMAS NEAL, J.I.C., April, 1843.

WARREN COUNTY: Lot 147-4 Coweta. Pers. app'd. JAMES PILCHER, who saith he was born and raised in the 151 Dist. and of sd. county and he knows of no widow named SOPHRONEY KITCHEN but believes that SOPHRONY KITCHENS, illigitimate of SARAH KITCHENS. Signed: James Pilcher bef. THOMAS NEAL, J.I.C., 22 May 1843.

WARREN COUNTY: Lot 147-1 Coweta. Pers. came MARTHY L.

BRASSEL, for herself and for SARAH ANN BRASSEL and NATHAN E. BRASSEL, to claim the lot they drew as illigitimates in Lee County, given in by LUCRITA BRASSEL of Jefferson County. Signed: MARTHY L. BRASSEL (by mark) before JAMES BRADDY, J.P., 29 June 1843. App't. of BRYANT J. HUNTER as att'y.

Lot 195-1 Coweta. "Cumming Ga. 5 Dec. 1848.
Dear Sir
  My Brother in Law ALSALEM THORNTON deceased short while before his death bought a lot of Lan No. 195-1st Dist. of Coweta of HARVEY MC CORMICK WAR illigitimate of formerly Raburn County but for many years past of Tennessee.By refering to copy grant (the original haveing been issued years ago), I find that said number purports to have been drawn by HENRY MC CORMICK from which circumstances Mr. Thornton before his death a short while, visited Milledgeville in order to get the grant &c. and there he found that the grant had issued in the name of HENRY MC CORMICK, he believes that an error had been committed in entering Drawers name &c. examined all the books on entry and found that a mistake had really been made and the grant should have issued in the name of HARVEY MC CORMICK WARD. He, Thornton had first commenced, when he was taken sick, to have the errors corrected, but so it is, he died before it was done, as such it will devolve upon me as his Admr. to do what he intended to have done I know Mr. Ward & he says he will swear that he has never sold said Lot of Land to any person save Thornton and it is only recently that he has become of age. Thornton a short while before his death wrote to Mr. S. G. ELDER of your neighborhood Relative to said Lot and was informed in Return by Letter that you was in possession of the Lot and laid Claim ot it, therefore you now can see the Reason Why I write to you. I wish you to write to me forthwith, if you please stating what you intend to do about it. I would be glad that the thing could be arranged without any difficulty. I think when you are satisfied that these statements are the facts of the case, you certainly will not contend for the lot. I know these are the facts and am advised by competent authority that there is no chance for you to hold the land. If you have bought and paid anything for the land I should regret to see you loose it, but filling the station of an Adm. you know that I shall be forced to proceed for the Land in case you are disposed to contend for it. I' hope you will let me hear from you without delay. I shall be down as soon as possible but cannot say when that will be
      yrs Respectfully
      PLEASANT G. LIGHT
Write to Cumming Forsyth Co. Ga."

COWETA COUNTY: Lot 50-2 Coweta. Pers. app'd. WM. D. MURPHY, one of the orphans of DANIEL MURPHY, as one of the three owners of lot 50, 2nd Dist. of Coweta County, to claim sd. lot for himself and the other two orphans, although he is the youngest of the orphans and has not yet reached age 21. Signed: Wm. D. Murphy bef. WM. B. SMITH, J.P., 2 Feb. 1846.

BALDWIN COUNTY: Lot 88-2 Coweta. Pers. came EBENEZER CALEF, one of the legal representatives of

LETHIA CALEF, to claim lot 88, 2nd Dist. of Coweta County. Signed: EBENEZER CALEF bef. CHAS. D. HAMMOND, J.I.C., 5 May 1843.

CHATHAM COUNTY: Lot 126-2 Coweta. Pers. app'd. BENJAMIN E. STILES, agent of MARY A. COOPER (the sister of MARGARET C. MC QUEEN), to claim the lot drawn by McQueen. Signed: Benj. Edwd. Stiles bef. R. RAIFORD, J.P., 9 May 1843. App't. of MILLER GRIEVE of Baldwin Co. as att'y.

BUTTS COUNTY: Lot 28-3 Coweta. We have appointed HENRY DILLON as att'y. to take out grants to the lot drawn by PAYNES offius (orphans?) and the lot drawn by TURNERs offius this lot being in Lee County No. 5 not recollected. also two fractional lots, nos. 59 and 60 at the Indian Spring Reserve. Signed: ABNER BANKS, JOHN H. PAYNE & SARAH BANKS bef. C. M. COODY, J.P., 2 June 1843. Includes signed statement of HENRY DILLON that he is the agent of WILLIAM PAINE, who drew lot 28-3 Coweta, 7 June 1843, bef. J. R. ANDERSON, J.I.C.

BALDWIN COUNTY: Lot 29-4 Coweta. Pers. came SUSAN HOLTZCLAW, natural guardian of WILLIAM H. and ELESHA PADGETTE (her children) to claim lot 29-4 of Coweta Co. Signed: Susan Holtzclaw bef. Alfred M. Horton, N.P. 21 June 1843.

COWETA COUNTY: Lot 96-4 Coweta. JAMES STOREY, JOHN STOREY, WILLIAM M. STOREY, GEORGE STOREY, MARGARET "PEGGY" STOREY, JANE WYATT, WILLIAM CHRISTOPHER (who married LILLY STOREY), ISHAM HUCKABY (who married HANNAH STOREY),& JACOB LAND (who married MARGERY STOREY), the heirs and distributees of NANCY STOREY, dec'd., do transfer fraction 96-4 of Coweta to CHRISTOPHER BOWEN for value received. Signed. Wm. M. Storey, Isham Huckaby (by mark), Jacob Land, Margaret Storey (by mark) Jane Wyatt (by mark), James Storey, W. Christopher, George Storey and John S. Storey bef. TYRE HARRIS, 20 Feb. 1844.

PULASKI COUNTY: Lot 60-14 Dooly. Pers. came ELIZABETH HARVEY to claim lot 60-14 of Dooly, drawn by JOHN H. HARVEY (her husband). Signed: Elizabeth Harvey bef. JOHN BOZEMAN, J.I.C., 14 June 1843. App't. of WILEY F. D. HOLDEN as att'y. Signed: Elizabeth Harvey bef. SARAH F. BOZEMAN & JOHN BOZEMAN, J.I.C., 14 June 1843.

"A return of the fractional Surveys in the Several Districts in the County of Duly County and the twelevth Deastrict of Houston County rented on the 26th February 1822:

Ds	County	Numbers	Persons names	$	Cts.
13	Duly				
15		228	THEOPELUS WILLIAMS	155	00
		232	WILLIAM T. SMITH	20	12½
		233	THOMAS SMITH	31	00
		231	THEOPELUS WILLIAMS	34	00
		254	WILLIAM DONALSON	34	00
		250	RUBIN MANNING	1	00
		247	THOS. MERE		50
16,69,12,10					
8		19	BENJAMIN POSEY	9	11
		21	DAVID BRIANTS	151	00
2					
4		297	JAMES D. SHANKS	10	00
		308	GEORGE KERNEGE	6	50
		303	JOHN SHEARRARD	50	00
		304	RICHARD GEANY	8	00
		305	JAMES BRACEWELL		50
		284	" "		50
		226	RICHARD B. WENJETT		50
		225	JOHN RALLS	11	00
		255	MOSES YARBOROUGH		50
12	Houston	285	WILLIAM FARNAL	51	00
		276	WILLIAM BARREN	5	00
		290	JOHN RALLS	86	00
		291	" "	1	50

Comnetion(?) on the above at 20 percent

```
                                                 66662½
                                                 13332½
                                                 53330
amount in notes Which We send you is             51882½
                                                  1447½
Cash Which amounts                               533300
```

given under our hands the day (illegible)
      ROBT. MORELAND
      FURNEY F. GALLEN Commishioners"

MERIWETHER COUNTY: Lot 29-15 Dooly. In person came HEZEKIAH S. WIMBISH, in right of his former wife, one of the distributees of the estate of GEORGE W. HEARD dec'd. and as a guardian, he claims two of the three remaining shares of the estate, including lot 29, 15 of Dooly Co. Signed: Hezekiah S. Wimbish bef. W. H. P. ADAIR, J.P., 23 Oct. 1848. Includes note by A. M. NISBET, cashier of the Central Bank of Georgia, that Geo. W. Heard paid for his fraction.

MORGAN COUNTY: Lot 244-14 Dooly. Pers. app'd. JOHN C. REES to claim lot 244-14 of Dooly Co. and also lots 1282 in 2 Dist., 3rd Sect. and lot 112, 11th Dist., 3rd Sec. of Cherokee. The latter two lots were drawn by SUSANNAH M. FURLOW widow, who REES has since married. Signed: Jno. C. Rees before ELIJAH E. JONES, J.I.C., 24 May 1843.

ELBERT COUNTY: Lot 88-14 Dooly. Pers. app'd. GEORGE J.

DYE, one of the orphans of THOMPSON DYE, to claim lot 88-14 of Dooly Co. App't. of Doctor WILLIAM G. ALLEN as att'y. Signed: GEORGE J. DYE bef. H. G. TATE and LINDSAY H. SMITH, J.P., 31 May 1843.

CHATHAM COUNTY: Lot 289-15 Dooly. Pers. app'd. ALLETHA SCRUGGS, mother and natural guardian of JOHN, FREDERICK & RICHARD S. SCRUGGS, orphans of JESSE SCRUGGS, to enter sd. orphans in the current land lottery. Signed: Allethis Scruggs bef. GEO. L..COPE, J.I.C.C.C., 7 Aug. 1821.

GREENE COUNTY: Lot 205-13 Dooly. Pers. app'd. JOHN R. EIDSON, the only lawful heir of THOMAS EIDSON, dec'd., to claim lot 205-13 of Dooly Co. Signed: John R. Eidson bef. (illegible) WILSON, J.P., 26 June 1843.

JASPER COUNTY: Lot 178-3 Dooly. Pers. app'd. JOHN WYNENS who saith that he was well acquainted with ELISHA SMART for many years before and after 1821 and that he knows of no one named SMART ELISHA. Signed: John Wynens before JOHN C. GIBSON, J.P., 26 April 1848.
JOSHUA HILL, Adm'r. of the estate of ELISHA SMART dec'd., saith that he has not found any grant for lot 178-13 of Dooly Co. Signed: Joshua Hill bef. PLEASANT M. COMPTON, J.P., 8 November 1848.

CHATHAM COUNTY: Lot 79-13 Dooly. Pers. app'd. RICHARD D. ARNOLD, Adm'r. of the estate of SARAH C. NOEL, dec'd., to claim lot 79-13 Dooly Co. App't. of SOLOMON COHEN as att'y. Signed: Richard D. Arnold bef. JOSEPH FELT, J.P. 1 June 1843.

COLUMBIA COUNTY: Lot 36-13 Dooly. Pers. came JOHN Y. TANKERSLY to claim lot 36-13 Dooly Co. The lot was drawn by JESSE ROBERTS and sold to LUKE F. CLARK. Tankersly is Adm'r. of the est. of Clark and also claims lot 283-6-2 Cherokee, as the guardian of the orphans of LUKE F. CLARK. App't. of WM. H. PRITCHARD of Milledgeville as att'y. Signed: John Y. Tankersly bef. DAVID HOLIMAN, J.P., 26 June 1843.

Lot 32-13 Dooly
"To His Excellency JOHN B. GORDON, Governor of Georgia.
The petition of M. B. MILLEN, Adm'r. de

bonis non cum testamento annexo of the last will and testament of MARY P. HARRIS, and of his own right respectfully showeth that lot of land number thirty two of the thirteenth district of Dooly County, of the state of Georgia, containing two hundred and two and one half acres, was granted to THOMAS GREENE on the 28th day of November, 1849, by sd. State of Georgia, as is shown by plat and grant hereto annexed as exhibit "A"; and that sd. lot of land has since been sold L. F. HARRIS and Petitioner as tenants in common, and that L. F. HARRIS has since died leaving his wife MARY P. HARRIS as heir to his interest in this lot of land, and your Petitoner is the Adm'r. of (de bonis non cum testamento annexo) sd. Mary P. Harris, who is also dead. Petitioner respectfully shows that a mistake was made in the grant of sd. lot to THOMAS GREENE in this, that the lot is described number thirty three instead number thirty two, while the plat describes the land as number thirty two. That the plat has the number correctly, and the grant incorrectly, is shown by the following evidence: Book B of reverted lots of Dooly county, which is a record of grants, on page 479 of sd. book shows the record of a grant of lot number thirty two to THOMAS GREENE, and on page 437 it shows a record of the grant of lot number thirty three, thirteenth district of Dooly county to JOHN FOSTER. In the record of the plats of Dooly Co. reverted lots page 253, it is shown that lot number thirty three was platted to JOHN FOSTER and that lot number thirty two was platted to THOMAS GREENE. The Numberical Book of Dooly county also shows that lot number thirty two of the thirteenth district of sd. county was granted to THOMAS GREENE and that lot number thirty three was granted to JOHN FOSTER. Therefore petitioner says that the error in the description of the lot is in the grant,and not in the plat, issued to Thomas Greene and he asks that your Excellency pass an order requiring the Secretary of State to issue a new grant to sd. Thomas Greene, describing the land in accordance with the plat, and that is number thirty two in the 13 dist. of Dooly co., in accordance with the Code of Georgia, Secs. 2352 and 2353. Petitioner hereby delivers up for cancellation the original grant made to Thomas Greene as aforesaid. Signed: M. B. Millen by TOMPKINS & BRAUDEN (no date)"

TALIAFERRO COUNTY: Lot 158-12 Dooly. Pers. app'd. ABNER DARDEN, one of the Ex'rs. of the estate of WILLIAM DARDEN, to claim lot 158-12 of Dooly Co. App't. of ALEXANDER H. STEPHENS as att'y. Signed: Abner Darden bef. A. J. LOCKETT & THOMAS PITTMAN, J.P., 13 June 1843.

JACKSON COUNTY: Lot 61-12 Dooly. Pers. came FRANCIS MARTIN for himself and the orphans of WILLIAM MARTIN, dec'd., to claim lot 61-12 Dooly. Signed: Francis Martin before JAMES MORRIS & WILLIAM BELL, J.P., 27 May 1843.

PIKE COUNTY: Lot 20-12 Dooly. Pers. came MARY T. GRIFFIN, Adm'trx. of the est. of ANDERSON GRIFFIN, dec'd., to claim lot 20-12 Dooly. App't. of JOHN W. COPPEDGE as att'y. Signed: Mary P. Griffin bef. A. A. GAULDING, J.P. 10 June 1843.

GREENE COUNTY: Lot 205-11 Dooly. Pers. app'd. WILLIAM
                       DANIEL, one of the Adm'rs. of F. H. WIL-
LIAMS, dec'd., to claim lot 205-11 Dooly County; for the orphans
of sd. dec'd., lot 143-20-2 and lot 647-11-1, Cherokee Co.; as
guardian of R. BENNETT's orphans, lot 201-23-3, Cherokee; and as
Adm'r. of the estate of WM. FOSTER, dec'd., lot 113-7-3, Troup
Co. He also applys for a lot as agent of WM. D. SANKEY. Signed:
William Daniel before E. SPARKS HUNTER, J.P., 15 June 1843.

CHATHAM COUNTY: Lot 196-11 Dooly. JOSEPH M. FOUNTAINE....
                       swears that he is a citizen of the United
States and that he has resided in Georgia three years prior to
the current land lotter but that he was away in the north at the
time of the drawing. He has no wife or child. Signed: Joseph M.
Fountaine bef. JNO. P. WILLIAMSON, J.I.C.C.C, 22 September 1821.

CHATHAM COUNTY: Lot 159-11 Dooly. Pers. app'd. J. T. PAT-
                       TON, agent of SARAH VOTEE (widow of DAVID
VOTEE), to claim lot 159-11 Dooly and lot 470-12-1 Cherokee Co.
App't. of JOHN M. EXLEY of Effingham Co. as att'y. Signed: J. T.
Patton bef. JOSEPH FELT, J.P., 1 June 1843.

GREENE COUNTY: Lot 143-10 Dooly. Pers. app'd. THOMAS J.
                       FINDLEY, one of the orphans of ROBERT FIND-
LEY, dec'd., to claim lot 143-10 Dooly. Signed: Thomas J. Findley
before J. R. HALL, J.I.C., 23 June 1843.

JASPER COUNTY: Lot 90-11 Dooly. Pers. app'd. BERRY T.
                       DIGBY to claim lot 90-11 Dooly Co. for
himself, LUCINDA LAMB, JOHN DIGBY & ELIZA MATHALL (orphans of
JOHN DIGBY, dec'd.). Signed: Berry T. Digby bef. THOS. Q. SMITH,
J.I.C., 25 June 1843.

JONES COUNTY: Lot 113-10 Dooly. THOMAS HUNT, son of WIL-
                       LIAM HUNT, dec'd., appoints JOSEPH DAY as
att'y. for himself and the other legatees to claim lot 113-10 of
Dooly. Signed: Thos. Hunt bef. ALEXANDER ODOM, J.P., 23 May 1843.

                       Lot 92-10 Dooly.
"April 16th 1836 Appling Columbia Co. Ga.
Mr. JAMES R. BUTTS, Esq.
        Dr. Sir
                       I received your letter a few days ago
which I now proceed to answer   you may State to your brother that

I will sell my lot 92 10th District in Dooly though I have never seen it. I will get some friend to look at it for me and let me know what it is worth if your brother will write to me immediately what he is willing to pay for the lot I will let him know whether I will take it or not. Please let me hear from you again in relation to the matter.
Respectfully Yours
SULLIVAN HARRISON"

Lot 87-9 Dooly. "Drayton 7th Decr. 1849
Mr. JAS. R. BUTTS
Dr Sir
Enclose you will find Three dollars. I wish you to have a coppy grant issued to lot land no. 87 in the 9th dist Dooly (drawn by GEORGE STRANS of Richmond County) please forward to me by mail to Drayton. It is with great pleasure I congratulate you in the success of your election we are all well hoping you and your family is enjoying good health, we have no news in these parts, more than occasionally we have a wedding. JOHN ISHAM ROYAL was married to a one of old man GODWIN's daughters last night, your friend HENRY PETTEE at (?) Doctor HAMES was married last sunday morning to Miss SPIVY allow me to call your attention to our unsettled business which we should (illegible line) I am wiling to settle it as much to your intent as I possibly can, to that I am not (illegible word) in any way.
H. PETTEE
PLEASANT H. KEY and muself was and has been negotiating for lot no. 69, in the 10th dist Dooly from a man in Franklin Cty., his name I now forget as Key has done the negotiations Key informed me that the owner of the lot would empower his members from Franklin County to sell during the Legislature, I think the lot was offered to Key at $150 or $200 I wish you would make inquiries of the members from Franklin County if the (illegible word) legally empowered to sell the lot...69 in the 10th dist of Dooly if so closed the trade immediately either in my name or Pleasant H. Key go as high as Two Hundred dollars each buy lower if you possibly can and inform me and I will send the money immediately my business is so confining I cannot leave home and Keys wife is in such a condition he cannot leave at present
H. PETTEE"

MUSCOGEE COUNTY: Lot F12-9 Dooly. Pers. app'd. JAMES F. BOZEMAN, son of JAMES BOZEMAN, dec'd. to claim several fractions in the 9th District of Dooly County: nos. 12,13 and 28. Signed: James F. Bozeman before A. G. FOSTER, J.I.C., 9 October 1848.

HOUSTON COUNTY: Lot 197-8 Dooly. Pers. came JAMES POWELL to claim lot 197-8 Dooly Co., having married one of the orphans of THOMAS PERKINS. Signed: James Powell bef. D. W. TAYLOR, J.P., 19 June 1843.

CHATHAM COUNTY: Lot 115-8 Dooly. Pers. app'd. MARY ELIZA LONG, widow and the surviving heir of ELIZABETH KEEN, to claim lot 115-8- Dooly Co. App't. of JAMES S. PARK of Baldwin Co. as att'y. Signed: Mary Eliza Long before LEVI

S. RUSSELL, 24 April 1843.

MC INTOSH COUNTY: Lot 86-8 Dooly. THOMAS MAGUIRE, Adm'r. of the estate of JOHN FOWLER, appoints J. E. TOWNSEND as att'y. to take out a grant to lot 86-8 Dooly County. Signed: Thomas Maguire before PDE. LE CHARTIEZ(?), J.I.C. 15 June 1843.

MERIWETHER COUNTY: Lot 5-8 Dooly. Pers. came HEZEKIAH S. WIMBISH who saith that in right of his former wife he is the distributee of the estate of GEORGE W. HEARD, dec'd. and as guardian he represents two of the other three heirs. Signed: Hezekiah S. Wimbish bef. W. H. P. ADIAR, J.P., 23 Oct. 1848.

BALDWIN COUNTY: Lot 103-6 Dooly. Pers. app'd. JAMES M. REYNOLDS, Ex'r. of the estate of ATTON PEMBERTON of Burke Co. dec'd. to claim lot 103-6 Dooly County. Signed: Jas. M. Reynolds bef. Alfred M. Horton, N.P. 19 June 1843

BURKE COUNTY: Certification that JAMES M. REYNOLDS is Ex'r. of the est. of ATTON PEMBERTON of Burke Co., dec'd. Signed: EDWARD GARLICK, C.O.B.C., 15 June 1843.

TROUP COUNTY: Lot 138-6 Dooly. Pers. app'd. NATHAN L. ATKINSON to claim lot 138-6 of Dooly Co. being a gift from MARTHA ATKINSON of Greene County. Signed: Nathan L. Atkinson bef. JAMES M. BEALL, J.I.C, 7 June 1843.

HOUSTON COUNTY: Lot 39-8 Dooly. Pers. app'd. ISAAC W. WEST one of the heirs of JOHN WEST, dec'd., to claim lot 39-6 of Dooly Co. Signed: Isaac W. West bef. D. M. BROWN J.P., 18 April 1843. App't. of JOHN W. BROWN as att'y. before W. BROWN & D. M. BROWN, J.P., 18 Apr. 1843.

Lot 245-5 Dooly. "Decatur, DeKalb County April 5th 1827
His Excellency G. M. TROUP
Sir
   I enclose to you as the head of the State house department a grant (which was issued from that department) for correction   I as the agent of my son ALLEN STOKER sent by Major HOOPER for a grant to him for Lot No. 245 in the 5 Dist Dooly and there appears to have been a mistake in the grant both as to the name of the granter & no of the lot the number must have been given correctily to the Surveyor Genl as the 5 appears (as you will see) to have been inserted and afterwards erased and all other circumstances of identity appear. As the error must have

originated in the statehouse officers I presume that the error can be corrected or a new grant issued without additional expence if it can be done please have it returned by mail as early as possible as the time has expired for me to execute title to said lot your obdt. Sert. WILLIAM STOKER"

MONROE COUNTY: Lot 191-5 Dooly. Pers. app'd. ALLEN G. FRAMBRO to claim lot 191-5 Dooly County. and also, for his dec'd. father, lot 556-21-2 Cherokee. App't. of WM. S. NORMAN as att'y. Signed: Allen G. Frambro bef. JAMES W. KNOTT, J.I.C., 15 June 1843.

CHATHAM COUNTY: Lot 154-4 Dooly. Pers. appd. JAMES P. SCREVEN, Adm'd. of the estate of DELIA BRYAN, to claim lot 154-4 of Dooly Co. Signed: James P. Screven bef. M. MYERS, J.I.C.C.C., June 1843.

CHATHAM COUNTY: Personally appeared JAMES P. SCREVEN Ex'r of the estate of JOHN SCREVENS, dec'd. to claim lot 168-31-1, Land Lottery of 1827. Signed: James P. Screven bef. M. Myers, J.I.C.C.C., 23 June 1843.

CHATHAM COUNTY: Lot 107-3 Dooly. Pers. app'd. Mrs. ELIZABETH S. SHICK, JANE C. CLINE & AGNES CLINE legal representatives of SARAH CLINE, dec'd., to claim lot 107-3 Dooly Co. Signed: Elizabeth S. Shick, Jane C. Cline and Agnes Cline before ISAAC RUSSELL, J.P., 16 June 1843.

WILKES COUNTY: Lot 205-2 Dooly. Pers. app'd. JAMES H. FLYNT, one of the orphans of JOHN FLYNT, to claim lot 205-2 of Dooly Co. Signed: James H. Flynt before JAMES F. HACKNEY, J.P., 27 June 1843. App't. of JOHN R. ANDERSON of Baldwin Co. as att'y.

CHATHAM COUNTY: Lot 178-2 Dooly. Pers. app'd. MARY MAXWELL to claim lot 178-2 Dooly Co., drawn by JAMES MC KAY MAXWELL. App't. of W. THOMAS BUTLER as att'y. Signed: Mary Maxwell bef. R. RAIFORD, J.P., 20 June 1843.

GLYNN COUNTY: Lot 111-2 Dooly. Pers. app'd. SAMUEL M. BURNETT, Adm'r. of the est. of WILLIAM F. BURNETT, to claim lot 111-2 Dooly Co. Signed: Samuel Burnett bef. A. G. BURNETT, J.I.C.G.C., 9 June 1843.

GLYNN COUNTY" SAMUEL M. BURNETT, Adm'r. of the estate of ABSOLEM HALL, pers. app'd. to claim lot

309-18-2, Cherokee County. Signed: SAMUEL BURNETT before A. G. BURNETT, J.I.C.G.C., 9 June 1843. App't. of W. A. SANFORD as attorney.

MUSCOGEE COUNTY: Lot 84-2 Dooly. Pers. app'd. GEORGE W. UNDERWOOD, Adm'r. of the estate of WINNFORD UNDERWOOD, dec'd. (widow) to claim lot 84-2 Dooly County. Signed: George W. Underwood before AUGUSTUS J. ABBOTT, J.P., 16 June 1843. App't. of JOHN W. A. SANFORD as att'y. Signed: Geo. W. Underwood bef. F. M. LIGON & Augustus J. Abbott, J.P., 28 June 1843.

OGLETHORPE COUNTY: Lot 67-2 Dooly. Pers. app'd. JOHN MARTIN, lawful agent of GIBSON MARTIN's orphans, to claim lot 67-2 Dooly County. App't. of WILLIAM H. PRITCHARD of Baldwin County as att'y. Signed: John Martin bef. FREDERICK W. BUTLER & JOHN CRAWFORD, J.I.C., 3 June 1843.

CHATHAM COUNTY: Lot 25-2 Dooly. Pers. app'd. MARY ELIZA LONG to claim lot 25-2 Dooly Co., drawn by her husband MICHAEL LONG. Signed: Mary Eliza Long before LEVI S. RUSSELL, J.P., 24 April 1843. App't. of JAMES S. PARK as att'y. of Baldwin County.

BALDWIN COUNTY: Lot 181-16 Dooly. Pers. app'd. JAMES P. GRAVES, one of the heirs and orphans of JOHN Y. GRAVES of Wilkes Co., to claim lot 181-16 Dooly County. and lot 212-11 of Dooly Co. Signed: James P. Graves before J. R. ANDERSON, J.I.C.B.C., 3 June 1843.

EFFINGHAM COUNTY: Lot 97-16 Dooly. Pers. app'd. JAMES A. COURVOISIE to claim lot 97-16 Dooly County drawn by his father (JOHN F. COUR<u>VOISE</u>) and lot 79-4-3 drawn by his mother (SARAH COURVOISE). App't. of D. B. STETSON as att'y. Signed: James A. Courvoisie bef. JOSH GNANN, J.P., 7 June 1843.

PIKE COUNTY: Lot 29-16 Dooly. MARIA DONOUGHO, formerly MARIA BUCHANAN, appoints LEBAN BECHAM as att'y. to take out a grant to lot 29-16 of Dooly Co., drawn by her late husband MARTIN G. BUCHANAN. Signed: Maria Donough_ bef. D. M. BLOODWORTH and ABRAM B. ADAMS, J.P., 24 Sept. 1844.

RICHMOND COUNTY: Lot 92-16 Dooly. Pers. app'd. ANDREW J.MIL-

LER (MILLEN?), Adm'r. of the estate of JAMES BALLARD, dec'd., to claim lot 92-16 Dooly County. App't. of WILLIAM H. PRITCHARD of Milledgeville. Signed: A. J. MILLER before HENRY A. CUMMING, N.P. 30 June 1843.

EARLY COUNTY: Lot 427F-28 Early. NOAH PHILLIPS of Early County, Georgia, sells to JOSHUA MC DONALD of the Territory of Florida, county of Gadsden, the following lots in Early County, for the sum of $6,000: lot 427-28-; lot 447-; lot 426. Signed: Noah Phillips before L. B. HOLLENGER and THOMAS SPEIGHT, J.I.C., 14 Sept. 1838. Recorded in Book E, page 123, 17 September 1838.

BALDWIN COUNTY: Lot 21-28 Early. Pers. app'd. DAVID ANGLIN to claim lot 21-28-Early County, for himself, ANNE BALLARD, AMELIA WAGGONER, & JOHN ANGLIN. Signed: David Anglin before Alfred M. Horton, N.P., 30 August 1841.

THOMAS COUNTY: Lot 102-23 Early. Pers. app'd. REBECCA REVELLS, Ex'trx. of the est. of RANDOLPH REVELLS, dec'd., to claim fractional lot 102-23-Early Co., purchased by Randolph Revell from MARADA BRASWELL. Signed: Rebecca Revill (by mark) bef. CHAS. H. REMINGTON, J.P., 1 May 1849.

Lot 8-20 Early. "Executive Dept. Georgia Milledgeville, 22d May 1823
It appeareing from the records of the third land lottery, that lot no. 8 in the 20th Dist. Early County was drawn in the name of the Rev'd. Mr. CRANSTON of Chattham County, and it appearing from the affidavit of ANTHONY PORTER, Esquire, that the Rev'd. WALTER CRANSTON of sd. County (who is no doubt the drawer of sd. lot of land, reference being had to the return of the names of persons entitled to draws from sd. County in the sd. lottery, where there appears to be but one person of the name of Cranston entered for a draw or draws, and which is enterd "Rev. W. Cranston") has deceased that the sd. Walter Cranston was a single man and that the only legal heir is a single sister of the sd. Walter Cranston now in the City of Savannah, by the name of MARY CRANSTON. Application being made for a grant for sd. lot of land to issue to the Heirs of the Rev'd. Walter Cranston, it is,
Ordered that a grant issue accordingly, Attest. ELISHA WOOD, Secretary."

PIKE COUNTY: Lot 22-18 Early. JOSHUA C. MILLER, one of the legal heirs and legatees of the est. of ALEXANDER MILLER, dec'd., of Pike County, formerly of Morgan County, appoints JOHN GRACE as att'y. to take out a grant for lot 22-18 of Early Co. Signed: Joshua C. Miller bef. D. M. BLOODWORTH, J.I.C., 19 August 1841.

TALIAFERRO COUNTY: Lot 140-16 Early. Pers. came MARTHA A.
                        WARD to claim lot 140-16 of Early County,
drawn by JOSEPH W. LUCKETT, dec'd.(Any relationship between Ward
and Luckett is not explained.) Signed: Martha A. Ward before SIL-
VESTER V. LUCKETT, J.I.C., 22 August 1841.

STEWART COUNTY: Lot 40-16 Early. In person came TOLIVA W.
                        MORE to claim lot 40-16 of Early County,
drawn by NICHOLAS DARBY, dec'd., of Twiggs County. (Any relationship between Moore and Darby is not explained). Signed: TALIA-
FERRO W. Moore bef. L. BRYAN, J.I.C., 7 June 1841.

GREENE COUNTY: Lot 147-15 Early. We certify that no Rev-
                        olutionary War soldier named WM. OWEN lives
in the 148 district of Greene county but that a Revolutionary
character named JOHN OWEN was probably intended. We have lived
in this district for a great many years. Signed: WILLIAM REDD,
JAMES K. REDD & J. H. RASSOE(?), 22 October 1830.

BALDWIN COUNTY: Lot 147-15 Early. Pers. app'd. THOMAS
                        STOCKS who saith that he was familiar for
many years with JOHN OWEN a Revolutionary War soldier in the 148
Dist. of Greene County and that he does not believe that any WIL-
LIAM OWEN has lived in that district in the last 15 years.Signed:
THOMAS STOCKS bef. ADAM G. SAFFORD, J.I.C.B.C., 1 November 1830.

                        Lot 288-8 Early. "Georgia Laurens Cty.
His Excellency GEORGE M. TROUP
                        Dr. Sir. The intention of these lines,is
to know of you; whether we are Intitled to give in for draws in
the present Contemplated Land Lottery or Not. the circumstances
is this; each of us has given in as indigent Revolutionars and
was allowed four Draws, two as residents of this State, and two
as Revolutioners. We did also drew two prizes each, but from the
face of the List of the Drawing that we have only drew our resident Draws; and not our Revolutionary Draws, youll please to let
us know whether we are intitled to give in for draws as Revolutionary Soldiers in the present contemplated Land Lottery. a few
lines in answer directed to Dublin Laurens County will lay us under an obligation, which we shall gratefully remember, we are respectfully &c.
                HOSEA CLEMENTS & WILLIS ROYALS"

JASPER COUNTY: Lot 293-7 Early. Pers. came PETER CARDELL
                        to claim lot 293-7 Early Co., drawn by ED-
MOND NIBLET of Jones County. CARDELL has married the widow of
NIBLET and he is guardian of NIBLET's children. Signed: Peter
Cardell bef. THOS. J. SMITH, J.I.C., 24 August 1841.

BALDWIN COUNTY: Lot 185-7 Early. Pers. app'd. THOMAS HAR-
                      PER, Ex'r. of the estate of ANNE TEMPLE,
dec'd. to claim lot 185-7 of Early Co. Signed: T. Harper before
Alfred M. Horton, N.P., 31 August 1841.

COLUMBIA COUNTY: Lot 152-5 Early. Pers. came ROBERT WALTON
                      and SARAH his wife who saith that for many
years a MARY SMITH lived with them on charity and that she died
with no relatives in the United States. She had drawn a lot in
the land lottery as the widow of MICHOOL SMITH, no. 152-5, Smiths
Creek, Early County. Before her death, she requested that the lot
be given to BENJAMIN T. REES and TALBOT REES, as her only heirs.
Signed: Robert Walton and Sarah Walton bef. CHARLES M. LIN, J.P.
7 November 1848.

HANCOCK COUNTY: Lot 244-18 Henry. WILLIAM D. CALHOUN claims
                      lot 244-18 of Henry County; lot 93-7 of
Gwinnette County; lot 1104-21-3 Cherokee, belinging to the est.
of the orphans of WOOTEN DRISKILL. The Adm'r. of the estate has
moved from Georgia and Calhoun is married to MILLY ANN DRISKILL,
entitled to one fifth of the above land. The other orphans are
under 21 years of age and have no guardian. Signed: Wm. B. Calhoun (by mark) bef. TUTTLE H. AUDAS and LEREN O. CULVER(?), J.P.
Includes app't. of WASHINGTON H. BRANTLY as att'y. 6 June 1843.

MERIWETHER COUNTY: Lot 172-17 Henry. Pers. came HEZEKIAH S.
                      WIMBISH, in right of his wife, one of the
distributees of the estate of GEORGE W. HEARD, dec'd., and as
guardian representing two of the three remaining shares of the
estate, to claim fractional lot 172-17, Henry Co. Signed: Hezekiah S. Wimbish before W. H. P. ADAIR, J.P., 23 Oct. 1848.

DEKALB COUNTY: Lot 82-15 Henry. THOMAS J. PERKERSON and
                      AUGUSTIN W. SILLAVEN, Adm'rts. of the est.
of DAVID R. SILLAVEN, dec'd., sold at auction on the steps of the
Dekalb County courthouse a lot to JAMES A. SILLAVEN, the highest
bidder. Signed: Thomas J. Perkerson and Augustin W. Sillaven before ELIJAH TURNER & GEO. CLIFTON, J.I.C., 6 Oct. 1829.

                      Lot 52-14 Henry.
"Attorney Genrls Office, State of Ga., Atlanta, Ga. Apr. 22d.1884
His Excellency HENRY D. MC DANIEL
            Governor &c   Sir.

CLEMENT R. HARVIS derives title to the portion of City lot No. 52 in the 14th District of Originally Henry now Fulton County (being the property recently condemned by the Capitol Commission) by deed from the Gate City National Bank as the successor of the Atlanta Savings Bank dated Jany. 28th 1880 & recorded Feby. 2d 1880. The Atlanta Savings Bank held a warranty deed to the property from SAMUEL B. HOYT dated June 17th 1878 & recorded June 19th 1878. Samuel B. Hoyt held under a warranty deed from W. J. WARD (by his attoryney in fact G. W. ADAIR) dated November 1870 & recorded June 19th 1878. (Your Excellency informed me that A. L. MILLER Esqr., one of the capitol commissioners had found this power of attorney on record and examined it, it being a power authorizing Mr. Adair to sell this & other property. You having informed me that Mr. Miller was satisfied with this power of Attorney, I did not examine it.) W. J. WARD held under a deed from DAVID YOUNG as Trustee for his children and Young as Trustee held under a deed (illegible) by himself individually, dated May 8th, 1865 (recorded in Book B(?) Minutes Fulton Superior Court p. 621) in which the sd. Young conveyed sd. property to CHAS. H. ELYEA to be held in trust for the sd. Youngs wife during her life and after her death to be conveyed by said Trustee to her children in equal proportions sd. Elyea to continue Trustee at the pleasure of Mrs. Young. Subsequently, WILLIAM EUCLID YOUNG (one of the children of DAVID & Mrs. YOUNG) having married and taken up his residence in the City of New York, made a deed to his share for interest in sd. property to MARCUS L. D. MC CRASKEY in trust for his (EUCLID YOUNG's) wife for her life and at her pleasure, to be conveyed in equal parts to their children. In September 1871 DAVID YOUNG in behalf of the family concerned, applied to Judge JOHN L. HOPKINS as Chancellor for leave to sell this property stating that the Trustee appointed in the deed (CHAS. H. ELYEA had been removed from sd. trust by his wife MAHALA YOUNG in his life time) and he (sd. DAVID YOUNG) appointed by her as Trustee in lieu of sd. ELYEA. An order of sale was then granted but subsequently, to wit, on January 15th 1872 a supplemental petition was filed...refering to the former petition and order, reciting the fact that WILLIAM EUCLID YOUNG had conveyed his share (one third) at the death of his mother to sd. McCraskey in trust for sd. Euclid Young's wife for life and at her death to be conveyed in equal parts to their children and stating that sd. William Euclid Young and wife then had two children both minors one being between two and three years old and the other less than a year old. This supplemental petition prayed a confirmation of the appointment of David Young as Trustee in lieu of Elyea, removed as aforesd....that a guardian ad litem be appointed to represent the sd. two minor children of Wm. Euclid Young and wife (then residents of New York) and that the former order authorizing a sale of the property be confirmed. These petitions stated also that Mrs. MAHALA YOUNG (wife of DAVID YOUNG) was dead. Judge Hopkins appointed a guardian ad litem for said minors, confirmed the substitution of David Young as Trustee and affirm the previous order of sale "when Wm. Euclid Young & his wife JULIA had given their assent in writing as the other parties have." It appears from the recorded proceedings that Wm. Euclid Young and wife as well as the others parties in interest including the sd. guardian ad litem and also the trustee (McCraskey) all assented to sd. sale. The deed from David Young Trustee (as appears from the copy on record) to W. J. Ward bears date Sept. 9th 1872 and is recorded in Book "CC" p. 227. David Young held under a deed from PAUL F. EVE dated Jany. 28th 1864 and recorded Feby. 3rd 1864. PAUL F. EVE held under deed from ATTICUS G. HAYGOOD et al Executors of GREEN B. HAYGOOD dated Aug. 15th 1865 & recorded in Book G p. 514. GREEN B. HAYGOOD held under deed from

JAMES CALDWELL and GERMANT M. LESTER dated Sept. 18th 1852 and recorded June 15th 1853. CALDWELL & LESTER held under deed from WILLIAM P. HIGGINS dated March 3d 1852 and recorded June 15th, 1853. This traces the title back over thirty years and so far as I have been able to discover from an examination of the indexes to the records of deeds and mortgages, there is no other deed or record adverse to the title under which Mr. HARRIS holds or do I find any incumbrance on the property on record. I herewith enclose a certificate of C. H. STRONG, Clerk Supr. Court, certifying that there is no judgement, mortgage or other incumbrance of record in his office against any of the parties; also certificate of the county and City tax Collectors and other officials and also the certification of several Justices of the Peace. The only delicate point connected with the title grows out of the sale by DAVID WM. EUCLID YOUNG. This point has given me some trouble an I have given it much reflection and examination. In addition, I have been recently informed that WM. EUCLID YOUNG & his wife have never had any other children than the two who were in esse when the order of sale was granted. If this is true (and I have requested Mr. Harris's attorney to obtain and file, in connection with this report, an affidavit showing the fact, if it exists) there would seem to be no probability of the birth of any other children interested in the property than the two who were represented by a guardian ad litem in the matter of the application for sale granted Judge HOPKINS. I am inclined to think, too, as the result of much reflection on the subject that the appointment of a guardian ad litem for the children in esse when the application was made was all that was practicable and that such a guardian represented after born children entitled jointly in remainder with those then in life. Such seems to be fairly inferable from the decision of the Supreme Court in the case of BOARDMAN, next friend &c. vs. TAYLOR et al 66th Ga. 638. If, therefore, satisfaction, proof is filed that WM. EUCLID YOUNG & wife have no children except the two living when the sale was made, I think the title of Mr. Harris may properly be considered as satisfactory. An affidavit of WM. A HAYGOOD relating to the occupancy of the property in former years, accompanies this report.
       Very respectfully,
       CLIFFORD ANDERSON , Atty Genl.
P.S. Since writing the foregoing, I have found two decisions of our Supreme Court which determine that the birth of a child, subsequent to an order to sell trust property, does not envolidate the sale...although the child is interested in the property sold. See 64th Ga. 670, 68th Ga. 402."

HOUSTON COUNTY: Lot 144-12 Henry. LEVI EZELL appoints JAS. M. HALL of Wilkinson County as att'y. for taking out a grant to lot 144-12 of Henry Co. He is part owner of same having married one of the orphans of JAMES ROACH of Pulaski Co. Signed: Levi Ezell bef. EZEKIEL EVANS, J.P. 17 June 1843.

CHATHAM COUNTY: Lot 4108 Henry. Pers. app'd. Mrs. ELIZA M. OSBORNE, who saith that she is a widow with two children and that she has resided in this state for the last three years. Signed: Eliza M. Osborne bef. THOS. M. MOREL, J.I.C.C.C., 24 Aug. 1821.

BALDWIN COUNTY: R. M. ORME testifies that ELIZA M. OSBORNE and her orphans are entitled to two draws in the land lottery, she being the widow of JAMES G. H. OSBORNE, dec'd. Signed: R. M. Orme bef. JAMES ROUSSEAU, J.P. 8 Jan. 1824.

JEFFERSON COUNTY: Lot 233-5 Henry. We do certify that we have lived in the 76th District for the last ten or twelve years and that we know CATHERINE KENNEY, a widow who has since married THOMAS HANNAH, and that no such person as CATHERINE KELLY lives in sd. district. Signed: JOHN SINING, J.P., JONATHAN ROBERSON, J.P., JAMES W. KIGNEY, B. VINING, & THOMAS WHIGHAM.

BENJAMIN GOBERT certifies that he was a justice of the inferior court for 1821 and that he qualified applicants for the land lottery while ROBERT B. SHELMAN registered names. He believes that an error was made in recording the name CATHERINE KELLY instead of CATHERINE KENNY. Signed: Benj. Gobert, J.I.C., 7 December 1826.

BALDWIN COUNTY: Lot 276-23 Muscogee. Pers. app'd. WILLIAM MITCHELL of Talbot County, Ex'r. of the estate of WILLIAM HOBBS, dec'd., of Talbot Co., to claim fractional lots 276 and 277, 23rd Dist. of Muscogee Co. Signed: William Mitchell before P. M. COMPTON, N.P., 24 October 1848.
"Treasury of Ga., 25th October 1848.
It appears from the Books of Fraction Sales on file in this office that Fractions Nos. 276 and 277 in the 23rd District Muscogee were purchased at the sale by JNO. P. BLACKMON and it further appears from entries opposite sd. numbers on the sd. Books, that the purchase money has been paid as I understand sd. entries. Signed: WM. B. FINSLEY, Treas.

Executive Department
Milledgeville 25 Oct. 1848

Let grants issue to JOHN P. BLACKMAN for fractions No. 276 and 277 in the 23rd District of Muscogee County. Signed: CHS. H.RICE, S.E.D."

GREENE COUNTY: Lot 110-23 Muscogee. Pers. app'd. HENRY COTTON who saith that he is entitled to an extra draw in the land lottery having served six months in Capt. SAFFORD's Company under General MC INTOSH at Mobile. Signed: Henry Cotton before THOMAS STOCKS, J.I.C., 11 July 1837.

FAYETTE COUNTY: Lot 152-22 Muscogee. Pers. app'd. SUSANNAH

SIMMONS, mother of LEWIS CAMPBELL, to claim lot 152-22 of Muscogee County as sd. orphan was 21 years old on 22 January 1844. Signed: Susannah Simmons before J. H. ELDER, J.P., 8 December 1844.

MORGAN COUNTY: Lot ------Muscogee. We the orphans of JNO. PRIOR dec'd. appoint THOMAS V. ALLEN as att'y. to take out the grant to the lot drawn by JOHN PRIOR in the land lottery. Signed: R. A. PRIOR, G. I. H. PRIOR, FELIX W. PRIOR, E. C. RADFORD, & M. P. EDWARDS (formerly PRIOR) before A. B. BOSTWICK, J.P., 5 May 1843.

HENRY COUNTY: Lot 141-22 Muscogee. Interrogation of WAID H. TURNER in the case of RANDOLPH MITCHELL vs. JONATHAN CHILDS, Harris County. Turner testifies that he does not know either of the parties involved. He did take down the name of GEORGE KILGORE, illegitimate, given by Kilgore's next friend JOHN OWENS at the home of REUBEN HAND. He also took down the name of RACHEL HAND, widow of a Revolutionary War soldier, at the home of Reuben Hand. Signed: Waid H. Turner before JAMES SELLERS, WM. GREER & A. V. SELLERS, 26 August 1835.

TATTNALL COUNTY: Lot 225-21 Muscogee. JOHN SIKES saith that he was given in for a draw in the land lottery by his brother JETREE(?) SILKES. Signed: John Sikes before ELHANAN MC CALL, J.P., 7 October 1828.

Lot 124-21 Muscogee.
"Governor
  It currently circulated and credited here at the time of giving in returns for draws in the last land Lottery that Adult Females as well as Males was Entitled to a draw; I therefore returned my daughter MARY ANNE BLUE, which came out a prize No.124-21st District Muscogee County when I found out that She was not entitled to a draw I then determined to have nothing more to do with it but let it revert to the State. Being however recently informed that in all probability it would be made out a fraudulent return, & seeing her name in the Gazette as having drawn the above No. 124 & the letter W affixed to it; either by an error of the press or by design: the inclosed Certificate on Oath will testify that I did not put the letter W, only Simply the Name. Captain ABRAHAMS of Wayne County having been in the Interior lately, Informed me ther were Interlopers, who would take out the grant in my daughters Name; & then return it a fraudulent draw this would be Swallowing publick Utility in private Enolument with a Vengeance. I lay no claim to the tract & never will; & I cannot concieve what right any one else has to take out Such grant without my Consent ...he that takes my purse take trash...But he that feltches from

me my Good name makes me poor Indeed. Should such a grant be presented for your signature; I hope & beg your Excellencey to refuse Signing thus you will save half of the tract to the State, and an Innocent man from the Odius Imputation of making fraudulent returns...With Sentiments of perfect Respect I remain.
       Your Excellencys
       Most Obedt
       And Very Humbl Servt, DANL. BLUE Senr."
Glynn County 13th Feby. 1828.

CRAWFORD COUNTY: Lot 128-20 Muscogee. Pers. app'd. LEWELLEN MORGAN, guardian of JAMES W. HILL (minor of NANCY HILL, widow, dec'd.), to claim lot 128-20 Muscogee Co. App't. of THOMAS B. STOKES as att'y. Signed: Lwellen Morgan bef. W. J. D. SMILEY & E. B. WALLACE, J.P., 29 May 1843.

CHATHAM COUNTY: Lot 135-20 Muscogee. Pers. app'd. Mrs. ELIZABETH S. SHICK, JANE C. CLINE & AGNES CLINE, orphans of JONATHAN CLINE, to claim lot 135-20-2 of the land lottery of 1827. Signed: Elizabeth S. Shick, Jane C. Cline, and Agnes Cline before ISAAC RUSSELL, J.P., 16 June 1843.

HARRIS COUNTY: Lot 348-20 Muscogee. Pers. app'd. JOHN PATTILLO to claim lot 348-20 Muscogee co. drawn by JAMES CARTER, a illegitimate whose name has been changed by act of legislature to JAMES OATS. App't. of ANDERSON W. REDDING of Baldwin Co. as att'y. Signed: John Pattillo before ELIJAH MULLINS, J.P. and JAMES PATTILLO, 17 Sept. 1845.

MUSCOGEE COUNTY: Lot F193-17 Muscogee. JAS. M. RENFROE & JAS. WHITTLE, Adm'rs. of the estate of ENOCH RENFROE, dec'd., legally advertised and sold a fractional lot at auction to THOS. GUICE for $300. Signed: J. M. Renfroe & Jas. Whittle bef. JOHN W. EDWARDS & WM. B. ROCKMORE, J.P. 5 Feb. 1850.

MC INTOSH COUNTY: Lot 55-13 Muscogee. EDMUND M. BLOUNT,Admr. of the estate of RICHARD GREEN, appoints J. E. TOWNSEND att'y. to take out a grant to lot 55-2 of Muscogee. Signed: E. M. Blount bef. ARMOND LEFETS, J.P. 15 June 1843.

MACON COUNTY: Lot 238-13 Muscogee. Pers. came GEORGE PATTEN, lawful agent of GIBBONS M. TAYLOR of Louisiana, to claim lot 238-13 and lot 194-3 of Muscogee Co. Signed: G. Patten bef. ELEZAR RUSS, J.P., 15 June 1843.

DOOLY COUNTY: Lot 94-13 Muscogee. Pers. app'd. JAMES M.
                         GRAHAM to claim lot 13-2 Muscogee drawn
by JOSEPH GRAHAM's orphans, as one of the owners. App't. of JAC-
OB WATSON as att'y.Signed: James M. Graham before CAROLINE E. WAT-
SON & WILLIAM B. CONE, J.I.C., 15 June 1845.

BULLOCH COUNTY: Lot 239-13 Muscogee. Pers. came WM. H.
                         ROWLS to claim lot 239-13 Muscogee and lot
919-1 & 2, Cherokee, drawn by GEORGE M. LOVE, orphan, for the benefit of GEORGE LOVE. Signed: W. H. Rowls before PETER CONE, J.I.
C.B.C., 18 May 1848.

PUTNAM COUNTY: Lot 46-14 Muscogee. POLLY MILLIRONS claims
                         lot 46-14 Muscogee drawn by her illegiti-
mate children SIMON and HARRIET MILIRONS, both of whom are under
eighteen years of age. Signed: Polly Millirons (by mark) before
B. W. CLARK, J.P., 13 October 1838.

EMANUEL COUNTY: Lot 102-14 Muscogee. Pers. app'd. WILLIAM
                         DOUGLAS, agent for HENRY S. ROBERTS (Ille-
gitimate of SARAH ROBERTS), who saith that the name was incorrectly given in as SARAH ROBERTS, illegitimate. Signed: William Douglas (by mark) before JAMES M. TAPLEY, J.P., 1 December 1851.
                         JAMES TAPLEY saith that he is acquain-
ted with HENRY S. ROBERTS, a illegitimate who was nine years old
in 1826 and the son of SARAH ROBERTS. Signed: James Tapley (by
mark) bef. JAMES M. TAPLEY, J.P., 1 Dec. 1851.

GWINNETT COUNTY: Lot 29-15 Muscogee. Pers. app'd. CHARITY
                         MATHEWS, widow of HENRY MATHEWS, dec'd.,
to claim lot 29-15 of Muscogee. Signed: Charity Mathews (by mark)
bef. LOT ROWDEN, J.P., 1 June 1843.

TALBOT COUNTY: Lot 145-14 Muscogee. Pers. app'd. DAVID
                         TERRELL, owner of one half and Adm'r. of
the estate of DAVID MONTFORT dec'd., who is the owner of the other half, to claim lot 145-14 Muscogee Co.; lot 497-4-3, Cherokee
Co.; lot 730-3-3, Cherokee Co.; and lot 170-11-1, Cherokee Co.
Signed: Dd. Terrell bef. RICHD. HATT, J.P., 19 June 1843.

                         Lot 139-15 Muscogee
"His Excellency the Govr.
                         Sir, I concieve it to be my duty to make

known to you, the following facts:
                    Mrs. ELIZABETH C. THOMAS of Clark (who has
since died) give in, for a draw, in the late land lottery, as the
widow of a Revolutionary Soldier. She drew two tracts of land,to
but one of which, I consider muself as her representative intitled to wit, the one she drew as the widow of a Revolutionary Soldier. I have thought proper to communicate the facts that such
disposition might be made of the other (Lot No. 139 in the 15th
district of Muscogee County) as might be considered best for the
public good.   Yours respectfully,
                            C. L. THOMAS
Milledgeville 7th Novr. 1827"

LOWNDES COUNTY: Lot 41-16 Muscogee. Per. app'd. JOHN G.
                        UNDERWOOD, Adm'r. of the ASA BAKER (one
of the orphans of Baker), to claim lot 41-16 Muscogee drawn from
Bulloch County. He is also the att'y. for MOSES SMITH & AARON
SMITH, owners of lot 373,14th Dist., 1st Sect., Cherokee County.
Includes app't. of Alfred M. Horten as att'y. Signed: John G.
Underwood before DUNCAN SMITH, J.I.C., 13 June 1843.

MONROE COUNTY: Lot 20-12 Muscogee. NAIL MC MULLEN, Ex'r.
                        of FIELDEN MC MILLEN, dec'd., appoints
WILLIAM S. NORMAN att'y. to take out grants to lot 20-12 of Mus-
cogee, drawn by PURIFY TINGLE: lot 179-28 of Early County, drawn
by JAMES B. ADAMS; and lot 267-7 Lee, drawn by FIELDEN MC MULLEN.
Signed: Nail McMullen before DALPHIN FLOYD and J. D. CALAWAY, J.
P., 12 June 1843.

CHATHAM COUNTY: Lot 102-12 Muscogee. Pers. app'd. JOHN C.
                        HUNTER, agent for the orphans of FLEMING
AKIN, to claim lot 102-12-Muscogee. Signed: John C. Hunter before
WM. THORNE WILLIAMS, J.I.C.C.C., 22 June 1843.

MUSCOGEE COUNTY: Lot 93-12 Muscogee. Pers. app'd. SAMUEL
                        LEWIS to claim lot 93-12 of Marion County
as part owner. Signed: Samuel Lewis bef. MICHAEL N. CLARKE, J.P.
12 Sept. 1844. The lot was drawn by James C. Lewis' orphans.

COLUMBIA COUNTY: Lot 118-1 Muscogee. Pers. app'd. W. A. L.
                        COLLINS, guardian of JOHN B. COLLINS, to
claim lot 118-1 of Muscogee Co. Signed: W. A. L. Collins before
JAMES M. DORSEY, J.I.C., 15 June 1843.

LOWNDES COUNTY: Lot 206-12 Muscogee. Pers. app'd. JAMES
                        A. GOLDWIN, Ex'r. of the est. of ELIZABETH

M. GREEN, widow, dec'd., to claim lot 206-12th Dist. Marion(?) County. Includes app't. of JOHN J. UNDERWOOD as att'y. Signed: James A. Goldwin before B. W. SINCLAIR & HAMILTON W. SHARPE, J.I.C., 14 February 1843.

MACON COUNTY: Lot 218-12 Muscogee. Pers. app'd. JOHN P. D. KELLY to claim lot 218-20th Dist. of Muscogee Co., as one of the heirs. Signed: J. P. D. Kelly before MOSES JOHNSON, J.P., 13 May 1843.

HENRY COUNTY: Lot 26-13 Muscogee. Pers. app'd. SARAH GRICE, widow of STEREN GUICE of Henry Co., dec'd., to claim lot 26-13 of Muscogee co.; lot 96-5 of Muscogee co.; and lot 1090-15-2 Cherokee. App't. of DUNCAN MCVICKER as attorney. Signed: Sarah Grice (by mark) before JOHN G. SYRUS, J.P. 4 May 1843.

BURKE COUNTY: Lot 219-11 Muscogee. Pers. app'd. ENOCH BYNE to claim the following: "I am Adm'r. of the Est. of WM. R. CALDWELL; I am still the owner of all lands drawn by me in the Lotteries; I am the owner of lot 946-12 dist. sst section (?) drawn by HAMILTON T. BOYD; I am the owner by purchase and have a bond for titles, for all the lands drawn by DEMSEY MURRY--Burke; I am the owner by purchase for two tracts drawn by PETER J. YORDY--Burke; I am the owner by purchase of 1 lot drawn by WILLIAM STRONGFELLOW; I am the owner by purchase of all the lands drawn by TIMOTHY MURRY--bond for titles--of Burke; I am part owner of a lot drawn by JOHN M. HILL--Burke; I am Plaintiff in Execution vs. JOSEPH ROE--Burke; I am owner of all lands drawn by EDWARD HUGHS--of Burke". Signed: Enoch Byne bef. GEO. W. EVANS, J.I.C.B.C., 5 June 1843.

Lot 220-11 Muscogee. "Bethel Aug. 19,1850
Mr. JAMES R. BUTTS
     Dear Sir
          I will give you all the information I can about the causes you addressed me about one you say was Drawn by MARTHA, MAY, JOHN, PAUL & CAROLINE DEMERE 25 Dist. of (illegible) they formerly resided on st symons Island MARY & MARTHA now reside at White Spring P office Fla. One of these is now the wife of Doct. KNIGHT who also resides there JOHN Resides near Darien P office McIntosh Co. PAUL DEMERE near Centerville Carroll Co. Ga. My impression is they have never sold their land of MARGARET HOLMES I know nothing but will try & find out & let you know THOMAS PENTON resides at Jacksonville Fla WILLIAM WHILLEMORE I never heard of any such person MAY F. SCOTT is now the wife of J. W. MOORE of Brunswick in this county she has never sold her tract in Cherokee asks 5¢ pr acre has been offered 2¢ by some one she says any further information at any time will be cheerfully given in my person if you can give me any information as regards the value of no 96 in 9th Dist of Carrol County Drawn by WILLIAM MANGO orphans I would be glad to receive it yours respectfully JOHN M. TISON".

HOUSTON COUNTY: Lot 234-9 Muscogee. Pers. app'd. JOHN C. MOUNGER of Macon County to claim a share of lot 234-9 of Muscogee Co. and lot 408-15-2, Cherokee, drawn by the orphans of JOSEPH GARTRELL, MOUNGER having married LUCY H. GARTRELL, one of the orphans. App't. of Alfred M. Horton of Baldwin Co. Signed: John C. Mounger bef. W. D. WHITEHEAD, J.I.C. 16 June 1843.

MARION COUNTY: Lot 260-4 Muscogee. In person app'd. WILLIAM WISENER, agent for NANCY & CAROLINE MOTES (illegitimates), to claim lot 260-4 of Muscogee Co. App't. of JOHN CAMPBELL as att'y. Signed: William Wisener (by mark) bef. R. W. MASTON, J.P., 8 June 1843.

MUSCOGEE COUNTY Lot 219-5 Muscogee. Pers. app'd. WM. R. RUSSELL to claim lot 449-2-1, Cherokee and as the lawful agent of DAVID RUSSELL, minor, claims lot 219-5 of Muscogee Co. App't. of THOMAS M. COOK of Baldwin Co. as att'y. Signed: WILLIAM R. RUSSELL before RICHARD B. CUFF & DANIEL HUFF, J.P., 17 June 1843.

BIBB COUNTY: Lot 246-5 Muscogee. Pers. app'd. THOMAS J. CARTER to claim lot 246-5, Muscogee County drawn by the orphans of TITUS WIMBERLY dec'd., to wit: LEWIS T. WIMBERLY, SAMUEL T. WIMBERLY, & AMELIA E. WIMBERLY. CARTER has married AMELIA E. WIMBERLY. Signed: THOS. J. CARTER bef. JESSE S. OWEN, J.P., 31 October 1843.

CLARKE COUNTY: Lot 115-7 Muscogee. Pers. came JOHN S. ROBISON, one of the orphans of JAMES ROBISON dec'd. to claim lot 115-7 of Muscogee Co. Signed: John S. Robison before THOMAS SIMONTON, J.I.C., 6 October 1845.

Lot 48-8 Muscogee.
"WILSON LUMPKIN Esqr. 27th April 1834
Dear Sir you will confer a singular favor on an old friend by having Lot no 48-8 Dist Muscogee drawn by ELIZA AN HAYS Illigitimate granted before the first Tuesday in May as it is to be Gold then if you see a convenient chance to send it by private conveyance do. if not mail it and much oblige
your friend truly
DAVID J. BRITT
After paying grant fee & postage remaining in my hands $1.50cts April 30th 1834.
WILSON LUMPKIN"

MONROE COUNTY: Lot 215-4 Muscogee. Pers. app'd. WILLIAM C. NUTT, JOHN C. NUTT, SAMUEL M. NUTT, ENOCH JACKSON, & ASHER JACKSON, who are the owners with HARRIETT NUTT & ELIZAR NUTT, of half of lot 215-4 Muscogee. Co. App't. of JOHN CAMPBELL as att'y. Signed: William C. Nutt, John C. Nutt, Samuel M. Nutt, Enoch Jackson, and Asher Jackson before FIELDING JACKSON, J.O. & S. R. NUTT, J.I.C., 22 May 1843.

MONROE COUNTY:		Lot 214-4 Muscogee. Pers. app'd. HARMAN E.
		D. CERESTER to claim lot 124-4 Muscogee
co. as half owner; and as lawful agent of SUSAN COURTER, guardian of SAMUEL H. COURTER, minor and owner of the other half,drawn by them as orphans of EDWARD D. COURTER. App't. of WILLIAM B.TINSLEY of Baldwin Co. as att'y. Signed: HARMON E. D. COURTER bef. R. RAIFORD, J.P., 11 May 1843.

MORGAN COUNTY:		Lot 66-4 Muscogee. We, the orphans of AUS-
		TIN CLEMENTS, dec'd., of Morgan County,
claim lot 66 in Muscogee Co. as we are all now of age. Signed: MATILDA WILLIS, PERMELIA BROOKS, NANCY WHITLOCK, ELIZABETH GIBBS, LILY ANN STEWART, & ROBERT H. CLEMENTS before CREZY(?) THOMPSON & R. A. PRIOR, J.P., 3 May 1843.

		Lot 42-4 Muscogee. "Dublin Sept. 3rd 1833
Dear Sir		Mr EDWARD SNELLGRAVE of our County sent by my Son for a grant to a tract of Land he drew in the Lottery before the last and on refering to the Books his name was entered SNEEGRAVE instead of SNELLGRAVE. I have lived in the County 18 years and know there never was a man living in it by the name of Sneegrave I have acted as Clerk of the differenct Courts for six years and the jury Box has been corrected three times since I came into office therefore have had every opportunity of knowing every man in the county and can say certainly there is no such man as Sneegrave in the county and never was. I am Dr Sir
		with much respect your obt servt
His Excellency WILSON LUMPKIN		THO. MOORE"

JEFFERSON COUNTY:	Lot 23-4 Muscogee. ANN M. KIRKLAND (form-
		erly ANN M. PENNINGTON) and MARY F. FAY
(formerly MARY F. PENNINGTON), the orphans of SIM PENNINGTON,deceased, appoints PHILIP S. LAMB as att'y. to take out grant to lot 23-4, Muscogee; and lot 501-19-3 Cherokee Co. Signed: Ann M. Kirkland and Mary F. Fay before BENIAH S. CARSWELL, J.P., 14 June 1843.

LINCOLN COUNTY:		Lot 82-2 Muscogee. Pers. app'd. HOGAN WADS-
		WORTH, guardian of the heirs of WILLIAM
ONEAL, to claim lot 82-2 Muscogee Co.; lot 197-10-3, Cherokee co.; lot 175-2-2, Cherokee Co.; and lot 11-5-1 Cherokee Co. App't. of HARVEY WHEAT as att'y. Signed: Hogan Wadsworth bef. ALEXR. JOHNSTON, J.I.C. and BURKE MOORE, 14 June 1843.

COLUMBIA COUNTY:	Lot 240-2 Muscogee. Came personally WIL-
		LIAM A. BAULDWIN, lawful representative of

WILLIAM WILEY, dec'd., to claim lot 240-2 Muscogee County. App't. of WILLIAM H. PRITCHARD of Baldwin Co. as att'y. Signed: WM. A. BALDWIN bef. H. W. MASSENGALE, J.I.C., 27 June 1843.

COLUMBIA COUNTY: Lot 176-10 Muscogee. Came personally BIRD PERRY, Ex'r. of JOHN PERRY, dec'd. (who intermarried with MARY G. PEARN), to claim lot 176-10 Muscogee county. App't. of WILLIAM H. PRITCHARD of Baldwin Co. as att'y. Signed: Bird Perry bef. H. W. Massengale, J.I.C., 17 June 1843.

DECATUR COUNTY: Lot 243-2 Muscogee. Pers. app'd. HANNAH LEE to claim lot 243-2, Muscogee Co. that she drew as HANNAH WATSON, widow. Signed: Hannah Lee (by mark) before SAMUEL MILLER, J.P., 10 June 1843.

MARION COUNTY: Pers. app'd. BURTON W. DOWD, Adm'r. of the estate of WILLIAM MOTE, dec'd., to claim Lot 219-3rd Dist., Muscogee Co. App't. of JOHN CAMPBELL as att'y. Signed: Burton W. Dowd bef. B. A. STACY & R. W. MASTON, J.P. 16 June 1843.

BALDWIN COUNTY: Lot 297-1 Muscogee. In person came A. D. KENDRICK, one of the Ex'rs. of JAMES A. EVERETT, dec'd., to claim lot 297-and 305, 1st Dist. of Muscogee. now Crawford County. Signed: A. D. Kendrick before S. B. BROWN, J.P., 18 July 1850.

BAKER COUNTY: Lot 22-2 Muscogee. Pers. app'd. JAMES A. NEWMAN, Adm'r. of the estate of EZEKIEL M. LENDON, dc'd., to claim lot 22-2 of Muscogee Co. Signed: James A. Newman bef. NELSON TIFT, J.I.C., 22 June 1843.

JONES (?) COUNTY: Lot 321-1 Muscogee. Pers. app'd. THOMAS S. HUMPHRES, one of the Ex'rs. of JAMES LOCK- ETT, dec'd., to claim lot drawn by HENRY CRASSWELL and sold to WILLIAM H. BUSBA and from him to SOLOMON S. CHAPMAN. From the ex- ecutors of sd. Chapman, the lot was sold to James Lockhart. It is lot 321-1, Muscogee. Signed: Thomas S. Humphries before JONA. PAR- RISH, J.I.C., 26 July 1850.

Lot 118-1 Muscogee. "Red Oak June 12th 1843 Dear Sir

JNO. B. COLLINS a younger brother during his minority drew a lot of land I think in the lottery of 1827 which from negligence I discover is still ungranted He is now in Alabama and probably unapprized that the time for granting expires on the 1st of next month. At the time of the lottery I was acting as his guardian and have made oath as required by the last Legislature. I have no recollection of the number or the locality of the lot that may be readily ascertained by an examination of the list of 1827 and the affidavit filled out The lot I understand is valuable and if you have any difficulty about the irregularity or informality of the papers pay them in the money which is enclosed and the errors may be rectified and the grant forwarded If your time do not admit attention to it if you will turn the papers over to Mr. CHARLES E. RYAN in the office of the Secty of State he will attend it for me   you attention will much oblige your friend
      W. A. L. COLLINS"

HENRY COUNTY: Lot 238-17 Lee. Pers. app'd. WILLIAM T. SUMMERLIN, one of the heirs of THOMAS SUMMERLIN, dec'd., to claim lot 238-17, Lee County. and lot 143-12 of Muscogee Co. App't. of FRANCIS E. MANSON as att'y. Signed: William T. Summerlin bef. THOS. E. HICKS, J.P., 10 June 1843.

BURKE COUNTY: Lot 117-19 Lee. Pers. app'd. ELI MC CROAN to claim lot 117-19, Lee County, which he purchased from the orphans of JAMES MC CROAN. Also lot 235-13-4 of Cherokee, as guardian of the heirs of EDMUND PCOR(?). Includes app't. of WM. H. PRITCHARD of Baldwin Co. as att'y. Signed: Eli McCroan before ELBERT D. TAYLOR, J.P. and N. W. TAYLOR, 16 June 1843.

TWIGGS COUNTY: Lot 46-21 Lee. Pers. came NANCY GANDY, widow of GRIFFIN GANDY, dec'd., to claim lot 46-21 of Lee Co. Signed: Nancy Gandy (by mark) bef. ABISHA ANDREWS, J.P., 12 June 1843.

BURKE COUNTY: Lot 46-20 Lee. Pers. came REBECCA SKINNER, mother of JOHN J. SKINNER, illegitimate, to claim lot 46-20-Lee Co. John has no legal guardian. Signed: Rebecca Skinner (by mark) bef. HOMER V. MULKEY, J.P., 13 June 1843.

GREENE COUNTY: Lot 98-21 Lee. Pers. app'd. HENRY C. SEYMON, Adm'r. of the est. of PHILIP GATEWOOD, to claim lot 98-21 of Lee. Signed: Henry C. <u>SYMORN</u> bef. J. R. Hall J.I.C., 26 June 1843.

      Lot 100-22 Lee. "Louisville Mar. 8, 1850

Mr. JAMES R. BUTTS
                Dear Sir
                        On my return home I saw Mr. RENFROE
(Mr. NATHANIEL RENFORE) who drew lot No 100-22d section originally Lee now Stewart two hundred Dollars he says is the least he
will take for it. May be to it might be bought for a fraction
lower. Do you know any thing about it. he has promised to give me
three weeks to answer him. I have also a tract of land in Dooly
that I want to know something about. it is No 136-11Dist Dooly.
My mother in Law is quite unwell. the Rest are Well; I do not expect to go atlanta next week. but will go to Savannah in Eight or
ten days. I write from Louisville because I do not expect id be
able to get to Fenns Bridge by next mail; as I have several jobs
of Surveying that must be attended to. Please say to Miss FANNY
that I am obliged to her for the Recipe & when the object intended is effected will most assuredly follow her advice my respects
to Mrs. BUTTS & the Ladies---accept the same yourself
                        your obt servt
                                JOHN C. HARMAN"

WARREN COUNTY: Lot 274-22 Lee. HOWEL H. HUNT, guardian of
                        AUGUSTUS B. DUNAWAY, illegitimate, to lay
claim to lot 274-22 now Stewart Co. and lot 247-5-1, now Lumpkin
Co. Signed: Howel H. Hunt bef. ELISHA BURSON, J.P., 26 Feb. 1843.

STEWART COUNTY: Lot 60-24 Lee. Pers. app'd. JNO. R. M.
                        WILLIAMSON, one of the orphans of JNO.
WILLIAMSON, dec'd. of Screven(?) County, to claim lot 60-2 of Lee
Co. Signed: John R. Williamson bef. JAMES CLARK, J.I.C., 22 July
1845.

GWINNETT COUNTY: Lot 81-24 Lee. Pers. came THOMAS A. GLEN
                        Adm'r. of the estate of GEORGE W. GLEN,
dec'd. to claim lot 81-24-Lee Co. App't. of JOHN G. PARK as attorney. Signed: Thomas A. Glen (by mark) bef. H. CRAWFORD and
W. S. IVIE, J.P., 29 June 1843.

GWINNETT COUNTY: Lot 81-24 Lee. Pers. came Thomas A. Glen
                        Adm'r. of the estate of ELISABETH GLEN,
dec'd., to claim lot 150-24-3, Cherokee. App't. of John G. Park
of Baldwin Co. as att'y. Signed: Thomas A. Glen (by mark) bef.
H. Crawford and W. S. Ivie, J.P., 24 June 1843.

RANDOLPH COUNTY: Lot 158-24 Lee. Pers. app'd. EMANUEL POS-
                        TON to claim lot 158-24 of Lee Co., having
married the widow who won sd. lot. Signed: E. Poston before EZEK-
IEL BRYAN, J.P., 19 June 1843.

MORGAN COUNTY: Lot 157-25-Lee. Pers. app'd. WILLIAM H.

WILSON to claim lot 157-25 of Lee County, drawn by the orphans of THOMAS STOVALL of Dekalb county. WILSON married one of the orphans. Signed: WILLIAM H. WILSON before JOHN J. WALKER, J.P., 10 June 1843

Lot 151-27 Lee. "Americus Jan 8th 1851
Mr. JAMES R. BUTTS
            Dear Sir
                    Upon inquiry I find that no 151 in the 27th dist one of the numbers you sent me has passed through a number of hands. It is said to have been drawn by an orphan girl named SALTER whose husband after marriage sold to JOHN PREEMAN. He sold to ENOCH CALLAWAY of this county who sold a few weeks since to WM. MASK(?) for six hundred and fifty dollars. Not knowing who Miss SALTER married I have not been able to trace the title on the record all the way. No 148 in the 26th dist is said to have been sold several times and regularly from the drawer to the present holder whose name I cannot at this moment recall No 140 in the 26th dist if you can find the owner we can get two hundred dollars for on a credit til next christmas
                    In haste yours &c
                    A. A. ROBINSON
140-26 SAMUEL W. NILSON Robertson Jones 1838
145-26 JONATHAN HOBBS Orphans"

WALTON COUNTY: Lot 18-29 Lee. Pers. came PETER G. MORROW, one of the heirs of JOSEPH MORROW, dec'd., of Morgan County, to claim lot 18-29 of Lee, now Marion County. App't. of WARREN J. HILL of Walton Co. as att'y. Signed: Peter G. Morrow bef. CHARLES SORRELLS and NEH. JOHNSON, J.I.C. 29 May 1843.

COLUMBIA COUNTY: Lot 63-29 Lee. JOHN H. SCOTT, husband of ELIZA HALLIMAN, now ELIZA SCOTT, claims lot 63-29, Lee Co. drawn by the orphans of ELISHA HOLLIMAN, dec'd. as half owner. He appoints CHARLES E. RYAN as att'y. Signed.John H. Scott before H. W. MASSENGALE, J.I.C., 13 Oct. 1846.
            "Wrightsboro Oct 13/46
Dear Charles
        Enclosed you find Five dollars and with the annexed affts. you are asked to take out the grant for sd. lot please attend to it and write to me your fees & they shall be remitted. This Lot may have been granted if so advise me yours very truly &c.   HENRY W. MASSENGALE"

WALTON COUNTY: Lot 100-29 Lee. Certification that EDWARD R. CAMP should have been EDWARD K. CAMP in the land lotteries. Signed: THOS. R. MITCHELL, J.I.C., 19

February 1828. "THOS. R. MITCHELL killed Oct. 22, 1838 by JOHN H. HENDRICKS (Proclamations 1823-53, p. 146)"

JONES COUNTY: Lot 201-29 Lee. Pers. came JOHN B. CHILDS Adm'r. of ROBERT CHILDS, dec'd. to claim lot 201-29 of Lee Co. Includes app't. of BENNETT BRIDGES as atty. Signed: J. B. Childs before LUCY DAVIS & JOHN WILLIAMSON, J.P. 13 June 1843.

                     Lot 9-1 Lee. "Burke County April 15h/51
Dear Mr. Butts
           I would have written to you long ago but was hoping to get some information that would be satisfactory to you, but in vain, some of the persons I have not been able to hear of yet. FUNDERBUSS died in this county, in 22 or 23, I have not yet been able to find out who has his land, he left no heir, GODBEE who drew No 9 1st Lee, has moved to Jonesboro, Georgia. I still am trying and may get some information ere long, when I do you shall know. I expect to spend a night in Scottsboro, my wife expects to accompany me, we will be anxious to get home as we shall have been a long time absent. Tell LOUISA that her name sake is a smart little girl. we hope she will get well, she improves. I received the papers you sent, I am sorry you had so much trouble as you sent several that was not in my section of the country I have not yet been enabled to get a good surveyor, I have been waiting on HARMON, but he has not yet come over I cannot say what other papers I may stand in need of until he comes. Give my love to LOUISA, I am anxious to see them all.
                     yours very truly
                     JOS. POLHILL"

PUTNAM COUNTY: Lot 40-1 Lee. Pers. app'd. ROBERT T. SANDERS, JULIA CAROLINE SANDERS, & MASSAURE ANN SANDERS, the illegitimate children of PENELOPE SANDERS, to claim lot 40-1 of Lee Co. Signed: Julia C. Sanders (by mark), Messour A. Sanders (by mark) and Robert T. Sanders before B. W. CLARK, J.P., 28 January 1844.

BALDWIN COUNTY: Lot 74-1 Lee. Pers. app'd. JOHN U. MC MATH Adm'r. of the estate of WILLIAM MC MATH, late of Jones County, dec'd., to claim lot 74-1 Lee County. Signed: John H. McMath before Alfred M. Horton, N.P., 29 June 1843.

MUSCOGEE COUNTY: Lot F6-33 Lee. "Georgia, Múscogee County
                     10th October 1850
To his Excellency GEO. W. TOWNS
           Through some mistake there is an omission made about a certain Fraction of land In 1848 I sent an affidavit and money by MANSFIELD TORRANCE to grant Fraction no 6 in the 33d of Lee County (as originally surveyed) after he returned home to Columbus he wrote to me that he had sent it by some person to me but could not recollect who by further I have M. Tor-

Rance Receipt for the money to grant said fraction I Reced a letter from M Torrence the 8th Inst from Milledgeville that the fraction was not marked granted. as I am uneasy about the case, not knowing who to write to for a grant only your Excellency I Implore your grace to grant said fraction or have it done by the proper authorities. I believe MANSFIELD TORRANCE honestly thought that he granted the Fraction, he had such a Multitude to grant that he thought that he granted all; and that omission was made through mistake please grant me the land as the state is satisfied for the money due I hope you cannot consider it forfeited as I have acted on my part every way prudent knowing the state was satisfied, please grant the Fraction enclose it and send it to me, to Ball Hill post office Muscogee County Ga I here inclose an affidavit and Money to grant the said Fraction No 6 in the 33 Lee
G. W. TOWNS   LITTLE MORGAN
P.S.
I granted Fraction No 5 for $1.50 I expect I have sent enough."
(Includes a signed affidavit.)

Lot 157-27 Lee. "Americus Dec 22d 1850
Your favor making inquiry about lot of land no 157 has been received upon examination of the records I find that JOHN LONG formerly of Habersham county now of Alabama conveyed a one half interest in said lot to ABSALAM HOLCOMB of Murry County who transfered his title to WILLIAM MIMS of this place. The other half lot has never been sold as yet so far as the second shows and is most likely still owned by the other orphan The deed from JOHN LONG to ABSALOM HOLCOMB was not recorded in time would take precedence of it However it would involve a lawsuit I would not attempt the purchase of the half which is already sold. It will not do to give more than two hundred dollars at the outside for the other half if that much for we could not sell it for more than three hundred anyway. I have examined 128 in the 27th district We may safely give two hundred for it I think we can sell it for four I have rode through 224-27th Dist. give much more than one hundred dollars for it. Nos 151 and 10 of the 27th District I will write you further about in a few days No 179 in the 16th dist GREEN WHEELER the Sheriff of this county says he has a regular chain of title to it I have made inquiry about each of the other lots and find that none of them sit where they will be easily marketable but I will go on to know more about them and write you as soon as I do so. I will have a little spare time now to look to them and will attend to it If you can buy 151-224 and the half of 157 at the prices above intimated do so I think we can make some thing respectable from them I have had no opportunity to me Mr. BENTON BYRD since you handed me the five dollars in Macon to settel your tax matter except once and that was at court when through press of other business I forgot to inquire of him for the receipts in his hands. I went to the tax collector and tried to settle with him for you but he was unwilling to take the five dollars except as in settlement for that amount still holding the balance open against you whereupon I refused to pay it over when I see Byrd and get the receipts he holds I will try again I will write you again in a little while yours &C   A. A. ROBINSON"

STEWART COUNTY: Lot 92-1 Lee. Pers. came JOHN P. DURHAM, one of the legatees of THOMAS DURHAM,deceased, to claim lot 92-1 Lee County, drawn by the orphans of THOMAS DURHAM. App't. of CHARLES S. BELL as att'y. Signed: John

P. Durham before ARCHIBALD NICHOLSON and WM. SIMS, J.P. 6 June 1843.

ELBERT COUNTY: Lot 159-1 Lee. Pers. came ENOS TATE, Ex'r. of the estate of ENOS TATE, SR., dec'd., to claim lot 159-1 Lee County. Signed: Enos Tate before Z.SMITH, J.P., 15 June 1843.

DEKALB COUNTY: Lot 7-3 Lee. Pers. came JNO. N. BELLINGER, Ex'r. of the estate of MILES PATY, dec'd., to claim lot 7-3 Lee County, drawn by JOHN PATY of Dekalb County, and lot 99-8-2, Cherokee County, drawn by MILES PATY, dec'd. Signed: J. N. Bellenger before J. B. WILSON, J.P., 31 May 1843.

BURKE COUNTY: Lot 110-3 Lee. Pers. came JAMES TINDALE, JR., son of JAMES TINDALE, SR., to claim lot 110-3 Lee Co., now Dooly Co. Signed: James Tindale, Jr. bef. DRURY CORKER, J.P., 14 June 1843. App't. of JAMES M. REYNOLDS as agent.

NEWTON COUNTY: Lot 129-3 Lee. SARAH REYNOLDS appoints JOHN ROSS as her attorney for taking out a grant to lot drawn by her five illegitimate children: HOLAND MATTERSON REYNOLDS, DICA REYNOLDS, ENILINE THOMPSON REYNOLDS, JAMES HENRY REYNOLDS, & ANN REYNOLDS. Signed: Sarah Reynolds (by mark) before DAVID KALB & WM. CONNANDY, J.P., 20 April 1843.

COBB COUNTY: Lot 134-3 Lee. Pers. came CYNTHIA BEASLEY, THOMAS MC GRIFF, & SARAH MC GRIFF (formerly S. BEASLEY), heirs and legatees of WILLIAM BEASLEY, dec'd., a Revolutionary War soldier, to claim lot 134-3 Lee County. Signed: Cynthia Beasley (by mark) Thomas McGriff (by mark) and Sarah McGriff (by mark) before THOMAS HOOPER, J.P. 9 Sept. 1844. App't. of W. H. MITCHELL of Baldwin Co. as att'y.

MUSCOGEE COUNTY: Lot 151-3 Lee. Pers. app'd. RICHARD LANGFORD, agent of ELIZABETH LANGFORD, to claim lot 151-3 Lee Co. App't. of KENNETH MC KENZIE as att'y. Signed: Richard Langford (by mark) bef. JOEL FORESTER & GEORGE W. TURENTINE, J.P., 9 June 1843.

TALBOT COUNTY: Lot 188-3 Lee. Pers. came JOHN H. WALTON, representative of the minors of WILLIAM

WALTON, to claim lot 188-3 Lee County. Signed: JOHN H. WALTON before JOSEPH JACKSON, J.P., 15 June 1843.

"To Mr. LEVI SMITH   Georgia Talbot County May the 19, 1843
Dr Sir - Enclosed I send you five dollars as the granting fee on a lot of land & I wish you to have the kindness, while visiting Milledgeville as a Delegate of the Democratick party. In the ensuing June Convention to be my authorized agent in granting the lot of Land Drawn by the minors of WILLIAM WALTON, dec'd. given in, in Lincoln County. Capt. PRATHERs District. no as far as recollected 188.3 of Lee, JAMES E. LADD, guardian verry Respectfully. Signed: JOHN H. WALTON before G.B. MAY, J.P."

RICHMOND COUNTY: Lot 191-3 Lee. Pers. app'd. WILLIAM BRUX, representative of "my son" ARMAND R. BRUX dec'd., to claim lot 191-3 Lee Co. Includes app't. of WILLIAM H. PRITCHARD as att'y. Signed: W. Brux before A. PRIQUET, N.P. 26 June 1843.

DEKALB COUNTY: Lot 24-4 Lee. Pers. app'd. JOHN WOODY to claim lot 24-4, Lee Co., drawn by HENRY WOODY's orphans. Signed: John Woody before HENRY M. WHITE, J.P. 17 February 1847.

FAYETTE COUNTY: Lot 32-4 Lee. Pers. came WILEY JONES to claim lot 32-4 Lee Co., drawn by ARTHUR DAVIS' orphans. Signed: Wiley Jones before HARRISON WALKER, J.P. 20 February 1847.

GREENE COUNTY: Lot 33-4 Lee. Pers. came ABSALOM JONES (JAMES?), one of the Ex'rs. of the estate of ARTHUR BUNCH, to claim lot 33-4 Lee Co. Signed: Absalom Jones before JAMES M. DAVIDSON, J.P., 15 June 1843.

RANDOLPH COUNTY: Lot 73-4 Lee. Pers. app'd. ELISHA FOLSOM to claim lot 73-4 Lee Co., as agent for the rest of the heirs (of whom is not explained). Signed: Elisha Folsom before JOHN MC INNIS, J.P., 20 May 1843.

WASHINGTON COUNTY: Lot 86-5 Lee. Pers. app'd. MORGAN BROWN, surviving Ex'r. of SYLVIA COKER, dec'd. to claim lot 86-5 Lee Co. Signed: M. Brown bef. SAMUEL ROBISON, J.I.C., 23 June 1843.

BIBB COUNTY: Lot 163-5 Lee. Pers. app'd. R. W. JENNISON
                         to claim lot 163-5 Lee, and lots no. 102-
17-1 of Cherokee Co., drawn by the orphans of HENRY JENNISON, deceased. Signed: Robt. W. Jennison bef. W. H. CALHOUN, J.I.C.
27 June 1843.

RANDOLPH COUNTY: Lot F57-4 Lee. Pers. app'd. BENJAMIN WIL-
                         LIAMS to claim fractional lots 57 and 58,
4th Dist. of Randolph Co. Signed: B. Williams bef. JOSEPH B. ELLIS, J.P., 31 July 1848.

RANDOLPH COUNTY: Inferior Court, November Term 1846. JAMES
                         L. SWEET and EDMUND W. HODGES were app'td.
adm'r. of the estate of JAMES BUCHANAN but were later annulled as they were unable to provide proper security. Therefore RANDALL C. GEIGER is appointed final adm'r. Signed: J. P. BEALL, J.I.C, (date illegible)

RANDOLPH COUNTY: Personally came RANDAL C. GEIGER, Adm'r.
                         of the estate of JAMES BUCHANAN, to claim
fractional lots 57 and 58, 4th Dist. of Lee Co., drawn by BENJAMIN WILLIAMS, purchased by BUCHANAN. Signed: Randall C. Geiger before S. L. ANDREWS, J.P., 29 August 1848.

RANDOLPH COUNTY: I, ZADOCK SAWYER, a justice of the infer-
                         ior court, certify that RANDAL C. GEIGER
is a gentleman of veracity and character and should be credited accordingly. Signed: MARGARET BUCHANAN and Zadock Sawyer, J.I.C. 29 August 1848.

PULASKI COUNTY: Lot F190-5 Lee. CHARLES E. TAYLOR, Adm'r.
                         of the estate of JOHN RAWLS, dec'd., to
claim fractional lot 191 and 190-5 of Lee Co., purchased from CHARLES INGRAM. Signed: Chas. E. Taylor before EDWARD ST. GEORGE, J.I.C., 18 Sept. 1850. DANIEL MATTHEWS certifies that the above statement is true. Signed: Daniel Matthews bef. Edward St. George J.I.C., 18 Sept. 1850.

CHATHAM COUNTY: Lot 65-6 Lee. Pers. app'd. Dr. J. C. HAB-
                         ERSHAM, guardian of the orphans of NATHAN-
IEL ADAMS, dec'd., to claim lot 65-6 Lee and lot 227-4 Lee. Includes app't. of WM. H. PRITCHARD of Baldwin Co. Signed: J. C. Habersham bef. R. RAIFORD, J.P., 27 June 1843.

PUTNAM COUNTY: Lot 59-7 Lee. Pers. app'd. LEROY SINGLETON one of the orphans of JAMES SINGLETON, deceased, to claim lot 59-7 Lee Co. Signed: LEROY SINGLETON before SAMUEL PEARSON, J.I.C., 5 June 1843.

CAMPBELL COUNTY: Lot 148-7 Lee. Pers. app'd. REUBIN C. BEAVERS, agent for SARAH BEAVERS (one of the children and lawful heirs of JOHN FLUKER, dec'd.) to claim lot 148-7 Lee Co. Includes app't. of JOHN CARLTON as att'y. Signed: R. C. Beavers and Sarah Beavers before R. A. BEAVERS and A. K. RICHARDSON, J.P., 27 May 1843.

COLUMBIA COUNTY: Lot 151-7 Lee. Pers. came THOMAS ROWLAND one of the representatives and distributees of JAMES ROLAND, dec'd., to claim lot 151-7 of Lee Co. Includes app't. of Wm. H. Pritchard as att'y. Signed: THOMAS ROLAND before STEPHEN DRAWE, J.P., 24 June 1843.

PULASKI COUNTY: Lot 202-7 Lee. Pers. app'd. JESSE BRYANT, legal guardian of SARAH & CHARITY MILLER (orphans), to claim lot 202-7 Lee Co. App't. of B. B. HAMILTON as att'y. to take out a grant to the lot drawn by WILLIAM MILLER orphans. Signed: Jesse Bryant bef. JAMES HENSON, J.P., 29 May 1843.

MUSCOGEE COUNTY: Lot 214-7 Lee. Pers. app'd. GEORGE W. ROSS one of the adm'rs. of the est. of GEORGE ROSS, dec'd., to claim lot 214-7 Lee Co. and lot 129-15 Lee Co. App't. of JAMES JOHNSON as att'y. Signed: George W. Ross before JNO. M. BETHUNE, J.I.C., 23 June 1843.

BIBB COUNTY: Lot 236-7 Lee. Pers. app'd. WILLIAM P. HARRIS, half brother of RILEY BAYSEMORE (idiot), dec'd., to claim lot 236-7 Lee Co. Signed: William P. Harris before HENRY NEWSOM, J.I.C., 26 May 1848.(1843?).

BURKE COUNTY: Lot 309-7 Lee Pers. came ISAAC MULKEY, Administrator of the estate of WILLIAM H. LEVERETTE, dec'd., to claim lot 309-7 Lee Co. Signed: Isaac Mulkey before WM. SAPP, J.P., 26 April 1843.

FORSYTH COUNTY: Lot 348-7 Lee. Pers. came HENRY BAGBY, son and one of the heirs of HARMON BAGBY, Revolutionary Soldier, dec'd., to claim lot 348-7th District of Lee County. Signed: HENRY BAGBY (by mark) before RICHARD HAYS, J.P. 19 September 1844.

WARREN COUNTY: Lot 78-8 Lee. Pers. app'd. LARKIN WELCHER, OLIF WELCHER, & FREDERICK WELCHER, to claim lot 78-8 Lee County, drawn by them as illegitimates. Includes app't. of ADAM JONES as att'y. Signed: Larkin Welcher, Olif Welcher (by mark) and Fredrick Welcher (by mark) before B. B. KITCHENS, J.P. and B. C. KITCHENS, 10 June 1843.

Lot 79-11 Wilkinson. "Executive Department Georgia   Milledgeveille 11 Dec. 1810 WILLIAM TATUM of the County of Hancock attended for the purpose of obtaining a grant for lot No 79 in the 11th Dist. of Wilkinson County drawn by his brother SETH TATUM of Hudson's district Hancock County and stated that his said brother had departed this life since the drawing of the last Land Lottery, it is therefore ORDERED that the Secretary of the State prepare a grant for and in the name of the Heirs of Seth Tatum dec'd. of Hudsons district Hancock County for the aforesaid lot of land. Attest
ANTHONY PORTER, Secretary"

Lot 10-2 Wayne. "Pendarvis Store 6 Feb. 1851.
Dear Sir Inclosed I send you six surveys and twenty Dollars ... please foreward the grants by mail I also send the warrants to grant these survey I hope you will pardon me for my Neglect.
CLOB(?)
I have made Delegent Inquiry for WILLIAM CLUB of Camden I cant hear of him I hear that there is a young man there by the Name of JAMES CLUB I think it is a son of WILLIAM you had better Rite to him and also Rite to Major DAVID BALEY who is an olde Resadenter and perhaps can give you Information. I refer you to JOHN M. TYSON of Glynn perhaps he may know of BARNARD NACOB I cannot hear of him. The family of DARTS some of them I feel Condedant Now Lives in Glynn but is some distance from here and I know but Little about them you may Rite to SAMUEL BURNETTE he live Near & can give you all information. In Riting to BURNETTE Direct to Brunswic Glynn Co. In Riting to Major BALEY Direct to Jeffersonton Camden Co. In Riting to J. M. TYSON Direct to Bethill Glynn Co. The Lots of Land Inquired for in Wayne in the 3rd District is

unimportant and very poore they are scarcely worth anything them in the first and second I know Nothing of as I have No map I dont even know where they Lye but I know both District to be poor land if they Lye on the sttiller they may in time be worth something for lumber or Turpentine   I give you my thanks for forwarding the Duplicate grant to No 10 in second District your obedient Servt
                                 CALEB PENDARVIS
To J. R. BITTS s.g.s.g."

Lot 223-1 Wilkinson

"Executive department Georgia 11th June 1806
                           This day came Col. JOHN PARKS and being duly sworn saith that there are two persons by the name of WILLIAM RICHARDSON in the Regiment commanded by him in Wilkes Co. that one of them is known by WILLIAM RICHARDSON JUNR. and that the other, who is the neighbor of Mr. ANDREW SHEPARD, is not designated or known in the Regiment by either Senior or Junior to best of his knowledge. JOHN PARKS
Sworn to in the presence of the governor
attest Signed: G. R. CLAYTON, Sectry."

Lot 10-4 Rabun. "Clayton (Rabun County)Ga. Nov. 13th 1914
Hon. JOHN M. SLATON   Atlanta Ga.
Dear Governor:-
                     I would appreciate it very much, if you would act on the matter of adjusting that part of lot No. 10 in the 4th district of Rabun with Dr. P. N. NORCOP, since the old man is very much worried over his title. As you will see by the papers left with the Attorney General by me a few days ago, this lot was sold in 1878 under fifa issued by the Comptroller General of this state, and the same has been held in good faith by the doctor and his predecessors in title. He is an Englishman by birth, though now nationalized, and is much worried over the fact that he should have been induced to buy land that had been sold by the State to which the State still claims title. Knowing the lands as I do I feel sure that he has paid much more for them than they are worth, and that a settlement with the State based on $50.00 is ample and should be accepted and closed up at once by you and the Attorney General. So I hope you can see your way clear to do this at once and put the old man's composure back at normal.
With sincerety, I remain,
                     Your friend,
                         R. E. HAMBY"
(Includes photo of R.E.A. Hamby, printed at the top of the stationary).

Lot 273-3 Wilkinson. ANTHONY GHOLSON of Hancock County, ex'r. of the estate of JOHN GHOLSON, certifys that he entered the orphans of JOHN GHOLSON in the land lottery and that he knows of no other orphans of John Gholson. Signed: Anthony Gholson before G. R. CLAYTON,Sec'y. E.D.   Sworn to in the presence of the Governor, Executive Dept. Louisville,   27 August 1806.

COLUMBIA COUNTY: Lot 61-4 Wilkinson. Pers. app'd. JOHN CASEY who saith that he and Capt. SNOWDEN

GRIFFIN called on Mr. LENARD THOMSON on Saturday the twenty sixth Instant to inquire respecting his father WILLIAM THOMSON having a draw in the late lottery. Thomson told them that his father had put in for a draw on the same day that he did. Signed: JOHN CASEY before JOS. TANKERSLEY, J.P., 31 October 1805.

RUSSELL COUNTY: Lot 284-2 Lee. Pers. came SARAH S. MORELAND, widow of TUTTLE H. MORELAND, to claim fractional lots 284, 285, 282, and 286, 3rd Dist. of Lee Co. Signed: Sarah S. Moreland before U. U. COWDERY, J.P., 22 May 1849

Lot 135-8 Lee. "Troup Co. Feb. 12th, 1834
Dear Sir
    pardon my troubling you a little as I have no acquaintances in Milledgeville that I know of except yourself and the distance is such (about 100 miles) and busy season commenced, I request you, if you please and will do so, to take out a plat & grant to lot no 135 in the 8th Dist. of Lee drawn by HARRISON W. ELDER as a particular friend of mine vis my son in law has given his bond to make a title to said lot in April as he and his brother H. W. ELDER went halves in the Lottery & JAMES P. ELDER has sold it by virtue of authority from his brother by sending said plot by mail to mountain creek P.O. Harris County you will sir very much oblige your humble servant
                                    ISAAC A. PARKER
I live in the 4th Troup but the above is the nearest Post office I inclose $5"

WILKES COUNTY: Lot 286-8 Lee. Pers. app'd. WILLIAM C. WRIGHT to claim lot 286-8 of Lee County, and fractional lot 680-1-3 Cherokee, drawn by ELVERA L. WRIGHT. He claims the lots as one of the owners. Includes app't. of HENRY T. ELLINGTON as att'y. Signed: William C. Wright before AUGUSTUS W. FLYNT, J.P., 17 June 1843.

MONTGOMERY COUNTY: Lot 335-8 Lee. Pers. app'd. WILLIAM A. BUTLER, one of the orphans of SHEM BUTLER, to claim lot 335-8 Lee Co. App't. of A. MC LOUD(?) as att'y. Signed: William A. Butler bef. MALCOM CURRIE, J.P., 26 November 1847.

COLUMBIA COUNTY: Lot 56-9 Lee. ADDISON HASSEL, formerly ADDISON KENDRICK (illegitimate child of JUDAH KENDRICK, now JUDAH GOING), his name having been changed by an Act of the General Assembly, 1826 session, see Dawsons Digest page 329, appoints Doctor NATHAN CRAWFORD as att'y. for himself and LITTLEBERRY A. KENDRICK of Alabama, to take out a grant to lot 56-9th Dist. Lee County. Signed: ADDISON HASSEL bef. JAMES D. GREEN, J.P., 15 June 1843.

Pers. app'd. Addison Hassel, formerly Addison Kendrick, to claim lot 56-9-1 of the 1827 lottery, drawn by Judah Greene's illegitimate children, which was in error when entered and should have been Judah Kendrick's illegitimate children. Signed: Addison Hassel bef. James D. Green, J.P., 15 June 1843.

HARRIS COUNTY: Lot 59-9 Lee. Pers. came JOHN L. STEPHENS for his wife (the former MARY E. BOOKER) and ANN C. BOOKER, to claim lot 59-9 Lee Co., drawn by the orphans of WILLIAM M. BOOKER. Signed: John L. Stephens and Ann C. Booker before A. H. SCOTT, J.P., 5 April 1843.

HARRIS COUNTY: Lot 71-9 Lee. Pers. app'd. JESSE O'NEAL to claim lot 71-9 Lee County, as part owner. App't. of WILLIAMSON O'NEAL as att'y. Signed: Jesse O'Neal before HAYWOOD BARROW and JAMES SMITH, J.P., 26 June 1843.

CHATHAM COUNTY: Lot 89-9 Lee. Pers. app'd. JANE L. LAMPE, widow and only heir of WILLIAM CHARLES CUTHBERT, dec'd., of McIntosh County (he had no children), to claim lot 89-9 Lee Co. Her present husband is CHRISTIAN LAMPE. She appoints WILLIAM H. PRITCHARD of Milledgeville as her att'y. Signed: J. L. Lampe and C. Lampe before R. RAIFORD, J.P. 21 June 1843.

JEFFERSON COUNTY: Lot 172-10 Lee. Pers. app'd. EDWARD H. W. HUNTER to claim lot 172-10 Lee Co., drawn by the orphans of EDWARD HUNTER, as one of the surviving children. App't. of Doctor P. L. LEMBE as att'y. Signed: E. H. W. Hunter before THOS. H. POLHILL, N.P., 12 June 1843.

LOWNDES COUNTY: Lot 250-9 Lee. HAMILTON W. SHARPE, Adm'r. of the estate of PENEVILL FOLSOM, dec'd., appoints HENDERSON GRAHAM as att'y. to take out grants to the following tracts:
```
250-9 dist. Lee        285-3 dist. 3rd Section
408-14 "    Early      317-1  "    1st    "
133-15 "    2nd Section 190-1 "    1st    "
578-2  "    4th   "    1185-3 "    1st    "
261-13 "    3rd   "    290-2  "    2nd    "
```
Signed: Hamilton W. Sharpe before WILLIAM H. PERRY and D. H. HOWLE, J.P., 1 April 1843

Lot 6-10 Lee.

"Sir
   this day JOHN PRESCOT returned to me on Oath the orphans of WILLIAM UMPHRIES dec'd. of Captn DENNIS LARK HOLLIDAYs district their names are as follows viz PENELOPE, REBEKAH, JOHN, AMOS, and THOMAS UMPHRIES it may be proper to observe that Mr. Prescot who is the guardian of the above named orphans did not know untill this morning that it was his duty to have returned them with great Respect & Consideration I have the Honour to be your most obt very Humble Servt   JAMES TORRANCE, J.I.C.B.C.
Burke County
9th April 1827
His Excellency Gov'ernor TROUP"

TALBOT COUNTY: Lot 228-10 Lee. ZACHARIAH B. TRICE, guardian of the minor orphans of CHESLY P. TRICE appoints JACOB MCLAINE as att'y. for taking out a grant to lot 228-10 Lee Co., and also lot 170-3-2 Cherokee Co. Signed: Z. B. Trice before WM. STALLINGS, J.I.C., 8 June 1843.

TALBOT COUNTY: Lot 232-10 Lee. Pers. app'd. SOLOMON H. KENYON to claim lot 232-10 Lee Co., having purchased it from the orphans of SARAH BALL, the orphans being of age when he made the purchase. Includes app't. of CHARLES H. STILLWELL and MARION BETHUNE as att'y's. Signed: Solomon H. Kenyon before H. A. CAMPBELL(?) and PHILIP ADAMS, J.P., 19 June 1843.

RICHMOND COUNTY: Lot 53-12 Lee. Pers. app'd. JOHN TAYLOR, one of the orphans of JOHN TAYLOR of Elbert County, to claim lot 53-12 Lee Co.; and also the lot he drew from Wilkes Co. as an orphan, lot 273-4-1. App't. of WILLIAM H. PRITCHARD of Baldwin Co. as att'y. Signed: John Taylor (by mark) before J. W. MEREDITH, J.P., 24 June 1843.

BALDWIN COUNTY: Lot 95-12 Lee. Pers. app'd. ROBERT THOMPSON, one of the heirs and representatives of SAMUEL THOMPSON, to claim lot 95-12-Lee Co. Signed: Robert Thompson bef. J. R. ANDERSON, J.I.C.B.C., 22 June 1843.

CHATHAM COUNTY: Lot 71-12 Lee. Pers. app'd. SUSAN MORRILL, formerly SUSAN BOND of Camden Co., to claim lot 71-12-Lee Co. App't. of William H. Pritchard of Baldwin Co. as att'y. Signed: Susan Morrill bef. R. RAIFORD, J.P., 29 May 1843.

CHATHAM COUNTY: Lot 78-12 Lee. Pers. app'd. ANN M. BOURKE, guardian of Miss ELIZABETH BOURKE, to claim lot 78-12th District of Lee County. Signed: Ann M. Bourke before R. RAIFORD, J.P., 10 May 1843.

BURKE COUNTY: Lot 172-12 Lee. Pers. app'd. ALEXANDER J. PERRY, Adm'r. of the estate of HARDY PERRY, dec'd., to claim lot 172-12 Lee County. Signed: A. J. Perry before JAS. W. JONES, J.I.C.B.C. and EDWARD GALLICK, clk., Co. B. C., 26 June 1843.

DEKALB COUNTY: Lot 14-13 Lee. Pers. app'd. ELIZABETH WARD Adm'rtx. of the est. of THORNTON WARD, deceased, to claim lot 14-13. Signed: Elizabeth Ward (by mark) bef. J. B. WILSON, J.P., 1 June 1843.

CHATHAM COUNTY: Lot 122-13 Lee. Pers. app'd. WILLIAM LAW to claim lot 122-13 Lee Co., drawn by ALETHA STARK, widow. Signed: Wm. Law bef. R. Raiford, J.P., 27 June 1843.

CRAWFORD COUNTY: Lot 140-13 Lee. HENRY ROWELL certifies that DAVENPORT LAWSON gave him $25 for taking out plats and grants to lot 140-13 and lot 157-2, belonging to the estate of JANE LAWSON, dec'd. of Wilkinson County, & he did take out sd. grants and apply for sd. lots. Signed: H. CROWELL, 22 February 1831.

MARION COUNTY: Lot 168-13 Lee. Pers. app'd. HAMILTON HATCHER, agent of the legatees of THOMAS HATCHER, dec'd., to claim lot 168-13-Lee Co., drawn by THOMAS HATCHER of Monroe Co., Signed: Hamilton Hatcher bef. RANDALL W. MASTON, J.P., 15 May 1843.

MEREIWETHER COUNTY: Lot 34-14 Lee. Pers. came NEWTON JENKINS, one of the orphans of (illegible) JENKINS dec'd., to claim lot 34-14 Lee Co. Signed: Newton Jenkins before ALLEN ROWE, J.P., 21 June 1843.

Pers. came HANNAH GROCE to claim lot 513-17-3-Cherokee Co. Signed: Hannah Groce before Allen Rowe, J.P., 21 June 1843.

Pers. came ELLISON GROCE to claim lot 242-22-2-Cherokee Co. Signed: Ellison Groce bef. Allen Rowe, J. P., 21 June 1843.

App't. of CHARLES H. NELSON of Baldwin Co.

as attorney. Signed: ELLISON GROCE, NEWTON JENKINS, & HANNAH GROCE (by mark) before ALLEN ROWE, J.P., 21 June 1843.

<u>STEWART COUNTY</u>: Lot 66-14 Lee. Pers. app'd. CAROLINE MATILDA(?) GACHET, legal representative of BENJAMIN GA<u>SHETT</u>, to claim lot 66-14-Lee Co. and lot 266-9-Lee. Signed: Caroline M. Gachet before JAMES L. WILLIAMS, J.P. 12 April 1843.

<u>UPSON COUNTY</u>: Lot 96-14 Lee. RICHARD RESPESS, son of NANCY RESPESS of Jasper County, appoints EVAN H. POWELL of Jasper County as att'y. for taking out grant to lot 96-14-Lee Co. Signed: Richard Respess bef. THOMAS K. WORTHY and DAVIS DAWSON, J.P., May 1843.

<u>FLOYD COUNTY</u>: Lot 115-14 Lee. Pers. came WESLEY PLEDGER to claim lot 115-14-Lee Co. that he drew while living in Elbert Co. Includes app't. of HOMER V. M. MILLER as att'y. Signed: Wesley Pledger bef. M. C. MARTIN, J.P. 26 May 1843.

Pers. came MICAJAH C. MARTIN to claim lot 84-26-3-Cherokee Co. Signed. M. C. Martin bef. D. M. MC CURRY, J.P., 26 May 1843.

<u>BIBB COUNTY</u>: Lot 182-14 Lee. Pers. came THOMAS R. PACE, one of the orphans of WILLIAM PACE, dec'd. to claim lot 182-14-Lee Co. Signed: Thomas R. Pace before KEELIN COOK, J.I.C., 29 March 1848.

Lot 70-15 Lee. (Signed letter SIMPSON WELLS, Atlanta, 27 December 1850 mentioning his attempts to buy lot 7-15 Lee and other lots. Mentions that Major NELSON is one of the heirs to lot 70-15. The letter is addressed to JAS. R. BUTTS, surveyor general.)

<u>UPSON COUNTY</u>: Lot 63-16 Lee. Pers. came THOMAS N. GIBSON to claim the undivided half lot 63-16-Lee Co., purchased from ALEXANDER QUICK, who had married NANCY WEEKS, one of the drawers of the lot. App't. of JAMES W. GRUM as att'y. Signed: Thomas N. Gibson bef. O. C. GIBSON & WM. A. COBB, J.P., 10 June 1843.

TALBOT COUNTY: Lot 87-16 Lee. Pers. came LEWIS WIMBERLY
                           to claim lot 87-16-Lee Co. and lot 824-
18-2-Cherokee, drawn by PERRY WIMBERLY of Houston Co. Includes
app't. of JACOB WILLIAMS as att'y. Signed: Lewis Wimberly before
CHARLES H. MC CALL, J.P., 15 June 1843.

COLUMBIA COUNTY: Lot 108-16 Lee. Pers. came ENOCH CRAWFORD
                           to claim lot 108-16-Lee Co., for himself
and JAMES CRAWFORD, illegitimates. Includes app't. of WM. H.
PRITCHARD of Baldwin Co. as att'y. Signed: Enoch Crawford (by
mark) before STEPHEN DRANE(?), J.P., 12 June 1843. Note on the
back shows that this document was mailed from Lombardy, Georgia.

MARION COUNTY: Lot 230-16 Lee. Pers. app'd. JORDON WIL-
                           CHER, father of MARY WILCHER (idiot), to
claim lot 230-16-Lee Co. App't. of JOHN CAMPBELL as att'y. JORDON
WELLS before S. R. NUTT, J.I.C. and BURTON DOWSE, 6 June 1843.

COBB COUNTY: Lot 28-17 Lee. Pers. app'd. HENRY HOPKINS,
                           one of the heirs of GEORGE HOPKINS, dec'd.
of Gwinnette Co., to claim lot 28-17-Lee Co. App't. of JOHN ROWE
as att'y. Signed: Henry Hopkins bef. J. W. MOORE, J.P. 8 June
1843.

PIKE COUNTY: Lot 11-1 Monroe. Pers. app'd. ABSALOM B.
                           BECKHAM, agent of the legatees of WILLIAM
GILBERT dec'd. to claim lot 11-1 Monroe Co. App't. of JOHN NEAL
as att'y. Signed: A. B. Beckham bef. J. N. MANGHAM, J.P. 27 May
1843.

ELBERT COUNTY: Lot 139-1 Monroe. Pers. app'd. THOMAS WAR-
                           SLOW (WANSLOW?) and JOHN WARSLOW, JR. who
saith that NATHAN WARSLOW removed from this state in 1818, as a
married man, and would have been entitled to two draws in the
1821 land lottery. They believe, however, that the lot of land
reported as won by NATHAN WARSLOW was actually won by NELSON WAR-
SLOW, a single man in the same militia district. Signed: Thomas
WANSLEY(by mark) and JOHN WANSLEY 2nd Jn. (by mark) bef. ABNER
WARD, J.P., 11 October 1830.
                           WILLIAM ROEBUCK testifies that he heard
NATHAN WARSLOW say that the lot of land reported that he won was
not his as he was not in the state at that time and did not give
in at the lottery. It must have been intended for NELSON WARLOW.

Signed: WM. ROEBUCK before JAMES BURKS, JR., J.P., 12 Oct. 1830.

<u>BALDWIN COUNTY</u>: Lot 107-4 Monroe. Pers. came CHARLES L. WALLER, who saith that WILLIAM & ELEANOR FREEMAN, orphans of Screven County, drew lot 107-4 Monroe Co. and that ELEANOR FREEMAN, the younger of the two, was 24 years of age in October past. Signed: Charles R. Waller before E. H.PIERCE J.P., 10 November 1830.

<u>BALDWIN COUNTY</u>: Lot 181-7 Monroe. I do certify that I have been for ten years past "well acquainted in Captain LUTHERs District" of Richmond County and I have never heard of a LEGAN WOODSON but I do know a WOODSON LIGAN. Signed: ROBERT WATKINS bef. CHARLES J. MC DONALD, judge, S.C., 20 Dec. 1825.

<u>FAYETTE COUNTY</u>: Lot 205-8 Monroe. WILLIAM G. SIKES, for his wife (formerly NANCY PADGETT), claims lot 205-8-Monroe Co., drawn by the orphans of JOHN PADGETT,dec'd. of Jones County. His wife is one of the sd. orphans. JOHN S.PARKS is appointed att'y. Signed: Wm. G. Sikes (by mark) before JOHN SIMMONS, J.P., 20 June 1843.

<u>HALL COUNTY</u>: Lot 110-10 Monroe. Pers. app'd. RODA BISHOP who saith that she was guardian and nearest friend of JONES BISHOP's orphan and in 1821 she put in for herself as the widow of JONES BISHOP and for the orphan of JONES BISHOP and that there is no other orphan of Jones Bishop in the county. Signed: Roda Bishop (by mark) before DAVID TANNER, J.P., 23 August 1836.

Lot 294-13 Monroe. "Columbia County 9th January 1822.
Dear Sir
permit me to introduce to your notice a particular friend and neighbor of mine SOLOMON HOGE Esqr. Mr. Hoge is a Merchant & holds a commission in the peace of this county and is a gentleman of respectability & integrity; and one that the most inplicit confedence can be placed in. He goes to Milledgeville for the purpose of endeavouring to have rectified a mistake which does appear clearly to me from the papers and certificates that he has in his possession have been made by the commissioners or the clerks of the late land Lottery. Mr. Hoge purchased of JAMES WALTER,who resides in the county of Captain SHAWs destrict No. 6, two draws, or chances in the sd. Lottery, when there is no such man as James Walter residing in the Shaws destrict No. 6, but there is a man by the name of JAMES C. WALKER, who does reside in the above destrict & who has drawn a lot land in sd. Lottery in his proper

name. Now it does appear clearly to me that the two lots of land drawn, and entered in the name of JAMES WALKER must be JAMES WALTER because JAMES C. WALKER was only entitled to two draws of course He cannot have three, consequently there cannot be any mistake made in the name of JAMES C. WALKER. Any attention or services rendered Mr. Hoge in the above business, will be thankfully acknowledged by your devoted friend. ZACH. WILLIAMS
His Excellency Governor CLARK."

MERIWETHER COUNTY: Lot 121-15 Monroe. Pers. came DAVID FRANKLIN, one of the orphans of NELSON FRANKLIN dec'd. of Oglethorpe County, to claim lot 121-15 Monroe County. Includes app't. of THOMAS WALTON as att'y. Signed: David Franklin before ALLEN ROWE, J.P., 23 June 1843.

MERIWETHER COUNTY: Lot F266-15 Monroe. Pers. came JEFFERSON ALFORD and JIMERSON ALFORD to claim fractional lots 266, 267, and 281, 15th Dist., Monroe Co. Signed: Jefferson Alford and Jemerson Alford before WM. C. ROPER, J.P. 21 October 1848.

HANCOCK COUNTY: Lot 142-3 Wayne. "NATHANIEL PERRITT being sworn saith that some time in the last spring JOHN BROWN of sandy run came to his house, and offered to sell him the tract of land drawn in the late Lottery in the name of JOHN BROWN of Barksdales district and that he informed this deponent that the dispute between him and the other JOHN BROWN of the same destrict was settled in his favour. sworn to before me this 4th August 1806
Signed: Natl. Perritt   JNO. CROWDER, J.I.C.
The truth of the above was acknowledged by JOHN BROWN of Sandy Run. Before WM. RABUN, J.I.C.   JNO. CROWDER, J.I.C."

Lot 102-4 Wilkinson. "Executive department Georgia Louisville 9th October 1805
This day two men by the name, as they sd. of JOHN VENSON of Hancock County came into this office for the purpose of settling a despute relative to a tract of land drawn by one of them in the late land Lottery. The tallest one of the two said he entered his name for draws in said Lottery on the first day assigned by the Justices of the Inferior Court of Hancock County for receiving names and the other acknowledged that the name first entered on the list, returned by the Inferior Crt. of Hancock Co., of persons entitled to draws in sd. lottery was the one against which the prize was drawn, the person who said he gave in on the second day appeared satisfied he had no claim to the prize & consented to the grants being delivered to the other person. Signed: G. R. CLAYTON, Sectry. E.D."

Lot 397-7 Wilkinson. "Executive department Georgia Louisville 11th August 1806

This day came JOSEPH OWENS of the County of Columbia and being duly sworn saith that on Saturday last he had a conversation with WM. THOMPSON of the County of aforesaid the father of LEONARD THOMPSON when the sd. Thompson told this deponent that he did not himself have his name entered for draws in the late land lottery but that he directed his son Leonard to have it done for him. this deponenet further saith that Leonard Thompson told him on tuesday last he would not swear that he had his fathers name entered for draws in the lottery aforesaid. and this deponent further saith that the aforesaid WILLIAM THOMPSON at the time aforesaid told this deponent that he should not pretend to claim the lot of land drawn against the name of WM. THOMPSON of Columbia County in the sd. lottery and desired to deponent to inform Capt. MARBURY to that effect. Signed: Joseph Owens (by mark) before G. R. CLAYTON secty. E.D."

Lot 278-8 Wilkinson
"Mr. JAMES BUTTS   Sept. 9th 1851
Dear Sir
I received yours a few days ago back and would of answered it sooner but I wanted to see one of my neighbors & get him to go with me and look at the no or track 278, in 8 dist, it is adjoining my lands and Genl JOHN COFFs to the lands of my Estate, I was mistaken in the location of it when I saw you I then thought it was a part in the (illegible) but not so it is Pine and bay Gall(?) some intruder has taken the Timber off (illegible) since I have shown you little to (illegible) and asked what they would go, not a bid as it ajoins me I will give $25 it is poor (illegible) to flatt if you ever hauled up thro (illegible) through Jacksonville you have been on the land near the timber of the tract 3 miles below Jacksonville I want you to look and see who Drew and granted lot 235 in the 8 Dist of Wilkerson now (illegible) and write me soon Genl MOREIS is trying to get that lot for me (the rest of the letter is illegible)

Lot 274-12 Wilkinson. "Augusta 15th July 1807.
Dear Sir
Your favour of the 23d ulto. came duly to hand, and in replying to it, as I supposed last week, in the hurry of business I directed my letter to Mr. CLAYTON, as he may be surprised at receiving an answer to a letter he never wrote, he may perhaps have observed my letter to you, and thereby have explained, what I shall now attempt myself. CHARLES WILLIAMSON an orphan, who was returned by me in Richmond, is the son of Mrs. HOBBY(?), he was at General CLARKs with his mother when I made his return and Gen. Clark, who was an executor to his fathers will, supposing that as he was absent, I might neglect to return his name, made a return for him in Wilkes County. The two returns are therefore for the same person, and the name can be taken off either from the names of Richmond or Wilkes list as (illegible) Charles is usually a member of my family and resides in Richmond, it might perhaps be as well to let his name remain under my return. The Governor's knowledge of the connection between myself and General Clarke, naturally suggested to him the true cause of the error of a double return (illegible) your letter to me on the subject please accept my acknowledgements. I am respectfully
your most obt sert
WM. HOBBY
If you have an opportunity (..) to Wm. CLAYTON the cause of my

writing him."

WARREN COUNTY: Lot 123-20 Wilkinson. "Whereas a certain AMBROSE CHAPMAN resident of the county & living in Capt. BAKERs Dist whose father Departed this Life some years past, his mother still Living and at the time of giving in for the Draws in the present Lottery, and said Ambroses age not being set Down the old Lady his mother telling said Ambrose that she supposed him to be of Age the young man to wit said Ambrose gave in his name in the usual form since that it Appearing by the age of a Relative in the Neighbourhood that sd. Ambrose was Not twenty one years of age at the time of his giving in the sd. Ambrose is willing and Disirous to Relinguish all his Claim as a citision. the sd. Ambrose at the time of making this Affidavit producing a tax Receipt for the year Eighteen hundred and six, which had the appearance of inosence on his part, Sworn to and Subscribed Before me this 17th September 1807
E. Hunt, J.I.C. AMBROSE CHAPMAN"

Warren County: "MILLEY CHAPMAN came before me and after being suly sworn saith that at the time of her son AMBROSE giving in his name for Draws in the Land Lottery sd. milley thought him to be of age. sworn to and subscribed before me this 17th sepr. 1807." Signed: Milley Chapman (by mark) before E. HUNT, J.I.C.

GREENE COUNTY: Lot 123-27 Wilkinson. Being applied to by Major JOSEPHUS LOVE to say what I know respecting the ages of orphans of Capt. WILLIAM BALLARD of Greene County dec'd. I do certify that I was personally acquainted with sd. Ballard in his lifetime and a general knowledge of his orphans and do not hesetate to say that HENRIETTA BALLARD is the youngest ----living and from a long acquaintance with her I have not a doubt that she is twenty three or four yrs of age given under my hand this 9th day of April 1822. Signed: ELIJAH JORDAN WM. GIBONEY, J.P."

Lot 135-28 Wilkinson. "Marion 17th January 1851.
JAMES R. BUTTS, Esqr. Dear Sir
yours of the 11th Inst. has been received at this time I am not prepared to say any thing about No. 135-28, but by refering to the records of my office and ascertaining the numbers of the forsyth plantation and others immediately around it. I feel satisfied that No 231 in 25 is entirely in the swamp and worth nothing though I will look further into the matter, checks of the 25 and 28 districts would greatly fascilitate the trouble of ascertaining where any particular number lay. you will send them to me, RANDAL BLACKSHEAR has resided in the state of Alabama for a number of years and at the time is in Dalle County I think, Mr. DANL. STUCKLY also removed to the state of Alabama

Seven years ago, and some 3 or 4 years ago as I learned from the Shff. of the county where he lived committed a murder and absconded from justice (bad chances)

your friend P. REYNOLDS"

CAMPBELL COUNTY: Lot 135-9 Fayette. Pers. app'd. DAVID D. SMITH who saith that under a deed from JORDON HEATH SENR. of Burke Co. to JOHN ADAM's dec'd.; one from DANIEL STONE, Adm'r. of the estate of sd. dec'd., to ALLEN LOVELESS, and one from LOVELESS to CHRISTOPHER NOLEN; and one from NOLEN to this deponent, claims lot 135, 9th Dist., Campbell Co. Signed: David D. Smith bef. EDWD. H. GLEENWORTH, J.P., 25 May 1843. Daniel Stone certifies that he sold the above lot to Allen Loveless.

BIBB COUNTY: Lot 131-9 Fayette. Pers. came MARGARET E. LANE to claim lot 131-9 Fayette Co. drawn by THOMAS LANE, formerly of Burke Co. and late of Sumter Co., Alabama. Signed: M. E. Lane before BARNETT WILLIAMS, J.P. 18 September 1844.

Lot 101-10 Habersham. "Executive Dept. Ga. Milledgeville 19 March 1823.
GEORGE F. WING of Hamiltons district in McIntosh County having drawn lot No. 101 in the 10th District of Habersham County and having since departed this life as appears from the affidavit of BUTLER WING and ELIZA U. WING, and application having been made for a grant in the name of the heirs of sd. dec'd., it is
Ordered that the aforesd. lot of land be granted to, "The heirs of GEORGE F. WING deceased" of Hamiltons district in McIntosh County. Attest
JNO. BURCH, Secy. E.D."

BALDWIN COUNTY: Lot 147-2 Troup. Pers. app'd. JAMES M. REYNOLDS, agent of DRURY CORKER (Adm'r. of the estate of L. SNEAD, dec'd.), to claim lot 147-2 Troup County. Signed: Jas. M. Reynolds bef. ALFRED M. HORTON, N.P. 19 June 1842.

Lot 196-3 Troup. "Milledgeville Geo. 1st April 1839
Information having been given through the Southern Recorder (a newspaper in the city of Milledgeville) by the following advertisement viz:
Executive Department,
Milledgeville, 2d October 1838.
UPON the application of THOMAS THOMPSON, POLLY THOMPSON's illegitimate, of Columbia County, by which it appears, that Lot number one hundred and ninety-six, (196) in the third (3d) District

of Troup County, was drawn by said illegitimate, and that the said lot has, through mistake, been heretofore granted to POLLY THOMSON's illegitimate children and that sd. Grant cannot be produced at this office for correction. It is ordered, that unless good cause be shown to the contrary, within six months, that an alias Grant do issue for sd. Lot, to the rightful drawer of the same; and that this notice be published in one of the public gazettes of this State for six months previous to issueing sd. alias Grant.

    By the Governor.
         BENJAMIN T. BETHUNE, Sec. E. Dep't.
Oct. 9, 1838.   38 mon.

         That a application had been made to the Ex Dept for the issuing of an alias grant for 196 of the 3rd of Troup and that sd. grant would issue unless good cause should be shown to the contrary. I WILLIAM L. ELLIS husband of MELINDA ELLIS, one of the illegitimate children of POLLY THOMSON of Culbreaths Dist. of Columbia do file the following objections in the Executive office against the issuing of sd. grant
         First that THOMAS THOMPSON the illegitimate child of POLLY THOMPSON is dead. That if he is not, he can only claim a third of the land. (Crossed out: "(For JAMES GAMBELL who gave in for POLLY THOMPSONs illegitimates gave in for two children)") whereas THOS. THOMPSON as appears from his application claims the whole of the land as the only illigetimate of Polly Thompson. It can be proven (by the Interrogatories served upon JAMES GAMBELL.) That a draw was given in for Polly Thompsons illegitimates all the offices in the state house have recorded the sd. illegitimates as the fortunate drawers which taken together render it probable that the illegitimate children rather than the illegitimate child, drew the lot of land in question.
         I also object to the issuing of sd. grant because the individual now claiming the land disclaims being a brother of MELINDA (now ELLIS) THOMPSON and LEROY THOMPSON, has no evidence of his name being given in for a draw except the word of the individual to whom he sold the land and because no other THOMAS THOMPSON lived in Columbia County at the time of giving for draws in 1827.
         I further object because of the acknowledgement of sd. Thomas Thompson now living in Oglethorpe that he came from Tennessee and that he would not positively swear that he ever lived in Columbia County.
         That the individual J. W. SHEPPERD who purchased the land from Thos. Thompson told Thompson that a draw had been given in Columbia for him (Thompson) of which Thompson says he knew nothing before being told of it by Shepperd. That Shepperd tried to but the land from me but not succeeding threatened to have (illegible) of me.
         WM. C. ELLIS"

COLUMBIA COUNTY: Lot 196-3 Troup. Pers. came JOHN GRAY who "saith that he has lived in sd. county and District for upwards of forty years, and that he has never known any person to reside within sd. destrict of the name of JAMES GAMBEL or any other Gambel and that he has frequently seen THOMAS THOMPSON who was reputed to be the illegitimate of POLLY THOMPSON and that he believes he lived with WM. B. LUKE and that he never knew any other illegitimate child or children of Polly Thompson and does believe that there was no other withing said District or that resided any where near at the time of giving in

for the lottery of eighteen hundred and twenty seven." Signed:
JOHN GRAY before WM. B. LUKE, 13 April 1839.

BALDWIN COUNTY: Lot 196-3 Troup. Pers. app'd. JOHN W.
                         SHEPHERD who "saith that he saw ARCHER
AVERY of Columbia County and THOMAS THOMPSON the applicant for
an Alias grant in Company together and that Sd. A. Avery informed
sd. deponent that sd. Thomas Thompson was the individual or person that he gave in for the Lottery of 1827.
                         And sd. deponent never saw Mr. WM. C. ELLIS (as he knew) until after he purchased the land of Thomas
Thompson and that sd. deponent never offered to purchase sd land
from Wm. C. Ellis and sd. deponent has been informed and does
believe that Wm. C. Ellis married MALINDA THOMPSON ill. who lived
in Monroe County Houses district at the time of the giving in for
draws in the Lottery of 1827." Signed: JOHN W. SHEPHERD before
J. T. CATCHING, J.P., 9 April 1839.

COLUMBIA COUNTY: Lot 196-3 Troup. Pers. came ARTHUR AVERY
                         who "saith that the sd. THOMAS THOMPSON
that he gave in a draw for in the lottery of 1827 visited him
during the last winter and that he knows him to be the sd. orphan
that he gave in for and that since that time he saw him Thompson
in Greenville in Merrewether County and that at the time I gave
in the draw the sd. Thomas Thompson resided in Culbreaths District in Columbia County and at the House of WM. B. LUKE and I
know of no other illegitimate of POLLY THOMPSON and that I have
lived in sd. District ever since it was formed having lived where
I now live 52 years and that I have never known a man to have
lived in the District of the name of GAMEL and there has appeared
to be but one belief in the District about the right of Thomas
Thompson to the lot drawn to the orphan of Polley Thompson so far
as I have heard in the Destrict." Signed: Archer Avery before
ALEXANDER PEARRE, J.P., 13 April 1839.

MERIWETHER COUNTY: Lot 196-3 Troup. HIRAM WARNER, judge of
                         the superior court, appoints Z. B. TRICE
and WILLIAM R. MAY to question AYRES GAMBELL and ELEANOR GAMBELL
as witnesses in <u>JOE DOE</u> on the demise of THOMAS THOMPSON,plaintiff vs. RICHARD ROE, cas. ejector & WILLIAM C. ELLIS, tenant in
possession. Signed: LEVI M. ADAMS, 20 August 1838. (Editor's note
...the following documents conatin examples of the sort of information that can be found in loose superior court records.):
"Interrog to be exhibited to AYRES GAMBELL & ELEANOR GAMBELL material witnesses for the defendant in the above stated case and
who resides without the limits of sd. county of Merriwether.
Interrog 1st were you acquainted withPOLLY THOMPSON formerly of
Columbia County in this state? Is sd. Polly in life or is she
dead? if dead when and where did she die? was she a single or
married Lady? was she ever married? did she have children at the
time of her death? if yea, how many and what their names and ages.
How many children did she have during the years 1825,1826 and
1827 what their names and ages? & where did they reside during
sd. years? did she have a son of the name of THOMAS THOMPSON? if
yea, what was the age and description of sd. son? where did he
live during the years 1824, 1826 and 1827? what became of sd. boy
what relation are you to sd. Polly Thompson?
Iterrog 3rd did the defendant Ellis marry one of the children of
sd. Polly Thompson? yea, which one did he marry?
Relate all that you know that will benefit the defendant
Signed: COLQUETT & HOLT, M.J. WILBORN, Defts. Atts.

First Int. Where did you and JAMES GAMMELL move from when you

came to Monroe County and at what time did you and he so move?
Did MALINDA THOMPSON now MALINDA ELLIS come with either of you
to sd. county? If so, where did she come from, who did she live
with, and who brought her to Monroe?
Second Int. who gave in for MALINDA THOMPSON for a Draw in the
Land Lottery of 1827? and in what county was her draw given in?
did you yourself ever draw any land in that lottery; if so state
what Lot of Land you drew, and where you gave in for it?
4th Int. Where did you move to, from Monroe Co. and where do you
now live?
5th Int. Did any of POLLY THOMPSON's children besides THOMAS
THOMPSON ever live in Cuthbreaths Dist. Columbia: if yea, please
state at what time they lived there and which of them?
6th Int. Did JAMES GAMMELL give in for a draw in the Land Lottery
of 1826-1827 for himself; if yea, state where he gave in and to
whom? and where he was living at that time?
7th Int. Who did you marry, and what relation are you to ELIZA-
BETH GEMMELL SENR. and ELIZABETH GAMMEL JUN.? and what relation
are you to WILLIAM C. ELLIS wife ?
8th Int. How old is MALINDA THOMPSON when came to Monroe County?
How many years did she live there? How long did she leave Monroe
before she was married? How many years has it been since she was
married?
9th Int. Did JAMES GAMBELL's wife have a child by the name of
JACKSON THOMPSON if yea was he an illegitimate child? Did he have
a draw give in for him in the Land Lottery of 1827 if yea who
gave in for him and in what county and district was it given in?
Did he draw land? if yea what Lot did he draw? Where and who did
JACKSON THOMPSON live with in the years 1826 and 1827.
Signed: ALFORD & BELL, Plffs. Attys."

"the examination of AYRES GAMBELL (GAMELL)
1st I know the defendant Mr. ELLIS
2nd I am acquainted POLLY THOMSON. POLLY THOMSON is dead. she
died in Lincoln County. she was a single Lady she never was married, had children at the time of her death. She had three to my
knowledge. One was named MALINDA. One LEROY. One THOMAS. MALINDA
I think is about twenty four or five years of age. LEROY is abt.
twenty three. THOMAS is about nineteen or twenty years old. she
had three children living in 1828,1827 and 1826 names and ages
are above stated by me before. MALINDA lived in 1827 at JAMES
GAMELs in Monroe County the other two LEROY and THOMAS that time
lived in Columbia County at the house of THOMAS HEIRS. she had
a son his giben name was THOMAS. age at the time I have stated.
he was fair skinned light haired and blue eyes. he lived in 1825
1826 & 1827 in Columbia County at the house of THOMAS HEIRS. I
do not know what has become of him. I married POLLY THOMPSONs
sister.
3rd The defendant ELLIS married POLLY THOMPSONs daughter. he
married MALINDY THOMPSON. I heard JAMES GAMEL say that he gave
in the Lottery in the purchase of the above named children.
1st I moved from Jasper County to Monroe. JAMES GAMEL moved from
Lincoln to Monroe I moved from Lincoln I think in 1811 or 1812
James moved about 1826 or 1827. she came with Brother James to
Monroe County from Lincoln. she lived with brother JAMES GAMEL.
2nd JAMES GAMEL gave in for them. I do not know but think it was
in Columbia County. I did draw lot in the first District of orig.
Muscogee Co., I give in Monroe Co., I moved from Upson. I now live
in Talbot. not that I know of. I do not know that James Gamel did
give in the Lottery. I married ELEANOR THOMPSON. I am her son.
I am her brother in law. she is my niece by marriage. she was ten
or twelve years old. she lived in Monroe Co. two years. about 3
years. about nine years. she did. he was. he did. AYERS GAMEL

in Monroe County Cooper's District, he did no 17 in fifth district originally Muscogee county. lived with his father JAMES GAMEL. Signed: AYERS GAMEL (by mark)."
(Signed testimony of ELEANOR GAMMELL, signed by mark, is identical to the above, except that she adds "my step mother told me that he left Columbia for some foreigh parts and she had .... heard that he was dead.")
"Interrogations to be exhibited to JAMES GEMBELL. a material witness on the part of the defendant and who resides without the County of Meriwether." Questions deal with whether Gamell placed POLLY THOMPSON's illegitimates in the 1827 land lottery in Columbia County. He replies that he did for MALENDA and LEROY THOMPSON the only two he knew of. MALENDA has married WILLIAM C. ELLIS. JAMES GAMELL now lives in Upson Co. Signed: James Gambell (by mark) before BURWELL HOWELL and BENJAMIN H. MARSH, commissioners. 30 December 1837.

Lot 288-3 Troup. "Meriwether County.
4th June 1850.
Gov. TOWNS,
I address you upon the subject of a grant to fraction no. 288 in the 3rd Dist. Meriwether Co. Geo. when this fraction was advertised for sale last year, according to your instructions to Maj. CLAPTON, I paid the price of the grant, and took his certificates which I sent to Milledgeville by Col. GASTON who deposited it with mr. JOHN T. SMITH, who I was told would attend to the granting of my fraction. I have recently recd a line from Mr Smith and your letter of rules imposing upon claimants certain injunctions, which as far as possible, I have endeavoured to conform to. I send Mrs. SHARP's affidavits and Mr. MILO B. MATTHEW's Mr. Mathrews is a county man of yours, and for the last ten years a neighbor of mine. In your instructions to Maj. Clapton last year, the receipt of payment, was acknowledged for fractions no. 287,288 and 289 in the 3rd dist. Meriwethers you are therefore, refered to the proper department to learn that fact. I send these by Mr. W. M. ARMAS, by whom please send my grant.
I have been 14 years in peaceable possession of this fraction, nor did I know anything was amiss till I was informed, in 1849 it was advertised for sale, by the sheriff of this county. I have been particular in my details hoping that this effort will not porve unavailing. With due respect. I am Sir yours,
MILES SCARBOROUGH"

Lot F231-5 Troup.
"Magnolia 24th January 18 1831 I do hereby transfer my interest in the above certificates which is one seventh to WM. FERRELL for value recd. Signed: SAML. WILLIAMS.
Magnolia Jany 24th 1831 I do hereby Transfer my part in the above certificate to P. A. CLAYTON value recd. Signed: MECKLEBURY FERRELL.
Magnolia 24th Jany 1831
I do hereby transfer the shear which I purchased from S. WOODFOLK which is one Seventh to P. A. CLAYTON for value recd. A.SEAB
I do hereby transfer my interest in the certificate to JOHN TAYLOR which is one seventh part August 5th 1833. ARNOLD SEAB
I do hereby trancefere my interest to the within certificate to ARNOLD SEAB which is one seventh part July 10th 1834. JOHN TAYLOR.
I transfer my interest in the within certificate which is one seventh part to CHARLEY B. HARDIN for value recd. June 18, 1835. ARNOLD SEAB.
I do hereby transfer the within certificate which is one seventh part to A Seab for value recd. 28 Sept. 1835. CHARLES B. HARDIN

I do hereby transfer the within certificate which is one seventh to P. A. CLAYTON for value recd. Signed: A. SEAB.
2d Nov. 1835
I do hereby transfer the within certificate which is one seventh to P. A. Clayton for value recd. 2 Nov. 1835. A. Seab agent for JOHN BAYBE
I do hereby transfer my interest which is one seventh of fraction 231 5th dist. 3d sect. to P. A. Clayton for value recd. 7 Nov. 1835. WILLIAM W. LUCAS."

MERIWETHER COUNTY: Lot F288-3 Troup. Pers. app'd. JUDY A. SHARP, widow of WM. SHARP, who saith that she cannot find the certificate for the purchase by her late husband to lot 288-3 Meriwether Co. Signed: Judy A. Sharp (by mark) before B. J. PARHAM, J.P., 3 June 1850.

Pers. app'd. MILO B. MATHEWS who saith that MILES SCRABOROUGH, the present owner of fraction 288, 3rd dist. has been in peaceful possession of the fraction for ten years or more. Signed: Milo B. Matthews before B. J. Parham, J.P. 3 June 1850.

Lot 212-7 Troup."Augusta 9th May 1827

I am requested by EDMUND BUGG Esquire to state to your Excellency that his sister OBEDEANCE BUGG has drawn a tract of land as an orphan in Lee County 6th District No 80 which she is not entitled to and requests her name may be reased as an orphan and the Lot or number returned to the wheel as Gdn. for his sister he returned her name as entitled to a draw, she being both deaf and dumb which drew fortunate she is entitled to the same   your obedient servant   JAMES M. LAWS
The above mistake occured by her mother making her return as her next friend and as an orphan without thinking her age would exclude her being over the age of Eighteen years my living in another district made the return as guardian being both Deaf and Dumb which Drawn she is Fairly Entitled to I thought this course most advisible to let the draw she was entitled to return back to the wheel which Tract is agreed to the numbers contained in the above. I am yours Respectfully. E. BUGG."

HALL COUNTY: Lot 81-9 Hall. Pers. came WILLIAM LITTON who "saith that in the Spring of 1834 he came to reside in the immediate neighborhood of WILLIAM ROBBINS in sd. county. that sd. Robbins was then in possession of fractions no. 81-82 and 84 in the 9th dist. of sd. county, his (sd. Robbins) house was situate near the line of fractions 81 and 84.

that his farm extended to, and was on each of the other fractions and that sd. ROBBINS claimed possession under JACOB J. HOLLINGSWORTH. Signed: WILLIAM SITTON before JAMES ROBERTS, J.I.C. 11 September 1850.

JASPER COUNTY: Lot 198-8 Troup. Petition to Governor JOHN FORSYTH that JOHN PERSONS drew lot 148-8 of Troup but that the only John Persons in this district died many years before the land lottery. The lot was probably drawn by BENJAMIN PERSONS who was entitled to draw in the last lottery. 9 December 1828. Signed: WM. HANCOCK, J.P., MORGAN COATS, EPHRAIM LYNCH, P. M. SPRATLIN, CHRISTOPHER DRESKILL, ZACHARIAH FAULKNER, PINKNEY PERSONS, WOODY DOZIER, J.I.C., HOMER HINDS, WALLACE N. LIMON, T. W. WRIGHT, SIMEON FREEMAN, JOHN FAULKNER, ZACHERY ESTES, JAMES BUTTS, J.P., R. C. ESTES, JORDAN COMPTON, EZEKIEL FEARS, RICHARD CROSS, ELBERT MOORE, JOHN HAYS, ALSEY DURHAM, JOHN MALON, JAMES H. ESTES and ALEXANDER ALLISON.
Includes signed certificate of JOHN B. DARDEN that no one named JOHN PERSONS was living in the district he commanded at the time of the land lottery.

MONROE COUNTY: Lot 72-9 Troup. Pers. app'd. JOHN BROWN to claim lot 72-9 Troup Co., drawn by him as a soldier of the War of "1814." Includes app't. of LEONARD T. DPYLE as att'y. Signed: Jno. Brown bef. GEORGE B. BIRD & C. RAIFORD, J.P. 16 June 1843.
Pers. app'd. JOHN BROWN, natural guardian of his son BENJAMIN BROWN, to claim lot 120-13-3 Cherokee Co. Signed: Jno. Brown bef. C. Raiford, J.P., 16 June 1843.

MONROE COUNTY: Lot 36-10 Troup. Pers. app'd. JESSE POPE to claim a lot drawn in the 10th Dist. of Troup, drawn by SARAH PINCKARD, dec'd., as legatee; lot 702-18-3, drawn by WILLIAM S. MILLER, dec'd., as agent for Miller's orphans and for Miller's widow, JULIAN A. MILLER; and lot 667-3-2 as legatee of SARAH PINCKARD, dec'd. Includes app't. of WILLIAM S. NORMAN as att'y. Signed: Jesse Pope bef. WARREN GOODNO (GOODNOW?) and JONA. JOHNSTON, J.P., 16 June 1843.

BALDWIN COUNTY: Lot 207-12 Troup. Pers. app'd. WILLIAM B. DASHER of Effingham Co. who saith that his father drew the within named lot of land and he claims it as Ex'r of his father's estate. His father transfered the title to the same (not signed).

EFFINGHAM COUNTY: Pers. app'd. JOHN ARNSTORPH to claim lot 207-12 Troup Co., as Ex'r. of the estate of GEORGE ARNSTORPH. App't. of WM. B. DAHSER as att'y. Signed: John Arnstorph (by mark) bef. JNO. CARLTON, clk. and GEORGE FOY, 26 June 1843.

CRAWFORD COUNTY: Lot 172-7 Houston. ELIZABETH FUDGE, Extrx of the estate of JACOB FUDGE, dec'd. appoints SAMUEL RUTHERFORD as att'y. for taking out a grant to lot 172-7 Houston Co.; lot 181 in the same co. and lot 827-4-1 in Cherokee. Signed: Elizabeth Fudge before JOHN W. ELLIS, J.P. and BENJAMIN F. PITSON(?). (no date)

PULASKI COUNTY: Lot F22-1! Houston. WILLIAM SIMPSON, for the estate of SUSANNAH STEVENS, sells to DEMPSY B. SMALL fractional lot 22-12 Houston Co., "sd. interest of WILLIAM SIMPSON being the interest of the heirs of MAJAMSEY MOORE" and "after the termination of the life estate of SUSANNAH STEVENS." Signed: William Simpson bef. HENRY ANDERSON and S. M. MANNING, J.I.C., 22 November 1854.

HARRIS COUNTY: Lot 1F-3 Troup. Pers. came ABEL NELSON who saith that WILLIAM NELSON purchased fractional lots one and thirty four in the 3rd district, Troup Co., and that he and William Nelson have lived there more than seven years. Signed: Abel Nelson bef. SAMUEL MC CANTS, J.P. 20 July 1850.

HARRIS COUNTY: Pers. came MIRIAM COCHRAN, widow of MARTIN COCHRAN, dec'd., who saith that she believes her husband paid the purchase money for the fractional lots 1 and 34, 3rd Dist., Troup Co. Signed: Miriam Cochran bef. W. H. C. DAVENPORT, J.I.C., 26 May 1849.

Includes order by B. F. GULLESS, secretary of Ex. Dept. for grants to issue for fractional lots 1 & 34,3- Troup Co.

Lot 104-16 Houston. "Representative Chamber, 21 Decr. 1822. The Subsribers Certify that by the returns from Richmond County for draws in the Land Lotteryes an error has been made in the name of one of the orphans of THOMAS SANDWICH, dec'd.; that there is but one family of that name in the County, and it is known to some of us, that the names of these orphans are: CAROLINA and MATTHEW; and not Caroline and Martha, as entered in the sd. return. Signed: J. HUTCHINSON, ROBERT WATKINS and LEWIS HARRIS.

TROUP COUNTY: Lot 106-2 Irwin. JAMES RICE of Chambers Co., Alabama, appoints JOSEPH EDGE of the same as att'y. for taking out a grant to lot 106-2, in Irwin Co. Signed: James Rice bef. MILES H. ESTES, J.P., 3 August 1841.

BALDWIN COUNTY: Lot 256-4 Irwin. Pers. came WILLIAM S. WHITWORTH who saith that he has lived in Madison Co. for 24 or 25 years and has never heard of anyone named BENJAMIN BORUN although he did know a Doctor BENJAMIN BORUM from the time he moved to sd. county until Borum's death. Borum lived in the village of Danielsville, in the district commanded in 1819 by Captain WILLIFORD. Signed: William S. Whitworth bef. Alfred M. Horton, N.P., 1 Dec. 1840.

GREENE COUNTY: Lot 187-7 Irwin. JOHN CURTRIGHT, Adm'r. of the estate of THOS. MALLORY dec'd., appoints JOHN MALLORY of Upson Co. as att'y. to take out a grant to lot 187-7 Irwin Co. Signed: John Curtright before PAUL DAVIDSON, J.P. and R. P. WRIGHT, 23 Aug. 1841.

MADISON COUNTY: Lot 236-7 Irwin. Pers. appd. LETTUCE MILLICAN, SENR., LETTUCE MILLICAN, JUNR., THOMAS MILLICAN and JOHN SCOTT (in right of his wife, the former JANE MILLICAN), heirs of ANDREW MILLICAN, SENR. dec'd. to claim lot 236-11 Irwin Co. Signed: Lettuce Millican Senr. (by mark), Lettuce Millican, Junr. (by mark), Thomas Millican (by mark), & John Scott bef. JAMES LONG, J.I.C., 23 Aug. 1841. Includes note from John Scott, Danielsville, 23 Aug. 1841, to JOHN R. ANDERSON, enclosing money for the grant.

HOUSTON COUNTY: Lot 360-7 Irwin. Per. came LEWIS POLLOCK, Ex'r. of the estate of his father JESSE POLLOCK, to claim lot drawn by his father. He sends money for the grant by JOHN BARTON. Signed: Lewis Pollock bef. THOMAS POLLOCK J.P., 28 August 1841.

TWIGGS COUNTY: Pers. came JOHN BARTON who saith he is the lawful agent of Lewis Pollock, Ex'r. of

JESSE POLLOCK. Signed: JOHN BARTON before PEYTON REYNOLDS, J.I.C. 30 August 1841.

JEFFERSON COUNTY: Lot 382-7 Irwin. MOSES BRINSON, guardian of the minor heirs of ISAAC BRINSON of Jefferson County, dec'd., appoints JESSE CONNEL as lawful att'y. to take out a grant to lot 382-7 Irwin Co. Signed: Moses Brinson, Junior before MARTHA M. CHEATHAM and JAMES L. CHEATHAM, J.P. 17 August 1841.

Lot 271-8 Irwin. "Fulton Post Office S. Carolina Oct. 17th 1822
Dear Sir,
A few days since I received information of my having drawn in the lottery (Land) of Georgia, lot No. 271 in the 8th District, Irwin County. my peculiar situation at this time prohibits my immediate attention to the requisites of clearances &c. may I, presume Sir, to trespass on a leisure moment & ask of you to give attention to its preservation for me? I am compelled to Charleston, from whence I shall go to Milledgeville ere the adjournment of your Legislature. when Sir t'will give me much pleasure to see you. Be pleased to offer my respectful compliments to your Lady and believe me
to be Dr. Genl. your most respectful
Governor CLARKE   obt. Sert. LAWRENCE MANNING"

WILKERSON COUNTY: Lot 235-9 Irwin. Pers. app'd. JOHN HOLLIMAN to claim lot 235-9 Irwin Co., drawn by SUSANNAH DEEN, widow, of Laurence (Laurens?) Co. Includes appointment of THOS. J. HOLLIMAN as att'y. Signed: John Holliman bef. ALLEN CANNON, J.P., 26 August 1841.

MC INTOSH COUNTY: Lot 270-10 Irwin. ELIZABETH C. DEXTER, widow of BENJAMIN W. DEXTER, saith that her husband died 21 January last. Signed: Elizabeth C. Dexter, JON. SAWYER, J.P. 1 Aug. 1822.
WILLIAM B. HOLZENDORF and JON. SAWYER certify that BENJAMIN W. DEXTER is the only person by that name in their district and county.

TWIGGS COUNTY: Lot 391-13 Irwin. THOMAS CHAPPELL, gdn. of the orphans of ROBERT REYNOLDS, dec'd. appoints THOMAS HAYNES of Baldwin County as his att'y. for taking out a grant to lot 391-13 Irwin County. Signed: THOS. S. CHAPPELL before PEYTON REYNOLDS, J.I.C., 25 August 1801. Includes a note to THOMAS HAYNES to ask Haynes to take out the above grant.

HALL COUNTY: Lot 81-9 Hall. WILLIAM A. BELL, Adm'r. of
                          the est. of JACOB J. HOLLINGSWORTH of
Stewart County, sells to DAVIS WELCHEL, SR. of Hall Co. a lot by WILLIAM ROBINS of CHARLES HULSEY; a lot orig. granted to JAMES PATTERSON; and fractional lots 81,82 and 84 in the 9th Dist. of Hall Co. Signed: William Bell, Adm'r. of the est. of Jacob J. Hollingsworth, dec'd., before JAMES LAW and M. W. BROWN, N.P. 10 Sept. 1845. Recorded on 22 January 1846.

The following are abstracted from several almost identical documents. Georgia. Chatham County.
                    I so solemnly swear, that I have been three years a Citizen of the United States, and have resided in this State three years immediately preceding the passage of the undermentioned Act, except absence on lawful business, and am now an inhabitant of the same place ---that I was eighteen years of age at the time of the passing of sd. Act---that I have not given in my name for any draw or draws in the present contemplated Land Lottery, in any other part of the State---that I have not drawn a Tract of Land in any of the former Land Lotteries, in my individual capacity, or as an individual Orphan, and that I did not, directly or indirectly, evade the service of this State or of the United States, in the late wars against Great Britain or the Indians; and that the cause of my not having entered my name in the Books of the proper Officers appointed to receive the ...... for the County of Chatham, in due course of time, was in consequence of my having....."
File Designation in
Surveyor General	/Name & date	/Excuse for absence and family Composition.
231-2 Monroe	JOHN PELLEGREN 24 Sept. 1821	absent to the North; wife and 2 children
188-7 Monroe	DANIEL SWEENEY 10 Sept. 1821	at work down the river; wife and 1 child
241-8 Monroe	JOHN SHEPARD 6 Sept. 1821	sick in the hospital; wife and 1 child
182-9 Monroe	CHARLES THOMAS* 13 Oct. 1821	absent from county; wife and family
230-11 Monroe	AUGUSTA GIBON* 20 Aug. 1821	ignorant of the law; wife
161-12 Monroe	WILLIAM TAYLOR 13 Oct. 1821	absent from county; wife & 2 children
153-13 Monroe	JOHN DERRICK* 22 Aug. 1821	absent from county; a male legitimate child, his wife is dead.
60-8 Monroe	JOHN AUGUSTUS RUSSELL	absent; wife & 4 children
100-2 Houston	T. MARSH(?) 29 Aug. 1821	mistakenly thought he had won in other lottery; wife and 1 child.
139-12 Houston	WILLIAM UNDERWOOD 6 Sept. 1821	at work in South Carolina; wife and 1 child

287-14 Houston	WILLIAM LYON* 18 Oct. 1821	absent from the county;wife	
287-14 Houston	WM. LACY* 2 Oct. 1821	been at St. Mary's; wife & 3 children	
41-15 Houston	WM. RADFORD* 24 Sept. 1821	river boating; wife and 2 children.	
77-15 Houston	ANTHONY STEVENS,JR. 20 Aug. 1821	can not read; wife and 2 children	
154-15 Houston	JOHN COUSTON* 20 Sept. 1821	sick; wife and 1 child	
78-15 Houston	GASPER WILLIAMS* 13 Aug. 1821	ignorant of the law; wife and 2 children	
269-1 Dooly	RICHARD BURR 18 Oct. 1821	north on business; wife & 1 child	
126-4 Dooly	HENRY MATTHEWS 17 Sept. 1821	absent from state; wife and 1 child	
132-3 Dooly	JOSEPH REVERS* 24 Aug. 1821	can not read	
89-3 Dooly	FREDERICK MERRELL 7 Sept. 1821	sick in the hospital; wife and 1 child	
30-2 Dooly(?)	JOSEPH MERIE 17 Sept. 1821	absent from state on business; wife and 2 children	
78-16 Henry	PETER WHITE* 19 Sept. 1821	no opportunity; wife and 1 child.	
127-15 Henry	ISAAC RODGERS* 2 Oct. 1821	been absent; wife and 2 children	
202-12 Henry	THOS. WATTS 1 Sept. 1821	travelling on the road; wife and 1 child	
208-11 Henry	FRANCES BROWN* 12 Sept. 1821	dragging business between Savannah, Darien and St.Mary has wife and 1 child.	
225-10 Henry	LAWRENCE ALDEN 1 Sept. 1821	ignorant of the law; wife and 2 children	
21-6 Henry	JOHN BARNEY* 4 Oct. 1821	been absent; wife and 5 children	
78-5 Henry	ALEXANDER C. A. LE PAGE	did not know cut off date; wife and 2 children	
161-6 Henry	JOHN BATISTE	absent from country; wife and 2 children	

(*indicates that petitioner signed by mark. Similar documents signed by individuals who had no wife or children are not included in this book.)

DOOLY COUNTY: Lot F232-15 Dooly. "This is to certify that I lived a neighbor to the lot WILLIAM T. SMITH (who signed his name WILL T. SMITH) and that I was well acquainted with him, that he owned the fractions now claimed by W. W. TYSON in the 15th Dist. of Dooly Co., that he was subject to fits of Drinking that he went from this place to Hawkinsville on business with the intention of returning in a few days, but that he was found dead in the streets of Hawkinsville one morning. That he was a man of property. As soon as his death was known here, the Post Master at this place wrote to his wife MARGARET SMITH, who in the Course of a few days came here with A. H. KENNEDY as her attorney and took possession of the Negroes and other property and the moveable part they took away with them. Then shortly after she came again with her son LAN(?) WILLIAM TOMPKINS and sold her cattle which run on the west side of Flint River & that she paid up all the debts in this neighborhood of her late husband amounting to some 3 or 4 hundred Dollars, and that the sd. Margaret Smith was the legal representative of the property,

that she has had possession of it ever since and I never heard
that any other person had ever made an effort to get it out of
her possession, that sd. SMITH, had a brother living then in
Twiggs County by the name of BENJAMIN SMITH, formerly a member
of the Legislature from that County. Sworn to and subscribed before me this 11th day of June 1848. Signed: A. WEBB before S.C.
LIPPITT, J.I.C., of Dooly County."

                    Lot F252-15 Dooly.
"We recollect being at WM. T. SMITHS in Dooly County some fourteen or fifteen years since as well acquainted with sd. Smith we
no he Exercised Owner Ship held and claimed Sertain fractions &
paid Tax for them to wit (nos.) 252,256,255 and 254 in the 15th
Distr Dooly. Mr. Smith started that morning to Milledgeville in
Order to grant his fractions I Saw his Negro woman Open his Trunk
by his Smiths order and hand him the Sertificates in order to get
his grants for Smith Said this was his business to Milledgeville
Mr. Smith Started and Some four or fives Days afterwards he Smith
was found Dead at Hawkinsville in Pulaski County no papers or any
of his money or Other matters has ever been Seen for Mr. Smith it
is supposed was murdered and the Papers no Doubt was destroyed
for fear it would Lead to Some descovery of his Death. the above
fractions is now Claim by WM. W. TISON.
The 15th 1848
S. C. LIPPITT J.I.C. of Dooly County   Signed: S. L. HOLLIDAY
                                              & ABNER HOLLIDAY"

                    Lot 217-5 Coweta
"To the Legislature of the State of Georgia
                    The petition of HENRY TAUNTON, Guardian of
the orphans of STEPHEN GILMORE deceased respectfully sheweth that
his Father NATHAN TAUNTON who was the grandfather of sd. orphans
gave in their names for draws in the land lottery of 1827 to one
BROWN who was appointed by the Inferior Court of Crawford County
for that purpose. That it was intended to give in said children
as the orphans of STEPHEN GILMORE and your petitioner who was
present at the giving in, heard sd. Brown ask the names of sd.
orphans and some one replied that the oldest was named HUGHEY.
The names were given in, in Dukes district Crawford County, and
during the drawings of the lottery lot of land no. 217 in the 5
District Coweta County was drawn by HUGHEY GILMORE's orphans in
Dukes district Crawford County
            Now as there has at no time been such orphans in sd. district your petitioner has been induced to belive
that a mistake was made by the person, Brown, who took down said
names and that sd. lot of land belongs to HUGHEY GILMORE and the
other orphans of STEPHEN GILMORE whose names were given in, in
sd.district. And your petitioner feels it his duty in behalf of
sd. orphans, to ask of your Honorable Body to pass an act authorized a grant to the orphans of Stephen Gilmore, to whom as he believes sd. lot of land rightfully belongs. And your petitioner
will ever pray swear to and subscribed before me this 29th day
of October 183_.   HENRY TANTON
before MOSES TULLIS, J.P."

The following are all counties in the State of <u>ALABAMA</u>:
<u>Chambers County</u>:   Lot 156-14-3 Cherokee. We, WILLIAM N. CURRY, in right of his wife LUCINDA (formerly LUCINDA FARRAR); JOHN SHARMAN in right of his wife ELIZABETH
JANE (formerly ELIZABETH JANE FARRAR); and PETER DARRAR, lawful

                              316

heirs of ROBERT FARRAR, dec'd. of Jones County, Georgia, appoint AMELIOUS TORRENCE of Baldwin County, Georgia, as their att'y. to receive the grant for lot 156-14-3, which they drew as orphans. Signed: WM. N. CURRY, JOHN SHARMAN and PETER FARRAR before GREEN D. BRANTLY, J.P., 8 March 1843.

COOSA COUNTY: Lot 337-4-2 Cherokee. SUSAN R. FULTON, widow and representative of SAMUEL FULTON, decd., appoints THOMAS M. COOK of Milledgeville as her att'y. to take out a grant for lot 337-4-2. Signed: Susan R. Fulton before JOHN H. CANANT, J.P., 12 April 1843.

RANDOLPH COUNTY: Lot 5-4-2 Cherokee. Pers. app'd. BENJAMIN TOWERS, who married widow ELIZABETH MARTIN of Dekalb County, to claim lot 5-4-2. Signed: Benjamin Towers before SAML. T. OWEN, J.P., 10 June 1843.

TALLAPOOSA COUNTY: Lot 223-27-2 Cherokee. Pers. app'd. AARON BROOKS to claim lot 223-27-2 drawn by THOMAS EWING, JOHN EWING, & SARAH EWING (orphans of JAMES EWING of Newton County) and purchased by Brooks from them, the orphans having come of age. Signed: A. Brooks bef. JOHN A. JOHNSON, J.P. 13 November 1852.

MACON COUNTY: Lot 116-22-2 Cherokee. GRANVILLE WHITE claims lot 116-22-2 for himself and, as guardian of WILLIAM H. STEPHENS, orphan of BERY STEPHENS of Dooly County, claims lot 282-13-3. Signed: Granville White before WM. B. FILES, J.P., 22 June 1843.

RUSSELL COUNTY: Lot 132-6-4 Cherokee. Pers. app'd. GEORGE C. KING, guardian for the heir of WILLIAM CLEMMOND dec'd. who sayeth that when the people of Jones County, he was a resident and gave in the names of ELIZABETH CLEMMOND & MARTHA CLEMMOND, the only children of William Clemmond, dec'd. as their stepfather and guardian. (He does not specify for which orphan he is claiming land.) Signed: George C. King bef. ABRAM P. WATT, J.P., 27 June 1843.

COOSA COUNTY: Lot 116-8-4 Cherokee. HARRIETT E. SMITH, Ex'trx. of the est. of JOSIAH BOSWELL, deceased. of Bibb Co., Georgia, appoints IVERSON L. HARRIS of Baldwin County as att'y. to take out a grant for lot 131-18-1. Signed by HARRIET E. SMITH bef. JAS. A. LAFTIN, JOHN H. CONANT, LEWIS KENNEDY, J.P., JOSEPH B. CLEVELAND, clerk, and EBENEZER POND, judge, 9 November 1844.

PIKE COUNTY: Lot 64-11-4 Cherokee. Pers. app'd. JOHN G. ROBERTSON to claim lot 64-11-4 in Dade co. Also, for his wife, the former JENNETT EVANS (orphan of STEPHEN EVANS dec'd.) lot 275-17-4. Signed: John G. Robertson before CHARLES A. DENNIS, J.I.C., 5 June 1843.

PIKE COUNTY: Lot 64-11-4 Cherokee. JOHN G. ROBERTSON appoints ANSALEM ROBERTSON att'y. for taking out a grant to lot 64-11-4 drawn by JOHN G. ROBERTSON of Morgan County, Georgia, and lot 275-17-4 drawn by JENNETT EVANS, orphan of LEVEN EVANS dec'd. of Green County. JENNETT EVANS is now the wife of JOHN G. ROBERTSON. Signed: John G. Robertson before ELI AMASON, J.R (by mark), 14 June 1843.

CHEROKEE COUNTY: Lot 300-8-2 Cherokee. Pers. app'd. P. J. CHISOLM, one of the orphans of ANDREW CHISOLM of Elbert County, to claim lot 300-8-2. Signed: P. J. Chisolm bef. JACKSON SMITH, J.P. and M. E. MC DANIEL, Judge of Probate, 18 October 1851.

RANDOLPH COUNTY: Lot 395-15-1 Cherokee. Pers. app'd. WILLIAM P. POOL, orphan of WILLIAM POOL, decd. to claim lot 395-15-1. Signed: William P. Pool bef. ZACHARIAH DARDIN, J.P., 15 June 1843.

CHAMBERS COUNTY: Lot 909-14-1 Cherokee. Pers. app'd. JAMES ANDERSON to claim lot 909-14-1. Signed: James Anderson bef. G. D. BRANTLY, J.P., 10 June 1843.

RUSSELL COUNTY: Lot 382-13-1 Cherokee. Pers. app'd. WILLIAM MYRICK to appoint BENJAMIN H. REYNOLDS as att'y. to take out the grant to lot 382-13-1 and lot 44-10-1. Signed: Wm. Myrick bef. F. J. ABBOTT and AUGUSTUS J. ABBOTT J.P., 13 May 1843.

BARBOUR COUNTY: Lot 156-12-1 Cherokee. Pers. app'd. JOHN W. RAINS to claim lot 156-12-1. Signed:

JOHN W. RAINS before Z. Y. DANIEL, 11 March 1843.

BARLOW(?) COUNTY: Lot 590-2-1 Cherokee. MILTON H. BROWDER appoints CHARLES H. NELSON of Milledgeville as att'y. to take out the grants for the lot he drew and the lot drawn by WILLIAM JONES of Wilkinson County and purchased by him from Jones. Lots 590-2-1 and 115-7-1. Signed: M. A. Browder bef. (illegible), N.P., 15 June 1843.

RUSSELL COUNTY: Lot 137-2-1 Cherokee. RICHARD T. LANKEY appoints General CHARLES NELSON of Milledgeville to take out the grant for lot 131-2-1. Signed: Richard T. Lankey bef. D. P. TOWNS and JAS. KELLOGG, N.P., 20 May 1843.

CHAMBERS COUNTY: Lot 237-9 Carroll. Pers. app'd. NICHOLAS GUYSE, JR. to claim lot 237-9 of Carroll County, drawn by NICHOLAS GUYSE, SR. of Lincoln County and lot 162-11-4 Cherokee County, drawn by NICHOLAS GUYSE, JR. of Lincoln County. Also lot 736-21-3 Cherokee County, drawn by JOHN BEVIN of Lincoln County. /signed: Nicholas Guyse before CALVIN PRESLEY, J.P., 23 June 1843.

MACON COUNTY: In person app'd. JOHN G. ROBERTS to claim lot 1265-3-2, drawn by JOHN RIGHT and lot 281-7 of Carroll County. Signed: John G. Roberts before ORREN D. COX, J.P., 22 May 1843.

MACON COUNTY: Lot 29-7 Carroll. Pers. came JAMES B. HOOTEN, one of the heirs of THOMAS WESTBROOK, dec'd. of Twiggs County, whose orphans are the drawers of lot 29-7 Carroll County, and lot 252-3 Muscogee County. Signed: James B. Hooten before WM. H. HAUGH, J.P., 26 Sept. 1847.

MACON COUNTY: Lot 186-24-3 Cherokee. Pers. app'd. CHARLES W. MOORE, for his brother JAMES S. MOORE, to claim lot 186-24-3. Signed: Chas. W. Moore bef. MATHEW PETERS, J.P., 10 Sept. 1844.

BARBOUR COUNTY: Lot 204-13 Early. JOHN W. RAINES appoints JOHN R. ANDERSON of Baldwin Co., Georgia as att'y. for taking out a grant to lot 204-13 of Early Co. purchased from SARAH T. RAINES. Signed: John W. Raines before GEO.

STINSON, EDWARD B. YOUNG and A. C. VANN EPPS, N.P., 16 Aug. 1841.

CHAMBERS COUNTY: Lot 242-6 Henry. "Mill Town P.O. Chambers Co. Ala. August 6th 1850
Sir
  Mr Father THOMAS MILES of Columbia County Geo. draw a lot of land and as well as I can recollect it was in 6th district of Henry County Geo. and granted it since which he died.
  The children has now come of age and are desirious of getting their rights tho it may be worth but little. Consequently you will do the orphans a favor by informing me by return mail, what lot he, THOMAS MILES, of Columbia County Geo. drew and much oblige
                    yours truly
                        JOHN W. MILES
To: The Surveyor Genrl
Milledgeville Geo   Mill Town P.O.
                                 Chambers County, Ala."

CHAMBERS COUNTY: Lot 132-1 Lee. Pers. app'd. THOMAS L.
THOMASON, agent of the owner, to claim lot 132-1 of Lee County, drawn by MAHALA EDMONSON, widow, and lot 726 1st Dist. 3rd section Cherokee County, drawn by JINEY(?) EDMONDSON, orphan. Signed: Thos. L. Thomason before G. D. BRANTLY, J.P. 10 June 1843.

The following counties are in the Territory of FLORIDA:
HAMILTON COUNTY: Lot 1115-21-2 Cherokee. Pers. app'd. ELIZA
ANN SMITH, formerly ELIZA ANN COUCH, to claim lot 1115-21-2. Signed: Eliza Ann Smith before WM. M. KIDD, J.P. and JOHN S. PURRANCE, clerk of the Circuit Court, 13 Feb. 1843.

LEON COUNTY: Lot 195-11-2 Cherokee. CHARLES H. NELSON
of Georgia is appointed attorney to take out the grant for the lot drawn by C. E. BARTLETT. Signed: C. E. Bartlett before J. ATKINSON, N.P., 13 May 1843.

JACKSON COUNTY: Lot 92-8-3 Cherokee. Pers. app'd. WILLIAM
E. FULGHAM, agent for the heirs of HARDY FULGHAM dec'd. of Burke County, to claim the lot drawn by HENRY FULGHAM, dec'd. Signed: William E. Fulgham bef. R. BALLARD, J.P. 2 June 1843.

HAMILTON COUNTY: Lot 103-5 Carroll. Pers. app'd. JAMES MC-
DONALD to claim lot 103-5 Carroll County. Signed: James McDonald bef. (illegible), 3 May 1843.

The following counties are in the State of MISSISSIPPI:

KEMPER COUNTY: Lot ......Dooly. JOHN HALL appoints JOHN HANCOCK of Crawford County, Georgia as att'y. to take out the grant for the lot in Dooly County that Hall drew as a citizen of Putnam County. Signed: John Hall before M. EVANS, JAMES F. BEHANNON, WM. G. GILL, clerk and LEWIS STOVALL, judge of probates, 12 May 1843.

HINDS COUNTY: Lot 948-15-2 Cherokee. Pers. app'd. H. F. DEES, for his wife, the former MARTHA HILL (the only surviving heir of HARBARD HILL), to claim lot 948-15-2. Signed: H. F. Dees bef. JAS. GRAY, J.P., 14 May 1853.

Following county in the state of NEW YORK:

NEW YORK: Lot 896-2-2 Cherokee. Pers. app'd. ALBERT O. PARMELIA who appoints ISAAC NEWELL of Milledgeville as his attorney to claim lot 896-2-2. Signed: Albert O. Parmelia before JOHN BISSELL, commissioner for Georgia. 19 June 1843.

The following counties are in the state of SOUTH CAROLINA:

GREENVILLE DISTRICT: Lot 317-2-2 Cherokee. Per. app'd. Mrs. HARRIET GARRISON, formerly HARRIET BROCK, an orphan of WELCHELs District, Hall County, to claim lot 317-2-2. Signed: Harriet Garrison bef. C. J. ELFORD, M.G.D. 18 Mar. 1852.

EDGEFIELD COUNTY: Lot 192-27-2 Cherokee. Per. app'd. DAVID G. TAYLOR to claim lot 192-27-2 as the only brother of ROBERT H. TAYLOR, dec'd. of Burke County. Includes app't. of WILLIAM H. PRITCHARD of Baldwin Co. as att'y. Signed: David G. Taylor bef. ROBERT ANDERSON, Magistrate, 19 June 1843.

EDGEFIELD DISTRICT: Lot 336-4-2 Cherokee. Pers. app'd. AUGUSTUS BLALOCK to claim lot 336-4-2 for his brother JOHN H. BLALOCK, orphan. App't. of THOMAS M. COOK of Milledgeville as att'y. Signed: Augustus Blalock bef. ROBERT ANDERSON, Magistrate, 15 Feb. 1847.

EDGEFIELD COUNTY: Lot 319-4-2 Cherokee. Pers. app'd. DANIEL TILLEY of Burke Co., one of the orphans of

GEORGE TILLEY of Burke County, dec'd., to claim lot 319-4-2 for himself, his brother WILLIAM TILLEY, and his sister MARGARET. Signed: Daniel Tilley (by mark) bef. SAMUEL JENKINS, BENJ. MILLS and ROBERT ANDERSON,N.P., 7 Apr. 1853.

PICKENS DISTRICT: Lot 193-15-3 Cherokee. Pers. app'd. JAMES RUSSELL, one of the orphans of WILLIAM RUSSELL, dec'd., of Gwinnett County, Georgia, to claim lot 193-15-3. Includes appointment of THOMAS M. COOK of Milledgeville as att'y. Signed. James Russell (by mark) bef. JOHN PERKINS, J.P. 15 July 1846.

CHARLESTON DISTRICT: Lot 36-21-3 Cherokee. Pers. app'd. JOHN R. HAYES, with JAMES T. HAYES & MARY HAYES Ex'rs. of the estate of GEORGE HAYES, dec'd. of Thomas County, to claim lot 36-21-3 and to appoint WILLIAM C. POWELL as att'y. Signed: Jno. R. Hayes bef. A. G. MAPERTH, Magistrate, 15 June 1843.

EDGEFIELD DISTRICT: Lot 78-11 Muscogee. Pers. came ARCHIBALD KEMP (formerly of Augusta, Ga.) to claim lot 78-11 Muscogee County, drawn by MURRAHA, as owner by marriage. Signed: A. Kemp bef. Robert Anderson, Magistrate, 18 May 1843.
     Pers. came ARCHIBALD KEMP to claim 268-17-3 of Cherokee County, drawn by ELIZABETH MURRAH, as owner by marriage. Signed: A. Kemp bef. Robert Anderson, Magistrate. 18 May 1843. Includes app't. of WILLIAM H. PRITCHARD of Baldwin Co. as att'y.

The following are counties in the state of TENNESSEE:
HARDEN COUNTY: Lot 4-28-3 Cherokee. Pers. app'd. ELIZA-BETH LARD, SARAH PALMORE & ELIZA SEVENFORD (the orphans of LUCINDA COCKRAN) to claim lot 4-28-3. They resided in the 4th Section of Cherokee Co. They have sold the lot to ROBERT S. CHURCH. Signed: Elizabeth Lard (by mark), Sarah Palmore (by mark) and Eliza Sevenford (by mark) bef. STEPHEN AUSTIN, J.P. 25 June 1853.

HARDEN COUNTY: Lot 4-28-3 Cherokee. RICHARD LARD and ELIZABETH LARD his wife (formerly ELIZABETH COCHRAN), JOHN PALMER and SARAH his wife (formerly SARAH COCHRAN) and BURNS LANGFORD and ELIZA his wife (formerly ELIZA COCHRAN) appoint ROBERT S. CHURCH as attorney to claim land on the waters of Chicamaugua Creek, in Walker County, on the Georgia-Tennessee border, having been a lot won by the heirs of LUCINDA COCHRAN, widow of JOHN COCHRAN. Signed: RICHARD LARD, ELIZABETH LARD, JOHN PALMER (by mark), SARAH PALMER (by mark), BURNS LUMFORD (by mark) and ELIZA LUMFORD (by mark) before D. A.STREET, G. C. CHURCH, JOHN DAVIS (by mark), and D. H. DUCKWORTH, clerk. 12 Dec. 1851.

GREENE COUNTY: Lot 16-16 Dooly. CAIN BROYLES purchased lot 16-16 of Dooly County, drawn by CLEVERLY PHILLIPS who sold it to AMOS W. HAMMOND; lot 242-10 of Irwin County, purchased from JOB HAMMOND, att'y. for JOHN HARBOR; lot 254-9-of Irwin County, purchased from RUSSELL J. DANIEL; and lot 294-6 of Lee County, from AMOS W. HAMMOND. GEORGE W. FOUTE is appointed att'y. for taking out grants to sd. lots. Signed: Cain Broyles bef. H. R. BAKER, G. JONES, JOHN MC KEE, M. LINCOLN, J.P. G. W. FOUTE,clerk, and CHARLES GASS, chairman. 22 May 1841.

LINCOLN COUNTY: Lot 307-3 Early. We do appoint JAMES RONER (ROVER?) as att'y to claim lot 307-3 Early County. Signed: RICHARD W. ROLIN (by mark) ELIZABETH ROLIN (by mark) and CHARLES ROLIN (by mark), 1 March 1841.

The following county is in the state of **VIRGINIA:**

BRUNSWICK COUNTY: Lot 833-11-1 Cherokee. Pers. app'd. THOMAS W. CLARK to claim lot 833-11-1, having bought sd. lot from ISAAC SCOTT. Also lot 47-13 of Marion County also bought from Scott. Includes app't. of HENRY W. COLEMAN of Hancock County as att'y. Signed. T. W. Clark before R. F. PRITCHETT, J.P., 10 June 1843.

Addendum:
RUSSELL COUNTY, ALABAMA:Lot 185-27 Early. JOHN TOWNSEND, formerly of Greene County, Georgia, appoints WILLIAM F. SCOTT of Baldwin County as att'y. to take out a grant to the lot he drew in Early County. Signed: John Townsend bef. W. D. TAYLOR and R. T. BLASINGAME, 23 Jan. 1841.

INDEX

Georgia Land Lottery Papers
Prepared by
Jim Herman
Ft. Worth, Tx.

(_)ellum, Robert 195
(---ile), Silas B. P. 44
(---), Edward 40
(---), Louisa 286
(---), Miss Fanny 284
(---), N. B. 43
(---), R. A. 36,53

Aaron, (Orphans) 50,60
  Elizabeth 50,60
  James C. 50,60
  John 50,60
  Susan Ann 60
  Susanann 50
  W. B. 50
  W. H. 50
  Wm. H. 60
Abbott, Augustine J. 136
  Augustus 98,204
  Augustus J. 126,150,203,
    204,219,255,256,268,318
  F. F. 136
  F. J. 318
  F. P. 204
Abercrombie, John 134
Abrahams, (Captain)...275
Adair, G. W. 272
  Madison L. 238
  W. H. P. 261,266,271
  Walter 232,233,254
Adams, Abram B. 268
  Danl. 86,156
  Geo. F. 215
  J. 204
  James B. 278
  John 304
  L. M. 46
  Levi M. 306
  Nathaniel 290
  O. F. 166
  Philip 296
  Seth K. 24,25
Adamson, Wm. C. 212
Adderhold, Isaac M. 135
Adison, Charles 61
  Charlotte 61
  Elizabeth 61
  Matilda 61
  Nancy 61
  William 61
Adkins, John 194
Adkinson, Lucy 54,251,252
Akin (Orphans) 278
  Fleming 278
Akins, Joseph 194
Aldadge, James R. 102
Alden, Lawrence 315
Aldridge, Thos. B. 124
Alexander, (Orphans) 31,
  170
  Adam 31,170
  Ann March 137
  Dr. 152
  James L. 31
  Jas. H. 170
  Jas. L. 81
  Martha 31,81,170
  Robert B. 137
  Thomas W. 122
  William 108,109,206
Alford, --- 307
  Jefferson 301
  Jemerson 301
  Jimerson 301
  Wilie 105
Alfriend, Abram 117

Alfriend, Sarah H. 117
Allen, (Orphans) 5,221
  Green 5,220,221
  Parham 174
  Rebecca 218
  Richard 3,36,41,54,98,
    131,147,171,210
  Richmond 121,122
  Thomas V. 2,275
  William 5,221
  William G. 151,225,238,
    262
  Willis 70,220,222
Allison, Alexander 310
  David 23,24,34,35,232
  Martha 232
  Reuben 34
Allman, Thomas 225
Alman, Ann 44
  Moses 222
  William 44
Almand, Ann 249,250
  Isaac 44,249,250
  William 44
Almond, Ann 44
Alston, Sarah D. 151
Alwell, Philip P. 157
Amason, Eli 318
Amores, Matthias 137
Amoros, Mathias 137
An(---), James 85
Andas, Tuttle H. 142
Anderson, (Orphans) 130
  (---) 155
  (---) 220
  Clifford 273
  Hary (?) P. 92
  Henry 311
  J. P. 23
  J. R. 3,82,99,166,167,
    168,170,193,201,245,260,
    268,296
  James 85,153,318
  James, Junr. 85
  James, Jr. 153
  James, Sr. 85
  James B. 207
  James R. 207
  John 97
  John J. 201
  John P. 23
  John R. 20,34,96,116,117,
    121,136,151,179,202,203,
    210,211,214,238,267,312,
    319
  Jordan 130
  Joseph J. 213
  Mary P. 231
  Robert 67,111,122,321,
    322
  Sarah Ann 207
  Viney 153
  William V. 217
Andrews, Abisha 7,283
  Eliza F. 73
  Joseph B. 184
  Montclaiborn 138
  S. Thos. 176
  S. L. 290
  William 224
  William G. 127,130,139,
    192
  Wm. G. 127,130
Andrus, Joseph B. 184
Angier, N. L. 209
Anglin, Abner 159

Anglin, Amelia 269
  Anne 269
  David 269
  Henry, Jr. 159
  John 269
Ansell, --- 58
Ansley, L. M. 140
Anthony, A. L. 23,179
Aorea, Bradley 176
  Margeret 176
  Margerett 176
Appleby, John 103,109
Applewhite, John 255
  Peter 255
Armas, W. M. 308
Armington, S. 121
Armor, P. M. 116
Arnett, Jabel 178
  Thomas 136
Arnold, (Orphans) 196
  Alston A. 257
  James 179
  Jno. B. 196
  John B. 196
  John T. 7,200
  Moses 7,200,203
  Richard D. 151,262
  Susan 7,199,200
  Thomas R. 7,200
  William B. 12
  William W. 196
Arnstorph, George 311
  John 311
Arnsworth, James 205
Asbury, Jesse 244
Ash, Geo. A. 143
  Sarah 143
  Sarah H. 30
Ashton, (Orphans) 203
  Henry 203
Ashurst, John M. 143
  Jno. M. 143
Askew, Benjamin F. 122
  James 122
  James M. 122
  John 122
  Richard 122
  Thos. 229
  William 122,123,236
Ataway, Sterling 45,250
Atkinson, Alex D. 162
  J. 320
  Lazaraus 130
  Martha 266
  Nathan L. 130,266
Attaway, Harley, Jr. 226
  Harley, Senr. 226
  Rebecca 200
Atwell, Philp. P. 86
Atwood, P. P. 86
Audas, Tuttle H. 271
Austell, Alfred 258
Austin, John C. 229
  Mary 183
  Stephen 322
Auston, Mary 183
Avera, David 216
Avery, (Orphans) 21
  A. 306
  Archer 306
  Arthur 306
  Charles 21
Aycock, Wm. M. 209

Bachus, (Children) 58
  Sarah 58,251

Bachus, William 58
Backus, (heirs) 258
  Sarah 251,258
  Western 58,251,258
  William 258,251
Bacous, John 117
Bagby, Harmon 291
  Henry 291,292
Baggs, William 169
Bagshaw, Catherine 30
Bailey, (Orphans) 214
  Charles 168
  David F. 147
  David J. 25
  Elizabeth W. 147
  James 118
  Joel 214
  Josiah 118
  Margaret 81
  Matthew 118
  Saml. A. 141
  Sarah W. 214
  Stephen 224,239
Bails, Emmer 61
Baizmore, Capt. 104
Baker, Capt. 303
  (Children) 128
  (Orphans) 278
  Asa 278
  Benjamin 128
  Daniel 224
  H. R. 323
  Hottory 88
  Jesse L. 34
  Jesse L. 170
  Mary 169,224
  T. H. 152
  Thos. S. 185
Baldwin, (Orphans) 147
  Christopher 159
  Christopher S. 159
  Owen 147
  Susan M. 137
  William D. 159
  William T. 137
  Wm. A. 282
Bales, William, Jr. 178
Baley, David 292
Balkcom, James 187
Ballard, (Orphans) 303
  Anne 269
  E. M. 200
  Ed. 6
  Henrietta 303
  James 269
  James M. 173
  R. 110,320
  W. J. 68
  William 166,303
Ballinger, Rebecca 22
Banardy, ---162
  Catherine 162
  Margaret 162
Banks, Abner 260
  Esther Ann 70,172
  Henry 149
  J. A. 70,172
  James 244
  Sarah 260
  Thomas 70,172
Bankston, John 114
  John, Sr. 114
  L. 180/Lanier 180
Banley, E. S. 99
Barber, William 21
Barclay, E. S. 240
Barefield, James 177
Baringer, Elizabeth 64
  Jane 64
  Jane S. 64
  Thomas 64
  William 64
Barksdale, (Orphans) 165

Barksdale, B. R. 165
  Beverly R. 164,165
  Henry 165
  Joseph C. 164,165
  William 165
Barlow, William W. 113
Barnes, (Orphans) 180
  Clarissa 97
  Franklin 97
  John T. 147
  John Thomas 147
  Joseph 180
  Joshua 66,185
  Nathan 66,185
  Noah 66,185
  Richard G. 147
Barnet, (Orphans) 77
  Joseph 77
Barnett, William W. 184
Barney, John 315
Barnlay, E. S. 151
Barnwell, William 97
Barren, James A. 24
  Jas. A. 24
  William 261
Barrnett, N. C. 222
Barron, Abington 135
  Barnabas 101
  Wiley 246
Barrow, Haywood 120,295
Bartlett, C. E. 310
Barton, Ellen 35,171
  John 312,313
  John B. 35,171
  W. H. 43
  William N. 43
Baselton, Thomas 88
Bass, Hartwell 140
  John 42,210,231
Baster, Reuben 255
Bateman, William M. 175
Bates, Mary 63
Batiste, John 315
Batley, Thomas W. 173
Battey, Thomas W. 18
Battle, Cullin L. 222,239
  O. S. 143
Baughn, Peyton 154
Bauldwin, William A. 281
Baxter, Candacey 255
  Charles 255
  Dacey 255
  Eli H. 169
  Elizabeth 255
  Felix 255
  Joseph W. 244
  Lethe 255
  Martha 244
  Mary 255
  Reuben 255
Baybe, John 309
Baynes, John 230
Baysemore, Riley 291
Bazeman, Humphrey 224
Beacham, ___ is 77
Beal, Elizabeth W. 147
  Jacob 147
Beall ------217
  ----, Jr. 90
  Adnastus 126
  Elizabeth 95
  Fredk. 126,249
  James M. 266
  J. P. 290
  Jas. M. 100,115,128,140,
    155,159,165
  Meremiah 90
  Saml. 49
  T. A. 90
  Thad. A. 90
Bealle, Frederick 52
Beard, Edmund C. 206
  Elizabeth W. 160

Beard, William 160
  Wm. F. 110
Beardin, John C. 138,139
Bearefield, Larkin 215
Bearfield, James 136
Beasley, (heirs) 288
  Abraham 153
  Cynthia 288
  S. 288
  Sarah 288
  William 288
Beaty, Hugh 235
Beavens, John F. 143
Beavers, (Orphans) 143
  Henry R. 95
  John F. 206
  R. A. 291
  R. C. 291
  Rebecca 95
  Reubin C. 291
  Sarah 291
  Silas N. 143
  William C. 95
Becham, Leban 268
Beck, Isaiah 33
Beckham, A. B. 299
  Absalom B. 299
Bedford, G. P. 144
  George P. 144
Bedingfield, Gideon 51
  Hiram 51
Bedington, Washington 65
  William 65
Beesley, Abraham 85,153
Behannon, James F. 321
Belcher, Obadiah 184
  Obadiah R. 184
Bell, --- 307
  (heirs) 210
  Augustus J. 26,172
  Catherine 210
  Charles A. 82
  Charles S. 287
  David 149
  Elizabeth 210
  Enock 202
  George 210
  Harriet 210
  Hester 246
  James 210,258
  John 214
  Margaret 26,172
  S. 258
  Sampson 206
  Sarah 296
  Simeon 4
  Thomas 149,214,225,238
  William 210,263,314
  William A. 314
Belle, H. A. T. E. J. 25
  171,172
Bellenger, J. N. 288
Bellinger, J. N. 56,76
  Jno. N. 22,288
  John H. 76
  John N. 248
Belton, Solomon D. 34
Bennett, (Orphans) 264
  Cooper L. 244
  D. 244
  Mitchell 244
  R. 264
  Samuel C. 40
Bennes, Thomas 239
Benson, J. A. 198
  Sarah 198
  William, Sr. 198
Bentley, Hiram 106,107
Benton, A. 63
  Francis L. 86
  Joseph 108
Berins, Thomas 222
Berren, J. W. M. 208

Berryhill, Wm. 170
  W. N. 46
  W. R. 46
Beth, Marion 56
Bethune, Benjamin T. 305
  Benjamin Y. 239
  Jno. M. 291
  Jno. W. 59,135,223,252
  John 106,223,228
  Mana 32
  Marion 10,190,296
Bettar, Solomon D. 170
Betten, Solomon D. 34
  Solomon P. 68
Better, Solomon D. 253
Bettison, John S. 28
  Samuel D. 28
  Sarah J. 28
  S. J. 28
Betts, Jonathan 15
Beuton, Francis L. 156
Bevil, W. D. 77,180
  William D. 77,180
Bevin, John 319
  Thomas 206
Bibb, Gross 156
  John H. 148
Bidingfield, Gidern 51
Billingslea, Francis B.217
  Frs. B. 217
Bird, George B. 310
  Lewis 64
  Sarah 64
Bishop, (Orphan) 300
  John D. 116
  Jones 300
  Roda 300
  William L. 175
  Wm. S. 175
Bissell, John 321
  Richard 239
Bitts, J. R. 293
Biven, Thomas 87
Black, James H. 21
  James W. 92,93
  Jas. H. 22,50,60,79,153,
    176,209
  Wm. A. 88
Blackman, John P. 274
Blackmon, Jno. P. 274
  John P. 198
Blackshear, Randal 303
Blake, (Orphans) 178
  G. W. 142
  K. H. 245
  Kennedy H. 102
  R. A. 216
  Sarah 178
Blaker, K. H. 102
Blalock, (Orphan) 321
  Augustus 321
  John H. 321
Blance, Joseph G. 174
Blanchard, (Orphans) 237
  Jeremiah 237
  Nancy 237
  Philip 237
  Zachariah 237
Bland, Micajah 141
Blandrum, Samuel 220
Blankett, --- 145
Blasingame, R. T. 323
Blewett, John 83,173,174
Bliss, Benjamin 115
Blissit, Benjamin 115
Blodget, Foster 122
Blois, (Orphans) 234
  F. H. 214
  James F. 234
  Peter 234
Bloodworth, D. M. 268
  D. M. 269
Blount, (Orphans) 155

Blount, E. M. 276
  Edmund M. 276
  F. W. 155
  Freeman W. 155
  James 83
  John 155
  Richard 158
  Selina 190
Blue, (heirs) 214
  Daniel, Sr. 214,276
  James 214
  Mary Anne 275
Blunt, David E. 71
Boaddy, James 177
Boardman, --- 273
Boen, A. (Alanson) 185
Boirdain, Mich. F. 157
Boisdain, Mich. F. 55
Bolan, Mary 8
  Michael I. 8
  Richard 8
Boles, L. B. 240
Bolton, Samuel 163
Bond, (Orphans) 96,117
  Ebenezer 318
  John M. D. 178
  Lucy 178
  Mark 96,117
  Susan 296
  Thomas 96,117
Bonds, William F. 49
Bone, Wm. 183
Bonner, Josiah M. 254
Booker, (Orphans) 295
  Ann C. 295
  Mary E. 295
  William M. 295
Boon, Elbert A. 32
  James O. 32
Booth, (Orphans) 28
  George 28
  George J. 28
Boring, Isaac 177
  John 176,177
Borum, Benjamin 312
Borun, Benjamin 312
Bostwick, Ab. 237
  Araviah 237
  A. B. 69,143,147,189,204,
    275
  Archibald B. 204
  Azariah B. 69
Boswell, Josiah 104,317
Bothwell, Ebenezer 18,214
Bottom, Davis 16
Bourke, Ann B. 215
  Ann M. 215,296
  Elizabeth 296
Bowden, Lot 178
Bowdoin, John W. 178
  Mary 178
Bowen, A. 66,74,180
  Alarson 66
  Christopher 260
Bowling, John W. D. 155
Bowman, Raymon 213
  Robert 213
Boyd, Eliza 161
  Eliza T. 161
  Hamilton T. 279
Boyle, Hannah 126
  Jno. 126
  John 126
Boynton, William 159
Bozeman, James 265
  James F. 265
  John 75,76,260
  Sarah F. 260
Bracewell, James 261
Brack, John 192
Braddy, James 20,136,259
  Linson 136
Bradley, Chs. 85

Brady, James 174
  Joseph 28,29
  Nancy 28,29
Brandon, James, Jr. 205
Branham, William T. 140
  Wm. T. 140
Brannon, Thos. A. 204
Brantley, Jeptha 150
  Jno. H. 201
  Solomon D. 31
  Washington H. 114
Brantly, G. D. 318,320
  Green D. 317
  W. H. 12
  Washington H. 271
Branttey, Solomon D. 227
Brassel, Lucrita 259
  Nathan E. 259
  Sarah Ann 259
  Marthy L. 258,259
Brasswell, G. C. 86,156
Braswell, Marada 269
Brauden, --- 263
Brean, Moses 70,71
Bremer, Stueart 220
Brewer, Catherine 25
  Charity 102,182
  Daniel 215
  James 25
  Mary 81,157
  Solomon 102,182
Brewster, Hugh 164
Brian, Moses 71
Briants, David 261
Brice, William 188
Bridgeman, Francis 235
  Judith 235
Bridges, Bennett 120,124,
    204,286
  Reuben 211
  Sarah 211
Brinberry, W. H. 51,117,
    250,225
Brimer, --- 220
  Stewart 220
Brinson, Isaac 313
  Moses 313
  Moses, Jr. 313
  Stephen 174
Britt, David J. 280
Broach, R. M. 140
  Robert M. 140
Brock, Harriet 321
  John 26
  Thomas 99
Broddus, Edward A. 184
  Th. C. 221
Brooke, William F. 128
Brookings, Nancy 3
Brookins, Haywood 90,147
Brookin, Haywood 155
Brooks, A. 110,317
  Aaron 109,317
  Chas. Y. 86,156
  Isam 116,140
  Jacob R. 144,145
  Joshua 230
  Laurena 188
  Laurenia 134
  Lutenia 188
  Permelia 2 ,281
  Philip H. 86,156
  Thomas 237
  W. H. 139,198,213
  Wm. F. 175
Broom, Edmund 97
  Moses 242
  Solomon 242
Brouch, A. J. 130
Broughton, John A. 238
Browder, M. A. 319
  Milton H. 319
Brown, --- 316,258

Brown, (Orphans) 48,80,87,
  153
  A. 70
  Benj. 146
  Benjamin 310
  Bennett W. 221
  Charles 87,153
  Charles W. 87,153
  C. W. 87,153
  D. H. 131
  D. M. 266
  Edwin R. 243
  Edmund 97
  Eliphalet E. 218
  Evan 257
  Frances 315
  Francis 181
  George A. 29,172
  Jno. 310
  Jno. U. 105,107
  John 23,310,301
  John D. 48,80
  John H. 29,129,172
  John U. 105,107
  John W. 266
  Josiah 118
  Lewis S. 218,37,125,151,
  179,203,238
  M. 100,289
  M. W. 314
  Morgan 100,147,289
  S. B. 199,282
  Sarah 90,134
  Sarah A. 240
  Sarah M. 257,258
  Thomas A. 86,157
  Thomas R. 181
  Thos. A. 86
  W. 266
  William 48,80,86,156
  William B. 173,217
  Wm. B. 32,101,164
Browne, Mary H. 241
Browning, J. R. 61
Broyles, Cain 323
Bruton, Nicholas 133
Brux, W. 289
  Armand R. 289
  William 289
Bry, W. M. 214
Bryan, (Orphans) 191
  David 218
  Delia 267
  Ezekiel 284
  James 229
  James E. 191
  Joseph 191
  L. 270
  Mary G. 191
  Susan P. 191
  Susannah 41
  Theophelus 239,240
  Thomas P. 240
  Thos. P. 240
Bryant, Jesse 291
Bryce, William 129,188
Brzman, John 113
Buchan, John 186
Buchanan, C. W. 189,190
  Charles W. 189
  G. F. 125
  George 102
  George F. 125
  James 204,290
  John D. 189
  Margaret 290
  Maria 268
  Martin G. 268
Buchannon, Joseph J. 91
  J. W. 91
  Thos. E. 91
Buckannon, James 239
  Joseph J. 91

Buckannon, Thos. E. 91
Buckley, Constantine W.132
  Elizabeth 255
  Jane T. 132
  John 255
Buckner, L. D. 89
Buckus, John 117
  John, Sr. 117
Buel, Wyllys 28
Buffington, Ezekiel 71,117
Buford, Henry 224
Bugg, E. 309
  Edmund 309
  Obedeance 309
Bull, O. H. 115
  O. K. 158
  Orville H. 159
Bullard, James M. 16,173
  N. 195
Bullock, R. H. 207
  Thomas 146
Bunch, Arthur 289
Burch, Jno. 304
  Mortin N. 62
Burchfield, Zachariah F.
  65
Burge, Rebecca 54,251
Burham, Lyman 88
  Sarah A. 88
  William L. 88
Burk, Saml. J. 49
Burke, Thomas 68,253
  Thomas J. 68,253
Burkhalter, --- 206
  D. H. 87
  D. N. 87,206
  N. 125
Burkhannon, (Orphans) 241
  John 241
Burlong, Henry 163
Burks, Elisha 193
  Fortune 23
  James, Jr. 300
  Robert 32
  Wiley P. 23
Burnett, A. G. 74,267,268
  Samuel 74,267,268
  Samuel M. 267
  Saml. M. 74
  William F. 74,267
Burnette, Samuel 292
Burney, R. 116
  Sylvanus W. 125
Burns, (Orphans) 207
  James 207
  Lard 207
  Mary 207
  Robert L. 207
Burr, Jason 57,251
  Richard 315
Burris, Wm. 141
Burrows, Jas. E. 141
Burson, B. F. 195
  Elisha 284
Burton, (Orphans) 143
  Charles 36
  Henry A. 143
  Nicholas 133
  Sarah 143
  Thomas 72
  Thomas S. 72
Busba, William H. 282
Bush, John B. 193,204
  John W. 175
  S. J. 70,136,242
  William W. 177
Butler, Dr. --- 228
  (Orphans) 294
  A. J. 17,103
  Frederick W. 268
  Joel 27
  John 103
  Phineus 82

Butler, Shem 294
  W. Thomas 267
  William A. 294
Butrume, Manar 159
Butt, John 205
  W. M. 258
Butts, Mrs. --- 284
  Mr. --- 286
  Arthur I. 134
  Celia 193
  Henry 150
  J. B. 257
  James 302,310
  James R. 253,257,264,
  279,284,285,303
  Jas. R. 265,298
  Joel W. 193
Byne, Enoch 279
Byrd, Benton 287
Byre, William 226
Byrn, Joseph T. 105
Byrom, Nancy 69
  William 69
  William H. 69
  Wm. H. 69
Byron, T. 196

Cain, John, Jr. 40
Caine, J. T. 91
Calaway, J. D. 54,278
Caldwell, (Orphans) 52
  Ann 52
  James 273
  John 189
  Margaret 52
  Robert 135
  Sarah 52
  William 52,232
  Wm. R. 279
Calef, Ebenezer 259,260
  Lethia 260
Calhoun, E. N. 179
  Ezekiel 38,56
  Milly Ann 271
  W. H. 45,290
  William D. 271
  Wm. B. 271
  Wm. H. 160
Callaway, (Orphans) 134
  140
  Anna 134
  Benjamin 134
  Daniel 134
  Enoch 285
  Felix 140
  Isaac 140
  J. D. 251
  Jonathan 134
  Josiah D. 134
  Levicy 134
  Nancy 134
  Sarah 134
  Thos. E. 167
  William 134
Callott, Cicero 43
Camack, James 6
Cameron, B. H. 182,217
  Benjamin H. 182,217
  James 217
Camfield, (Orphans) 130,
  131
  Abiel 3,131
  Elizabeth I. 3
  Elizabeth J. 131
  John 3,131
  Lydia 131
  Lydia Octavia 3
  Mary 3,131
  Octavious 131
  Rebecca 3,130,131
  Sarah 3,131
  William A. 41,111
Camp, Edward K. 285

Camp, Edward R. 285
  H. H. 240
Campbell, Edward 148
  Edward H. 155
  Griffith 8,212
  H. A. 296
  John 125,144,280,282,
    299
  John S. 148,155
  Joseph 211
  Lewis 275
  Susannah 275
  Virginia 8,212,213
  William D. 73,74,160
Camson, Robt. 239
Canant, John H. 317
Candler, (Orphans) 174
  S. C. 154
  Samuel C. 121
  W. S. 154
  William Mc. 174
Cannon, --- 107
  Allen 244,313
  James 107
  Jane 107
Cans, Susan Ann 30
Cant, Susan Ann 30
Cants, (Orphans) 43
  Alexander F. M. 43
  Andrew M. 43
Cape, Marion T. F. 19
  T. F. M. 19
Caper, Temple F. 53
Caraway, (Orphans) 176
  James 176
  Sarah Ann 176
  Thomas 176
  William R. 176
Cardell, --- 270
  Peter 270
Careton, Dickson 175
Cargile, Augustus 75,211
  224
  J. I. W. 117
  John 106
  Joseph I. W. 117
  R. B. M. 117
  Runn B. M. 117
Cargill, Augustus 178,239
Carleston, Stephen 99
Carleton, John M. 99,158
  Stephen 158
Carlston, John M. 99
Carlton, John 45,239,291,
  311
Carmichael, John 159,160
Carn, Joseph 201
Carnes, R. W. 139
  Robert W. 13
Carpenter, W. W. 169
Carr, John 49
Carrington, Augustus G.149
  Henson 149
  Mary 44
  Orsburn 44
Carruthers, Joseph 213
Carswell, Beniah S. 281
  Sarah 242
  W. E. 242
  William E. 242
Cartarpher, James T. 132
Carten, Mary 56
Carter, Amelia E. 280
  Farish 209
  James 239,276
  Mary 122
  Thomas J. 280
  Wiley 93,96,121
Case, Duncan 120
  Dunly 120
  Martha 100
  Robert 120
  Thomas 100
Casey, John 293,294

Cash, Howard 240
  Nelson 240
Cason, James McC. 174
  Myriott 31
  Susan 161
  Wyriott 161
Casper, Temple F. 78
Cass, Mary 86
Castens, Mary 56
Caster, Peter 191
Castleberry, (heirs) 218
  Mark 218
  William 41,50,60,191
  William M. 218
  Wm. S. 218
Catching, J. T. 306
Cates, Amanda 94,154
  Ladawick M. 154
  Lodowick M. 94
  Robert H. 152
Caully, Betsy Jane 197
  Robert 197
Cavender, Clemmeth 134
  Rebecca 134
Caveness, DeMarcus A. La-
  fayette 141
  Henry 141
  Napoleon Bonapart 141
  Sarah 141
Cawley, Cornelius 177
Cawthorn, Orville 165
Cerester, Harman E. D.281
Chaffin, Stephen 105
Chain, Fauntleroy F. 67
  253
Chamberless, Char. V. 116
Chambers, ...215,245
  Elizabeth 215
  Hardin 245
  Nicy 129
Chambliss, Henry 212
  Lawson G. 212
  L. G. 212
Chandler, Authaniul 58
  Bailey 195
Chapman, ---303
  Ambrose 303
  G. M. 219
  Giles M. 218
  James A. 118,190,226
  Joseph 58,59
  Milley 303
  Samuel 218
  Solomon S. 282
  William 244
Chappell, Joseph J. 122
  Thomas 313
  Thos. S. 314
Charlston, Jno. 182
  Charlton, John 63
  Jno. 63
Chartiez, Pde. Le 266
Chastain, Benjamin T. 33
  171
  E. W. 33
  J. S. 33
  John B. 206
  Madison C. 33,170,171
Chatham, E. M. 236
Cheany, Francis A. 26,172
Cheatham, James L. 313
  Martha M. 313
Cheny, F. A. 26,172
Chester, William P. 239
Chestnut, Ann 93,94,154
  Daniel 93,154
  Isaac 154
Chesnut, Mary 175
Childs, Henry 99,120,204
  J. B. 286
  Jonathan 275
  John B. 286
  Robert 286
Childress, Holman 200

Chinniaker, --- 47
Chisolm, (Orphans) 318
  Andrew 318
  Edward D. 174
  P. J. 318
Christian, (Orphans) 124
  Elijah W. 76,156
  Elijah W., Jr. 76,156
  William 76,156
Christopher, Lilly 260
  William 260
Church, G. C. 323
  Robert S. 322,323
Churchill, (Orphans) 208
  Joseph J. 208
  Sarah 216
  Simon 216
Cicker, John M. 141
Cinson, D. R. 227
Clapp, J. P. 223
  Julius R. 223
Clapton, Maj....308
Clark, General...302
  Governor...301
  (Heirs) 121
  (Minors-5) 192
  (Orphans) 73,74
  A. S. 74
  Arthur S. 73
  B. W. 277,286
  David 74
  Davies 73
  Eliza F. 73
  George 247
  James 105,108,192,284
  Jno. M. 128,148
  John L. 130
  Luke F. 262
  Mary 121,122
  Peter 99
  Sarah 192
  Seaborn J. 118
  T. W. 323
  Thomas 121,122
  Thomas C. 217
  Thomas R. 247
  Thomas W. 323
  William 121,122
  William F. 75
  Z. H. 240,241
Clarke, General...302
  Governor...313
  A. S. 73
  Arthur S. 74
  L. D. 67
  Michael N. 278
Claxton, James 110
Clay, G. B. 190
Clayton...163
  G. R. 293,301,302
  Milton 21
  P. A. 308,309
  Wm. 302
Cleghord, William H. 228,
Cleghorn, William H. 227,
  228
Clements, W. L. 146
Clemen/Clements, ..2,281
  Austin 2,281
  Elizabeth 281
  George 152
  Hosea 270
  Lilly Ann 2
  Lily Ann 281
  Matilda 2,281
  Nancy 2,281
  Permelia 2,281
  Robert H. 2,281
Clemmond, Elizabeth 104,105
  317
  Martha 104,105,317
  William 104,317
Cleveland, Benj. 16,235
  Joseph B. 318

Cleveland, Robert W. 238
Clevelin,...144
Clifton, Geo. 271
  Thomas 131
  William 131
Cline, Agnes 8,267,276
  Elizabeth S. 267,276
  Jane C. 8,267,276
  Jonathan 8,276
  Sarah 267
Clinton, Lawson 131
Clob...292
Cloud, J. M. 238
  John M. 238
  William 238
Clower, Thomas 142
Club, James 292
  William 292
Coats, Morgan 310
Cobb...7
  Edward 88
  Lewis 203
  Lues 200
  T. W. 228
  Wiley 88
  Wily 88
  Wm. A. 193,298
Cochran, Eliza 322
  Elizabeth 322
  John 323
  Lucinda 323
  Martin 311
  Miriam 311
  Sarah 322
  Thomas G. 175
Cockran, Eliza 322
  Elizabeth 322
  Lucinda 322
  Sarah 322
  Sarah W. 214
Cody, Peter 190,199
Coff, John 302
Coffe, Genr...231
Coffee, Cleveland 37,38
  Edward 38,44
  Joel 38
Coffery...144
Coffey...144
Coffie, Peter H. 254
  Susan A. 254
Cogburn, John A. 128
  John A. 176
Cohen, Solomon 151,262
Coker, Daniel 166
  Sylva 147
  Sylvia 289
Cockran, John R. 175
Colbert, John G. 37
  John S. 37
  Thomas 200
Coldwell, Ann 249
  Margaret 249
  Sarah 249
  William 249
Cole, Carleton B. 123
  C. B. 248
  James 71,86
  Samuel M. 187
Coleby, John 174
Coleman, Daniel T. 200
  Henry W. 323
  James L. 120
  Sarah 120
  Thomas 117,142,175
Collat, Cicero L. 87
Collatt, Cicero L. 87
  John 87
Collet, Cicero L. 43
Colley, John 192
  Zachariah 193
Collier, C. C. 83
  Chloe C. 83
  Edward W. 150

Collier, James 220
Colliers, Elisha 248
Collins, Henry 39,40
  Jno. B. 283
  John B. 278
  Nancy 29
  W. A. L. 278,283
Collot, Cicero L. 81
Collot, Collott...43,80
  Cicero L. 80
  John 43
Colly, James 142
  Martha 142,143
Colquett...306
Colquitt, John H. H. 107
  John N. N. 105
Colston, Charles 13,125
  Charles H. 13,125
Comer, Hugh M. 137
  John F. 137
Compton, Jordan 310
  P. M. 77,105,129,146,
  160,162,166,167,188,
  208,244,247,274
  Pleasant M. 262
Conant, John H. 104,318
Condon, William 91,92
Cone, Peter 277
  William B. 277
Connandy, Wm. 288
Connaway, Wm. 42,222
Connel, Jesse 313
Connely, Patrick B. 37
Conner, Edward 173,221
  John 4
Conyers, B. H. 131
Coody, C. M. 260
Cook, F. T. 189
  Francis T. 189
  Harriet M. 22
  Hugh 254
  Isaken 247
  James 222
  Joab 30,126,247
  Judy 222
  Keelin 29,87,153,208,
  241,298
  Olive 132
  Thomas M. 30,46,106,117,
  280,317,321,322
  Thos. M. 180
  Thos. W. 179
  William L. 70,172
Cooke, Harriet M. 22
  Nathaniel M. 22
Cooksy, Caleb 188
  Ferribe 187,188
Cool, James 71
Cooly, James J. 231
Coombs, Martha A. 16
Coonce, Benj. 156
Cooper, George W. 177
  James 147
  Joseph M. 101
  Marthy 177
  Mary A. 260
  Samuel 147
  Temple F. 165,207
Cope, Geo. L. 262
Copeland (Illegitimates)
  221
  Lucy 187
  Mary Ann 138
  Nancy 221
  Stephen 187
Coppedge, Charles R. 181
  John W. 31,81,170,176,
  181,248,263
  Lewis 248
Corb, Peter 162
Cordell, Wm. H. 118
Cordemon, Fredrick 56
  Frederick 252

Cordemon, Martha 56,252
Corker, Drury 288,304
Corley, Davenport 173
  Elizabeth 173
  Jeremiah 173
  John C. 147
Corner, Benj. 86
Corr, John 49
  Joseph 49
Corry, A. 134
Cottle, Ebenezer J. 113
  John J. 113
Cotton, Abraham 176
  Henry 274
Couch, Eliza Ann 320
Courter, Edward D. 281
  Harmon E. D. 281
  Samuel H. 281
  Susan 281
Courvoise, John F. 268
  Sarah 268
Courvoisie, James A. 268
Couston, John 315
Cowdery, U. U. 294
Cowen, James 221
  Martha 221
Cowles, E. M. 64
Cox, Cary 102,251
  George 85
  James 85,142
  Orren D. 319
  Stephen 143
  William B. 178
Coxe, Cary 54
Coxwell, Benjamin 206
  John 206
  Mitchell 206
Cozart, H. W. 116
  Hubbard W. 116
Craddick, Mary 68,249
Craig, Jno. 168
Cramer, Elisha 232
Crane, Reoss 122
Cranston, Mary 269
  W. 269
  Walter 269
Crapon, Wm. 111
Crasswell, Henry 282
Craun, John 132
Craven, John 47,79
Crawford, A. J. 106
  Elijah 185
  Elisha 152
  Enoch 299
  James 185,299
  Jefferson 185
  H. 284
  John 268
  Nathan 294
Cray, Scott 181
Crenshaw, S. P. 208
Crew, Eliza 126
Crocker, Elijah E. 5,221
Croft, Deward 109
  Edward 108
Crofton, Bennet 18
  Bennett 173
Crompton, David 61,155
Crosby, B. R. 134
Cross, Richard 310
Crossley, Edward 81,157
  Jno. 81,157
  Lemuel 81
  Lemuel P. 157
  Mary 81,157
Crow, Abner 211
  Ann 203
  Burns 126
  Eli 203
  Isaac 226
  Martin 211
Crowd, Wm. 77,180
Crowder, Jno. 301

Crowder, Thomas 193
Crowell, E. S. 241
  Elisha S. 241
  H. 297
Crowley, Mary 140
  Spencer 140
Crumney, Nancy 123
  Rebecca 123
Crutchfield, Hilliard 123
Cuff, Richard B. 280
Culberson, James 138
Culbertson, Jefferson 27
  Wm. P. 27
  Wm. T., Jr. 27
Culpepper, Benjamin 203
  David 205
  Dickerson 205
  Rachel 75
  Washington 160,161
Culver, Leren O. 271
Cumming...164
  Andrew 164
  Gideon 18
  Henry A. 269
Cummings, Alahala 149
  Gideon 149
  Thomas 18,149
Cummins, Gideon 18
  Jos. 203
  Joseph 203
Cunningham, Joseph 197
  Joseph T. 136
  Sarah 94,154
  Thomas M. 94
  Thomas W. 154
Cureton, Dickson 218
Curney, Major...233
Currcy, Ben. F. 145
Currey, Benjamin F. 181
Currie, Malcom 294
Currs, Elijah 230
Curry, B. F. 228
  John 127
  Lucinda 316
  William N. 316
  Wm. N. 317
Curtright, John 312
Curyler, Thomas H. 91
Cuthbert, John A. 146
  William Charles 295
Cuty, Richmd. 126

Dabney, Anderson W. 110, 111
Daggett, Ezra 67,253
Dahser, Wm. B. 311
Dalonville, Joseph 194
Dane, Henry G. 135
  John B. 135
Danforth, Saml. 223,211
Daniel...164
  Cunningham 200
  James P. 165
  Jno. W. S. 164
  Russell J. 323
  Thos. E. 159
  William 264
  Wm. 145
  Z. Y. 319
Danielly, Francis 102.103
Darby, Nicholas 270
Darden, Abner 263
  Jethro 151
  John B. 310
  William 263
Dardin, Zachariah 318
Darley, John 139
Darracott, F. W. 211
Darts, ...292
Dasher, William B. 310
Daugharty, Charles 6
Davenport, John 246
  Richard 182

Davenport, W. H. C. 311
  Wm. 18
David, John W. 40,61
Davidson, Asa 127
  Benjamin R. 158
  J. H. 127
  James M. 289
  John H. 127,158
  Paul 312
Davies, James W. 66
Davis, (Orphans) 51,134, 152,250,289
Davis,...95
  A. 198
  Abraham 198
  Arthur 289
  B. A. 39,60
  Benjamin 28
  Benjamin A. 39,60
  Dawson 152
  Elizabeth 117
  Elizabeth J. 47
  Elizabeth T. 202
  H. L. 157
  Isaac 124
  Isaiah 198
  James 223
  James M. 28
  James W. 66,185
  Jane 95
  Jno. 110
  John 28,110,323
  John F. 131
  Lewis 193,204
  Lewis L. 134
  Lucy 286
  Maria 28
  Maria R. 62,185,186
  Prier L. 55
  S, Newton 95
  Silas N. 95
  Thomas 128,142
  Thomas J. 128
  William 142
  Wm. H. 51,250
  Wm. J. 179
  Wm. P. 237
Davison, Cary 137
  Davis 32
  James M. 130
Dawson...231
  Davis 298
  Jno. R. 255,256
  W. C. 99
  William A. 148
Day, Joseph 214,264
  Stephen 246
Deadwyler, John G. 221
Dean, Archibald 246
  Elijah 246
  Mary 246
  Nimrod 117
  Shadrack 117
Deavours, John 234,235
Deen, Susannah 313
Dees, H. F. 321
  Martha 321
Delanney, John D. 161
DeLeGal, E. W. 202
  Edward J. 202
  Edward W. 202
  Embrie 202
  Henry 202
  Thomas 202
Delongs, Elisha 24
DeLouch, William 205
Demere, Caroline 279
  John 279
  Martha 279
  Mary 279
  May 279
  Paul 279
Demers, Dennis 192

Demerst, David 21
Demorest, David 189
Dempsy...227
Denard, John A. 151
Denham, R. S. 77,180
  Robert S. 77,180
Denmark, M. 71,72
  Malachi 179
Dennard, Kanzada 136
  Thomas W. 136
Dennis, Allen 241
  Charles A. 104,318
  E. W. 213
  Elizabeth 241
  Jacob 128
  Jasper N. 109
Dennuad, Edward 113
Denster, Henry L. 13
Dent, Benj. B. W. 53
  Joseph E. 118
  William B. W. 249
  Wm. B. W. 118,225
Denton...253
  James 82,99,180
  John 125
DeOlanney, J. D. 161
Depriest, Susan A. 221
Derby, (Orphans) 52,249
  Richard 52,249
Dernerast, David 41
Derrick...314
  John 314
Derrycoat, Francis W. 210
  Garland W. 210
Dexter, Benjamin W. 313
  Elizabeth C. 313
Dial, Doctor W. 32,66,185
  Temperance 32
Dibble, Samuel 197
Dickerson, Alpheous 47,202
Dickinson, C. 16
Dickson, G. W. 138
  John 183
  Martha 129
  Michael 256
Digby, Berry T. 264
  Eliza 264
  John 264
  Joseph 2
  Lucinda 264
Dill, Robert S. 96
  Robert S. 153,154
  Robt. S. 97
  William H. 96
  Wm. H. 97,153
Dillard, James 73,160
  Moses 237
  Nancy 237
Dillatonyn, Jno. S. 253
Dillon, Henry 260
  M. O. 42
  Mildred Ann 10,125
  Robert 114
  William C. 10,125
Dimon, Abel 89,194
  William T. 89,194
Dinson, William T. 194
Dives, Elizabeth J. 47
Dixon, Roger K. 183
D'Lynn, Abraham 72
  Anna 72
  Isaac 72
  Levi S. 72
  M. S. 72
  Mordecai J. 72
  Rebecca 72
D'Lyon, Abraham 124
  Anna 124
  Isaac 124
  Levi S. 124
  M. S. 124
  Mordecai S. 124
  Rebecca 124

Dobbs, Jesse 92,39
Dodd, John J. 208
   John S. 196
Dodson, C. M. 65
   John P. 65
   Lidia 72
Doe, Joe 306
Doke, John 75,76
Donalson, William 261
Donoho, James 197
Donohao, James 198
Donough_, Maria 268
Donougho, Maria 268
Dooly, Thomas 235
Dorsey, James M. 278
Doss, Azariah 212
Dossey, Edmund 140-141
   Martha 141
Doster, Benjamin 218
   Mary 218
Doty, Mary 37
Dougherty, Wm. 158
   William 158
Douglas, George 236,47,250
   John 100
   William 277
Douglass, John 101
Doures, Shelby 92-93
Dowd, Burton W. 282-144
Downe, Thomas 177
Downing, John 198
Downs, Captain...258
   Jesse M. 179,180
Downey, William M. 135
Dowse, Burton 299
   Elizabeth M. 205
   Saml. 205
Doyal, Leonard T. 103
   Leonard Y. 251
Doyle, Leonard T. 54
   Nancy 183
   William 53
Dozier, Woody 310
Dpyle, Leonard T. 310
Drake, Amillia 130
   Elias 130
   John C. 192
   Joshua 144
   Mary Ann 192
   Milly 130
   Thomas 130
Drane, Stephen 231-299
Drawe, Stephen 291
Drawhorn, Rich. 86-156
Driskill, Milly Ann 271
   Wooten 271
Dregors, Jacob 169
Dreskill, Christopher 310
Drew, Runion 77
Drysdale, Alex. 72-124
Duckworth, D. H. 323
Duffy, Thos. 179
Dufus, Leon G. 252
Dugas, P. 150
Dugger, John, Jr. 63-182
Duke, Gipson D. 118
   James 51-238
   Lucinda L. 118
   Lucinda S. 118
   R. T. 238
   Robert T. 238
   Samuel P. 238
Dukes, Matthew C. 50-51
   79
Dumass, D. 207 (David)
   E. B. 78
Dunagan, Joseph 121
Dunagane, Joseph 199
Dunagun, Joseph 126
Dunaway, Augustus B. 284
Dunbar, Hiram 188
Duncan, James 127
   John 145

Duncan, Susan M. 127
   W. D. 185
Dunham...58
   A. C. 57,58
   Cleon 58
   J. H. 57,58
   Jacob H. 58
Dunn, Ann H. 130
   Francis C. 130
   Thomas 228
   William 215
Durham, Alsey 310
   John P. 287,288
   Samuel D. 130
   Sanders W. 230
   Shelman 230
   Thomas 287
Durden, William 237
Durton, James 184
Dwine, John J. 239
   Mary 239
   W. D. 239
   W. F. 239
Dye, Benjamin 98,210
   Elizabeth 98,210
   George J. 261,262
   Thompson 262
Dyer, Edwin 230
   H. 151
   Hezekiah 151
   Nicholas 106
   Sarah D. 151
   Simpson C. 229
   Wiley 232
Dyess, Winafred 234
   Winnefried 234
Dykes, Burwell B. 204
   George 45,250
   Henry 45,250
Dyson, George 121,136
   John 136,151
   John N. 121,136,151
   Martha 136
   Wm. 226

Easco, George 27
Easley, J. I. 143
   Joseph I. 143
Eason, Wynett 183
Easter, Peter 191
Easty, J. I. 206
Eaverson, Allen 190
   Vienna 190
Eaves, William 99,158
Eberhart, James 41,42,251
Eberheart, Jacob 27
Echols, Jenkins 229
   Joseph 181,203
   Joseph H. 7,177,200,
      202
Echols, Tompkins 155
Ector, Louisa M. 132
   Mathew D. 132
   Mathus D. 132
Edgar, (Orphans) 220
Edge, John 46
   John M. 46
   Joseph 2,312
Edmondson, Jiney 320
   Mahala 320
Edv, John M. 170
Edward, Allen 199
Edwards, (Orphans) 208
   Allen 155,196
   Andrew 208
   Ann 218
   Beal 63,182
   David R. 149
   Elizabeth A. 149
   George R. 214
   James W. 30
   John W. 276
   Levicy 134

Edwards, Littleberry 30
   M. P. 275
   Martha 30
   Milsey L. 43
   Thomas J. 30
   William Y. 30
Edy, John 170
   John W. 169,170
Eidson, John R. 262
   Thomas 262
Elands, Alex. W. 161
   William 161
Elder, (Orphans) 38,60
   Eliza 38,60
   H. 217
   H. W. 294
   Harrison W. 294
   J. H. 275
   James 38,60
   James P. 294
   John L. 131
   S. G. 259
Eleg, John W. 161
Elford, C. J. 321
Elisha, Smart 262
Ellington, Henry T. 294
Elliot, James S. 141
   Jas. S. 141
Ellis, G. B. 217
   J. B. 205
   James M. 40,140,242
   John W. 311
   Joseph B. 290
   Malinda 307
   Melinda 305
   William C. 306,307,308
   William L. 305
   Wm. C. 305,306
Ellison, Matthew 186
Elmore, David 228
El(um?), Mark S. 105
Elry, John W. 135
Elyea, Chas. H. 272
Embrey, Joe 59
   Joel 49,50,59
   Johannah 49,50,59
English, Jonathan 147
   Sarah 175
Eppinger, Hannah E. 113
   James 113,194
   Jas. 113,114,194
Epps, A. C. Vann 320
Esley, John W. 151
Espy, James 235
Estes, James 126,191
   James H. 310
   Mary 126,191
   Miles H. 312
   R. C. 310
   Simeon 191,238
   Zachery 310
Estill, W. H. 107
   Wm. H. 107
Eubank, Edward 127
   Nancy C. 127
Eubanks, Nancy C. 127
Evans, Ardew 189
   Charles 116
   Elizabeth 159
   Ezekiel 273
   Geo. W. 5,279
   James 48,79
   Jennett 104,318
   John 220
   John P. 189
   Jos. M. 243
   Joseph M. 243
   M. 321
   Stephen 318
   William 183
   William G. 48,79
Evanson, Viena 190
   Alan 190

Eve, Paul F. 272
Evens, Steven 104
Everett, James A. 282
Evertson, John 127
  Laura 127
Ewing, James 109-317
  John 109-317
  Sarah 317
  Sarah V. 109
  Thomas 109-317
Exley, John 234
  John M. 264
Exeey, John W. 52
Exley, John W. 30-37-97+
  98-143-161-162-186-196-
  219-227-257
Ezell, Levi 273

Fair, Peter 219
Fanch, Jonas 48,80
Fannin, Abraham B. 64
  Abraham Baldwin 72-124
  Abram B. 22
Farell, James 192
Farley, Alexander 136
  John 229
  Mathew 136
  Matthew T. 136
  Samantha J. 136
Farman, Joel C. 172
  James 172
Farmer, F. 246
  Frederick 245
Farnal, William 261
Farrar, Jesse C. 154
Farrow, Jesse C. 132
Farrar, Elizabeth Jane 316
  Jesse 93
  Lucinda 316
  Peter 316,317
  Robert 317
Farrell, James 192
Fauch, Jonas 48
Faulk, James G. 167
Faulkner, John 310
  Zachariah 310
Fay, Mary F. 281
Fears, Ezekiel 310
Fedrick, Austin 164-165
Felt, Joseph 62-71-186-234
  262-264
Felton...164
  Robert 217
Felwood, James 234
Fergerson, John G. 6
Ferguson, John G. 125
Ferrell, Mecklebury 308
Ferrel, Michlebury 138
Ferrell, Wm. 308
Ferrill, Benjn. 199
  Edy 192
Few, Emily E. 244
Fielder, William 227
Fields, Charles 228
  Sarah 48-79-80
Files, Wm. B. 107-317
  Wm. R. 107
Finch, Burdit 181
Findlay, Robert 49-59-264
Findley, Roleet 153
  Samuel 153
  Samuel M. 49-59-153
  Thomas J. 264
Finley, Saml. 209
Finney, James 162
Finsley, Wm. B. 274
Fish, Geo. W. 248
  William 248
Fithean, Isaac 245
Fitten, Isaiah C. 215
  John C. 215
Fittes...229
Fitzgerald, John 240
  Joshua 240

Fitzpatrick, Jackson 69
Fleck, Michael 36,171
Fleming, Cela 119
  James 61,119
  Perry H. 136
  Porter 138
  Samantha J. 136
  W. T. P. 61
Fletcher, John 108
Flewellen, Abner H. 155
  Mary Ann 192
  William 155
Fling, John 180
Flournoy, Geo. W. 27
  George W. 26
  Saml. W. 223
Flowers, James M. 159
Flows, James M. 159
Floyce, Dolphin 212
Floyd, Alexander 66-185
  Dolphin 278
  Dalphin 70
  John G. 37
Fluker, B. F. 40-242
  Caroline 208
  John 291
  S. Q. 242
  Sarah 291
  Sarah Q. 40-242
  William T. 208
Flynn, Patrick W. 132
Flynt, Augustus W. 294
  James H. 267
  John 267
Follom, Mary 91
Folsem...100
  P. 101
  Elisha 289
Folsom, Penevill 295
  Penseville 207
Fondren, John G. 64
Forbes, Catharine 101-182
  John M. 101-102-182
Ford, John 24
Forester, Joel 288
Forsyth...303
  John 310
Forter, Robert G. 25
Foster, A. G. 265
  Elijah 135
  Joel 258
  John 263
  John S. 113
  N. G. 87
  Paintan S. 139
  Peggy 25
  Robert G. 25
  Thomas M. 139
  William 121-264
Foule, Hezekiah W. 111
Fouler, William 115
Fountaine, Joseph M. 264
Foute, G. W. 323
Fowler, Dennis 70
  Eda 173
  John 266
  Nicy 36
  Wiley 36
  William 7-8-178-232
  Zaphaniah 7-8
Foy, George 311
Fraeme, Jas. 197
Frambro...267
  Allen G. 267
Frank, ...150
Franklin, David 301
  Marcus A. 218
  Nelson 301
Frars, Richard 142
Fraser, S. 57 (Simon)
Freeman, Eleanor 300
  Hugh 228
  Jacob 100
  James 228

Freeman, James, Jr. 228
  James, Sr. 228
  John 285
  Simeon 310
  William 300
French, Sarah 49,62,80
  William 49,62,80
Fret, Joseph 95
Fridges, Malinda 54-55
  Stephen 54
Frierson, J. D. 133
Frost, Saml. 122,133,212,
  222
Fudge, Elizabeth 311
  Jacob 311
Fulgham, Hardy 110,320
  Harry 110
  Henry 320
  William E. 110,320
Fuller, John 65
  Simeon, Jr. 243
  Spivey 49,80-118
  Spivy 62
  William 227
Fullom, James 91
  Joseph 91,92
  Luke 91,92
  Mary 91
Fulton, Dillion D. 235
  Elizabeth C. 97
  James 235
  R. L. 115
  Samuel 317
  Sarah 115
  Susan R. 317
  Thomas 97
  Thomas L. 97-98
  William D. 115
Funderbuss...286
Furlason, Daniel 232
Furlow, C. M. 36
  Charles 35,36
  Charles M. 35
  David 46,81
  Edward A. 35
  Margaret M. 35
  O. S. 165
  O. T. 46-81
  Osborn S. 46-81-165
  Rebecca A. 35
  Susannah M. 3-261

Gable, ...172
  Henry 26-172
Gachet, Caroline M. 298
Gaines, Liveston P. 175
  Mary E. 175
Gallen, Furney F. 261
Gallick, Edward 297
Gambel, James 305
Gambell, Ayres 306-307
  Eleanor 306
  James 305-
Gamble, James 189
  R. L. 247
Gamel...306
  Ayers 308
  James 307-308
Gamell, Ayres 307
  James 308
Gammell, Eleanor 308
Gammell, Elizabeth, Jr. 307
Gammell, James 306-307
Gandy, Griffin 7-283
  Nancy 283
Ganier, Elizabeth 198
Gardner, Ezekeil 196
  James 201
  James, Jr. 201
Garlick, Edward 162-255
  266
  John 162
  Judah 162
Garner, Harriet 140

Garner, Osborn 210
Garratt, William 190-191
Garrett, Abraham 100
   James 241
   Lumpkin J. 241
Garrison, David 143
   Elizabeth 143
   Harriet 321
   Thos. W. H. 38
Gartrell, Joseph 280
   Lucy H. 280
Garvin, James 239
Gashett, Benjamin 298
Gaslin, Simon 240
Gass, Charles 323
Gaston...308
Gates, James 166-212
   James, Jr. 17
   James, Sr. 17
   Thos. 166
Gatewood, Philip 283
   Sary 49
Gathright, M. H. 33
Gatlin, L. M. 150-176-245
   Thomas M. 204
Gaulding, A. A. 83-176-190-263
Gawtaw, William 140
Gay, Francis 191
   William S. 191
Geany, Richard 261
Geiger, Armon H. 94
   H. H. 94
   Harman H. 94
   Randal C. 290
Gellesbee, Samuel 141
Gembell, James 308
Gemmell, Elizabeth Sr. 307
George, Alfred M. 110
   Forney 56
Gerald, H. W. 6-200
Gholson, Anthony 293
   John 237-293
Gibbs, Elizabeth 281
Gibon...314
   Augusta 314
Giboney, Wm. 303
Gibs, A. 76
Gibson, ...230
   John C. 262
   O. C. 298
   Polly 230
   Shadrack A. 5-200
   Thomas 205
   Thomas N. 298
Giddens, Edward 190
Gilbert, Allen 47-201
   Elizabeth 47-201
   Elizabeth J. 47-202
   Wiliam 299
Giles, William L. 229
Gill, Wm. G. 321
Gilleland, Allen 100
Gillis, Norman 225
Gilmer, Elizabeth 70-71
   James 71
   Silas 178
   William G. 168
Gilmon, Lucinda 29-191
   William G. 191
   Wm. G. 29
Gilmore, Hughey 316
   Pamilia 178
   Silas 178
   Stephen 316
Gilstrap, R. W. 131
   Rial 131
Ginn, Margaret 94
   William H. 94
Girens, ...60
Giriam, William H. 154
   Margaret 154
Gist, Richard 191

Givens,...39
Glascock, Thomas 163-169
Glass, William P. 115
Glaze, Jacob 122
   Jospeh 122
Glazier, Franklin H. 211
Gleenworth, Edwd. H. 304
Glen, George W. 284
   Elisabeth 284
   Thomas A. 284
Glenn, Andrew J. 149
   Ann. Sr. 94 95
   Franklin 174
Glore, George W. 39
Glove, George W. 39=60
Glover, Allen 178
   H. 156
   J. 86
   Martha A. 16
   Mary 86-156
   Robert D. 16
   Sabetha F. 156
   Saliba F. 86
   Wiley 233
Gnann, Josh 268
Gober...145
   Asa 77-180
   William Y. 180
   Wm. Y. 77
Gobert, Benj. 274
Godard, Daniel 139-184
Godbee...286
Godkin, Jas. W. 23-47
   Pas. W. 209-232
Godley, James M. 239
   John M. 239
Godwin...250-265
   Barnabas 43-250
   Henry 43
   Henry A. 250
   Henry F. 43-250
   Henry J. 43
   J. H. 43-250
   Jonathan H. 43-250-170
Goggins, Abraham 39-78
Gogley, John M. 239
Going, Judah 294
Golden, Joseph 218
Goldwin, James A. 278-279
Goodman, Aaron 120
   John 96
Goodno, Warren 310
Goodnow, Warren 310
Goodwins, J. A. 98
Goolsby, C. L. 75
   Elizabeth 222
   Wm. 168
Goodwin, J. C. 190
Gorden, Elizabeth 62
   John 92
Gordon, John 92
   John B. 56-58-262
Goss, Riley 83-84
   William S. 198
Goulding, A. A. 124
   Peter J. 121
   Thomas A. 121
Grace, John 269
   Matthew 18-173
Graham, Henderson 295
   Joseph 277
   Martin 237
   Peter 120
Grant, Ambrose H. 47-202
   Aug. S. 140
   James 222
   John 177
   John O. 175
   Joseph 146
   Nathan 61
   Nathaniel 61 155
Graves, Barzellai 165
   James P. 268

Graves, John Y. 268
   More 141
Gray, A. 137-236
   Archibald 235
   Daniel 192
   Frances 29
   James 54-235-252-321
   John 305-306
   John H. 68
   John J. 68-192-253
   Joseph 4
   Rebecca 192
   Rebecca E. 192
   Sanders W. 182
   William S. 29-168
Graybill, John W. 127
Greathouse, Abraham 231-232
Gregory, Reuben 221
Green, (Orphans) 20
   Curtis 33-171-183-219
   Elizabeth M. 278-279
   Isaac 199
   J. C. 81-138
   James A. 52-183-249
   James B. 295
   John 20=123
   N. B. 77-84-162
   Napoleon B. 84
   R. A. 254
   R. D. 53
   Richard 276
   Richard N. 123
   Robert D. 53
   Thomas 20-82-199
   Thomas F. 193
   Wm. C. 239
Greene, James W. 22
   James W. 176
   Judah 295
   R. A. 181-219
   Thomas 263
   Thomas B. 176
Greenwood, Benjamin L. 127
   L. A. G. 127
   Lithitia A. G. 127
Greer, Gilbert D. 217
   James 223
   John 217
   Jno. C. 125
   M. C. 6
   William C. 15-18-88-171-172-213
   Wm. 275
Gresham, Archd. 128
   Davis C. 46-179
   Edmond B. 4
   Edward 205-211
   S. H. R. 242
   Sterling H. R. 242
   Young H. 45-250
Grice, Sarah 279
Grieve, Miller 260
Griffin...83
   Andrew B. 13
   Anderson 263
   Edward 245
   J. S. 217
   Mary P. 263
   Mary T. 263
   Robt. F. 81-157
   Snowden 293-294
Griffith, Henry W. 150
   Mary 17
   Nancy M. 150
Griffis, Junipher 234
   Junniper 234
Grimes, Striband 39
   Stribland F. 78
   Stribling F. 38-39
   Stubind F. 78
   Thomas P. 38-78
Grist, Richard 41-191
Groce...157

Groce, Ellison 297-298
  Lewis J. 184
  Hannah 297-298
  Solm. 86-157
  Solomon 86-156
Groover, Chas. E. 96
  D. B. 96
  David 40
  David, Sr. 71
  S. E. 96
Grove, Solomon 85
Groves, Catherine 227
  Charles 227
  Eliza 227
  James W. 76-180-196
Gross, Thos. 125
Grubbs, Hannah 214
  J. 218
  Silas 127
Grum, James W. 298
Gudger, William 144
  Wm. 144
Guest, Thomas 116
Guice, Steren 279
  Thos. 276
Gulless, B. F. 311
Gunn, Elizabeth 178
  G. A. 227
  Jane 178
  Mary 178
  Nelson 178
  Pamilia 178
  William 234
  William C. 234
  William H. 139
Guthright, M. H. 117-122
Guyse, Nicholas4 Jr. 319
  Nicholas, 319
Gwinn, Mary 220

Ha---, Barnett 86
Habersham, J. C. 290
Hackney, James F. 267
Haddock, Caswell 105
  Cynthia 105
  Emily 175
  J. B. 105
  Sarah 175
Hagan, Calvin 208
Hail, John 121-135-212-241
Haile, Elizabeth 256
Hale, Enoch 115
  Mark A. 142
Hall, Absolem 267
  Alexander 240
  Asa 20-81
  Asoph 188
  Benj. 9-66-18,
  Cincinnatus 237
  George 47
  Henry 164
  Hugh 164
  Hugh, Sr. 164
  J. R. 48-49-59-80;
  153-158-174-242-264-283
  James 152
  James C. 113
  James H. 209
  Jas. M. 273
  John 321
  Mary 243
  Seaborn 188
  Thomas 209
Hallaway, James 209
Halliman, Eliza 285
Halls, Absolum 74
Hamby, R. E. 293
  R. E. A. 293
  Thomas 241
  Thomas 241-242
Hamle, J. H. 101
Hames...265

Hamelton, Calvin 190
  Adeir 190
  Irwin 190
  Joseph 190
  Sarah Ann 190
Hamer, Seth 149
Hamilton, B. B. 291
  Caroline 184-185
  David 184
  Duke 187
  E. 187 Evirard 187
  George N. 246
  James 169
  Joseph J. 71
  Mary 184
  Sarah 61-155
  T. T. 184-185
  Thomas P. 246
Hammoc, Mary 176
Hammock, Hope H. 237
Hammond, Amos. W. 323
  C. S. 90
  Chas. D. 260
  Job 323
  M. C. M. 168
  Marcus C. M. 168
Hampton, F. A. 51
  James 3
  Nancy 3
Hana, Isaiah 247
Hannah, Catherine 274
  Thomas 274
Hanberry, Henry 195
  Moses 195
Hancock, John 321
  Wm. 310
Hand...275
  Hannah L. 126
  Isaiah 30-126
  Rachel 275
  Reuben 275
Handley, Sarah Ann 51-79
Hanes, Joshua 243
  James, Sr. 243
Hanks, James B. 148-149
  Mary A. 148
Hannock, H. H. 203
Hansell, Augustin H. 113
Hanson, James 226
Haralson, H. A. 101
  Hugh A. 101
Harbour, John 323
Harbuck, James 235
Hardaway, Thomas E. 167
Hardeman, Arabella R. 137
  Benj. F. 116-137
Harden, James 218
  John 76-165-156
  Nicholas 100-127
Hardiman...233
Hardin...218 -233
  Charles A. 55-255
  Charles B. 308
  Charley B. 308
  James 218
  Jas. 44,48,80,119
  Wm. 254
Hardman, B. S. 233
  Parks 215
Hardy, William P. 35,196
Harton, Charlotte A. 139
Hargett, Flynn 178,149
Hargrave, A. N. 239
Harman, John C. 284
  Zach. 32,255
Harmon...286
Harrell, John 199
  Simeon 199
Harrington, J. M. 92,231
Harper, David 75
  Elizabeth 34,120
  George 20,171
  Hannah 75

Harper, James 82,150,179
  Sexton 75
  T. 271 Thomas 271
  William, Se. 171
  William, Jr. 171
  Wm. Junr. 20
  Wm. Senr. 20
Harris,...100
  Alfred 133
  Ann March 137
  Arabella R. 137
  Augustus 141
  Barnett 157
  Benjamin 31,30,227
  Benjamin T. 142
  Buckner 238
  Caroline 208
  Churchill 227
  Churchwell 30,31
  Clara 100
  David 246
  Elias 183
  Ellen 179
  Eunice 238
  Giles 141
  Isom 246
  Iverson L. 104,110.111
  167,317
  J. Z. C. 105
  James A. 178
  James J. 246
  Joel N. 246
  John 132,208
  L. F. 263
  Lewis 312
  Mary A. 179
  Mary Ann 179
  Mary H. 246
  Mary P. 263
  Michael 179
  Robert 208
  Sanburn 183
  Stephen 257
  S. L. W. 257
  Stephen L. W. 157
  Stephen W. 137
  Susan M. 137
  Thomas E. R. 137
  Tyre 260
  Wiley 30,31,227
  William 208
  William G. 166,167
  William P. 291
  William Y. 246
Harrison, Benjamin 207
  H. R. 32
  Hillsberry R. 38,61-173-252
  J. 205
  John 200
  John B. 165-207
  Jonathan 204
  Sullivan 265
  Tilmon 126
  William 122
  William M. 172
Hart, Edmund S. 160
  Elizabeth W. 160
Harton, Augustus C. 139
  Wm. H. 204
Harts, Jonathan 127
Harvey, Elizabeth 260
  Jeremiah C. 123
  John H. 260
  John P. 86,156
Harvin, Peeter 181
Harvis, Clement R. 272,273
Harwell, J. F. 57
  T. B. 50,79,143,179
  Thomas B. 40,57
Haskins, Joseph 213
  Maria 213
  Mary Jane 200

Haskins, Selvinus 213
Hassel, Addison 294-295
Hatcher, Hamilton 297
   John 24
   Thomas 297
Hathaway, H. B. 113
   Henry B. 113
Hatt, Richd. 186-277
Haugh, Wm. H. 319
Hawthorn, Nathaniel 130
Hayes, Geo.rge 111-322
   James T. 111-322
   John R. 111-322
   Jno. R. 111-322
   Mary 111-322
Haygood, Atticus G. 272
   Green B. 272
   Wm. A. 273
Hayles, Fr. A. 188
   John M. 121
Hayman, Elisha 192
   Stephen 192
Haynes, A. O. 104
   Alvin O. 103
   Thomas 313-314
Hays, Eliza An 280
   George 191-238
   John 310
   R. 216 Richard 218-292
Head, Isaac 134
   William 15
   William J. 15
Heard, Falker 41
   George 115
   Geo. W. 261
   George F. 115
   George W. 261-266-271
   Joseph 41
Hearn, Francis S. 8-213
   William S. 221
   Wm. 258
Heary, Rose 248
Heath, Irvin D. 45-250
   Jordon, Sr. 304
   Margaret 40-57
   Margant 40-57
Heflen, William 188
Heggens, Eliza 57
   Eliza A. 57
Hemphill, Henrietta 36
Heirs, Thomas 307
Helst, Cornelius 223
Hemphill, Henryetta 36
   John 209
   Robert 209
Henderson, A. H. 186
   Brockman W. 227
   David 25
   Ferte 223
   John 249
   H. A. T. E. J. 25-171-172
   J. H. 25-172
   Jeremiah W. 25-171
   John 52
   Robert, Jr. 52-249
   Robert S. T. 25-171
Hendrick, G. 75-133(George)
   H. W. 123
   Jamiah 135
Hendricks, John H. 286
Henry, Albert 116
   Derricks 30
   Joseph 116
   Robert A. 232
Henson, James 291
Herb, George 196
   Jno. F. 229
Herd, Elizabeth 122
Heringdine, Thomas R. 204
Herndon, James 207=208
   Mary 207
Herren, Edmund R. 209

Herren, Elbert 209
   Peter 148
Hester, Wm. B. 220
   W. R. 64
   William R. 64
Hesterly, Francis 63
Hewet, George J. 190
Hibberts, C. 122
Hibler, I. A. 154
   Isaac A. 154-252
   Judith S. 154
Hichcock...207
   John 207
Hick, Eli 233
Hicks, Daniel 153
   Susan 153
   Thos. E. 121-135-283
   William 254
   Wm. 181
Hickle, Jesse 73
   Thomas 73
Hicks, Daniel 79
   Susan 79
   T. E. 73
Higdon, John B. 190
   John S. 190
Higgins, C. A. 83
   John J. 99
   Wiley G. 146
   William P. 273
   Sterling T. 143
High, John 119
Highsmith, Henry 242
   J. H. 39
   Jacob 242
   James 194-242
   John 242
   Sarah 242
Hightower, Echols 239
   James 86-156
   Jesse 168
Hiles, Hirum 62
Hill, Abner R. 119
   Adaline L. 118
   Benjamin J. 198
   Benjamin 231
   Charles M. 53-252
   Dorothy 118
   Edward Y. 221
   Elizabeth 231
   Frances C. V. 53
   Francis C. V. 252
   Harbard 321
   James W. 276
   John M. 279
   Joshua 262
   Martha 321
   Middleton 189
   Mountain 118
   Nancy 276
   Oliver P. 231
   Pressley 169
   Priscey 169
   Rachel 169
   Sarah A. 231
   Sion 15
   Susan 231
   Theophilus 118
   Thomas 257
   Warren H. 250
   Warren J. 51-198-223-285
   William M. 257
Hiller, Isaac A. 53
Hillhouse, Elijah 70
Hilliard, Francis 76
   Levi 239
   Maniy 239
   Nancy 239
   Quintine 239
   Robert 239
   Tilletha 239
   William 239

Hills, J. M. 200
Hinds, Homer 310
Hines, William 207
Hinton, Henry 138
   W. P. 143
Hitchcock, Raiford E. 55
Ho(---), Joel 86
Hobbs, Elizabeth 204
   Jonathan 285
   William 274
Hobby...302
   Wm. 302
Hobkirk, Sarah Jane 135
Hodges, Edmund W. 290
   Foreman 141
   John 141,242
   John J. 131
Hoge, Solomon 300,301
Hogan, John 136
   Shadrack 136
Hogon, John 136
Holcomb, Absalam 287
   Martin 121
Hold, Richd. 43
Holden, A. J. 239
   Wiley F. D. 260
Holder, Eliza 13,125
   William 13
Holiman, David 262
Holland, Charity 102,182
   James 102,182
   Joseph L. 247
Hollands, William 52,249
Hollaways, William 75
Hollenger, L. B. 269
Holley, James 176
   John 109,154
   John G. 109
   Mary M. 109
   Presley 93,154
   Presly 109
Holliday, Abner 316
   Allen 179
   Dennis Lark 296
   Nancy 179
   Richd. F. 179
   S. L. 316
   William D. 179
Holliman, David 72
   Elisha 285
   James 211
   John 313
   Samuel B. 211
   Thos. J. 313
Hollingsworth, D. G. 191
   Jacob J. 310,314
   Rebeca A. 35
Holloway, Anthony 165
   Edward 139,140
Holmes, Margaret 279
   Robert 218
Holms, Isaac 181
Hols, Presley 109
Holsombake, Lewis D. 135
Holt...306
   Asa 161
   Richd. 12
   Wm. 102,182
Holton, Nathaniel J. 166
   Stephen 69,249
   Van 69,70,248,249
Holtzclaw, Susan 260
Holzerdorf, Eveline 181
Holzendorf, William B. 313
Hones, James W. 252
Hood, Elizabeth 86,156
   Martha 141
   Nathaniel R. 89
Hooper...266
   Charles G. 236
   John M. 236
   John W. 177
   Johnson M. 236

Hooper, Thomas 288
  Thos. 142
Hooten, James B. 319
Hopkins, George 299
  Henry 299
  John L. 272,273
Hopper, Jos. F. 106
Hopson, Briggs W. 148-181
Horn, Benj. H. 30
  John 239
  Josiah 30
Horne, I. M. 67
  J. U. 42,209
Hornsby, Elizabeth 255
  John 255
Horton, A. M. 63-82-88-92
  123-148-152-186-219-
  Alfred 121
  Alfren M. 196
  Alford M. 206
  Alfred M. 2-3-15-18-20)
  31-34-50-60-72-83-85-
  88-94-101-115-117-120-
  124-127-129-130-131-
  133-134-138-139-150-
  153-155-159-165-166-
  167-169-170-171-174-
  179-186-187-188-194-
  201-212-213-214-215-
  240-242-243-244-245-
  246-255-260-266-269-
  271-278-280-286-304-
  312
  John 72
  Judge 86
Hott, Richd. 236
Houghton, Alfred M. 106
  222
House, John G. 15
  Samuel C. 181
Houston, M. M. 107
  Samuel 58-63-251
Howard, Allen 193
  Caroline Eliza 224
  Eliza 224
  Michael 193
  Nehemiah M. 223
  Nathan 244
  Samuel 152
  Thomas 232
Howel, James 125
Howell, B. 204
  Benjamin 204
  Burwell 308
  Daniel W. 244
  David 100
  James 125
  James, Sr. 125
  John J. 185
  John P. 66
  Meshack 114
  N. N. 244
  N. W. 208
  R. 204 Robert 204
  Thomas 204
  Thomas B. 193-204
Howle, D. H. 295
Howlkeld, Tulley 149
Hoyl, Geo. L. 133
  Geo. S. 85
Hoyt, Samuel B. 272
Hubard, Rial 197
Hubbard, Elijah 221
  Jacob 236
  Stephen 221
  Woodson 186
Huckaby, Hannah 260
  Isham 260
Hudgins, James 16
  Littleberry 74-180
  Phillip 16
Hudles, Penelope 78
Hudson, Charles 159

Hudson, David N. 149
  Elizabeth A. 149
  Irby 204
  Ivy 143
  John 115
  John L. 127
  John R. 158-159
  Madison 149
  W. S. 253
  William 149
Huey, John M. 253
Huff, Charles 221
  Daniel 280
  James 117
Hughs, Edward 279
Hughes, W. W. 5
Huling, James 163
Hulsey, Charles 314
  Galathill 235
Humber, Robert 120
Humphres, Thomas S. 282
Humphrey, Calvin 29
Humphries, Calvin 29
  Thomas S. 282
Hunt, Daniel 100
  E. 303
  Edmund S. 160
  Elizabeth W. 160
  Howel H. 284
  John F. 138
  Judkins 159
  Thomas 264
  Thomas G. 159
  William 264
Hunter, Bryant J. 259
  Edward 295
  E. H. W. 295
  E. Sparks 264
  John C. 278
  Nicholas P. 136
  Samuel B. 139,236
  William 93
Huntin, George R. 139
Hurdin, Wm. 145
Hurst, George J. 38,60
Hussey, J. J. 108
  James S. 108
  John J. 108
Hust, Wm. 205
Hutcheson, Peter W. 24
Hutchings, Charles 71
  Elbert 127
  Seaborn 55
Hutchins, N. L. 186
Hutchinson, J. 312
Hutson, Robert 119
Hylton, Wm. 102

Indan, Chas. S. 161
Ingraham, Riley G. 194
Ingram, Charles 290
  William A. 234
Irby, John 53
Irwin, Duwin 113
  Francis 113
  Joseph 230
Ivie, W. S. 122,218,284
Ivey, William 129,215

Jackson, ...255
  Amanda 214
  Asher 280
  Edmond 194
  Edmund 194
  E. L. 239
  Enoch 280
  Ephraim 138
  Fielding 280
  Francis 203
  J. B. 177
  James 198
  John 214
  John M. 149

Jackson, Joseph 9,56,137,
  159,196,289
  Joseph J. 10
  Jourdan 39
  Lucy 214
  Mark P. 34
  Mary 31,32,255
  Samuel 232
  Thomas 199
  Thos. 138
  William 203
  William E. 47,78
Jacobs, Lemuel 241
James, A. G. 22
  Absalom 289
  David N. 22
  John 31,32,255
  John M. 190
  Joseph 190
  Littleberry 256
  Mary 32,255
  Micael 256
  Thomas G. 167
Jameson, J. J. 137
  J. I. 84
Jamison, J. J. 84
Jarr, N. C. 138
Jarratt, William A. 160
  William D. 160
Jarvis, James 168
  Jane 161
Jeffers, Mary 255
  John 255
Jefferson, Youngs 65
Jenkins, Elizabeth 12
  Francis 195
  Joseph 95
  Newton 297,298
  Owen 114
  Polly 242
  Samuel 322
  William 114
Jennings, Henry 133
  James M. 231
  William G. 177
Jennison, Henry 290
  R. W. 290
Jernigan, Albert 33
  John E. 33
Jeter, Francis M. 228
  Jeremiah C. 228
  William 228
Jinkins, Francis 195
Johnson,...173
  Ahab 204
  Alex. 86,156
  Alfred 218
  Allen E. 73
  Andrew 16,173
  E. W. 126
  Elizabeth 149
  Ellen 179
  Ellen B. 179
  Gilbert D. 132
  Hosea 203,204
  Isaac 149
  Isaac Daniel 149
  J. B. Troy 173
  J. W. 237
  James 56,291
  James W. 237
  Jas. H. 247
  Jas. W. P. 200
  Jo. A. 109,110
  Joel 152
  John 34,119
  John A. 317
  John H. 212,258
  Jonas 113
  Joseph A. 110
  Land 149
  Lucy H. 45
  M. B. 188

Johnson, Mary 149,150
  Melandor B. 188
  Moses 279
  Nathan B. 241
  Neh 198,285
  Nehemiah 95
  Richard 237
  Robert 45,160
  Samuel 208
  Snellin 218
  Thomas 114
  W. M. 44
  William 160
Johnston, Alex 7,281
  Benjamin 144
  Bushrod W. 237
  J. 151
  J. B. troy 18
  J. M. A. 95
  James 6,7,133
  John 6,7
  Jona 212,310
  Little 15
  N. B. 241
  R. A. 240
  T. 237
  Thomas 237
  Th. Jef. 133
  William C. 237
  Wm. D. 192
Joiner, John 6,125
Joines, Jabez 76
Jones...86,151,184
  A. G. 125
  Absalom 289
  Adam 8,20,178,232,292
  Ann 43,250
  Anthony 31
  Augs. Seaborn 114
  Charles 210
  David N. 125
  E. E. 37
  E. K. 76
  Edward L. 76
  Elijah E. 3,21,36,41,
    48,79,176,192,261
  Ezra B. 219
  F. M. 219
  Francis M. 219
  G. 323
  G. W. 178
  H. P. 195
  Henry P. 195
  Isaac 86,156
  Isaac W. 5,6,200
  J. P. 63
  James 44,45,156,250
  Jas. 3
  Jas. W. 3,297
  James W. 53
  Joel 156
  Jesse P. 63
  John, Jr. 43,44,250
  John A. 134
  Jno. H. 41,191
  Lewis J. 240
  M. T. 86,156
  Martha 177,178,184
  R. W. 232
  Richard M. 238,239
  Robert 200
  Robertson 285
  Russell 36,246
  Seaborn 140
  Stephen 178
  Tallaver 174
  Thomas 178
  Thomas F. 97
  Thomas W. 151
  Thos. D. 173
  Thos. P. 243
  Walter 5,6
  Wiley W. 151

Jones, Wiley 289
  William 319
Jordan, Charles 117
  Daniel M. 80,48
  Elijah 303
  Elisabeth L. 62
  Elizabeth 62
  James 50,79
  Matthew J. 69,216
  Sterling G. 237
  Wiley B. 62
  William J. 249
Jorden, James 222
  Judy 222
Jordon, James 174
  Joshua R. 174
  Wiley B. 62
Joyner, C. 216
  E. 69,70,249
Judan, Chas. 120,221
Juhan, Daniel B. 114
  Francis P. 114
  Julian A. 114
Jumon, Joshua 189

Kalb, David 288
Keel, Loven J. 16,151,235,
  240
Keen, Elizabeth 265
Keg, Thos. H. 171
Keith, John W. 133
  M. A. 133
  Matthew 133
  McAnderson 133
Kelley, Barnaba 163
  Mary A. 16
  William H. 16
Kellett, John 115
Kellogg, Jas. 319
Kellum, Dexter 191
Kelly, Catherine 274
  J. P. D. 279
  Mary A. 144
  W. H. 144
  Wm. S. 115,192
Kelm...89
Kemp, A. 322 (Archibald)
  Clarborn 186
  Solomon 84
Kempsey, John J. 235
Kenan, A. H. 215
Kendall, Elizabeth 139
  Henry 139
Kendrick, A. D. 282
  Ephr. 67
  Judah 294,295
  Littleberry A. 294
  Addison 294,295
Kennedy...191
  A. H. 315
  J. A. R. 187
  L. 104 (Lewis),318
  Mary 183
  Philip 191
Kennemuer, Mary 84
Kenney, Catherine 274
Kenon, A. H. 93
Kent, William 200
Kenyon, Solomon H. 296
Kerby, James 98
Kernege, George 261
Key...265
  Pleasant H. 265
  Thos. H. 18,213,239
  Thos. J. 88
Kidd, Wm. M. 320
Kigney, James W. 274
Kilgore, George 275
  Peter W. 198
Killingsworth, D. G. 29
  168
Killum, Dexter G. 191
Kilpatrick, Hugh P. 195

Kimball, Henry 139
Kimbell, William 140
Kimberly, Anson 148
King, Agnes B. 133
  Alfred P. 106,222,223
  Barrington 57,128,129
  Benjamin 146
  G. C. 9,46,56,78,92,191,
    251,252,253
  G. W. 133
  George C. 104,317
  James 144
  Jane 178
  John 4
  John H. 35
  John M. 196,209
  John P. 55,157
  Permelia 4
  Roswell 128,129
  Sarah 133
  Thomas 19,36,83,144,209
  William 88,178
Kingsley, Sanford 159,160
Kinrick, Eli O. 140
Kinslow, Levi 247
Kirby, James 98
Kird, Wiley 220
Kirk, Sarah A. W. 57,251
  Thomas 57,251
Kirkland, Abraham L. 77
  Ann M. 281
Kirkpatrick, T. M. 132
Kitchen, Sophroney 258
  Wm. K. 150
Kitchens, B. B. 292
  Sally 258
  Sarah 258
  Sophrany 258
  Thomas 195
Knight, ...279
  Enoch 55,157
  Gazamay B. 55
  Mary M. 55,157
  N. B. 215
  Noel B. 65,81
  Susan 55,157
  William 55,157
  Woodard 55,157
Knott, David 73
  James 73
  James W. 267
Knox, David 106
  Samuel 67,68,230
  Samuel, Jr. 67,230
  Samuel, Sr. 68,230
Kolb, David 42
Krath, Harriet 154
  Judith S. 154
  Tarlton F. 154
Kruger, Thos. H. 97

Lacklin, James B. 225
  Wm. L. 198,225
Lacy, Wm. 315
Ladd, James E. 289
Ladson, Cynthia 202
Laen, Catherine 162
Laftin, Jas. A. 318
LaGaste, A. G. 109
LaLaste, A. G. 109
  Andw. G. 103
Lamar...119
  James 119
  Peter 241
Lamb, ...264
  H. K. 125
  Lucinda 264
  Philip S. 281
Lambert, Anderson 130
Lampe, Christian 295
  J. L. 295
  Jane L. 295
Lampp, Lewis 175

Land, Jacob 260
  Margery 260
Landrum, Jeptha 173
  Whitefield 52,249
Lane, M. C. 110
  M. E. 304
  Marcus C. 110
  Margaret E. 304
  Richard A. 152
  Robt. C. 232
  Saml. 95,178
  Thomas 304
Lanford, John W. A. 150
Lang, George 202
  Richard 202
Langford, Allen 237
  Bedford 53,54,252
  Burns 322
  Eliza 322
  Elizabeth 288
  Richard 288
Langly, John 194
Langston, Winney D. 152
Lanier, Augustus 96
  Geo. M. 54,226
  Patrick 179
  Thos. C. 102
Lankey, Richard T. 319
Lansford, John B. 232
Lanton, Horace 51,79
Lard, Elizabeth 142,322,
  323
  Richard 322,323
  Samuel 142
Lark, Arch. P. 162
  Mildred Ann 10,125
  W. G. 10,126
Laslie, Charles 204
  Daniel 204
  Mary Jean 204
  Rachel 204
LaTarte, A. G. 224
Latham, Thomas A. 257
Latimer, Benjamin F. 114
  William 59,100,256
Latimor, Wm. 148
Laurence, Elijah M. 102
  Seaborn 242
Laventen, W. James 3
Law, James 213,314
  Joseph 161,213
  William 297
Lawrence, E. G. 2
  E. M. 182
  Elijah M. 102,182
  Elizabeth G. 2
  Julia Ann 182
  Robert 235
  S. A. F. 241
  Silas 114
  William 2
Laws, James M. 309
Lawson, Davenport 297
  David 217
  Jane 297
  Ruffin 217
  W. I. 125
  W. J. 199
Lawton, Horace 130,131
  William J. 162
Leachman, William 138
Leary, Calvin 41
Le Chartiez, Pde. 266
Lecklin, James V 198
Ledbetter, J. 105,108
  John 108
Lee, B. B. 258
  Bennett 258
  George 168
  Hannah 282
  James 183,195
  Joshua 44
  Larkin D. 212

Lee, Mary 183
  Seabern A. 65
Lefets, Armond 276
Lefils, Armound 190,202
Lefitz, Armond 194
Leitner, John C. 133
Lemh, Daniel 183
  Philip S. 183
Lemle, Babb L. 73
  Philip S, 161
  P. L. 295 (Lempe)
Lendon, Ezekiel M. 282
LePage, Alexander C. A.
  315
Lequeux, Martha 5
  Peter 5
Lervis, Thos. J. 176
Lesils, Armound 169
Lessester, William 130
Lesseter, William 130
Lester, Germant M. 273
  William M. 72
Levens, Robert 108
Leveretz, Pherely 245
Leverette, Amanda 245
  Ferley 245
  Herely 245
  James 245
  William 245
  William H. 291
Lewis, Berrien M. C. 115
  Curtis 83
  Evan 200
  Francis 115
  Green B. 68
  James C. 278
  John L. 233
  Samuel 239,278
  Wiley 115
Liddell, Moses M. 91
Ligan, Woodson 300
Light, Obadiah 17
  Obediah 16
  Pleasant G. 259
Lightfoot, John 178
  Thomas M. 89
  Thos. M. 89
Ligon, F. M. 268
  Robert 124
Likes, Jacob 109
Lill(es), Martin 27
Limon, Wallace N. 310
Lin, Charles M. 271
Linch, Lewis H. 194
Lincoln, M. 323
Lindly, James 223
Lindsay, David W. 77,180,
  196
  Jacob 183
  Sarah 70
Lindsey, David W. 77,180
  Frances 27
  Isaac 70
  John 77,180
  Martha D. 27
  Palmyria 27
  Samuel 27
  Sarah 70
  Thomas 27
Lingo, Elijah 122
Lippitt, S. C. 316
Lipscomb, Nathan 155
Little, Joseph C. 195
  Nahume 236
  Wiley 236
  Zabud 126
Littleton, William 161
  217
Litton, William 309
Lloyd, Jared G. 24
  Jared J. 24
  Lewellen W. 24
  Mary 24

Lockett, A. J. 263
  James 282
Lockhart, Henry 199
  James 282
Locklar, James 225
Locklin, James Z. 117
Loflin, John 241
  William 241
Loftin, Jas. A. 104
Logan, James L. 181
Long, Alfred 31
  James 312
  John 160,287
  Lemuel 22,124,125
  Mary Eliza 265,268
  Michael 268
  Stafford 22,125
Loolsby, H. 90
Lot, N. P. 52
Loughridge, J. C. 184
  Wilford R. 184
Love, George M. 277
  John 64
  Josephus 303
Loveless, Allen 304
Low, John H. 249
  John H., Sr. 52
Lowe, Thomas F. 226
Lowery, J. B. 91,158
  Polly 158
Lowrey, A. B. 91
  Polly 91
Loyd, James C. 198
  James L. 209
  Martha S. 209
  William H. 209
Lucas, William W. 309
Lucis, C. C. 132
Luck, M. P. 83
Luckett, Joseph W. 270
  Silvester V. 270
Luckey, R. H. 246
  Reuben H. 246
Luke, Wm. B. 305,306
Lumford, Burns 323
  Eliza 323
Lumpkin...233
  John W. 169
  Jno. H. 25,228
  Samuel 181
  W. 247,257
  Wilson 146,228,232,280
  281
  Wilson H. 230
Lumpkins, Wilson 144
Lunday, McLin 195
  Robert 195
Lundy, Henry 136
Lunies, Geo. M. 252
Lunsden, John 175
  John G. 177
Lurch, Lewis H. 138
Luther, ...300
Lutt, A. H. 240
Lutton, C. H. 168
Lylar, O. William 148
Lynch, Ephraim 310
  Margaret 212
Lyon, William 315
Lyons, Robert 217

Mabley, E. W. 84
Mabry, Hinchey P. 102
Mackay, Eliza J. 131
  John T. 131
  Littleton P. 131
Mac Intyre, Hannah 19,216
  John 19
  John L. 19,216
Mack, J. H. 239
Mackenzie, Kenneth 216
Madden, James M. 171
  Martha 97

Madden, W. D. 97
Maddin...103
Maddon, Martha 97
Maddox, A. A. 184
   George B. T. 81
   H. D. 151
   Hamilton D. 151
   Henry 82
   James A. 85
   Martha 81
   Nancy 151
   Nancy J. 151
   Tabitha 151
   William 151
   William S. 151
Magee, Ephraim 84
   Reuben 84
Maguire, R. L. 26
   Thomas 266
Maiene, J. M. 15
Malfoon, John 164
Mallory, John 312
   Thos. 312
Malon, John 310
Malone...177
   Maria Louise 177
   T. L. 177
   Thomas 177
   Thomas L. 177
Mancey, Jesse 116
Maner, Eli 75
Mangham, J. N. 299
Mango, William 279
Mann, Baker 171
   S. A. 171
   Thomas M. 50,60,215
Manning, Lawrence 313
   Mary 220
   Reubin 261
   S. M. 311
   Thos. 84
   Wm. R. 68,69,249
Manson, Francis E. 283
   Hugh 31
   Margaret 31
Maperth, A. G. 322
Marbury...302
Marchman, Nathan 42,251
Marcus, William E. 235
Mark, J. H. 239
Marlow, Paul 182
Marsh...162,314
   Benjamin H. 308
   John 234
   Malford 225
   Mulford 41,162
   T. 314
Marshall, William 20
   (Orphans) 189
Marlow, Paul 63
Martin, Asa 204
   Elizabeth 317
   Francis 263
   George 200,201
   Gibson 268
   James, Sr. 114
   J. G. 214
   John 82,99,180,268
   John L. 19,20,174
   John S. 19,20
   Joseph 17
   M. C. 298
   Micajah 114
   Micajah C. 298
   Robert 118
   Samuel 77,180
   Tamsa 174
   Tamsey 20
   Tamsy 19,174
   William 263
Mask, Wm. 285
Massengale, H. W. 147,211,
   224,226,282,285

Massey, John B. 190
Masters, Bartholomew 113
Maston, R. W. 87,125,144,
   206,280,282
   Randal W. 87,297
Mathall...264
   Eliza 264
Mathews, Charity 277
   Geo. G. 80
   George G. 48,80
   Henry 277
   Milo B. 308,309
Mathis, Robert 198
Matthews, A. M. 202
   Daniel 290
   Henry 315
   Levan C. 237
   Milo B. 309
   Rebecca 202
Mattox, Wm. 128
Maupus, L. N. 151
   M. 151
Maughum, J. N. 173
Mavuth, A. C. 111
Maxey...231
Maxwell, James 57,251
   James Mckay 267
   Mary 267
   Sarah A. W. 57,251
   Wylie 179
May, Edmund, Sr. 127
   Jethro 127
   Reuben 127
   William R. 306
   Wm. 144
Mayes, Cyntha A. 203
   John 203
Mayo, Cyprian 33
   R. P. 94
Mays, James H. 80
   Jas. H. 48
   John 98
   Mary 48,80
McArthur, Alexander 119
McBee, Jeremiah 148
McBride, Wm. G. 141
McCall, C. H. 6,7,299
   Elhanan 26,275
   Elkanan 192
   F. S. 232
   Sarah Ann 137
McCalla, James R. 142,245
   Jas. R. 34,170
McCallough, Sarah 214
McCant, Martha F. 45,250
McCants, Samuel 311
McCantz, A. 12
   J. C. 186
McCarley, Wm. M. 96,117
McCarty, ...13,14,225
   Daniel 202
   Michael 225
   Michael J. 13,14
   Sampson 3,13,14,225
   Sherod 202
McCollough, Sarah 214
McCord, J. R. 211
   James R. 211
   Jesse C. 208
McCormick, Henry 259
McCoullough, Sarah 214
McCoy, A. C. 175
   Henry 185
   Leroy 79,153,171
McCrary, (Orphans) 186
   Bartley 12
   Ezra 232
   Jonathan B. 237
   M. Bartley 12
   Matthew 237
   T. K. 203
   Thomas K. 203
   William 186

McCraskey, Marcus L. D.
   272
McCroan, (Orphans) 283
   Eli 283
   James 283
McCullars, Nancy 161
McCulloch, John J. 55
   John L. 221
   Jno. I. 221
McCurdy, James 40,43,61,
   149,251
   John W. 212
McCurry, Angus, Sr. 92
   D. M. 298
McDanell, H. W. 93,154
McDaniel, Henry 154
   Henry D. 271
   Henry W. 109
   M. E. 318
   Wm. 213
McDill, Newton 248
McDonald, Alexander 197
   Alexandria 197
   Alexandria P. 196
   Anderson 31
   Catherine 42
   Charles 73
   Charles J. 300
   Chas. J. 162
   D. M. 168
   George, Jr. 169
   James 196,197,320
   John, Jr. 208
   Joshua 269
   Maria 42
   Mary 169
McDougald, Alexander 136
McDow, Jonathan 160
McDowel, William 137
McDowell, Daniel 127
   Mary Ann 127
McDowele, Baptist 162
McDowelle, William 137
McElroy, Robert G. 32
   Sarah 32
   William 32
   William M. 32
McFail, D. C. 102
McGammer, F. 110
McGee, (Heirs) 129
   (Orphans) 220
   Eliza 126
   George W. 128
   Henry 129
   Henry H. 129
   Levin 128
   Samuel 126
   William 220
McGehee, R. D. 138
   R. F. 158
McGehn, Mary 220
   R. F. 220
   Robert F. 220
McGhee, Geo. W. 128
   Mary 128
McGinnes, James 152,248
   William 152
McGlammary, Jeptha 137
   John 137
McGowen, Margaret 151
McGraw, James 184
   Melley 184
McGriff, Sarah 288
   Thomas 288
McGuine, Lea R. L. 172
   Richen L. 172
McGuire, Richard L. 26
McIntosh, ...274
McInnis, John 204,289
McJunkin, Dwaties 200
McKannon, Lany 168
McKee, Eveline A. 243
   John 323

McKenden, John J. 153
McKendon, John J. 124
McKendre, John J. 87
McKendree, John J. 140
McKendue, John J. 239
McKenzie, James 213
  Kenneth 89,141,194,
  228,288
McKey, Edw. D. 242
McKinne, Ann 11,229
  B. 229
  B. M. 11
  Barna 11,229
  Jno. Jr. 11,229
McKinney, Hinchen 125
McKinnie, Barna 229
McKinon, Archibald 232
McKinsey, John 163
McKissack, William 115
McKoy, James 257
McL------, William R. 11
McLaine, Jacob 296
McLarty, Emily S. 253
  L. W. 253
McLaws, James 141,142
  William R. 96,97,142,
  154,210,229
McLean, John 119
McLendon, Benjamin 68,69,
  249
  Isaac A. 73,198
McLemore, Kenneth 89
McLendon, Mary 68,249
McLin, G. W. 254
  Robert N. 45,250
McLoud, A. 294
McMahan, Greenberry 225
  Susan 225
McMath, John H. 286
  John U. 286
  William 286
McMichael, W. G! 178,212
McMickle, William 171,198
McMillen, Fielden 278
McMullen, Fielden 278
  Nail 278
McNeal, William 229
McNoble, Taylor 92
McQueen, Margaret C. 260
McQuire...146
McRae, Christopher 119
McVicker, Duncan 279
McWhorter, A. M. 182,246
  James 232
  Saml. 232
Mead, Heman 83
Meadows, Wiley 174
Meal, R. A. 83
Meeks, Josiah 235
  Wiley 48,80
Megan, Sophia E. 197
  Sophia M. 197
Melton, Moses 226
Mendenhall, Marmaduke F.
  159
Meran, John 160
Mercer, Levi 210
Mere, Thos. 261
Meredith, J. M. 14
  J. W. 11,26,47,73,78,
  172,296
Merewether, Ths. 90
Merie, Joseph 315
Meriwether, David 90,91
  Thos. 91
Merrell, B. S. 223
  Frederick 315
Merrill, James 148,181
Merritt, A. 243
Merry, Bradford 236
Merwether, David 90
Mesency, Benjamin 249
Mesley, Garland 138

Mesley, Sarah 138
Methvin, Daniel 131
Meuene, J. M. 15
Meyers, M. 71
Micklejohn, R. 16,29,39,
  78,129,147,160,170,172
  173,181,184,201,204,
  219,236,248,
Middlebrook, James H. 114
  Mary 198
Middlebrooks, Thos. J. 99
  120
  Zachariah 198
Middleton, Nancy 177
  William 177
Miers, Joseph J. 206
Migill, John 34
Mitchell, Alexander 169
Miles, John W. 320
  Lewis 45
  Thomas 320
  William 9,191
Milirons, Harriet 277
  Simon 277
Mill...19
Milledge, John 226
Millen, A. J. 114,268,269
  George 229
  M. B. 262,263
  McPherson B. 229
  Robert 114
Miller, ...33,191,269,291,
  310
  A. J. 8,190,269
  A. L. 272
  Alexander 269
  Andrew J. 268,269
  Ann 43,250
  Charity 291
  Dennis 189
  Frances 29
  Francis 191
  G. J. 183
  H. V. M. 170
  Henry 29,168,191
  Homer V. M. 298
  James 43,250
  Joseph N. 240
  Joshua C. 269
  Julian A. 310
  Lewis 29,191
  Lucinda 29,191
  Lucretia 29,191
  N. V. M. 46
  Richard 33
  Samuel 282
  Sarah 291
  T. W. 114,154
  Thomas 29,168,191
  William 291
  William S. 310
Millican, Andrew, Sr. 312
  Jane 312
  John 119
  Lettuce, Jr. 312
  Lettuce, Sr. 312
  Thomas 312
Milligan, Joseph 41,111
Millirons, Polly 277
Mills, (Heirs) 83
  (Orphans) 139
  Alexander 139
  Benjamin 322
  Elisha 139
  Green 139
  Jesse 139
  John 83,122
  Martha 139
  Moses 139
  Nancy 139
  Nelly 139
  Rutha 83
  Susannah 139

Milner, (Orphans) 236
  John B. 236
Milton, (Orphans) 247
  Eliza 247
Mimms, Wm. 113
  William 45,96,250,287,
  Wright 96
Misoney, Benjamin 52
Mitchell, Alexander 169
  D. B. 168
  Peter 255
  Randolph 275
  Robert F. 212
  Thos. F. 138
  Thos. R. 285,286
  W. H. 16,288
  W. N. 93
  W. U. 146
  Walter H. 39
  William 274
  William L. 212
  William W. 78
Mixon, Michael 215
  Silpha 215
Mizell, John 123,170
Mobley, Daniel A. 14
  E. W. 84
Molden, Catherine 78
Monroe, Jackson A. 98,204
  James 136
  John 136
  L. D. 98,204
Montfort, David 277
  Peter T. 236
Montgomery, Hugh 126
  John 24,115
Moon, Robert 15
Moor, John 16
Moore, Alexander 198
  Ben B. 96,117
  Burke 281
  Charles W. 319
  Daniel 195
  Daniel Q. 195
  Elbert 310
  Elijah 221
  Elizabeth 198
  I. J. 117
  J. W. 279,299
  Jackson J. 198
  James 46,81,165
  James S. 319
  John 138
  John C. 176
  Joseph 176
  Joshua G. 177
  Loverd 193
  Majamsey 311
  Mary 198
  May F. 279
  Robert 195
  Taliaferro W. 270
  Tho. 281
  Thomas H. 95
  Thomas J. 198
  Toliva W. 270
  W. B. 116,117
  W. S. 208
  Walter H. 39
  Will A. 181
  William 93
  William B. 116
  William J. 198
Mure, Tuliva W. 270
  Wiliam 282
Moreis,...302
Morel, Ths. M. 273
Moreland, Robt. 261
  Sarah S. 294
  Turner 140
  Tuttle H. 294
  William 54,157,251,252
Morgan, A. 204

Morgan, Edward A. 204
  Elizabeth 221
  James W. 221
  John 120
  Lewellen 276
  Little 287
  Lwellen 276
  P. E. 140
Morgin, Jhn David 55
Morison, L. B. 202
Morrill, Susan 296
Morris, B. 198
  Charles 128
  G. 128
  Gustavus 127
  James 239,263
  Jas. 144
  Laura 127
  Peter 127
  Simon 128
  Simon, Jr. 128
  Thomas 175,210,241
  Thos. 165,175,201,207, 241
Morrison, M. 207
Morrow, David 49
  Joseph 285
  Peter G. 285
  Robert G. 100
Moseby, John 216
Mosely, Samuel 27
  Samuel, Jr. 27
Moss, Alexander 236
  E. W. 73
  Elizabeth W. 73
  James S. 108
  John 73
  Reese H. 204
Mossey, O. W. 211
  Orren W. 211
Mossler, Thomas L. 32
Mote, William A. 154
Motes, Nancy 280
  Caroline 280
Mott, Joseph 238
Mound, John C. 13
Mounger, E. 67,253
  John C. 280
  Lucy H. 280
Mulkey, David 195
  Elizabeth 195
  Homer 160
  Homer V. 130,192,283
  I. J. 183
  Isaac 291
Mullikin, B. 125
Mullins, Elijah 276
  Miles 95
Murcheson, William 183
Murchison, Colen 101,183
  William 101,183
Murphey, Jesse 154,173,186, 220,238,244
  John 179
Murphy...191
  Daniel 259
  Elizabeth 256
  James W. 26
  Jaw S. 65
  Jesse 94
  John 191
  John C. 256
  Josiah 159
  Wm. D. 259
Murrah, Elizabeth 322
Murraha...322
Murray, Geo. W. 194
  Geo. W. M. 209
  W. W. 141
Murry, Demsey 279
  Hartwell 190
  Timothy 279
  Vienna 190

Muselwhite, Nancy 164
  Wm. 164
Myers, Henry 77,162
  John 207
  J. A. J. 207
  John A. J. 207
  M. 41,77,162,181,267
  Mordica 40
Myrick, William 318

Nabers, J. B. 21,54,68, 72,91
  James B. 55,72,215
  William 6,125
Nabus, J. B. 189,217,222, 230
Nacob, Barnard 292
Nail, R. A. N. 114
Nash, Elijah 21
  Reubin 133
  Rubin 21
Nations, Israel 167
Naylor, John 255
  Thomas J. 255
Neal, John 114,299
  John T. 158
  R. A. P. 165
  R. A. R. 175,201,207, 209,241
  Thomas 258
Neays, George 126
Neel, R. A. R. 64,65
  William M. C. 243
Neese, Andrew 168
Nelm...57
  Elizabeth 57
Nelms, Thomas 15
  William B. 99,100
Nelson...298
  Abel 311
  Charles 36,319
  C. H. 132,164,213,218
  C. N. 58
  Charles A. 19,216
  Charles H. 114,132,134, 142,143,148,152,165, 173,202,206,217,235, 240,297,319,320
  John 140,150
  John A. 28
  Mary 69
  Matthew 150
  William 311
Nesbitt, Eleanor L. 66, 185
Newell, Isaac 16,144,321
Newhall, George 161
Newman, James A. 282
Newsom, Robert 244
  Rebecca 95
  Henry 291
Newton, Charles 235
  E. L. 235
  Levi 66,185
  Nesbets 89
Nial, Arthur 59
Niblack, S. J. 91
  S. L. 91
  William M. 91
Niblet, ..270
Niblock, Augustin 197
Niblet, Edmond 270
Niblock, S. J. 197
  Thomas 197
Nichols, Julius 212
  Marthy 248
  Ransom 212
Nicholson, Archibald 288
Nilsen, C. H. 223
  Samuel W. 285
Nisbet, A. M. 261
  Eugenius A. 69
  Miles C. 69

Nisht, ...170
  Eugenius A. 170
  Eugenus A. 170
  Miles 170
  Miles C. 170
Nix, Delatha 250
Noble, Taylor M. 92
Nock...148
  John 148
Noel, Sarah C. 262
Nolan, Thos. 143
Nolen, Christopher 304
Norcop, P. N. 293
Norman, Emma 135
  Ewena 135
  William S. 212,278,310
  Wm. S. 267
Norris, James 4,47,139, 236,250
Northern, George 86,156
Northingtor, Jas. F. 127
Norton, Alfred M. 67
  M. V. 120
Nowden, Lot 77
Nox, Delitha 45
Nunallee, John 133
Nutt, Elizar 280
  Harriet 280
  John 19,250
  John C. 280
  Jno. 44
  S. R. 280,299
  Samuel M. 280
  William C. 280

Oates, Samuel S. 37
  William W. 229
Oats, James 276
Odell, Catherine 215
Oden, Alexander 20
Odena, John A. 194
Odom, Alexander 264
Offutt, Nathaniel 76
Oglesby, Lindsay 118,119
  Thomas 119
O'Kelley, George W. 55
O'Kelly, Richard 202
Old Friend (Indian) 234
Oliver, Benjamin 4,247
  Charles 247
  Saml. 40
  Saml. K.57,129
  Thomas J. 185
  Zilphay 247
  Zilpheha 247
Oneal, ...281
O'Neal, Benjamin 199
  Edmund 199
  Jesse 295
  Williamson 295
Oneal, Henry 20
  William 281
Oquin, Nancy 123
  Silas 123
Orme, R. M. 273,274
Osborne, Eliza M. 273
  James G. H. 274
  Joseph 113
O'Shields, John 15
Outlaw, Brutley 124
  Joice E. 124
  Matilda M. 124
  Sanders D. 123,124
Owdonis, J. 106
  S. 106 (Samuel)
Owen, Allen F. 32,159
  J. L. 245
  Jesse L. 69,140,170
  Jesse S. 280
  John 270
  Mary 32
  Saml. T. 317
  William 270

Owens, Andrew 86,156
  Eliza 133
  John 275
  Jno. Tho. 211
  Joseph 302
  Purnel W. 165
  Susan 133
Ozburn, Charles 42
  Elias 42

Pace...86,298
  Columbus D. 15,97,123,
    136,193,231
  Elizabeth 180
  Thomas R. 298
  William 298
  William H. C. 231
  William H. E. 97
  William W. C. 123
Padgett, (orphans) 300
  John 300
  L. D. 78
  Nancy 300
Padgette, Elesha 260
  Susan 260
  William H. 260
Pafford, William O. 113
Page, Columbus D. 97
  Jesse 106
  McKenneth 137,243
Pain, Wm. W. 232
  William 260
Painter, Ezekiel 235
  Joel 235
Palmar, John W. 239
Palmer, Jas. M. 55
  John 322,323
  Sarah 322,323
  William W. 130
Palmore, Sarah 322
Palmour, Silas B. 195
  T. B. 196
Pannell, James 54
Parham, B. J. 309
Paris, Albert 129
Park...11,143,155,220,229
  Andrew 143
  J. G. 84
  James S. 203,265,268
  John C. 142
  John G. 17,108,216,225,
    284
Parker, Isaac A. 294
  John B. 187
  Joseph R. 172
  Lewis 158
  Robertson 243
  Sarah 158
  William 254
Parkerson, T. J. 211
Parkes, Sylvanius E. 138
Parks...131
  John 293
  John S. 300
  Welcome 131
  Wm. J. 186
Parmelia, Albert O. 321
Parnell, Thomas 25
Parr, Daniel W. 182
  Wm. S. 182
Parrish, Eliza 194
  Jona. 282
  William H. 194
Parsons, Evan 120
Pass, Thomas 92
  Thomas S. 92
Pate, Samuel 246
Pates, David 23
Patrick, Joshua 238
  Robert 237,238
  Sintha 237
Patten, G. 276
  George 276

Patterson, James 314
  Wm. 55
Pattillo, James 276
  John 276
Patton, J. T. 264
Paty, John 288
  Miles 288
Paul, Brice 39
  James 27
  Price 39
Paulk, John 136
  Micajah 135,136
Paullen, Ann 95
  John 95
Payne, John H. 260
Pcor, Edmund 283
Peabody, J. D. 134
Peacock, A. P. 150,190
Pearn, Mary G. 282
Pearre, Alexander 306
Pearson, Griffin G. 7
  Jeremiah 75
  John 214
  John T. 214
  Samuel 291
Peavy, John 186
Peddy, Nancy 118
  William 118
Peebles, Abram 176
  Albert 176
Peel, James G. 82
Pellegren...314
  John 314
Pelt, Joseph 196
Pemberton, Atton 266
Pendarvis, Caleb 293
Pender, William 40
Pendergast, Pierce B. 113
Pendergrass, N. A. 237
  N. H. 74,180
Pendue, Benjamin R. 121
Pennington, Ann M. 281
  Mary F. 281
  Sim 281
Pennuad, Edward 113
Penson, J. J. 101
Penton, Thomas 279
Perkerson, Thomas J. 271
Perkins, Eldridge 152
  John 322
  Joseph 152
  Thomas 265
Perritt, Nathaniel 301
Perry...101
  A. J. 297
  Bird 282
  Hardy 297
  John 282
  K. W. 131
  Mary C. 282
  Oscar F. 208
  William H. 295
Perryman, A. G. 7
  Elisha 134
Persons, Benjamin 310
  John 310
  Pinkney 310
Peterman, George 162
  John 162
Peters,...106
  B. 151 Balaam 59
  Mathew 319
  William 106
Pettee, Henry 265
Petus, Balaam 39
Pew, Ann 121
  Isaac 121
Phail, D. C. 182
Phalan, John 179
Pharr, Alexander 61
Phelps, Glenn 217
  Harriet 217
  James 157

Phelps, Sarah 157
Philip, Alexr. 140
Philips, Alex'r. 150
  David 152
Phillips, Cleverly 323
  David R. 168
  Edmund G. 132
  Emily M. 132
  Jane L. 132
  Louisa M. 132
  Mary 131,132
  Noah 269
  Viney 85,153
  William 176
  Zachariah 132
  Zachariah, Jr. 131,132
Philpot, William H. 27
Phinizy, Ferdinand 232
Phulips, Benjamin 163
Picket, William 144
Pierce, E. H. 300
  Ezekiel 192
  Thomas W. 227
  William 192
Pilcher, James 258
  John J. 118,199
Piles, Robt. S. 240
Pinckard, Sarah 310
Pinkston, Evans W. 175
  Jesse M. 174,175
Pinson, Mary 93,96
Pitman, I. 187
  Dempsey 187
Pitson, Benjamin F. 311
Pittman, Thomas 263
Pitts, E. 76
  Hardy 205
  Joseph 35
  Lizza 76
  Liza 120
  Nancy 76,99,120
Platt, G. F. 249
  George F. 137
Pledger, Wesley 298
Plott, F. 52
Poe, William 140
Poerter, Joel L. 230
Polbe, James 192
Polhill,...286
  Jos. 286
  T. 74
  Thomas H. 74,295
Polk, Evan 158
  T. A. 158
Pollard, ...176
  Leroy 176
Pollock, Jesse 312,313
  Lewis 312
  Thomas 312
Ponder, James 15
Pool, William 238,318
  William P. 318
Pooler, Rbt. W. 128
Poore, William 98
  Wilson 98
Pope, Henry 140
  Jesse 310
  Walter R. 115
Porter, Anthony 269,292
  Edwin R. 14
  Henry J. 47,78
  John S. 47,78
  Sarah F. 47,78
  Sylvester 14
  William S. 14
Posey, Benjamin 261
Poss, Christopher 162
Poston...284
  E. 284 (Emanuel)
Pothill, H. 73
Potter, Abraham 162
Potts, Francis M. 222
  Samuel 221,222

Powel, Kader 110
   Kader J. 110
   Mary 110
Powell, Eleany 110
   Evan H. 298
   G. B. 244
   Green B. 56,58,244
   James 213,214,265
   Kader P. 110
   Mary 217
   Millington 217
   Ransom 181
   William C. 111,322
   William F. S. 101
   Wm. C. 5
   Wm. F. S. 131
Power, William W. 40,61
Poythes, Geo. 226
Prather...289
Pratt, Hillary M. 4
   Permelia 4
Preer, T. C. 206
Prescot, John 296
Presley, Calvin 319
Preston, Archibald 204
   Elisha J. 224
   Elisha T. 224
   Gillim 94
   Gillum 224
   Thomas 204
Price, Arriaia 197
   Betsy Jane 197
   David Solomon 197
   Geo. Washington 197
   James 197
   Jesse 44
   Joshua 197
   Mary Elkins 197
   Nancy 197
   Nancy Ann 197
   Rebecca 44
   Sarah 197
Prichard, William H. 25
Prior, E. C. 275
   Felix W. 275
   G. I. H. 275
   Jno. 275
   M. P. 275
   R. A. 2,147,204,275, 281
Priquet, A. 289
Pritchan, Wm. H. 55
Pritchard, W. A. 135
   William 218
   William H. 9,10,11,66, 72,91,114,120,126,137, 183,185,197,200,211, 212,223,268,269,282, 289,295,296,321,322
   Wm. H. 41,55,65,73,147, 185,198,200,222,229, 262,283,290,291,299,
Pritchett, R. F. 323
Prosser, Cynthia 105
   John 105
Proudfoot, Hugh W. 169
Prudhomme, Louis 163
Pruett, Henry 216
   Jacob 216
Pruitt, Robert 68
Pryor, Felix 147
Psalmonds, Thomas 20,171
Puckett, Aaron B. 95
   Robert M. 95
Pulliam, William 85,252
Pullum, Thos. 91
Purcell, Abraham 53
   Jaceb L. 53
   Jacel 53
Purcell, Jarrett 53
Purdy, Samuel 218
Purrance, John S. 320
Purvis, Bennett 248

Purvis, Jeptha 102
   Wm. 102
Puryman, Elisha 188
Pussas, Leon P. 53
Putnam, Jacob C. 228
   James Cob 156
   James Cole 86

Quarterman, Edward 58
   F. W. 213
   Sarah L. 57
   T. N. 57
Quick, Alexander 298
   Nancy 298
Quillian, D. 148
Quinn...89
   Alfred 89

Rabun, John 189
   Wm. 301
Rachel, Wm. 19
   Zadock 188,201
Radford, E. C. 275
   Wm. 315
Rae, Robert 164
Rafield, Mary 175
   Nelson 175
Ragland, Adam 21,46,155, 180
Raiford...16,17,22,58
   B. 93,97,98
   C. 310
   Campbell 134,166
   R. 64,137,143,144,148, 182,183,197,215,224, 234,255,257,,260,267, 281,290,295,296,297,
   Roberts 57
Raines, John W. 319
   Sarah T. 319
Rainey, Elizabeth 241
   John 241
   Mathew 38,101
   Matthew 61,252
   Wootsen 252
   Wootson 38,61,101
Rains, John W. 318
   Josiah 179
Ralls, John 261
Ramey, Abr. 226
Ramsay, Allen C. 137
   James 137
   Nancy 101
Ramsey, R. H. 90
Ramsay, Randolph H. 137
Randall, Chas. 202
Randolph, J. H. 215
Ranew, Timothy, Jr. 96
Ransom, B. B. 198
   C. W. 66
   G. W. 185
   George W. 66
Rassoe, J. H. 270
Ratchford, Ezekiel 235
Raulerson, Herod 23
Rawkins, Robert C. 189
Rawlings, William 41
Rawls, John 290
   Silus 98
Ray, A. J. 38,61
   Benjamin 217
   Christina 163
   Dempsey I. 12
   Jacob 163
   John A. 236
   Jonas 163
   Sanders W. 223,236
   Saunders H. 220
   Young W. 12
Reaves, Elizabeth 38,61
   J. F. 251
   Josiah F. 46,250,251
Red. G. B. 3 (Green B.)

Redd, James K. 270
   William 270
Reddick, Jacob 160
   Sarah 160
Redding, A. W. 123,142
   Anderson W. 123,276
Redman...239
Reece, D. A. 254
Reed, Sam. 103
Rees, Benjamin T. 271
   Jno. C. 3,261
   Susannah M. 3,261
   Talbot 271
   D. A. 75
Reese, ...66,185
   D. A. 75
   F, M. 66,185
   Hugh 226
   Jordan 116,214,126
   Redman 66,185
Reeve, James W. 248
   Green 230
Reeves, J. F. 46
   John D. 116
   Polly 230
Reid, David 147
   James W. E. 142
   Robert A. 147
   Samuel 103
Reilly, John 179
Remington, Chas. H. 269
Remsnia, H. C. 245
Rendrick, Ephr. 253
Renew, Timothy 96
Renfore, Nathaniel 284
Renfroe, Enoch 276
   J. M. 276
   Nathaniel 284
Renishart, W. 161
Respess, Nancy 298
   Richard 298
Revells, Randolph 269
   Rebecca 269
Revers, Joseph 315
Revill, Rebecca 269
Reynolds, Ann 288
   Benjamin H. 318
   Dica 288
   Eniline T. 288
   Holand M. 288
   James H. 288
   Jas. H. 141
   James M. 266,288,304
   P. 304
   Peyton 5,122,167,221, 313,314
   Pudmedus 257
   Puomedus 185
   Robert 313
   Sarah 288
Rhaton, Martin R. 148
Rhodes, James 136
   J. Y. 92,231
   Rebecca 92,231
   Sarah 136
   Thomas 136
Rice, B. J. 16,17
   Benjamin H. 238
   Charles H. 67,253 ,274
   Charles S. 253
   David L. 238
   James 135,210,312
Richards, Evan G. 108
   William B. 146
Richardson, A. K. 291
   David 64
   Richard 124
   Samuel 64
   William 293
Ricks, John 230
Riddle, A. A. J. 129
Ridgway, Thos. P. 220
Ridley, Robert A. Y. 220

Rigby, Jonathan 244
Rigdon, Robert 30
Right, John 319
Riley, Harriet L. 220
  John P. 13
  Mary A. 220
  S. W. 220
  Spencer 23,28,87,153,
    176,183,199,206,241
Rinehart, A. H. 25
  A. K. 25,172
Rise, Sophia 161
Roach, James 273
Roath, Alfred 199
Robbardes, Henry R. R.183
Robbins, George 215
  James M. 215
  William 309,310
Roberson, Catherine 41
  James R. M. 35
  Jonathan 274
Roberts, Absolem V. 137
  B. M. 186
  Benjamin 240
  Benson 81
  Bryant 70
  Burch M. 186
  Delila 137
  Elijah 114,199
  Elisha 224
  Elizabeth 137
  Henry S. 277
  James 310
  Jefferson 199
  Jesse M. 8
  Jesse 262
  John 114,125,199
  John A. 162,200,255
  John G. 224,319
  L. 104 Lurana 137
  Mary 224
  P. B. 99,158
  Sarah 277
  William 70,137,195
  Zimri 137
Robertson, Ansalem 318
  Charles 147
  Edny T. 123
  Henry 147
  Jennett 318
  Jemima 222
  Jennett 104
  John 248
  John G. 104,318
  William 222,
Robins, William 314
Robinson, A. A. 285,287
  Benjamin P. 182
  Bolling H. 41,191
  E. B. 56
  Hezekiah 52
  John 52,159,160,249
  M. D. 53,249
  Monoah D. 52
  Menorah D. 249
  Robert 158
  William 42,57,248
Robison, James 280
  John S. 280
  Samuel 148,207,289
Robsen, John 193
Robson, John 90,157
Rockmore, Wm. B. 276
Rodes, Willis 240
Rodgers, Isaac 315
  James H. 182
Roe, Joseph 279
  Richard 306
Roebuck, James 193
  Luallin 193,204
  Martha 193
  Martha N. 193
  William 299,300

Rogers, (Children) 51
  Henry 159
  Jacob 121
  James A. 254
  John 4,253,254
  John A. 48,79,153
  Pleasant H. 116
  Thos. 51
  Washington 89
Rollins, William 18
Rogers, Wm. 121
  W. S. 179
Roland, James 291
  John 239
  William 239
Rolin, Charles 323
  Elizabeth 323
  Richard W. 323
Rollins, David 173
  Nicholas 173
  William 173
Romans, Alexander 142
  Elizabeth 142
Roney, Francing 134
  Fransey 188
Roner, James 323
Roney, Robert 134,188
Rooks, John 22
  Mary 22,23
Roper, Wm. C. 230,301
Rose, Milton B. 237
Rosier, John A. 218
Ross, A. B. 118
  Benj. F. 238
  D. W. 43,81,87
  David 166
  George 291
  George W. 291
  Henry E. 245
  Henry G. 245
  Henry H. 133
  John 233,254,288
  Larkin 166
Roundtree, Arthur 18
Rounsaville, Robert 209
Rountree, Arthur 171
  Raby 243
  Mills 18,171
Rousseau, James 274
Rover, James 323
Row...126
Rowan, John 121
Rowden, Lot 180,277
Rowe, Allen 297,301
  Eliza 57
  Eliza A. 57
  John 120,299
Rowell, Joab T. 15,172
  Oliver H. 15,172
  Phreny 297
  Richard 15,172
Rowland, Thomas 291
Rowlins, David 173
Ruwls, W. H. 277
Rownee, Ilsey A. 135
Royal, John Isham 265
Royals, Willis 270
Royston, Richard W. 135
Rozar, Mary 169
Rucker, R. B. 215
Rucks, William 107
Rue, Joel B. 215
Ruff, Lemon 18,173
  M. L. 84
Ruffin, R. N. C. 75
  R. V. C. 154
Rumsnia, J. C. 245
Run, D. A. 91
Runnells, (Children) 59
  (Orphans) 252
Runnels, Benjamin 210
Runnells, Prudence 59,252
  Richard 59,252

Runnells, William 252
Rupell, Benjamin B. 10
Ruse, D. A. 90
Rushing, Eli 216
Russ, Elezar 276
Russell, ...314
  Benjamin 245
  Benjamin B. 126,142,
    212,248
  David 280
  Isaac 8,115,149,151,
    202,219,267,276
  James 322
  James, Sr. 189
  James M. 199
  John Augustus 314
  John M. 181
  L. S. 135
  Levi S. 151,265,266,
    268
  Philip 199
  William 322
  William R. 280
Rutherford...85
  Samuel 311
Rutledge, Edny T. 123
  William C. 123
Ryan, Charles E. 2,138,
  283,285
  Charles Eaton 224
Rylin, James 237

Saffold, Adam G. 14,200
  William Oliver 200
Safford...274
  Adam G. 200,270
Safitte, Genevieve R. 9
  James B. 9
Salcruon, Mabry 51
Salmon, Hezekiah 249
Salter...285
  T. B. 90
  Thomas 90
  Thomas S. 90
Salters (see above)
Sanders, Aaron 196,197
  Ann G. 12,201
  Bridger 193
  Charles H. 193
  Denis D. 12,201
  Ephraim 234
  James 193
  Julia C. 286
  Massaure Ann 286
  Menyard 197
  Penelope 286
  Rachel 193
  Richard 193
  Robert T. 286
  S. H. 143
  Seaborn 193
Sandwich...311
  Carolina 312
  Caroline 312
  M. H. 209
  Martha 312
  Matthew 312
  Thomas 311
Sanfor_, J. M. A. 84
Sanford, B. W. 139,177
  Bush--d W. 40
  Bushrod W. 57
  D. 152 Daniel 152
  Henry 167
  J. W. 40
  J. W. A. 109,236,126,
    142,268 (John W. A.)
  O. W. 42
  R. 158 Raymon 17
  Thomas 63
  Thomas G. 50,79
  V. O. W. 251
  W. A. 74,268

Sangester, Elizabeth J. 193
  John 193
  Robert 193
  Peter 193
  Washington 193
St. George, Edward 290
Sankey,..256
  Wm. D. 264
Sammons, Martha 175
  Nancy 155
  Seaborn 155
  Wiley 175
Sapp, Delany 88,152
  John G. 88,152
  Wm. 245,291
Sappington, Caleb 210
Sargent, Harrison J. 124
Sasnett, Joseph R. 142
  Richard Philip 142
Satter, R. L. 175
Savage, Daniel 25
  William B. 25
Sawyer, John L. 195
  Johnson 195
  Jon. 313
  Zadock 43,290
Scales, Fanny 196
  Joel 196
Scarborough, Absley 207
  Agnes 207
  David 207
  Drury F. 76
  Ivey 207
  Miles 148,155,207,308
  P. F. 164
Scearcey, Benjamin R. 17
Schly, William 36,171
Schroder, Harriet M. 22
Scogin, Gillum 101,102,182
Scott, A. H. 88,242,250, 257,295
  A. M. 225
  A. W. 50,59
  Anderson C. 143
  Archibald 88
  Daniel 89
  Eliza 285
  Henry 225,226
  Isaac 323
  James C. 34,170
  Jane 312
  John 254,312
  John H. 285
  Joseph 190
  May F. 279
  William 231
  William F. 323
Scraborough, Miles 309
Scranton, D. T. 224
  Mary 224
Screven, James P. 267
  John 267
Scruggs, Alletha 262
  Frederick 262
  John 262
  Jesse 262
  Richard S. 262
Se----, James M. 34
Seab, A. 308,309 (Arnold)
Seavey, William 84
Sebastian, Edmund 49
Seeon, Nancy 130
Sellers, A. V. 275
  James 275
Sentell, Mary 123
  Nathan 123
Sessions, Joseph 205
Sevenford, Eliza 322
Sewell, Green B. 64
  Joseph 72
  Levi 36,83
  Samuel 64,65
Seymon, Henry C. 283

Shamblin, A. 235
Shankle, Jas. W. 186
Shanks, James D. 261
Sharman, Elizabeth Jane 316
  John 316,317
Sharp...14,308
Sharpe, Hamilton W. 101, 115,
  Judy 309
  Lucretia 14,15
  Nathan J. 32
  Wm. 309
  Wm H. 207
Sharpe, Hamilton W. 100, 207,209,295,
Shau, W. S. 55
Shaw...300
  George 217
Shearrard, John 261
Sheats, M. M. 124
Sheet, Sam M. 148
Sheets, Tarlton 258
Sheffield, Wm. 96
Shelman, Robert B. 274
Shepard...314
  Andrew 293
  John 314
Shepherd, Curten/Carter 26
  James M. 119
  John W. 306
Sheppard, Carter 204
  John 224
Shepperd, J. W. 305
Sheptan, Canton 172
Sheridan, John 19
Sherils...87
  Thomas 87
Sherman, Eli G. 199
Sherrard, Julia Ann 102, 182
Shi, James H. 184
Shick, Elizabeth S. 8,267 276
Shields, Mathew 190
Shivener, Thos. J. 216
Shivers, Thos. W. 190
Shly, John 3,14,201,225
Sholars, John 189
Shorter, Eli S. 124
  Gen....146
  James H. 124
  Sophia H. 124
Shuman, James 17
Shvits, Thomas 206
Sikes, Henry 138
  John 275
  Nancy 300
  William G. 300
  William H. 138
Silkes, Jetree 275
Sillaven, Augustin W. 271
  David R. 271
  James A. 271
Simmons, Geo. F. 116
  J. K. 44
  James P. 122
  John 300
  John F. 75
  Lazarus 241
  Samuel 116
  Susannah 274,275
  Thomas R. 211
  William 44
Simms, Andrew G. 121
Simons, George F. 116
Simonton, A. S. 236
  Albert A. 236
  Thomas 280
  William G. 89
Simpson, ...253
  William 311
Sims...55

Sims, Frederick 205
  James M. 235
  Joannah 53,54,252
  Robert 53,252
  Susan 205
  Thomas 210
  Wiley 55
  William 69,288
Sinclair, B. W. 279
Singleton...291
  James 291
  Leroy 290,291
Sinning, John 274
Sitton, William 310
Skidmore, Crosby S. 158
Skidmon, Jett T. 166
Skidmore, Jett T. 165,166
Skinner, John J. 283
  Rebecca 283
Skidmore, Samuel W. 158
Slappy, Jno. G. 133
Slaton, John M. 293
Slaughter, Henry 184
  Isaac 184
  John 47
  M. Y. 258
  Mary 24
  Thomas K. 184
  Thomas P. 24
  William A. 184
Sledge, Robert H. 235,246
Slill, Nancy 145
Slone, Elizabeth 188
Smart...207
  Elisha 262
  Henry T. 42,119,194, 251
  James M. 207
Smiley, W. J. D. 276
Smith...131
  A. T. 69
  A. W. 196
  Aaron 278
  Aaron M. 115
  Alexander 223,254
  Ann 210
  B. 208
  B. B. 23,99
  Babin 227
  Benajah 208
  Benj. B. 86,156
  Benjamin 42,223,251, 315
  Benjamin B. 98,235
  Caroline V. 135
  Charles 131
  David 244
  David C. 243,304
  Dempsy B. 311
  Duncan 278
  E. T. 107
  Easaw 113
  Eliza Ann 320
  Elizabeth 244
  F. M. 232
  Gideon 137
  Hamson 157
  Harriett E. 104,317,318
  Harrison 54
  Henry B. 210
  Henry Montgomery 135
  J. C. 23,176
  Jackson 318
  James 82,160,295
  James B. 117
  James D. 19
  James M. 48,80,202
  Jesse C. 23
  John 209,216
  John A. 148
  John T. 308
  John W. 210
  L. W. 35,171

Smith, Lindsay H. 151,202, 225,238,241,262
  Levi 289
  Lovel 129
  Margaret 315
  Margaret Ian 135
  Marion Helen 135
  Mary 271
  Michool 271
  Millington 79
  Moses 278
  Moses C. 176
  R. 135
  Robert W. 238,239
  Phinias 197
  Sarah 197
  Selina 190
  Shaddrack 190
  Sibby A. 251
  Silbey A. 42
  Silly A. 42
  Silly S. 43
  Simon 47,48,79,153
  Singleton W. 202
  Stephen 141
  Sterling W. 54,157
  Stoddard W. 13,118, 125,161,190
  Thomas 47,79,258,261
  Thomas J. 209,184,270
  Thos. Q. 264
  Walter 135
  Wesley F. 62
  William 120,223,226
  William B. 95,101,182
  William E. 210
  William S. 134
  William T. 261,315
  Willimington 153
  Willington 47,79
  Wm. 120,226
  Wm. B. 259
  Wm. E. 138
  Wm. T. 316
  Z. 74,160,244,252,288 85
Snead, L. 304
Sneed, Wm. 227
Sneegrave, Edward 281
Snellgrave, Edward 281
Snellings, John 149
Solomon, D. 166,174
  Henry 51
  Lewis 122
  Maria Louise 177
  Peter 177
Sorrow, Andrew J. 121
  George P. 121
  John S. 27
  Joshua 121
  Lucinda 121
  Perry D. 121
  Susan 121
Sorrells, Charles 285
Sour, John H., Sr. 52 226
  N. P. 52
  Thomas F. 52,249
Southall, Seaborn 166
Sowden, Wm. 164
Spain, Nelson 118
Sparks, ...136
  Kanzada 136
  Leven 136
  Louisa 136
  Sanford 136
Speakman, John 62,185
  Maria R. 62,185
Spear, William A. 58,63 258
Speer, A. M. 125
  Thomas D. 8,212
  Wm. A. 251

Speight, Thomas 269
Speir, Allison 113,180
Spence, Barry 235
  D. W. 94,154
  George 129
  Jane 48,80
  Sophia 94,154
  Susannah 235
Sperghts, M. H. 245
Spiers, Elizabeth E. 169
  Lucy Ann 169
Spink, G. H. 71
Spinks, Garrett H. 71
Spivy...265
Spratlin, P. M.,310
Spraybury, H. J. 166
Sprights, Levi 240
Springer, William G. 227
  Wm. 227
  Wm. G. 219,182,233,234
  Wm. C. 233
Spurgers, E. R. 136
Srach, Benjamin W. 229
Stacy, B. A. 282
Stallings, James 123,186
  Sarah 139
  Wm. 191,296
Stanton, B. S. 227
  Burrel 71
  James 71
  John 71
  Jonathan 71
  (Family) 163
Stapleton, James 122
Stapler, Jno. A. 2
  Thomas L. 133,138
  William N. 133
Stapleton, C. M. 82
  James 85
  L. D. 82
Stark, Aletha 297
Starr, John C. 203
Stebbins, (Orphans) 58
  C. A. 58
  Catherine A. 58
  Edward 58
  F. C. 58
  Frances C. 58
  Octavia J. 58
Steed, Sion P. 220
Steen, James 92,252
  Tabitha 92,252,253
Stephens...233,247
  A. H. 242
  Alexander H. 116,128, 197,211,263
  Benjamin 250
  Bery 107,317
  John L. 295
  Josiah 247
  Mary E. 295
  Nancy 161
  Nathan 161
  William H. 317
  William N. 107
Stephenson, James L. 10
Steptoe, Thos. 226
Sterling, Willis B. 128
Stetson, D. B. 268
Stevens, (heirs) 204
  Anthony, Jr. 315
  Benjamin 51,250
  Benjamin B. 51
  Gallatin 142
  John A. 142
  N. 204 (Needham)
  Susannah 311
Stewart, (Orphans) 84
  (heirs) 174
  A. 174,177
  Alexander 78,174,189
  David M. 84,174
  Edmund 101,183

Stewart, Elias F. 242
  Emely Savannah 253
  Esther 161
  Jesse 187
  Joseph J. 103
  Lilly Ann 2,281
  Lucy 187
  Nancy 253
  Robert 223
  Thomas J. 103
Stibbs, John Henry 234
Stiles, Benjamin 260
  Benj. Edwd. 260
Stillwell, Charles 190
  Charles H. 296
Stinsell, Lin T. 161
Stinson, George 146,319, 320
  James 146
Stocks, Susan 126
  Thomas 25,274,270
Stockton, W. M. 133
Stoker, Allen 266
Stokes, F. R. 151
  Frederick R. 151
  Silas A. 167
  Thomas B. 276
Stoker, William 267
Stokes, Wm. F. 159
  Wm. S. 166
  Wm. Y. 200
Stone, (Orphans) 77,162
  Charles W. 77,162
  Daniel 304
  Joshua 77,162
  Walter 190
  William H. 124
Storey, George 260
  Hannah 260
  James 260
  Jane 260
  John 260
  John J. 232
  John S. 260
  Lettleton B. 143,144
  Margaret "Peggy" 260
  Margery 260
  Nancy 260
  William M. 260
Storrs, Seth P. 107,157
Story, Abigail 11
  B. A. 144
  Benjamin A. 143
  Thad. S. 12
  Thaddeus S. 11
Stoval, Thomas 6
Stovall, (Orphans) 6,285
  David 245
  James 43,210,250
  Lewis 52,249,321
  Thomas 285
  William 52,249
Stowers, Francis G. 175
  Mary E. 175
Strans, George 265
Stratton, Henrietta 219
Strawn, Hiram 212
Street, D. A. 323
Streetman, Isaac L. 159
Stressell, Lin T. 227
Strickland, Cary 21,22
  Milzy 21,22
  Peter 179
Stringer, (heirs) 174
  Beliea 174
Strong, (Orphans) 225
  Allen B. 47,236,250
  C. H. 273
  Lewis P. 225
  Nancy C. 47,236,250
  Sherrod 225
Strongfellow, William 279
Strozer, (Orphans) 30

Strozer, John 30
　Reuben J. 29,30
Strut, Saml. M. 63
Stuart, Robert 223
Stubblefield, G. G. 238
Stubbs, F. P. 164
　James A. 164
　James W. 164
　Lucinda 164
　Thomas 164
　Thos. B. 58
Stuckly, Danl. 303
Studdard, James 189
Stull, John 221
Stunter, Sparks 244
Sturdivant (heirs) 206
　Edward 206
　James G. 206
Sturges, Elizabeth 93
　Joseph 204
Sullivan, F. J. 51
　Frances 27
　James 27
Sumerall, N. W. 26
　Neil W. 26,192
Summerall, Jesse 26,192
Summerlin, (heirs) 283
　Thomas 283
　William T. 283
Summers, George W. 12
Sumner, Elizabeth 58
Swank, Luther 164
Swann, Lee 196
Swain, Canneth W. T. 26
　172
Swan, Lee 35
Swarm, Josoph B. 123
Sweademan, Michael 150
Swearingin, Edward 39,78,
　170
Sweeney...314
　Daniel 314
Sweet, James L. 290
Swinnamon...150
Sylar, William 63
Symorn, Henry C. 283
Syrus, John G. 279

Talbot, John 215
Taliagerro, Z. 167
Tally, Joseph J. 214
　Joseph T. 215
　Russell 214
Tankersly, John Y. 262
Tankersley, Jos. 294
Tanner, David 300
Tansley, S. B. 90
Tant, (children) 212
　Elizabeth 212
　Thomas 212
Tanton, Henry 316
Tapley, James 277
　James M. 277
Tarell, James 21
Tarman, James 26
Tarmean, James 26
　Joel C. 26
Tarrell, James 21
Tarrett, Nathaniel C. 32
Tarver, (orphans) 150
　Benjamin P. 150
　Elijah 150
　Milton J. 150
Tarvin, Wm. J. 254
Tate, (orphans) 225,238
　Enos 288
　H. G. 225,238,262
　Hannah 67
　Heratio G. 225,238
　Zimm 225,238
Tatum, (heirs) 292
　Seth 292
　William 292

Taunton, Henry 316
　Nathan 316
Taylor, (orphans) 10,219
　Daniel 10
　Hillis 70
　(Heirs) 65,185
　(Orphans) 273,296,314
　Absalom 65,185
　Charles E. 290
　D. W. 265
　Daniel 219
　David G. 321
　Elbert C. 66
　Elbert D. 185,255,283
　Elbert L. 65
　Francis C. 187
　G. L. 123
　Gibbons M. 276
　J. 195
　John 10,11,296,308
　N. W. 66,185,283
　Peterson 34
　Richard 147,148
　Robert H. 321
　Sarah 123
　W. D. 323
　William 147,148,314
　William P. 65,185
　Willis 126,249
Teasby, Isham 201
　John A. 201
Teat, James J. 141
Tebeau, F. E. 196
　F. G. 162
　Frederick E. 196
　Frederick G. 161
Tefft, I. K. 203
Temple, Anne 271
Tennsend, E. A. 194
Terhum, A. A. 100
　Cornelius D. 100
Terhune, C. D. 231,233,234
Terrell, Catherine W. 201
　David 277
　Dd. 163,277
　Edy 21
　James C. 201
Terrentin, Geon 194
Terry, Daniel 178
　David 178
　Elizabeth 178
Tevhune, C. D. 124
Thacker, Ezekiel 173
Thercott, John Y. 251
Thigpin, Claborn 136
Thobrook, R. K. 229
Thomas...198,278,314
　C. L. 278
　Charles 314
　Elizabeth 198
　Elizabeth C. 278
　George 248
　John B. 55
　John M. 131
　John S. 90
　P. M. 236
　Rose 248
　Sary 49
　Stephen 165
　Thomas W. 236
　Woodley A. 49
　Y. L. 168
　Zachariah 135
Thomason, Thomas L. 320
Thompkins, Giles S. 118
Thompson...2,201,307
　Charles 189
　Crezy 281
　Eleanor 307
　G. W. 2
　Henry 81
　Hiram 183
　Jackson 307

Thompson, James 34,170,
　208
　John 201
　Joseph K. 40
　Leonard 302
　Leroy 305,308
　Malinda 307
　Polley 306
　Polly 304,305,306,307,
　308
　Robert 296
　Robert M. 186
　Samuel 201,296
　Thomas 304,305,306,307
　William 302
Thompsons, Malenda 308
Thomson (illegitimates)
　305
　Hudson A. 228,229
　Lenard 294
　Leroy 307
　Melinda 305,306,307
　Polly 305,307
　Thomas 307
　William 294
Thornton, Alsalem 259
　Absalom 222
　Benjamin 99,100,158
　Elsey B. 175
　John 99,100,158
　Martha 100
　Peggy 45
　Thomas J. 100
　William D. 200
Thorp, C. I. W. 169
Thrasher, Barton 256
　Isaac 143
Threlkill, J. W. 109
Thurman, David 76
Thurmond, John 164
　Samuel P. 124
Thweatt, John G. 82
　John T. 57
　M. W. 81,82
　Peterson 82
Tift, Nelson 282
Tillars, Frederick 6,125
Tilley, Daniel 321,322
　George 322
　Margaret 322
　Nathaniel G. 168
　William 322
Tilly, Elizabeth 203
　N. G. 168
Tillman, Aaron S. 9
　Joseph 165
　Sarah 165
Tilman, Aaron 9,191
Timmons, J. K. 44
　Mary 42
　William 44
　Z. T. 178
Tindale, James, Jr. 288
　James, Sr. 288
Tingle, Purify 278
Tinsley, J. W. 39,170
　James W. 78,201
　T. W. 78,201
　W. 78
　William B. 160,281
Tison, John M. 279
　Wm. W. 316
Titcombe, George 219
　Samuel 219
Todd, Henry B. 147,214
Tolerman, Henry 51
Tolleson, B. 95
Tomlin, Z. D. F. 56
　Zach. L. F. 56
Tomme, D. W. 2
Tompkins...105,108,263
　G. 225
　Giles L. 221

Tompkins, Giles S. 178
  Lan. William 315
  William 88
Toombs, Robert A. 143,210
  Robert 179,217
Torrance, James 296
  M. 286,287
  Mansfield 286,287
Torrence, Amelious 317
  John E. 150
  Septemus 150 ,217
Towers, Benjamin 317
  Elizabeth 317
Towns, ...255,256,308
  Benjamin 222
  D. P. 319
  Drury 255,256
  G. W. 287
  Geo. W. 286
  George W. 9,10
  George W. B. 10
  James 222
  John 9,10
  William 198
Townsend, I. E. 169
  J. E. 169,255,266,276
  Jos. E. 190
  John 323
Trammel, D. L. 50
  Elisha 21
Trammell, D. L. 60,78,79, 153
  Drakeford L. 50,60,153
Trawick, Frederick 129
Traylor, William 140
Treadaway, James M. 33
Treadwell, Burton 240
  Isaac 240
Trible, Richard T. 93
Trice...296
  Chesly P. 296
  Ezekiel 171,190
  Thomas A. 190
  Thos. C. 190
  Z. B. 296,306
  Zachariah 190
  Zachariah B. 296
Trimble, Amanda 107
  James 107,157
  Sarah Amanda 157
Trother, Branson 213
Trotter, Bronson 8
Troup...296
  G. M. 266
  George M. 224,270
Trout, J. F. 126
  Sarah 126
Truitt, Robert 230
Truston, J. A. 211
Trylor, William 139
Tuck, Thomas A. 54,93,203
Tucker, C. B. 167
  Crawford 21
  John R. 141
Tuggle, Lodowich 91
  Thomas S. 91
  T. P. 91
Tullis, Moses 316
Tumm, James 136
Turentin, Geon 210
Turentine, G. W. 56
Turrentine, G. W. 78
Turentine, George W. 38, 288
Turenton, Geo. W. 89
Turk, Cyntha J. 203
  Phiney A. 230
  Pleney A. 67,203
  Pleyney A. 68,230
  Pliney A. 67,68,203
  Thomas 252
  William 203
Turman, G. A. 12

Turman, Martin 12
  Milton C. 12
  Nancy W. 12
  Thomas J. 85,252
Turner, Amanda 94,154
  Elijah 271
  Gregory J. 236
  Henry G. 106,107
  James 208
  James, Jr. 169
  John W. 94,154
  Luke 143
  Margaret 94,154
  Nathan 257
  Philip 142
  Sarah 94,154
  Sherrod W. 237
  Sophia 94,154
  Waid H. 275
  Wm. 187
  Z. G. 95
Tutend, Ezekiel P. 208
Tutt, A. H. 44
Twilley, James 33
Tyner, Jackson 211
  Jackson, Jr. 211
  Jackson, Sr. 211
Tyson, J. M. 292
  John M. 292
  W. W. 315

Umphries, Amos 296
  John 296
  Penelope 296
  Rebekah 296
  Thomas 296
  William 296
Underwood...268,314
  A. A. 194
  Isaac 194
  James 148
  Josiah 94
  George W. 268
  Lawson 94
  John G. 278
  John J. 279
  William 314
  Winnford 268
Upchurch, Camp 177

Vabus, J. B. 68
Valbeau, Henry G. 229
Valentine, Andrew 204
  Thomas 140
Valentino (uro), Luis 17
Vance, Harriet 154
Vandegraft, John 211
Vann, Joseph 233
  Polly 233
Vann Epps, A. C. 320
Vardaman, Ed--y L. 29
  Edwy. L. 202
Varnum, Asa 122
  W. M. 196
  William M. 122
Varnell, M. 39,60
Vaughn, Benjamin 119
  John, Jr. 4 (Sr. 4)
Veal, Asa W. 116
Veitch, Mary Ann 217
  Walker 217
Venable...74
  John 74,180
  Nathaniel 74,180
Venson, John 301
Verdery, Thomas J. 177
Vestal, Wm. A. 45
Vester, Bolevre J. 151
Vial, Asa W. 116
Vincent, Nancy 236
  William 236
Vining, B. 274
Votee, David 264

Votee, Sarah 264

Wade...222
  Hudson 36
  James H. 199
  Jesse 222
  Mary 36
  Moses 222
Wadkins, Nancy 152
Wadly, Edwd. C. 177
Wadsworth, Hogan 281
  Walter 155
Waggoner, Amelia 269
Walden, Pleasant 155
Walker...206,223
  Benj. 206,223
  Freeman 159
  George 82,99,109,154, 180
  Harrison 289
  James C. 300,301
  John F. 183
  John H. 152,224
  John J. 6,10,61,113, 219,285
  John L. 36
  John S. 14,105
  Joseph 178,179
  Marshal 245
  Marshal D. 245
  Mary M. 109,154
  Philip 205
  William 206
Wall, Daniel D. 119
  Jesse M. 119
  William D. 119
Wallace, C. J. 32
  Dolly 17
  E. B. 132,,276
  John H. 17
  Turner M. 17
  Walter 135
Waller, Charles L. 300
Wallhall, Furman 94
Walls, John A. 221
Walpole, John 123
Walter, James 300,301
Walthall, Charles F. 50, 60
Walton...163,289
  Abner R. 223
  Augustus G. 163
  Elizabeth 163
  Francing 134
  John H. 288,289
  Joseph W. 113
  Mary 113
  Lurenia 134
  Robert 163,271
  Sarah 271
  Thomas 163,301
  Thos. L. 117
  Uriah 134
  William 288,289
Ward, Ann 51,52
Wansley, John 299
  Thomas 299
Wanslow, John, Jr. 299
  Thomas 299
War, Harvey McC. 259
Ward, Abner 299
  Amos 184
  B. F. 120
  Elizabeth 297
  Harvey McC. 259
  John M. 178
  Lucy 178
  Martha A. 270
  Pascal E. 119
  Thornton 297
  W. J. 272
Wardlaw, Joseph M. 189
Ware, James 134

Ware, James M. 134
Warlow, Nelson 299
Warner, Hiram 306
Warren...120,149
    Bray 149
    Dredsil 149
    J. T. 105
    Jeremiah S. 141,201, 244
    Jesse T. 106
Warslow, John Jr. 299
    Nathan 299
    Nelson 299
    Thomas 299
Warton, Alford M. 177
Washington, James A. 75
    James H. R. 71,160
Wasson, John F. 122
Watehall, Furman 94
Water, George M. 219
Waters, James Y. 214
Watkins, A. L. 216
    Claiborn A. 115
    James 109
    Jno. D. 133
    John R. 115
    Robert 300,312
Watson, Caroline E. 277
    Fransey 188
    Hannah 282
    Jacob 277
    Laurena 188
    Lurenia 188
    Moses 193
    Uriah 188
Watt, Abram P. 104,317
Watts...211,162
    Daniel S. 217
    Elizabeth 46
    John 162
    Jubal 211
    Thos. 315
Way...199
    John, Sr. 199
    N. J. 199
    Rachel 98
Weathers...219
    Allen 10,219
Weaver, Frederick 247,248
    James B. 210
    Marthy 248
    Thos. B. 248
Webb, A. 316
    John 195,222
Weeks, Jesse 237
    Nancy 298
    Rufus G. 237
Welborn, James 244
    Sarah 244,245
Welchel, Davis, Sr. 314
Welchels...321
Welcher, Frederick 292
    Jeremiah 258
    Larkin 258,292
    Olif 292
Wellborn, Adaline L. 118
    J. W. 93
    Marshall H. 118
    Marshall N. 118
    William J. M. 33
Wellbourne...233
Wellbron, Wm. J. W. 97
Welmaker...37,203
    Felix 37,202,203
    John 37,203
Wells, Eliza 194
    John D. 45,184,250
    Jordon 299
    Samuel 254
    Simpson 298
Wenderweedle, Jane B. 167
Wenget, Amos 138
    Mary Ann 138
Wenjett, Richard B. 261

Wesley, John 62
West...266
    Isham 50,60,215
    John 266
    Jos. 245
    Isaac W. 266
    Moses S. 245
    William 163
Westbrook...319
    Thomas 319
Wethers, William 240
Whatley, Amanda 107
    James 98
    Michael 107,157
    Sarah Amanda 157
Wheat, Francis A. 139
    Francis Henry 139
    Harvey 281
    Moses 108
Wheeler, Green 287
    Phinny 132
Wheeless, Charlotte 27
Whelchel, John 199
Whidden, Green 224
Whigham, Thomas 274
Whillemore, William 279
Whipples...39
Whisenhunt, John 246
Whitaker, H. 70
Whitdon, Green 90
White...208
    A. J. 238
    Albert T. 208
    Granville 107,317
    Henrietta 219
    Henry 218
    James R. 44
    John, Sr. 113
    Kenny 218
    Nathaniel 56
    Peter 315
    P. S. W. 219
    Reuben H. 238
    Thos. H. 72
    Timothy 132
    William 208
Whitehead, Amos P. 205
    W. D. 280
Whiteman, Cullen 39
Whitfield...164
    M. A. 164
    Mary A. 164
    Mat. 94,95
    Matthew 141
    William 204
    William S. 164
    Wm. 204
Whithead, Elizabeth M. 205
Whitley, Bird 42
    Byrd 251
Whitlock, Nancy 2,281
Whirly, Bird 251
Whitman, Christopher 39, 59
    Cullen 39,59,236
Whitsett, Francis 140
    John 140
Whitten, Alvan E. 241
    William 176
Whittich, Lovick L. 90
Whittle, Jas. 276
Whitworth, William S. 55 312
Wicker, Allen 155
    James 155
Widdon, Green 197
Wiggins, George W. 168
Wilborn, M. J. 306
Wilcher, Jordon 299
    Mary 299
Wild, William 206
Wilder, Holmon 86
Wiley, J. M. Caleb 105
    Johnson 197

Wiley, Wesley 197
    Westley 197
    William 282
Wilkerson, Celia 193
    Irwin 156
Wilkins, James S. 137
Wilkinson...39,197
    B. N. 82
    Benjamin N. 82
    Cain 197
    Elisha 210
    J. F. 197
    James 197
    Margaret 138
    Signal A. 210
Wilky, Lunceford 30
Willcox, Ebenesar 206
    Thomas 63
William...191
    Jno. 145
Williams...143,234,264
    Absalom 16
    Andrew J. 27
    B. 290
    Barnett 304
    Benjamin 290
    Crawford B. 39
    E. H. 27
    F. H. 264
    Gasper 315
    Godfrey 197
    Gren B. 99
    Isham 192
    Jacob 299
    James L. 298
    Jno. 145
    John 42,94,149,150,154, 211
    Joseph M. 223
    Luke 209
    Mary 98,150
    Mary Elikins 197
    Pike 115
    Robert 191
    Robert, Sr. 192
    Thomas 234
    Saml. 308
    Theopelus 261
    William 26,143,192
    Wm. T. 52
    Wm. Thorne 278
    Zach. 301
Williamson...284
    ---- J. 255
    Anow E. 52
    Anne E. 249
    Charles 302
    Emily M. 132
    G. B. 76
    Green 193
    Green B. 76,120,193, 204,236,
    Jno. 284,255
    Jno. P. 264
    Jno. R. M. 284
    John 123,193,236,255
    John G. 165
    John R. 284
    John 286
    John N. 216
    Thomas E. 52,249
    William 174
    William J. 132
    William T. 131,132
Williford...312
    Maxfield H. 238
Willis, ..243
    George W. 25
    James 243
    Jane 209
    John A. 209,210
    Matilda 2,281
    Nathl. 163

Willis, Richard J. 25
Wills, Abner 133
  James H. 133
Willson, Leroy M. 141
Wilmot...172
  Esther Ann 70,172
  Isaac 70,172
Wilson...172,251,262,285
  Abel P. 161
  Abel S. 161
  Benjamin 19
  J. B. 53,67,155,179,
    200,222,288,297
  James B. 137
  Jas. 35
  Jas. B. 200
  John 147
  Joseph 46,251
  Joseph A. 161
  Miles 137
  Nancy 46,251
  Sarah 55
  T. R. 172
  Thomas 46,251
  William H. 6,284,285
  William L. 19
  William P. 46,251
Wily, J. M. Caleb 108
Wimberly, Amelia E. 280
  Dennis D. 211
  Lewis 299
  Lewis T. 280
  Perry 299
  Samuel T. 280
  Titus 280
Wimbish...266
  Hezekiah 261
  Hezekiah S. 266,271
Winderwedle, Jane B. 167
Windham, Daniel 76
  Permelia 76
Wing...304
  Butler 304
  Eliza U. 304
  George F. 304
Wingate...18,173
  Amos 18,173
  P. A. 202
  Pamella 202
Wingfield, A. J. 203
  A. S. 37,121,136
  James L. 214
Winn Elisha 145
  George A. 139
  Geo. A. 139
Winship, J. 211
Wipper, Jaboc N. 185
Wisener, William 280
Wisenhunt, John 246
Wisunant, Jacob 138
Withors, G. 195
Witt, Jacob 20
  Martin 20
  Middleton 222
Wittich, Lovick L. 157
Wjite, Henry M. 289
Wofford, Charles 145
Wolfe, John 148
  Mary A. 148
Wolfolk, Sowel 240
Wood, ..173,253
  Charles 173
  Elisha 269
  Elizabeth 68,253
  Green B. 253
  Isaac S. 182,220,223
  John 68,253
  Joseph 68,253
  Laica 253
  Lovica 68
  Nathaniel R. 89
  Robert 173
  Robert, Sr. 234

Wood, Susannah 173
  Thomas 235
  William 220,223
Woodall, Abner 128
  Jesse 116,117,172,197,
    211
  Sarah 128
Woodfolk, S. 308
Woodruff, Canot 87
  Carnot 87,153
  Philip D. 153
  Philo. D. 87
  Richard 116
Woods...72 -
  Elizabeth 188
  Timothy C. 235
  W. M. 188
  William 72
Woodson, Legan 300
Woodward, Irwin H. 119
  John L. 120
  Owen 119
  Owen S. 119
Woody...289
  Henry 289
  John 289
Wooly, Andrew F. 113
Wooten, Henry 119
Wootten, Henry 119
Wornack, Jason 37
  Bugil 37
  Burgis 37
Worrill, Simeon S. 15
Worthington, M'. C. 135
  Margaret C. 135,182
  Peter 135,182
Worthy, Jane 182
  Thomas 41,182
  Thomas K. 298
Wright...59,227
  Cassandra 217
  Charlotte A. 139
  Elvera L. 294
  James 180,217
  Jas., Jr. 77
  John 139,224
  Lauson D. 50
  Lawson D. 50,60
  Millicent 50,60
  Moses 7,200,203
  R. P. 312
  Robert M. 123
  Samuel 74,180
  T. W. 310
  William C. 294
Wyatt...260
  Elijah 115
  Jane 260
  Lorana 42,251
  Lovena 139
  Thomas M. 42,119,194,
    251
  Thomas W. 139
  Thos. M. 89
Wyche, Henry 204
  John R. 89
  Littleton 204
  Susanah 89
  Thomas C. 204
Wyley, Leonidas 91
Wylly, Elisha 161
  Leonidas 20,82,91,92,
    161,162,241
  Leonidas W. 30
  Oliver C. 148
  Toroidas 229
Wynen, Elisha T. 218
Wynens, John 262
Wynn, C. R. 32,159
  Sarah 167,168
  Thomas H. 187
  Threewiss 226

Yarborough, Moses 261
Yarbrough, N. 177
Yarby, George 130
Yates, W. H. 212
Yerby, George 130,131
  Mary 131
Yonells, Walter 242
Yonge, Philip R. 71
Yopp, J. H. 65
  Jeremiah H. 65
Yordy, Peter J. 279
Young, ...272,
  A-------- 12
  Allen C. 98,210
  Alzor-- 12
  Cuyler W. 116
  David 272
  David W. E. 273
  Earnest L. 75
  Earnest S. 75
  Edward B. 320
  Elizabeth 98,210
  Henry F. 16
  Julia 272
  Mahala 272
  Miles N. 17
  William Euclid 272,273
  William U. 237
  Wm. P. 237
Youngblood, J. T. 127

Zachary, Clemont R. 128

www.ingramcontent.com/pod-product-compliance
Lightning Source LLC
Chambersburg PA
CBHW050613300426
44112CB00012B/1492